Hong Kong

"All you've got to do is decide to go
and the hardest part is over.

So go!"

TONY WHEELER, COFOUNDER – LONELY PLANET

THIS EDITION WRITTEN AND RESEARCHED BY
Emily Matchar,
Piera Chen

Contents

(left) Golden pagoda at Nan Lian Garden (p134)

(above) Fishmonger, Bowrington Road Market (p111)

(right) Figurines for sale, Cat Street (p83)

Kowloon
p128

Hong Kong Island:
Central
p66

Hong Kong Island:
The Peak &
the Northwest
p79

Hong Kong Island:
Wan Chai &
the Northeast
p99

Hong Kong Island:
Aberdeen &
the South
p120

Welcome to Hong Kong

Hong Kong welcomes with an iconic skyline, a legendary kitchen, and lush, protected nature where rare birds and colourful traditions thrive.

Neighbourhoods & Islands

Hong Kong's enchanting neighbourhoods and islands offer a sensory feast. You may find yourself swaying along on a historic double-decker tram, cheering with the hordes at the city-centre horse races, or simply gazing out at the glorious harbour. More than 70% of Hong Kong is mountains and sprawling country parks, some also home to geological and historical gems. Escape the city limits on one of the world's smoothest transport systems and spend your day wandering in a Song-dynasty village, hiking on a deserted island or kayaking among volcanic sea arches.

Cuisine

One of the world's top culinary capitals, the city that worships the God of Cookery has many a demon in the kitchen, whether the deliciousness in the pot is Cantonese, Sichuanese, Japanese or French. So deep is the city's love of food and so broad its culinary repertoire that whatever your gastronomic desires, Hong Kong will find a way to sate them. The answer could be a bowl of wonton noodles, freshly steamed dim sum, a warm pineapple bun wedged with butter, a pair of the sweetest prawns, your first-ever stinky tofu, or the creations of the latest celebrity chef.

Shopping

From off-the-rack Chinese gowns to bespoke speciality knives (and vice versa), the sheer variety of products in Hong Kong's shops is dizzying. Every budget, need and whim is catered for in 'can do' spirit by a similarly impressive assortment of venues: glitzy malls where the moneyed shop; chic side-street boutiques and vintage dens where fashionistas find their gems; nerdy gadget bazaars; and a mix of markets where you can haggle to your heart's content. The city has no sales tax so prices are generally attractive to visitors.

Culture

Underneath the glass and steel of Hong Kong's commercial persona is a dynamic cultural landscape where its Chinese roots, colonial connections and the contributions of its home-grown talent become intertwined. Here you're just as likely to find yourself applauding at Asia's top film festival as joining in dawn taichi or reading the couplets of a local poet to the drumbeat of a dragon boat. Culture could also mean indie music by the harbour or Chinese opera in a bamboo theatre, not to mention the thousands of shows staged year-round at the city's many museums and concert halls.

Why I Love Hong Kong

By Piera Chen, Writer

Hong Kong has a complexity that defies definition. It's the only place where I can be searching for colonial military relics near the Chinese border, lunching with a Buddhist at a Sikh temple, trying to decipher the aesthetics of Chinese Revival architecture, or splurging on a set of knives – all within five hours – followed by a night of Cantonese opera, karaoke or poetry, anywhere I choose. Hong Kong is so intense and so full of possibilities that I'm glad there's the rule of law (and an awesome transport system) to stop it from whirling into chaos.

For more about our writers, see p320

For more about our writers, see p320

Top: Hong Kong cityscape at sunset

Hong Kong's
Top 16

Star Ferry (p69)

1 A floating piece of Hong Kong heritage and a sightseeing bargain, the legendary Star Ferry was founded in 1880 and plies the waters of Victoria Harbour in the service of regular commuters and tourists. At only HK$2.50, the 15-minute ride with views of Hong Kong's iconic skyline must be one of the world's best-value cruises. While the vista is more dramatic when you're Island-bound, the art deco Kowloon pier, resembling a finger pointing at the Island, is arguably more charming.

⊙ *Central*

The Peak (p81)

2 Rising above the financial heart of Hong Kong, Victoria Peak offers superlative views of the city and the mountainous countryside beyond. Ride the hair-raising Peak Tram, Asia's first cable funicular, in operation since 1888 – to the cooler climes at the top, as skyscrapers and apartment blocks recede into the distance. At dusk Victoria Harbour glitters like the Milky Way on a sci-fi movie poster, mysterious and full of promise, as the lights come on. BELOW: PEAK TRAM

⊙ *The Peak & the Northwest*

DANIEL FUNG / SHUTTERSTOCK ©

GAGLIARDIIMAGES / SHUTTERSTOCK ©

Mong Kok Markets (p150)

3 With its eclectic speciality markets Mong Kok is your best bet for a rewarding shopping crawl. Ladies' Market has a mile-long wardrobe covering everything from 'I Love HK' rugby shirts to granny swimwear. Exotic seeds and gardening tools sit next to buckets of fragrant florals in the flower market. Stalls displaying colourful aquatic life in softly humming, UV-lit tanks line the streets of the goldfish market. There are vertical markets too – a buzzing computer mall, and a multistorey gadget-lovers' heaven.

🏠 *Kowloon*

Man Mo Temple (p82)

4 Experience Chinese folk religiosity in Soho. Permanently wreathed in sandalwood smoke from the hanging incense coils, the famous temple is dedicated to Man (literature) and Mo (war) and the gods who govern them. Formerly a cultural and political focal point for the local Chinese, the temple now commands a following beyond conscientious students and the martially inclined, as locals and tourists come to perform age-old rites and have their fortunes told.

⊙ *The Peak & the Northwest*

Wan Chai Dining (p108)

5 If you were to hurl yourself, eyes closed, into a random neighbourhood and expect to emerge smacking your lips, you'd stand the best chance if you were in Wan Chai. The district is home to a great many restaurants suiting a range of pocket sizes. Regional Chinese cooking, European cuisines, Asian kitchens, East–West fusion, classy, midrange, hole in the wall... Just name your craving and head on down to the Wanch; you're certain to find it there.

✗ *Wan Chai & the Northeast*

Temple Street Night Market (p132)

6 Beneath the glare of naked bulbs, hundreds of stalls sell a vast array of booty, from sex toys to Nepalese daggers. You can browse for handy gadgets or quirky souvenirs, and test your bargaining skills. Nearby, fortune-tellers beckon in English from dimly lit tents, and Cantonese opera singers strike a pose. If you're hungry, the many open-air stalls offer snacks or a seafood feast. Sure it's touristy, but its mesmerising and impenetrable aura makes everyone – including locals – feel like a welcome visitor.

🔒 *Kowloon*

Hong Kong Wetland Park (p160)

7 Surreally nestled under an imposing arc of apartment towers, this 61-hectare ecological park in crowded Tin Shui Wai is a swampy haven of biodiversity. This is urban/nature juxtaposition at its best and, curiously, most harmonious. Precious ecosystems in this far-flung yet easily accessible part of the New Territories provide tranquil habitats for a range of waterfowl and other wildlife. Try to forget the human-made world for a moment and delve into a landscape of mangroves, rivers and fish-filled ponds.

👁 *New Territories*

Shopping in Tsim Sha Tsui *(p149)*

8 An afternoon's visit to Tsim Sha Tsui's shopping quarters should yield a few gems. If you're seeking Chinese-style gifts, comb the streets near the southern end of the area for that silk gown, teapot or trinket. If glamour is what floats your boat, join the über-wealthy mainland tourists for a card-swiping marathon in the mile-long block of luxury malls along Canton Rd. Want something unique? Head over to Granville Rd for that super-sized orange blazer or a micromall nearby for those asymmetrical earrings and thigh-high boots.

🛍 *Kowloon*

Big Buddha (p175)

9 A favourite with local day trippers and foreign visitors alike, the world's biggest outdoor seated Buddha lords over the western hills of Lantau Island. Visit this serene giant via the Ngong Ping 360 cable-car. Negotiate the 268 steps to the three-platform altar on which it is seated and check out the three halls along the way. Reward yourself with some monk food at the popular vegetarian restaurant in Po Lin Monastery below. Buddha's Birthday in May is a colourful time to visit this important pilgrimage site.

⊙ *Outlying Islands*

Happy Valley Races (p105)

10 Every Wednesday night the city horse-racing track in Happy Valley comes alive, with eight electrifying races and a carnival of food and beer. You can try your luck at betting or simply enjoy the collective exhilaration and the thunder of ironed hooves. Races were first held here in the 19th century by European merchants who imported stocky stallions from Mongolia, which they rode themselves. Now there are races every week except in the sweltering months of July and August.

⊙ *Wan Chai & the Northeast*

9

Riding the Trams *(p263)*

11 Nicknamed 'ding dings' by locals, trams have been sedately chugging back and forth between the Eastern and Western districts of the Island since 1904. A century later the world's largest fleet of still-operating double-decker trams continues to negotiate pathways through the city's heavy traffic. Board a ding ding – Hong Kong's low-carbon transport option – and watch the city unfold like a carousel of images as you relax and ponder tomorrow's itinerary. It's the fun option, too: high fives between passengers on passing trams are not unheard of.

⊙ *Transport*

Tsim Sha Tsui East Promenade (p131)

12 Gleaming skyscrapers lined up between emerald hills and a deep-blue harbour with criss-crossing boats – Hong Kong's best-known imagery is of the Island but, like a hologram, its beauty only shimmers into view when you're looking from the Tsim Sha Tsui East Promenade in Kowloon, especially after sundown. Home to windswept museums and a world-class concert venue, the promenade offers pockets of culture as you stroll its length, as intimate with one of the world's best views as you can get without falling into the water.

⊙ *Kowloon*

Hiking the Hong Kong Trail (p60)

13 Once you've made it past the windy Dragon's Back ridge, the Hong Kong Trail sweeps you into rolling hills, secluded woodland and lofty paths that afford sumptuous views of the rugged south and its wavy shore. Starting from the Peak, the 50km route snakes across the entire length of Hong Kong Island, past beautiful reservoirs, cobalt bays and WWII battlefields. Spread over five country parks, this wonderful trail invites both easy perambulations and harder hikes.

🏃 *Sports & Activities*

Exploring Lamma (p176)

14 If there were a soundtrack for the island of Lamma, it would be reggae. The island's laid-back vibe attracts herb-growers, musicians and New Age therapists from a rainbow of cultures. Village shops stock prosecco, and island mongrels respond to commands in French. If you hike to the nearest beach, your unlikely compass will be three coal-fired plants against the skyline, looking more trippy than grim. Then, in the glow of the day's final rays, head back for fried calamari and beer by the pier.

🏃 *Outlying Islands*

13

14

Walled Villages of Yuen Long *(p159)*

15 Let Yuen Long's walled villages take you back over half a millennium to a wild and windy time when piracy was rife along the South China coast. Isolated from China's administrative heart, Hong Kong, with its treacherous shores and mountainous terrain, was an excellent hideout for pirates. Its earliest inhabitants built villages with high walls, some guarded by cannons, to protect themselves. Inside these walls today you'll see ancestral halls, courtyards, pagodas, temples and ancient farming implements – vestiges of Hong Kong's precolonial history, all carefully restored.

◉ *New Territories*

MARVAIG / SHUTTERSTOCK ©

ILONGVEKING / SHUTTERSTOCK ©

Ruins of the Church of St Paul, Macau *(p193)*

16 Macau's answer to the Eiffel Tower or Statue of Liberty is a dramatic gate perched on a hill 26m above sea level, smack in the middle of the city. A sweep of stairs with landings and balustrades takes you to it, and then to nowhere. Once part of a 17th-century Jesuit church destroyed in a fire, the facade, with fine carvings and detailed engravings featuring Christian, Chinese and Japanese influences, is a captivating historical fragment and a document in granite of Macau's unique Mediterrasian culture.

◉ *Macau*

What's New

Hong Kong Global Geopark

The government will step up facilities at this breathtaking geopark – Unesco listed since 2011 – including accessibility, certain pier facilities and training of professional guides. (p155)

Lai Chi Wo

A 400-year-old village and freshwater wetland, Lai Chi Wo is undergoing an agricultural revival that may serve as a model for other country park enclaves. It's also part of Hong Kong Geopark. (p155)

Hong Kong Craft Beer

Suddenly everyone is making craft beer in Hong Kong and bars are selling them. Young Master Ales has a brewery that's open to the public on Saturday mornings. (p122)

Caroline Haven

This old gritty residential area on the outskirts of Causeway Bay has become a haven for shop owners, designers and restaurateurs attracted by the lower rent and the old-fashioned neighbourhood vibe. (p100)

Pok Fu Lam Village

There are tours now at PFL Village, one of Hong Kong Island's last remaining villages, after it was declared a 'heritage site under threat' by an international watchdog. (p122)

TUVE

A strongly design-oriented boutique hotel in an old and quiet corner of a largely residential neighbourhood. Design freaks will be right at home among the steel, glass and concrete. (p221)

Simple Dishes Refined

Restaurants making refined versions of familiar Chinese chow have sprung up on the island: Fortune Kitchen and Choi's Kitchen. (p111)

Desserts

Dessert shops, including high-end Atum Desserant and budget Master Low Key Food Shop, are blossoming in the city that traditionally believes the best compliment one can give to cake is 'It's not sweet'. (p110, p113)

Restaurants by Family of Old Establishments

Family feuds and other exciting matters at some of the most revered names in Hong Kong's culinary landscape have spawned new, smaller and more affordable outlets that live up to their heritage – respectively Seventh Son, Kam's Kitchen and Kam's Roast Goose. (p109, p111, p108)

Campus Hong Kong

A dormitory for students with access to the luxuries of a serviced apartment complex run by the same company. Perks include a swimming pool, a gym and awesome views. Backpackers can book when the students are away. (p226)

For more recommendations and reviews, see **lonelyplanet .com/china/hong-kong**

Need to Know

For more information, see Survival Guide (p257)

Currency
Hong Kong dollar (HK$)

Language
Cantonese, English

Visas
Not required for British passport holders for stays up to 180 days; citizens of Australia, Canada, the EU, Israel, Japan, NZ and the US for up to 90 days; holders of many African (including South African), South American and Middle Eastern passports for visits of 30 days or less. Others must apply at a Chinese embassy or consulate before departure.

Money
ATMs are widely available. Credit cards are accepted in most hotels and restaurants; some budget places only take cash.

Mobile Phones
Any GSM-compatible phone can be used in Hong Kong.

Time
Hong Kong Time (GMT/UTC plus eight hours)

Tourist Information
Hong Kong Tourism Board (p272) Helpful staff, and reams of information – most of it free.

Daily Costs

Budget: Less than HK$800
➡ Guesthouse HK$180–450
➡ Meals at a *cha chaan tang* (tea house) or *dai pai dong* (food stall): HK$60–150
➡ Museums (free Wednesdays); night markets (free); horse races (HK$10)
➡ Bus, tram, ferry ticket: HK$2.50–15

Midrange: HK$800–HK$1800
➡ Double room in a hostel or budget hotel: HK$550–1100
➡ Chinese dinner with three dishes: HK$350
➡ Drinks and live music: HK$300

Top end: More than HK$1800
➡ Double room in a boutique or four-star hotel: HK$2000
➡ Dinner at top Chinese restaurant: from HK$800
➡ Cantonese opera ticket: HK$400

Advance Planning

Two months before Check dates of Chinese festivals; book accommodation, tickets for major shows, and a table at a top restaurant.

One month before Check listings and book tickets for fringe festivals; book nature tours and a table at a popular restaurant.

Two weeks before Book harbour cruises; sign up for email alerts from events organisers.

One week before Check the weather forecast.

Useful Websites

Discover Hong Kong (www.discoverhongkong.com) The Hong Kong Government's user-friendly website for travel information.

Urbtix (www.urbtix.hk) Tickets to movies, shows and exhibitions.

Time Out Hong Kong (www.timeout.com.hk) What to eat, drink and do in Hong Kong and Macau.

Hong Kong Observatory (www.hko.gov.hk) Weather information including forecasts.

Lonely Planet (lonelyplanet.com/china/hong-kong) For all your travel needs.

WHEN TO GO

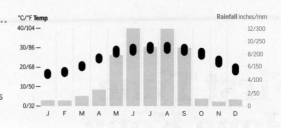

°C/°F **Temp**   Rainfall inches/mm

October to early December is the best time to visit. June to August is hot and rainy. Beware of typhoons in September.

Arriving in Hong Kong

Hong Kong International Airport Airport Express MTR train to city centre from 5.54am to 12.48am, HK$90 to HK$100; buses to various parts of Hong Kong from 6am to 12.30am, HK$19 to HK$48; taxi to city centre HK$220 to HK$360.

Lo Wu and Lok Ma Chau MTR train to city centre from 5.55am to 12.30am (Lo Wu), from 6.38am to 10.55pm (Lok Ma Chau), HK$37 to HK$48.

Hong Kong-Macau Ferry Terminal MTR train (Sheung Wan) to city centre from 6.05am to 12.46am, HK$4.50 to HK$13; taxi HK$20 to HK$100.

China Ferry Terminal MTR train (Tsim Sha Tsui) to city centre from 6.11am to 12.54am, HK$4.50 to HK$12; taxi HK$20 to HK$100.

For much more on **arrival** see p258

Useful Tours

Gray Line Tours (p266) More than 20 different tours.

Little Adventures in Hong Kong (www.littleadventuresin hongkong.com) Everything from food crawls to history walks.

Handmade in Hong Kong tour (www.hstvl.com) An eight-hour tour from 9.15am on Tuesday, Wednesday and Thursday for HK$850 per person. The tour will show you Hong Kong's age-old handicrafts such as shoe making, neon-sign making and bespoke tailoring.

Land Between Tour (www.grayline.com.hk) Full-/half-day tours for HK$620/460 that take you on hikes to walled villages, monasteries, fish farms and the like in the New Territories.

Hong Kong Foodie Tour (www.hongkongfoodietours.com) A mouth-watering food crawl in Central and Sheung Wan departing 2.15pm Monday to Saturday for adult/child HK$690/490.

HKTB Island Tour (p265) Includes Man Mo Temple, the Peak, Aberdeen, Repulse Bay and Stanley Market.

For much more on **getting around** see p260

Sleeping

Hong Kong offers a full range of accommodation, from closet-sized rooms to palatial suites. Most hotels on Hong Kong Island are between Central and Causeway Bay; in Kowloon, they fall around Nathan Rd, where you'll also find budget places. During low seasons prices fall sharply, particularly the midrange and top-end options, when booking online can get you discounts of up to 60%.

Useful Websites

Lonely Planet (lonelyplanet. com/china/hong-kong/hotels) Book LP's top accommodation picks online.

Hotel.com (www.hotels.com/ hong-kong) Specialises in cheap lodgings.

Discover Hong Kong (www. discoverhongkong.com) Provides a hotel search based on location and facilities.

Asia Travel (www.hongkong hotels.com) Offers better deals than others.

For much more on **sleeping** see p217

First Time Hong Kong

For more information, see Survival Guide (p257)

Checklist

➡ Make sure your passport is valid for at least one month past your intended stay

➡ Inform your debit-/credit-card company

➡ Arrange for appropriate travel insurance

➡ Check if your mobile phone service provider has roaming agreement with a Hong Kong operator

What to Pack

➡ Good walking shoes for the city and the countryside

➡ Light rain gear – Hong Kong has a subtropical climate with monsoons in summer

➡ Mosquito repellent, sunscreen and sunglasses in summer

➡ Travel electric adapter for Hong Kong

➡ A small day pack

Top Tips for Your Trip

➡ Hong Kong's efficient Mass Transit Railway (MTR) system and buses can take you to most of the sights and allow you to pack a lot into a day. Most rural areas are no more than 1½ hours away from the city centre by public transport.

➡ If you have more than two days, visit the countryside or outlying islands. It will give you a completely different impression. Hong Kong is much more than just skyscrapers.

➡ Some of the world's best Chinese food is to be had in Hong Kong. Indulge in at least one excellent Chinese meal during your visit.

➡ To get a feel for local culture, explore the main areas of the city by foot.

➡ Take the Star Ferry and the trams at least once. They are living heritage and are well connected to some of the main sights.

What to Wear

Hong Kong has its share of fashion-obsessed people, but in general, Hong Kongers are casual. Many would go to dinner at a fancy restaurant in jeans (though not flip-flops). Central and Causeway Bay have the best dressed.

Summer is hot and humid. Dress lightly but bring a jacket for air-conditioned facilities. The air-con can be strong on empty buses and certain indoor areas.

When hiking in summer, pack your swimsuit and goggles for an impromptu dip.

Be Forewarned

Hong Kong is a very safe city, but you should always exercise common sense.

➡ Always be careful of your valuables when in crowded areas.

➡ When using a taxi, always make sure the driver starts the meter.

➡ Some shops and restaurants are closed on the first and second days of the Lunar New Year, some for a longer period of time.

Money

Credit cards are accepted in most hotels and restaurants; some budget places accept only cash. ATMs are widely available.

For more information, see p270.

Taxes

There is no value-added tax (VAT) or sales tax in Hong Kong.

Etiquette

Though informal in their day-to-day dealings, Hong Kong people do observe certain rules of etiquette.

➡ **Greetings** Just wave and say 'Hi' and 'Bye' when meeting for the first time and when saying goodbye.

➡ **Dining** At budget places, people think nothing of sticking their chopsticks into a communal dish. Better restaurants provide separate serving spoons with each dish; if they're provided, use them. Don't be afraid to ask for a fork if you can't manage chopsticks.

➡ **Queues** Hong Kongers line up for everything. Attempts to 'jump the queue' are frowned upon.

➡ **Bargaining** Haggling over the price of goods is not expected in shops. Do bargain when buying from street vendors (but not in food markets).

Shopping on Cat Street (p83)

Tipping

➡ **Hotels** A HK$10 or HK$20 note for the porter; gratuity for cleaning staff at your discretion.

➡ **Restaurants** Most eateries, except very cheap places, impose a 10% to 15% service charge, but it is normal to still tip a little (under 5%) if you're happy with the experience. At budget joints, just rounding it off to the nearest HK$10 is fine.

➡ **Pubs and cafes** Not expected unless table service is provided, then something under 5% of your bill.

➡ **Taxis** Tips are never expected.

Language

Most people in Hong Kong speak some level of English. Don't be afraid to ask for directions in English. Most restaurants have English menus.

If you know Mandarin, you can try using it in Hong Kong. Most people understand the dialect; some speak it reasonably well.

For more language terms and a useful glossary, see p274.

Getting Around

For more information, see Transport (p258)

Metro

Hong Kong's Mass Transit Railway (MTR) system covers most of the city and is the easiest way to get around. Most lines run from 6am to after midnight.

Bus

Relatively fast, buses are an indispensable form of transport to places not reachable by the MTR or after midnight.

Ferry

The Star Ferry connects Hong Kong Island and Kowloon Peninsula via Victoria Harbour. Modern ferry fleets run between Central and the outlying islands.

Tram

Slow, but the upper deck offers great views. Runs along the northern strip of Hong Kong Island, from 6am to midnight.

Taxi

Cheap compared to Europe and North America. Most taxis are red; green ones operate in certain parts of the New Territories; blue ones on Lantau Island. All run on meter.

Public Light Buses (Minibuses)

Green- or red-roofed vans supplement bus routes and go beyond. Green ones take Octopus cards; red ones are cash-only

Key Phrases

MTR The Mass Transit Railway runs nine lines serving Hong Kong Island, Kowloon and the New Territories; the Airport Express to and from the airport; a light rail network in Northwestern New Territories; and trains to Guǎngdōng, Běijīng, and Shànghǎi.

Octopus Card A rechargeable 'smart card' that can be used on most forms of public transport, and allows you to make purchases at convenience stores and supermarkets.

Cross-Harbour Taxi A taxi going from Hong Kong Island to Kowloon Peninsula or vice versa that requires passengers to pay the cross-harbour toll for a single trip.

Central-Mid-Levels Escalator A long, covered escalator that links up areas built on slopes in Central, Sheung Wan, and Western District.

Key Routes

Star Ferry The scenic option.

MTR Island Line Covers Central, Admiralty, Wan Chai and Causeway Bay.

MTR Tsuen Wan Line Connects Central and Tsim Sha Tsui.

Peak Tram A funicular railway that takes you to the highest point on the island.

Tram 'Heritage' vehicles that run along the northern coast of the island.

Taxi Etiquette

➡ Look for a stationary or approaching cab with a lit 'For Hire' sign.

➡ When the car is approaching, stand in a prominent place on the side of the road and stick out your arm. The driver should pull over when he sees you.

➡ Taxis do not stop if there are double yellow lines on the side of the road, or at bus stops.

TOP TIPS

➡ Use the tram or walk if your destination is one MTR station away.

➡ Download the app for the MTR system before you leave home.

➡ If short of time, combine the MTR with taxis for destinations that are some walking distance from MTR stations.

➡ Carry your hotel's business card with its name in written in Chinese characters so you can show your taxi driver.

When to Travel

➡ Avoid rush hours (8am to 9.30am and 5.30pm to 7pm), when the MTR's interchange stations (Central, Admiralty, Tsim Sha Tsui, Kowloon Tong) are jam packed.

➡ Vehicular traffic on major roads and the cross-harbour tunnels can also be painfully slow during peak hours.

Etiquette

➡ Have your ticket or Octopus Card ready before you go through the barrier in the MTR station. Or feel the impatience at your back if you slow down the human traffic by three seconds.

➡ Stand on the right side of the escalator or risk being asked to move aside by commuters in a hurry – plenty in Hong Kong.

➡ Drinking and eating on MTR and buses is not allowed.

➡ Let passengers disembark first before entering the MTR carriage. The train won't leave the station until all doors are properly closed.

➡ Priority seats are clearly marked on buses and the MTR.

➡ Hong Kongers are not very good at giving up their seats to pregnant women and the elderly.

Tickets & Passes

➡ A prepaid Octopus Card can be used on most forms of public transport. They can be bought at any MTR station, and topped up at MTR stations and convenience stores.

➡ If visiting for over two days, buy an Octopus Card; it will save you up to 5% per trip and you won't have to buy tickets and pay exact fares on buses.

➡ For shorter stays, buy a one-day or three-day pass for unlimited rides on the MTR. Available at any MTR station.

For much more on **getting around** see p260

Top Itineraries

Day One

The Peak & the Northwest (p79)

 Catch the legendary Peak Tram up to **Victoria Peak** for stunning views of the city. Then descend and walk to **Sheung Wan**, checking out the shopping options along the way. Stop at **Man Mo Temple** for a taste of history and explore the burgeoning community on **Tai Ping Shan St**.

> ✕ **Lunch** Elegant Luk Yu Tea House (p89) serves great dim sum.

Kowloon (p128)

Take the **Star Ferry** to Kowloon. Enjoy the views along **Tsim Sha Tsui East Promenade** and savour your stroll to the **Museum of History** where you'll get some context on your day's impressions.

> ✕ **Dinner** Dunk and dip Hong Kong–style at Woo Cow (p142).

The Peak & the Northwest (p79)

 Take the tram to **Soho** for drinks, dancing and live music. If there's an indie gig on at **Hidden Agenda**, head over there by MTR, grab a few beers from a nearby convenience store, and hang with the hipsters.

Day Two

Wan Chai & the Northeast (p99)

 Embrace (manufactured) nature at lovely **Hong Kong Park**, not forgetting to check out the **Museum of Teaware**, then head over to **Queen's Rd East** to explore the sights and streets of this older part of Wan Chai. Then take the tram to **Causeway Bay** for some shopping. Don't miss the speciality shops of **Caroline Haven**.

> ✕ **Lunch** Fortune Kitchen (p111) serves delicious Cantonese homecooking.

Kowloon (p128)

Take a peek inside **Chungking Mansions**. Then relax and people-watch at the **Tsim Sha Tsui East Promenade** if construction has finished, or the **Middle Road Children's Playground** if you have a child, before taking afternoon tea in style at the **Peninsula**. If the queue is too long, the **InterContinental Lobby Lounge** serves tea too, with excellent harbour views. After that bus it north to **Yau Ma Tei**, where you can check out **Tin Hau Temple**, the **Jade Market** and traditional shops along **Shanghai Street**.

> ✕ **Dinner** Temple Street Night Market (p132) for cheap food under the stars.

Kowloon (p128)

 Have your fortune told and catch some Cantonese opera at **Temple Street Night Market**. Then it's on to atmospheric **Butler** for a crafted Japanese cocktail or two.

SAHACHATZ / SHUTTERSTOCK ©

Largo do Senado, Macau

Day Three

Aberdeen & the South (p120)

 Take the bus to Aberdeen for a cruise on the lovely **Aberdeen Harbour**. Follow with shopping (for bargain designer furniture and clothing) at Horizon Plaza on the island of **Ap Lei Chau**. Coffee and cakes are available at several of the furniture shops here. If it's a Saturday, take a boozy tour of Hong Kong's own brewery, **Young Master Ale**.

> **Lunch** Jumbo Kingdom (p125) for dim sum at a 'floating' restaurant.

New Territories (p153)

Make your way from Aberdeen to **Sai Kung** after lunch. Check out Sai Kung Town or hop on a ferry at the waterfront to a nearby **beach** for a late afternoon dip.

> **Dinner** Loaf On (p171) for excellent seafood.

Kowloon (p128)

 If it's a clear night, hit the Ritz Carlton for stellar drinks at **Ozone**, the world's highest bar. If it's cloudy, **Aqua** in Tsim Sha Tsui is a fabulous alternative. After a few drinks, late-night dim sum at **One Dim Sum** may be music to your ears.

Day Four

Macau (p192)

 Hop on an early boat to Macau. When you arrive, take a bus or a cab to the legendary **Long Wa Teahouse**. Have dim sum for breakfast. Buy some tea leaves from them before you go and explore the bustling **Red Market** next door. Have a leisurely stroll to the cultural parts of **Northern Macau Peninsula** to work off your breakfast. Check out the designer shops and the cobbled streets of the atmospheric **St Lazarus District**, and buy a few souvenirs.

> **Lunch** Clube Militar de Macau (p206) for old-school Portuguese dining.

Macau (p192)

Explore the sights around the **Largo do Senado**. Walk along Rua Central through much of the Unesco-listed **Historic Centre of Macau**, including the ruins of the Church of St Paul. Nibble on Portuguese egg tarts and almond cookies as you do so. Then head to lovely **Taipa Village** for a look.

> **Dinner** António (p214) dishes up sumptuous Portuguese classics.

Macau (p192)

 Check out the brand-new **Studio City** casino complex. Try your hand at the tables or just have a drink at the bar. Then head back to Macau Peninsula to catch the ferry back to Hong Kong.

If You Like...

Views

Victoria Peak Pilgrims the world over come here for unbeatable views of the city. (p81)

Sevva A million-dollar view in every sense. (p76)

Tsim Sha Tsui East Promenade Lap up Hong Kong's iconic skyline from the water's edge. (p131)

InterContinental Lobby Lounge Afternoon tea and late-night drinks come with some of the best harbour views in Kowloon. (p146)

High Island Reservoir East Dam Climb the dramatic East Dam to survey this engineering feat and the polygonal rock formations below. (p172)

Tai Long Wan Hiking Trail Gasp and whip out your camera every time a bay comes into view. (p172)

Tai Po Waterfront Park Telescopes at the viewing tower rein in views of the hills and retro factory premises. (p164)

Tai Mo Shan Gaze across the New Territories from Hong Kong's highest mountain. (p158)

Amah Rock Visit the city's all-seeing guardian in Sha Tin for its cross-harbour study of population density. (p168)

Pak Nai Drink in the sunset at this westernmost edge of Hong Kong. (p161)

Traditional Culture

Tai O Visit the stilt-houses in Hong Kong's southwestern corner for a glimpse of the city's fishing culture. (p185)

TUNGCHEUNG / SHUTTERSTOCK ©

View from the Dragon's Back (p60)

Aberdeen & Ap Lei Chau The Water People's culture is palpable at the markets and food stalls, and on dragon boats. (p120)

Walled Villages Dotted around the New Territories, they preserve traces of an agricultural way of life. (p155)

Folk voodoo In full swing every March after the first (mythological) thunder of the year rouses the animal world. (p105)

Cantonese opera The endangered Unesco-listed art is conserved at the Sunbeam and Yau Ma Tei theatres. (p115)

Pok Fu Lam Village This 'urban' village features an old way of life among relics of a dairy and a fire dragon. (p122)

Sheung Wan See some of the last surviving executors of traditional funereal culture in Hong Kong. (p84)

Tsim Sha Tsui TST's little-known side comprises colonial-era recreation clubs and the homes of early Shanghainese migrants. (p135)

North Point Hong Kong's Little Fujian since the turn of the last century. (p107)

Yau Ma Tei Kowloon's grass-roots street culture is still very much alive here. (p138)

Unusual Eats

French toast, Hong Kong–style Popular comfort food, liberally served at *cha chaan tangs* (tea houses). Try it at Sei Yik. (p126)

Snake soup A winter favourite trusted for its warming properties. Served at Ser Wong Fun. (p88)

Oyster omelette A Chiu Chow favourite of gooey shellfish and egg fried in lard until crisp. Served at Chan Kan Kee. (p90)

Cow innards Cheap and nutritious, simmering away in vats of stock behind steamy noodle-shop windows. Try City Hall Maxim's Palace. (p72)

Turtle jelly A mildly bitter concoction of turtle shell and Chinese herbs. Good for skin. Available at Kung Lee. (p93)

Yin Yeung Born of colonialism, the quintessential Hong Kong drink of tea mixed with coffee. Served at Mido Café. (p144)

Stinky Tofu Fermented, bacterium-rich goodness. Smells more pungent than it tastes. Available at Chuen Cheong Foods. (p109)

Roast pigeon 'Rat of the sky' never tasted so good. Find it at Lung Wah Hotel. (p169)

Lui Seng Chun This common bitter drink the colour of wrath will cool your system. Enjoy at Lui Seng Chun. (p140)

Hiking

Tai Long Wan Hiking Trail Emerge from the luxuriant mountains to find the idyllic Tai Long Wan beach. (p172)

Dragon's Back A popular see-the-sea ramble that undulates to the somnolent village of Shek O. (p60)

Lamma Island Take a gentle 4km hike across the leafy island to the embrace of waterside seafood restaurants. (p176)

High Island Reservoir East Dam The only volcanic site of Hong Kong Geopark that humans (and stray cattle) can access on foot. (p172)

Lai Chi Wo Any walk from Wu Kau Tang or Luk Keng passes this ancient Hakka village surrounded by woodlands and mangroves. (p155)

Hong Kong Cemetery Wander through this hilly, overgrown,

For more top Hong Kong spots, see the following:
➡ Eating (p39)
➡ Drinking & Nightlife (p46)
➡ Entertainment (p50)
➡ Shopping (p53)
➡ Sports & Activities (p58)

PLAN YOUR TRIP IF YOU LIKE...

deeply atmospheric resting place of Hong Kong's good and naughty. (p105)

Pok Fu Lam Reservoir to the Peak A picturesque ascent past dense forests, waterfalls and military ruins. (p81)

Ng Tung Chai Waterfall Pack a picnic and aim for the waterfall amid the lush greenery. (p165)

Tai Mo Shan Several hiking trails thread up and around Hong Kong's tallest mountain. (p158)

Chinese Architecture

Man Mo Temple Now dwarfed by skyscrapers, this stunning complex is Hong Kong's most famous temple. (p82)

Tang Clan Ancestral Hall Hong Kong's most magnificent ancestral hall sits in Ping Shan alongside other worthy village structures. (p160)

Tin Hau Temple A fine Tin Hau Temple that has kept much of its original elements, including the elaborate roof ornaments. (p104)

Tsz Shan Monastery An impressive ancient-inspired modern Buddhist complex in Tai Po. (p165)

Chi Lin Nunnery A meticulous modern replica of Tang dynasty Buddhist architecture. (p134)

Colonial Architecture

Former Legislative Council Building The most imposing colonial edifice left in town, though perhaps not the most beautiful. (p70)

Government House Residence of Hong Kong's British governors (1855 to 1997). An elegant, rare Georgian–Japanese hybrid. (p71)

Former Marine Police Headquarters Even blatant commercialism cannot detract from the poise and beauty of this neoclassical monument. (p135)

Tao Fong Shan Christian Centre Christian buildings with Buddhist characteristics designed by a Dane sit on a hill in Shatin. (p168)

Murray House This Victorian confection was moved brick by brick from Central to Stanley. (p123)

Central Police Station & Central Magistracy The stern cousins trace the history of law enforcement in Hong Kong. (p83)

Lui Seng Chun A surprisingly harmonious marriage between a Chinese 'shophouse' and an Italian villa. (p140)

St John's Cathedral Criticised for blighting the colony's landscape when it was first built, today it's a reminder of dear old Blighty. (p70)

Béthanie Two octagonal cow sheds plus a neo-Gothic chapel equal a new performing-art space. (p122)

Parks & Gardens

Victoria Peak Garden The peak above the Peak. This landscaped haven of calm commands untrammelled views. (p85)

Tai Po Waterfront Park A charming park by the Tolo Harbour with picnic lawns and a viewing tower. (p164)

Kowloon Walled City Park The former sin city par excellence reincarnated as a traditional Jiāngnán (southern Yangtze) garden. (p140)

Nan Lian Garden A splendid Tang-style garden at Chi Lin Nunnery, adorned with a pagoda, tea pavilion, koi pond and Buddhist pines. (p134)

Hong Kong Zoological & Botanical Gardens Enveloped by skyscrapers, this stronghold of nature has graced the city since 1871. (p70)

Hong Kong Park A rainforest-like aviary and the city's oldest colonial building lie in this man-made leisure space. (p101)

Ocean Park A huge aquarium and thrilling rides draw families to this highly popular amusement park. (p122)

Middle Road Children's Playground A sprawling park and playground with views of the Tsim Sha Tsui Waterfront. (p138)

Astropark This park appeals to the stargazer within, with Chinese and Western astronomical instruments. (p172)

Kowloon Park An oasis of green off Nathan Rd. (p135)

Month By Month

February

The marquee of clammy clouds may seal up the city in perfect hibernation mode, but nothing can dampen the spirits around Chinese New Year, the most important festival on the cultural calendar.

✨ Chinese New Year

Vast flower markets herald the beginning of this best-loved Chinese festival. Wear red and be blessed at Sik Sik Yuen Wong Tai Sin Temple (p133). Then find a spot by Victoria Harbour (or failing that, a TV) and be awed by fireworks.

✨ Spring Lantern Festival

Lovers are the focus this month as colourful lanterns glowing under the first full moon of the lunar year mark the end of New Year celebrations, and a day known as Chinese Valentine's Day.

✨ Hong Kong Arts Festival

Lasting five to eight weeks, Hong Kong's premier cultural event (p50) scintillates with a feast of music and performing arts, ranging from classical to contemporary, by hundreds of local and international talents.

🏃 Hong Kong Marathon

In 2016, 61,000 athletes competed in this top Asian marathon (www.hkmarathon.com). The annual event also includes a half-marathon, a 10km race and a wheelchair race.

March

Rain and warm weather return, triggering the whirr of dehumidifiers in every home and office – as flowers and umbrellas bloom across the city.

◉ 'Beat the Little Man'

Witness folk sorcery performed by rent-a-curse grannies under the Canal Rd Flyover in Wan Chai or at Yau Ma Tei's Tin Hau Temple. Rapping curses, they pound cut-outs of clients' enemies with a shoe.

✨ Hong Kong International Film Festival

One of Asia's top film festivals, the four-decade-old, two-week-long HKIFF (p51) screens the latest art-house and award-winning movies from Asia and around the world.

◉ Hong Kong Flower Show

For approximately 10 days, Victoria Park turns into a colourful sea of fragrant floral displays as horticulturalists from over 20 countries experiment with their green fingers.

☆ Hong Kong Sevens

Hong Kong's most famous sporting event – and probably its most original – this eternally popular tournament promises fierce competition, as well as a reliable glut of carnivalesque partying from the fans (www.hksevens.com.hk).

⭐ Art Basel

Hong Kong becomes the epicentre of the international art world for three days as the world's top art fair takes the Hong Kong Convention and Exhibition Centre by storm (www.artbasel.com/hong-kong).

May

The city steams up, especially in the urban areas, as the long summer months begin. The first heavy showers of the year cleanse the air as religious celebrations heat up the mood.

⭐ Birthday of Tin Hau

A festival dedicated to the patroness of fisherfolk and one of the harbour city's most popular deities. Key celebrations include a colourful float parade in Yuen Long and traditional rites at the 'Big Temple' in Joss House Bay.

⭐ Cheung Chau Bun Festival

This unique, week-long festival (p191) on Cheung Chau climaxes on Buddha's birthday when children 'float' through the island's narrow lanes dressed up as mythological characters and modern-day politicians, while the more daring townsfolk scramble up bun-studded towers at midnight.

⭐ Buddha's Birthday

Devotees stream to Buddhist monasteries and temples all over the territory on the eighth day of the fourth lunar month to pray to the revered founder of Buddhism and bathe his likenesses with scented water.

⭐ Le French May

Misleadingly named, this celebration of all things Gallic often starts in April and ends in June – so much the better, as it returns with a rich arts program of consistently high quality, plus the obligatory fine food and wine (www.frenchmay.com).

June

The heavens are truly open, the mercury spikes and strong air-conditioning switches on citywide to soothe the nerves of locals and visitors alike.

☆ Dragon Boat Festival

Thousands of the world's strongest dragonboaters meet in Hong Kong over three days of intense racing and partying at Victoria Harbour, while smaller but equally heart-stopping races happen in waterways all over the city.

August

Seven million souls palpitate and perspire in the sweltering heat. Torrential downpours are common but there is always a sun-toasted beach near you in this sprawling archipelago of 260-plus islands.

⭐ Hungry Ghost Festival

Restless spirits take leave from hell to roam the earth during the seventh moon. Hell money, food and earthly luxuries made of papier mâché are burned to propitiate the visitors.

Fascinating folk traditions come alive across the city.

September

Good old summer lingers but the humidity factor starts to recede. Continue to hug the ocean coastlines for free respite as school kids swap their buckets and spades for mighty dunes of homework.

⭐ Mid-Autumn Festival

Pick up a lantern and participate in a moonlit picnic on the 15th night of the eighth lunar month. This family occasion commemorates a 14th-century anti-Mongol uprising with much cheerful munching of the once-subversive 'mooncakes'.

November

At long last Hong Kong mellows. Temperatures sensibly cool down to around 22°C (72°F) and rainfall ceases significantly, much to the delight of ramblers and other countryside merrymakers.

🏃 Oxfam Trailwalker

What began as a fundraising exercise drill by local Ghurkha soldiers in 1981 is today a celebrated endurance test challenging hikers in teams of four to complete the 100km MacLehose Trail in 48 hours (www.oxfamtrailwalker.org.hk).

⭐ Hong Kong International Literary Festival

Held over 10 days in autumn, the festival features

(Top) Chinese New Year celebrations (p29)

(Bottom) Display at the Hong Kong Flower Show (p29)

ANTHONY KWAN / GETTY IMAGES ©

EXPOSE / SHUTTERSTOCK ©

established and emerging writers from around the world. Past authors include luminaries Seamus Heaney and Louis de Bernières (www.festival.org.hk).

🎤 Clockenflap Outdoor Music Festival

Hong Kong's largest outdoor music festival (p51) incorporates international, regional and local live music of a mostly indie variety, as well as art installations and pop-ups. Acts that have played the festival include New Order, The Libertines, A$AP and Primal Scream.

December

Arguably the best time of the year to visit the city. Sunny days and clear blue skies reign. The delightful weather is perfect for all outdoor activities, though brace for the Christmas shopping crowds.

🎤 Hong Kong Winterfest

Rejoice as neon Yuletide murals appear on the Tsim Sha Tsui harbourfront. Ferry across to Statue Sq to see illuminated Christmas trees and fake snow. Join teenage revellers around Times Sq to ring in Christmas day.

☆ Hong Kong International Races

Billed as the Turf World Championships, master horsemen and equine stars from across the planet descend on the beautifully set Sha Tin Racecourse (p169; http://racing.hkjc.com) to do battle. Expect fanatical betting from the 60,000-plus who pack the stands.

With Kids

Hong Kong is a great destination for kids, though the crowds, traffic and pollution might take a little getting used to. Food and sanitation are of a high standard. The city is jam-packed with things to entertain the young ones.

Folklore performance, Ocean Park

Child-Friendly Museums

Hong Kong Science Museum

The three storeys of action-packed displays at Hong Kong's liveliest museum are a huge attraction for toddlers to teens. There's a theatre where staff in lab coats perform wacky experiments. (p136)

Hong Kong Museum of History

This excellent museum brings the city's history to life in visually and aurally colourful ways. Kids will enjoy the 'Hong Kong Story' exhibition with its splendid replicas of local traditions, and a life-sized fishing junk. (p130)

Hong Kong Space Museum & Theatre

Kids eager to test their motor skills will go berserk – there are buttons to push, telescopes to peer through, simulation rides and computer quizzes. Older kids will enjoy the Omnimax films shown on the convex ceiling of the theatre. (p136)

Hong Kong Maritime Museum

Even if the exquisite ship models at this museum don't do the trick, there's plenty to fire junior's imagination – gun-toting pirate mannequins, real treasures salvaged from shipwrecks, a metal diving suit, fog-horn music, a digitised ancient map... (p70)

Hong Kong Railway Museum

Thomas and his friends jolt to life at this open-air museum converted from a historic railway station; it comes complete with old coaches and a train compartment. (p164)

Hong Kong Heritage Museum

Though some youngsters may appreciate the displays, the real gem is the hands-on children's discovery gallery where they can dress up, play puzzle games and enjoy an exhibition of vintage toys. (p168)

Kid-Perfect Parks

Ocean Park

Hong Kong's premier amusement park offers white-knuckle rides, a top-notch aquarium, real giant pandas and a cable-car ride overlooking the sea. (p122)

Hong Kong Park

Ducks, swans and turtles inhabit the ponds here, and the massive forest-like aviary has an elevated walkway that lets visitors move through the tree canopy to spy on the birds. (p101)

Hong Kong Zoological & Botanical Gardens

After a visit to this park, your offspring will have seen the American flamingo, the Burmese python, the two-toed sloth and may even be able to tell a buff-cheeked gibbon from a cheeky child. (p70)

Middle Road Children's Playground

This breezy playground, with swings and slides for all ages, is a utopia of sorts, where you'll see kids of different ethnicities and social classes united in the language of play. (p138)

Hong Kong Wetland Park

Patience may be required for appreciation of the wetland habitats, but not for the themed exhibition galleries, the theatre and 'Swamp Adventure' play facility. (p160)

Kowloon Park

This large verdant venue has plenty of running room, lakes with waterfowl, two playgrounds, swimming pools and an aviary. (p135)

Hong Kong Disneyland

The latest attraction at this famous theme park is Toy Story Land. (p180)

Tips for Visiting Theme Parks

Here are some tips if you're visiting Ocean Park (p122) or Disneyland (p180) with young ones in tow.

Practicalities

➡ Both parks are extremely popular with mainland Chinese tourists. For a quieter visit, avoid Chinese public holidays, in particular Labour Day (1 May) and the ensuing two days,

NEED TO KNOW

➡ **La Leche League Hong Kong** (☑Caroline 852 6492 7606, Jenny 852 2987 7792, Molly 852 5303 6164; www. lll-hk.org) English-speaking breastfeeding support group.

➡ **Nursing rooms** Available in large malls and most museums.

➡ **Rent-a-Mum** (☑852 2523 4868; www.rent-a-mum.com; per hr from HK$180) Babysitting for a minimum of four hours.

➡ **In Safe Hands** (☑852 2323 2676, 852 9820 3363; www.insafehands.com. hk; per hr from HK$280, plus transport costs) Childcare agency that provides full-time and part-time nanny services, and evening babysitting (minimum four hours).

National Day holidays (1 to 7 October), Ching Ming Festival in April, and Chinese New Year in January or February. The summer months of July and August are also very busy.

➡ At the weekend, Sunday is slightly less busy than Saturday.

➡ Some of the rides have height restrictions.

➡ There's plenty of decent Chinese and Western food at both parks.

Ocean Park

➡ Most teens and grown-ups will prefer Ocean Park to Disneyland; it's much bigger, has a lot more to offer, and the rides are more intense.

➡ Ocean Park consists of two parts – Waterfront near the entrance, and Summit on the headland. You can't walk between the two, but you can take the scenic Cable Car or the subterranean Ocean Express train. The former is busiest in the morning and just before closing. To avoid long lines, take the Ocean Express up and the Cable Car down.

➡ Younger children may like Whisker's Harbour, the age-appropriate play area, and Pacific Pier where they can look at and feed seals and sea lions. Note that it may seem like a lovely idea but animal welfare groups suggest interaction with sea mammals held in captivity creates stress for these creatures.

Disneyland

➡ Though Hong Kong Disneyland is comparatively small, do bring a stroller if you have one. It's great for moving tired kids around and stowing your bags. It's stroller-friendly with parking near the rides. The park also has a limited number of strollers for rent.

➡ There are lockers on Main Street, USA, where many of the shops are located.

➡ Fantasyland is by far the best for the very young set. Here's where you'll find Dumbo, Mad Hatter's Teacups, It's a Small World and the Many Adventures of Winnie the Pooh.

➡ The highly popular Toy Story Land and Grizzly Gulch usually have the longest lines.

➡ Taking the train on Disneyland Railroad is nice if you're tired, but remember that seats are few. Also it does not take you all the way around the park. There are two stops – at the entrance and in Fantasyland.

➡ There's no need to stake out a position to watch the fireworks that come on at 8pm, unless you're looking to take awesome photos. On the other hand, watching near the entrance will allow a quick exit.

➡ Going to Disneyland in the afternoon may let you make flexible use of your time and avoid long lines. The park also takes on a special magic in the twilight hours (6pm to 9pm). For example, the Jungle Cruise ride becomes a 'night safari', the Orbitron flying saucers at Tomorrowland are lit up and the constellation globe and the planets will be twinkling with fibre-optic stars.

Boats & Trams

Peak Tram

Children may be fascinated by the ride on the gravity-defying Peak Tram. (p70)

Star Ferry

Cruise liner, barge, hydrofoil, fishing junk... Your mini-mariner will have a blast naming passing vessels, as their own tugboat nimbly dodges the swipes of a gigantic dragon in tempestuous Victoria Harbour. (p69)

Trams

Looking out the window on the top deck of a narrow vehicle that rattles, clanks and sways amid heavy traffic can be exhilarating.

MTR

The metro is interestingly colour-coded and full of myths and features of interest.

Symphony of Lights

Children will be awestruck by the dance of laser beams projected from skyscrapers on both sides of the harbour, to accompanying music. Bring the Darth Vader costume.

Shopping with Kids

Horizon Plaza (p127) has megastores selling kids' books and clothing. Tai Yuen St is known for traditional toy shops catering to youngsters of all ages.

For dozens of outlets dedicated to children, head to the ground floor of Ocean Terminal (p137) at Harbour City, level 2 of **Festival Walk** (又一城; www.festivalwalk.com.hk; 80-88 Tat Chee Ave, Kowloon Tong; ⊙11am-10pm; MKowloon Tong, exit C), level 9 of Times Square (p118) or level 2 of Elements mall (p152).

Dolphin-Watching

See the second-smartest animal on earth in the wild – and it's in bubble-gum pink! Hong Kong Dolphinwatch runs three four-hour tours a week to waters where Chinese white dolphins may be sighted. (p152)

Ice Skating

Elements (p152), Festival Walk (p34) and **Cityplaza** (太古城; ☑852 2568 8665; www. cityplaza.com.hk; 18 Tai Koo Shing Rd, Tai Koo Shing, Quarry Bay; MTai Koo, exit D2) malls have indoor ice rinks. Check the websites for the latest rates and opening hours.

Like a Local

Certain values and habits permeate everyday life in Hong Kong, but while they're prevalent, your experience of the city's cultural mores depends on the locals who cross your path – not everyone is the same. Here are some tips to help you navigate the social seas of this metropolis.

Dim sum restaurant (p36)

Cultural Etiquette

Greetings

Some locals find hugging and cheek kissing too intimate; others secretly wish for more. Generally speaking, a simple 'Hello, how are you?' and a light handshake will do. Remove your shoes before entering someone's home.

Face

The cornerstone of human relations in this part of the world. Think status and respect: be courteous and never lose your temper in public.

Gifts

If you present someone with a gift, they may appear reluctant for fear of seeming greedy, but insist and they'll give in. Don't be surprised if they don't unwrap a gift in front of you, though; to do so is traditionally considered impolite.

Dining Out

Most Hong Kongers like to 'go Dutch' when dining out with friends. The usual practice is to split the bill evenly, rather than for each person to pay for what they ordered, or asking for separate cheques.

Colours

Red symbolises good luck, happiness and wealth (though writing in red can convey anger and unfriendliness). White is the colour of death in Chinese culture, so think twice before giving white flowers or attending an elderly person's birthday celebration in white.

Table Manners

Sanitary Consumption

Dishes are meant to be shared at Chinese meals. Expensive eateries provide serving chopsticks or spoons with each dish; most budget places don't, but you can ask for them.

Mind Your Chopsticks

Don't stand your chopsticks upright in the middle of a bowl – that resembles two incense sticks at a graveside offering. Nearly all restaurants have forks; don't be afraid to ask for one.

Spirit of Sharing

Take a few pieces of food from a communal dish at a time, preferably those nearest to you. It is not necessary to shove half the dish into your bowl in one go. For shared staples, it is fine to fill your whole bowl up.

Tea Language

When someone refills your dainty teacup, you can tap two fingers (index and middle) gently on the table twice instead of saying thank you with your mouth stuffed. Mastering this (allegedly) centuries-old gesture will endear you to your hosts.

Bones & Tissues

Your plate is the preferred spot for bones, but at budget places diners put them on the table beside their plates or bowls. If you find that disconcerting, place a tissue under or over your rejects.

Food Obsessions

Swallow & Scribe

Legions of food critics, amateur or otherwise, post reports and photos on the user-driven, bilingual restaurant-review website www.openrice.com every day.

Dim Sum – a Fact of Life

Morning dim sum is a daily ritual for many retirees and a tasty excuse for a family reunion at the weekend. Now family and food vie for attention with smartphones.

Tea Break

When mid-afternoon comes, *cha chaan tangs* (tea houses) are full of elderly folks debating the morning's meat prices and stock-market fluctuations. These holes-in-the-wall function as community focal points for the aged and housewives to swap gossip and commentary. They're also boltholes for many a stressed office worker.

Late-Night Sweets

After dinner, locals like to head to a dessert shop for sweet soups and other Chinese-style or fusion desserts, such as black sesame soup and durian crepes.

Steamy Winter

In winter a hotpot at a *dai pai dong* (food stall) or even a restaurant is a soul-warming, convivial experience. Dip slivers of meat, seafood and vegetables in a vat of steaming broth. Consume and repeat.

Local 'Hoods

Full-scale gentrification has yet to arrive in these areas, but urban development is already changing their character.

Aberdeen & Ap Lei Chau

Go on a boat-ride in the city's most famous typhoon shelter, watch the dragon boat races, and explore the markets and temples of Hong Kong's 'People of the Water'. (p120)

Yau Ma Tei

Stroll Shanghai St for traditional barbers, Chinese wedding costume–makers and artisans of other time-honoured crafts.

Sham Shui Po

Find flea markets, 1930s shophouses, post-war housing estates and even an ancient tomb in this resilient working-class district.

Queen's Road West

The pungent smells of dried seafood and Chinese herbal medicine lead you into this parade of industrious small traders.

Money Matters

Jockey Club

Step into any Jockey Club off-course betting centre (often found in public housing estates, near markets or in transport terminals) on any race day or night, and you'll be assailed by a maelstrom of emotions as punters struggle to defy the odds. Occasionally you'll hear a squeal of joy, but more often than not invective peppers deep sighs of desperation as numerals streak across the TV screens every 30 minutes. Outside, high rollers squat on the pavement en masse, heads buried in race cards, in search of the forever elusive winning formula.

Stocks & Shares

Similarly, look out for the hole-in-the-wall brokerage firms on any weekday and you'll find crowds of (not all small-time) investors deeply engrossed in the live stock-market updates on the wall-mounted panels.

For Free

Hong Kong is not a cheap place to visit and prices creep up at every opportunity, as any local can testify. But with a bit of planning and some imagination, you can still indulge yourself for little money.

Hong Kong Heritage Museum

Museums & Galleries: Free on Wednesdays

Hong Kong Museum of Art
A treasure trove of Hong Kong and Chinese art. (p135)

Hong Kong Museum of History
A good place to get context for what you see during your stay. (p130)

Hong Kong Heritage Museum
Featuring exhibits on folk traditions, the life of Bruce Lee and Cantonese opera. (p168)

Hong Kong Science Museum
The basics of physics, chemistry and biology made fun and for kids. (p136)

Hong Kong Space Museum
Kids will enjoy seeing how celestial bodies roll. The Space Theatre is not free. (p136)

Museum of Coastal Defence
A museum next to a fort detailing Hong Kong's coastal defence over six centuries. (p107)

Dr Sun Yat-Sen Museum
Dedicated to the man sometimes called Father of Modern China. (p85)

Museums & Galleries: Free Always

Museum of Tea Ware
An elegant showcase of vintage tea ware inside Hong Kong Park. (p101)

Railway Museum
Featuring Hong Kong's railway history with disused train carriages for the kids. (p164)

Para Site
Long-standing indie institution focusing on art with a social bent, now in North Point. (p105)

SORBIS / SHUTTERSTOCK ©

Blindspot Gallery

Specialising in showing the works of Hong Kong and Asian **photographers** (刺點畫廊; Map p312, D1; ☎852 2517 6238; www.blindspotgallery.com; 15th fl, Po Chai Industrial Bldg, 28 Wong Chuk Hang Rd, Aberdeen; ⊙10am–6pm Tue-Sat, by appointment only Sun & Mon; ☒70, 90, 590, 72, 42, 38).

PMQ

Locally designed homeware, fashion and an exhibition or two. (p83)

Tours

Asia Society Hong Kong Centre

A former explosives magazine that stages top-notch exhibitions. (p102)

Heritage of Mei Ho House Museum

Shows the development of public housing in Hong Kong with photos and replicas. (p140)

Tai O Heritage Hotel

This former police station guarded the coast against pirates. (p227)

Tsz Shan Monastery

An elegant antiquity-inspired modern Buddhist monastery. Access only by tour. (p165)

Lui Seng Chun

An old building with a Chinese medicine clinic. Access only by tour. (p140)

Festivals & Events

Dragon Boat Races

Dragon boat racing against a backdrop of decorated fishing junks. (p30, p59)

Hungry Ghost Festival

Elaborate rites to appease roaming spirits in the seventh lunar month when the gates of hell are believed to be open. (p30)

Fire Dragon Dance

A smoky dance by a straw dragon stuck with glowing incense sticks during the Mid-Autumn Festival on the 15th night of the eighth lunar month.

Cheung Chau Bun Festival

Modern reenactment of a Qing ritual where climbers scramble up bun towers and try to pocket as many buns as possible. (p191)

Freespace Happening

Monthly kaleidoscope of live music, film, dance, parkour and handicrafts (www.westkowloon.hk/en/freespacehappening).

Nature Escape

Hills

Hike, cycle or take long walks in Hong Kong's beautiful countryside.

Beaches

Hong Kong's beaches come with lifeguards; just bring sunblock and beer.

Hong Kong street-food scene

 **Eating**

One of the world's most delicious cities, Hong Kong offers culinary excitement whwether you're spending HK$20 on a bowl of noodles or HK$2000 on a seafood feast. The best of China is well represented, be it Cantonese, Shanghainese, Northern or Sichuanese. Similarly, the smorgasbord of non-Chinese – French, Italian, Spanish, Japanese, Thai, Indian – is the most diverse in all of Asia.

NEED TO KNOW

Opening Hours

➡ Lunch 11am–3pm

➡ Dinner 6pm–11pm

Some restaurants are open through the afternoon, while others are also open for breakfast. Most restaurants open on Sunday and close for at least two days during the Lunar New Year.

Price Ranges

The prices below are based on a two-course meal with a drink.

$	Less than HK$200
$$	HK$200–500
$$$	More than HK$500

Reservations

Most restaurants (midrange or above) take reservations. At very popular addresses booking is crucial, especially for weekend dinners. Popular restaurants may serve two or even three seatings a night.

How Much?

HK$40 will buy you noodles and some greens, or a set meal at a fast-food chain.

A sit-down lunch in a midrange restaurant costs at least HK$80, and dinner HK$150. Dinner at upmarket restaurants will set you back at least HK$600.

Many restaurants in Central have lunch specials.

Tipping

Tipping is not a must as every bill includes a 10% service charge, but this almost always goes into the owner's coffers, so if you're happy with the service, tip as you see fit. Most people leave behind the small change.

Cantonese Cuisine

The dominant cuisine in Hong Kong is Cantonese and it's easily the best in the world. Many of China's top chefs fled to the territory around 1949; it was therefore here and not in its original home, Guǎngzhōu, that Cantonese cuisine flourished.

This style of cooking is characterised by an insistence on freshness. Seafood restaurants display tanks full of finned and shelled creatures enjoying their final moments. Flavours are delicate and balanced, obtained through restrained use of seasoning and light-handed cooking techniques such as steaming and quick stir-frying.

REGIONAL VARIETIES

Cantonese cuisine refers to the culinary styles of Guǎngdōng province, as well as Chiu Chow (Cháozhōu) and Hakka cuisines. Chiu Chow dishes reflect a penchant for seafood and condiments. Deep-fried soft-boned fish comes with tangerine oil; braised goose with a vinegar and garlic dip. Hakka cuisine is known for its saltiness and use of preserved meat. Salt-baked chicken and pork stewed with preserved vegetables fed many hungry families and famished workers back in leaner times.

MODERNISATION

Hong Kong's chefs are also an innovative bunch who'll seize upon new ingredients and find wondrous ways of using them. For example, dim sum has expanded to include mango pudding, and shortbread tarts stuffed with abalone and chicken. Black truffles – the kind you see on French or Italian menus – are sometimes sprinkled on rolled rice sheets and steamed. And it works.

Dining Local

DIM SUM

Dim sum are Cantonese tidbits consumed with tea for breakfast or lunch. The term literally means 'to touch the heart' and the act of eating dim sum is referred to as yum cha, meaning 'to drink tea'.

In the postwar period, yum cha was largely an activity of single males, who met over their breakfast tea to socialise or exchange tips about job-seeking. Soon yum cha became a family activity.

Each dish, often containing two to four morsels steamed in a bamboo basket, is meant to be shared. In old-style dim-sum places, just stop the waiter and choose something from the cart. Modern venues give you an order slip, but it's almost always in Chinese only. However, as dim sum dishes are often ready-made, the waiters should be able to show you samples to choose from.

SOY SAUCE WESTERN

'Soy sauce Western' (si yau sai chaan) features Western-style dishes prepared with a large dollop of wisdom from the Chinese

Above: Wonton noodles

Right: Ap Lei Chau Market Cooked Food Centre (p124)

kitchen. It's said to have emerged in the 1940s when the ingenious chef of Tai Ping Koon decided to 'improve' on Western cooking by tweaking recipes, such as replacing dairy products with local seasoning – lactose intolerance is common among East Asians – and putting rice on the menu.

His invention met its soulmate in White Russians, who had fled to Shànghǎi after the Bolshevik Revolution and sought refuge in Hong Kong in 1949; they soon cooked up what's known as Shanghainese–Russian food.

The two schools of Western-inspired cuisine offered affordable and 'exotic' dining to locals at a time when authentic Western eateries catered almost exclusively to expatriates. Eventually the two styles mingled, spawning soy sauce Western as we know it today. Popular dishes include Russian borscht, baked pork chop over fried rice and beef stroganoff with rice.

CHA CHAAN TANG

Teahouses (茶餐廳, *cha chaan tangs*) are cheap and cheery neighbourhood eateries that appeared in the 1940s serving Western-style snacks and drinks to those who couldn't afford Earl Grey and cucumber sandwiches. Their menus have since grown to include more substantial Chinese and soy sauce Western dishes.

Some teahouses have bakeries creating European pastries with Chinese characteristics, such as pineapple buns (菠蘿包, *bo law bao*), which don't contain a trace of the said fruit; and cocktail buns, which have coconut stuffing (雞尾包, *gai may bao*).

Dai Pai Dongs

A *dai pai dong* (大牌檔) is a food stall, hawker-style or built into a rickety hut crammed with tables and stools that sometimes spill out onto the pavement. After WWII the colonial government issued food-stall licences to the families of injured or deceased civil servants. The licences were big so the stalls came to be known as *dai pai dong* (meaning 'big licence stalls').

Dai pai dong can spring up anywhere: by the side of a slope, in an alley or under a tree. That said, these vintage places for trillion-star dining are fast vanishing; most have now been relocated to government-run, cooked-food centres.

The culinary repertoire of *dai pai dong* varies from stall to stall. One may specialise in congee while its neighbour whips up seafood dishes that give restaurants a run for their money. In places where there's a cluster of *dai pai dong*, you can order dishes from different operators.

International Cuisine

From monkfish-liver sushi to French molecular cuisine, Hong Kong has no shortage of great restaurants specialising in the food of other cultures. The variety and quality of Asian cuisines is outstanding, surpassing even that of Tokyo. Then there's the exceptional array of Western options. Hong Kong's affluent and cosmopolitan population loves Western food, especially European. This is evidenced by the number of international celebrity chefs with restaurants here, such as Joël Robuchon and Pierre Gagnaire. Prices at these and other

---

HOW HONG KONGERS EAT

Many busy Hong Kongers take their breakfast and lunch at tea cafes. A full breakfast at these places consists of buttered toast, fried eggs and spam, instant noodles and a drink. The more health-conscious might opt for congee, with dim sum of rolled rice sheets (*chéung fán*) and steamed dumplings with pork and shrimp *(siù máai)*.

Lunch for office workers can mean a bowl of wonton noodles, a plate of rice with Chinese barbecue or something more elaborate.

Afternoon tea is popular at the weekends. On weekdays it is the privilege of labourers and ladies of leisure (*tai-tais*). Workers are said to vanish, Cinderella fashion, at 3.15pm sharp for their daily fix of egg tarts and milk tea. For *tai-tais*, tea could mean scones with rose-petal jam with friends or a bowl of noodles at the hairdresser's.

Dinner is the biggest meal of the day. If prepared at home, what's on the table depends on the traditions of the family, but usually there's soup, rice, veggies and a meat or fish dish. Everyone has their own bowl of rice and/or soup, with the rest of the dishes placed in the middle of the table for sharing. Dining out is also extremely common, with many families eating out three to five times a week.

VEGGIES BEWARE

There are 101 ways to accidentally eat meat in Hong Kong. A plate of greens is probably cooked in meat stock and served with oyster sauce. Broth made with chicken is a prevalent ingredient, even in dishes where no meat is visible. In budget restaurants, chicken powder is used liberally. The safe bet for vegetarians wanting to go Chinese is to patronise vegetarian eateries or upmarket establishments.

top addresses can be steep, but there's also a burgeoning number of excellent eateries specialising in rustic French or Italian that cater to food lovers with medium-sized pockets.

Cooking Courses

Hong Kong is a good place to hone your skills in the art of Chinese cookery. Try these:

Home's Cooking (www.homescookingstudio. com; classes HK$600) This highly rated cooking class, run out of the owner's home, offers three-hour morning or afternoon sessions. Students cook a three-course Chinese meal: think spring rolls, lotus-leaf chicken and ginger pudding. Classes include a trip to a local wet market and lunch or dinner.

Martha Sherpa (p119) Expert Cantonese home-cook Martha Sherpa (her last name comes from her Nepali husband) has taught the likes of former Australian PM Julia Gillard how to cook dim sum and Hong Kong favourites. Small group classes cover topics like wok cookery, dim sum and vegetarian Chinese. Half-day, full-day and evening classes are available.

Publications

The popular website Open Rice (www.open rice.com) has restaurant reviews penned by the city's armchair gourmands.

Time Out (www.timeout.com.hk) An authoritative fortnightly guide and listings of what's on.

Good Eating (www.scmp.com) The restaurant guide and directory of a local English-language newspaper.

WOM Guide (www.womguide.com) A guide to the city's dining scene.

Self-Catering

The two major supermarket chains, **Park'N'Shop** (www.parknshop.com) and **Wellcome** (www.wellcome.com.hk), have megastores that offer groceries as well as takeaway cooked food.

Eating by Neighbourhood

➜ **Hong Kong Island: Central** Power lunch spots for business wheelers and dealers, plus international food of all stripes.

➜ **Hong Kong Island: the Peak & the Northwest** Tourist traps around the Peak give way to low-key local spots further west.

➜ **Hong Kong Island: Wan Chai & the Northeast** Everything from the world's best *char siu* (roast pork) to ultra-authentic sushi in Hong Kong's foodie heart.

➜ **Hong Kong Island: Aberdeen & the South** Laid-back beach cafes and British-style pubs dot the island's sunny south side.

➜ **Kowloon** Cheap Indian dives sit next to glittering Cantonese banquet halls along Kowloon's screaming neon boulevards.

MEGAN EAVES / LONELY PLANET ©

Steamed pork buns (dim sum; p40)

Lonely Planet's Top Choices

Choi's Kitchen (p111) Claypot rice with choice ingredients and Cantonese dishes prepared with heart.

Kam's Roast Goose (p108) The crispiest, juiciest roast goose in the territory.

Fortune Kitchen (p111) Cantonese homecooking refined but still affordable.

Aberdeen Fish Market Yee Hope Seafood Restaurant (p124) Seafood feast inside a wholesale fish market.

Atum Desserant (p110) Delicious desserts presented as paintings right before you.

Lung King Heen (p74) Exquisite dim sum, pristine service and sweeping harbour views.

Best by Budget

$

Sun Kwai Heung (p112) Excellent low-key Cantonese barbecue.

Tai Cheong Bakery (p87) Serving Hong Kong's favorite egg tarts for half a century.

$$

Fortune Kitchen (p111) Cantonese soul food done right.

Choi's Kitchen (p111) Masterful take on claypot rice and common Cantonese.

$$$

Seventh Son (p109) Top-notch dim sum and Cantonese fare.

Chairman (p91) Perfectly executed Cantonese classics.

Best for Dim Sum

City Hall Maxim's Palace (p72) The most famous of Hong Kong's dim-sum palaces.

Seventh Son (p109) An excellent Fook Lam Moon spin-off.

Luk Yu Tea House (p89) This venerable teahouse was once an artist's haunt.

Lin Heung Tea House (p72) Old-school cart dim sum in no-frills setting.

Tim Ho Wan, the Dim Sum Specialists (p72) The first-ever budget dim-sum place to earn a Michelin star.

Fook Lam Moon (p143) Celeb haunt with swanky menu but reasonably priced dim sum.

Best for Noodles

Ho To Tai Noodle Shop (p161) Shrimp-filled wonton noodles earn a devoted following.

Tasty Congee & Noodle Wonton Shop (p72) Shrimp wontons, prawn congee and more in luxe IFC mall.

Mak's Noodle (p88) Beloved shrimp-wonton shop with multiple locations.

Ho Hung Kee (p110) Making noodles, wontons and congee for 68 years.

Best for Seafood

Aberdeen Fish Market Yee Hope Seafood Restaurant (p124) Seafood in a wholesale fish market; preordering required.

Ap Lei Chau Market Cooked Food Centre (p124) Seafood you buy from the market below is prepared here.

Lei Yue Mun (p146) Seafood village drawing crowds.

Loaf On (p171) Low-key but high-end seafood in seaside village of Sai Kung.

Chuen Kee Seafood Restaurant (p171) Classic seafood palace on Sai Kung waterfront.

Sam Shing Hui Seafood Market (p159) Bustling working seafood market in New Territories.

Best for Non-Cantonese Asian

Din Tai Fung (p142) Prepare to queue for soup dumplings at this wildly popular Taiwanese chain.

Chicken HOF & Soju Korean (p141) Shockingly good spicy Korean-style fried chicken.

Spring Deer (p142) This old-timer of northern Chinese cooking always delivers.

Woodlands (p141) Join South Asian families here for hearty South Indian vegetarian.

Best Dai Pai Dongs

Sing Kee (p72) One of few surviving *dai pai dong* (food stalls) in Central.

Gi Kee Seafood Restaurant (p112) Gourmet seafood above a wet market.

Sei Yik (p126) Queues form for breakfast toast at this half-hidden Stanley mainstay.

Ap Lei Chau Market Cooked Food Centre (p124) Where the fisherfolk hang out.

Best Teahouses

Australia Dairy Company (p144) Beloved for fab egg sandwiches and brusque service.

Lan Fong Yuen (p88) *The* place to sample Hong Kong's famous milk tea.

Capital Cafe (p109) Fluffy eggs and spam noodles draw crowds.

Mido Café (p144) A charmingly retro spot overlooking the Tin Hau temple.

Best for Vegetarian

Pure Veggie House (p108) Standout veggie dim sum and Cantonese classics.

Chi Lin Vegetarian (p145) Delightful Buddhist cuisine in a gorgeous nunnery.

Queen of the East (p45) A lower-price version of Pure Veggie House.

Woodlands (p141) The South Indian vegetarian dishes here are a perennial favourite.

Bookworm Cafe (p178) Beloved hippie haunt on laid-back Lamma.

Best for Sweets

Atum Desserant (p110) Confectionary presented as art.

Master Low Key Food Shop (p113) Arguably the town's best eggettes.

Yuen Kee Dessert (p91) Glutinous Cantonese confections.

Tai Cheong Bakery (p87) The ultimate in Hong Kong egg tarts.

Honeymoon Dessert (p171) HK-based chain serving up sweet soups and icy treats.

Best for Southeast Asian

Cheong Fat (p145) Chiang Mai noodles in Hong Kong's Little Bangkok.

Chom Chom (p90) Trendy Vietnamese and cocktails next to a slope.

Bêp (p89) Vietnamese classics in stylish Soho.

Chachawan (p89) Thai street-food-hipster style.

Best Dining Away from the Crowds

Rainbow Seafood (p179) A rainbow of fish and crustaceans at the end of Lamma's Family Trail hike.

Black Sheep (p126) Eclectic hippie cafe down a quiet back alley in beachside Shek O.

Chi Lin Vegetarian (p145) Veggie cuisine on the grounds of a stunningly landscaped nunnery.

Yue Kee Roasted Goose (p158) Primo roast goose in a far-flung village.

Mavericks (p185) A chill beachfront cafe on the Lantau coast.

Best English-Language Food Blogs

That Food Cray (www.thatfood cray.com)

Sassy Hong Kong (www.sassy hongkong.com)

E-Ting (www.e-tingfood.com)

Food Craver (www.foodcraver.hk)

Hungry Hong Kong (http://hungryhk.blogspot.hk)

Best for Spicy Food

Megan's Kitchen (p109) Sìchuān hot pot has a real kick.

San Xi Lou (p108) Well-regarded Sìchuān in a Mid-Levels tower building.

Cheong Fat (p145) Spicy Thai in Little Bangkok neighborhood.

Woodlands (p141) Sweat-producing veggie Indian.

Best for Japanese

Sogo (p111) Decadent Japanese food hall.

Go Ya Yakitori (p111) Tasty skewers in trendy Tai Hang.

Inagiku (p75) Sumptuous sushi, grilled meat and tempura in the Four Seasons.

Best for French

Bistronomique (p92) Yummy down-home Gallic specialities.

Upper Modern Bistro (p91) Fine Asian-inspired French in a chic setting.

Serge et le Phoque (p110) Creative modern French cooking opposite a wet market.

Pierre (p75) Big-name, Michelin-star French cuisine.

Best for Italian (or New York Italian)

Otto e Mezzo Bombana (p75) Considered by many the finest Italian in Hong Kong.

Motorino (p88) Crowds feast on killer Neapolitan-style pizza at this hip New York import.

Grissini (p110) Worthy veteran in Hong Kong's fine Italian dining scene.

Best for North American

Beef & Liberty (p108) Solid North American fare in Wan Chai.

Mavericks (p185) Eco- and health-conscious burgers and sausages in Lantau.

Flying Pan (p89) Breakfast in Soho at any time of the day.

Drinking & Nightlife

Energetic Hong Kong knows how to party and does so visibly and noisily. Drinking venues run the gamut from British-style pubs through hotel bars and hipster hang-outs, to karaoke bolt-holes aimed at a young Chinese clientele. The last few years have seen a heartening surge in the number of wine bars and live-music venues, catering to a diverse, discerning and fun-loving population.

Wine & Whisky Bars

A growing number of bars are dedicated to connoisseurship of whisky, gin or other spirits. Expect hand-carved ice, obscure bottles and nerdily expert bartenders.

Another recent trend is whisky drinking, and a growing number of bars are devoted to savouring the amber liquid, including a couple of stylish Japanese whisky bars.

Cafes

Though still dominated by Starbucks and Pacific Coffee (essentially Hong Kong's home-grown Starbucks), Hong Kong has lately sprouted a very decent independent coffee-house scene, complete with organic beans, micro-roasters and cupping events.

Cha Chaan Tang

Teahouses (茶餐廳; *cha chaan tangs*) are perhaps best known for their Hong Kong-style 'pantyhose' milk tea (奶茶; *nai cha*) – a strong brew made from a blend of several types of black tea with crushed egg shells thrown in for silkiness. It's filtered through a fabric that hangs like a stocking, hence the name, and drunk with evaporated milk. 'Pantyhose' milk tea is sometimes mixed with three parts coffee to create the quintessential Hong Kong drink, tea-coffee or *yin yeung* (鴛鴦), meaning 'mandarin duck', a symbol of matrimonial harmony.

Karaoke

Karaoke clubs are as popular as ever with the city's young citizens, with a sprinkling of clubs in Causeway Bay and Wan Chai, and local dives in Mong Kok. The aural wallpaper at these clubs is most often Canto-pop covers, compositions that often blend Western rock or pop with Chinese melodies and lyrics, but there is usually a limited selection of 'golden oldies' and pop in English.

Dance

SALSA

Hong Kong's salsa community holds weekly club nights that are open to anyone in need of a good time. Check out www.dancetrinity.com or www.hongkong-salsa.com. The annual **Hong Kong Salsa Festival** (香港沙沙節; www.hksalsafestival.com; ◷Mar), held around February, features participants from the world over. The website has details of events including the after-parties.

SWING

If you like swing, there are socials with live jazz bands (and sometimes free beginners' class) at least six times a month. The calendar on www.hongkongswings.com has more.

TANGO

Hong Kong has a small but zealous community of tango dancers, usually white-collar workers, professionals and expats. Tango Tang (www.tangotang.com), the most prominent of all the schools, has all tango events, including those by other organisers, posted on its website. You can join any of the many *milongas* (dance parties) held every week at restaurants and dance studios all over town.

Happy Hour

During certain hours of the day, most pubs, bars and even certain clubs give discounts on drinks (usually from a third to half off) or offer two-for-one deals.

Happy hour is usually in the late afternoon or early evening – 4pm to 8pm, say – but times vary widely from place to place. Depending on the season, the day of the week and the location, some happy hours run from noon until as late as 10pm, and some start up again after midnight.

LGBT Hong Kong

While Hong Kong's gay scene may not have the vibrancy or visibility of cities like Sydney, it has made huge strides in recent years and now counts more than two dozen gay bars and clubs.

Useful resources include the following:

Dim Sum (http://dimsum-hk.com) A free, monthly gay magazine with listings.

Les Peches (☑852 9101 8001; lespechesinfo@ yahoo.com) Hong Kong's premier lesbian organisation has monthly events for lesbians, bisexual women and their friends.

Utopia Asia (www.utopia-asia.com/hkbars.htm) A website with listings of gay-friendly venues and events in town.

Drinking & Nightlife by Neighbourhood

➡ **Hong Kong Island: Central** Imbibe in the plush environs of a hotel bar.

➡ **Hong Kong Island: The Peak & the Northwest** The epicentre of Hong Kong's partying scene attracts trendsetters, professionals and expats.

➡ **Hong Kong Island: Wan Chai & the Northeast** A delicious cocktail of the classy, the hidden and the hip alongside hostess bars from another era.

➡ **Hong Kong Island: Aberdeen & the South** Options are slim as we head south, but bring a bottle to the waterfront and you have your own party.

➡ **Kowloon** Waterholes with a local flavour abound in Tsim Sha Tsui.

NEED TO KNOW

Opening Hours

➡ Bars open noon or 6pm and stay open until 2am to 6am; Wan Chai bars stay open the latest.

➡ Cafes usually open between 8am and 11am and close between 5pm and 11pm.

Price Ranges

➡ Beer from HK$45 per pint

➡ Wine from HK$50 per glass

➡ Whisky from HK$50 per shot

➡ Cocktails HK$80–200

➡ Cover charge for dance clubs HK$200–700 (including one drink)

Dress Code

Smart casual is usually good enough for most clubs, but patrons wearing shorts and flip-flops will not be admitted. Jeans are popular in Hong Kong and these are sometimes worn with heels or a blazer for a more put-together look. Hong Kong's clubbers can be style-conscious, so dress to impress!

How Much?

It's not especially cheap to drink in Hong Kong. An all-night boozy tour of the city's drinking landscape can set you back at least HK$800. That said, it's possible to cut corners while still soaking up the atmosphere – lots of youngsters do that. Buy your drinks from a convenience store and hang out with the revellers standing outside the bars. The alley near a convenience store in Soho is called 'Cougar Alley' for a reason

Latest Information

➡ **Time Out** (www.timeout.com.hk)

Lonely Planet's Top Choices

Ping Pong Gintoneria (p95) Gin swigging in a former ping-pong hall.

Tai Lung Fung (p113) Cocktails and old-fashioned flamboyance.

MO Bar (p75) Keep your eyes peeled for Cantopop stars.

Executive Bar (p114) Exclusive whisky and cocktail bar where you can catch serious Japanese mixology in action.

Club 71 (p92) Where all the activists, artists, musicians and the socially conscious go to rant and revel.

Best for Views

Sevva (p76) See (both beautiful people and a beautiful harbour) and be seen atop the Prince's Building.

Ozone (p147) Head up to the highest bar in Asia.

Ben's Back Beach Bar (p126) Overlooking a deserted Shek O beach.

Sugar (p115) Dizzying views from atop an Island East hotel.

Intercontinental Lobby Lounge (p146) Floor-to-ceiling glass overlooks Victoria Harbour.

Best for Cocktails

Butler (p146) Japanese cocktail bar in quiet part of TST.

Executive Bar (p114) It's appointment-only at this swanky whisky lounge.

Bar 42 (p94) Expats and locals mix it up with board games.

Tai Lung Fung (p92) Charming retro setting awash in pink neon light.

Ping Pong Gintoneria (p95) Gin-based concoctions in an old ping-pong hall.

Quinary (p92) Creative Asian-inspired cocktails in an elegant setting.

Best for a Cuppa

Peninsula Hong Kong (p225) The most elegant afternoon tea in the territory.

Cafe Corridor (p115) An intimate den with a lot of regulars.

Teakha (p94) Wake up and smell the jasmine at this elegant tea lounge.

Elephant Grounds (p115) Great brews including 'bulletproof coffee' and much-loved ice-cream sandwiches.

Lan Fong Yuen (p88) The classic spot to try Hong Kong's famous milk tea.

Best for People-Watching

Peak Cafe Bar (p94) Watch the Mid-Levels elevator roll by from this Soho spot.

China Bear (p187) Watch the ferry crowds come and go in sleepy Mui Wo village.

Club 71 (p92) A mainstay of artists and writers.

Senses 99 (p76) Venue of choice for the hipster observer.

Best for Clubbing

Dragon-I (p93) Swanky and celeb-filled hot spot.

Dusk Till Dawn (p114) The place to be rocking out to live music when the other bars close.

Tazmania Ballroom (p93) Grind with models on their night off.

Best Pubs

Smugglers Inn (p126) Cosy pub in British-influenced Stanley.

Delaney's (p126) Spacious Irish pub perfect for a pint.

Dickens Bar (p114) A colonial classic that never stops to re-invent itself.

Best for Local Vibes

Utopia (p147) Play darts with local office workers.

Buddy Bar (p114) Hang in Tai Hang with locals and their dogs.

Club 71 (p92) Talk politics with local radicals or chat up the artist on the next bar stool.

Ben's Back Beach Bar (p126) When the beach crowds leave, this waterfront spot is locals only.

Best for Quirky Vibes

Ned Kelly's Last Stand (p147) Dixieland jazz, Aussie decor and expat crowds.

Wanch (p115) Rock out with tourists, locals, sailors, junkies and other assorted weirdos at this live-music spot.

Best for Unpretentious Drinking

Pier 7 (p76) Postdinner drinks atop Star Ferry Pier.

Club 71 (p92) As unpretentious as you can get in the Soho area.

Buddy Bar (p114) A low-key neighbourhood pub in hip but friendly Tai Hang.

Best for Whisky

Butler (p146) It's either whisky or cocktails here, or whisky-based cocktails.

Angel's Share Whisky Bar (p92) It's all about this whisky here.

Executive Bar (p114) The Japanese mixologist knows his whisky.

Best for Wine

MyHouse (p113) Organic wines and vinyl in Causeway Bay.

Les Copains D'Abord (p179) Far-flung French cafe on an outer island.

Central Wine Club (p94) Baroque bar with fine European wines.

Best for Bar Food

Dickens Bar (p114) Stuff yourself on Indian curry then watch the rugby.

Classified (p171) Scrummy cheese plates go perfectly with a glass of red.

Stone Nullah Tavern (p113) Solid North American fare.

Ted's Lookout (p114) Great burgers.

Best for Watching Sports

Amici (p114) Football fans' fave thanks to big screens and beer on tap.

King Ludwig Beerhall (p147) Football and rugby on the screen at this German joint.

Dickens Bar (p114) This British-style pub plays any rugby and football to be found.

Delaney's (p126) An Irish pub with TVs and friendly crowds.

EDUCATION IMAGES / UIG / GETTY IMAGES ©

Chinese opera performer

 # Entertainment

Hong Kong's arts and entertainment scene is healthier than ever. The increasingly busy cultural calendar includes music, drama and dance hailing from a plethora of traditions. The schedule of imported performances is nothing short of stellar. And every week, local arts companies and artists perform anything from Bach to stand-up to Cantonese opera and English versions of Chekhov plays.

The Arts

Local Western music ensembles and theatre troupes give weekly shows, while famous foreign groups are invited to perform often, particularly at the **Hong Kong Arts Festival** (香港藝術節; www.hk.artsfestival.org; from HK$150; ☺Feb-Mar). The annual event attracts world-class names in all genres of music, theatre and dance, including the likes of the Bolshoi Ballet, Anne-Sophie Mutter and playwright Robert Wilson.

Cantonese Opera

Hong Kong is one of the best places on earth to watch Cantonese opera. The best time to watch it is during the Hong Kong Arts Festival (p50) and the Mid-Autumn Festival, when outdoor performances are staged in Victoria Park. You can also catch a performance at the Temple Street Night Market (p132) or during Chinese festivals.

There are daily performances at the Sunbeam Theatre (p115) and at the new **Yau Ma Tei Theatre** (油麻地戲院; ☎852 2264 8108, tickets 2374 2598; www.lcsd.gov.hk/ymtt; 6 Waterloo Rd, cnr Reclamation St, Yau Ma Tei; Ⓜ Yau Ma Tei, exit B2). If you don't speak Cantonese, the best way to book tickets for the Sunbeam Theatre is through Hong Kong Ticketing, Urbtix or **Cityline** (☎852 2317 6666; www.cityline.com.hk).

Cinema

Hong Kong is well served with cinema, screening both mainstream and art-house films. Cinemas usually show local productions and Hollywood blockbusters. The vast majority of films have both English and Chinese subtitles. Book tickets and seats online or in person well before the show.

Cinema buffs from all over Asia make the pilgrimage to the **Hong Kong International Film Festival** (香港國際電影節; www.hkiff.org.hk; from HK$45; ⊘Mar & Apr) held each year in March/April. **Cine Fan** (www.cinefan.com.hk), run by the same folks, has offerings all year round.

AVENUE OF STARS

Much of Kowloon's prime waterfront is dedicated to stars of the Hong Kong cinema, honoured through statues and hand prints. Though foreigners may not recognise many of the names, everyone loves to pose in front of the Bruce Lee statue. The giant bronze pig, in case you're wondering, is McDull, a beloved Hong Kong children's cartoon.

Live Music

Hong Kong's live-music scene has seen a growing number of venues hosting independent musicians (imported and local) several nights a week. The options range from a smooth evening of jazz to a raucous night of goth metal, not to mention dub step, post-rock drum 'n' bass and electronica.

The Fringe Club (p95) and Grappa's Cellar (p76) are popular venues. And don't miss the clandestine dive Hidden Agenda (p148).

The **Hong Kong International Jazz Festival** (www.hkijf.com; from HK$200; ⊘Sep, Oct or Nov) caters to jazz lovers.

Hong Kong is a stop on the big-name concert circuit, and a growing number of internationally celebrated bands and solo artists perform here. These include mainstream acts and those on the edge of the mainstream – from U2, Robbie Williams and Red Hot Chilli Peppers, to Kings of Convenience, Deerhoof and Mogwai.

The highlight in Hong Kong's live-music calendar is the excellent multi-act outdoor music festival known as **Clockenflap** (www.clockenflap.com; tickets HK$600-1800; ⊘Nov

NEED TO KNOW

Price Ranges

Expect to pay around HK$80 for a seat up the back for a local ensemble and from about HK$600 for a performance by big-name international acts or an international musical such as *Chicago*.

Movie tickets cost between HK$65 and HK$100, but can be cheaper at matinees, at the last screening of the day (usually 11.30pm), on weekends and on holidays, or on certain days of the week. Almost all non-English-language films have both Chinese and English subtitles.

Tickets & Reservations

Urbtix (☎852 2734 9009; www.urbtix.hk; ⊘10am-8pm) and **Hong Kong Ticketing** (☎852 3128 8288; www.hkticketing.com; ⊘10am-8pm) have tickets to every major event in Hong Kong. You can book through them or purchase tickets at the performance venues.

What's On

➡ **Artmap** (www.artmap.com.hk)

➡ **Artslink** (www.hkac.org.hk)

➡ **Time Out** (www.timeout.com.hk)

or Dec). The three-day event has featured dozens of local, regional and international acts performing at the West Kowloon promenade.

Entertainment by Neighbourhood

➡ **Hong Kong Island: Central** Central's boisterous Lan Kwai Fong (LKF) is one of Asia's legendary party streets.

➡ **Hong Kong Island: the Peak & the Northwest** The hip Sheung Wan neighbourhood is the place for laid-back bars and speakeasies.

➡ **Hong Kong Island: Wan Chai & the Northeast** A former red light district, Wan Chai is still synonymous with all-night indulgence.

➡ **Hong Kong Island: Aberdeen & the South** Though it has a few great pubs, quiet Southside is more about beaches than bars.

➡ **Kowloon** Sing karaoke until the sun comes up in the peninsula that never sleeps.

Lonely Planet's Top Choices

Hong Kong International Film Festival (p51) Asia's top film festival features both esoteric titles and crowd pleasers.

Clockenflap Outdoor Music Festival (p51) Everyone in town attends this massive rock festival.

Hong Kong Arts Festival (p50) Hong Kong's most exciting outdoor music festival.

Hidden Agenda (p148) The city's most visible clandestine live-music venue.

Street Music Concert Series (p116) Free under-the-stars live music, from Bach to original jazz.

Best for Live Music

Peel Fresco (p95) Groovy jazz and arty crowds in a tiny club.

Hidden Agenda (p148) HK's most famous music dive has a line-up of solid indie acts.

Wanch (p115) Wan Chai's venerable live-music spot is tops for rock, jazz and lots of beer.

Grappa's Cellar (p76) This Italian restaurant turns to rock, jazz and comedy.

Fringe Club (p98) Jazz, world music and more play inside this Victorian building.

Best Movie Theatres

Broadway Cinematheque (p149) Hong Kong's best art-house theatre shows indie films that don't play elsewhere.

AMC Pacific Place (p116) In the plush Pacific Place mall, watch Hollywood and Hong Kong releases in comfort.

Agnès b. Cinema (p116) In the Hong Kong Arts Centre, this small space plays festival releases on a limited basis.

Best for Theatre

Hong Kong Arts Centre (p115) Theatre, dance and more.

Hong Kong Academy for the Performing Arts (p115) All manner of performances grace this school's stage.

Hong Kong Cultural Centre (p149) If it's culture, it's here.

Fringe Club (p95) Think of it as Hong Kong's off-Broadway.

Cattle Depot Artist Village (p140) Esoteric performance art in a former slaughterhouse.

Best Underground Vibe

XXX (p148) A dive bar with indie bands.

Cattle Depot Artist Village (p140) A Kowloon slaughterhouse turned artists' village and music venue.

Hidden Agenda (p148) *The* underground music spot in Hong Kong, so cool the government wants to shut it down.

Shopping

Everyone knows Hong Kong as a place of neon-lit retail pilgrimage. This city is positively stuffed with swanky shopping malls and brand-name boutiques. All international brands worth their logo have outlets here. These are supplemented by the city's own retail trailblazers and a few creative local designers. Together they are Hong Kong's shrines and temples to style and consumption.

Antiques

Hong Kong has a rich and colourful array of Asian (especially Chinese) antiques on offer, but serious buyers will restrict themselves to reputable shops and auction houses only. Forgeries and expert reproductions abound. Remember that most of the quality pieces are sold through auction houses such as Christie's, especially at its auctions in spring and autumn.

Most of Hong Kong's antique shops are bunched along Wyndham St and Hollywood Rd in Central and Sheung Wan. The shops at the western end of Hollywood Rd tend to carry cheaper paraphernalia, including magazines, Chinese propaganda posters and badges from the Cultural Revolution.

For old-style Chinese handicrafts, the main places to go are the large emporiums.

Art

An increasing number of art galleries in Hong Kong sell paintings, sculptures, ceramic works and installations – some very good – by local artists. Like antique and curio shops, most of the city's commercial art galleries are found along Wyndham St and Hollywood Rd in Central and Sheung Wan.

Art Basel (p30) and Le French May (p30) offer great opportunities to acquire art or simply acquaint yourself with the city's interesting visual-arts scene.

Bargaining

Sales assistants in department or chain stores rarely have any leeway to give discounts, but you can try bargaining in owner-operated stores and certainly in markets.

Some visitors believe that you can always get the goods for half of the price originally quoted. But if you can bargain something down that low, perhaps you shouldn't be buying it from that shop anyway. Remember you may be getting that DSLR cheap but paying high mark-ups for the memory card, or worse, it may have missing components or no international warranty.

Don't be too intent on getting the best deals. Really, what's HK$2 off a souvenir that's being sold for HK$20? Probably not much to you, but it may mean a lot to the old lady selling it.

Cameras

One of the best spots in Hong Kong to buy photographic equipment is Stanley St in Central. Everything carries a price tag, though some low-level bargaining may be possible. Never buy a camera without a price tag. This will probably preclude many of the shops in Tsim Sha Tsui. That said, Tsim Sha Tsui has a couple of places on Kimberley Rd dealing in used cameras, and there are plenty of photo shops on Sai Yeung Choi St in Mong Kok.

Watches

Shops selling watches are ubiquitous in Hong Kong and you can find everything from a Rolex to Russian army timepieces and diving watches. Avoid the shops without price tags. The big department stores and City Chain are fine, but compare prices.

NEED TO KNOW

Opening Hours

➡ Central: generally 10am to 8pm

➡ Causeway Bay: 11am to 9.30pm or 10pm

➡ Tsim Sha Tsui: 11am to 8pm

➡ Most shops open on Sunday

➡ Winter sales in January; summer sales in late June and early July

Duty-Free

There's no sales tax in Hong Kong so ignore the 'Tax Free' signs in some stores. However, you will pay duty on tobacco, perfume, cosmetics and cars. In general, almost everything is cheaper when you buy it outside duty-free shops.

Refunds & Exchanges

Most shops won't give refunds, but they can be persuaded to exchange purchases if they haven't been tampered with and you have a detailed receipt.

Service

Service is attentive and credit cards are widely accepted.

Shipping Goods

Many shops will package and post large items for you, but check whether you'll have to clear the goods at the country of destination. Smaller items can be shipped from the post office or try DHL (www.dhl. com.hk/en).

Warranties & Guarantees

Some imported goods have a Hong Kong–only guarantee. If it's a well-known brand, you can return the warranty card to the Hong Kong importer to get one for your country. Grey-market items imported by somebody other than the official agent may have a guarantee that's valid only in the country of manufacture, or none at all.

Defensive Shopping

Hong Kong is not a nest of thieves just waiting to rip you off, but pitfalls can strike the uninitiated.

Whatever you're in the market for, always check prices in a few shops before buying. The most common way for shopkeepers to cheat tourists is to simply overcharge. In some of the electronic stores in the tourist shopping district of Tsim Sha Tsui, many goods do not have price tags. Checking prices in several shops therefore becomes essential. Sometimes stores will quote a reasonable or even low price on a big-ticket item, only to get the money back by overcharging on accessories.

Spotting overcharging is the easy part, though. Sneakier (but rarer) tricks involve merchants removing vital components that should have been included for free (and demanding more money when you return to the shop to get them). Another tactic is to replace some of the good components with cheaper ones.

Clothing

DESIGNER BRANDS & BOUTIQUES

The best places to find global designer brands and luxury stores are in malls such as IFC and the Landmark in Central, Pacific Place in Admiralty and Festival Walk in Kowloon Tong. Some of these shops such as Prada have outlets at Horizon Plaza in Ap Lei Chau selling off-season items at discounted prices.

There's also an embarrassment of midrange malls showcasing second- or thirdtier brands, fast-fashion outlets such as Mango and Zara and local retailers such as Giordano.

For something unique, there are cool independents opened by local designers and retailers in Sheung Wan, Wan Chai and Tsim Sha Tsui. You'll see some brilliant pieces but the range of styles is limited, simply because these places are few and far between.

STREET MARKETS & MINIMALLS

The best hunting grounds for low-cost garments are in Tsim Sha Tsui at the eastern end of Granville Rd, and Cheung Sha Wan Rd in Sham Shui Po. The street markets on Temple St in Yau Ma Tei and Tung Choi St in Mong Kok have the cheapest clothes. You may also try Li Yuen St East and Li Yuen St West, two narrow alleyways linking Des Voeux Rd Central with Queen's Rd Central. They are a jumble of inexpensive clothing, handbags, backpacks and costume jewellery.

For a truly local shopping experience, the minimalls in Tsim Sha Tsui are teeming with all things young and trendy, both locally designed and imported from the mainland or Korea. Usually you can negotiate a lower price when you purchase more than one item. And if you have a good eye, you can end up looking chic for very little.

THE LOW-DOWN ON HIGH-TECH SHOPPING

Hong Kong has a plethora of shops specialising in electronic and digital gadgets, but the product mix and prices may vary. Similarly, vendors' command of English can range from 'enough to close a deal' (Mong Kok, Sham Shui Po) to 'reasonable' (the rest). Shopkeepers are generally honest but some have been known to sell display or secondhand items as new ones. All things considered, Wan Chai is your safest bet, but if you're a bit of a geek, the malls and flea market in Sham Shui Po are worth exploring.

Gems & Jewellery

The Chinese attribute various magical qualities to jade, including the power to prevent ageing and accidents. The Jade Market in Yau Ma Tei is diverting, but unless you're knowledgeable about jade, limit yourself to modest purchases.

Hong Kong also offers a great range of pearls – cultured and freshwater. Retail prices for other precious stones are only marginally lower than elsewhere. The more reputable jewellery-shop chains – and there are many in Tsim Sha Tsui and Mong Kok catering to tourists from the mainland – will issue a certificate that states exactly what you are buying and guarantees that the shop will buy it back at a fair market price.

Handicrafts and Souvenirs

For old-school Chinese handicrafts and other goods such as hand-carved wooden pieces, ceramics, cloisonné, silk garments and place mats, head to the large Chinese emporiums, such as Chinese Arts & Crafts.

You'll also find a small range of similar items (but of a lesser quality) in the alleyways of Tsim Sha Tsui, but remember to check prices at different vendors and bargain.

If you prefer something in a modern Chinese style, Shanghai Tang (the fashion boutique with branches all over town) has a range of cushions, tableware, photo frames and other home accessories.

The furniture store G.O.D. has a wide range of homewares and contemporary office products but with a cheeky Hong Kong twist.

Leather Goods & Luggage

All the brand names – such as Louis Vuitton, Samsonite and Rimowa – are sold at Hong Kong department stores, and you'll also find some local vendors in the luggage business. The popularity of hiking and travel has triggered a proliferation of

outdoor-products shops that carry high-quality backpacks. If you're looking for a casual bag or daypack, check out Li Yuen St East and Li Yuen St West in Central or Stanley Market.

Local Brands & Designers

Hong Kong doesn't have a profusion of quirky, creative one-offs or unique vintage items as in London, New York or Copenhagen. (Have you seen the rent landlords charge here?) But the city has a small, passionate band of local designer boutiques offering value, character and style across a range of goods, especially in fashion and furniture.

Soho, Wan Chai, Causeway Bay and Tsim Sha Tsui are the best places to find them. Some stores, such as Homeless, carry a smattering of chic, design-oriented goods (local and imported) while others, such as furniture store G.O.D. and fashion boutiques Shanghai Tang and Initial, have in-house design teams.

Shopping by Neighbourhood

➡ **Hong Kong Island: Central** Posh malls and designer brands abound in Hong Kong's business district.

➡ **Hong Kong Island: the Peak & the Northwest** Trendy Sheung Wan is fast becoming the go-to spot for quirky boutiques and homewares shops.

➡ **Hong Kong Island: Wan Chai & the Northeast** From street markets to fancy malls to funky hipster enclaves, Wan Chai has it all.

➡ **Hong Kong Island: Aberdeen & the South** Ap Lei Chau is the place for outlet hauls; Stanley has a fun outdoor souvenir market.

➡ **Kowloon** Shop for designer goodies and knock-offs galore along with half of China.

Lonely Planet's Top Choices

G.O.D (p127). Awesome lifestyle accessories, homewares and gifts – Hong Kong to the bone with a whiff of mischief.

Wattis Fine Art (p96) Antique maps and nostalgic photographs of Hong Kong and Macau.

Gallery of the Pottery Workshop (p96) Excellent ceramic works by Hong Kong's home-grown artists.

Chan Shing Kee (p97) Classical Chinese furniture and decorative objects.

Lane Crawford (p77) Luxury department store specialising in stylish clothing, homewares and accessories.

Best Markets

Stanley Market (p127) Touristy streets market, good for souvenirs.

Ap Liu Street Flea Market (p151) Massive electronics flea market.

Temple Street Night Market (p132) Iconic night market of kitsch and souvenirs.

Ladies' Market (p150) Clothing, mobile-phone covers, knock-off purses and more.

Ap Lei Chau Market (p124) A seafood extravaganza just a floor below the Ap Lei Chau Cooked Food Centre.

Wholesale Fruit Market (p138) The oldest market buildings in Hong Kong.

Best for Antiques

Lam Gallery (p96) Sculptures from Neolithic to Qing, and ancient Chinese art in other genres.

Andy Hei (p97) Rare Chinese antique furniture.

Capital Gallery (p97) Tiny shop selling curios from several thousand years ago.

Chan Shing Kee (p97) *The* place for classical Chinese furniture.

Ngai Tile Wave (p98) Figurines, pottery and porcelain.

Picture This (p77) Vintage maps, books and posters.

Best for Art

Grotto Fine Art (p96) Featuring works by predominantly Hong Kong artists.

Karin Weber Gallery (p97) Antiques and contemporary Asian art.

C&G Artpartment (p140) Edgy local art.

Pearl Lam Galleries (p96) Contemporary Hong Kong and Asian art.

Best for Gifts

Temple Street Night Market (p132) Everything from chop-sticks to jewellery – bargain hard.

Chinese Arts & Crafts (p116) Expensive but authentic handicrafts.

Stanley Market (p127) Carved name chops, satin baby shoes and more in a touristy but fun street market.

Picture This (p77) Cool vintage posters and antique books.

Mountain Folkcraft (p96) Folk crafts from Chinese minorities and Southeast Asian countries.

Lam Kie Yuen Tea Co (p97) Venerable tea shop with huge selection.

Best for Food & Beverages

Tak Hing Dried Seafood (p151) Trustworthy dried-seafood shop.

Shanghai Street (p138) Woks, mooncake molds and other cooking implements galore.

Citysuper (p78) Huge variety of international gourmet groceries.

Sogo (p118) Basement food hall with every type of Japanese snack food imaginable.

Papabubble (p118) Hard candies in a variety of quirky local flavors.

Best for Beauty Products

Two Girls (p118) Hong Kong's cheap-and-cheerful local beauty brand, with fun vintage packaging.

Joyce (p116) High-end beauty products and scents from across the world.

Muji (p117) Elegantly packaged Japanese toiletries.

Hysan Place (p117) The 6th floor Garden of Eden is a paradise for hard-to-find, youth-oriented Asian cosmetics.

Best for Books

Flow (p96) Used books hidden inside a Soho building.

Eslite (p117) Massive Taiwanese bookshop-cafe-gallery–toy shop.

Hong Kong Reader (p151) Bilingual bookstore with an intellectual edge.

Kubrick Bookshop Café (p147) Excellent selection of highbrow fiction, art books and literary journals.

Basheer (p118) Grand selection of architecture and design titles.

Best for Fashion

Joyce (p116) Hong Kong–born multi-designer department store.

Numb Workshop (p118) Sleek black and locally designed minimalism.

Vivienne Tam (p152) High-fashion dresses and more from a Hong Kong–bred designer.

Kapok (p116) Hipster fashions from local and international designers.

Horizon Plaza (p127) Cut-rates on luxury goods and clothing in a 27-floor warehouse.

Cuffs (p118) Bespoke shirts at a reasonable price point.

Best for Gadgets

Wan Chai Computer Centre (p116) A warren of all things electronic.

Golden Computer Arcade (p151) Computers and components for extra low prices.

Apliu Street Flea Market (p151) A huge digital-products flea market.

Sin Tat Plaza (p151) Everything mobile phone.

Mong Kok Computer Centre (p151) Cheap computer mall.

Best Malls

IFC Mall (p77) Swanky and always crowded Central mall.

Pacific Place (p116) Ultra-luxe international clothing and accessories.

Elements (p152) One of Kowloon's fanciest shopping centres.

Festival Walk (p34) More than 200 shops plus an ice rink.

Rise Shopping Arcade (p149) Cheap, fun shopping mall.

Hysan Place (p117) The finest in Japanese and Korean fashions.

Best for Quirky Items

Sino Centre (p151) Geek out at this anime mall.

Chan Wah Kee Cutlery Store (p150) One of Asia's few remaining master knife sharpeners.

Picture This (p77) Antique books, posters and maps.

Cat Street (p83) Junk shops hawk communist kitsch at this touristy street market.

Island Beverley Mall (p117) Eye-popping Japanese youth fashions.

Sports & Activities

Hong Kong offers countless ways to have fun and keep fit. From golf and soccer to cycling and windsurfing, you won't be stumped for something active to do or somewhere to do it – for lists of fields, stadiums, beaches, swimming pools, water-sports centres etc, including equipment for hire, check the website or call the Leisure and Cultural Services Department. There are also gyms, yoga studios and spas offering everything from aromatherapy to foot massage. If you prefer watching people play, the world's most exciting dragon boat racing takes place right here!

Hiking

Many visitors are surprised to learn that Hong Kong is an excellent place for hiking. Lengthy wilderness trails criss-cross the territory and its islands through striking mountain, coast and jungle trails. The four main ones are the **MacLehose Trail**, at 100km the longest in the territory; the 78km-long **Wilson Trail**, which runs on both sides of Victoria Harbour; the 70km-long **Lantau Trail**; and the Hong Kong Trail (p60), which is 50km long. Hong Kong's excellent public-transport network makes it feasible to tackle these trails a section at a time.

For full details and advice on routes and suggested itineraries, invest in one of the excellent hiking guides that are widely available in Hong Kong bookshops. Before heading out it's also a good idea to consult the official Hong Kong hiking website (www.hkwalkers.net) for updates on weather and the condition of the trails (landslides can sometimes mean route closures or diversions). Hikers can camp on some remote beaches.

SNAKE WARNING

Take care when bushwalking in the New Territories, particularly on Lamma and Lantau Islands. Poisonous snakes, the most common being the bamboo pit viper, are a hazard, although they will not attack unless surprised or provoked. Go straight to a public hospital if bitten; private doctors do not stock antivenene.

Horse Racing

Horse racing is Hong Kong's biggest spectator sport. There are two racecourses: one in Happy Valley (p105) and one at Sha Tin (p169). Attending one of the Wednesday race meetings (7pm, HK$10 entrance fee) at Happy Valley during the racing season (September to June) is a great way to experience horse racing in Hong Kong.

Spa Treatments & Therapies

Whether you want to be spoilt rotten with thousand-dollar caviar facials or have a simple foot rub, Hong Kong's extensive pampering sector can assist. Most of the top hotels operate their own spas. For less elaborate routines, you'll find plenty of places in Central and Kowloon offering spa treatments, massages and reflexology. Be aware that some massage venues, especially in Wan Chai, may be 'happy ending' establishments.

Martial Arts

Hong Kong has a glut of martial-arts programs, but only a few have special arrangements for English-speaking visitors.

Hong Kong Shaolin Wushu Culture Centre (p188) offers overnight stays.

Wan Kei Ho International Martial Arts Association (p98) has a local and foreign following.

Dragon Boat Racing

Hong Kong is possibly the best place in the world to watch dragon boat racing because the traditions underlying the practice are still very much alive. The city has more than 20 races a year with most taking place from May to July. The Hong Kong Tourism Board (www.discoverhongkong.com) has information on the main events.

Running

The best places to run on Hong Kong Island include Harlech and Lugard Rds on the Peak, Bowen Rd above Wan Chai, the track in Victoria Park, and the Happy Valley racecourse – as long as there aren't any horse races! In Kowloon a popular place to run is the Tsim Sha Tsui East Promenade. Lamma makes an ideal place for trail runners, with plenty of paths and dirt trails, great views and, best of all, no cars.

Gyms & Yoga Studios

Yoga and fitness are big business here, with the largest slices of the pie shared out among a few big names. Pure Fitness (p78) has comprehensive gym facilities.

Cycling

Hong Kong's natural terrain makes for some fabulous cycling.

The longest bicycle track runs from Sha Tin through Tai Po to Tai Mei Tuk, taking you through parks, and past temples and the waterfront. The Hong Kong Cycling Alliance (http://hkcyclingalliance.org) has information on road rules and safety for cyclists.

You need a (free) permit for mountain biking. Check with the Mountain Biking Association (www.hkmba.org) for permit details.

Football (Soccer)

Hong Kong has a fairly lively amateur soccer league. Games are played at the Happy Valley Sports Ground (p119), a group of pitches inside the Happy Valley Racecourse, and at **Mong Kok Stadium** (旺角大球場; Map p319; ☑852 2380 0188; 37 Flower Market Rd, Mong Kok; Ⓜ Prince Edward, exit B1). For match schedules and venues, check the sports sections of the English-language newspapers or check the Hong Kong Football Association website (www.hkfa.com). For information on casual football matches, visit http://casualfootball.net.

NEED TO KNOW

Maps

The Map Publications Centre sells excellent maps detailing hiking and cycling trails; buy online (www.landsd.gov.hk/mapping/en/pro&ser/products.htm) or at major post offices.

Information & Facilities

In addition to the following, check the sports sections of English-language newspapers.
Environmental Protection Department (www.epd.gov.hk) Lists of country and marine parks.

Hong Kong Tourism Board (www.discoverhongkong.com) Has a full list of what's on.

Leisure & Cultural Services Department (www.lcsd.gov.hk) Lists of fields, stadiums, beaches, swimming pools, water-sports centres etc, including equipment for hire.

South China Athletic Association (p119) Has sports facilities for hire.

Enjoy Hiking (http://hiking.gov.hk) A government site with comprehensive information; select trails by area, level of difficulty, duration etc.

More Ideas

Birdwatching (www.hkbws.org.hk)

Dolphin-watching Try Hong Kong Dolphinwatch (p152).

Hiking and kayaking trips Try Kayak and Hike (p266).

Outdoor Sports (www.hkoutdoors.com)

Golf

Hong Kong has only one public golf course, but some private clubs open their doors on weekdays for a green fee.

The **Hong Kong Golf Association** (☑852 2504 8659; www.hkga.com) has a list of driving ranges and tournaments held in the territory, including the **Hong Kong Open Championships**, one of Asia's leading professional golf tournaments (usually played in November or December).

Rugby

The **Rugby World Cup Sevens** (www.hksevens.com.hk; ⊙late Mar or early Apr) sees teams

THE HONG KONG TRAIL

If you want to hike without exerting yourself too much, the **Hong Kong Trail** (港島徑) on Hong Kong Island is a great choice. The 50km route comprises eight sections of varying difficulty, beginning on the Peak (take the tram up to the Peak and follow the signs) and ending near Shek O, on Island South.

One of the easiest and most scenic sections runs for about two hours along a mountain ridge called **Dragon's Back**. It takes you past woods, then up to the windy spine of the dragon where there are views of sun-drenched beaches and billowing hills streaked with cloud shadow. Then it's all the way down to Shek O Rd, where you can hoof it or bus it to Shek O's beach for a rewarding meal, a swim or a game of frisbee.

from all over the world come together in Hong Kong for three days of lightning-fast 15-minute matches at the 40,000-seat Hong Kong Stadium (p115) in So Kon Po. Even those who are not rugby fans scramble to get tickets, because the Sevens is a giant, international, three-day party, complete with costumes and Mardi Gras levels of drunkenness.

Climbing

Hong Kong is peppered with excellent granite faces and volcanic rocks in some striking wilderness areas. The best place to climb is on Tung Lung Chau, which has a technical wall, a big wall and a sea gully. Shek O beach has some excellent bouldering as well.

The Hong Kong Climbing website (www. hongkongclimbing.com) is a handy resource for climbers.

Scuba Diving

Hong Kong has some surprisingly worthwhile diving spots, particularly in the far northeast, and there is certainly no shortage of courses. One of the best sources of information for courses and excursions is Sai Kung–based **Splash Hong Kong** (☑852 2792 4495; www.splashhk.com; courses from HK$1200).

Windsurfing, Kayaking & Canoeing

The best time for windsurfing is October to December. Check the Leisure and Cultural

Services Department website (www.lcsd.gov. hk) for government-run watersports centres providing canoes, windsurfing boards, kayaks and other equipment for hire, some only to holders of the relevant certificates.

Wakeboarding

Most operators of this popular sport are based in Sai Kung (New Territories) and Tai Tam (Hong Kong Island). Rates are about HK$700 per hour.

Sports & Activities by Neighbourhood

➡ **Hong Kong Island: Central** Hong Kong's business district is the place for relaxation, with some of the world's most relaxing spas.

➡ **Hong Kong Island: the Peak & the Northwest** Climbing (or riding) up the Peak is an essential experience.

➡ **Hong Kong Island: Aberdeen & the South** Southside is all about beaches and family fun, with the city's biggest amusement park.

➡ **Kowloon** City parks are perfect for people-watching on this crowded peninsula.

➡ **New Territories** The mountains of Hong Kong's biggest region contain some of the world's finest hiking.

➡ **Outlying Islands** Are you in Fiji? Hawaii? Nope, these golden sands are pure Hong Kong.

Lonely Planet's Top Choices

Dragon boat racing (p30, p59) Feel the heart-pounding excitement of these atmospheric races that evolved from an ancient ritual.

Hiking Hong Kong's trails A palette of hills, history, grottoes and rural culture.

Horse racing in Happy Valley (p105) The thunderous action at this urban racecourse makes for an unforgettable experience.

Rugby Sevens (p59) Join rugby fans for three days of lightning matches and wild partying.

Kayaking in Sai Kung (p172) Paddle in clear waters surrounded by hills and geological wonders.

Best Day Hikes

Lion Rock Country Park (p168) A steep climb past forests of monkeys to a craggy, lion-shaped peak.

Dragon's Back (p60) Hong Kong Island's best scenery.

The Morning Trail A shady paved path around the Peak, with stunning city views.

Sunset Peak (p187) On Lantau, Hong Kong's third-highest peak.

Lamma Island Family Trail A two-hour stroll between this outer island's two main villages.

Best for Treating Yourself

Spa at the Four Seasons (p78) Luxury, luxury and more luxury.

Ten Feet Tall (p78) Foot massages, pressure points and aromatherapy.

Happy Foot Reflexology Centre (p98) Hong Kong's go-to foot-rub spot.

Best for Scenery

Tai Long Wan Hiking Trail (p172) A glorious hike to an even more glorious beach.

Plover Cove Reservoir (p166) Cycling around the shimmering blue waters.

Eastern Nature Trail (p119) An easy day hike.

Tai Tam Waterworks Heritage Trail (p127) Nature and history come together.

Best for Martial Arts

Hong Kong Shaolin Wushu Culture Centre (p188) Teaches ancient Shaolin style of martial arts.

Wan Kei Ho International Martial Arts Association (p98) Kung fu for locals and foreigners.

Wing Chun Yip Man Martial Arts Athletic Association (p152) Runs six-week intensive courses.

Best for Swimming

Lamma Island Small and laid-back.

Lantau Island Large, remote and good for water sports.

Cheung Chau Island (p191) Tops for windsurfing.

Sai Kung Scuba, kayaking and blue water galore.

Island South (p124) Sometimes crowded but gorgeous waters around Stanley and Shek O.

Best for Socialising

Rugby Sevens (www.hksevens. com.hk) Epic annual spring debauchery.

Football (playing it) Get to know the Anglo expat crowd.

Dragon boat races (p30, p59) Down post-row beers with your team.

Best One-Stop Sports Facilities

South China Athletic Association (p119) A gym and other sports facilities.

Victoria Park (p119) Tennis, swimming, jogging track and more.

Kowloon Park (p135) Taichi, running, swimming, martial arts and beyond.

Explore Hong Kong

HONG KONG'S TOP SIGHTS

Neighbourhoods at a Glance

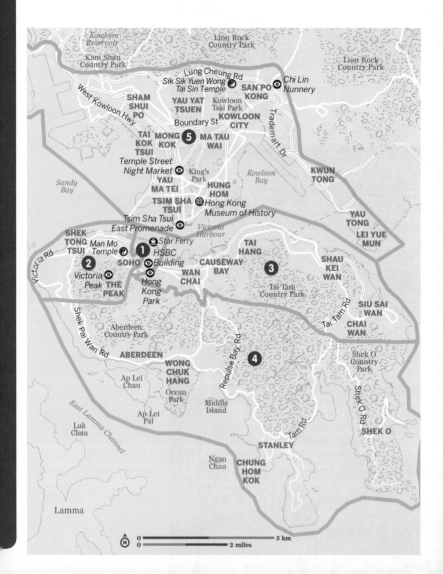

❶ Hong Kong Island: Central (p66)

The minted heart of Asia's financial hub comes replete with corporate citadels, colonial relics and massive monuments to consumerism. It's where you'll find the stock exchange, the Four Seasons, Prada and award-winning restaurants, all housed in a compelling mix of modern architecture, alongside graceful remnants of the city's colonial history. Dynamic during the day, it retires soon after sundown.

❷ Hong Kong Island: The Peak & the Northwest (p79)

Victoria Peak, soaring above the luxury residences in the Mid-Levels, offers a great vantage point from which to gaze back on Hong Kong. Down below, the charming old neighbourhoods of Sheung Wan, Sai Ying Pun and Western District have, between them, something for everyone, whether it's history, antiques and fine art, stylish hedonism or a generous slice of local life as it has been in these 'hoods for decades.

❸ Hong Kong Island: Wan Chai & the Northeast (p99)

Versatile Wan Chai is a showcase of the arts and folk traditions, and a god of cookery. You'll also find here some better examples of Hong Kong's preservation efforts. To its west, Admiralty is home to government headquarters and mind-blowing hill-and-sea views, and offers quality over quantity for your shopping, dining and lodging needs. In the shopping mecca of Causeway Bay, traffic, malls and restaurants jockey for space with a racecourse and a cemetery, while at its periphery, old meets new and East greets West in pockets of tranquillity.

❹ Hong Kong Island: Aberdeen & the South (p120)

The southern district is not only a showcase of history – Pok Fu Lam has the island's last surviving village alongside vestiges of a Victorian dairy – but Aberdeen and Ap Lei Chau are also the homes of Hong Kong's boat-dwelling fishermen. As such, Aberdeen and Ap Lei Chau offer tasty seafood and boat-rides to a bygone era, while Ap Lei Chau also offers art and shopping. The district is also the island's backyard playground – from the beaches of Repulse Bay to Stanley Market (the waterfront bazaar) and Ocean Park (an amusement park).

❺ Kowloon (p128)

Tsim Sha Tsui is endowed with an unbeatable harbour setting, four museums and all the superlatives Central has to offer on a more human scale. Other assets include leafy parks, colonial gems and the most diverse ethnic mix in all of Hong Kong. Indigenous Yau Ma Tei is a mosaic of night markets, guesthouses and martial-arts dens, while Mong Kok's distinguishing feature is its sardine-packed commercialism. In New Kowloon a Buddhist nunnery and a Taoist temple beckon the spiritually inclined.

Hong Kong Island: Central

Neighbourhood Top Five

❶ Star Ferry (p69) Cruising on iconic mid-century green-and-white ferries that cross Victoria Harbour all day and into the night.

❷ Skyscrapers (p70) Getting personal with skyscrapers you saw in *The Dark Knight* by checking out buildings like the Bank of China Tower.

❸ Cantonese Cuisine (p74) Enjoying top-notch Cantonese food at Lung King Heen, the world's first Chinese restaurant to snag three Michelin stars.

❹ IFC Mall (p77) Shopping with the wealthy (or watching the wealthy shop) at Central's premier mall, a sleek multistorey shopaholic's paradise at the base of the IFC towers.

❺ Zoological & Botanical Gardens (p70) Taking your morning constitutional and paying the animals a visit at this leafy zoo and public park on the slope of Victoria Peak.

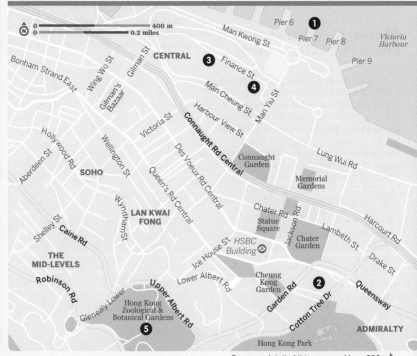

For more detail of this area see Map p298 ➡

Explore: Central

Whatever time of the day you plan on visiting Hong Kong's CBD, it's worth remembering that shops here close relatively early (6pm or 7pm), and that by mid-evening the dust has settled. It's also advisable to have lunch outside the noon-to-2pm insanity when hordes of hungry suits descend on every table in sight.

Travelling on the MTR, take the Statue Sq exit and spend an hour looking around the Former Legislative Council Building and other memorials to Hong Kong's past. In the next couple of hours, check out the architecture in the vicinity – glass-and-steel modernity like the HSBC Building and colonial-era survivors like the Gothic St John's Cathedral.

Head over to the Zoological and Botanical Gardens for some hobnobbing with the rhesus monkeys. Recharged after an hour, make a beeline for the harbour for some retail therapy at the IFC Mall. Take as long as you like, then hop on the Star Ferry to Kowloon.

Local Life

➡ **Lil' Manila** Every Sunday, Filipina domestic helpers take over Statue Square (p71) and the nearby pavements to eat, sing, chat and read the Bible.

➡ **Hang-outs** On weekdays at 3pm, well-coiffed ladies of leisure congregate at Sevva (p76) for Marie Antoinette's Crave (it's a cake).

➡ **Shopping** World-Wide Plaza (p72) is handy for stocking up on affordable toiletries and snacks.

Getting There & Away

➡ **MTR** Central station on the Island and Tsuen Wan lines.

➡ **Airport Express** Hong Kong station below IFC Mall connects (by underground walkway) with Central MTR station on one side and Central Piers on the other.

➡ **Star Ferry** Ferries from Tsim Sha Tsui in Kowloon arrive at Central Pier 7.

➡ **Bus** Buses start and end their journeys at Central Bus Terminus below Exchange Sq.

➡ **Tram** Runs east and west along Des Voeux Rd Central.

➡ **Outlying Islands Ferry** Ferries to Discovery Bay, Lamma, Cheung Chau, Lantau and Peng Chau run from Central Piers 3 to 6.

➡ **Central Escalator** Runs from the former Central Market to the Mid-Levels.

➡ **Peak Tram** Runs from the lower terminus (33 Garden Rd) to the Peak.

Lonely Planet's Top Tip

To enjoy Central's top-notch French and Italian restaurants without breaking the bank, go for the midday specials. Most restaurants offer these for the convenience of business-lunch eaters and frugal foodies. Some may even serve breakfast and/or afternoon tea, weekend lunch buffets or sell gourmet sandwiches at a takeaway station. Remember to book in advance if you're dining in for lunch.

 Best Places to Eat

➡ Lung King Heen (p74)
➡ Otto e Mezzo Bombana (p75)
➡ Amber (p75)
➡ Tasty Congee & Noodle Wonton Shop (p72)

For reviews, see p72 ➡

 **Best Places to Drink**

➡ Sevva (p76)
➡ MO Bar (p75)
➡ Pier 7 (p76)

For reviews, see p75 ➡

 Best Places to Shop

➡ Shanghai Tang (p77)
➡ Armoury (p77)
➡ Lane Crawford (p77)
➡ Picture This (p77)

For reviews, see p77 ➡

HONG KONG ISLAND: CENTRAL

TOP SIGHT
HSBC BUILDING

The stunning HSBC headquarters, designed by British architect Sir Norman Foster in 1985, is a masterpiece of precision, sophistication and innovation. And so it should be. On completion in 1985 it was the world's most expensive building (costing over US$1 billion). The building reflects the architect's wish to create areas of public and private space, and to break the mould of previous bank architecture. A lighting scheme fitted later enabled the building to stand out at night.

The two bronze lions guarding the main entrance were designed for the bank's previous headquarters in 1935; the lions are known as Stephen – the one roaring – and Stitt, after two bank managers from the 1920s. The Japanese used the lions as target practice during the occupation; both bear shrapnel scars. Rub their mighty paws for luck.

The 52-storey glass and aluminium building is full of examples of good feng shui (Chinese geomancy). There's no structure blocking its view of Victoria Harbour because water is associated with prosperity. The escalators are believed to symbolise the whiskers of a dragon sucking wealth into its belly. They're built at an angle to the entrance, supposedly to disorient evil spirits, which can only travel in a straight line.

The ground floor is public space, which people can traverse without entering the bank. From there, take the escalator to the 3rd floor to gaze at the cathedral-like atrium and the natural light filtering through its windows.

DON'T MISS

➡ Lighting scheme at night
➡ Stephen and Stitt
➡ Feng shui features
➡ The atrium

PRACTICALITIES

➡ 滙豐銀行總行大廈
➡ Map p298, D6
➡ www.hsbc.com. hk/1/2/about/home/ unique-headquarters
➡ 1 Queen's Rd, Central
➡ admission free
➡ ⏰escalator 9am-4.30pm Mon-Fri, 9am-12.30pm Sat
➡ Ⓜ Central, exit K

TOP SIGHT
STAR FERRY

You can't say you've 'done' Hong Kong until you've taken a ride on a Star Ferry, that legendary fleet of electric-diesel vessels with names like *Morning Star* and *Twinkling Star*. At any time of the day the ride, with its riveting views of skyscrapers and soaring mountains, is one of the world's best-value cruises. At the end of the 10-minute journey, watch as a crew member casts a hemp rope to his colleague who catches it with a billhook, the way it was done in 1880 when the first boat docked.

The Star Ferry was a witness to major events in Hong Kong history, including on Christmas Day 1941, when the colonial governor, Sir Mark Aitchison Young, took the ferry to Tsim Sha Tsui, where he surrendered to the Japanese at the Peninsula.

Take your first trip on a clear night from Tsim Sha Tsui to Central. It's less dramatic in the opposite direction. That said, you can turn to face the rear and bid adieu to the glorious view as it slips away from you. If you don't mind the noise and diesel fumes, the lower deck (only open on the Tsim Sha Tsui–Central route) is better for pictures.

The pier you see on Hong Kong Island is an uninspiring Edwardian replica that replaced the old pier (late art-deco style with a clock tower) at Edinburgh Pl that was demolished despite vehement opposition from Hong Kong people. The Kowloon pier remains untouched.

The Star Ferry operates on two routes – Tsim Sha Tsui–Central and Tsim Sha Tsui–Wan Chai. The first is more popular. The coin-operated turnstiles do not give change but you can get it from the ticket window.

DON'T MISS

➡ The views
➡ Kowloon pier
➡ The hemp rope and billhook routine

PRACTICALITIES

➡ 天星小輪
➡ Map p298, F2
➡ 📞852 2367 7065
➡ www.starferry. com.hk
➡ adult HK$2.50-3.40, child HK$1.50-2.10
➡ ⊙every 6-12min, 6.30am-11.30pm
➡ Ⓜ Hong Kong, exit A2

◉ SIGHTS

STAR FERRY FERRY
See p69.

HSBC BUILDING NOTABLE BUILDING
See p68.

PEAK TRAM TRAM
Map p298 (☏852 2522 0922; www.thepeak.com.
hk; Lower Terminus, 33 Garden Rd, Central; one-
way/return adult HK$28/40, child 3-11yr & seniors
over 65yr HK$11/18; ⊗7am-midnight; ⓂCentral,
exit J2) The Peak Tram is not really a tram
but a cable-hauled funicular railway that has
been scaling the 396m ascent to the highest
point on Hong Kong Island since 1888. A
ride on the tram is a classic Hong Kong experience, with vertiginous views over the city
as you ascend up the steep mountainside.
The Peak Tram runs every 10 to 15 minutes
from 7am to midnight. Octopus cards can be
used. On clear days, expect long lines.

**HONG KONG MARITIME
MUSEUM** MUSEUM
Map p298 (香港海事博物館; ☏852 3713 2500;
www.hkmaritimemuseum.org; Central Ferry
Pier 8, Central; adult/child & senior HK$30/15;
⊗9.30am-5.30pm Mon-Fri, 10am-7pm Sat & Sun;
▮; ⓂHong Kong, exit A2) Relocation and ex-
pansion have turned this into one of the
city's strongest museums, with 15 well-
curated galleries detailing over 2000 years
of Chinese maritime history and the development of the Port of Hong Kong. Exhibits
include ceramics from China's ancient sea
trade, shipwreck treasures and old nauti-
cal instruments. A painted scroll depicting
piracy in China in the early 19th century
is one of Hong Kong's most important historical artefacts, and, like the rest of the
museum, a real eye-opener.

The museum is located, as it should be,
right next to Victoria Harbour. After leaving the MTR, walk towards the pier along
Man Yiu St.

ST JOHN'S CATHEDRAL CHURCH
Map p298 (聖約翰座堂; ☏852 2523 4157; www.
stjohnscathedral.org.hk; 4-8 Garden Rd, Central;
⊗7am-6pm; ▯12A, 40, 40M, ⓂCentral, exit K)
FREE Services have been held at this Anglican cathedral since it opened in 1849, with
the exception of 1944, when the Japanese
army used it as a social club. It suffered
heavy damage during WWII, and the front
doors were subsequently remade using tim-

ber salvaged from HMS *Tamar,* a British
warship that guarded Victoria Harbour. You
walk on sacred ground in more ways than
one here: it is the only piece of freehold land
in Hong Kong. Enter from Battery Path.

Note the stained-glass windows, which
show scenes of vernacular Hong Kong life,
such as a fisherwoman holding a net. Note
also the tattered regimental flags hanging
from the ceiling; these were buried during WWII to hide them from the Japanese.
Outside you'll see the grave of RD Maxwell,
a British soldier killed during the Battle of
Hong Kong and buried in the nearest convenient spot.

**HONG KONG ZOOLOGICAL &
BOTANICAL GARDENS** PARK
Map p298 (香港動植物公園; www.lcsd.gov.hk/
parks; Albany Rd, Central; ⊗terrace gardens 5am-
10pm, greenhouse 9am-4.30pm; ▮; ▯3B, 12)
FREE This Victorian-era garden has a welcoming collection of fountains, sculptures
and greenhouses, plus a zoo and some fabulous aviaries. Some 160 species of bird reside
here. The zoo has a large collection of monkeys, sloths, lemurs and orangutans, and is
also one of the world's leading centres for the
captive breeding of endangered species. Albany Rd divides the gardens, with the plants
and aviaries to the east, close to Garden Rd,
and most of the animals to the west.

**FORMER LEGISLATIVE
COUNCIL BUILDING** HISTORIC BUILDING
Map p298 (前立法會大樓; 8 Jackson Rd, Central;
ⓂCentral, exit G) The colonnaded and domed
building (c 1912) was built of granite quar-
ried on Stonecutters Island, and served as
the seat of the Legislative Council from 1985
to 2012. During WWII it was a headquarters of the Gendarmerie, the Japanese version of the Gestapo, and many people were
executed here. Standing atop the pediment
is a blindfolded statue of Themis, the Greek
goddess of justice and natural law.

BANK OF CHINA TOWER NOTABLE BUILDING
Map p298 (中銀大廈, BOC Tower; 1 Garden Rd, Central; ⓂCentral, exit K) The awesome 70-storey
Bank of China Tower, designed by IM Pei,
rises from the ground like a cube, and is then
successively reduced, quarter by quarter,
until the south-facing side is left to rise on
its own. Some geomancers believe the four
prisms are negative symbols; being the opposite of circles, these triangles contradict what
circles suggest: money, union and perfection.

The lobby of the BOC Tower features the **Prehistoric Story Room** (⊘9am to 6pm, closed Tue), a small exhibition depicting Earth's life history through fossil displays.

OLD BANK OF CHINA BUILDING
NOTABLE BUILDING

Map p298 (1 Bank St, Central; ⓂCentral, exit K) Constructed in 1950, the old BOC building now houses the bank's Central branch and, on its top floors, the exclusive **China Club**, which evokes the atmosphere of old Shanghai. BOC headquarters are now in the awesome Bank of China Tower to the southeast.

TWO INTERNATIONAL FINANCE CENTRE
NOTABLE BUILDING

Map p298 (國際金融中心; Two IFC; 8 Finance St, Central; ⓂHong Kong, exit A2 or F) A pearl-coloured colossus resembling an electric shaver, this is the tallest building on Hong Kong Island. You can't get to the top, but you can get pretty high by visiting the Hong Kong Monetary Authority Information Centre. The building sits atop IFC Mall (p77), which stretches to the lower levels of its sister building, the much-shorter **One IFC** (國際金融中心; Map p298; 1 Harbour View St, Central; ⓂHong Kong, exit A2 or F).

GOVERNMENT HOUSE
HISTORIC BUILDING

Map p298 (禮賓府; ☑852 2530 2003; www.ceo. gov.hk/gh; Upper Albert Rd, Central; ⓂCentral, exit G) Parts of this erstwhile official residence of the chief executive of Hong Kong, and previously the colonial governors, date back to 1855. Other features were added by the Japanese, who used it as military headquarters during the occupation of Hong Kong in WWII. It's open to the public three or four times a year, notably one Sunday in March when the azaleas in the gardens are in full bloom.

STATUE SQUARE
SQUARE

Map p298 (皇后像廣場; Edinburgh Pl, Central; ⓂCentral, exit K) This leisurely square used to house effigies of British royalty. Now it pays tribute to a single sovereign – the founder of HSBC. In the northern area (reached via an underpass) is the **Cenotaph** (Map p298; 和平紀念碑; Chater Rd; ⓂCentral, exit A), built in 1923 as a memorial to Hong Kong residents killed during the two world wars. On the south side of Chater Rd, Statue Sq has a pleasant collection of fountains and seating areas, with tiling that's strangely reminiscent of a 1980s municipal washroom.

To the east a building resembling a swimming stingray houses a prestigious club that didn't accept Chinese members until well after WWII.

HONG KONG OBSERVATION WHEEL
FERRIS WHEEL

Map p298 (www.hkow.hk/en/; Hong Kong Central Piers; adult/child HK$100/70; ⊘10am-11pm; ♿; ⓂCentral exit A) In the perpetually under-construction waterfront area near Central Piers, this 60m enclosed Ferris wheel is hardly the highest spot in Hong Kong, but is still fun for a cheerful spin, with views over the water and Kowloon.

EXCHANGE SQUARE
SQUARE

Map p298 (交易廣場; 8 Connaught Pl, Central; ⓂCentral, exit A) This complex of office towers houses the Hong Kong Stock Exchange and the offices of global financial corporations. The main draw is the attractive and relatively peaceful open-air space, featuring fountains, and sculptures by Henry Moore and Ju Ming. Access is via a network of overhead walkways stretching west to Sheung Wan and linked to buildings on the other side of Connaught Rd.

HELENA MAY
HISTORIC BUILDING

Map p298 (梅夫人婦女會主樓; ☑852 2522 6766; www.helenamay.com; 35 Garden Rd, Central; ☒23) The Helena May was opened in 1916 by the wife of a governor as a social club for working, single European women, for whom the colony had little to offer by way of 'respectable' entertainment like ballet lessons and tea parties. The colonial building, with features of the Palladian and beaux-arts styles, was used to stable horses during the Japanese Occupation.

Currently a private club and hostel, it runs 20-minute tours in English and Chinese one Saturday a month (10am to noon; see the website for dates). Reservations are compulsory and accepted a month in advance.

FORMER FRENCH MISSION BUILDING
HISTORIC BUILDING

Map p298 (前法國外方傳道會大樓; 1 Battery Path, Central; ⓂCentral, exit K) This handsome red brick building was built in the mid-1800s and renovated to its current Edwardian glory in 1917 by the French Society of Foreign Missions. Until 2015 it was home to Hong Kong's Court of Final Appeal. It's now awaiting repurposing.

WORLD-WIDE PLAZA
NOTABLE BUILDING

Map p298 (環球商場; 19 Des Voeux Rd, Central; MCentral, exit G) A slice of Manila in Hong Kong's financial heart, the rabbit warren of tiny shops in this '80s-style shopping arcade caters to the needs of the Filipina domestic helpers working in Hong Kong, who, on Sundays, like to congregate in the streets around this area. Products for sale include food, toiletries and phone cards.

JARDINE HOUSE
NOTABLE BUILDING

Map p298 (怡和大廈; 1 Connaught Pl, Central; MHong Kong, exit B2) This 52-storey silver monolith punctured by 1750 porthole-like windows was Hong Kong's first true 'skyscraper' when it opened in 1973. Inevitably the building has earned its own irreverent nickname: the 'House of 1000 Arseholes'.

HONG KONG CITY HALL
NOTABLE BUILDING

Map p298 (香港大會堂; www.cityhall.gov.hk; 5 Edinburgh Pl, Central; ⊙9am-11pm; MCentral, exit K) The City Hall, built in classic Bauhaus style in 1962, was Hong Kong's first large-scale civic centre. It remains a major cultural venue today, with concert and recital halls, a theatre and exhibition galleries. Within the Lower Block, entered to the east of City Hall's main entrance, the **City Gallery** (⊙10am to 6pm) may awaken the Meccano builder in more than a few visitors.

EATING

★TIM HO WAN, THE DIM SUM SPECIALISTS
DIM SUM $

Map p298 (添好運點心專門店; ☑852 2332 3078; www.timhowan.com; Shop 12a, Podium Level 1, 8 Finance St, IFC Mall, Central; dishes HK$50; ⊙9am-8.30pm; MHong Kong, exit E1) Opened by a former Four Seasons chef, Tim Ho Wan was the first ever budget dim sum place to receive a Michelin star. Many relocations and branches later, the star is still tucked snugly inside their tasty titbits, including the top-selling baked barbecue pork bun. Expect to wait 15 to 40 minutes for a table.

CITY HALL MAXIM'S PALACE
DIM SUM $

Map p298 (美心皇宮; ☑852 2521 1303; 3rd fl, Lower Block, Hong Kong City Hall, 1 Edinburgh Pl, Central; meals from HK$150; ⊙11am-3pm Mon-Sat, 9am-3pm Sun; ☜⛟; MCentral, exit K) This 'palace' offers the quintessential Hong Kong dim sum experience. It's cheerful, it's noisy

and it takes place in a huge kitschy hall with dragon decorations and hundreds of locals. A dizzying assortment of dim sum is paraded on trolleys the old-fashioned way. There's breakfast on Sunday from 9am, but people start queuing for a table at 8.30am.

A seat by the window will let you see the harbour or, a more common sight, land reclamation in progress.

LIN HEUNG TEA HOUSE
CANTONESE, DIM SUM $

Map p298 (☑852 2544 4556; 160-164 Wellington St, Central; meals from HK$100; ⊙6am-11pm, dim sum to 3.30pm; MSheung Wan, exit E2) In the morning, this famous tea house is packed, just as it was in 1926, with older men reading newspapers. Dim sum (from HK$12), served from trolleys, is quickly snapped up, so hover near the kitchen if you want more choices.

The big bun and liver siu mai are coveted items, prized more for their nostalgic value than their taste. But the lotus-root patties and the braised stuffed duck (HK$150; advance booking required) live up to their reputation.

TASTY CONGEE & NOODLE WONTON SHOP
NOODLES $

Map p298 (正斗粥麵專家; ☑852 2295 0101; Shop 3016, Podium Level 3, 8 Finance St, IFC Mall, Central; dishes HK$90-200; ⊙11am-10.45pm; MHong Kong, exit E1) This clean and affordable eatery in the ultra-posh IFC Mall has a long line at lunchtime. So learn from the ladies of leisure – shop first, eat later. Delayed gratification also means you'll be able to sample more of the Michelin-crowned deliciousness – shrimp wontons, prawn congee, stir-fried flat noodles with beef...

PIERRE HERMÉ
BAKERY $

Map p298 (www.pierreherme.com; Shop 1019c, Level 1, 8 Finance St, IFC Mall, Central; boxes of macarons from HK$210; ⊙10am-9pm; MHong Kong Station, exit A1 or A2) Hong Kongers are in the midst of a love affair with macarons, so when this legendary French patissier opened in IFC Mall there were lines for days. Stop in to pick up a box of these jewel-like treats, in flavours ranging from the classic (chocolate, pistachio, raspberry) to the avant garde (olive, foie gras, white truffle).

SING KEE
DAI PAI DONG $

Map p298 (盛記; ☑852 2541 5678; 9-10 Stanley St, Soho; meals HK$200; ⊙11am-3pm & 6-11pm; ⛟; MCentral, exit D2) In the fine-dining

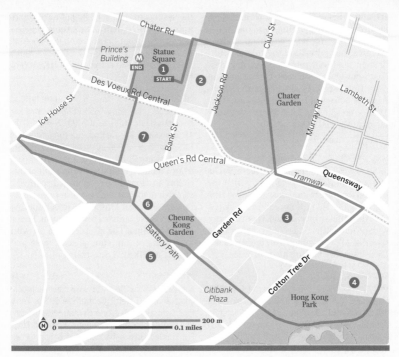

Neighbourhood Walk
Exploring Hong Kong's Heart

START STATUE SQ
END CENTRAL MTR STATION
LENGTH 1.5KM, 45 MINUTES

Begin the walk at **1 Statue Square** (p71) and take in the handsome outline of the neoclassical **2 Former Legislative Council Building** (p70), one of the few colonial-era survivors in the area and the former seat of Hong Kong's modern legislature.

Walk southwest through Chater Garden park and cross over Garden Rd to the angular, modern lines of the **3 Bank of China Tower** (p70), which has amazing views from the 43rd floor.

Duck into Hong Kong Park for the free **4 Flagstaff House Museum of Tea Ware** (p101), displaying valuable pots, cups and other elegant tea ware. Sample some of China's finest teas in the serene cafe.

From here take elevated walkways west over Cotton Tree Dr, through Citibank Plaza, over Garden Rd and through Cheung Kong Garden to **5 St John's Cathedral** (p70), dating from 1849. It is a modest building to earn the title of cathedral, especially with the towering corporate cathedrals now surrounding it, but it is an important historic Hong Kong monument all the same.

Follow Battery Path past the **6 Former French Mission Building** (p71) to Ice House St. Cross over and walk right (east) along Queen's Rd Central to the **7 HSBC building** (p68) and up the escalator (if it's open) to the large airy atrium. Walk through the ground-floor plaza to pat Stephen and Stitt, the two lions guarding the exit to Des Voeux Rd Central.

The closest Central MTR station entrance is a short distance to the north along the pedestrian walkway between Statue Sq and Prince's Building.

enclave of Soho, finding a good and cheap meal can be tricky. Sing Kee, one of the few surviving *dai pai dong* (food stalls) in the area, has withstood the tide of gentrification, and still retains a working-class, laugh-out-loud character. Go-tos here include Hong Kong classics like garlic prawns, fried noodles and sweet-and-sour pork. There's no signage. Look for the crammed tables at the end of Stanley St.

YUE HING
DAI PAI DONG $

Map p298 (裕興; 76-78 Stanley St, Soho; meals HK$25-40; ⊗8.15am-2pm; ⓂCentral, exit D2) One of a gang of *dai pai dong* (food stalls) earmarked for preservation, easygoing Yue Hing reinvents the Hong Kong sandwich by topping the usual suspects (ham, spam and egg) with peanut butter and cooked cabbage. And it works! Allow 15 minutes for preparation as these wacky wedges are made to order.

OLIVER'S, THE DELICATESSEN
SUPERMARKET $

Map p298 (☑852 2810 7710; www.oliversthedeli.com.hk; 201-205, Prince's Bldg, 10 Chater Rd, Central; meals HK$80-150; ⊗8am-9pm Mon-Fri, 8.30am-8pm Sat & Sun; ⓂCentral) The grab-and-go gourmet salads and sandwiches at this high-end international grocery store are popular with Central workers looking for a desk meal. Great place to stock up on picnic supplies.

LEI GARDEN
CANTONESE, DIM SUM $$

Map p298 (利苑酒家; ☑852 2295 0238; www.leigarden.hk/en/; Shop 3007-3011, Level 3, 8 Finance St, IFC Mall, Central; meals HK$180-900; ⊗11.30am-3pm & 6-11pm; 🛜📶; ⓂHong Kong, exit E1) Military-like control of food quality has earned a number of the 24 Lei Garden outlets, including this one, a Michelin star, but this branch at the IFC Mall has the most contemporary environment and the most professional staff. Signature dishes include roast meats, dim sum and the award-winning dessert – sweet sago soup with mango and pomelo. Booking essential.

ISLAND TANG
CANTONESE, DIM SUM $$

Map p298 (港島廳; ☑852 2526 8798; www.islandtang.com; Shop 222, 9 Queen's Rd Central, Galleria, Central; set lunch from HK$308, dinner from HK$400; ⊗noon-2.30pm & 6-10.30pm; 🛜; ⓂCentral, exit D1) Island Tang can easily be a place where, as the Chinese say, one goes to 'devour the decor' – the 1930s art deco interior is sheer elegance. But admirably,

the restaurant has kept its culinary standards extremely high. The exquisite selections range from Cantonese home-cooking to banquet-style seafood dishes, which means a meal can set you back HK$300 or HK$3000.

HEICHINROU
CANTONESE $$

Map p298 (聘珍樓; ☑852 2868 9229; www.heichinrou.com; G05 & 107-108, Nexxus Bldg, 41 Connaught Rd, Central; lunch/dinner from HK$200/350; ⊗10.30am-midnight; 🛜📶; ⓂCentral, exit C) It's everything you'd expect from a modern Cantonese restaurant of this calibre in Hong Kong – polished service, a somewhat formal ambience, refined cooking and good tea. This makes its self-touting as the 'oldest Chinese restaurant in Japan' a little baffling. The afternoon tea set with four kinds of dim sum, snack, staple and dessert for HK$128 is a steal.

WATERMARK
EUROPEAN $$

Map p298 (☑852 2167 7251; www.cafedecogroup.com; Shop L, Level P, Central Pier 7, Star Ferry Pier, Central; lunch & brunch from HK$400, dinner HK$600; ⊗noon-2.30pm & 6pm-late Mon-Fri, 11.30am-3pm & 6pm-late Sat & Sun; 🛜📶; ⓂHong Kong, exit A2) With its location on the Star Ferry Pier, Watermark commands panoramic views of Victoria Harbour. It's airy during the day and romantic at night, and you can feel the sway of the waves at some of the tables. Dry-aged rib-eye and seafood are the highlights of its solid European menu. Weekend brunch is a big draw.

★ LUNG KING HEEN
CANTONESE, DIM SUM $$$

Map p298 (龍景軒; ☑852 3196 8888; www.fourseasons.com/hongkong; Four Seasons Hotel, 8 Finance St, Central; lunch HK$200-500. dinner HK$500-2000; ⊗noon-2.30pm & 6-10.30pm; 🛜; ⓂHong Kong, exit E1) The world's first Chinese restaurant to receive three Michelin stars still retains them. The Cantonese food, though by no means peerless in Hong Kong, is excellent in both taste and presentation, and when combined with the harbour views and the impeccable service, provides a truly stellar dining experience. The signature steamed lobster and scallop dumplings sell out early.

★ CAPRICE
MODERN FRENCH $$$

Map p298 (☑852 3196 8888; www.fourseasons.com/hongkong; Four Seasons Hotel, 8 Finance St, Central; set lunch/dinner from HK$540/1740; ⊗noon-2.30pm & 6-10.30pm; 🛜; ⓂHong Kong, exit E1) In contrast to its opulent decor, Caprice, with two Michelin stars, has a straightforward menu. The meals are masterfully crafted from ingredients flown in daily from France. The selections change, but experience says anything with duck, langoustine or pork belly is out of this world. Their artisanal cheeses, imported weekly, are the best you can get in Hong Kong.

AMBER
MODERN EUROPEAN $$$

Map p298 (☑852 2132 0066; www.mandarin oriental.com/landmark; Mandarin Oriental, 15 Queen's Rd, Central; set lunch HK$598-1288, set dinner HK$2068; ☺noon-2.30pm & 6.30-10.30pm; Ⓜ Central, exit G) With dusk-like lighting and 3000 hanging 'organ pipes', it feels a tad formal, but once you've sampled Chef Ekkebus's masterful modern takes on traditional French dishes, you'll warm to this two Michelin–star restaurant. Changing menus never fail to surprise and delight – think Hokkaido sea urchin with lobster jelly and seaweed waffles or duck foie gras with daikon radish fondant.

L'ATELIER DE JOËL ROBUCHON
MODERN FRENCH $$$

Map p298 (☑852 2166 9000; www.robuchon.hk; Shop 401, 15 Queen's Rd Central, Landmark, Central; set lunch HK$598-858, set dinner HK$2080, à la carte mains HK$440-1000; ☺noon-2.30pm & 6.30-10.30pm; ☏; Ⓜ Central, exit G) One-third of celebrity chef Joel de Robuchon's Michelin-crowned wonder in Hong Kong, this red-and-black workshop has a tantalising list of tapas (from HK$350) and a 70-page wine list. If you prefer something more formal, visit Le Jardin in the next room. Le Salon de The, one floor down, has the best sandwiches and pastries in town for dine-in or takeaway.

OTTO E MEZZO BOMBANA
MODERN ITALIAN $$$

Map p298 (☑852 2537 8859; www.ottoemezzo bombana.com; Shop 202, 18 Chater Rd, Landmark Alexandra, Central; lunch/dinner from HK$700/1380; ☺noon-2.30pm & 6.30-10.30pm Mon-Sat; ☏; Ⓜ Central, exit H) Asia's only Italian restaurant with three Michelin stars lives up to its name, and Chef Bombana is here, sleeves rolled, to see that it does. 'Eight and a Half' is the place for white truffles, being the host of the local bidding for these pungent diamonds. To eat here though you'll need the tenacity of a truffle hound – book two months ahead.

DUDDELL'S
CANTONESE $$$

Map p298 (都爹利會館; ☑852 2525 9191; www. duddells.co; Level 3 & 4 Shanghai Tang Mansion, 1 Duddell St, Central; lunch HK$500-800, dinner HK$800-1600; ☺noon-2.30pm & 6-10.30pm Mon-Sat; ☏; Ⓜ Central, exit G) Light Cantonese fare is served in riveting spaces enhanced by artwork – a graceful dining room awash in diffused light; a marble-tiled salon in modernised '50s chic; a leafy terrace. Saturday brunch (HK$680; noon to 3.30pm) with free-flowing champagne and all-you-can-eat dim sum is a welcome treat, especially given the usually petite serving portions.

INAGIKU
JAPANESE $$$

Map p298 (稲菊日本餐廳; ☑852 2805 0600; www.fourseasons.com/hongkong; Four Seasons Hotel, 8 Finance St, Central; lunch/dinner from HK$600/900; ☺11.30am-3pm & 6-11pm; Ⓜ Central, exit A) Inagiku, meaning 'rice chrysanthemum', is perfection. It's a formal place with subtle interiors and stunning views of the harbour, and attention is lavished on every dish. You can choose to sit at one of the sushi, teppanyaki or tempura bars and watch the chefs work their magic, or bask in the romantic privacy of a table. If money's no an issue, order the *kaiseki*, a multicourse meal comprising seasonal ingredients from Japan, prepared with finesse and plated like art.

PIERRE
MODERN FRENCH $$$

Map p298 (☑852 2825 4001; www.mandarin oriental.com/hongkong; Mandarin Oriental, 5 Connaught Rd, Central; set lunch HK$498-598, set dinner HK$998-1598; ☺noon-2.30pm Mon-Fri, 6.30-10.30pm Mon-Sat; ☏; Ⓜ Central, exit F) The godfather of fusion, Pierre Gagnaire, has created a provocative menu in the city that embodies the concept. Amuse-bouche might be a marshmallow sprinkled with shrimp powder, dessert a caramelised rocket salad – and it works. The decor, with portholes and chandeliers, is reminiscent of a cruise liner, especially when adding the harbour view. Pierre has two Michelin stars.

🍷 DRINKING & NIGHTLIFE

MO BAR
BAR

Map p298 (☑852 2132 0077; 15 Queen's Rd Central, Landmark, Central; ☺7am-1.30am; ☏; Ⓜ Central, exit D1) If you want to imbibe in the quiet or to catch up with a chat, the swish MO Bar, attached to the Mandarin's swanky outpost at the Landmark Oriental (p220), offers peace, soft lighting and a first-rate drinks list of wines and cocktails.

GOOD SPRING CO
HERBAL TEA

Map p298 (春回堂; ☑852 2544 3518; 8 Cochrane St, Soho; tea HK$7-30; ◷8.45am-8pm; MCentral, exit D2) This Chinese medicine shop has a counter selling herbal teas – for detoxing, getting rid of water, cooling the body or treating colds. The most popular is the bitter 24-herb tea. There's also the fragrant chrysanthemum infusion. If you like, the English-speaking herbalist will take your pulse and prescribe a (black and bitter) medicinal soup.

SEVVA
COCKTAIL BAR

Map p298 (☑852 2537 1388; www.sevva.hk; 25th fl, Prince's Bldg, 10 Chater Rd, Central; ◷noon-midnight Mon-Thu, to 2am Fri & Sat; ☎; MCentral, exit H) If there was a million-dollar view in Hong Kong, it'd be the one from the balcony of ultra-stylish Sevva – skyscrapers so close you can see their arteries of steel, with the harbour and Kowloon in the distance. At night it takes your breath away. To get there, though, you have to overcome expensive drinks and patchy service.

Book ahead if you want a table on the balcony, but even if you don't, you can go out to take pictures.

RED BAR
BAR

Map p298 (☑852 8129 8882; www.pure-red.com; Level 4, 8 Finance St, Two IFC, Central; ◷noon-midnight Mon-Wed, to 1am Thu, to 3am Fri & Sat, to 10pm Sun, happy hour 6-9pm; ☎; MHong Kong, exit E1) Red Bar's combination of alfresco drinking and harbour views is hard to beat. Expect to meet lots of smartly dressed finance types from the corporate offices nearby. DJs playing funk and jazz turn up the volume as the weekend approaches.

Hint: if you're on a budget, grab some beers at 7-Eleven and take one of the rooftop tables adjacent to Red; it's public space.

BEER BAY
BAR

Map p298 (Hong Kong Central Ferry Pier 3, Central; ◷3pm-midnight; MHong Kong, exit A1 or A2) Still wearing your sightseeing grubbies and don't feel up to the glam nightspots of Central? Head to this ultra-local open-air beer bar at the ferry pier, a favourite of outer-island-dwellers looking for a quick tipple before heading home. Grab one of Beer Bay's affordable British imports and sit on the concrete steps watching the water.

CAPTAIN'S BAR
BAR

Map p298 (船長吧; ☑852 2825 4006; www.mandarinoriental.com.hk; Mandarin Oriental, 5 Connaught Rd Central, Central; ◷11am-2am Mon-Sat, to 1am Sun; ☎; MCentral, exit F) Captain's Bar has been attracting drinkers with its clubby atmosphere and polished service for half a century. Though looking slightly old-fashioned now, it still makes some of the best martinis in town and serves ice-cold draught beer in chilled silver mugs. It's a good place to talk business, at least until the cover band strikes up at 9pm.

PIER 7
BAR

Map p298 (☑852 2167 8377; www.cafedecogroup.com; Shop M, Roof Viewing Deck, Central Pier 7, Star Ferry Pier, Central; ◷9am-midnight, happy hour 6-9pm; ☎; MHong Kong, exit A1) Sitting atop the Star Ferry terminal, Pier 7 has a large outdoor terrace with views of neighbouring skyscrapers, the hills of Kowloon and a sliver of the harbour. It's an unpretentious spot for a quiet pre-movie (or post-dinner) drink and some light refreshments. On random weekends there are reggae DJs in the house and the vibe turns shaggy.

⭐ ENTERTAINMENT

GRAPPA'S CELLAR
LIVE MUSIC

Map p298 (☑852 2521 2322; http://elgrande.com.hk/restaurant/grappas-cellar/; 1 Connaught Pl, Central; ◷9pm-late; MHong Kong, exit B2) For at least two weekends a month, this subterranean Italian restaurant morphs into a jazz or rock music venue – chequered tablecloths and all. Call or visit the website for event and ticketing details.

SENSES 99
LIVE MUSIC

Map p298 (☑852 9466 2675; www.sense99.com; 2nd & 3rd fl, 99 Wellington St, Soho; ◷9pm-late Fri & Sat; MSheung Wan, exit E2) This two-floor speakeasy inside a pre-WWII building has all the features of a tasteful mid-century residence – high ceilings, balconies overlooking a quiet street, folding screen doors and distressed couches. Music sessions begin after 10pm, but before that you can take charge of the drum set and electric guitar on the 3rd floor to start a jam session or join one.

PALACE IFC CINEMA

Map p298 (☎852 2388 6268; Podium Level 1, 8 Finance St, IFC Mall, Central; Ⓜ Hong Kong, exit F) This eight-screen cinema complex in the IFC Mall is arguably the most advanced and comfortable in the territory. But you can't pull up the armrests if you're seated in the back row.

🛍 SHOPPING

★**SHANGHAI TANG** CLOTHING, HOMEWARE

Map p298 (上海灘; ☎852 2525 7333; www.shanghaitang.com; 1 Duddell St, Shanghai Tang Mansion, Central; ⊘10.30am-8pm; Ⓜ Central, exit D1) This elegant four-level store is the place to go if you fancy a body-hugging *qipao* (cheongsam) with a modern twist, a Chinese-style clutch or a lime-green mandarin jacket. Custom tailoring is available; it takes two weeks to a month and requires a fitting. Shanghai Tang also stocks cushions, picture frames, teapots, even mah-jong tile sets, designed in a modern chinoiserie style.

★**LANE CRAWFORD** DEPARTMENT STORE

Map p298 (連卡佛; ☎852 2118 3388; www.lanecrawford.com; Podium Level 3, 8 Finance St, IFC Mall, Central; ⊘10am-9pm; Ⓜ Central, exit A) The territory's answer to London's Harrods, Lane Crawford (c 1850) was Hong Kong's original Western-style department store, and one that, admirably, has succeeded in rejuvenating itself while remaining classy over the decades. This flagship store sells everything from fashion to crockery. There are four other branches in town.

★**KOWLOON SOY COMPANY** CHINESE CONDIMENTS

Map p298 (九龍醬園; ☎852 2544 3695; www.kowloonsoy.com; 9 Graham St, Soho; ⊘8am-6.15pm Mon-Fri, to 6pm Sat; Ⓜ Central, exit D1) *The* shop (c 1917) for artisanal soy sauce, premier cru Chinese miso and other high-quality condiments; it also sells preserved eggs (*pei darn,* 皮蛋) and pickled ginger (*suen geung,* 酸姜), which are often served together at restaurants. Did you know that preserved eggs, being alkaline, can make young red wines taste fuller-bodied? Just try it.

★**PICTURE THIS** GIFTS & SOUVENIRS

Map p298 (☎852 2525 2803; www.picturethiscollection.com; 13th fl, 9 Queen's Rd, Central; ⊘10am-7pm Mon-Sat, noon-5pm Sun; Ⓜ Central, exit H) The vintage posters, photographs, prints and antique maps of Hong Kong and Asia on sale here will appeal to collectors or anyone seeking an unusual gift. There's also an assortment of antiquarian books related to Hong Kong. Prices are not cheap but they guarantee all maps and prints to be originals.

★**ARMOURY** CLOTHING

Map p298 (☎852 2804 6991; www.thearmoury.com; 307 Pedder Bldg, 12 Pedder St, Central; ⊘11am-8pm Mon-Sat; Ⓜ Central, exit D1) The Armoury can help any man look like a dapper gentleman, whatever his build – the elegant shop is a specialist in refined menswear sourced from around the world. You can choose from British-, Italian- and Asian-tailored suits, and a high-quality selection of shoes and ties to match. Still not good enough? Ask about their bespoke suits and custom footwear.

★**BLANC DE CHINE** FASHION & ACCESSORIES

Map p298 (源; ☎852 2104 7934; www.blancdechine.com; Shop 123, Prince's Bldg, 10 Chater Rd, Central; ⊘10.30am-7.30pm Mon-Sat, noon-6pm Sun; Ⓜ Central, exit H) This sumptuous store specialises in Chinese men's jackets and silk dresses for women, both off-the-rack and made-to-measure. A gorgeous sequinned gown takes about four weeks to make, including one fitting. If you're not in Hong Kong after a month, the shop will ship it to you. The satin bed linens are also exquisite (as are the old ship's cabinets in which they are displayed).

IFC MALL MALL

Map p298 (☎852 2295 3308; www.ifc.com.hk; 8 Finance St, Central; Ⓜ Hong Kong, exit F) Hong Kong's most luxurious shopping mall boasts 200 high-fashion boutiques linking the One (p71) and Two (p71) IFC towers and the Four Seasons Hotel (p220). Outlets include Prada, Gucci, Céline, Jimmy Choo, Vivienne Tam, Zegna...we could go on. The Hong Kong Airport Express Station is downstairs.

FOOK MING TONG TEA SHOP FOOD & DRINK

Map p298 (福茗堂; ☎852 2295 0368; www.fookmingtong.com; Shop 3006, Podium Level 3, 8 Finance St, IFC Mall, Central; ⊘10.30am-8pm Mon-Sat, 11am-8pm Sun; Ⓜ Central, exit A) Tea-making accoutrements and carefully chosen teas of various ages and grades are available here, from gunpowder to Nanyan Ti Guan Yin Crown Grade – costing anything from HK$10 to HK$9000 per 100g.

CITY'SUPER
FOOD & DRINKS

Map p298 (www.citysuper.com.hk; Shop 1041-1049, Level 1, 8 Finance St, IFC Mall, Central; ☻10.30am-9.30pm; MHong Kong, exit F) This gourmet grocery store sells a range of top-notch, hard-to-find ingredients from all over the world, as well as natural and organic foods. The prices, of course, are on the high side.

LANDMARK
MALL

Map p298 (置地廣場; ☎852 2525 4142; www.centralhk.com; 1 Pedder St, Central; MCentral, exit G) The most central of all shopping centres, the Landmark has high fashion and good eating in a pleasant, open space. It has become a home almost exclusively to the very high-end fashion brands and boutiques (Gucci, Louis Vuitton, TODs etc).

SPORTS & ACTIVITIES

TEN FEET TALL
FOOT MASSAGE

Map p298 (☎852 2971 1010; www.tenfeettall.com.hk; 20th & 21st fl, L Place, 139 Queen's Rd, Central; ☻11am-midnight Mon-Thu, 10.30am-1.30am Fri & Sat, 10.30am-12.30am Sun; MCentral, exit D2) This sprawling comfort den (745 sq metres) offers a range of treatments from foot reflexology and shoulder massage to hardcore pressure-point massage and aromatic oil treatments. The interiors were created by French restaurant designers.

SPA AT THE FOUR SEASONS
SPA

Map p298 (☎852 3196 8900; www.fourseasons.com/hongkong/spa.html; Four Seasons Hotel, 8 Finance St, Central; ☻8am-11pm (last appointment 10pm); MHong Kong, exit F) A 1860-sq-metre, ultra-high-end spa with a comprehensive range of beauty, massage and health treatments, plus ice fountain, hot cups, moxibustion and even a 'herbal cocoon room'.

IMPAKT MARTIAL ARTS & FITNESS CENTRE
MARTIAL ARTS

Map p298 (☎852 2167 7218; www.impakt.hk; 110-116 Queen's Rd Central, 2nd fl, Wings Bldg, Central; ☻7am-10pm Mon-Fri, 8am-7pm Sat, 10am-5pm Sun; MCentral, exit D2) Impakt is one of the few martial arts centres with female trainers. They teach muay Thai, kickboxing, jiu jitsu, karate etc to GI Jane wannabes and experienced fighters alike. You can walk in for a one-off class or to use the gym facilities for HK$250. You can book personal private training for upwards of HK$325 per person per hour.

PURE FITNESS
GYM

Map p298 (☎852 8129 8000; www.pure-fitness.com; Level 3, 8 Finance St, IFC Mall, Central; ☻6am-midnight Mon-Sat, 8am-10pm Sun; MHong Kong, exit F) A sleek urban gym offering comprehensive facilities and classes for cardio-strength training, cycling, kickboxing, yoga, Pilates and dance fitness. It's a favourite among the professionals working in the area. In addition to this location, there are seven others throughout the city. Pure offers short-term contracts, ideal for travellers on a longer stay or those who pop in and out of Hong Kong.

Hong Kong Island: The Peak & the Northwest

LAN KWAI FONG & SOHO | SHEUNG WAN | MID-LEVELS & THE PEAK | WESTERN DISTRICT

Neighbourhood Top Five

1 **Victoria Peak** (p81) Taking the white-knuckle ascent to Victoria Peak on the Peak Tram for night views from the summit.

2 **Sheung Wan** (p86) Strolling the streets of Sheung Wan to uncover the fascinating history of 19th-century Hong Kong.

3 **Lan Kwai Fong** (p92) Bar-hopping your way over the inviting slopes of 'LKF', as it's known to local party animals, the centre of Hong Kong Island's bar scene.

4 **Luk Yu Tea House** (p89) Enjoying delicious food under ceiling fans and stained-glass windows at this 1933 Hong Kong staple.

5 **Soho** (p83) Trawling through the galleries and boutiques of Soho, the centre of the city's gallery world.

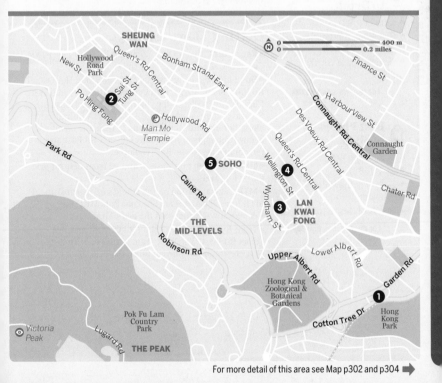

For more detail of this area see Map p302 and p304 ➡

Lonely Planet's Top Tip

Besides partying in Lan Kwai Fong and Soho, don't miss the neighbourhood around Tai Ping Shan St in Sheung Wan. The area is a burgeoning boho haven, with cafes, galleries and boutiques – all quite low-key and tasteful – mushrooming alongside weather-beaten shrines.

 ### Best Places to Eat

- Luk Yu Tea House (p89)
- Chachawan (p89)
- Dumpling Yuan (p87)
- The Boss (p89)

For reviews, see p87

 ### Best Places to Drink

- Club 71 (p92)
- Ping Pong Gintoneria (p95)
- Angel's Share Whisky Bar (p92)

For reviews, see p92 ➡

 ### Best Places to Shop

- Grotto Fine Art (p96)
- PMQ (p83)
- Gallery of the Pottery Workshop (p96)
- Goods of Desire (p95)

For reviews, see p95 ➡

Explore: the Peak & the Northwest

Begin by exploring Sheung Wan's old neighbourhoods in the morning when the temples and the dried seafood shops get into full swing. Sample some local fare in the area before heading to Hollywood Rd to browse the antique shops and art galleries. If time allows, trek up to the Mid-Levels to check out the museums and religious monuments. Take the Peak Tram in Central to Victoria Peak; wait to see the lights come on in the city. Descend and return to Sheung Wan for dinner, followed by pub crawling in Lan Kwai Fong and Soho.

Local Life

➡ **Hang-outs** For intellectual banter and a bohemian vibe, head to Club 71 (p92), the haunt of activist-artist types.

➡ **Shopping** Li Yuen St East and West, two alleyways that link Des Voeux Rd Central with Queen's Rd Central, have a jumble of inexpensive clothing, handbags and jewellery.

➡ **Old Chinese Quarter** The area around Tai Ping Shan St is where the old Chinese quarter used to be in the 19th century; you'll see temples and shops specialising in funeral-related services.

Getting There & Away

➡ **Escalator** Caine Rd and Robinson Rd (Mid-Levels) via Central–Mid-Levels Escalator (p84).

➡ **Bus** Lan Kwai Fong and Soho bus 26 along Hollywood Rd links Sheung Wan with Central, Admiralty and Wan Chai; Western District bus 3B from Jardine House in Central and buses 23, 40 and 40M from Admiralty stop along Bonham Rd; the Peak bus 15 from the terminus below Exchange Sq runs along Queen's Rd East and terminates below the Peak Galleria.

➡ **Minibus** Green minibuses 8 and 22 from Central pass Caine Rd (Mid-Levels).

➡ **MTR** Central station on the Island and Tsuen Wan MTR lines. Sheung Wan, Sai Ying Pun, HKU and KennedyTown stations on the Island line.

➡ **Tram** Runs along Des Voeux Rd Central and Des Voeux Rd West. The Peak Tram (p265) runs from the lower terminus on Garden Rd to the Peak Tower.

MATHEE VORAN / SHUTTERSTOCK ©

 TOP SIGHT
VICTORIA PEAK

Standing at 552m, Victoria Peak is the highest point on Hong Kong Island. The Peak is also one of the most visited spots by tourists in Hong Kong, and it's not hard to see why. Sweeping views of the vibrant metropolis, verdant woods, easy but spectacular walks – all are reachable in just eight minutes from Central.

The best way to reach the Peak is by the 125-year-old gravity-defying **Peak Tram** (p265). Rising almost vertically above the high-rises nearby, Asia's oldest funicular clanks its way up the hillside to finish at the Peak Tower. The lower terminus in Central has an interesting gallery that houses a replica of the earliest carriage. The Peak Galleria (p85), adjoining the anvil-shaped Peak Tower (p84), has an admission-free viewing deck, though its harbour views are obscured.

Some 500m to the northwest of the upper terminus, up steep Mt Austin Rd, is the site of the old governor's summer lodge, which was burned to the ground by Japanese soldiers during WWII. The beautiful **gardens** remain, however, and have been refurbished with faux-Victorian gazebos and stone pillars. They are open to the public.

The dappled **Morning Trail**, a 3.5km circuit formed by Harlech Rd on the south, just outside the Peak Lookout, and Lugard Rd on the northern slope, which it runs into, takes about 45 minutes to cover. A further 2km along Peak Rd will lead you to Pok Fu Lam Reservoir Rd. Hatton Rd, reachable by Lugard or Harlech Rds, on the western slope goes all the way down to the University of Hong Kong. The 50km Hong Kong Trail also starts on the Peak.

DON'T MISS

→ Peak Tram
→ Peak Trails
→ Victoria Peak Garden

PRACTICALITIES

→ 維多利亞山頂
→ ☑852 2522 0922
→ www.thepeak.com.hk
→ admission free
→ ⊙24hr
→ 🚌bus 15 from Central, below Exchange Sq, 🚋Peak Tram Lower Terminus

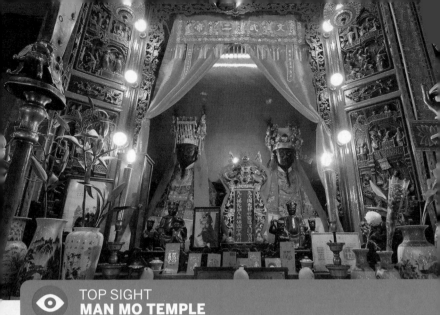

SASIMOTO / SHUTTERSTOCK ©

TOP SIGHT
MAN MO TEMPLE

One of Hong Kong's oldest temples, atmospheric Man Mo Temple is dedicated to the god of literature ('Man'), who's always holding a writing brush, and the god of war ('Mo'), who wields a sword.

Built in 1847 during the Qing dynasty by wealthy Chinese merchants, it was, besides a place of worship, a court of arbitration for local disputes when trust was thin between the Chinese and the colonialists. Oaths taken at this Taoist temple (often accompanied by the ritual beheading of a rooster) were accepted by the colonial government.

Outside the main entrance are four **gilt plaques** on poles that used to be carried around at processions. Two describe the gods being worshipped inside, one requests silence and a show of respect within the temple's grounds, and the last warns menstruating women to keep out of the main hall. Inside the temple are two 19th-century sedan chairs with elaborate carvings, which used to carry the two gods during festivals.

Lending the temple its beguiling and smoky air are rows of large earth-coloured spirals suspended from the roof, like strange fungi in an upside-down garden. These are incense coils burned as offerings by worshippers.

Off to the side is **Lit Shing Kung**, the 'saints' palace', a place of worship for other Buddhist and Taoist deities. Another hall, **Kung Sor** ('Public Meeting Place'), used to serve as a court of justice to settle disputes among the Chinese community before the modern judicial system was introduced. A couplet at the entrance urges those entering to leave their selfish interests and prejudices outside. Fortune-tellers beckon from inside.

DON'T MISS
➡ The main temple
➡ Lit Shing Kung
➡ Fortune-tellers

PRACTICALITIES
➡ 文武廟
➡ Map p302, A2
➡ ☏852 2540 0350
➡ 124-126 Hollywood Rd, Sheung Wan
➡ admission free
➡ ⊘8am-6pm
➡ 🚌26

◉ SIGHTS

◉ Lan Kwai Fong & Soho

GRAHAM STREET MARKET
MARKET

Map p302 (嘉咸街; Graham St, Central; ☻8am-6pm; 🚇5B) This busy street market has been providing Central Hong Kong with fruit, veggies, tofu, duck eggs and all variety of fermented beans and sauces for nearly 200 years. Sadly Graham St is in peril, as urban authorities plan to replace it with hotels and apartments in coming years. But for now this is one of the most convenient places to see Hong Kong street life in action, from ancient grannies weighing carrots on rusted scales to market cats sleeping atop beds of pak choy.

PMQ
ARTS CENTRE

Map p302 (元創方; ☎852 2870 2335; www.pmq. org.hk; S614, Block A, PMQ, 35 Aberdeen St, Soho; ☻building open 7am-11pm, most shops open noon-8pm; 🚇26, Ⓜ Central, exit D2) This new arts hub occupies the modernist buildings and breezy courtyard of the old married police quarters (c 1951). Dozens of small galleries and shops hawk hip handmade jewellery, leather goods, prints, clothing, housewares and more, making the PMQ a terrific place to hunt for non-tacky souvenirs. There are also several restaurants and bakeries, and a large exhibit space with a rotating variety of free shows.

LIANGYI MUSEUM
MUSEUM

Map p302 (兩依博物館; ☎852 2806 8280; www.liangyimuseum.com; 181-199 Hollywood Rd, Soho; admission HK$200; ☻10am-6pm Tue-Sat; Ⓜ Central, exit D2) This private three-floor museum houses two exquisite collections – antique Chinese furniture from the Ming and Qing dynasties, and Chinese-inspired European vanities from the 19th and 20th century. The former is one of the world's best. The 400 pieces of precious *huanghuali* and zitan furniture are shown in rotating exhibitions that change every six months. The only way to visit is by contacting the museum at least a day in advance to join a small tour.

CENTRAL POLICE STATION
HISTORIC BUILDING

Map p302 (10 Hollywood Rd, Lan Kwai Fong; 🚇26, Ⓜ Central, exit D2) Built between 1841 and 1919, Hong Kong's oldest symbol of law and order is this now-disused, police-magistracy-prison complex modelled after London's Old Bailey. The large compound is currently being redeveloped into an arts hub with cinema, museum and boutique shopping mall.

◉ Sheung Wan

MAN MO TEMPLE
TAOIST TEMPLE

See p82.

PAK SING ANCESTRAL HALL
TEMPLE

Map p304 (廣福祠; Kwong Fuk Ancestral Hall; 42 Tai Ping Shan St, Sheung Wan; ☻8am-6pm; 🚇26) In the 19th century, many Chinese who left home in search of better horizons died overseas. As it was the wish of traditional Chinese to be buried in their home towns, this temple was built in 1856 to store corpses awaiting burial in China, and to serve as a public ancestral hall for those who could not afford the expense of bone repatriation. Families of the latter have erected 3000 memorial tablets for their ancestors in a room behind the altar.

Pak Sing Ancestral Hall also functioned as a clinic for Chinese patients refusing treatment by Western doctors. The words *pak shing* mean 'people' – it was a temple for the people.

CAT STREET
AREA

Map p302 (摩囉街; Upper Lascar Row, Sheung Wan; ☻10am-6pm; 🚇26) Just north of (and parallel to) Hollywood Rd is Upper Lascar Row, aka 'Cat Street', a pedestrian-only lane lined with antique and curio shops and stalls selling found objects, cheap jewellery and newly minted ancient coins. It's a fun place to trawl through for a trinket or two, but expect most of the memorabilia to be mass-produced fakes.

PALACE OF MOON & WATER KWUN YUM TEMPLE
BUDDHIST TEMPLE

Map p304 (水月觀音堂; 7 Tai Ping Shan St, Sheung Wan; ☻9am-6pm; 🚇26) Not to be confused with Kwun Yum Temple (p84) nearby, this dimly lit temple honours Kwun Yum of a Thousand Arms. Kwun Yum (aka Guanyin) is the Goddess of Compassion. According to legend, Buddha gave her a thousand arms so she could help everyone who needed it. For a small donation, you can give the small wooden windmill at the entrance a spin; it will presumably change your luck.

WESTERN MARKET
HISTORIC BUILDING

Map p304 (西港城; ☑852 6029 2675; 323 Des Voeux Rd Central & New Market St, Sheung Wan; ⊙9am-7pm; 🚇Sheung Wan, exit B) Textile vendors driven off nearby streets in the 1990s moved into this renovated market building (1906) with its red-and-white facade, four-corner towers and other Edwardian features. Now bolts of cloth flank the corridors of the 1st floor. Souvenir shops and the **Grand Stage** (大舞臺飯店; Map p304; ☑852 2815 2311; 2nd fl, Western Market, 323 Des Voeux Rd Central, Sheung Wan; lunch/dinner from HK$120/200; ⊙11.30am-3pm & 7pm-midnight; 🎏; 🚇Sheung Wan, exit E2) restaurant occupy the ground and top floors.

KWUN YUM TEMPLE
BUDDHIST TEMPLE

Map p304 (觀音廟; 34 Tai Ping Shan St, Sheung Wan; ⊙9am-6pm; 🚌26) Built in 1840, Sheung Wan's oldest temple honours Kwun Yum, the Goddess of Mercy. It's a quaint-looking structure, with a magnificent and intricate brass carving just above the doorway. The temple has been renovated with funky structural additions – orange iron railings and a yellow awning printed with Buddhist swastika symbols.

TAI SUI TEMPLE
BUDDHIST TEMPLE

Map p304 (太歲廟; 9 Tai Ping Shan St, Sheung Wan; ⊙9am-6pm; 🚌26) A quirky temple featuring statuettes of deities governing the different Chinese zodiac animals (there are 12 altogether). For less than HK$100 and four red packets (of any amount), they will help you burn incense and offer prayers to bless your animal, which will translate into blessings for you.

MAN WA LANE
AREA

Map p304 (文華里; Man Wa Lane, Sheung Wan; ⊙10am-6pm; 🚇Sheung Wan, exit A1) Kiosks in this alley just east of the Sheung Wan MTR station specialise in name chops: a stone (or wood or jade) seal with the owner's name carved in Chinese on its base. It's combined with Chinese red ink or cinnabar paste to make a seal imprint that can be used in lieu of a handwritten signature. Tell the shop owner your name and he will create an auspicious Chinese version for you.

LEUNG CHUN WOON KEE
SHOP

Map p302 (梁津煥記; www. leungchunwoonkee.com; 17 Square St, Sheung Wan; ⊙9am-5.30pm Mon-Sat; 🚌26) Leung Chun Woon Kee (1904) is one of the last remaining burial garment producers in Hong Kong. White, black, brown or blue are the preferred colours for the clothing, but never red. The Chinese believe only those who want revenge on the living depart in red. Sleeves cover the hands completely – exposed hands make beggars of one's descendants. The outfits also come without pockets to prevent the dead from taking money or luck from their family. It's not permitted to take photos in the shop.

◉ Mid-Levels & the Peak

VICTORIA PEAK
PEAK

See p81.

JAMIA MOSQUE
MOSQUE

Map p302 (些利街清真寺; Lascar Mosque; ☑852 2523 7743; 30 Shelley St, Mid-Levels) Also called Lascar Mosque, Hong Kong's oldest mosque was erected in 1849. Non-Muslims can only admire the mint green facade from the terrace out the front. Jamia Mosque is accessible from the Central–Mid-Levels Escalator.

CENTRAL–MID-LEVELS ESCALATOR
ESCALATOR

Map p302 (⊙down 6-10am, up 10.30am-midnight) The world's longest covered outdoor people-mover zigzags from Central's offices to the homes near Conduit Rd. Embark and let the streets unveil themselves around you – Stanley and Wellington with their glamour and tradition; Gage and Lyndhurst where florists and prostitutes once hawked their wares; Hollywood, Hong Kong's second oldest street; Staunton, whose porcelain shops made way for Soho; then Shelley, named unromantically after an infamous auditor-general.

PEAK TOWER
NOTABLE BUILDING

(凌霄閣; ☑852 2849 0668; 128 Peak Rd, Victoria Peak; ⊙10am-11pm Mon-Fri, 8am-11pm Sat, Sun & public holidays; 🚋Peak Tram) The anvil-shaped Peak Tower makes a good grandstand for great views of the city and harbour. On Level P1 you'll find an outpost of Madame Tussauds (p85), which houses eerie wax likenesses of international stars and local celebrities.

There is an open-air **viewing terrace** (adult/child $30/15) on Level 5.

HONG KONG MUSEUM OF
MEDICAL SCIENCES
MUSEUM

Map p304 (香港醫學博物館; ☑852 2549 5123; www.hkmms.org.hk; 2 Caine Lane, Mid-Levels; adult/concession HK$20/10; ◎10am-5pm Tue-Sat, 1-5pm Sun; ☐3B) This small museum features medical accoutrements, including an old autopsy table and herbal medicine chests, plus a rundown of how Hong Kong coped with the 1894 bubonic plague, and exhibits comparing Chinese and Western medical approaches. Equally interesting is the building, a breezy Edwardian-style, brick-and-tile structure (1905) fronted by bauhinia trees.

From the Central–Mid-Levels Escalator exit on Caine Rd, walk west to Ladder St; descend one flight of steps and turn left. If you take the bus, alight at the Ladder St bus stop on Caine Rd.

OHEL LEAH SYNAGOGUE
SYNAGOGUE

Map p304 (莉亞堂; ☑852 2589 2621; www.ohel leah.org; 70 Robinson Rd, Mid-Levels; ◎by appointment only 10.30am-7pm Mon-Thu, services 7am Mon-Fri, 6pm Mon-Thu; ☐3B, 23) This Moorish Romantic temple, completed in 1902, is named after Leah Gubbay Sassoon, the matriarch of a philanthropic Sephardic Jewish family. It's Hong Kong's earliest synagogue. Be sure to bring ID if you plan on visiting the sumptuous interior. Those who keep kosher can call ahead to shop at the Kosher Mart, Hong Kong's only dedicated kosher grocery store.

DR SUN YAT-SEN
MUSEUM
HISTORIC BUILDING

Map p302 (孫中山紀念館; ☑852 2367 6373; http://hk.drsunyatsen.museum; 7 Castle Rd, Mid-Levels; adult/concession HK$10/5, Wed free; ◎10am-6pm Mon-Wed & Fri, to 7pm Sat & Sun; ☐3B) The museum, dedicated to the father of modern China, is housed in an Edwardian-style building, which is arguably more interesting than the solemn displays of archival materials. Built in 1914, the mansion belonged to Ho Kom-tong, a tycoon from a Eurasian family. It was converted into a Mormon Church in 1960, and became a museum in 2006. If you're taking the bus, alight at the Hong Kong Baptist Church on Caine Rd.

HONG KONG CATHEDRAL OF THE
IMMACULATE CONCEPTION
CHURCH

Map p304 (香港聖母無原罪主教座; ☑852 2522 8212; www.cathedral.catholic.org.hk; 16

THE PEAK OF THE PEAK

While the commercialised part of **Victoria Peak** has scrumptious views, it's not truly the highest point of the mountain. To get as high as possible, walk up Austin Rd to Victoria Peak Garden and take the path up the hill towards the control towers.

Just west of Victoria Peak is the 494m **High West**, a mountain offering tremendous panoramic views with a fraction of the crowds. The only caveat? You have to hike to get here. Take the path from the junction of Hatton, Harlech and Lugard Rds, and prepare for a steep climb. Bring water and decent shoes and expect a one- to 1½-hour round trip.

Caine Rd, Mid-Levels; ◎9.30am-5.30pm Mon-Fri, to 12.30pm Sat, mass 9.30am Sun; ☐23) This Gothic-revival cathedral was built in 1888 and financed largely by the Portuguese faithful from Macau. If taking the bus, alight at Caritas Centre on Caine Rd.

PEAK GALLERIA
VIEWPOINT

(山頂廣場; 118 Peak Rd, Victoria Peak; ☐15) The building is designed to withstand winds of up to 270km/h, theoretically more than the maximum velocity of a No 10 typhoon. The only attraction here is the admission-free viewing deck, which is larger than the one in the Peak Tower (p84) but doesn't have a good view of the harbour. If taking the bus, alight at the stop between Stubbs Rd & Peak Rd

MADAME TUSSAUDS
MUSEUM

(☑852 2849 6966; www.madametussauds.com/ hong-kong/en; Peak Rd, Victoria Peak; adult/child HK$250/180; ◎10am-10pm; ☐15, ☐Peak Tram) Most people go to the Peak for the views or the thrill of ascending Hong Kong's highest point at a preposterous incline on the Peak Tram. But there are some other lures, including this attraction in the Peak Tower (p84), with eerie (and scary) wax likenesses of international stars as well as local celebrities such as Jackie Chan, Andy Lau, Michelle Yeoh, Aaron Kwok and Cecilia Cheung. There are lots of packages available as well. You'll save big if you buy tickets online in advance.

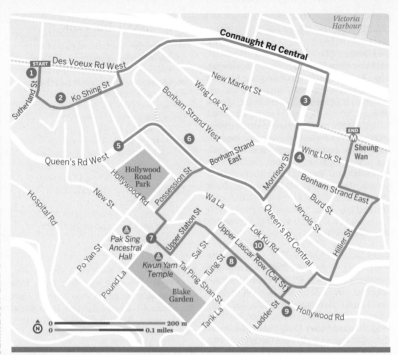

🏃 Neighbourhood Walk
Hong Kong's Wholesale District

START SUTHERLAND ST STOP, KENNEDY TOWN TRAM
END SHEUNG WAN MTR STATION, EXIT B
LENGTH 1.9KM; ONE HOUR

Set off from the Sutherland St stop of the Kennedy Town tram. Have a look at (and a sniff of) Des Voeux Rd West's many ❶ **dried seafood shops** piled with all manner of desiccated sea life. Walk south on Sutherland St to Ko Shing St to browse the medieval-sounding goods on offer from the ❷ **herbal-medicine traders**.

At the end of Ko Shing St, re-enter Des Voeux Rd West and head northeast. Continue along Connaught Rd West, where you'll find the attractive colonial building that houses the ❸ **Western Market** (p84).

At the corner of Morrison St, walk south past Wing Lok St and Bonham Strand, which are both lined with ❹ **shops selling ginseng root and edible birds' nests**. Then turn right onto Queen's Rd Central to the ❺ **incense shops** (p87) selling paper funeral offerings for the dead.

Retrace your steps, and if you're hungry, progress to Queen's Rd West for a quick Chiu Chow meal at ❻ **Chan Kan Kee** (p90). Climb up Possession St, then take a left into Hollywood Rd, before turning right to ascend Pound Lane to where it meets Tai Ping Shan St. Here you'll see four charming ❼ **temples** (p83).

Head southeast down Tai Ping Shan St, then left to descend Upper Station St to the start of Hollywood Rd's ❽ **antique shops**. There's a vast choice of curios and rare, mostly Chinese, treasures.

Continuing east on Hollywood Rd brings you to ❾ **Man Mo Temple** (p82), one of the oldest and most significant temples in the territory.

Take a short hop to the left down Ladder St to Upper Lascar Row, home of the ❿ **Cat Street Market** (p83), which is well stocked with inexpensive Chinese memorabilia. Ladder St brings you back to Queen's Rd Central. Cross the road and follow Hillier St to Bonham Strand. Sheung Wan MTR station is due north.

⊙ Western District

QUEEN'S ROAD WEST
INCENSE SHOPS SHOP

Map p304 (Queen's Rd W, Sheung Wan; ⊘8am-7pm; 🚌26) At 136–150 Queen's Rd West, there are shops selling incense and paper offerings for the dead. The latter are burned to propitiate departed souls and the choice of combustibles is mind-blowing – dim sum, iPad, Rolexes, Viagra tablets and – the latest – solar-powered water heaters. You may buy them as souvenirs, but remember that keeping these offerings meant for the dead (rather than burning them) is supposed to bring bad luck.

UNIVERSITY OF HONG KONG UNIVERSITY

(香港大學; ☎852 2859 2111; www.hku.hk; Pok Fu Lam Rd, Pok Fu Lam; 🚌23, 40 from Admiralty) Established in 1911, HKU is the oldest university in Hong Kong. The **main building**, completed in the Edwardian style in 1912, is a declared monument. Several other early 20th-century buildings on the campus, including the **Hung Hing Ying** (1919) and **Tang Chi Ngong Buildings** (1929), are also protected.

UNIVERSITY MUSEUM & ART GALLERY MUSEUM

(☎852 2241 5500; www.hku.hk/hkumag; Fung Ping Shan Bldg, 94 Bonham Rd, Pok Fu Lam; ⊘9.30am-6pm Mon-Sat, 1-6pm Sun; 🚌23, 40M) 🆓 The University of Hong Kong Museum & Art Gallery houses collections of ceramics and bronzes spanning 5000 years, including exquisite blue-and-white Ming porcelain; decorative mirrors from the Warring States period to the Qing dynasty; and almost 1000 small Nestorian crosses from the Yuan dynasty, the largest such collection in the world. It also hosts temporary exhibitions from around the world – recent favourites include Picasso and Botticelli.

The museum is to the left of the university's Main Building and opposite the start of Hing Hon Rd.

SAI YING PUN
COMMUNITY COMPLEX HISTORIC BUILDING

(西營盤社區綜合大樓; ☎852 2540 2812; 2 High St, Western District; ⊘9am-5.30pm; 🚌12M, 13, 14M) A high-rise imposed on Victorian remains make up this complex that's fondly nicknamed the High Street Haunted House. The grey stone facade and arched verandah, both heritage structures (c 1892), were part of a nurses' dormitory, then a mental asylum and an execution hall during the Japanese Occupation. Rumours of men bursting into flames, women wailing and decapitated spirits spread in the 20 years the building was abandoned. Fires subsequently swallowed everything, except what you see today.

WESTERN DISTRICT
COMMUNITY CENTRE HISTORIC BUILDING

(西區社區中心; ☎852 2119 5001; 36A Western St, Western District; ⊘9am-10.30pm; 🚌37A, 90B) NGO offices and amenity rooms occupy this red-brick Georgian house at the junction of Western St and Third St. The listed building was opened in 1922 as the Tsan Yuk Maternity Hospital to offer obstetrics and gynaelogical services and to train midwives for the British colony.

✗ EATING

✗ Lan Kwai Fong & Soho

★DUMPLING YUAN NORTHERN CHINESE $

Map p302 (餃子園; ☎852 2541 9737; 98 Wellington St, Soho; meals from HK$40; ⊘11am-10.30pm Mon-Sat; ✐; 🚌40M) Locals and visitors from the north flock to this little shop for its nine varieties of juicy bundles of heaven, more commonly known as lamb and cumin, pork and chives, egg and tomato or vegetarian dumplings.

★TAI CHEONG BAKERY BAKERY $

Map p302 (泰昌餅家; ☎852 8300 8301; 35 Lyndhurst Tce, Central; pastries from HK$8; ⊘7.30am-9pm Mon-Sat, 8.30am-9pm Sun; 🚌40M) Tai Cheong was best known for its lighter-than-air beignets (deep-fried dough rolled in sugar; *sa yung* in Cantonese) until former governor Chris Patten was photographed wolfing down its egg-custard tarts. Since then 'Fat Patten' egg tarts have hogged the limelight.

★KAU KEE RESTAURANT NOODLES $

Map p302 (九記牛腩; ☎852 2850 5967; 21 Gough St, Sheung Wan; meals from HK$40; ⊘12.30-7.15pm & 8.30-11.30pm Mon-Sat; Ⓜ Sheung Wan, exit E2) You can argue till the noodles go soggy about whether Kau Kee has the best beef brisket in town. Whatever the verdict, the meat – served with toothsome noodles in a fragrant beefy broth – is hard to beat. During the 90 years of the shop's existence, film stars and politicians have joined the queue for a table.

Besides regular brisket, you can order – and many of the locals do – the chewier butterfly brisket (爽腩; *song laam*), and beef tendon (牛筋; *ngau gun*) served in a curry sauce.

★ LAN FONG YUEN
CAFE $

Map p302 (蘭芳園; ☑852 2544 3895, 852 2854 0731; 2 & 4A Gage St, Soho; meals from HK$60, cover charge HK$20; ⊙7am-6pm Mon-Sat; ☐5B) This rickety facade hides an entire *cha chaan tang* (tea cafe). Lan Fong Yuen (1952) is believed to be the inventor of the 'pantyhose' milk tea. Over a thousand cups of the strong and silky brew are sold daily alongside pork-chop buns, tossed noodles and other hasty tasties. Watch staff work their magic while you wait for a table.

BUTAO RAMEN
JAPANESE $

Map p302 (豚王; ☑852 2530 0600; www.butao ramen.com; 69 Wellington St, Central; ramen from HK$85; ⊙11am-11pm; MCentral, exit D2) From the line of customers waiting out the front, you have to believe that this street-side joint serves the best ramen in town. Choose from the signature rich Butao (pork) broth, the spicy Red King, the fusion-y Parmesan-enhanced Green King, or the squid inky Black King. You can customise how long the noodles should be cooked and the intensity of the broth. Just put a tick in the right boxes on the order sheet.

MAK'S NOODLE
NOODLES, CANTONESE $

Map p302 (麥奀雲吞麵世家; ☑852 2854 3810; 77 Wellington St, Soho; noodles HK$32-48; ⊙11am-8pm; ☐40M) At this legendary shop noodles are made the traditional way with a bamboo pole and served perched on a spoon placed over the bowl so they won't go soggy. The beef brisket noodles are equally remarkable.

YAT LOK
CHINESE $

Map p302 (一樂燒鵝; ☑852 2524 3882; 34-38 Stanley St, Soho; meals HK$45-80; ⊙10am-9pm Mon-Sat, to 5.30pm Sun; MCentral, exit D2) Be prepared to bump elbows with locals at this tiny joint known for its roast goose. Anthony Bourdain gushed over the bird. Foodies prefer it to fowls from pricey 'goose specialists'. Our favourite cut is the leg, over rice or slippery rice noodles. Order it unchopped and rip it – crispy skin, tender flesh and all!

MOTORINO
PIZZA $

Map p302 (☑852 2801 6881; www.motorinopizza. com; 14 Shelley St, Soho; meals HK$150-380; ⊙noon-midnight; ☎☝; MCentral, exit D2) The buzzing debut outpost of the famed NYC pizzeria puts out charcoal-kissed Neapolitan pies with a bubbly and flavourful crust that will give your jaws a delectable workout. The Brussels sprout and smoked pancetta pizza is especially glorious. Reservations accepted for lunch.

SHARKIE'S
SNACKS $

Map p302 (鯊仔記; ☑852 2530 3232; 8-12 Wo On Lane, Lan Kwai Fong; snacks HK$5-25; ⊙11.30am-6am; MCentral, exit D2) On your left as you make your way down short Wo On Lane from D'Aiguilar St, Sharkie's sells Hong Kong–style snacks, such as curry fish balls and egg waffles. Like the convenience stores in the neighbourhood, it's earned the reputation of being a 'cougar hot spot' because of its – presumably – young, hungry and male following.

SER WONG FUN
CANTONESE $

Map p302 (蛇王芬; ☑852 2543 1032; 30 Cochrane St, Soho; meals HK$70; ⊙11am-10.30pm; MCentral, exit D1) This snake-soup specialist whips up old Cantonese dishes that are as tantalising as its celebrated broth, and the packed tables attest to it. Many regulars come just for the homemade pork-liver sausage infused with rose wine – perfect over a bowl of immaculate white rice, on a red tablecloth. Booking advised.

WANG FU
NORTHERN CHINESE $

Map p302 (王府; ☑852 2121 8089; 65 Wellington St, Soho; meals HK$40; ⊙11am-3pm & 6-10pm Mon-Sat; ☐40M) At this cosy eatery, you'll see visitors from the mainland demolishing plate after plate of dumplings. There are nine delicious varieties (HK$31 to HK$44), as well as hearty noodles and Northern-style appetisers.

MANA! FAST SLOW FOOD
VEGAN $

Map p302 (☑852 2851 1611; www.mana.hk; 92 Wellington St, Soho; meals HK$100-200; ⊙10am-10pm; ☎☝; MCentral, exit D2) ✿ A vegan and raw food haven that whips up smoothies, salads and desserts for the professional crowd. Flat breads (available gluten-free) are baked in-shop by the cheerful staff then smothered with organic veggies and Mediterranean dips. Besides tasty, guilt-free food, Mana offers a hippy vibe that makes one forget its physical smallness and not-so-bohemian prices.

FLYING PAN AMERICAN $

Map p302 (☑852 2140 6333; www.the-flying-pan.com; 9 Old Bailey St, Soho; breakfast combos HK$78-146; ⊙24hr; ⊛; ☐26) Fancy eggs Benedict, chocolate waffles, even a full English breakfast for dinner? No problem. Breakfast is served 24/7 in a 1950s-American-diner setting at the Flying Pan.

BÊP VIETNAMESE $

Map p302 (☑852 2581 9992; www.bep.hk; 88-90 Wellington St, Soho; mains HK$58-118; ⊙noon-4.30pm & 6-11pm; Ⓜ Central, exit D2) Offering quick, fresh Vietnamese fare in a stylish setting, Bêp has rapidly become a Soho standby. The pho is solid, but we especially love the tangy goi bo beef salad and the spring rolls. Expect a line at peak hours; it usually moves quickly.

★LUK YU TEA HOUSE CANTONESE $$

Map p302 (陸羽茶室; ☑852 2523 5464; 24-26 Stanley St, Lan Kwai Fong; meals HK$300; ⊙7am-10pm, dim sum to 5.30pm; ⊛; Ⓜ Central, exit D2) This gorgeous teahouse (c 1933), known for its masterful cooking and Eastern art-deco decor, was the haunt of opera artists, writers and painters (including the creator of one exorbitant ink-and-brush gracing a wall) who came to give recitals and discuss the national fate. The food is old-school Cantonese fare such as sweet-and-sour pork, prawn toast and a variety of dim-sum dumplings and pastries.

★CHACHAWAN THAI $$

Map p304 (☑85225490020; http://chachawan.hk; 206 Hollywood Rd, Sheung Wan; meals HK$200-450; ⊙12-2.30pm & 6.30pm-midnight; Ⓜ Sheung Wan, exit A2) Specialising in the spicy cuisine of northeastern Thailand's Isaan region, this hip little spot is always packed and plenty noisy. No curries or pad thai here, just scads of bright, herb-infused, chilli-packed salads (we like the green papaya with pork belly) and grilled fish and meat.

HO LEE FUK MODERN CHINESE $$

Map p302 (☑852 2810 0860; http://holee fookhk.tumblr.com/; 1-5 Elgin St, Soho; meals HK$250-500; ⊙6-11pm Sun-Thu, to midnight Fri & Sat; Ⓜ Central, exit D2) As irreverent as its name suggests, this buzzy underground spot does a winkingly modern take on retro Chinatown cuisine. Prawn toasts are served with a dollop of Kewpie mayo and savoury bonito flakes, the char siu is up-market with Kurobuta pork, and prawn lo mein is spangled with crunchy bits of fried garlic and slicked with shellfish oil. The atmosphere is very see-and-be-seen, despite nightclub-level darkness.

LITTLE BAO ASIAN $$

Map p302 (☑852 2194 0202; www.little-bao.com; 66 Staunton St, Sheung Wan; meals HK$200-500; ⊙6-11pm Mon-Fri, noon-4pm & 6-11pm Sat, noon-4pm & 6-10pm Sun; Ⓜ Central, exit D2) A trendy diner that wows with its bao (Chinese buns) – snow-white orbs crammed with juicy meat and slathered with a palette of Asian condiments. The signature pork-belly bao comes with hoisin ketchup, sesame dressing, and a leek and shiso salad. If spot-on flavours and full-on sauces appeal, go early – they don't take reservations.

YUNG KEE RESTAURANT CANTONESE $$

Map p302 (鏞記; ☑852 2522 1624; www.yung kee.com.hk; 32-40 Wellington St, Lan Kwai Fong; lunch HK$150-400, dinner from HK$450; ⊙11am-10.30pm; ⊛; Ⓜ Central, exit D2) The roast goose here, made from fowl raised in the restaurant's own farm and roasted in coal-fired ovens, has been the talk of the town since 1942. Celebrities and well-to-dos are regulars at this well-illuminated and welcoming place, and its lunch dim sum is popular with the Central workforce.

★THE BOSS MODERN CANTONESE $$$

Map p302 (波士廳; ☑852 2155 0552; www.the boss1.com; Basement, 58-62 Queen's Rd Central, Central; lunch/dinner sets from HK$230/680; ⊙11.30am-midnight Mon-Sat, from 11am Sun; ☎; Ⓜ Central, exit D2) Awarded one Michelin star, the Boss is a perfectionist. The flawless service, austere modern decor, and meticulous kitchen point to high expectations being imposed. The old-school Cantonese dishes are impressive, notably the deep-fried chicken pieces with home-fermented shrimp paste, and the baked-crab casserole. Dim sum, made with first-rate ingredients, is available at lunch.

CARBONE ITALIAN $$$

Map p302 (☑852 2593 2593; http://carbone. com.hk/; 9th fl, LKF Tower, 33 Wydham St, Soho;

dinner HK$400-800; ⊘noon-2.30pm Mon-Sat, 6-11.30pm Sun-Thu, to midnight Fri & Sat) The only foreign outpost of the over-the-top New York Italian-American joint, Carbone makes you feel like Frank Sinatra having dinner in 1963. Walls are panelled in dark wood, chairs are red leather, waiters rock maroon tuxedos, and desserts come on a rolling cart. Retro classics include a very solid Caesar salad with ricotta salata, a bigger-than-your-head veal Parmesan and a huge, satisfying tangle of spaghetti and meatballs.

SUSHI KUU
JAPANESE $$$

Map p302 (☑852 2971 0180; 1st fl, 2-8 Wellington St, Wellington Pl, Lan Kwai Fong; lunch/dinner from HK$200/800; ⊘noon-11pm Mon-Thu & Sun, noon-12.30am Fri & Sat; ⓂCentral, exit D2) If you order the *omakase* ('I'll leave it to you') at this elegant sushi bar, the chef will lavish you with a multicourse meal prepared with the sweetest fruits of the sea available. Though not cheap at HK$1500 per person, it's excellent value for jet-fresh seafood of this quality. The lunch sets are also much raved about. Bookings essential for weekend dinners.

✖ Sheung Wan

CHAN KAN KEE
CHIU CHOW $

Map p304 (陳勤記鹵鵝飯店; ☑852 2858 0033; 11 Queen's Rd W, Sheung Wan; meals HK$50; ⊘11am-10pm; ᦥ5) For an authentic Chiu Chow treat, this family-run eatery serves hearty marinated goose, baby oyster omelette and duck soup. It's jam-packed during lunch hours. Chiu Chow is a city in the northeastern part of Guǎngdōng province, but its cooking is so refined and distinctive that it's often mentioned separately from Cantonese cuisine.

TIM'S KITCHEN
CANTONESE $$

Map p304 (桃花源; ☑852 2543 5919; www.tims kitchen.com.hk/; 84-90 Bonham Strand, Sheung Wan; lunch HK$130-500, dinner HK$300-1300; ⊘11.30am-3pm & 6-11pm; ᦥ; ⓂSheung Wan, exit A2) This two-floor restaurant is considered one of Hong Kong's best – as evidenced by the Michelin honour and the praises lavished by local gourmets. It serves extraordinarily delicate and subtle Cantonese fare, each dish as spare and elegant as a gem on a clean white plate. Signature items such as the crab claw poached with wintermelon (HK$270) require preordering. The crystal king prawn

and braised pomelo skin with shrimp roe should not be missed. Reservations essential.

ABC KITCHEN
EUROPEAN $$

Map p304 (☑852 9278 8227; Shop 7, Queen St Cooked Food Centre, 1 Queen St, Sheung Wan; meals HK$150-400; ⊘7-10.30pm; ⓂSheung Wan, exit B) Serving elegant European cuisine in the unexpected environs of a local wet market's food court, ABC Kitchen is an experience you won't find elsewhere. And the food's terrific too – the menu changes, but reliable favourites include the mahogany-skinned suckling pig, the house-made risotto and the dessert souffles (pistachio, if you're lucky). Reservations essential; save money by bringing your own wine.

MRS POUND
ASIAN $$

Map p304 (☑852 3426 3949; www.mrspound. com; 6 Pound Lane, Sheung Wan; meals HK$150-400; ⊘noon-2.30pm & 5-11pm; ⓂSheung Wan) On the outside, Mrs Pound looks like a traditional Sheung Wan stamp shop. But press the right stamp in the display window (hint: it glows) and a door swings open to reveal a faux dive bar serving up cheeky twists on Asian street food.

Even if the painfully hip vibe is not your thing, you'll appreciate sriracha-drizzled corn on the cob, fluffy bao filled with Indonesian beef rendang and mac 'n' cheese stuffed with shreds of Singaporean chilli crab. Later on it becomes one of the area's more fun bars. No reservations.

CHOM CHOM
VIETNAMESE $$

Map p302 (☑852 2810 0850; www.chomchom. hk; 58-60 Peel St, Soho; meals HK$250-500; ⊘4pm-late Wed-Sun, from 6pm Mon & Tue; ☎; ⓂCentral, exit D1) Lively Chom Chom recreates Vietnamese street food with bold flavours and charcoal grills, which are best washed down with their craft beers on tap. The corner location makes for great people-watching – al fresco by a slope or indoors from a marble-topped bistro table. *Pho* fans take note: noodles are only served in a (refreshing) roll with beef and peppermint. Expect lines and crowds.

YARDBIRD
JAPANESE $$

Map p302 (☑852 2547 9273; www.yardbird restaurant.com; 33-35 Bridges St, Sheung Wan; meals HK$300; ⊘6-11.45pm Mon-Sat; ᦥ26) Yardbird is a hipster's ode to the chicken. Every part of the cluck-cluck, from thigh to gizzard, is seasoned, impaled with a stick then grilled, *yakitori* style. The resulting skewers are flavourful with just the right consistency. The highly popular eatery doesn't take reservations, so sample the sakes in the convivial bar area while you wait for a table.

ABERDEEN ST SOCIAL
MODERN BRITISH $$

Map p302 (☑852 2866 0300; www.aberdeen streetsocial.hk; Ground fl, PMQ, 25 Aberdeen St, Central; meals downstairs HK$150-300, upstairs HK$300-750; ◎11.30am-midnight; ⓂSheung Wan) Run by British celebrity chef Jason Atherton, trendy Aberdeen St Social is really two restaurants in one. Downstairs is an all-day cafe where hip Sheung Wan–dwellers eat avocado toast and fancy fish 'n' chips on the patio. Upstairs is elegant, avant-garde dining (think smoked eel with foie gras). Both are very good, but for our money we dig the relaxed ambience of downstairs.

CHAIRMAN
CANTONESE $$$

Map p302 (大班樓; ☑852 2555 2202; www.the chairmangroup.com; 18 Kau U Fong, Sheung Wan; lunch/dinner from HK$200/560; ◎noon-3pm & 6-11pm; ☎; ⓂSheung Wan, exit E2) Understated faux-retro decor and warm service impart a homely feel at this upmarket place serving Cantonese classics with a healthy twist. Ingredients are sourced locally; cured meat and pickles are made at their own farm. The website even has a manifesto! No surprise – almost all the dishes hit all the right notes, from flavour to presentation. Reservations absolutely essential.

UPPER MODERN BISTRO
MODERN FRENCH $$$

Map p304 (☑852 2517 0977; 6-14 Upper Station St, Sheung Wan; lunch HK$180-450, dinner from HK$850; ◎noon-10.30pm Mon-Sat; ⓂCentral, exit D2) Bland menu descriptions belie the complexity of flavours and clever Asian touches in the cooking here. Likewise, the 'bistro' label falls short of the chic interiors that include a whimsical ceiling overlaid with petal-like 'eggs'. Michelin-starred Philippe Orrico's latest take on haute French cuisine is full of surprises. Go with an open mind.

✖ Mid-Levels & the Peak

PEAK LOOKOUT
INTERNATIONAL, ASIAN $$

(太平山餐廳; ☑852 2849 1000; www.peaklook out.com.hk; 121 Peak Rd, The Peak; lunch/dinner from HK$250/350; ◎10.30am-11.30pm Mon-Fri, from 8.30am Sat & Sun; ☐15, ☐Peak Tram) This 60-year-old colonial establishment, with seating in a glassed-in verandah and on an outside terrace, has more character than all the other Peak eateries combined. The food is excellent – especially the Indian and Western selections – as are the views.

✖ Western District

BA YI RESTAURANT
CHINESE $

(巴依餐廳; ☑852 2484 9981; 43 Water St, Sai Ying Pun; meals from HK$100; ◎noon-3pm & 6-10pm Tue-Sun; ⓂCentral, exit B, ☐green minibus 55) In a city where gamey tastes are often tamed to please Cantonese palates, this rustic halal restaurant serving the cuisine of northwestern China's Xinjiang province is a lamb lovers' paradise. Here you can savour mutton in all its glory – grilled, braised, fried or boiled with lashings of spices. Take minibus 55 outside the United Chinese Bank Building (Des Voeux Rd Central) and disembark at St Paul's College. Bookings essential; specials such as roasted lamb leg require advanced order.

YUEN KEE DESSERT
DESSERTS $

(源記; ☑852 2548 8687; 32 Centre St, Sai Ying Pun; meals from HK$25; ◎noon-11.30pm; ☐101, 104) This old-timers' favourite has been whipping up its famous sweet mulberry mistletoe tea with lotus seeds and egg (桑寄蓮子雞蛋茶) since 1855. It pairs well with the eggy sponge cake.

KWUN KEE RESTAURANT
CANTONESE $

(坤記煲仔小菜; ☑852 2803 7209; Wo Yick Mansion, 263 Queen's Rd W, Sai Ying Pun; meals from HK$80; ◎11am-2.30pm & 6-11pm Mon-Sat, 6-11pm Sun; ☐101) Hong Kong's top brass make pilgrimages to this local place for its claypot rice (HK$40 to HK$60, available only at dinner) – a meal-in-one in which rice and toppings such as chicken are cooked in claypots over charcoal stoves until the grains are infused with the juices of the meat and a layer of crackle is formed at the bottom of the pot.

SUN HING RESTAURANT
DIM SUM $

(新興食家; ☑852 2816 0616; 8C Smithfield Rd, Kennedy Town; meals HK$50; ◎3am-4pm; ☐101) Many a drunken Soho reveller has trudged westward after a long night seeking cheap dim sum, but to no avail. Then just before they pass out, there appears, vision-like, Sun Hing in all its scrumptious glory! They weep. True story, though some say tears are shed over the runny custard bun. Ask the HKU students sharing your table.

CAFE HUNAN HUNAN $

(書湘門第; ☎852 2803 7177; Koon Wah Bldg, 420-424 Queen's Rd W, Sheung Wan; lunch/dinner HK$50/180; ◷noon-3pm & 5.30-10pm; MSheung Wan, exit A1) Honest prices, a neat environment and the culinary genius of young Chef Huang have won Cafe Hunan a well-deserved mention in the Michelin guide. But even before this, discerning foodies had been raving about the earthy dishes prepared with spices from Hunan, a province known for its chillies and Chairman Mao. Try the chilli-spiked fish head, the smoky tofu and the spicy potato strips.

BISTRONOMIQUE FRENCH $$

(☎852 2818 8266; Ground fl, 1B Davis St, Kennedy Town; lunch/dinner from HK$150/400; ◷noon-2.30pm & 6-10pm Tue-Sun, 6-10pm Mon; ᖫ5B, 5X from Central) High-ceilinged Bistronomique fulfils the market's need for affordable yet expertly made French food. The menu is decidedly rustic and features bone marrow, frogs legs and pig's ears alongside more commonplace ingredients – all cooked in a homey Gallic kind of way. The set lunches are incredibly good value.

🍷 DRINKING & NIGHTLIFE

🍺 Lan Kwai Fong & Soho

★ANGEL'S SHARE WHISKY BAR BAR

Map p302 (☎852 2805 8388; www.angelsshare. hk; 2nd fl, Amber Lodge, 23 Hollywood Rd, Lan Kwai Fong; ◷3pm-2am Mon-Thu, to 3am Fri & Sat; MCentral, exit D1) One of Hong Kong's best whisky bars, this clubby place has more than 100 whiskies from the world over – predominantly Scottish, but also French, Japanese and American. The 23-year-old Macallan, comes straight out of a large 180L oak barrel in the centre of the room. If you're hungry, there's a selection of whisky-inspired dishes.

★CLUB 71 BAR

Map p302 (Basement, 67 Hollywood Rd, Soho; ◷3pm-2am Mon-Sat, 6pm-1am Sun, happy hour 3-9pm; ᖫ26, MCentral, exit D1) This friendly bar with a bohemian vibe is named after a protest march on 1 July 2003. It's a favourite haunt of local artists and activists who come for the beer and jamming sessions. In the garden out the front, revolutionaries plotted to overthrow the Qing dynasty a hundred years ago. Enter from the alley next to 69 Hollywood.

★QUINARY COCKTAIL BAR

Map p302 (☎852 2851 3223; www.quinary.hk; 56-58 Hollywood Rd, Soho; ◷5pm-2am Mon-Sat; MCentral exit D2) A sleek, moodily-lit cocktail bar, Quinary attracts a well-dressed crowd to sip Asian-inspired cocktail creations such as the Quinary Sour (whisky, licorice root, Chinese black sugar), the Oolong Tea Collins (vodka, oolong tea cordial) or the Checkers (vodka, black sesame syrup, vanilla ice cream). Prices are high, making this a good place to start the evening before moving on to cheaper and less elegant environs.

★STOCKTON COCKTAIL BAR

Map p302 (☎852 2565 5268; www.stockton.com. hk; 32 Wyndham St, Lan Kwai Fong; ◷6pm-late Mon-Sat; MCentral, exit D2) Stockton evokes the ambience of a private club in Victorian London with Chesterfield sofas, dark-wood panelling and the odd candelabra. These are cleverly arranged to form intimate corners that are best for sipping their rum- and whisky-based cocktails with a date. Make a reservation if you're coming after 9pm on a weekend.

From the big iron gate diagonally across the road from the Fringe Club, walk three steps west and turn left into an alleyway. Go to the back and up the stairs to Stockton.

TAI LUNG FUNG CAFE

Map p302 (☎852 2572 2886; 1st fl, shop H107, PMQ, 35 Aberdeen St, Central; ◷11am-11pm; MSheung Wan) Amid the galleries and boutiques of the PMQ (p83) building, Tai Lung Fung rocks a retro 1960s Hong Kong vibe, with a tiled bar and vintage public works posters on the walls. An arty crowd sips home-brewed liqueurs in flavours such as osmanthus and pu-er tea, while attacking plates of old-school nibbles including shrimp toast.

GLOBE PUB

Map p302 (☎852 2543 1941; www.theglobe.com. hk; 45-53 Graham St, Soho; ◷10am-2am, happy hour 10am-8pm; MCentral, exit D1) Besides an impressive list of 150 imported beers, including 13 on tap, the Globe serves T8, the first cask-conditioned ale brewed in Hong Kong. Occupying an enviable 370 sq metres, the bar has a huge dining area with long wooden tables and comfortable banquettes. It's also popular for its very decent British pub grub.

T:ME
GAY

Map p302 (☑852 2332 6565; www.time-bar.com; 65 Hollywood Rd, Soho; ⊙6pm-2am Mon-Sat; ⓜCentral, exit D1) This small, chic gay bar is located in a residential back alley facing a small park; drinks are a bit on the pricey side but it has happy hour throughout the week. Enter through the alley off Peel St just north of Hollywood Rd.

KUNG LEE
JUICE

Map p302 (公利真料竹蔗水; ☑852 2544 3571; 60 Hollywood Rd, Soho; juice from HK$11; ⊙11am-11pm; ☐26) This institution in the heart of Soho has been quietly selling herbal teas and fresh sugarcane juice since 1948 – their quality is unchanged, as are the charming vintage tiles, posters and signs.

DRAGON-I
BAR, CLUB

Map p302 (☑852 3110 1222; www.dragon-i.com. hk; upper ground fl, the Centrium, 60 Wyndham St, Lan Kwai Fong; ⊙noon-late, terrace happy hour 3-9pm Mon-Sat; ☐26, ⓜCentral, exit D2) This fashionable venue has both an indoor bar and a terrace over Wyndham St filled with caged songbirds. Go after midnight and watch Ukrainian models and Cantopop stars sipping Krug and air kissing, as DJs fill the dance floor with hip hop, R&B and jazz. Go early or dress to kill if you want to be let in.

STUDIO
LOUNGE

Map p302 (www.studioclub.asia; 1st fl, On Hing Bldg, 1 On Hing Tce, Central; ⊙6pm-4am; ⓜCentral, exit D2) The house jazz band fires up every night at 9pm at Studio, a 1950s-inspired jazz lounge in Lan Kwai Fong. Warm wood walls and dramatic lighting give the open space a glamorous, theatrical vibe. Post-band DJs spin until late, late, late. Cocktails are pricey, but the whisky menu is one of the better ones around.

VARGA LOUNGE
LOUNGE

Map p302 (☑852 2104 9697; http://vargalounge hk.com; 36 Staunton St, Soho; ⊙6pm-3am; ⓜCentral D2) This little jewelbox of a cocktail bar pays homage to pin-up girls of yore, with vintage decor to match: tur-

'SECRET' PUBLIC GARDEN

If you want a change of air during your pub crawl, come to the amphitheatre at the end of Wo On Lane in Lan Kwai Fong. An open secret of sorts, it's the hang-out of young expats who buy smokes and drinks from convenience stores nearby and come to play charades or shoot the breeze. You can do the same – you might might even meet some beautiful strangers. The official name is **Lok Hing Lane Park**.

quoise walls, velvet sofas, leopard-print pillows. The gimlets are grand, and the vibe is welcoming – a typical crowd is a mix of gay 30- and 40-somethings, hipsters on dates and women on ladies' nights out.

VOLAR
CLUB

Map p302 (☑852 2810 1510; Basement, 38-44 D'Aguilar St, Central; ⊙6pm-6am; ⓜCentral, exit D2) A staple of the Lan Kwai Fong nightlife scene, this futuristically lit underground (literally) club grinds out the jams until the sun comes up. Expect a sweaty, international crowd of 20-somethings partying hard.

TAZMANIA BALLROOM
CLUB

Map p302 (☑852 2801 5009; www.tazmania ballroom.com; 1st fl, LKF Tower, 33 Wyndham St, Lan Kwai Fong; ⊙5pm-late, happy hour 5-8pm; ⓜCentral, exit D2) Skipped the gym? This sophisticated cavern whips out ping-pong tables every Tuesday, Thursday and Sunday night. The dress code, however, is casual glam, not Chinese national team. You can also shoot pool with bankers at a gold-plated table, join model types for verbal back-and-forth on the balcony, or groove to jazzy house music on the sleek dance floor.

ROUNDHOUSE TAPROOM
BAR

Map p302 (☑852 2366 4880; www. roundhouse.com.hk; 62 Peel St, Soho; ⊙noon-11pm, happy hour noon-8pm; ⓜCentral, exit D1) This is one of the best places in town to get microbrews on tap – there are 24 from all over the world! Roundhouse is small and brightly lit. If you want more atmosphere, pick your brew from the iPad menu and savour it on the steps just outside the bar. They also serve some of the most authentic Texas-style barbecue this side of the globe.

CENTRAL WINE CLUB
WINE BAR

Map p302 (☑852 2147 3448; www.thecentral wineclub.com; 3rd fl, Sea Bird House, 22-28 Wyndham St, Lan Kwai Fong; ☉2pm-2am Mon-Fri, 4pm-2am Sat, happy hour 3-9pm; Ⓜ Central, exit D1) If you're serious about your tipple and don't mind over-the-top modern baroque decor, CWC is a great place to sample fine old-world wines. The bar's iPad wine list features more than 500 bottles, in addition to Cognac and whisky. Blues and jazz provide the soundtrack to your evening. Non-members incur a 15% service charge.

TIVO BAR
BAR

Map p302 (☑852 2116 8055; www.aqua.com. hk; 43-55 Wyndham St, Lan Kwai Fong; ☉6pm-midnight Sun-Thu, to late Fri & Sat; Ⓜ Central, exit D2) Sophisticated Tivo delights with open frontage, an exuberant crowd and *aperitivo*-style snacks. On the first and third Sunday of the month, lovely drag hostesses take over from 7pm and whip up the action for the Tivo Tea Dance.

BAR 42
BAR

Map p302 (42 Staunton St, Soho; ☉happy hour 4-8pm; Ⓜ Central, exit D2) This cosy lounge with a small courtyard at the back attracts a cool mix of locals and expats. The board games are at the ready to get your brain functioning.

BAR 1911
BAR

Map p302 (逸日會; ☑852 2810 6681; www.sbs. hk/1911.html; 27 Staunton St, Soho; ☉5pm-midnight Mon-Sat, happy hour 5-9pm; 🚇26) This small bar with fine details (stained glass, burl-wood bar, ceiling fan) has a 1920s old Hong Kong vibe. The name commemorates the year Dr Sun Yatsen overthrew the Qing monarchy. You'll see a likeness of the man inside the bar. It's usually a tad less crowded than competitors nearby, which makes for quiet drinking.

TASTINGS
WINE BAR

Map p302 (☑852 2523 6282; www.tastings.hk; Basement, Yuen Yick Bldg, 27 & 29 Wellington St, Lan Kwai Fong; ☉5pm-2am Mon-Sat; Ⓜ Central, exit D2) This bar, on a side street off Wellington, offers 40 wines from 'enomatic' wine dispensers that pour, by a few millilitres, a half-glass or a full glass. This allows you to taste rare varietals without bankrupting yourself. You create a tab by handing over your credit card in exchange for a smart card that you use to operate the machines.

PEAK CAFE BAR
BAR

Map p302 (☑852 2140 6877; www.cafedeco group.com; 9-13 Shelley St, Soho; ☉11am-2am Mon-Fri, 9am-2am Sat, 9am-midnight Sun, happy hour 5-8pm; 🚇13, 26, 40M) This welcoming bar with great cocktails is decorated with the charming fixtures and fittings of the old Peak Cafe from 1947, which was replaced by the Peak Lookout (p91). The cafe comprises two parts, both next to the Central–Mid-Levels Escalator, with a courtyard linking the two. Plant yourself by the window and watch the world go by.

🍷 Sheung Wan

CAFE DEADEND
CAFE

Map p304 (☑852 6716 7005; www.cafedead end.com; 72 Po Hing Fong, Sheung Wan; meals HK$100-200; ☉9.30am-6pm Tue-Sun; 🚇23, 40) In Sheung Wan's leafy 'PoHo' neighbourhood of quiet boutiques and galleries, this tucked-away little cafe is one of the best places in Hong Kong to have a peaceful cup of coffee and read a book.

TEAKHA
TEA

Map p304 (茶家; ☑852 2858 9185; http:// teakha.com; Shop B, 18 Tai Ping Shan St, Sheung Wan; ☉11am-7pm Tue-Sun; 🕿; 🚇26) Fancy organic tea concoctions are best enjoyed with the homemade scones in this oasis, just off the main street in the impossibly hip Tai Ping Shan St area. The cute teaware makes a good souvenir.

THREE MONKEYS
PUB

Map p302 (☑852 3151 7771; http://threemon keys.hk; 151-155 Hollywood Rd, Sheung Wan; ☉5pm-1am Mon-Thu, to 2am Fri, 2pm-2am Sat, noon-1am Sun; Ⓜ Sheung Wan) Billing itself as a Japanese gastropub, this friendly two-storey spot has an excellent list of craft sakes and Japanese beers. Large tables make it a good place to come with a group. Start with tasty nibbles such as crab croquettes, edamame and cheese mochi, and stay all night.

BARISTA JAM
COFFEE

Map p304 (☑852 2854 2211; www.baristajam. com.hk; Shop D, ground fl, 126-128 Jervois St, Sheung Wan; ☉8am-6pm Tue-Fri, from 10am Mon & Sat; 🕿; Ⓜ Sheung Wan, exit A2) Connoisseurs should make the pilgrimage to this grey-walled institution that also sells coffee beans and professional coffee-making equipment.

Western District

★**PING PONG GINTONERIA** BAR
(☏852 9835 5061; www.pingpong129.com/; 135 Second St, Sai Ying Pun; ⊙6-11.30pm; Ⓜ Sai Ying Pun, exit B2) An unmarked red door leads you downstairs into a cavernous former ping-pong hall, now one of Hong Kong's coolest bars. The drink here is gin – the bar stocks more than 50 types from across the globe, served in a variety of cocktails both classic and creative. Crowds here are artsy, and the decor is even artsier – look out for original work by infamous Hong Kong graffiti artist the King of Kowloon.

 ENTERTAINMENT

★**PEEL FRESCO** JAZZ
Map p302 (☏852 2540 2046; www.peelfresco.com; 49 Peel St, Soho; ⊙5pm-late Mon-Sat; ☒13, 26, 40M) Charming Peel Fresco has live jazz six nights a week, with local and overseas acts performing on a small but spectacular stage next to teetering faux-Renaissance paintings. The action starts around 9.30pm, but get there at 9pm to secure a seat.

FRINGE CLUB LIVE MUSIC, THEATRE
Map p302 (藝穗會; ☐theatre bookings 852 2521 9126, 852 2521 7251; www.hkfringe.com.hk; 2 Lower Albert Rd, Lan Kwai Fong; ⊙noon-midnight Mon-Thu, to 3am Fri & Sat; Ⓜ Central, exits D1, D2 & G) The Fringe, housed in a Victorian building (c 1892) that was part of a dairy farm, offers original music in the Dairy several nights a week, with jazz, rock and world music getting the most airplay. The intimate theatres host eclectic local and international performances. The Fringe sits on the border of Lan Kwai Fong.

SHEUNG WAN CIVIC CENTRE THEATRE, LIVE MUSIC
Map p304 (上環文娛中心; ☐bookings 852 2853 2678, enquiries 852 2853 2689; www.lcsd.gov.hk/en/swcc/; 5th fl, Sheung Wan Municipal Services Bldg, 345 Queen's Rd Central, Sheung Wan; ⊙9am-11pm, box office 10am-6.30pm; Ⓜ Sheung Wan, exit A2) This government-run performance venue shares a building with a wet market and cooked food centre. Its year-round program leans towards drama by local theatre troupes – some engagingly experimental – and concerts by independent musicians and bands.

CULTURE CLUB LIVE MUSIC
Map p302 (☏852 2127 7936; www.cultureclub.com.hk; 15 Elgin St, Soho; ⊙2.30-10pm Mon-Thu, to 11pm Fri & Sat, tango workshops some Sundays; ☒26) Besides the tango *milongas* that take place here some Sundays, this multi-purpose venue is where amateur musicians hold their debut performances. It also features photography exhibitions, and the occasional Chinese music performance such as the blindman *nányīn* (a vanishing genre of Cantonese music).

TAKEOUT COMEDY CLUB COMEDY
Map p302 (☏852 6220 4436; www.takeoutcomedy.com; Basement, 34 Elgin St, Soho; ☒26) In need of some LOL? Hong Kong's first full-time comedy club, founded by Chinese-American Jameson Gong, has stand-up and improv acts in English, Cantonese and Mandarin. It also hosts visiting comedians from overseas. See website for program.

 SHOPPING

Lan Kwai Fong & Soho

★**PMQ** HANDICRAFTS, JEWELLERY
Map p302 (☏852 2870 2335; www.pmq.org.hk; 35 Aberdeen St, Central; ⊙most shops 11am-7pm) The modernist building that was once the police married quarters is now one of the best places in Hong Kong to shop for pieces by local designers, jewellery makers and artisans, with dozens of shops and boutiques occupying the old apartments. Top picks include the hip streetwear of Kapok, Hong Kong-themed gifts at HKTDC Design Gallery, industrially inspired jewellery at The Little Finger, and bamboo kitchenware at Bamboo Home.

★**GOODS OF DESIRE** GIFTS, HOUSEWARES
Map p302 (G.O.D.; ☏852 2805 1876; http://god.com.hk/; 48 Hollywood Rd, Soho; ⊙11am-9pm) Goods of Desire – or G.O.D. – is a cheeky local lifestyle brand, selling housewares, clothes, books and gifts with retro Hong Kong themes. Fun gets include aprons printed with images of Hong Kong's famous neon signs, strings of fairy lights resembling the red lampshades ubiquitous in Hong Kong wet markets, and bed linen with themes like koi fish, vintage Hong Kong mailboxes or double happiness signs.

★ **GALLERY OF THE POTTERY WORKSHOP** ART, HOMEWARES

Map p302 (樂天陶社; ☑852 9842 5889, 852 2525 7949; www.potteryworkshop.com.cn; 3rd fl Hollywood House, 27-29 Hollywood Rd, Soho; ⏱1-6pm Tue-Sun; ⛟26) This gallery showcases playful ceramic objects made by local ceramic artists and artisans from the mainland and overseas. The lovely pieces range from crockery to sculptures.

★ **GROTTO FINE ART** ART

Map p302 (嘉圖; ☑852 2121 2270; www.grotto fineart.com; 2nd fl, 31C-D Wyndham St, Lan Kwai Fong; ⏱11am-7pm Mon-Sat; Ⓜ Central, exit D2) This exquisite gallery, founded by a scholar in Hong Kong art, is one of very few that represents predominantly local artists. The small but excellent selection of works shown ranges from painting and sculpture to ceramics and mixed media. Prices are reasonable, too.

★ **WATTIS FINE ART** ANTIQUES

Map p302 (www.wattis.com.hk; 2nd fl, 20 Hollywood Rd, Lan Kwai Fong; ⏱10.30am-6pm Mon-Sat; ⛟26) This upstairs gallery has a great collection of antique maps for sale. The selection of old photographs of Hong Kong and Macau is also impressive. Enter from Old Bailey St.

HONEYCHURCH ANTIQUES ANTIQUES

Map p302 (☑852 2543 2433; 29 Hollywood Rd, Lan Kwai Fong; ⏱9am-6.30pm Mon-Sat; ⛟26) This fine shop, run by an American couple for 30-plus years, specialises in antique Chinese furniture, jewellery and English silver. There's a wide range of stock, with items from the early Chinese dynasties right up to the 20th century.

ARCH ANGEL ANTIQUES ANTIQUES

Map p302 (☑852 2851 6848; 53-55 Hollywood Rd, Lan Kwai Fong; ⏱9.30am-6.30pm Mon-Sat, to 6pm Sun; ⛟26) Though the specialities are ancient porcelain and tombware, Arch Angel packs a lot more into its three floors: it has everything from mah-jong sets and terracotta horses to palatial furniture.

PEARL LAM GALLERIES ART

Map p302 (藝術門; ☑852 2522 1428; www. pearllam.com; 601-605 Peddar Bldg, 12 Pedder St, Central; ⏱10am-7pm Mon-Sat; Ⓜ Central, exit H) This elegant space showcases mainland Chinese, Hong Kong and Asian contemporary art – mostly paintings and sculptures.

The owner, Pearl Lam, has been a fervent promoter of Chinese contemporary art and design since the 1990s. She also has galleries in Shanghai and Singapore.

MOUNTAIN FOLKCRAFT GIFTS & SOUVENIRS

Map p302 (高山民藝; https://mountainfolkcraft. com; 12 Wo On Lane, Soho; ⏱Mon-Sat; Ⓜ Central) This is one of the nicest shops in the city for folk craft. It's piled with bolts of batik and sarongs, clothing, wood carvings, lacquerware and papercuts made by ethnic minorities in China and other Asian countries.

LAM GALLERY ANTIQUES

Map p302 (松心閣; ☑852 2554 4666; 61 Hollywood Rd, Lan Kwai Fong; ⏱10.30am-6.30pm Mon-Fri, 11am-6pm Sat; ⛟26, Ⓜ Central, exit D2) Arguably the best shop in the area for sculptures, this is the largest of several stores owned by the Lam family on Hollywood Rd. Sculpted pieces from the Neolithic period to the Qing dynasty predominate. Other products include ceramics, bronze, paintings, gold and silverware. Lam is known by collectors and auction dealers worldwide, and offers restoration services.

L PLUS H CLOTHING

Map p302 (☑852 2923 2288; www.lplush.com; 17th fl, 11 Stanley St, Soho; ⏱10am-7pm Mon-Sat; Ⓜ Central, exit D2) Founded by a group of socially driven entrepreneurs, L Plus H teams up with local designers to create a 100% 'Designed and Made in Hong Kong' label. Classic-looking, highly wearable knitwear is its forte.

FANG FONG PROJECTS CLOTHING

Map p302 (69 Peel St, Lan Kwai Fong; ⏱11am-8pm Sun-Thu, noon-9pm Fri & Sat; ⛟26) Wu Laifan's very wearable dresses are a clever mix of vintage fabric and 1980s silhouettes. The shop also carries some of her own designs.

FLOW BOOKS

Map p302 (☑852 2964 9483, 852 9278 5664; www.flowbooks.net; 7th fl, 1A Wing On Bldg, 38 Hollywood Rd, Lan Kwai Fong; ⏱noon-7pm; ⛟26) A sprawling jumble of secondhand English titles covers almost every inch of Flow. You'll need some patience to find whatever you're seeking; alternatively, let the friendly owner, Lam Sum, guide you to the right shelf.

10 CHANCERY LANE GALLERY ART

Map p302 (10 號贊善里畫廊; ☑852 2810 0065; www.10chancerylanegallery.com; 10 Chancery

Lane, Soho; ⏱10am-6pm Tue-Sat; Ⓜ Central, exit D2) Located in hidden-away Chancery Lane, this gallery focuses on thought-provoking works by promising Asian, mainland Chinese and Hong Kong artists. It also runs seminars and art walks.

ANDY HEI ANTIQUES
Map p302 (研木得益; ☎852 3105 2002; www.andyhei.com; 84 Hollywood Rd, Lan Kwai Fong; ⏱10am-12.30pm & 1.30-6pm Mon-Sat; Ⓑ26, Ⓜ Central, exit D2) This world-class furniture dealer specialises in classical Chinese furniture from the Ming and Qing dynasties, and scholar's objects. It also restores rare *huanghuali* wood and *zitan* pieces. Hei is the founding chairman of Fine Art Asia (www.fineartasia.com), which showcases art and antiquities of Asian heritage.

LINVA TAILOR FASHION & ACCESSORIES
Map p302 (年華時裝公司; ☎852 2544 2456; 38 Cochrane St, Soho; ⏱9.30am-6.30pm Mon-Sat; Ⓑ26) Fancy a *cheongsam* aka *qipao* (body-hugging Chinese dress)? Bring your own silk or choose from the selection here. If you're pushed for time, the bespoke tailors, Mr and Mrs Leung, are happy to mail the completed items to you.

KARIN WEBER GALLERY ANTIQUES
Map p302 (☎852 2544 5004; www.karinwebergallery.com; 20 Aberdeen St, Soho; ⏱11am-7pm Tue-Sat, by appointment Sun; Ⓑ26) Karin Weber has an interesting mix of Chinese country antiques and contemporary Asian artwork. She can arrange antique-buying trips to Guǎngdōng for serious buyers.

INDOSIAM BOOKS, ANTIQUES
Map p302 (☎852 2854 2853; 1st fl, 89 Hollywood Rd, Soho; ⏱1-7pm; Ⓑ26) Hong Kong's first truly antiquarian bookshop deals in rare titles relating to Asian countries, with Thailand, China and the former French colonies being its areas of strength. Indosiam also sells vintage newspapers and old Chinese prints.

LI YUEN STREET EAST & WEST MARKET
Map p302 (Li Yuen St E & W, Central; ⏱10am-7pm; Ⓜ Central, exit C) The two narrow, crowded alleyways linking Des Voeux Rd Central with Queen's Rd Central are called 'the lanes' by Hong Kong residents, and were traditionally the place to go for fabric and piece goods. Most vendors have now moved to Western Market (p84) in Sheung Wan, and while it's no great retail hunting ground you'll still find cheap clothing, handbags, backpacks and costume jewellery.

🏠 Sheung Wan

★CHAN SHING KEE ANTIQUES
Map p302 (陳勝記; ☎852 2543 1245; www.chanshingkee.com; 228-230 Queen's Rd Central, Sheung Wan; ⏱9am-6pm Mon-Sat; Ⓑ101, 104) This shop with a three-storey showroom is run by Daniel Chan, the third generation of a family that's been in the business for 70 years. Chan Shing Kee is known to collectors and museums worldwide for its fine classical Chinese furniture (16th to 18th century). Scholar's objects, such as ancient screens and wooden boxes, are also available.

LAM KIE YUEN TEA CO FOOD & DRINKS
Map p304 (林奇苑茶行; ☎852 2543 7154; www.lkytea.com; 105-107 Bonham Strand E, Sheung Wan; ⏱9am-6.30pm Mon-Sat; Ⓜ Sheung Wan, exit A2) This shop, which has been around since 1955, is testament to just how much tea there is in China. From unfermented to fully fermented, and everything in between, there's simply too much to choose from. But don't panic – the owner will offer you a tasting.

CAPITAL GALLERY ANTIQUES
Map p304 (長安美術; ☎852 2542 2271; 27E Tung St, Sheung Wan; ⏱10am-6pm Mon-Sat, by appointment Sun; Ⓑ26, Ⓜ Central, exit D2) Located on a slope between Upper Lascar Row and Hollywood Rd, this tiny shop is crammed with sculptures, ceramics and other curios dating from 4000 to 5000 years ago. Highlights include Silk Road pieces, such as minority textiles from northwest China, and jewellery.

L'S FINE ARTS ANTIQUES
Map p304 (松心閣; ☎852 6606 1818, 852 2540 5569; Room G8, Hollywood Centre, 233 Hollywood Rd, Sheung Wan; ⏱noon-6pm Mon-Sat; Ⓑ26, Ⓜ Central, exit D2) L's is littered with curios worth between HK$5000 and HK$200,000, including early Chinese ceramics and Tang dynasty figurines. The reputable shop, located in the drab-looking Hollywood Centre, also sells consigned items for collectors worldwide.

SIN SIN FINE ART
ART

Map p304 (☑852 2858 5072; www.sinsin. hk; 53-54 Sai St, Sheung Wan; ⊙9.30am-6.30pm Mon-Sat; Ⓜ Sheung Wan, exit A2) This eclectic gallery owned by a fashion designer with a flair for ethnic designs shows good-quality Hong Kong, mainland Chinese and Southeast Asian art – mostly edgy paintings and photography.

NGAI TILE WAVE
ANTIQUES

Map p304 (藝雅廊; ☑852 2517 2586; 172 Hollywood Rd, Sheung Wan; ⊙11am-6pm Mon-Sat; ☐26, Ⓜ Central, exit D2) You can find Tang figurines, tricoloured ancient pottery, and porcelain from the Ming and Qing dynasties costing between HK$1000 and HK$100,000 in this shop. Older and more expensive artefacts are kept in a room upstairs. Tell the staff what you're looking for and they'll let you know if they have it.

WING ON DEPARTMENT STORE
DEPARTMENT STORE

Map p304 (永安百貨; ☑852 2852 1888; www. wingonet.com; Wing On Centre, 211 Des Voeux Rd Central, Central; ⊙10am-7.30pm; Ⓜ Sheung Wan, exit E3) The last truly one-stop-shop department store in Hong Kong. Sure, it's a little old-fashioned, but you can find almost everything you need here, from garden hoses to iPhone covers, and baby pacifiers to Italian leather jackets. And there are super-friendly women to help you.

SPORTS & ACTIVITIES

WAN KEI HO INTERNATIONAL MARTIAL ARTS ASSOCIATION
MARTIAL ARTS

Map p304 (尹圻灝國際武術總會; ☑852 2544 1368, 852 9506 0075; www.kungfuwan.com; 3rd fl, Yue's House, 304 Des Voeux Rd Central, Sheung Wan; ⊙10am-8pm Mon-Fri, 9am-1pm Sat & Sun; Ⓜ Sheung Wan, exit A) English-speaking Master Wan teaches northern Shaolin Kung Fu to a wide following of locals and foreigners. Classes are offered in the evenings from Monday to Thursday. Depending on how many classes you take, the monthly fees may range from HK$350 to HK$1600.

HAPPY FOOT REFLEXOLOGY CENTRE
SPA

Map p302 (知足樂; ☑852 2522 1151; www.happy foot.hk; 19th & 20th fl, Century Sq, 1 D'Aguilar St, Lan Kwai Fong; ⊙10am-midnight; Ⓜ Central, exit D2) Receiving intense, Chinese-style foot massages is a regular treat for many hard-driving Hong Kong business people. Foot/body massage starts at HK$200/250 for 50 minutes at this popular reflexology spa.

FLAWLESS HONG KONG
SPA

Map p302 (☑852 2869 5868; www.flawless. hk.com; 4th fl, Sea Bird House, 22-28 Wyndham St, Lan Kwai Fong; ⊙10am-10pm; Ⓜ Central, exit D1) This award-winning spa attracts a youngish clientele with its homey setting and vast array of no-nonsense treatments for the face (from HK$580 up) and nails (manicures from HK$160). They use sophisticated 'age-combating' serums, but nothing too airy-fairy such as flowers or pebbles.

HONG KONG PUB CRAWL
DRINKING TOUR

(www.hongkongpubcrawl.com; ticket HK$100) Hong Kong Pub Crawl organises an event every Thursday night that lets you experience Hong Kong's nightlife and meet new friends.

FRINGE CLUB
COURSE

Map p302 (☑852 2521 7251; www.hkfringe.com. hk; 2 Lower Albert Rd, Lan Kwai Fong) The Fringe Club offers any number of courses and workshops centred on visual arts.

Hong Kong Island: Wan Chai & the Northeast

ADMIRALTY | WAN CHAI | CAUSEWAY BAY | HAPPY VALLEY | ISLAND EAST

Neighbourhood Top Five

1 Blue House (p102) Combing the streets around Queen's Rd East and Johnston Rd for heritage architecture like the Viva Blue House cluster, where you'll also find temples, hipster bars, wet markets and open-air bazaars.

2 Happy Valley Racecourse (p105) Feeling your adrenaline soar at an urban racecourse on a Wednesday night, beer in hand.

3 Flagstaff House Museum of Tea Ware (p101) Experiencing culture, history and gastronomy at the museum and its resident restaurant, Lock Cha Tea Shop.

4 Fashion Walk (p118) Trawling through the streets and malls for fashion among the hordes of teenyboppers in Causeway Bay.

5 Street Music Concert Series (p116) Catching one of these professional-quality street concerts outside the Hong Kong Arts Centre and other venues in Wan Chai.

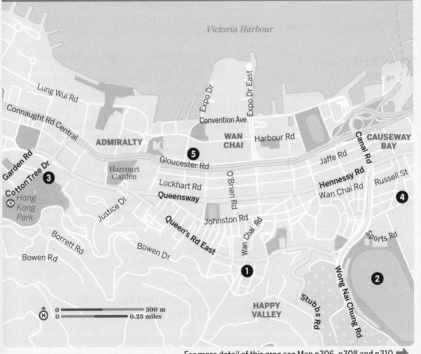

For more detail of this area see Map p306, p308 and p310 ➡

Lonely Planet's Top Tip

Viewing the Island's east districts from a moving tram imparts a charming cinematic quality to your impressions, as these primarily residential areas can underwhelm on foot. Add speed to the uniformity of housing blocks and you get rhythm and pattern. The bonus is that you can hop off when something tickles your fancy. The district is served by some 30 stops on the eastbound tramline.

Best Places to Eat

➡ Choi's Kitchen (p111)

➡ Sun Kwai Heung (p112)

➡ Lock Cha Tea Shop (p107)

➡ Atum Desserant (p110)

➡ Pure Veggie House (p108)

For reviews, see p107 ➡

Best Places to Drink

➡ Tai Lung Fung (p113)

➡ Elephant Grounds (p115)

➡ MyHouse (p113)

➡ Stone Nullah Tavern (p113)

For reviews, see p113 ➡

Best Places to Shop

➡ GOD (p117)

➡ Cuffs (p118)

➡ Basheer (p118)

➡ Kapok (p116)

➡ Eslite (p117)

For reviews, see p116 ➡

Explore: Wan Chai & the Northeast

Stroll through the Pacific Place mall connected to Admiralty MTR station and pay a leisurely two-and-a-half hour visit to Hong Kong Park and Asia Society Hong Kong Centre. Head over to Queen's Rd East nearby. Spend two hours exploring the 'old' Wan Chai area. Continue your journey to 'new' Wan Chai (closer to the harbour), where you can visit the Wan Chai Computer Centre or stroll further north to the Hong Kong Convention & Exhibition Centre. Dine on nouveau Hong Kong food in Wan Chai or in Causeway Bay, a tram ride away (arrive after the lunch crowds). Shop for books and fashion, sit under a tree in Victoria Park, or head to nearby Tai Hang to people-watch at a cafe. Enjoy happy-hour drinks in up-and-coming 'Caroline Haven' or hop on an eastbound 'ding ding' and play it by ear.

Local Life

➡ **Lil' Jakarta** Indonesian maids gather at Victoria Park (p104) on Sundays to eat, sing and pray.

➡ **Toy shops** Gen-Xers bring their kids to the Tai Yuen St toy shops (p116) to relive childhood innocence, and buy lanterns during the Mid-Autumn Festival.

➡ **Next coolest thing** The area around Caroline Hill Rd and Haven St (aka 'Caroline Haven') is where hipsters, collectors and garage mechanics hang out.

➡ **Neighbourly charm** The leafy streets of Tai Hang are full of hole-in-the-wall galleries and intimate corner cafes.

➡ **Fujian Town** North Point is the stronghold of Hong Kong's Fujianese community.

Getting There & Away

➡ **Tram** To Causeway Bay and Happy Valley, catch Central-bound or Shau Kei Wan–bound trams along Hennessy Rd and Yee Wo St; catch trams along Percival St to Happy Valley, and along Wong Nai Chung Rd to Causeway Bay, Central, Kennedy Town and Shau Kei Wan. Chai Wan–bound trams cover Island East.

➡ **Bus** From Admiralty and Central to Causeway Bay and Happy Valley, buses 5, 5B and 26 stop along Yee Wo St. Green minibus 40 from Stanley stops along Tang Lung St and Yee Wo St.

➡ **MTR** Admiralty station: Island and Tsuen Wan lines. Wan Chai station: Island line. Happy Valley and Tai Hang are reachable from Causeway Bay and Tin Hau stations (Central line).

➡ **Star Ferry Wan Chai ferry pier** (灣仔碼頭; Map p308; Ⓜ Wan Chai, exit C) to Tsim Sha Tsui, Kowloon.

TOP SIGHT
HONG KONG PARK

Designed to look anything but natural, Hong Kong Park emphasises artificial creations such as its fountain plaza, conservatory, waterfall, playground, taichi garden and viewing tower. Yet the 8-hectare park is beautiful and, with a wall of skyscrapers on one side and mountains on the other, makes for dramatic photographs.

The best feature of Hong Kong Park is the **Edward Youde Aviary** (尤德觀鳥園; Map p306; ⊙9am-5pm). Home to more than 600 birds representing some 90 species, it's like a rainforest planted in the middle of the city. Visitors walk along a wooden bridge suspended some 10m above the ground and at eye level with tree branches. The **Forsgate Conservatory** (霍士傑溫室; Map p306; 10 Cotton Tree Dr, Admiralty; ⊙9am-5pm) **FREE** overlooking the park is the largest in Southeast Asia.

The exquisite **KS Lo Gallery** (羅桂祥茶藝館; Map p306; ☑852 2869 0690; 10 Cotton Tree Dr, Admiralty; ⊙10am-6pm Wed-Mon) **FREE** contains rare Chinese ceramics and stone seals owned by the eponymous collector.

At the park's northernmost tip is **Flagstaff House Museum of Tea Ware** (旗桿屋茶具文物館; Map p306; ☑852 2869 0690; www.lcsd.gov.hk/CE/Museum/Arts/en_US/web/ma/tea-ware.html; 10 Cotton Tree Dr, Admiralty; ⊙10am-6pm Wed-Mon) **FREE**. Built in 1846, it now houses a collection of antique Chinese tea ware. The ground-floor cafe is a great place to recharge over a pot of fine tea and vegetarian dim sum.

DON'T MISS

➡ Edward Youde Aviary
➡ Flagstaff House Museum of Tea Ware
➡ KS Lo Gallery
➡ Forsgate Conservatory

PRACTICALITIES

➡ 香港公園
➡ Map p306, C4
➡ ☑852 2521 5041
➡ www.lcsd.gov.hk/parks/hkp/en/index.php
➡ 19 Cotton Tree Dr, Admiralty
➡ admission free
➡ ⊙park 6am-11pm
➡ 🚻
➡ Ⓜ Admiralty, exit C1

◉ SIGHTS

◉ Admiralty

HONG KONG PARK
PARK

See p101.

ASIA SOCIETY HONG KONG CENTRE
HISTORIC BUILDING

Map p306 (亞洲協會香港中心; Hong Kong Jockey Club Former Explosives Magazine; ☑852 2103 9511; www.asiasociety.org/hong-kong; 9 Justice Dr, Admiralty; ⊙gallery 11am-5pm Tue-Sun, to 7pm last Thu of month; Ⓜ Admiralty, exit F) An architectural feat, this magnificent site integrates 19th-century British military buildings, including a couple of explosives magazines, and transforms them into an exhibition gallery, a multipurpose theatre, an excellent restaurant and a bookshop, all open to the public. The architects Tod Williams and Billie Tsien eschewed bold statements for a subdued design that deferred to history and the natural shape of the land. The result is a horizontally oriented site that offers an uplifting contrast to the skyscrapers nearby. Experience it with a meal at AMMO (p108).

TAMAR PARK
PARK

Map p306 (添馬公園; Harcourt Rd, Admiralty; Ⓜ Admiralty, exit A) This harbour-front park on the site of the New Central Government Offices (新政府總部) is an inviting sprawl of verdant lawns where you can sunbathe while watching the ships go by. It's part of a 4km promenade along the northern shoreline of Hong Kong Island, from Central Piers, outside the IFC mall, past Wan Chai, all the way to North Point. Concerts and art events take place here occasionally, as did the major protest known as the Umbrella Movement in 2014.

The HMS *Tamar* was a British naval vessel moored in Victoria Harbour that served as the operational headquarters of the Royal Navy until 1946. The New Central Government Offices comprise the headquarters of the HKSAR government, the legislature and the Chief Executive's Office.

◉ Wan Chai

BLUE HOUSE
ARCHITECTURE

Map p308 (藍屋; ☑852 2835 4376; http://houseofstories.sjs.org.hk; 72-74A Stone Nullah Lane, Wan Chai; ☐6, 6A) The Blue House, built in the 1920s, and its neighbours **Yellow House** (黃屋; Map p308; 2-8 Hing Wan St, Wan Chai) and **Orange House** (橙屋; Map p308; 8 King Sing St, Wan Chai), make up a heritage cluster known as 'Viva Blue House' (We 嘩藍屋). The star of the lot, Blue House is a graceful four-storey tenement building featuring cast-iron Spanish balconies reminiscent of New Orleans. It is being restored and will reopen around mid-2017 with a dessert shop, a renovated osteopathy clinic, and toilets for its dozen residents. During its closure, House of Stories (p119) will relocate to Yellow House.

HUNG SHING TEMPLE
BUDDHIST TEMPLE

Map p308 (洪聖古廟; 129-131 Queen's Rd E, Wan Chai; ⊙8.30am-5.30pm; ☐6, 6A, Ⓜ Wan Chai, exit A3) Nestled in a nook on the southern side of Queen's Rd East, this dark and rather forbidding temple is built atop huge boulders that used to overlook the harbour. It was erected around 1850 in honour of a deified Tang-dynasty official known for his virtue (important) and ability to make predictions of value to traders (ultra-important).

A narrow staircase leads to the upper floor, where a fortune-teller can divine your future for HK$880. Do bring an interpreter.

KING YIN LEI
HISTORIC BUILDING

(景賢里; ☑852 2848 6230; www.heritage.gov.hk; 45 Stubbs Rd, Wan Chai; ☐15, 15B on Sun & public holidays) **FREE** This stunning 17,000-sq-ft mansion (c1937) owes its unique appearance to the Chinese Renaissance style associated with the 1920s when the Chinese government called for a revival of traditional culture, and architects in Shanghai set about merging Eastern and Western styles. Among Hong Kong's few surviving Chinese Renaissance structures, King Yin Lei is arguably the most successful at fusing eclectic elements into an aesthetic whole. Email for opening days – currently several days a year, but these may increase.

PAK TAI TEMPLE
TAOIST TEMPLE

Map p308 (北帝廟; 2 Lung On St, Wan Chai; ⊙8am-5pm; Ⓜ Wan Chai, exit A3) A short stroll up Stone Nullah Lane takes you to a majestic Taoist temple built in 1863 to honour a god of the sea, Pak Tai. The temple, the largest on Hong Kong Island, is impressive. The ceramic roof ridge ornaments depicting scenes from Cantonese opera were made in Shiwan – a beautiful example of Lingnan architecture in

Hong Kong. The main hall of the temple has a formidable 3m-tall copper likeness of Pak Tai cast during the Ming dynasty.

KHALSA DIWAN SIKH TEMPLE
SIKH TEMPLE

Map p308 (☎852 2572 4459; www.khalsadiwan.com; 371 Queen's Rd E, Wan Chai; ⏰5am-8pm; 🚌10) Sitting quietly between a busy road and a cemetery is Hong Kong's largest Sikh temple, a descendant of a small original built in 1901 by Sikh members of the British army. The temple in white with blue accents welcomes people of any faith, caste or colour to join in its services. Sunday prayer (9am to 1.30pm) sees some 1000 believers and non-believers in worship; there's fewer at the daily prayers, 6am to 8.30am and 6.30pm to 8pm.

One of the many signs of the temple's hospitality is the handing out of free vegetarian meals (11.30am to 8.30pm), a simple dal or *sabzi* (vegetable stew) to anyone walking through its gates. You could return the favour by helping to wash the dishes.

COMIX HOME BASE
MUSEUM

Map p308 (☎852 2824 5303; www.comixhomebase.com.hk; 7 Mallory St, Wan Chai; ⏰10am-8pm; MWan Chai, exit A3) FREE Housed in 10 historic buildings from the 1910s, this airy museum shines a spotlight on Hong Kong's talented comic-book artists, including a few international-award winners. A library, exhibitions, video footage and workshops introduce visitors to the city's rich comic-book history, from classics depicting wartime struggles *(Renjian Pictorial)* and satires on life in a British colony *(Old Master Q)*, through Ma Wing-shing's martial-arts comics, to the pensive creations of younger artists such as Chi Hoi.

POLICE MUSEUM
MUSEUM

(警隊博物館; ☎852 2849 7019; www.police.gov.hk/ppp_en/01_about_us/pm.html; 27 Coombe Rd, The Peak; ⏰2-5pm Tue, 9am-5pm Wed-Sun; 👪; 🚌15) FREE Crime-thriller fans should make a trip to this small museum in lush Wan Chai Gap. The protagonist in this former police station is the Hong Kong police force, formed in 1844, but the real stars are the Triads (ie Hong Kong Mafia). The eye-opening **Triad Societies Gallery** uncovers their secret rituals. Equally intriguing are the well-supplied **Narcotics Gallery** and the historical account of Kowloon Walled City. Kids will enjoy the weaponry display.

LOVERS' ROCK
LANDMARK

(姻緣石; off Bowen Rd, Wan Chai; 🚌green minibus 24A) Lovers' Rock or Destiny's Rock (Yan Yuen Sek) is a, well, phallus-shaped boulder on a bluff at the end of a track above Bowen Rd. It's a favourite pilgrimage site for women with relationship or fertility problems. It's busy during the **Maidens' Festival**, held on the seventh day of the seventh moon (mid-August).

The easiest way to reach here is to take green minibus 24A from the Admiralty bus station. Get off at the terminus (Shiu Fai Tce, 肇輝台) and walk up the path behind the housing complex.

GOLDEN BAUHINIA SQUARE
MONUMENT

Map p308 (金紫荊廣場; 1 Expo Dr, Golden Bauhinia Sq, Wan Chai; 🚌18, MWan Chai, exit A5) A 6m-tall statue of Hong Kong's symbol stands on the waterfront in front of the Hong Kong Convention & Exhibition Centre to mark the establishment of the Hong Kong SAR in 1997. The flag-raising ceremony, held daily (except the first day of each month) from 7.50am to 8.03am, and conducted by the Hong Kong police, is a must-see for mainland tourist groups. On the first, the ceremony starts at 7.45am and is followed by a short pipe-band performance.

CLOCK OF COLOURS

Central Plaza in Wan Chai, the lanky skyscraper sticking out from behind the Hong Kong Convention & Exhibition Centre when you're looking from Kowloon, is one of the world's biggest clocks. Between 6pm and midnight daily, there are four illuminated lines shining through the glass pyramid at the top of the building.

The bottom level indicates the hour: red is 6pm, white 7pm, purple 8pm, yellow 9pm, pink 10pm and green 11pm. When all four lights are the same colour, it's right on the hour. When the top light is different from the bottom ones, it's 15 minutes past the hour. If the top two and bottom two are different, it's half-past the hour. If the top three match, it's 45 minutes past the hour.

So what time is it now?

◉ Causeway Bay

TIN HAU TEMPLE
TEMPLE

Map p310 (天后廟; 10 Tin Hau Temple Rd, Causeway Bay; ⊙7am-5pm; ⓂTin Hau, exit B) Hong Kong Island's most famous Tin Hau (Goddess of the Sea) temple has lent its name to an entire neighbourhood, a metro station and a street. It has been a place of worship for 370 years and, despite renovations, imparts an air of antiquity, particularly in the intricate stone carvings near the entrance and the ceramic figurines from Shiwan decorating the roof. The main altar contains an effigy of the goddess with a blackened face.

LIN FA TEMPLE
BUDDHIST TEMPLE

Map p310 (蓮花宮; Lin Fa Kung St W, Tai Hang; ⊙8am-5pm; ⓂTin Hau, exit B) You'll recognise this unusual-looking temple by its semi-octagonal hall and its verandah with Western-style balustrades, both of which have survived several renovations since the 1860s. Important relics inside include an altar to its patron, the goddess of mercy, a fresco of a dragon that evokes the Fire Dragon Dance in Tai Hang, and an ancient boulder jutting into the rear hall on which the goddess is said to have appeared.

ST MARY'S CHURCH
CHURCH

Map p310 (聖馬利亞堂; ☏852 2576 1768; http://dhk.hkskh.org/stmary/; cnr Tung Lo Wan Rd & Ka Ning Path, Causeway Bay; ⓂCauseway Bay, exit F) This outlandish Anglican church was born in the 1930s through an apparent marriage between a Chinese temple and a Christian house of worship. Its red-brick walls are embellished with Chinese eaves and pillars, behind which are stained-glass windows. Inside, the Chinese cloud motif is liberally applied to pews and walls to evoke a (Christian) heaven. The church, especially its interior, is attractive despite being an eccentric representative of what's sometimes called the Chinese Renaissance style.

VICTORIA PARK
PARK

Map p310 (維多利亞公園; www.lcsd.gov.hk/en/ls_park.php; Causeway Rd, Causeway Bay; ⊙park 24hr; ⓕ; ⓂTin Hau, exit B) **FREE** Built on land reclaimed from the **Causeway Bay Typhoon Shelter** (銅鑼灣避風塘; Map p310; off Hung Hing Rd, Causeway Bay; ⓂCauseway Bay, exit D1), Victoria Park is the biggest patch of public greenery on Hong Kong Island. The best time to go is on a weekday morning, when it becomes a forest of people practising the slow-motion choreography of taichi. The park becomes a flower market just before the Lunar New Year and a lantern museum during the Mid-Autumn Festival (p30). The swimming pool (previously outdoor), built in 1957, was Hong Kong's oldest.

NOONDAY GUN
HISTORIC SITE

Map p310 (香港怡和午炮; 221 Gloucester Rd, Causeway Bay; ⊙7am-midnight; ⓂCauseway Bay, exit D1) A colonial tradition dating back to the mid-1800s, the daily firing of this Hotchkiss 3-pounder naval gun was made famous by its mention in the Noël Coward song 'Mad Dogs and Englishmen'. The gun stands in a small garden opposite the Excelsior Hotel on the waterfront, where its noon-on-the-dot firing always draws a small crowd.

The Noonday Gun is tricky to find – it's accessible via a tunnel through the basement car park in the World Trade Centre, just west of the Excelsior Hotel. From the taxi rank in front of the hotel, look west for the door marked 'Car Park Shroff, Marina Club & Noon Gun'.

LOCAL KNOWLEDGE

VICTORIA PARK'S ANGRY UNCLES

Victoria Park has always been associated with freedom of expression, a reputation owed mainly to the candlelight vigil that takes place here on 4 June, but also to the current-affairs debate 'City Forum', which turns it into a mini–Hyde Park every Sunday.

Spanning two MTR stations and with multiple entrances, the park provides a leafy detour and short cut for many locals. Among the regulars are a group of retired, pro-communist old men who, during 'City Forum' on Sundays (noon to 1pm), hang out near the venue and holler against speechifying pro-democracy politicians to drown them out.

These men came to be known as the 'Uncles of Victoria Park' (維園阿伯), but the term has since evolved to include any politically minded old man with a gripe. And Hong Kong certainly has no shortage of these.

RENT-A-CURSE GRANNIES

Under the Canal Rd Flyover between Wan Chai and Causeway Bay, you can hire elderly women to beat up your enemy. From their perch on plastic stools, these rent-a-curse grannies will pound paper cut-outs of your romantic rival, office bully or whiny celeb with a shoe (their orthopaedic flat or your stilettos – your call) while rapping rhythmic curses. All for only HK$50. Hung Shing Temple (p102) has a 'master' who performs the same with a symbolic 'precious' sword for the exorbitant sum of HK$100.

Villain hitting or villain exorcism (打小人; *da siu yan*) is a practice related to folk sorcery. It's performed throughout the year, but the most popular date is the **Day of the Awakening of Insects** when the sun is at an exact celestial longitude of 345° (usually between 5 and 20 March on the Gregorian calendar). It's believed to bring reconciliation or resolution, though that too could be symbolic.

◉ Happy Valley

HAPPY VALLEY
RACECOURSE
HORSE RACING

Map p310 (跑馬地馬場; ☑852 2895 1523; www.hkjc.com/home/english/index.asp; 2 Sports Rd, Happy Valley; HK$10; ⊙7-10.30pm Wed Sep-Jun; 🚃Happy Valley) An outing at the races is one of the quintessential Hong Kong things to do, especially if you happen to be around during one of the weekly Wednesday evening races here. The punters pack into the stands and trackside, cheering, drinking and eating, and the atmosphere is electric.

The first horse races were held here in 1846. Now meetings are held both here and at the newer and larger (but less atmospheric) Sha Tin Racecourse (p169) in the New Territories. Check the website for details on betting and tourist packages. Take the eastbound Happy Valley tram to the final stop and cross the road to the racecourse.

HONG KONG CEMETERY
CEMETERY

Map p308 (香港墳場; www.fehd.gov.hk/english/cc/introduction.html; Wong Nai Chung Rd, Happy Valley; ⊙7am-6pm or 7pm; 🚻; Ⓜ️Causeway Bay, exit A) Crowded and cosmopolitan, dead Hong Kong is no different from the breathing city. Tombstones jostle for space at this Christian cemetery (c 1845) located alongside the Jewish, Hindu, Parsee and Muslim cemeteries, and St Michael's Catholic Cemetery. Burial plots date from the mid-1800s and include colonialists, tycoons and silverscreen divas.

F11 PHOTOGRAPHIC MUSEUM
MUSEUM

(F11攝影博物館; ☑852 6516 1122; http://f11.com; 11 Yuk Sau St, Happy Valley; ⊙by appointment Tue-Sat; 🚃Happy Valley) FREE This photography museum inside a restored 80-year-old art deco residence specialises in the works of big-name international photographers. Exhibitions are held three or four times a year on two floors of the beautiful three-storey space. Shows have featured Elliott Erwitt, Bruno Barbey and Robert Capa. It also has a library and a display of vintage Leica cameras. Visits are by appointment only (made on the museum's online calendar) and are accompanied by a guided tour.

◉ Island East

PARA SITE
GALLERY

(☑852 2517 4620; www.para-site.org.hk; 22/F, Wing Wah Industrial Bldg, 677 King's Rd, Quarry Bay; ⊙noon-7pm Wed-Sun; Ⓜ️Quarry Bay, exit C) From this new address in Quarry Bay, the respected independent art space Para Site continues to mount exhibitions of contemporary art that question the very values of society and contemporary existence. The exhibitions usually have a Hong Kong or Asian focus but universal relevance.

HONG KONG FILM ARCHIVE
MUSEUM

(香港電影資料館; ☑bookings 852 3761 6661, enquiries 852 2739 2139, resource centre 852 2119 7360; www.filmarchive.gov.hk; 50 Lei King Rd, Sai Wan Ho; ⊙10am-8pm, box office noon-8pm, resource centre 10am-7pm Mon & Wed-Fri, to 5pm Sat, 1-5pm Sun; Ⓜ️Sai Wan Ho, exit A) FREE The archive is a cinephiles' heaven. Its resource centre has over 6300 reels and tapes, as well as magazines and scripts related to Hong Kong cinema through the ages. You can browse through its comprehensive bilingual online catalogue before visiting. The archive also holds thematic exhibitions

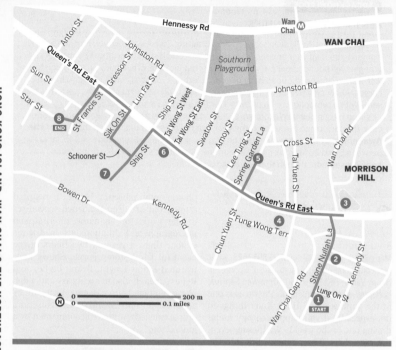

Neighbourhood Walk
Old Wan Chai's Forgotten Streets

START PAK TAI TEMPLE
END STAR ST
LENGTH 1.2KM; TWO HOURS

A short stroll from the main bus routes and Wan Chai metro (exit A3), you'll start to get a feel for the neighbourhood as it was in the 19th century at ❶ **Pak Tai Temple** (p102), a stunning temple built 150 years ago by local residents. Further down the slope, the ❷ **House of Stories** (p119) will show you what life was like in Wan Chai in the last century.

The Streamline Moderne exterior of the historic ❸ **Wan Chai Market** (p117) is all that remains of the place, which now fronts a shopping centre. Once the hub of the neighbourhood, the market was used as a mortuary by Japanese forces in WWII. Just to the west, the pocket-sized ❹ **Old Wan Chai Post Office** is Hong Kong's oldest post office.

Take a quick look at ❺ **Spring Garden Lane**, one of the first areas developed by the British, and imagine what it was like when prostitutes solicited here in the 1900s. Then head along Queen's Rd East to peep inside the mysterious ❻ **Hung Shing Temple** (p102), once a seaside shrine.

Just west of the temple turn up the hill along Ship St and stand before the now derelict ❼ **Ghost House** at 55 Nam Koo Tce. Its history is a wretched one: it was used by Japanese soldiers as a brothel housing 'comfort women' in WWII.

The ❽ **Star Street neighbourhood** is a quiet little corner of town that manages to contain the old, including a family-run *dai pai dong* (food stall) on St Francis St, and the new, in the form of quaint boutiques and restaurants. On 31 Wing Fung St is a six-storey balconied building in art deco style. Admiralty MTR can be reached by an escalator and underground travelator entered at the bottom of Wing Fung St.

and has regular screenings in its **cinema**. Check online for programs. From the MTR station, walk north on Tai On St and west on Lei King Rd.

STATE THEATRE BUILDING
HISTORIC BUILDING

(皇都戲院大廈; 279-291 King's Rd, North Point; **M**North Point, exit B4) Look past the billboards and you'll see flying buttresses on the roof, like a whale carcass. State Theatre is the last of Hong Kong's post-WWII luxury theatres. It opened in 1952 with *Just for You* starring Bing Crosby and Jane Wyman, and for years, catching a flick here was a big deal. The buttresses in a Soviet Constructivist style served to hold the roof from above, allowing for a large pillarless hall, a truly avant-garde design at the time.

AO VERTICAL ART SPACE
GALLERY

(AO Vertical 藝術空間; ☑852 2976 0913; www.aovertical.com; Photo Book Centre, 1-14th fl, Asia One Tower, 8 Fung Yip St, Chai Wan; ⊙10am-6pm, Mon-Sat; ☑788) **FREE** *The* place to see the works of Hong Kong's brilliant photographers and images of the region by Asian and international artists, this vertical gallery stretching 10 floors inside an industrial building mounts excellent exhibitions in its stairwell. The ground-floor bookshop has a strong collection on the region's art and photography; it's open by appointment. Make contact before you go.

Bus 788 from Central stops at the corner of Fung Yip St. The stop is called 'Kailey Industrial Building'. Express Bus 789 from Canal St in Causeway Bay also takes you here. Minibus 47M from Chai Wan MTR station stops at Fung Yip St, right in front of the bookshop. Tell the driver you're getting off at 'Asia One Tower' (宏亞大廈).

CHUN YEUNG STREET MARKET
MARKET

(春秧街街市; Chun Yeung St, North Point; ⊙8am-6pm; **M**North Point, exit A4) Hop on an eastbound tram, and past Fortress Hill you'll turn into an old narrow street teeming with market stalls and old tenement buildings. This is the famous Chun Yeung Street Market, and at 5pm it's so busy you wonder why no one ever got hit by the tram. Many stores here sell foodstuffs from Fújiàn that you can't find anywhere else in Hong Kong. North Point has a huge Fujianese community and you'll hear their dialect spoken on Shun Yeung St.

HONG KONG MUSEUM OF COASTAL DEFENCE
MUSEUM

(香港海防博物館; ☑852 2569 1500; http://hk.coastaldefence.museum; 175 Tung Hei Rd, Shau Kei Wan; adult/concession HK$10/5; ⊙10am-6pm Mar-Sep, to 5pm Oct-Feb, closed Thu; ☑; **M**Shau Kei Wan, exit B2) This museum occupies a knockout location in the Lei Yue Mun Fort (1887), which has sweeping views down to the Lei Yue Mun Channel and southeastern Kowloon. Exhibitions in the old redoubt cover Hong Kong's coastal defence over six centuries. There's a historical trail through the gun fortifications, tunnels and observation posts almost down to the coast.

ISLAND EAST MARKET
MARKET

(www.hkmarkets.org; Tong Chong St, Quarry Bay; ⊙11am-5.30pm Sat & Sun spring-autumn; **M**Quarry Bay, exit A) Hong Kong Island's largest farmers' market, inaugurated in 2012, has dozens of booths of organic produce, local snacks, craft makers and street musicians, all in a typically Hong Kong setting in a busy urban plaza. Check website for opening days. It can be closed for months at a time.

ARTIFY
GALLERY

(☑852 3543 1260; www.artifygallery.com; Unit 7, 10th fl, Block A, Ming Pao Industrial Centre, 18 Ka Yip St, Chai Wan; ⊙10am-7pm Tue-Fri, 11am-7pm Sat & Sun, closed Mon; ☑minibus 62, 62A) From its venue inside an industrial building overlooking the sea, Artify specialises in contemporary Asian art in print and paper, which includes paintings, etchings, colour viscosity prints, lithographs, even sculpture. Minibus 62 or 62A from Heng Fa Chuen MTR station, takes you to Ming Pao Industrial Centre. Tell the driver you're getting off at Ming Pao Industrial Centre (明報工業中心).

EATING

Admiralty

★LOCK CHA TEA SHOP
VEGETARIAN, CHINESE $

Map p306 (樂茶軒; ☑852 2801 7177; www.lockcha.com; Ground fl, KS Lo Gallery, 10 Cotton Tree Dr, Hong Kong Park, Admiralty; dim sum HK$15-28, tea from HK$25; ⊙10am-8pm, closed second Tue; ☑; **M**Admiralty, exit C1) Set in the lush environs of Hong Kong Park, Lock Cha offers fragrant teas and tasty vegetarian dim sum in a replica of an ancient scholar's study. It also hosts Chinese music performances on Saturday (7pm to 9pm) and Sunday (4pm to 6pm). Do call to reserve a seat. The music is popular; the tea shop is dainty.

GREAT FOOD
HALL   SUPERMARKET, INTERNATIONAL $

Map p306 (☑852 2918 9986; www.greatfood hall.com; Basement, Two Pacific Place, Admiralty; meals from HK$100; ⊙10am-10pm; ⊠Admiralty, exit F) In the basement of the swish Pacific Place shopping mall, Great Food Hall is one of the nicest gourmet supermarkets in Hong Kong. It has its own burger joint and Spanish tapas restaurant, as well as a stellar array of cheeses, takeaway sushi and hearty create-your-own salads.

BEEF & LIBERTY   BURGERS $

Map p306 (☑852 2811 3009; www.beef-liberty. com/hk; 2nd fl, 23 Wing Fung St; burgers HK$92-118; ⊙11.30am-10.30pm Mon-Fri, 11am-11pm Sat & Sun; ⊠Admiralty, exit F) For our money, this trendy spot has the best burgers in town. Juicy Tasmanian beef is cooked any way you like, and topped with bacon jam, green chilli, pickled onions and other goodies. Sweet potato fries are killer, and boozy spiked milkshakes add to the fun. Book ahead during peak times. Enter through the elevator in the pizza restaurant downstairs.

⭐PURE VEGGIE
HOUSE   VEGETARIAN, CHINESE $$

Map p306 (心齋; ☑852 2525 0556; 3rd fl, Coda Plaza, 51 Garden Rd, Mid-Levels; meals HK$250-500; ⊙10.30am-10.30pm; ☑; ⊠12A from Admiralty MTR) This Buddhist restaurant goes way beyond the usual tofu 'n' broccoli to serve innovative and delicious vegetarian dishes – fried rice with black truffle and pine nuts, seaweed-wrapped tofu rolls, and the city's best vegetarian Sichuan dishes prepared by its sister restaurant a few floors up, San Xi Lou (p108). Excellent all-veggie dim sum, served at lunch, will please even dedicated carnivores.

SAN XI LOU   SICHUAN $$

Map p306 (三希樓; ☑852 2838 8811; 7th fl Coda Plaza, 51 Garden Rd, Mid-Levels; meals HK$200-400; ⊙11am-10.30pm; ⊠12A from Admiralty MTR) Fresh ingredients and complex use of spices make this Hong Kong's best Sichuan restaurant. Indecisive chilli heads can go

for the hotpot, but hardcore fans of the cuisine should try the 'water-cooked fish' (水煮魚), which consists of fish slices and shredded vegetables swimming in a vermilion broth infused with dried chillies and Sichuan peppercorns. Many restaurants are known to use frozen fish for this fiery dish, but here you can actually taste the delicate sweetness of the fresh fish and feel its silken texture through the heat.

AMMO   MEDITERRANEAN $$

Map p306 (☑852 2537 9888; www.ammo.com. hk; Asia Society Hong Kong Centre, 9 Justice Dr, Admiralty; mains HK$118-400; ⊙noon-midnight Sun-Thu, to 1am Fri & Sat; ⊠Admiralty, exit F) Awash in a coppery light, this sleek glass-walled cafe at the Asia Society Hong Kong Centre (p102) features chandeliers and copper panels evoking the site's past as an explosives magazine. The modern menu is well thought out, with a selection of mostly Italian mains, which include excellent homemade pasta and fashionably deconstructed desserts. Tapas are available from 5pm. Bookings essential.

✕ Wan Chai

KAM'S ROAST GOOSE   CANTONESE $

Map p308 (甘牌燒鵝; ☑852 2520 1110; www.krg. com.hk; 226 Hennessy Rd, Wan Chai; meals HK$70-200; ⊙11.30am-9pm; ⊠Wan Chai, exit A2) One of two spin-offs from Central's famed Yung Kee Restaurant (p89), Kam's clearly still upholds the same strict standards in the sourcing and roasting of the city's most glorified roast goose. Besides the juicy crisp-skinned fowl (of which the best cut is the leg), other barbecued meats such as roast suckling pig are well worth sinking your teeth into.

JOY HING ROASTED MEAT   CANTONESE $

Map p308 (再興燒臘飯店; ☑852 2519 6639; 1C Stewart Rd, Wan Chai; meals HK$30-60; ⊙10am-10pm; ⊠Wan Chai, exit A4) This basic stall is one of your best bets for Cantonese barbecue (the Michelin inspectors think so too) – succulent slivers of barbecued pork, goose, chicken and liver over freshly steamed rice. The menu is simply cards stuck on the wall. Just see what your neighbours are having and point.

WING WAH   NOODLES $

Map p308 (永華雲吞麵家; 89 Hennessy Rd, Wan Chai; noodles from HK$50; ⊙noon-2am, to 1am Sun; ⊠Wan Chai, exit A3) This unpretentious noodle shop has been making Cantonese noodles the traditional way for 50 years. The dough is kneaded daily with a bamboo pole in a workshop to make the noodles al dente; the wontons are small, as they should be, with silken wrappers that trail in the broth. Tossed noodles with shrimp roe and dessert soups are their other specialities.

CAPITAL CAFE
CHA CHAAN TANG **$**

Map p308 (華星冰室; ☑852 2666 7766; Shop B1, ground fl, Kwong Sang Hong Bldg, 6 Heard St, Wan Chai; meals HK$35-50; ⊙7am-11pm; Ⓜ Wan Chai, exit A2) Designed to resemble a vintage *cha chaan tang* (tea house), but cleaner and more gimmicky, this joint owned by the founder of an eponymous Canto-pop record label serves good old classics like toast with fluffy scrambled eggs and iced red-bean drink, as well as fancier laced-with-black-truffle versions.

CHUEN CHEONG FOODS
CHINESE **$**

Map p308 (泉昌美食; ☑852 2575 8278; 150 Wan Chai Rd, Wan Chai; 2 pieces of stinky tofu HK$12; ⊙12.30-9pm Mon-Sat; Ⓜ Wan Chai, exit A4) So you're walking through Wan Chai and you smell something...wait, is there a *horse stable* nearby? Nope, that's just the manure-like stench of stinky tofu, a paradigmatic case of 'tastes better than it smells'. This popular street stall (no English sign) serves the beloved snack Hong Kong–style, which means deep-fried and slathered with chilli sauce and sweet 'hoisin' sauce.

★ SEVENTH SON
CANTONESE **$$**

Map p308 (家全七福; ☑852 2892 2888; www.seventhson.hk; 5 & 6th fl, Kwan Chart Tower, 6 Tonnochy Rd, Wan Chai; meals from HK$350; ⊙11.30am-3pm & 6-10.30pm; Ⓜ Wan Chai, exit C) Worthy spin-off from the illustrious Fook Lam Moon (p143; aka Tycoon's Canteen), Seventh Son reproduces to a tee FLM's homestyle dishes and a few extravagant seafood numbers as well. The food here is excellent, plus you get the treatment FLM reserves for regulars. Moot point, though – you wouldn't know how regulars are treated at FLM unless you are one.

22 SHIPS
TAPAS **$$**

Map p308 (☑852 2555 0722; www.22ships.hk; 22 Ship St, Wan Chai; tapas HK$88-198; ⊙noon-3pm & 6-11pm; Ⓜ Wan Chai, exit B2) This tiny, trendy spot is packed from open to close. But the long wait (the restaurant doesn't take reservations) is worth it for exquisite, playful

small plates by much-buzzed-about young British chef Jason Atherton.

Molecular gastronomy techniques are on display in many of the Asian-influenced Spanish dishes, like crispy fish skin with dollops of foamy cod mousse. Others, like a jamon, manchego and truffle toasty, topped with a fried quail's egg, are pure luxe comfort food.

KIN'S KITCHEN
CANTONESE **$$**

Map p308 (留家廚房; ☑852 2571 0913; 5th fl, W Square, 314-324 Hennessy Rd, Wan Chai; meals HK$180-450; ⊙noon-3pm & 6-11pm; Ⓜ Wan Chai, exit A2) Art critic-turned-restaurateur Lau Kin-wai infuses his artistic sense and passion for local ingredients into this under-stated restaurant specialising in Cantonese classics with a twist. Lau, looking quite the *bon vivant* with silver hair and rosy cheeks, is sometimes seen discussing the merits of the four kinds of white rice on the menu with customers.

HONG ZHOU RESTAURANT
HANGZHOU **$$**

Map p308 (杭州酒家; ☑852 2591 1898; 1st fl, Chinachem Johnston Plaza, 178-188 Johnston Rd, Wan Chai; HK$200-800; ⊙11.30am-2.30pm & 5.30-10.30pm; Ⓜ Wan Chai, exit A5) A food critics' favourite, this establishment excels at Hángzhōu cooking, the delicate sister of Shanghainese cuisine. Dishes such as shrimp stir-fried with tea leaves show how the best culinary creations should engage all your senses. Its version of Dongpo pork (東坡肉), a succulent braised pork belly dish named after a gluttonous poet, is cholesterol heaven.

PAWN
BRITISH **$$**

Map p308 (☑852 2866 3444; www.thepawn.com.hk; 62 Johnston Rd, Wan Chai; HK$250-1000; ⊙11am-2am Mon-Sat, to midnight Sun; Ⓜ Wan Chai, exit A3) The Pawn has relaunched in the same handsome block that used to house a century-old pawn shop. The menu, designed by British star chef Tom Aikens, is as refreshing in its take on classics like fish pie – halibut with skin seared paper-thin is paired with slow-cooked octopus and dried sakura shrimp.

MEGAN'S KITCHEN
CANTONESE, HOTPOT **$$**

Map p308 (美味廚; ☑852 2866 8305; www.meganskitchen.com; 5th fl, Lucky Centre, 165-171 Wan Chai Rd, Wan Chai; hotpot per person HK$200-300; ⊙noon-3pm & 6-11.30pm; Ⓜ Wan Chai, exit A3) Broth choices like *tom yum* and 'lobster borscht' make for a modern twist on the classic hotpot experience at Megan's, though standbys like spicy Sichuan soup are just as good. The vast menu of items runs the gamut from the standard (mushrooms, fish slices, tofu) to the avant garde (don't miss the fabulous rainbow cuttlefish balls).

Like all hotpot restaurants, Megan's is best visited with a crowd of at least four. Subdivided hotpots mean you can sample up to three broths, so the more the merrier. Call ahead for reservations, especially on weekends.

BO INNOVATION CHINESE $$$
Map p308 (廚魔; ☑852 2850 8371; www.bo innovation.com; 2nd fl, 60 Johnston Rd, Wan Chai; lunch set/tasting menu HK$430/730, dinner tasting menu HK$1680-2380; ⊘noon-2pm Mon-Fri, 7-10pm Mon-Sat; Ⓜ Wan Chai, exit B2) Bo takes classic Chinese dishes apart and reassembles them in surprising ways using the sci-fi techniques of molecular gastronomy. The barbecue pork bun *(cha siu bao)* is a wobbly blob of pork-infused soup encased in a wrapper that explodes in the mouth. Chilli crab is served in a baby-food bottle complete with Hello Kitty baby spoon. The lift entrance is at 18 Ship St.

GRISSINI ITALIAN $$$
Map p308 (☑852 2588 1234; www.hongkong. grand.hyattrestaurants.com/grissini; Grand Hyatt Hotel, 1 Harbour Rd, Wan Chai; lunch/dinner from HK$400/$800; ⊘noon-2.30pm Sun-Fri, 7-10.30pm daily; ☑; Ⓜ Wan Chai, exit A1) Fluffy, chewy and addictive, the foot-long *grissini* here are – appropriately – the best in town. Leave room for the Milanese specialities and pair them with a bottle from the 1000-strong cellar. With floor-to-ceiling windows and a chic '90s look, Grissini stays in the game with solid cooking, warm service, occasional celebrity chefs and special truffle menus.

SERGE ET LE PHOQUE MODERN FRENCH $$$
Map p308 (☑852 5465 2000; Shop B2, ground fl, Tower 1, The Zenith, 3 Wan Chai Rd, Wan Chai; dinner set from HK$700; ⊘6-10.30pm; Ⓜ Wan Chai, exit A3) Expect to see wet-market butchers chopping meat through the floor-to-ceiling windows (it's harder for them to look in) as you savour the perfect French beef or giant Japanese scallops in casual cool-toned luxury, pondering which side of the gentrification debate you're on. The restaurant, open only for dinner, is dimly lit by milk-white orbs from the '60s.

✖ Causeway Bay

★ ATUM DESSERANT SWEETS $
Map p310 (☑852 2956 1411, 852 2377 2400; www. atumhk.com; 16th fl, The L Square, 459-461 Lockhart Rd, Causeway Bay; desserts from HK$138; ⊘2.45pm-midnight Mon-Thu, from 1pm Fri-Sun; Ⓜ Causeway Bay, exit C) Hop onto a stool, hook your bag under the counter and watch museum-worthy desserts materialise with some help from liquid nitrogen and the owner's years as a pastry chef at the Mandarin Oriental. Improvisation (HK$348 for two) is confectionery, fruits and ice-cream arranged like a Jackson Pollock crossbred with a Monet. And it's not just for show – flavours are surprisingly well balanced.

Booking advised.

HO HUNG KEE NOODLES $
Map p310 (何洪記; ☑852 2577 6028; 12th fl, Hysan Place, 500 Hennessy Rd, Causeway Bay; noodles from HK$40; ⊘11.30am-11.30pm; Ⓜ Causeway Bay, exit F2) The tasty noodles, wontons and congee at this 70-year-old shop are cooked according to the Ho's heirloom recipes, and clearly they still work, as do the dim sum and Cantonese classics newly included in the menu. Though the location lacks character, Ho Hung Kee is always packed during lunch, even before it was awarded one Michelin star.

QUEEN OF THE EAST CHINESE $
Map p310 (東后齋; ☑852 2377 7733; 25/F Circle Tower, 28 Tang Lung St, Causeway Bay; mains HK$78-168; ⊘11am-10pm; ☑; Ⓜ Causeway Bay, exit A) The cheaper, smaller and more centrally located sibling of Admiralty's exquisite Pure Veggie House (p108), this Buddhist restaurant also minimises reliance on gluten mock meats in favour of creativity in the cooking of shrooms, pulses and veggies. The dim sum, available till 5pm, are a hardcore dimsummer's nirvana, vegetarian or otherwise.

GUN GEI HEALTHY VEGETARIAN CHINESE $
Map p308 (根記健康素食; ☑852 2575 7595; No 6 Bowrington Rd Market & Cooked Food Centre, 21 Bowrington Rd, Wan Chai; dishes HK$32-70; ⊘8.30am-2.30pm & 5.30-9.30pm Mon-Sat; ☑; Ⓜ Causeway Bay, exit A) The cleanest *dai pai dong* inside Bowrington Road Market (p111) makes simple but delicious vegetarian dishes. There are more choices at dinner, but it's best to have a Chinese-speaker help

you book a table and pre-order dishes – this place is usually packed. The lunch special has two or three dishes, one soup and as much rice as you need.

DELICIOUS KITCHEN
SHANGHAI $

Map p310 (☑852 2577 8350; 9-11B Cleveland St, Causeway Bay; meals HK$70-100; ☺11am-11pm; Ⓜ Causeway Bay, exit E) The Shanghainese rice cooked with shredded Chinese cabbage is so good at this *cha chaan teng* (teahouse) that fashionistas are tripping over themselves to land a table here. It's best with the legendary honey-glazed pork chop. Fat, veggie-stuffed wontons and perfectly crispy fried tofu are also winners.

LAB MADE ICE CREAM
DESSERTS $

Map p310 (分子雪糕專門店; ☑852 9355 4476; www.labmade.com.hk; 6 Brown St, Tai Hang; ice-cream from HK$41; ☺2pm-midnight, to 11pm Sun; Ⓜ Tin Hau, exit B) A very delicious science experiment, the ice cream at Lab Made is created with liquid nitrogen and a mixer, each scoop made to order and emerging with a puff of vapour. A rotating menu offers four flavours daily, a blend of the prosaic (chocolate, mango) and the only-in-Hong-Kong magical (condensed milk with crispy toast bits, purple yam, mooncake).

SOGO
JAPANESE, SELF-CATERING $

Map p310 (☑852 2833 8338; www.sogo.com.hk; Basement, 555 Hennessy Rd, Causeway Bay; snacks from HK$20; ☺10am-10pm; Ⓜ Causeway Bay, exit D3) In the basement of the landmark Sogo Japanese department store, this frantically packed supermarket and foodhall is the place to come for all manner of Japanese snacks. Look for *onigiri* (fish-stuffed rice balls), fresh crepes with fillings like green-tea ice cream, fried-octopus pancakes, and almost-too-pretty-to-eat *mochi* (sweet glutinous rice cakes).

BOWRINGTON ROAD MARKET
MARKET $

Map p308 (鵝頸街市; 21 Bowrington Rd, Causeway Bay; ☺6am-8pm; Ⓜ Causeway Bay, exit A) A multistorey indoor wet market with a cooked-food centre open till 2am. You'll see fish and vegetable vendors on the street leading up to it. A delight to wander in if you like markets.

★ KAM'S KITCHEN
CANTONESE $$

Map p310 (甘飯館; ☑852 3568 2832; 5 Mercury St, Tin Hau; lunch HK$50-300, dinner from HK$200; ☺11.30am-3pm & 6-10.30pm; Ⓜ Tin Hau, exit A1) A family feud at the venerable Yung Kee in Central has created this excellent-value spin-off. Kam's Kitchen serves classic, labour-intensive Cantonese dishes like prawn stuffed with crab roe and braised goose web. And, of course, the famous goose is still here, as a roasted bird or with its fat drizzled into fried rice.

Booking advised.

★ CHOI'S KITCHEN
CANTONESE $$

Map p310 (私房蔡; ☑852 3485 0501; Shop C, ground fl, Hoi Kok Mansion, 9 Whitfield Rd, Tin Hau; mains from HK$128; ☺11am-3pm & 6-10pm; Ⓜ Tin Hau, exit A) This charming shop refines common Cantonese dishes by using only fresh, high-quality ingredients and restraint in seasoning. The signature claypot rice is made to order and is only available at dinner. Decor is understated faux-retro to reflect the restaurant's origin as a *dai pai dong* (大牌檔; food stall). Prices are a far cry from those days, but the (well-heeled) customers keep coming.

Booking advised, or go early.

★ FORTUNE KITCHEN
CANTONESE $$

Map p310 (盈福小廚; ☑852 2697 7317; 5 Lan Fong Rd, Causeway Bay; mains HK$100-500; ☺11.30am-5pm & 6-10.30pm; Ⓜ Causeway Bay, exit A) Despite the old-fashioned Chinatown name, Fortune Kitchen is decorated like an old tea house and serves homey but sophisticated Cantonese at wallet-friendly prices. The owner was a sous-chef at a Michelin-star restaurant and his culinary skills are evident in dishes such as the signature steamed chicken with dried scallops and the eponymous fried rice. Booking advised.

SUSHI FUKU-SUKE
JAPANESE $$

Map p310 (鮨福助; ☑852 2955 0005; www.fukusuke.com.hk; 11th fl, Macau Yat Yuen Centre, 525 Hennessy Rd, Causeway Bay; meal sets HK$200-1300; ☺noon-11pm; Ⓜ Causeway Bay, exit D4) An elegant sushi bar with clean lines and pine wood like you'd find in Tokyo, which is where the chef/owner used to work. If you're not too hungry, there's a reasonable lunch set for HK$200. The *omakase* (chef's menu) at dinner comprises fresh sushi or sashimi and carefully prepared hot dishes for about HK$800.

GO YA YAKITORI
JAPANESE $$

Map p310 (五谷串燒; ☑852 2504 2000; 21 Brown St, Tai Hang; meals from HK$200; ☺6-11.30pm daily, also noon-2.30pm Sun; Ⓜ Tin Hau, exit B) This wood-panelled *yakitori* joint in cosy Tai Hang makes you feel like you're in a Japanese village. After your complimentary cup of sake and amuse-bouche, choose from dozens of skewers – popular picks include chicken with cartilage and *kurobuta* pork. Beer comes from an artisan Japanese brewery.

Don't panic when you see the prices – they're listed in Japanese yen!

YEE TUNG HEEN DIM SUM, CANTONESE **$$$**
Map p310 (怡東軒; ☑852 2837 6790; 2nd fl, Excelsior Hotel, 281 Gloucester Rd, Causeway Bay; lunch/dinner from HK$200/$500; ⊘noon-3pm & 6-10pm) This elegant and under-hyped restaurant is an expert at haute Cantonese cuisine. Managed by the Mandarin Oriental, it delivers MO-quality food and service at two-thirds of the price; it's easier to book too. The best ingredients are painstakingly prepared and presented to impress, as exemplified by lunchtime dim sum offerings like eggplant pastry and the award-winning mushroom assortment.

FORUM CANTONESE, DIM SUM **$$$**
Map p310 (富臨飯店阿一鮑魚; ☑852 2869 8282; 1st fl, Sino Plaza, 255-257 Jaffe Rd, Causeway Bay; meals HK$500-1600; ⊘11am-2.30pm & 5.30-10.30pm; Ⓜ Causeway Bay, exit D4) Fans from across the world flock to this posh eatery for its abalone dishes prepared from a recipe by restaurant owner and award-winning chef Yeung Koon-yat. If you want to try the braised abalone, your cheapest bet is the HK$1380 per person six-course set meal that includes a king prawn and a 'two-head' abalone.

WEST VILLA CANTONESE, DIM SUM **$$$**
Map p310 (西苑酒家; ☑852 2882 2110; www. westvillahk.com; 5th fl, Lee Gardens One, 33 Hysan Ave, Causeway Bay; meals from HK$350; ⊘11am-11.30pm; Ⓜ Causeway Bay, exit E) This elegant restaurant does the *char siu* (barbecued pork) job well – slightly charred at the edges, with a golden lean-to-fat ratio. It also makes a stellar soy-sauce chicken and Duke's Soup (爵士湯), which comprises chicken, conch, honeydew melon and a dozen other ingredients its competitors would kill to know. The delectable soup, originally concocted for a knighted local, requires pre-ordering. Dim sum, served at lunch, is also exquisite.

✕ Happy Valley

GI KEE SEAFOOD
RESTAURANT DAI PAI DONG, CANTONESE **$**
(鉄記海鮮飯店; ☑852 2574 9937; Shop 4, 2nd fl, Wong Nai Chung Municipal Services Bldg, 2 Yuk Sau St, Happy Valley; meals from HK$150; ⊘5.30-10pm; 🚌1 from Des Voeux Rd Central) Reserve a table or expect to queue for a plastic stool at this *dai pai dong* perched above a wet market. Chan Chung-fai, the man in the kitchen who turns out tantalising dishes such as chicken with fried garlic, is an award-winning cordon bleu chef with a huge fan following that includes the likes of Zhang Ziyi and Jackie Chan.

✕ Island East

TUNG PO SEAFOOD
RESTAURANT DAI PAI DONG, CANTONESE **$**
(東寶小館; ☑852 2880 5224; 2nd fl, Municipal Services Bldg, 99 Java Rd, North Point; meals HK$100-250; ⊘5.30pm-midnight; Ⓜ North Point, exit A1) Atop the Java Rd wet market, Tung Po has revolutionised *dai pai dong* cooking. Beer is served in chilled porcelain bowls to be downed bandit style. The staff strut around in rubber boots, serving Cantonese dishes with a twist. Book ahead (reservations 2.30pm to 5.30pm) or go before 7pm.

Must-tries include crispy chicken topped with heaps of fried garlic (風沙雞), rice with duck jus baked in lotus leaves (鴨汁荷葉飯) and fried pig's trotters with red fermented bean curd (南乳炸豬手).

SIU WA KITCHEN CANTONESE **$**
(紹華小廚; ☑852 8199 8188; Shop CF3, Aldrich Bay Market Cooked Food Centre, Aldrich Bay, Shau Kei Wan; claypot rice from HK$55; ⊘6.30-10pm; Ⓜ Shau Kei Wan, exit B3) A humble stall that prepares claypot rice the old way using charcoal, which cooks more evenly than gas and gives a beautiful layer of crust. More unusual ingredients include taro with pork (芋茸肉碎飯) and mutton and cumin (疆土羊肉). After drizzling the sweet soy sauce, wait a few minutes for it to caramelise with the rice crackling. Your taste-buds will thank you.

SUN KWAI HEUNG CHINESE **$**
(新桂香燒臘; ☑852 2556 1183; 17, Kam Tam Yun House, 345 Chai Wan Rd, Chai Wan; meals from

HK$37; ☉8am-9pm; ⓂChai Wan, exit C) 🍴 This off-the-beaten-track shop has unbeatable Cantonese barbecue and none of the lines of better-known places. *Char siu* (barbecued pork) emerges from the roaster several times a day. Get a Cantonese-speaker to call and ask when the next batch is ready, and feast on a succulent cut with above-par *char* on your visit.

MASTER LOW KEY FOOD SHOP SWEETS $
(低調高手大街小食; ☏852 6986 8500; 76A Shau Kei Wan Main St E, Shau Kei Wan; eggettes from HK$16; ☉noon-10pm Mon-Fri, 11am-10pm Sat & Sun; ⓂShau Kei Wan, exit B1) Master Low Key's eggettes, aka egg waffles (雞蛋仔), are among the town's best. These fluffy balls of goodness with a golden exterior and a melty, eggy centre are Hong Kong's favourite snack. The Master also does 'Belgian' waffles, which come drizzled with peanut butter and condensed milk, Hong Kong style, or with jam.

The shop is located at the left-back corner of exit B1 of Shau Kei Wan MTR station.

🍷 DRINKING & NIGHTLIFE

🍸 Admiralty & Wan Chai

⭐MYHOUSE WINE BAR
Map p308 (☏852 2323 1715; www.myhousehk. com; 26th fl, QRE Plaza, 202 Queen's Rd E, Wan Chai; ☉6pm-2am Tue & Wed, to 3am Thu-Sat, closed Sun; ⓂWan Chai, exit A3) 🍴 MyHouse brings together vinyls and natural wine in a spacious Euro-chic setting. Furniture is made from natural wood, illuminated wine bottles hang alongside cured meats, and guests can take their pick from a vinyl library, slip it on individual turntables, and kick back with an organic, chemical-free Beaujolais, or surrender to the whims of a resident DJ (analogue, of course).

⭐TAI LUNG FUNG BAR
Map p308 (大龍鳳; ☏852 2572 0055; 5-9 Hing Wan St, Wan Chai; ☉noon-1am Mon-Thu, to 1.30am Fri & Sat, happy hour noon-9pm; ⓂWan Chai, exit A3) This capriciously retro bar takes its name from a 1960s Cantonese opera troupe. In common parlance, Tai Lung Fung (Big Dragon Phoenix) means 'much

ado'. Appropriately the decor is fabulously over-the-top. Tai Lung Fung attracts artsy types who prefer its funky aesthetics and quiet environment to a more conventional partying vibe. Cocktails, less adventurous than the decor, are the speciality.

SKYBAR BAR
Map p308 (☏852 3926 3888; www.ihg.com; 29th fl, Hotel Indigo, 246 Queen's Rd E, Wan Chai; ☉4pm-1am, happy hour 5-8pm; ⓂWan Chai, exit A3) Skybar on the top floor of Hotel Indigo is richly decked out in burgundies and purples, with accents in the eponymous colour. The centrepiece here is a 300-drawer Chinese herbal cabinet that has drawers half-pulled out to form the Chinese character for 'sky'. The terrace has plush banquettes where you can relax with an Asia-inspired cocktail at sunset.

BOTANICALS BAR
Map p308 (☏852 2866 3444; www.thepawn.com. hk; 62 Johnston Rd, Wan Chai; ☉4pm-12.30am; ⓂWan Chai, exit A3) Botanicals draws after-work imbibers with real vegetation, chic furnishings in a green-compatible palette, craft beer, inventive cocktails flavoured with herbs from its rooftop farm, and reinvented pub food. Opening hours may change, so call before going to be safe.

STONE NULLAH TAVERN BAR
Map p308 (☏852 3182 0128; www.stonenullah tavern.com; 69 Stone Nullah Lane, Wan Chai; ☉noon-1am; ⓂWan Chai, exit A3) A fancified American 'farmhouse' tavern that stocks an impressive range of American whiskeys and bourbons, bottles from Francis Ford Coppola's vineyard, and Californian ale – all to be enjoyed amid white-tiled walls, vintage wine cabinets and a mule-deer taxidermy mount. French windows capitalise on the bar's location in a scenic and historic part of Wan Chai.

MANSON'S LOT CAFE
Map p308 (☏852 2362 1899; www.mansonslot. com; 15 Swatow St, Wan Chai; ☉8am-6.30pm Mon-Fri, from 8.30am Sat, closed Sun) Australian roasted brews and a tranquil environment are the attractions of this pretty little cafe. Some interesting trivia as you enjoy your flat white – in the 19th century, the ground under you belonged to the founder of Hong Kong's first dairy farm, a Scottish surgeon called Patrick Manson.

AMICI
SPORTS BAR

Map p308 (☑852 2866 1918; www.amicihong kong.com; 1st fl, Empire Land Commercial Centre, Lockhart Rd, Wan Chai; ☺noon-1am Sun-Thu, to 2am Fri & Sat; Ⓜ Wan Chai, exit C) The champion of Wan Chai sports bars features ample screens, five beers on tap, decent pizza and a long happy hour. A few local football supporters' clubs have made Amici their base, and it's easy to see why. The atmosphere during live broadcasts of big sporting events is contagious.

TED'S LOOKOUT
BAR

Map p306 (☑852 5533 9369; Moonful Court, 17A Moon St, Wan Chai; ☺5-11pm Mon-Fri, noon-11pm Sat & Sun; Ⓜ Admiralty, exit F) Ted's is hip. The concrete facade features theatre tip-up seats and the bar's name in marquee lights, while white-tiled walls and gas lanterns decorate the interior. It's also laid-back – neighbours like to nurse a beer here in easy clothes, especially during the day. The burgers are good too, but you can smell them being fried in the open kitchen.

DJIBOUTII
BAR

Map p306 (☑852 9449 0777; www.djiboutii. squarespace.com; 2 Landale St, Wan Chai; ☺noon-11pm; Ⓜ Wan Chai) Awash in aquamarine and purple neon lights, Djiboutii is hidden in a back alley away off Landale St. Choose your perch – wooden stools at the bar or chaise longue in the alley, under a crystal chandelier or North African-inspired copper lamps – from which to enjoy one of its signature tea-infused cocktails. Music is mostly reggae.

CHAMPAGNE BAR
BAR

Map p308 (☑852 2584 7722; Ground fl, Grand Hyatt Hotel, 1 Harbour Rd, Wan Chai; ☺5pm-1am Mon-Wed, to 2am Thu-Sun; Ⓜ Wan Chai, exit A1) Take your fizz in the sumptuous surrounds of the Grand Hyatt's Champagne Bar, kitted out in art deco furnishings to evoke Paris of the 1920s. Most evenings, a live jazz band entertains its moneyed clientele, comprising hotel guests and theatre-goers from the Arts Centre or the Academy for Performing Arts nearby.

LAWN
BAR

Map p306 (☑852 2918 1838; www.upperhouse. com/en/Inside-and-Out/Inside-the-Hotel/The-Lawn.aspx; 6th fl, The Upper House, 88 Queensway, Admiralty; ☺noon-10pm; Ⓜ Admiralty, exit F) Atop the Upper House boutique hotel, this secret garden of a roof bar is the place for cooling your heels with a Pimm's Cup beneath a lacquered parasol. Occasional Sunday DJ parties are see-and-be-seen events.

DUSK TILL DAWN
LIVE MUSIC

Map p308 (☑852 2528 4689; Ground fl, 76-84 Jaffe Rd, Wan Chai; ☺noon-5am Mon-Fri, 3pm-7am Sat & Sun, happy hour 5-11pm; Ⓜ Wan Chai, exit C) True to its name, when the other bars begin to peter out, Dusk Till Dawn is just getting started. A noisy Filipino rock band keeps the eclectic crowd of locals, expats and backpackers dancing until the sun comes up.

Causeway Bay

EXECUTIVE BAR
LOUNGE

Map p310 (☑852 2893 2080; http://executive bar-com-hk-1.blogspot.hk; 27th fl, Bartlock Centre, 3 Yiu Wa St, Causeway Bay; ☺5pm-2am Mon-Thu, to 5am Fri & Sat, closed Sun; Ⓜ Causeway Bay, exit A) You may not be served if you just turn up at this clubby, masculine bar – it's 'by appointment only' – although you can take your chances. This exclusive place is known for its whisky. Several dozen varieties are served here, in large brandy balloons with large orbs of ice hand-chipped by the Japanese proprietor to maximise the tasting experience.

DICKENS BAR
BAR

Map p310 (☑852 2837 6782; www.mandarin oriental.com/excelsior/dining/dickens_bar; Basement, Excelsior Hong Kong, 281 Gloucester Rd, Causeway Bay; ☺noon-1am Mon-Thu, to 2am Fri & Sat, happy hour 4-8pm; Ⓜ Causeway Bay, exit D1) Dickens has been popular with expats and locals for decades. The British pub lookalike has a long beer list, which includes rare selections like Black Sheep Ale from the UK, and Gweilo, a fruity pale ale crafted in Hong Kong. It also offers big-screen sports coverage and an ever-popular curry buffet at lunch.

BUDDY BAR
BAR

Map p310 (☑852 2882 9780; 22 School St, Tai Hang; ☺5.30pm-2.30am; Ⓜ Tin Hau, exit B) This low-key neighbourhood bar is the kind of place where everybody knows your name (or they would, if you lived in Tai Hang) and your dog is welcome to snooze at your feet while you down a pint of Belgian ale. Last call is 1.30am.

ELEPHANT GROUNDS
CAFE

Map p310 (852 2253 1313; www.elephant grounds.com; Shop C, 42-48 Paterson St, Fashion Walk, Causeway Bay; Causeway Bay, exit D2) With a chilled-out ambience, young upbeat staff, spot-on coffee, and branches in Sheung Wan and Aberdeen, Elephant Grounds is easily Hong Kong's hottest new coffee hang-out. The popularity of its brews is surpassed only by that of its chunky ice-cream sandwiches. Its food menu is also fancier than most cafe chow – eggs Benedict comes in a taco for instance.

CAFE CORRIDOR
CAFE

Map p310 (852 2892 2927; 26A Russell St, Causeway Bay; 8am-10pm Mon-Thu, to 11pm Fri, 10am-11pm Sat & Sun; Causeway Bay, exit A) Tucked away in the back of a narrow corridor, this nifty 15-year-old cafe with a dozen seats offers handcrafted Yirgacheffe coffee and all-day breakfast to regulars or anyone seeking respite from the Times Square drama across the street. Dim lighting and a feature wall keep it cosy. And people come to chat – the cafe has no wi-fi.

FRITES
BEER HALL

Map p310 (852 2142 5233; 38 Haven St, Causeway Bay; 11am-midnight, happy hour to 7pm; Causeway Bay, exit D4) Located on up-coming Haven St, this Belgian beer bistro has high ceilings, sports coverage and a selection of Belgian brews from Stella Artois on tap to bottled cherry-sweet Lindemans Kriek. To soak up the alcohol, there are mussels (Hoegaarden-tinged) and the eponymous fries with mayo (these are our preference).

Island East

SUGAR
LOUNGE

(852 3968 3738; www.sugar-hongkong.com; 32nd fl, East Hotel, 29 Taikoo Sing Rd, Quarry Bay; 5pm-1am Mon-Sat, noon-midnight Sun; Tai Koo, exit D1) This sleek bar inside a business hotel has illuminated floors and a deck that maximises the impact of the superb East Island views – silvery high-rises on one side and the old Kai Tak airport runway on the other. On a clear night, it's a stunning backdrop to your rendezvous, so understandably tables fill up fast.

Make a reservation or go at 6pm.

ENTERTAINMENT

FOCAL FAIR
LIVE MUSIC

Map p310 (www.facebook.com/focalfair; 28th fl, Park Avenue Tower, 5 Moreton Terrace, Causeway Bay; Tin Hau, exit A1) Finally a conveniently located indie music venue – Focal Fair is right by the Hong Kong Central Library! It hosts several gigs a month, and everyone from Canadian hardcore punks Career Suicide to local noise artists Dennis Wong and Eric Chan have played here. See the Facebook page for the latest.

WANCH
LIVE MUSIC

Map p308 (852 2861 1621; www.thewanch.hk; 54 Jaffe Rd, Wan Chai; Wan Chai, exit C) Decked out in old Hong Kong paraphernalia, the Wanch, which derives its name from what everyone calls the district, has live music (mostly rock and folk with the occasional solo guitarist thrown in) nightly from 9pm. Jam night is Monday from 8pm. No cover charge. Happy hour from 5pm to 9pm.

HONG KONG ARTS CENTRE
DANCE, THEATRE

Map p308 (香港藝術中心; 852 2582 0200; www.hkac.org.hk; 2 Harbour Rd, Wan Chai; Wan Chai, exit C) A popular venue for dance, theatre and music performances, the Arts Centre has theatres, a cinema and a gallery.

HONG KONG STADIUM
STADIUM

Map p310 (香港大球場; 852 2895 7926; www.lcsd.gov.hk/stadium; 55 Eastern Hospital Rd, So Kon Po; office 8.45am-5.45pm, Mon-Fri; Happy Valley) The 40,000-seat Hong Kong Stadium in So Kon Po, a division of Causeway Bay, is Hong Kong's largest sports venue. The **Hong Kong Sevens rugby tournament** (www.hksevens.com.hk) takes place here.

SUNBEAM THEATRE
THEATRE

(新光戲院; 852 2563 2959, 852 2856 0161; www.sunbeamtheatre.com/hk; 423 King's Rd, Kiu Fai Mansion, North Point; North Point, exit A4) Cantonese opera is performed at this vintage theatre throughout the year. Performances generally run five days a week from 7.30pm for about a week, with occasional matinees at 1pm or 1.30pm.

HONG KONG ACADEMY FOR THE PERFORMING ARTS
DANCE, THEATRE

Map p308 (香港演藝學院; 852 2584 8500; www.hkapa.edu; 1 Gloucester Rd, Wan Chai; Admiralty, exit E2) The APA is a major performance venue for dance, music and theatre.

STREET MUSIC CONCERT SERIES

The **Street Music Concert Series** (街頭音樂系列; http://hkstreetmusic.com) comprises a number of wonderful outdoor concerts thrown by eclectic musician Kung Chi-shing, and have entertained everyone from street sleepers to consul generals with their balance of tight, professional curation and fizzy spontaneity. Genres range from indie rock to Cantonese opera, Bluegrass to Bach. You're bound to find something you like, even if it's just the captivating atmosphere. Concerts happen monthly at the Arts Centre (p115) from 5.30pm to 8pm on the third Saturday of the month, at Comix Home Base (p103) from 3pm to 4.30pm every fourth Sunday, and at Blue House (p102) from 7.30pm to 9pm on the second Thursday of the month, with occasional concerts in other parts of town. See the website for the latest.

PUNCHLINE COMEDY CLUB COMEDY

Map p308 (☑bookings 852 2111 5333, enquiries 852 2598 1222; www.punchlinecomedy.com/hongkong; Tamarind, 2nd fl, Sun Hung Kai Centre, 30 Harbour Rd, Wan Chai; ☐18) A veteran on the scene, the Punchline hosts local and imported acts every month from 8pm or 9pm to 11pm. Tickets are around HK$350. Book online or call. Get off the bus at Wan Chai Sports Ground.

AMC PACIFIC PLACE CINEMA

Map p306 (☑852 2265 8933; www.amccinemas.com.hk; 1st fl, 1 Pacific Pl, Admiralty; ⓂAdmiralty, exit F) This cinema inside the Pacific Place mall in Admiralty screens some of the more interesting current releases.

AGNÈS B. CINEMA CINEMA

Map p308 (☑852 2582 0200; Upper basement, Hong Kong Arts Centre, 2 Harbour Rd, Wan Chai; ☐18) The place for classics, revivals, alternative screenings and travelling film festivals.

🛍 SHOPPING

🛍 Admiralty & Wan Chai

★WAN CHAI COMPUTER CENTRE ELECTRONICS

Map p308 (灣仔電腦城; 1st fl, Southorn Centre, 130-138 Hennessy Rd, Wan Chai; ⓉMon-Sat, noon-8pm Sun; ⓂWan Chai, exit B2) This gleaming, beeping warren of tiny shops is a safe bet for anything digital and electronic.

★KAPOK FASHION & ACCESSORIES

Map p306 (☑852 2549 9254; www.ka-pok.com; 5 St Francis Yard, Wan Chai; Ⓣ11am-8pm, to 6pm Sun; ⓂAdmiralty, exit F) In the hip Star St area, this boutique has a fastidiously edited selection of luxe-cool local and international clothing and accessory labels. Look for the Kapok-label made-in-HK men's shirts, and graphic Mischa handbags by local designer Michelle Lai. A sister boutique is around the corner at 3 Sun St. It also has a corner at Eslite (p117) bookstore.

JOYCE BOUTIQUE

Map p306 (☑852 2523 5944; www.joyce.com; Shop 232, Pacific Place, 88 Queensway, Admiralty; Ⓣ10.30am-8pm Sun-Thu, to 8.30pm Fri & Sat; ⓂAdmiralty, exit F) This Pacific Place outlet of one of Hong Kong's most famous luxury fashion retailers features a shrewdly curated collection of international brands that strikes a balance between the popular and the edgy.

TAI YUEN STREET TOY SHOPS TOYS

Map p308 (太原街玩具店; 14-19 Tai Yuen St, Wan Chai; Ⓣ10am-7.30pm; ⓂWan Chai, exit A3) Tai Yuen St is known as 'toy street' thanks to a handful of shops that carry every toy, game and knick-knack your child could ever want – not to mention party gear. The quality is no better than Toys R Us, but prices are cheaper and choices are overwhelming. A couple of these shops stock vintage mechanical tin collectibles behind glass. Bring a shopping bag.

PACIFIC PLACE MALL

Map p306 (太古廣場; ☑852 2844 8988; www.pacificplace.com.hk; 88 Queensway, Admiralty; ⓂAdmiralty, exit F) Pacific Place mall has a couple of hundred outlets, dominated by high-end men's and women's fashion and accessories. It also has a Lane Crawford (p117) department store and a Joyce (p116) boutique.

CHINESE ARTS & CRAFTS DEPARTMENT STORE

Map p308 (中藝; ☑852 2827 6667; 2nd fl Causeway Centre, 28 Harbour Rd, Wan Chai; Ⓣ10.30am-7.30pm; ⓂWan Chai, exit A5) This huge mainland-owned store is a good place to buy jade jewellery, porcelain chopsticks and other Chinese trinkets. It's positively an Aladdin's cave of souvenirs. Branches in Admiralty, Central and Tsim Sha Tsui.

LANE CRAWFORD
DEPARTMENT STORE

Map p306 (連卡佛; ☑852 2118 2288; level 1, Pacific Place, 88 Queensway, Admiralty; ⊙10am-9pm; MAdmiralty, exit F) This is the homeware and lifestyle speciality store of uber-stylish Lane Crawford, the city's original Western-style department store and its answer to Harrod's in London.

KUNG FU SUPPLIES
SPORTS & OUTDOORS

Map p308 (功夫用品公司; ☑852 2891 1912; www.kungfu.com.hk; Room 6A, 6th fl, Chuen Fung House, 192 Johnston Rd, Wan Chai; ⊙10am-7pm Mon-Sat, 1-6pm Sun; ☒6, 6A, 6X) If you need to stock up on martial-arts accessories, including uniforms, nunchakus and safety weapons for practice, or just want to thumb through a decent collection of books and DVDs, this is the place. Helpful staff.

WAN CHAI MARKET
MARKET

Map p308 (灣仔街市; Zenith, 258 Queen's Rd E, Wan Chai; ⊙6am-8pm; MWan Chai, exit A3) Vendors in the old Wan Chai Market, built in Streamline Moderne style in 1937, have relocated to this new complex occupying the lower floors of the Zenith, a residential property. The market is cleaner than most markets and the air-con is always at full blast. You can still see the facade of the old Wan Chai Market at 246 Queen's Road East.

LOCKHART RD MARKET
MARKET

Map p308 (駱克道街市; 225 Lockhart Rd, Wan Chai; ⊙6am-8pm; MWan Chai, exit A2) A large wet market occupying the ground and 1st floors of a government building that also houses a public library, sports facilities, and a cooked-food centre that opens till 2am.

🏠 Causeway Bay

★ESLITE
BOOKS

Map p310 (誠品; ☑852 3419 6789; 8th-10th fl, Hysan Place, 500 Hennessy Rd, Causeway Bay; ⊙10am-10pm Sun-Thu, to 11pm Fri & Sat; ☒; MCauseway Bay, exit F2) You could spend an entire evening inside this swanky three-floor Taiwanese bookstore, which features a massive collection of English and Chinese books and magazines, a shop selling

gorgeous stationery and leather-bound journals, a cafe, a bubble-tea counter, and a huge kids' toy and book section.

GOD
HOMEWARES, CLOTHING

Map p310 (Goods of Desire; ☑852 2890 5555; www.god.com.hk; 9 Sharp St E, Causeway Bay; ⊙noon-10pm; MCauseway Bay, exit A) Re-opened Causeway Bay branch of this playful born-in-Hong Kong store is great for getting those vintage mailbox fridge magnets and velour 'Hong Kong Team' hoodies for your friends. GOD has a large outlet in Stanley.

MUJI
CLOTHING, HOUSEWARES

Map p310 (無印良品; ☑customer service 852 2694 9309; www.muji.com/hk-en/; 3rd fl, Lee Theatre, 99 Percival St, Causeway Bay; ⊙11am-10.30pm; MCauseway Bay, exit F1) The Hong Kong flagship of the cult-hit Japanese brand, this two-storey Muji is chock-full of charmingly minimalist, neutral-toned clothing, housewares, stationery and toys. The section of Japanese snacks, like sour plum candy and animal-shaped seaweed crackers, is irresistible.

GUM GUM GUM
CLOTHING

Map p310 (☑852 3486 7070; http://gum-gum.com; 8-10 Cleveland St, Fashion Walk, Causeway Bay; ⊙noon-10pm; MCauseway Bay, exit D2) This cool outlet carries dozens of local and international fashion and lifestyle labels, and does occasional cross-overs with brands like Columbia. The clothes are young, street and wearable, with a few tailored pieces you could sport at work. Indie gigs and other hipster pop-up events also happen here. Check the website for updates and hit them up.

HYSAN PLACE
MALL

Map p310 (☑852 2886 7222; www.hp.leegardens.com.hk; 500 Hennessy Rd, Causeway Bay; ⊙10am-10pm Sun-Thu, to 11pm Fri & Sat; MCauseway Bay, exit F2) This shiny 17-storey mall is filled with hundreds of ever-trendy Japanese, Korean and local clothing and beauty brands in a more upmarket environment than other local teeny-bopper havens, but more affordable than most malls in Causeway Bay. The supermarket, Jason's Food & Living, in the lower basement, has an awesome bakery.

ISLAND BEVERLEY MALL
MALL

Map p310 (金百利商場; 1 Great George St, Causeway Bay; MCauseway Bay, exit E) Crammed into cubicles, up escalators and in the back lanes of this unassuming mall next to Sogo are microshops selling local designer threads, garments, toys, and cosmetics from Japan and Korea, not to mention a kaleidoscope of kooky accessories. Great place to get those Jimmy Choo lookalikes to go with your jeans. Shops are open from afternoon till late.

TWO GIRLS COSMETICS

Map p310 (雙妹嚜; www.twogirls.hk; Shop 283, 2-10 Great George St, Causeway Place, Causeway Bay; ⊙noon-10pm; Ⓜ Causeway Bay, exit E) Hong Kong's first cosmetics brand has been selling fragrant, highly affordable creams and potions since 1898. The pretty, retro packaging featuring two cheongsam-clad beauties makes these excellent gifts. We like the spicy Florida Water cologne.

FASHION WALK CLOTHING

(www.fashionwalk.com.hk; ⊙office 10am-11pm; Ⓜ Causeway Bay, D4) A mostly street-level fashion-shopping mecca spanning four streets in Causeway Bay – Paterson, Cleveland, Great George and Kingston. It's where you'll find big names like Paul Smith, Comme des Garcons and Kiehl's, but also up-and-coming local brands, and shops with off-the-rack high-street labels.

NUMB WORKSHOP CLOTHING

Map p310 (☑852 2312 7007; www.numbwork shop.com; 25 Haven St, Causeway Bay; ⊙1-10pm; Ⓜ Causeway Bay, exit A) A stark minimalist shop that stocks androgynous monochrome garments that will hide your love handles or have you looking like a stylish ninja, depending on the style and your shape. We particularly liked the details on the black twill zip trousers.

TIMES SQUARE MALL

Map p310 (時代廣場; www.timessquare.com.hk; 1 Matheson St, Causeway Bay; Ⓜ Causeway Bay, exit A) The 13 floors of retail are slightly less high-end than in Central, and have a whole floor devoted to kids' products. There are restaurants on the 10th to 13th floors, a cinema next door, and snack bars, cafes and a supermarket in the basement, then more restaurants and shops in the lower basement.

YIU FUNG STORE FOOD

Map p310 (么鳳; ☑852 2576 2528; Shop A, 2 Pak Sha Rd, Causeway Bay; ⊙11am-10.30pm; Ⓜ Causeway Bay, exit A) Hong Kong's most famous store (c 1960) for Chinese pickles and preserved fruit features sour plum, liquorice-flavoured

lemon, tangerine peel, pickled papaya and dried longan. Just before the Lunar New Year, it's crammed with shoppers.

SOGO DEPARTMENT STORE

Map p310 (崇光; ☑852 2833 8338; www.sogo.com.hk; 555 Hennessy Rd, Causeway Bay; ⊙10am-10pm; Ⓜ Causeway Bay, exit B) This Japanese-owned store, in the hub of Causeway Bay, has 12 well-organised floors and more than 37,000 sq metres of retail space. The range is mind-boggling: over 20 brands of ties just for starters. Eclectic departments include the Barbie Counter and the Character's Shop. The big sales (check the website) are when prices drop dramatically and the store's a madhouse.

CUFFS CLOTHING

Map p310 (☑852 2413 6033; www.cuffs.hk; 2/F, 27 Lee Garden Rd, Causeway Bay; ⊙1-9pm) The funkiest of Hong Kong's new generation of tailoring stores for men, Cuffs offers fashion-forward fabrics and custom-makes not only suits, shirts and tux, but 'cool-dry' chinos as well. There's even a Shirt Bar and a Suit Bar to guide dithering dandies to their desired look. A two-piece suit starts from HK$4200. The shop stocks off-the-rack garments and accessories too.

HOLA CLASSIC CLOTHING

Map p310 (☑852 2870 0246; 11A Caroline Hill Rd, Causeway Bay; ⊙12.30-9pm; Ⓜ Causeway Bay, exit A) This nifty little shop is known for its highly affordable made-to-measure suits, jackets and shirts for men. Don't expect impeccable fabrics (they don't dress the British monarchy), but a two-piece suit starts from only HK$2280. Hola can even make Oxfords, with purple tassels too if that's how you roll. The shoe shop is 30 seconds away at 13A Haven St.

PAPABUBBLE FOOD

Map p310 (☑852 2367 4807; www.papabubble.com.hk; 34 Tung Lo Wan Rd, Tai Hang; ⊙11am-10pm; Ⓜ Tin Hau, exit B) This Spanish artisan candy company sells flavours unique to Hong Kong, such as lemon tea and durian, featuring local designs like Chinese zodiac animals and the character for 'double happiness'. Great gifts. Kids love watching the hot sugar being pulled behind the counter.

BASHEER BOOKS

Map p310 (書得起; ☑852 2126 7533; www.basheer.com.hk; Flat A, 1/f, Island Bldg, 439-441

Hennessy Rd, Causeway Bay; ⊙11am-10pm Mon-Fri, from noon Sat & Sun; Ⓜ Causeway Bay, exit B) Haunt of architects and designers, Basheer has a strong collection on everything that's designed, from animation and architecture to product and jewellery.

🔒 Island East

WAH FUNG CHINESE
GOODS CENTRE   DEPARTMENT STORE
(華豐國貨公司; ☑852 2856 0333; Kiu Kwan Mansion, 395-421 King's Rd, North Point; ⊙10.30am-9.30pm; Ⓜ North Point, A4) This very local Chinese department store has everything from ginseng to silk baby slippers and acupuncture models to calligraphy brushes. Crowded, dusty and entirely non-English – in fact many of its staff speak Fujianese – it's a fun place to poke around for gifts without the hassle of bargaining.

MOUNTAIN SERVICES   SPORTS & OUTDOORS
Map p310 (名峰行; www.mshk.com.hk; Shop 1, 52–56 King's Rd, Fortress Hill; ⊙11am-7pm Mon-Sat; Ⓜ Fortress Hill, exit A) This excellent shop sells climbing and hiking gear and pretty much everything you need for tackling Hong Kong's hills and country parks. Turn left when you exit the MTR station and walk for three minutes.

🏃 SPORTS & ACTIVITIES

EASTERN NATURE
TRAIL   HIKING
(東區自然步道) Stage 5 of the Hong Kong Trail (p60), this 9km, three-hour nature trail, known for the indigenous trees and migratory birds it passes, starts on Mount Parker Rd in Quarry Bay and ends on Wong Nai Chung Gap Rd in Tai Tam. The trail also features WWII military relics and a former sugar refinery.

You'll pass beautiful Tai Tam Country Park on your descent to Tai Tam Reservoir. Following Tai Tam Reservoir Rd, you'll reach Wong Nai Chung Gap Rd. To get to the starting point, take exit B from Tai Koo MTR station, head 600m west and turn into Quarry St. The start of the trail is near the Quarry Bay Municipal Services Building at 38 Quarry St.

HONG KONG HOUSE OF
STORIES   LOCAL TOUR, MUSEUM
Map p308 (香港故事館; ☑852 2835 4376; http://houseofstories.sjs.org.hk; 74 Stone Nullah Lane, Wan Chai; ⊙11am-6pm Thu-Tue; ☒6, 6A) Opened by fans of Wan Chai, this tiny museum is located in the historic Blue House (p102) but will relocate to Yellow House (p102) during the former's closure until mid-2017. It runs private tours in English, covering historical sites, restaurants and other places of interest in Wan Chai. Email a month in advance to arrange. A two-hour tour is HK$600, so the more of you, the cheaper. Note, however, that the 'tram' tour is HK$6000.

MARTHA SHERPA   COOKING
(☑852 2381 0132; www.marthasherpa.com; Flat F, 14th fl, Wah Lai Mansion, 62-76 Marble Rd, North Point; courses HK$1680; Ⓜ North Point, exit A2) Expert Cantonese home-cook Martha Sherpa (her last name comes from her Nepali husband) has taught the likes of former Australian PM Julia Gillard how to cook dim sum and Hong Kong favourites. Small group classes cover topics like wok cookery, dim sum and vegetarian Chinese. Half-day, full-day and evening classes are available.

VICTORIA PARK   TENNIS
Map p310 (Hing Fat St, Causeway Bay; ⊙6am or 7am-11pm; Ⓜ Causeway Bay, exit E) The park has 13 standard tennis courts, two lawn-bowls greens, and swimming pools, as well as football pitches, basketball courts and jogging trails.

HAPPY VALLEY SPORTS
GROUND   FOOTBALL
Map p310 (☑852 2895 1523; 2 Sports Rd, Happy Valley; Ⓜ Causeway Bay, exit A) This group of pitches inside the Happy Valley Racecourse is where most amateur soccer action in Hong Kong takes place. For match schedules and venues, check http://casualfootball.net.

SOUTH CHINA ATHLETIC
ASSOCIATION   GYM
Map p310 (南華體育會; ☑enquiries 852 2577 6932, membership 852 2577 4427; www.scaa.org.hk; 5th fl, South China Sports Complex, 88 Caroline Hill Rd, Causeway Bay; visitor membership per month HK$60; ⊙8am-9.30pm; ☒31) The SCAA has a 1000-sq-metre gym, with modern exercise machinery and an aerobics room, as well as a sauna, a steam room and a massage room.

Hong Kong Island: Aberdeen & the South

ABERDEEN | POK FU LAM | DEEP WATER BAY | REPULSE BAY | STANLEY | SHEK O

Neighbourhood Top Five

❶ Aberdeen Promenade (p122) Watching the goings-on onboard moored boats then hopping on a sampan to cross the typhoon shelter the way it was done decades ago.

❷ Ap Lei Chau Market Cooked Food Centre (p124) Gorging on seafood without busting a hole in your pocket in Aberdeen or Ap Lei Chau.

❸ Béthanie (p122) Revisiting a time in Hong Kong history when French missionaries crossed paths with dairy cowboys and a fire dragon in Pok Fu Lam.

❹ Stanley (p126) Downing a pint or two at the British-style pubs in this seaside town and taking a dip at one of its beaches.

❺ Shek O Beach (p124) Lounging on the shaded sand at this laid-back, cliff-framed beach village

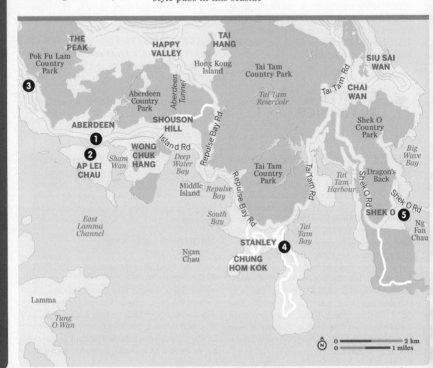

For more detail of this area see Map p312 and p313 ➡

Explore: Aberdeen & the South

The long coastline along the south of the island means you'll need at least half a day (if not a full day) to explore each of the areas listed below. Beach hopping is doable.

Aberdeen's theme park, Ocean Park, is a store of fun for kids and adults alike. Expect a full day there. More sedentary travellers can opt for a boozy brunch or a hearty seafood lunch in Aberdeen. Treasure hunters can find designer bargains in Ap Lei Chau.

Beach suburb Repulse Bay has Hong Kong's most famous beach and is home to some of its richest residents. People-watch before walking to the less-crowded beaches of Middle Bay and South Bay for a swim.

Stanley, with a lively market, friendly beaches and a fascinating mix of museums and heritage sites, certainly deserves a full day of exploration.

On Hong Kong Island's far southeast, Shek O is a laid-back village that oozes old-world charm. It has one of the best (and quietest) beaches on the island.

Local Life

→**Drinking** After dinner in Ap Lei Chau or Aberdeen, grab drinks from a convenience store and head to the seafront promenade for an after-party.

→**Shopping** When shopping in the mammoth Horizon Plaza (p127), wear sensible shoes like the locals, and have the number for a **taxi call-centre** (☑852 2368 1318) ready.

→**Seafood** IBuy your own seafood in a wet market and have it cooked in a *dai pai dong* (food stall) of choice for a by-weight cooking fee. Try Ap Lei Chau Market and its associated Cooked Food Centre (p124).

→**Swimming** Glowing algae is common in the waters of Stanley, Middle Bay and Repulse Bay during the summer months. They're completely harmless and you can see them sliding off your skin (or your paddle) like fireflies.

Getting There & Away

→**Bus for Shek O** Bus 9 from Shau Kei Wan MTR station (exit A3).

→**Bus for Stanley** Bus 14 from Shau Kei Wan Rd, near the MTR station. Buses 6, 6A, 6X, 66 and 260 head here via Repulse Bay from Central, below Exchange Sq; buses 6, 6A, 6X, and 260 stop at Stanley Market Bus Terminus.

→**Bus for Aberdeen** Buses 73 and 973 from Stanley call at Repulse Bay and Aberdeen Main St. Bus 107 from Kowloon Bay stops at Aberdeen Bus Terminus. Green minibus 40 runs from Tang Lung St (Causeway Bay) to Stanley via Ocean Park.

→**Bus for Pok Fu Lam** Buses 40 and 40M leave from Wan Chai Ferry Pier via Admiralty. Buses 7, 90B and 91 link Pok Fu Lam with Aberdeen Praya Rd in Aberdeen

→**Bus for Deep Water Bay** Bus 6A, 6X or 260 from Central, below Exchange Sq.

✖ Best Places to Eat

→ Ap Lei Chau Market Cooked Food Centre (p124)

→ Aberdeen Fish Market Yee Hope Seafood (p124)

→ Chu Kee (p124)

→ Pak Kee (p124)

→ Hoi Kwong Seafood Restaurant (p124)

For reviews, see p124 ➡

🍷 Best Places to Drink

→ Young Master Ales (p122)

→ Ben's Back Beach Bar (p126)

→ Smugglers Inn (p126)

→ Delaney's (p126)

For reviews, see p126 ➡

🔒 Best Places to Shop

→ G.O.D. (p127)

→ Horizon Plaza (p127)

For reviews, see p127 ➡

◉ SIGHTS

◉ Aberdeen

ABERDEEN PROMENADE
WATERFRONT

Map p312 (香港仔海濱公園; Aberdeen Praya Rd, Aberdeen) **FREE** Tree-lined Aberdeen Promenade runs from west to east on Aberdeen Praya Rd across the water from Ap Lei Chau. On its western end is sprawling **Aberdeen Wholesale Fish Market** (香港仔魚市場; Map p312; Aberdeen Promenade, Aberdeen) with its industrial-strength water tanks teeming with marine life. It's pungent and grimy, but 100% Hong Kong. Before reaching the market, you'll pass berthed house boats and seafood-processing vessels. (We detected a karaoke parlour or two as well.)

YOUNG MASTER ALES
BREWERY

Map p312 (少爺麥啤; www.youngmasterales. com; Units 407-9, Oceanic Industrial Centre, 2 Lee Lok St, Ap Lei Chau; ⊙noon-5pm Sat, or by appointment; ❑671, 90B) You can visit Hong Kong's own craft brewery most Saturday afternoons, but email ahead to inform them you're coming. It's possible to arrange a tasting tour on other days. YMA offers a selection of non-filtered, chemical-free ales that range from crisp to robust. We enjoyed the limited edition Mood for Spring with its floral infusions.

OCEAN PARK
AMUSEMENT PARK

(海洋公園; ☎852 3923 2323; www.ocean park.com.hk; Ocean Park Rd; adult/child 3-11yr HK$385/193; ⊙10am-7.30pm; ❸; ❑629 from Admiralty, ❑973 from Tsim Sha Tsui, ❑6A, 6X, 70, 75 from Central, ❑72, 72A, 92 from Causeway Bay) Despite the crowd-pulling powers of Disneyland on Lantau, for many Ocean Park remains the most popular theme park in Hong Kong. Constant expansion, new rides and thrills, and the presence of four giant pandas and two rare red pandas ensure the park remains a huge draw for families. Be aware that in part of the park, Marine World, cetaceans are kept in captivity and performances involving dolphins and orcas are a feature, which scientific studies suggest is harmful to these animals.

The park is divided into two main sections. The main entrance is on the Waterfront (lowland) side and is linked to the main section on the Summit (headland) via a scenic **cable car ride** and a marine-themed funicular train called the **Ocean Express**.

The major attractions at the Waterfront are **Amazing Asian Animals** and **Aqua City**. The **Grand Aquarium**, which boasts the world's largest aquarium dome, is home to 5000 fish representing over 400 species. **Old Hong Kong** is a replica of the old buildings that once graced Wan Chai and older parts of Kowloon. To the north is **Whiskers Harbour**, which thrives on an assortment of kid-oriented rides.

On the Summit, the **Thrill Mountain** has plenty of white-knuckle rides, such as the celebrated roller coaster, Hair Raiser. Meanwhile, the **Chinese Sturgeon Aquarium** showcases a living gift from the mainland.

◉ Pok Fu Lam

BÉTHANIE
HISTORIC BUILDING

(伯大尼; ☎852 2854 8918; www.hkapa.edu/asp/ general/general_visitors.asp; 139 Pok Fu Lam Rd, Pok Fu Lam; HK$33; ⊙11am-6pm Mon-Sat, from noon Sun; ❑7, 40, 40M, 90B, 91) Perched on hilly Pok Fu Lam, a college and residential area northwest of Aberdeen, this beautiful restoration is a highlight in this part of town. The complex, which now houses a film school, was built by the French Mission in 1875 as a sanatorium for priests from all over Asia to rest and recover from tropical diseases before they returned to their missions.

The 20-minute guided tour includes a visit to the neo-Gothic **Béthanie Chapel**, a **theatre** in the two octagonal Dairy Farm cowsheds, and a tiny **museum** housed in a converted wine cellar, which displays the history of the mission. Tours are run hourly and it's wise to call ahead, as some venues may not be accessible if they've been hired. The nearest bus stop is at the junction of Pok Fu Lam Reservoir and Pok Fu Lam Rd.

POK FU LAM VILLAGE
VILLAGE

(薄扶林村; ☎852 6199 9473; www.pokfulam village.org; ❑7, 40, 40M, 90B, 91) Built on a sloping hillside, peaceful Pok Fu Lam Village looks like a shantytown compared to the high-density middle-class residences around it. Though no stunner, it's valued by historians not only for the famous fire dragon dance at the Mid-Autumn Festival, but equally for its ties to Hong Kong's dairy industry. Other highlights include Bethanie and Li Ling Pagoda.

As the sites are scattered, the best way to see them all is to join a walking tour.

◉ Deep Water Bay

DEEP WATER BAY   BEACH
(深水灣; 🚌6, 6A, 6X, 260) A quiet little inlet with a beach flanked by shade trees, Deep Water Bay is a few kilometres northwest of Repulse Bay. There is a handful of places to eat and have a drink, and some barbecue pits at the southern end of the beach. If you want a dip in the water, this spot is usually less crowded than Repulse Bay. Deep Water Bay beach is a centre for wakeboarding.

◉ Repulse Bay

REPULSE BAY   BEACH
(淺水灣; 🚌6, 6A, 6X, 260) The long beach with tawny sand at Repulse Bay is visited by Chinese tourist groups year-round and, needless to say, is packed on weekends in summer. It's a good place if you like people-watching. The beach has showers and changing rooms and shade trees at the roadside, but the water is pretty murky.

Middle Bay (中灣) and **South Bay** (南灣), about 10 and 30 minutes to the south respectively, have beaches that are much less crowded. Middle Bay is popular with gay beachgoers, while French expats are drawn to South Bay.

KWUN YAM SHRINE   TAOIST TEMPLE
(觀音廟; 🚌6, 6A, 6X, 260) Towards the southeast end of Repulse Bay beach is a colourful shrine dedicated to Kwun Yam, the goddess of mercy. In the surrounding area, you'll find an assembly of deities and figures – goldfish, rams, the money god, and statues of Tin Hau – expressed in gloriously garish cartoon kitsch. Most of the statues were commissioned by local personalities and businessmen in the 1970s.

◉ Stanley

ST STEPHEN'S COLLEGE   HISTORIC SITE
Map p313 (聖士提反書院文物徑; ☑852 2813 0360; www.ssc.edu.hk/ssctrail/eng; 22 Tung Tau Wan Rd, Stanley; 🚌6, 6A, 6X, 260) FREE WWII history buffs can visit the beautiful campus of St Stephen's College, which sits right next to Stanley Military Cemetery. Founded in

1903, the school was turned into an emergency military hospital on the eve of the Japanese invasion of Hong Kong in 1941 and became an internment camp after the city fell. The two-hour guided tour by students takes you to eight sites in the campus.

STANLEY MILITARY CEMETERY   CEMETERY
(赤柱軍人墳場; ☑852 2557 3498; Wong Ma Kok Rd, Stanley; ⊙8am-5pm; 🚌14, 6A) South of Stanley Market, this cemetery for armed forces personnel and their families is a highlight in Stanley. The oldest graves, dating back to 1843, are an intriguing document of the colonial era. The earlier mounds show just how great a toll disease took on European settlers, while the number of graves from the early 1940s serves as a reminder of the many who died during the fight for Hong Kong and subsequent internment at the hands of occupying Japanese forces.

ST STEPHEN'S BEACH   BEACH
(聖士提反灣泳灘; 🚌6A, 14) A short walk south of Stanley village is this great little bolt-hole that handily comes with a cafe, showers and changing rooms. In summer you can hire windsurfing boards and kayaks from the water-sports centre.

MURRAY HOUSE   HISTORIC BUILDING
Map p313 (美利樓; Stanley Bay; 🚌6, 6A, 6X, 260) Across the bay from Stanley Main St stands this three-storey colonnaded affair. Built in 1846 as officers' quarters, it took pride of place in Central, on the spot where the Bank of China Tower now stands, for almost 150 years until 1982. It was re-erected here stone by stone and opened in 2001. Today it's home to a number of restaurants, many with lovely sea views.

THE BUILDING WITH THE HOLE

Anyone passing through Repulse Bay can't help but notice the enormous residential tower with the giant square hole in the middle, like an architectural doughnut. According to feng shui principles, it's unlucky to block the dragon who lives in the mountain from being able to access the sea. If he can't get through, he might just knock the building down. The hole accommodates the dragon, and keeps the building, called **The Repulse Bay**, standing.

STANLEY MAIN BEACH BEACH

Map p313 (赤柱正灘; ⊟6A, 14) Stanley Main Beach is crammed with sun-worshippers, passing windsurfers, and a few serious swimmers. Dragon boat teams practising here on weekends paddle 5km east to **To Tei Wan** and back.

TIN HAU TEMPLE TEMPLE

Map p313 (天后廟; 119 Stanley Main St, Stanley; ⊟6, 6A, 6X, 260) At the western end of Stanley Main St, past a tiny **Tai Wong shrine** (大王廟; Map p313) and through the Stanley Plaza shopping complex, is a Tin Hau temple. Though built in 1767, its appearance has completely changed over the years and it's now a concrete pile. The walk here is worthwhile for the sea views.

◉ Shek O

SHEK O BEACH BEACH

(石澳; ⊟9 from Shau Kei Wan MTR station, exit A3) Shek O beach has a large expanse of sand, shady trees to the rear, showers, changing facilities and lockers for rent. It's not quiet by any means, except on typhoon days, but the laid-back beach framed by rocky cliffs is quite pleasant.

BIG WAVE BAY BEACH

(大浪灣; Ⓜ Shau Kei Wan station, exit A3, Shek O-bound minibus) This fine, often deserted beach located 2km to the north of Shek O is little known outside the surfing community. To get there, follow the road north out of town, travel past the 18-hole Shek O Golf & Country Club, then turn east at the roundabout and keep going until the road ends. One of eight prehistoric rock carvings discovered in Hong Kong is located on the headland above Big Wave Bay.

✖ EATING

✖ Aberdeen

★ AP LEI CHAU MARKET COOKED FOOD CENTRE SEAFOOD $

Map p312 (鴨利洲市政大廈; 1st fl, Ap Lei Chau Municipal Services Bldg, 8 Hung Shing St, Ap Lei Chau; dishes HK$45-70; ⊟minibus 36X from Lee Garden Rd, Causeway Bay) Above an indoor market, *dai pai dong* (food stall) operators

cook up a storm in a sprawling hall littered with folding tables and plastic chairs. Pak Kee (p124) and Chu Kee (p124) offer simple but tasty seafood dishes. You can also buy seafood from the wet market downstairs and pay them to cook it for you the way you want. It's packed and noisy on weekends.

Every evening fishermen and dragon boaters come here for the cheap beer and food. You can reach the market from Aberdeen Promenade by taking a sampan.

CHU KEE SEAFOOD $

Map p312 (珠記; ☎852 2555 2052; 1st fl, Ap Lei Chau Municipal Services Bldg, 8 Hung Shing St, Ap Lei Chau; seafood dinner from HK$160; ⊗6pm-midnight; ⊟minibus 36X from Lee Garden Rd, Causeway Bay) One of six cheap and cheery *dai pai dong* (food stalls) in the Ap Lei Chau Market Cooked Food Centre, Chu Kee offers solid seafood and stir-fries. If you buy seafood from the market downstairs, they'll cook it for you for an additional cooking fee of about HK$80 per catty (600g). Things get frantic when they're busy.

PAK KEE SEAFOOD $

Map p312 (栢記; ☎852 2555 2984; 1st fl, Ap Lei Chau Municipal Services Bldg, 8 Hung Shing St, Ap Lei Chau; seafood dinner from HK$160; ⊗6pm-midnight; ⊟minibus 36X from Lee Garden Rd, Causeway Bay) A cheap and cheery *dai pai dong* (food stall) in the Ap Lei Chau Market Cooked Food Centre, Pak Kee serves up seafood and stir-fries.

HOI KWONG SEAFOOD RESTAURANT CANTONESE, SEAFOOD $

Map p312 (海港食家; ☎852 2552 6463; 71 Ap Lei Chau Main St, Ap Lei Chau; mains HK$40-220; ⊗11.30am-2.30pm & 6-11.30pm) This hole-in-the-wall with sea life in tanks and styrofoam boxes at the entrance has a repertoire of a hundred-plus dishes, over half of which involve seafood. They keep prices down by not offering expensive and exotic varieties, but whatever they do have is always fresh and always local. Bookings essential. Be prepared to rub elbows with the next table.

★ ABERDEEN FISH MARKET YEE HOPE SEAFOOD RESTAURANT CANTONESE, SEAFOOD $$

Map p312 (香港仔魚市場二合海鮮餐廳; ☎852 5167 1819, 852 2177 7872; 102 Shek Pai Wan Rd, Aberdeen; meals from $350; ⊗4am-4pm; ⊟107) Hidden in Hong Kong's only wholesale fish market, this understated eatery run by

BEACH BBQ, HONG KONG–STYLE

Show up at any Hong Kong beach or country park on a weekend and you'll see dozens, if not hundreds, of locals enthusiastically brandishing long sharp metal forks. Ancient Hong Kong ritual? Sort of. Here in the SAR, barbecue parties at public beaches and parks replace the kind of indoor or backyard entertaining done in countries where the average home size is larger.

Throwing your own barbecue is surprisingly easy and makes for a great day out. Here's a list of items to bring:

➡ Barbecue forks (sold at most supermarkets for around HK$3)

➡ Tin foil and paper plates

➡ Meat: pre-marinated chicken wings, fish balls, beef cubes and more are sold at most supermarkets

➡ Veggies (corn and mushrooms are good, easy picks)

➡ Salt, oil and condiments of your choice

➡ 'Barbecue honey': this thick syrup is sold at supermarkets, and is used to baste grilled bread, chicken wings, corn and much more

➡ Bread

➡ Charcoal and a lighter

➡ Beer

Just show up early enough to claim a pit in a public area, start your fire, and you're on your way to barbecuing like a local!

fishers is truly an in-the-know place for ultrafresh seafood. There's no menu, but tell them your budget and they'll source the best sea creatures available, including ones you don't normally see in restaurants, and apply their Midas touch to them.

The restaurant serves as a canteen for the fishers in the market and you'll see men in gumboots dropping in for beer, Hong Kong–style French toast and other *cha chaan tang* (tea house) staples throughout the day. Walk-in customers can do the same. There's no English sign; look for the nondescript one-storey yellow building with a green roof at end of the fish market.

You'll need a Cantonese-speaking friend to help you if you'd like to book a table; organise at least two days in advance (two weeks for weekends).

JUMBO KINGDOM FLOATING RESTAURANT
CANTONESE **$$**

Map p312 (珍寶海鮮舫; ☑852 2553 9111; www. jumbo.com.hk; Shum Wan Pier Dr, Wong Chuk Hang; meals from HK$200; ☺11am-11.30pm Mon-Sat, from 9am Sun; ☒90 from Central) Recently refurbished, Jumbo Kingdom comprises two restaurants – Jumbo Floating Restaurant and Tai Pak Floating Restaurant. The three-storey 'floating' extravaganzas (they're fastened by concrete) look like Běijīng's Imperial Palace crossbred with

Macau's Casino Lisboa – so kitsch they're fun. Eschew the overpriced Dragon Court on the 2nd floor and head to the 3rd floor for dim sum.

✕ Repulse Bay

SPICES RESTAURANT
SOUTHEAST ASIAN **$$**

(香辣軒; ☑852 2292 2821; www.therepulsebay. com; 109 Repulse Bay Rd, Repulse Bay; meals from HK$300; ☺noon-2.30pm & 6.30-10.30pm Mon-Fri, 11.30am-10.30pm Sat & Sat; ☒6, 6A, 6X, 260) The high ceilings, rattan chairs and sparkling wooden flooring evoke the romantic vibes of a beachfront hang-out in Bali. The decor is tropical colonial, as is the menu, which runs the gamut of seafood, satay and British Indian curry.

VERANDAH
INTERNATIONAL **$$$**

(露台餐廳; ☑852 2292 2822; www.therepulse bay.com; 1st fl, 109 Repulse Bay Rd, Repulse Bay; meals from HK$600; ☺noon-2.30pm, 3-5.30pm & 7-10.30pm daily, brunch 11am-2.30pm Sun; ☒6, 6A, 6X, 260) A meal in the grand Verandah, run by the Peninsula (p135), is a special occasion indeed. The large restaurant is dripping with colonial nostalgia, what with the grand piano at the entrance, the wooden fans dangling from the ceiling, and the marble staircases with wooden banisters.

The Sunday brunch is famous (HK$700) and the afternoon tea is the best this side of Hong Kong Island. Book ahead.

✕ Stanley

TOBY INN
CANTONESE, DIM SUM $

Map p313 (赤柱酒家; ☑852 2813 2880; U1-U2, 126 Stanley Main St, Stanley; meals HK$60-200; ⏰5.30am-10pm; 🚌6, 6A, 6X or 260) This humble place is Stanley's neighbourhood restaurant, with elderly people dropping in for dim sum at the crack of dawn, dragon boaters feasting on good-value seafood after practice, and families coming in for simple dishes throughout the day.

SEI YIK
CANTONESE $

Map p313 (泗益; ☑852 2813 0507; 2 Stanley Market St, Stanley; meals from HK$30; ⏰6am-4pm Wed-Mon; 🚌6, 6A, 6X, 66) Weekenders flock to this small tin-roofed *dai pai dong* (food stall), right opposite the Stanley Municipal Building, for its fluffy Hong Kong–style French toast with *kaya* (coconut jam) spread. There's no English sign; look for the long queue of pilgrims and the piles of fruits that hide the entrance.

KING LUDWIG BEER HALL
GERMAN $$

Map p313 (King Ludwig 德國餐廳; ☑852 2899 0122; www.kingparrot.com; Shop 202, Murray House, Stanley; meals from HK$180; ⏰noon-midnight; 🚌6, 6A) This absurd medieval-themed German restaurant has five locations in Hong Kong, but this one has the advantage of being in historic Murray House, with its killer verandah views over the ocean. After a long hike, you just might be able to finish King Ludwig's famous enormous pork knuckle. The all-you-can eat weekend brunch is massively popular.

✕ Shek O

HAPPY GARDEN
THAI $

(石澳樂園; ☑852 2809 4165; 786 Shek O Village; mains HK$70-200; ⏰11.30am-11pm; 🚌9 from Shau Kei Wan MTR station, exit A3) This laid-back mum-and-dad operation makes everyone happy with fresh seafood, authentic Thai fare and decent prices. Upstairs, the terrace offers some views of the ocean. The restaurant is in front of the car park by the beach.

BLACK SHEEP
INTERNATIONAL $

(黑羊餐廳; ☑852 2809 2021; 330 Shek O Rd, Shek O; meals from HK$180; ⏰6-9pm Mon-Fri, noon-9pm Sat & Sun; 🖉; 🚌9 from Shau Kei Wan MTR station, exit A3) With batik tablecloths, a plant-filled patio and dim lighting, this back-alley bistro exudes a hippie vibe, but it's busy and service can be less than friendly. Pizzas (from HK$150) and seafood (from HK$180) are favourites, but the moussaka and boiled artichoke hearts are also popular, and there's always a veggie option.

DRINKING & NIGHTLIFE

DELANEY'S
PUB

(☑852 2677 1126; Shop 314, 411, 501 & 601 The Arcade, 100 Cyberport Rd, Pok Fu Lam; ⏰noon-late, happy hour 4-9pm; 🚌30X, 42C, 73, 73P, 107P, 970) The Wan Chai institution closed down after 21 years but fans can reminisce in far-flung Cyberport. The clientele are mainly folks from nearby offices and luxury residences. The St Patrick's Day menu and the Sunday roast may be gone, but the laid-back vibe is still there and with added ocean views.

SMUGGLERS INN
PUB

Map p313 (☑852 2813 8852; Ground fl, 90A Stanley Main St, Stanley; ⏰10am-midnight Mon-Thu, to 1am Fri-Sun; 🚌6, 6A, 6X or 260) When you're in an ever-renewing tourist hot spot like Stanley, it's nice to step into a place where fads have made little impact over the years. You can still have Sex on the Beach next to currency-plastered walls or outdoors on the waterfront, or play darts for free beers against fellow drinkers. There's even a jukebox.

BEN'S BACK BEACH BAR
BAR

(石澳風帆會; ☑852 2809 2268; Shek O back beach, 273 Shek O Village; ⏰7pm-midnight Tue-Fri, 2pm-midnight Sat & Sun; 🚌9 from Shau Kei Wan MTR station, exit A3) Hidden on the quiet Shek O back beach, locals and expats munch burgers and sip cold brews beneath a rustic awning. A sea-facing shrine stands right next to this rugged ensemble. Enjoy reggae beats and the sound of the lapping waves while sipping beer.

From Shek O bus terminal, turn right into the path that leads to an abandoned school and a health centre. The beach is at the end of the path.

🛍 SHOPPING

★G.O.D. CLOTHING, HOUSEWARES

Map p313 (Goods of Desire; ☑852 2673 0071; www.god.com.hk; Shop 105, Stanley Plaza, 22-23 Carmel Rd, Stanley; ⊙10.30am-8pm Mon-Fri, to 9pm Sat; ☐6, 6A, 6X, 260) One of the coolest born-in-Hong Kong shops around, G.O.D. does irreverent takes on classic Hong Kong iconography. Think cell phone covers printed with pictures of Hong Kong housing blocks, light fixtures resembling the ones in old-fashioned wet markets, and pillows covered in lucky koi print.

There are a handful of G.O.D. shops in town, but this is one of the biggest.

STANLEY MARKET MARKET

Map p313 (赤柱市集; Stanley Village Rd, Stanley; ⊙9am-6pm; ☐6, 6A, 6X or 260) No big bargains or big stings, just reasonably priced casual clothes (including big sizes and children's wear), bric-a-brac, souvenirs and formulaic art, all in a nicely confusing maze of alleys running down to Stanley Bay. It's best to go during the week; on the weekend the market is bursting at the seams with tourists and locals.

HORIZON PLAZA MALL

Map p312 (新海怡廣場; 2 Lee Wing St, Ap Lei Chau; ⊙10am-7pm; ☐90 from Exchange Sq in Central) Tucked away on the southern coast of Ap Lei Chau, this enormous outlet housed in a converted factory building boasts more than 150 shops over 28 storeys. Most locals come here to buy furniture, but you'll also find Alexander McQueen on offer and Jimmy Choos at knock-down prices. Heaps of kiddies' stuff as well, from books and toys to clothing and furniture.

🏃 SPORTS & ACTIVITIES

TAI TAM WATERWORKS HERITAGE TRAIL HIKING

(大潭水務文物徑) This scenic 5km trail runs past reservoirs and a handsome collection of 20 historic waterworks structures – feats of Victorian utilitarian engineering that include bridges, aqueducts, valve houses, pumping stations and dams, many still working. The trail, which ends at Tai Tam Tuk Raw Water Pumping Station, takes about two hours. Enter at Wong Nai Chung Gap near the luxury flats of Hong Kong Parkview, or at the junction of Tai Tam Rd and Tai Tam Reservoir Rd. On weekends you'll see residents taking a walk with their dogs, kids, maids, chauffeurs and nannies.

From Admiralty MTR station, bus 6 takes you to Wong Nai Chung Reservoir. Walk east along Tai Tam Reservoir Rd.

HONG KONG YACHTING BOATING

Map p312 (☑852 2526 0151; www.hongkong yachting.com; 18A Gee Chang Hong Centre, 65 Wong Chuk Hang Rd, Aberdeen; ⊙9am-6pm Mon-Sat; ☐4C, 90) Hong Kong Yachting has vessels for hire to various stops in Hong Kong and the outlying islands from Aberdeen Harbour. You can buy tickets to a tour or organise a private tour with your friends.

HONG KONG AQUA-BOUND CENTRE WATER SPORTS

Map p313 (☑852 8211 3876; www.aquabound. com.hk; ☐6A, 14) This outdoor company near the southern end of Stanley Main Beach offers tuition and equipment rental for windsurfing, wakeboarding, kayaking and standup paddle-boarding.

ABERDEEN BOAT CLUB BOATING

Map p312 (香港仔遊艇會; ☑852 2552 8182; www.abclubhk.com; 20 Shum Wan Rd, Aberdeen; 5-day course from HK$4000; ☐70, 73, 793) This boat club offers sailing courses to both members and nonmembers.

Kowloon

TSIM SHA TSUI | YAU MA TEI | MONG KOK | NEW KOWLOON

Neighbourhood Top Five

1 Symphony of Lights (p135) Watching this kitschy but impressive light show against the backdrop of Victoria Harbour.

2 Peninsula Lobby (p135) Enjoying scones and a cup of Earl Grey in the lobby of the elegant Jazz Age Peninsula hotel, as a string quartet saws away.

3 Temple Street Night Market (p132) Taking in the intoxicating mix of sights, sounds and smells at the this lively night market.

4 Sik Sik Yuen Wong Tai Sin Temple (p133) Experiencing a Taoist ceremony or having your fortune told at this colourful temple.

5 Yuen Po Street Bird Garden & Flower Market (p138) Admiring the songbirds and blossoms at this sweet little market, where elderly locals 'walk' their caged songbirds among vendors selling intricate bamboo cages and a rainbow of birds.

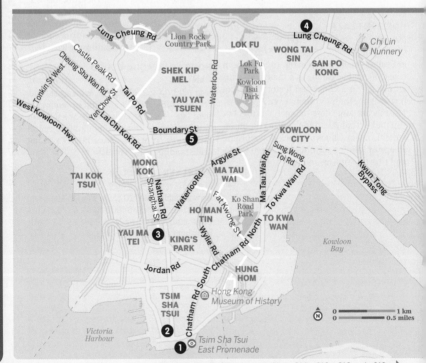

For more detail of this area see Map p314, p316, p318 and p319 ➡

Explore: Kowloon

Start your day by spending an hour or two at the Museum of History, then take a leisurely half-hour stroll to the Star Ferry Concourse via the scenic Tsim Sha Tsui East Promenade (parts of which are closed until 2018; detour on Salisbury Rd). Check out the sights along the way, such as the Cultural Centre and the clock tower, and follow up with lunch at an Indian or Shanghainese restaurant.

Walk to Yau Ma Tei, stopping at St Andrew's Church and Kowloon British School along the way. Spend an hour or so exploring Tin Hau Temple, the Jade Market and Shanghai St. Then do any one or two of the following: take the MTR to Prince Edward for the Yuen Po St Bird Garden & Flower Market followed by a visit to Mong Kok; visit Sham Shui Po and the Apliu Street Flea Market; or go to Diamond Hill to immerse yourself in the tranquillity of Chi Lin Nunnery.

Have dinner at one of the roadside stalls in Yau Ma Tei, then it's on to the Temple Street Night Market. Wrap up your day with drinks in Tsim Sha Tsui (TST).

Local Life

→**Hang-out** Film buffs and the artsy crowd like to chill on the upper floor of Mido Café (p144).

→**Shopping** Fashionistas seek affordable additions to their wardrobes at the Rise Shopping Arcade (p149) and street-level shops at Granville Circuit.

→**Singalong parlours** College kids like to celebrate birthdays in Yau Ma Tei's singalong parlours, such as Canton Singing House (p148).

Getting There & Away

→**Bus** Depart the Star Ferry Bus Terminal for points across Kowloon, Hong Kong Island and the New Territories: N21 goes to the airport, 5A goes to Kowloon City and 8 goes to Kowloon Station. Eternal East Cross Border Coach buses leave from various points in Tsim Sha Tsui.

→**Boat** Macau Ferries depart from the China Ferry Terminal on Canton Rd (Tsim Sha Tsui). Star Ferries leave from the Tsim Sha Tsui concourse at the western end of Salisbury Rd.

Lonely Planet's Top Tip

Ethnic pockets abound in Kowloon, especially in Tsim Sha Tsui, resulting in a diverse and exciting eating scene. Head to the streets around Chungking Mansions (p225) to find the best Indian grocery stores; Kimberley St and Austin Ave for Korean eateries and minimarts; the streets around Temple Street Night Market in Yau Ma Tei for Nepalese; and Kowloon City for Thai eateries.

KOWLOON

✖ Best Places to Eat

→ Chi Lin Vegetarian (p145)

→ Chicken Hof & Soju Korean (p141)

→ Spring Deer (p142)

→ Sun Sin (p144)

→ Yè Shanghai (p142)

For reviews, see p141

🍷 Best Places to Drink

→ InterContinental Lobby Lounge (p146)

→ Butler (p146)

→ Aqua (p146)

→ Kubrick Bookshop Café (p147)

For reviews, see p146

🔒 Best Places to Shop

→ Yue Hwa Chinese Products Emporium (p150)

→ Temple Street Night Market (p132)

→ Rise Shopping Arcade (p149)

→ Shanghai Street (p150)

For reviews, see p149 →

○ TOP SIGHT
HONG KONG MUSEUM OF HISTORY

If you have time for only one museum, make it the Hong Kong Museum of History. Its whistle-stop overview of the city's natural history, ethnography and indigenous culture provides some lively context to your impressions of Hong Kong. There are free guided tours in English at 11am on weekends.

The eight galleries of the **Hong Kong Story** exhibition take you on a fascinating walk through the territory's history, starting with the natural environment and prehistoric Hong Kong (about 6000 years ago), and ending with the territory's return to China in 1997. Interestingly, there's hardly anything on life post-1997.

You'll encounter colourful replicas of a Chinese marriage procession, and the dwellings of the Tanka boat people and the Puntay, who built walled villages. You'll see traditional costumes and re-created shophouses from 1881, and board a tram from 1913. You'll watch WWII footage that features interviews with Chinese and foreigners taken prisoner by the Japanese.

The section devoted to Hong Kong urban culture contains replicas of a retro grocery store, a soda fountain and the interiors of a poor man's home. There's a cinema decorated in '60s style with three screenings daily (11am, 2pm and 4pm) of old Cantonese films.

DON'T MISS

➜ The Hong Kong Story
➜ Special exhibitions

PRACTICALITIES

➜ 香港歷史博物館
➜ Map p316, B2
➜ ☑852 2724 9042
➜ http://hk.history.museum
➜ 100 Chatham Rd South, Tsim Sha Tsui
➜ adult/concession HK$10/5, Wed free
➜ ⊙10am-6pm Mon & Wed-Sat, to 7pm Sun
➜ 🛜♿
➜ Ⓜ Tsim Sha Tsui, exit B2

DANIEL FUNG / SHUTTERSTOCK ©

TSIM SHA TSUI EAST PROMENADE

The resplendent views of Victoria Harbour make this walkway one of the best strolls in Hong Kong. Go during the day to take pictures and visit the museums. Then after sundown, revisit the views, now magically transformed, with the skyscrapers of Central and Wan Chai decked out in neon robes.

The promenade is packed during the **Chinese New Year** fireworks displays in late January/early February and in June during the **Dragon Boat Festival**.

A good place to begin your journey is at the Former Kowloon-Canton Railway (KCR) Clock Tower (p136), a landmark of the age of steam, near the Star Ferry Concourse. In 1966 thousands gathered here to protest against a fare increase. The protest erupted into the 1966 riot, the first in a series of social protests leading to colonial reform.

Passing the Cultural Centre and the Museum of Art, you'll arrive at the Avenue of Stars (p136), Hong Kong's lack-lustre tribute to its once-brilliant film industry. The highlight here is a 2.5m tall bronze statue of kung fu icon Bruce Lee. Most of this area is closed for renovation until late 2018.

Every evening from the promenade you can watch the Symphony of Lights (p135), the world's largest permanent laser light show projected from atop dozens of skyscrapers.

The walk takes you past the hotels of the reclaimed area known as Tsim Sha Tsui East, and past that to the **Hong Kong Coliseum** and the Hung Hom train station. The further north you go, the quieter it gets, and tourists and pleasure boats are replaced by container barges and men angling for fish.

Parts of the promenade are closed until 2018; detour on Salisbury Rd.

DON'T MISS

➡ The views
➡ Clock Tower
➡ Symphony of Lights

PRACTICALITIES

➡ 尖沙嘴東部海濱花園
➡ Map p316, B6
➡ Salisbury Rd, Tsim Sha Tsui
➡ Ⓜ Tsim Sha Tsui, exit E

TOP SIGHT
TEMPLE STREET NIGHT MARKET

Hong Kong's liveliest night market, Temple St extends from Man Ming Lane in the north to Nanking St in the south, and is cut in two by the historic Tin Hau Temple (p138). It's a great place to go for the bustling atmosphere, the smells and tastes of the dai pai dong (food stalls), the free Cantonese opera performances, and fortune-telling. The market is at its best from about 7pm to 10pm, when it's clogged with stalls and people.

For alfresco dining, head for Woo Sung St, running parallel to the east, or to the section of Temple St north of the temple. You can get anything from a bowl of wonton noodles to oyster omelettes and Nepalese curries. There are also seafood and hotpot restaurants in the area. For an unusual experience, take a seat at a **singalong parlour** and order delivery.

Every evening a gaggle of **fortune-tellers** sets up tents in the middle of the market where they make predictions about your life (for HK$100 up) by reading your face and palm, or based on your date of birth. Some keep birds that have been trained to pick out 'fortune' cards. Most operators speak some English.

If you're in luck, you'll catch snippets of a Cantonese opera performed under the stars. Some of the most famous stars of the opera stage began their careers in this humble fashion – or so they say.

To get here from Yau Ma Tei MTR station, follow Man Ming Lane.

DON'T MISS

➤ Shopping
➤ Street food
➤ Fortune-tellers
➤ Temple St singalong parlours

PRACTICALITIES

➤ 廟街夜市
➤ Map p318, C2
➤ Temple St, Yau Ma Tei
➤ ⏲6-11pm
➤ Ⓜ Yau Ma Tei, exit C

OSTILL / SHUTTERSTOCK ©

SIK SIK YUEN WONG TAI SIN TEMPLE

An explosion of pillars, roofs, and lattice work in bright colours, this busy Taoist temple is a destination for all walks of life, from pensioners to young professionals. Some come simply to pray, others to divine the future with *chìm* (bamboo 'fortune sticks'), which are shaken out of a box onto the ground and interpreted by a fortune-teller.

The busiest times at the temple are around Chinese New Year, Wong Tai Sin's birthday (23rd day of the eighth month – usually in September) and on weekends.

The complex, built in 1973, is dedicated to a deified healer named Wong Tai Sin who, as a shepherd in Zhèjiāng province, was said to have transformed boulders into sheep. In fact, the whole district is named after him – ironic given he is said to have been a hermit. When he was 15 an immortal taught Wong how to make a herbal potion that could cure all illnesses. He is thus worshipped both by the sick and those trying to avoid illness. The term 'Wong Tai Sin' is sometimes used to describe people who are generous to a fault.

Taoist ceremonies take place at the **main altar**. The image of the deity was brought to Hong Kong from Guǎngdōng province in 1915. Behind the main altar and to the right are the **Good Wish Gardens**, replete with pavilions (the hexagonal **Unicorn Hall**, with carved doors and windows, is the most beautiful), zigzag bridges and carp ponds.

DON'T MISS

➡ The architecture
➡ *Chìm*
➡ The main altar
➡ Ceremonies
➡ Good Wish Gardens
➡ Unicorn Hall

PRACTICALITIES

➡ 嗇色園黃大仙祠
➡ ☎852 2351 5640, 852 2327 8141
➡ www.siksikyuen. org.hk
➡ 2 Chuk Yuen Village, Wong Tai Sin
➡ donation HK$2
➡ ⊙7am-5.30pm
➡ Ⓜ Wong Tai Sin, exit B2

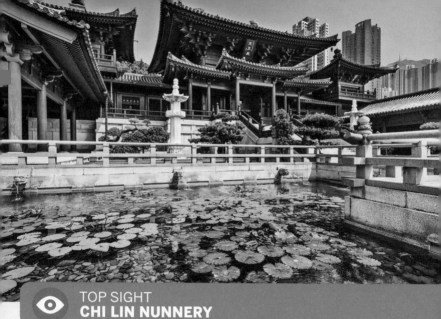

TOP SIGHT
CHI LIN NUNNERY

One of the most beautiful and arrestingly built environments in Hong Kong, this large Buddhist complex, originally dating from the 1930s, was rebuilt completely of wood in the style of a Tang-dynasty monastery in 1998. It's a serene place with lotus ponds, bonsai tea plants, bougainvillea and silent nuns delivering offerings of fruit and rice to Buddha or chanting behind intricately carved screens.

Built to last a thousand years, Chi Lin Nunnery is the world's largest cluster of handcrafted timber buildings, exhibiting a level of artistry rarely found in other faux-ancient architecture. The design, involving interlocking sections of wood joined without a single nail, is intended to demonstrate the harmony of humans with nature.

You enter through the **Sam Mun**, a series of 'three gates' representing the Buddhist precepts of compassion, wisdom and 'skilful means'. The first courtyard, which contains the delightful **Lotus Pond Garden**, gives way to the **Hall of Celestial Kings**, with a large statue of the seated Buddha surrounded by deities. Behind that is the **Main Hall**, containing a statue of the Sakyamuni Buddha.

Connected to the nunnery is **Nan Lian Garden**, a Tang-style garden featuring a golden pagoda, a koi pond and a collection of bizarre rocks.

To get here from Diamond Hill MTR, go through Hollywood Plaza and turn east on to Fung Tak Rd.

DON'T MISS

➡ Faux-Tang architecture
➡ Sam Mun
➡ Lotus Pond Garden
➡ Hall of Celestial Kings
➡ Main Hall
➡ Nan Lian Garden

PRACTICALITIES

➡ 志蓮淨苑
➡ ☏852 2354 1888
➡ www.chilin.org
➡ 5 Chi Lin Dr, Diamond Hill
➡ admission free
➡ ⊙nunnery 9am-4.30pm, garden 6.30am-7pm
➡ ⓜDiamond Hill, exit C2

⦿ SIGHTS

⦿ Tsim Sha Tsui

**TSIM SHA TSUI EAST
PROMENADE** HARBOUR
See p131.

**HONG KONG MUSEUM OF
HISTORY** MUSEUM
See p130.

KOWLOON PARK PARK
Map p314 (九龍公園; www.lcsd.gov.hk; Nathan
& Austin Rds, Tsim Sha Tsui; ⊙6am-midnight; 🚻;
MᵀTsim Sha Tsui, exit C2) Built on the site of a
barracks for Indian soldiers in the colonial
army, Kowloon Park is an oasis of greenery
and a refreshing escape from the hustle and
bustle of Tsim Sha Tsui. Pathways and walls
criss-cross the grass, birds hop around in
cages, and ancient banyan trees dot the
landscape. In the morning the older set
practise taichi amid the serene surrounds,
and on Sunday afternoon Kung Fu Corner
stages martial-arts displays.

SYMPHONY OF LIGHTS LIGHT SHOW
(Kowloon waterfront; ⊙8-8.20pm) This kitschy
but classic light and music show takes place
every single night of the year at 8pm, with
classical Chinese songs playing in time to
the sight of the Hong Kong Island skyscrapers flashing their lights across the harbour.
Get to the waterfront a few minutes early to
secure a good position. Best on clear nights.

PENINSULA HONG KONG HISTORIC BUILDING
Map p314 (香港半島酒店; www.peninsula.com;
cnr Salisbury & Nathan Rds, Tsim Sha Tsui; MᵀEast
Tsim Sha Tsui, exit L3) The Peninsula (c 1928),
housed in a throne-like building, is one of
the world's great hotels. Once called 'the
finest hotel east of Suez', the Pen was one
of several prestigious hotels across Asia, lining up with (but not behind) the likes of the
Raffles in Singapore and the Cathay (now
the Peace) in Shànghǎi. Taking afternoon
tea here is a wonderful experience – dress
neatly and be prepared to queue for a table.

HONG KONG MUSEUM OF ART MUSEUM
Map p314 (香港藝術館; ☑852 2721 0116; http://
hk.art.museum; 10 Salisbury Rd, Tsim Sha Tsui;
adult/concession HK$10/5, Wed free; ⊙10am-
6pm Mon-Fri, to 7pm Sat & Sun; 🚢Star Ferry,
MᵀEast Tsim Sha Tsui, exit J) This excellent

museum is currently closed as it undergoes
a multimillion-dollar renovation. When
open, it has seven galleries spread over six
floors exhibiting Chinese antiquities, fine
art, historical pictures and contemporary
Hong Kong art. Highlights include the
Xubaizhi collection of painting and calligraphy, contemporary works, and ceramics
and other antiques from China.

NATHAN ROAD STREET
Map p314 (彌敦道; Tsim Sha Tsui; MᵀTsim Sha
Tsui, Jordan) Named after Hong Kong's
only Jewish governor, Matthew Nathan,
Kowloon's main drag is a bit of a traffic-
and pedestrian-choked scrum of jewellery
stores and fashion boutiques. It's nonetheless an iconic Hong Kong scene where
guesthouses rub shoulders with luxury
hotels. And it's completely safe – which is
just as well since you won't be able to avoid
using it if you spend any time in the area.

**KOWLOON MOSQUE &
ISLAMIC CENTRE** MOSQUE
Map p314 (九龍清真寺; ☑852 2724 0095; 105
Nathan Rd, Tsim Sha Tsui; ⊙5am-10pm; MᵀTsim
Sha Tsui, exit C2) This structure, with its
dome and carved marble, is Hong Kong's
largest mosque. It serves the territory's
70,000-odd Muslims, more than half of
whom are Chinese, and accommodates up
to 3000 worshippers. The mosque was originally established to serve the Indian Muslim troops of the British army who were
stationed at what is now Kowloon Park.
Muslims are welcome to attend services,
but non-Muslims should ask permission to
enter. Remember to remove your footwear.

**FORMER MARINE POLICE
HEADQUARTERS** HISTORIC BUILDING
Map p314 (前水警總部; ☑852 2926 8000, tour
reservation 852 2926 1881; www.1881heritage.
com; 2A Canton Rd, Tsim Sha Tsui; ⊙10am-
10pm; 🚢Star Ferry, MᵀEast Tsim Sha Tsui, exit L6)
FREE Built in 1884, this gorgeous Victorian
complex is one of Hong Kong's four oldest
government buildings. It was used continuously by the Hong Kong Marine Police, except during WWII when the Japanese navy
took over. The complex is now a nakedly
commercial property called 'Heritage 1881'.
Some of the old structures are still here,
including stables, pigeon houses and bomb
shelter. Why 1881? Because '4' has a similar
pronunciation to 'death' in Chinese, and the
developer was superstitious.

ⓘ COPY WATCH, MADAM?

As with much of the tip of Kowloon, when walking on the promenade (p131) expect to be approached by touts offering 'copy watch', 'copy bag' or 'tailor'. If you want to buy a knock-off Rolex or Prada handbag, feel free to look at their wares (usually displayed in a laminated book). Bargain heavily. But if you're looking for a decent suit, you're probably better off going with a reputable tailor.

AVENUE OF STARS   WATERFRONT

Map p314 (星光大道; Tsim Sha Tsui East Promenade, Tsim Sha Tsui) The Avenue of the Stars, located on the spectacular Tsim Sha Tsui East Promenade, pays homage to the Hong Kong film industry and its stars, with hand prints, sculptures and information boards. It's a brave, but ultimately lacklustre, effort to celebrate Hong Kong's film and TV industry.

The Avenue of the Stars is currently closed for renovation, with an expected reopening date of 2018. However, some areas may be open throughout the construction process so it's worth stopping by.

HONG KONG SCIENCE MUSEUM   MUSEUM

Map p316 (香港科學館; ☑852 2732 3232; http://hk.science.museum; 2 Science Museum Rd, Tsim Sha Tsui; adult/concession HK$25/12.50, Wed free; ☉10am-7pm Mon-Wed & Fri, to 9pm Sat & Sun; 🔊🚻; ⓂTsim Sha Tsui, exit B2) Illustrating the fundamental workings of technology, with practical demonstrations of the laws of energy, physics and chemistry, the Hong Kong Science Museum is a great hands-on experience capable of entertaining adults as well as children from toddlers to teens.

INTERNATIONAL COMMERCE CENTRE   NOTABLE BUILDING

(環球貿易廣場, ICC; www.shkp-icc.com; 1 Austin Rd W, Tsim Sha Tsui; Sky100 adult/concession HK$168/118; ☉from 10am; ⓂKowloon, exit C) At 118 stories, the sleek ICC is Hong Kong's tallest building and one of the 10 tallest in the world. As well as the Ritz-Carlton (p226) and Elements (p152), it houses, on its 100th floor, a panoramic observation deck – **Sky100**. And 60 seconds is all it takes for the high-speed elevators to whisk you there for stunning views of Kowloon and part of the island. From Element's 2nd floor ('Metal Zone'), look for signage for Sky100. Last entry 8pm.

SIGNAL HILL GARDEN & BLACKHEAD POINT TOWER   PARK

Map p316 (訊號山公園和訊號塔; Minden Row, Tsim Sha Tsui; ☉tower 9-11am & 4-6pm; ⓂEast Tsim Sha Tsui, exit K) The views from the top of this knoll are quite spectacular, and if it were the 1900s the ships in the harbour might be returning your gaze – a copper ball in the handsome Edwardian-style tower was dropped at 1pm daily so seafarers could adjust their chronometers. The garden is perched above the Middle Road Children's Playground (p138). Enter from Minden Row (Mody Rd).

HONG KONG SPACE MUSEUM & THEATRE   MUSEUM

Map p314 (香港太空館; ☑852 2721 0226; www.lcsd.gov.hk; 10 Salisbury Rd, Tsim Sha Tsui; adult/concession HK$10/5, shows HK$24/12, Wed free; ☉1-9pm Mon & Wed-Fri, 10am-9pm Sat & Sun; 🔊🚻; ⓂEast Tsim Sha Tsui, exit J) This golf-ball-shaped building on the waterfront houses two exhibition halls and a planetarium with a large screen on the ceiling. The museum has a dated feel, but the Omnimax films, the virtual paraglider and the 'moon-walking' simulator hold a timeless fascination for kidults. The museum shop also sells dehydrated 'astronaut' ice cream in three flavours.

FORMER KCR CLOCK TOWER   HISTORIC BUILDING

Map p314 (前九廣鐵路鐘樓; Tsim Sha Tsui Star Ferry Concourse, Tsim Sha Tsui; 🚢Star Ferry, ⓂEast Tsim Sha Tsui, exit J) This 44m-high clock tower (1915) in red-brick and granite on the southern tip of Salisbury Rd was once part of the southern terminus of the Kowloon–Canton Railway (KCR). It was demolished in 1978 after operations moved to the modern train station at Hung Hom, but you can see what it looked like at the Hong Kong Railway Museum in Tai Po. The clocks began ticking on the afternoon of 22 March 1921 and have not stopped since, except during the Japanese Occupation.

HONG KONG CULTURAL CENTRE   NOTABLE BUILDING

Map p314 (香港文化中心; www.lcsd.gov.hk; 10 Salisbury Rd, Tsim Sha Tsui; ☉9am-11pm; 🔊; 🚢Star Ferry, ⓂEast Tsim Sha Tsui, exit J) Overlooking the most beautiful part of the harbour, the aesthetically challenged and windowless Cultural Centre is a world-class venue (p149) containing a 2085-seat concert hall, a Grand Theatre that seats 1750, a studio theatre for up to 535, and rehearsal studios. On the building's south side is the beginning of a viewing platform from where you can gain access to the Tsim Sha Tsui East Promenade (p131).

FORMER KOWLOON BRITISH SCHOOL
HISTORIC BUILDING

Map p314 (前九龍英童學校; www.amo.gov.hk; 136 Nathan Rd, Tsim Sha Tsui; MTsim Sha Tsui, exit B1) The oldest surviving school building for expat children is a listed Victorian-style structure that now houses the **Antiquities and Monuments Office** (古物古蹟辦事處). Established in 1902, it was subsequently modified to incorporate breezy verandahs and high ceilings, prompted possibly by the fainting spells suffered by its young occupants.

OCEAN TERMINAL BUILDING
NOTABLE BUILDING

Map p314 (www.oceanterminal.com.hk; Salisbury Rd, Tsim Sha Tsui; ⊙10am-9pm; ⑤Star Ferry, MEast Tsim Sha Tsui, exit J) This building jutting 381m into the harbour is a cruise terminal and a shopping mall. Originally Kowloon Wharf Pier (c 1886), it was rebuilt and reopened in 1966 as the Ocean Terminal – then the largest shopping centre in all of Hong Kong. Today it's part of the Harbour City (p149) complex that stretches for half a kilometre along Canton Rd and offers priceless views of the waterfront. You enter it at the western end of the Former KCR Clock Tower.

HONG KONG OBSERVATORY
HISTORIC SITE

Map p316 (香港天文台; ☑852 2926 8200; www. hko.gov.hk; 134a Nathan Rd, Tsim Sha Tsui; MTsim Sha Tsui, exit B1) This lovely historical monument, built in 1883, is sadly not open to the public, except for two days in March every year (see website for dates). It continues to monitor Hong Kong's weather and sends out frightening signals when a typhoon is heading for the territory.

ROSARY CHURCH
CHURCH

Map p316 (玫瑰堂; ☑852 2368 0980; http://rosarychurch.catholic.org.hk; 125 Chatham Rd S, Tsim Sha Tsui; ⊙7.30am-7.30pm; MJordan, exit D) Kowloon's oldest Catholic church was built in 1905 with money donated by a Portuguese doctor in Hong Kong, initially for the benefit of the Catholics in an Indian battalion stationed in Kowloon, and later for the burgeoning local Catholic community.

Rosary Church features a classic Gothic style with a yellowish facade reminiscent of churches in Macau.

KOWLOON UNION CHURCH
CHURCH

Map p318 (九龍佑寧堂; ☑852 2367 2585; www. kuc.hk; 4 Jordan Rd, Tsim Sha Tsui; ⊙9am-5pm Mon-Fri; MJordan, exit B2) This red-brick church with Protestant roots was constructed in 1930 with money from an English businessman of Armenian descent. It was built in a Neo-Gothic style – quite unusual for Kowloon – and features a Chinese-tiled pitched roof (which makes it typhoon-proof), a battlemented tower, and windows with Gothic tracery. Sunday service starts at 10.30am.

FOOK TAK ANCIENT TEMPLE
BUDDHIST TEMPLE

Map p314 (福德古廟; 30 Haiphong Rd, Tsim Sha Tsui; ⊙6am-8pm; MTsim Sha Tsui, exit C2) Tsim Sha Tsui's only temple is a smoke-filled hole in the wall with a hot tin roof. Little is known about its ancestry except that it was built as a shrine in the Qing dynasty and renovated in 1900. Before WWII, worshippers of its Earth God were the unskilled labourers from Kowloon Wharf nearby, where the Ocean Terminal (p137) now stands. Today most incense offerers are octogenarians – the temple specialises in longevity.

ST ANDREW'S ANGLICAN CHURCH
CHURCH

Map p314 (聖安德烈堂; ☑852 2367 1478; www. standrews.org.hk; 138 Nathan Rd, Tsim Sha Tsui; ⊙7.30am-10.30pm, church 8.30am-5.30pm; MTsim Sha Tsui, exit B1) Sitting atop a knoll, next to the Former Kowloon British School, is this charming building in English Gothic style that houses Kowloon's oldest Protestant church. St Andrew's was built in 1905 in granite and red brick to serve Kowloon's Protestant population; it was turned into a Shinto shrine during the Japanese

ⓘ BEWARE FAKE MONKS

Real monks never solicit money. But during your stay, you may be approached by con artists in monk outfits who try to make you part with your money. Some may even offer Buddhist amulets for sale, or force 'blessings' on you then pester you for a donation. When accosted, just say 'no' firmly and ignore them.

Occupation. Nearby you'll see the handsome former vicarage with columned balconies (c 1909). Enter from the eastern side of Nathan Rd via steps or a slope.

MIDDLE ROAD CHILDREN'S PLAYGROUND
PARK

Map p316 (中間道兒童遊樂場; Middle Rd, Tsim Sha Tsui; ⊙7am-11pm; 🚇; MEast Tsim Sha Tsui, exit K) Accessible via a sweep of stairs from Chatham Rd South, this hidden gem atop the East Tsim Sha Tsui MTR station has play facilities, shaded seating and views of the waterfront. On weekdays it's the quiet backyard playground of the residents nearby, but on weekends it's filled with children and picnickers of as many ethnicities as there are ways to go down a slide (if you're eight).

👁 Yau Ma Tei

TEMPLE STREET NIGHT MARKET
MARKET

See p132.

SHANGHAI STREET
STREET

Map p318 (上海街; Yau Ma Tei; MYau Ma Tei, exit C) Strolling down Shanghai St will take you back to a time long past. Once Kowloon's main drag, it's flanked by stores selling Chinese wedding gowns, sandalwood incense and Buddha statues, as well as mah-jong parlours and an old pawn shop (at the junction with Saigon St). This is a terrific place for souvenirs – fun picks include wooden mooncake moulds stamped with images of fish or pigs or lucky sayings, bamboo steamer baskets, long chopsticks meant for stirring pots and pretty ceramic bowls.

The main business here is kitchen goods. Check out dozens of shops hawking woks, cleavers, tree-trunk carving boards and other necessities of Chinese cookery.

TIN HAU TEMPLE
TAOIST TEMPLE

Map p318 (天后廟; ☎852 2385 0759; www.ctc. org.hk; cnr Temple & Public Square Sts, Yau Ma Tei; ⊙8am-5pm; MYau Ma Tei, exit C) This large, incense-filled sanctuary built in the 19th century is one of Hong Kong's most famous Tin Hau (Goddess of the Sea) temples. The public square out front is Yau Ma Tei's communal heart where fishers once laid out their hemp ropes in the sun next to Chinese banyans that today shade chess players and elderly men.

CHIN WOO ATHLETIC ASSOCIATION
MARTIAL ARTS SCHOOL

Map p318 (精武體育館; ☎852 2384 3238; www. chinwoo.com.hk/; Flat B & C, 13th fl, Wah Fung Bldg, 300 Nathan Rd, Yau Ma Tei; ⊙2.30-9pm; MJordan, exit B1) This is the 88-year-old branch of the Chin Woo Athletic Association, founded 100 years ago in Shanghai by the famed kung-fu master Huo Yuanjia (霍元甲). The Shanghai school was featured in Bruce Lee's *Fist of Fury* and Jet Li's *Fearless*. You can visit the school during opening hours. Classes, however, are taught mainly in Cantonese.

WHOLESALE FRUIT MARKET
MARKET

Map p318 (油麻地果欄; cnr Shek Lung & Reclamation Sts, Yau Ma Tei; ⊙2-6am; MYau Ma Tei, exit B2) This historic and still operating market, founded in 1913, is a cluster of one- and two-storey brick and stone buildings with pre-WWII signboards. It is a hive of activity from 4am to 6am when fresh fruit is loaded on and off trucks, and bare-backed workers manoeuvre piles of boxes under the moon. Non-night owls can still wander the area, where a number of fruit vendors set up during the day.

The market is bounded by Ferry St, Waterloo Rd and Reclamation St with Shek Lung St running through it.

To get here from Yau Ma Tei MTR exit B2, turn right.

YAU MA TEI POLICE STATION
HISTORIC BUILDING

Map p318 (油麻地警署; 627 Canton Rd, Yau Ma Tei; MYau Ma Tei, exit C) A stone's throw from Tin Hau Temple (p138) is this handsome Edwardian police station (c 1922) with arcades and arches. You may have caught a glimpse of it in the film *Rush Hour 2*. Some of its architectural features have been adapted for feng shui reasons – crimefighting is a high-risk profession. For instance, the portico at the main entrance is set in an indented corner to better protect the building's inhabitants.

👁 Mong Kok

YUEN PO STREET BIRD GARDEN & FLOWER MARKET
PARK

Map p319 (園圃街雀鳥花園, 花墟; Yuen Po & Boundary Sts, Mong Kok; ⊙7am-8pm; MPrince Edward, exit B1) In this enchanting corner of Mong Kok, you will find a handful of old

Neighbourhood Walk
Kowloon's Teeming Market Streets

START YUEN PO STREET BIRD GARDEN
END JORDAN MTR STATION, EXIT A
LENGTH 4.5KM; TWO HOURS

A 10-minute walk away from Prince Edward station (exit A), ❶ **Yuen Po Street Bird Garden** (p138) is the gathering place for older men who air their caged birds here. A little further along, Flower Market Rd is lined with fragrant and exotic blooms.

At the end of Flower Market Rd, take a left turn onto Sai Yee St, then a right onto Prince Edward Rd West and then a left turn onto Tung Choi St. Walk two blocks to the ❷ **Goldfish Market**, a dozen or so shops trading in these extravagantly hued fish. You'll see an amazing variety, with the real rarities commanding high prices.

Sharpen your elbows. ❸ **Tung Choi St market** (p150), also known as the Ladies' Market, is crammed with shoppers and stalls selling mostly inexpensive clothing.

Beneath the naked light bulbs, hundreds of stalls at the ❹ **Temple Street Night Market** (p132) sell a vast array of booty from sex toys to luggage. Coming from Tung Choi St, turn right on Dundas St and then left into Shanghai St, cut down Hi Lung Lane to Temple St and turn right. The market runs right down to Jordan Rd.

Fragrant smoke curls from incense spirals at ❺ **Tin Hau Temple** (p138). Fortune-tellers nearby use everything from tarot cards to palmistry and even tame sparrows to deliver their predictions.

A good place to pick up an inexpensive trinket, the large covered ❻ **Jade Market** (p151) contains dozens of stalls selling jade of all grades. At Jordan Rd turn east, then south into Nathan Rd to find Jordan MTR station.

KOWLOON

men out 'walking' their caged songbirds. Stick around long enough and you should see birds being fed squirming caterpillars with chopsticks. There are also feathered creatures for sale, along with elaborate cages carved from teak (an excellent souvenir, in our opinion). Adjacent to the garden is the flower market, which theoretically keeps the same hours, but only gets busy after 10am.

Don't miss shops choked with thousands of multihued orchids, all cheap as chips.

LUI SENG CHUN HISTORIC BUILDING

Map p319 (雷春生堂; ☑852 3411 0628; http://scm.hkbu.edu.hk/lsctour; 119 Lai Chi Kok Rd, cnr Tong Mi Rd, Mong Kok; ☉guided tour 2.30pm & 4pm Mon-Fri, 9.30am & 11am Sat, consultation 9am-1pm & 2-8pm Mon-Sat, 9am-1pm Sun; MPrince Edward, exit C2) FREE Hugging a street corner is this beautiful four-storey Chinese 'shophouse' belonging to a school of Chinese medicine. Constructed circa 1931, it features a mix of Chinese and European architectural styles – deep verandahs, urn-shaped balustrades and other fanciful takes on a neoclassical Italian villa. The ground floor, which has a herbal tea shop, is open to the public. Free guided tours to the upper-floor clinics is available by registration. They're in Cantonese, but exhibits have bilingual labels.

English tours can be arranged for groups of more than four. Make an appointment if you want to have your pulse taken by a Chinese doctor.

HERITAGE OF MEI HO HOUSE MUSEUM MUSEUM

(美荷樓生活館; ☑852 3728 3500; Block 41, Shek Kip Mei Estate, 70 Berwick St, Sham Shui Po; ☉9.30am-5pm Tue-Sun; ☒A2, MSham Shui Po, exit D2) FREE This museum inside the Mei Ho House Youth Hostel introduces the history of Mei Ho House, which was among the first batch of resettlement blocks built to house the survivors of a devastating blaze that broke out in 1953 and left nearly 58,000 homeless. Mei Ho House marked the beginning of Hong Kong's public housing policies. Using artefacts and replicas of old residences, the museum introduces the way of life and culture in Hong Kong during the 1950s to 1970s.

C&G ARTPARTMENT GALLERY

Map p319 (☑852 2390 9332; www.candg-artpartment.com; 3rd fl, 222 Sai Yeung Choi St S, Mong Kok; ☉2-7.30pm Thu, Fri, Sun & Mon, from

11am Sat; MPrince Edward, exit B2) Clara and Gum, the founders of this edgy art space behind the Pioneer Centre (始創中心), are passionate about nurturing the local art scene and representing socially minded artists. They close late when there are events. See website for the latest.

LEI CHENG UK HAN TOMB MUSEUM MUSEUM

(李鄭屋漢墓博物館; ☑852 2386 2863; www.lcsd.gov.hk; 41 Tonkin St, Sham Shui Po; ☉10am-6pm Fri-Wed; MCheung Sha Wan, exit A3) FREE Don't expect a Terracotta Army, but for those interested in the area's ancient history, this is a significant burial vault dating from the Eastern Han dynasty (AD 25–220). The tomb consists of four barrel-vaulted brick chambers set around a domed central chamber. It's encased in a concrete shell for protection and visitors can only peep through a plastic window.

◉ New Kowloon

CHI LIN NUNNERY BUDDHIST NUNNERY

See p134.

SIK SIK YUEN WONG TAI SIN TEMPLE TAOIST TEMPLE

See p133.

CATTLE DEPOT ARTIST VILLAGE VILLAGE

(牛棚藝術村; 63 Ma Tau Kok Rd, To Kwa Wan; ☉10am-10pm; ☒106, 12A, 5C, 101, 111) This century-old slaughterhouse has been reincarnated into an artists' village, its redbrick buildings now housing studios and exhibition halls. There are some 20 art organisations inside, including On and On Theatre Workshop (p148). The nonprofit visual art organisation **1a Space** (☑852 2529 0087; www.oneaspace.org.hk; Unit 14, Cattle Depot Artist Village; ☉11am-7pm Tue-Sun) holds regular exhibitions of high-quality local and international art, as well as concerts and theatrical performances.

The village itself is an interesting place to visit even when there's nothing happening. Its next to a Town Gas storage facility, in the northern part of To Kwa Wan, an area on Kowloon's east coast.

KOWLOON WALLED CITY PARK PARK

(九龍寨城公園; ☑852 2716 9962; www.lcsd.gov.hk; Tung Tau Tsuen, Tung Tsing, cnr Carpenter

& Junction Rds, Kowloon City; ⊙park 6.30am-11pm, exhibition 10am-6pm, closed Wed; ☐1 from Star Ferry pier) This attractive park was the site of the mysterious Kowloon Walled City, a Chinese garrison in the 19th century that technically remained part of China throughout British rule. Neither government wanted to have anything to do with the 3-acre enclave, so it became a lawless slum infamous for its gangs, prostitution and drug dens. The British eventually relocated the 30,000 residents and built a park in its place. There's a model of it on display at the park. If you're taking the bus, alight opposite the park at Tung Tau Tsuen Rd.

EATING

Tsim Sha Tsui

★CHICKEN HOF & SOJU KOREAN
KOREAN $

Map p316 (李家; Chicken; ☑852 2375 8080; Ground fl, 84 Kam Kok Mansion, Kimberley Rd, Tsim Sha Tsui; meals from HK$150; ⊙5pm-4am; ⓂJordan, exit D) This place with darkened windows may look dodgy from the outside, but in fact it's a Korean gastropub with a friendly owner who'll holler a greeting when customers enter. The excellent fried chicken, made with a light and crispy batter, comes in five versions. Traditional fare such as Korean barbecue is also available. If you need to ask directions, locals often refer to this place as 'Lee Family Chicken'. A long queue is the norm.

TAK FAT BEEF BALLS
NOODLES $

Map p314 (德發牛肉丸; Haiphong Rd, Tsim Sha Tsui; beef ball noodles HK$28; ⊙9am-8pm; ⓂTsim Sha Tsui, exit A1) This famous *dai pai dong* (food stall) is one of a handful operating in the Haiphong Rd Temporary Market. Pick a seat in the cacophonous sprawl and order the beef ball noodles, famed for their bounce and hint of dried mandarin peel. The market is next door to Fook Tak Ancient Temple. Venture past the florists and halal meat stalls to reach the *dai pai dong*.

WOODLANDS
INDIAN $

Map p316 (活蘭印度素食; ☑852 2369 3718; Upper ground fl, 16 & 17 Wing On Plaza, 62 Mody Rd, Tsim Sha Tsui; meals HK$70-180; ⊙noon-3.30pm & 6.30-10.30pm; ☑ ☑; ⓂEast Tsim Sha Tsui, exit P1) Located above a department store, good old Woodlands offers excellent-value Indian vegetarian food to compatriots and the odd local. Dithering gluttons should order the *thali* meal, which is served on a round metal plate with 10 tiny dishes, a dessert and bread. Dosai are excellent.

PEKING DUMPLING SHOP
NORTHERN CHINESE $

Map p316 (北京水餃店; ☑852 2368 3028; Shop A2, 15B Austin Ave, Tsim Sha Tsui; servings HK$10-40; ⊙11.30am-11.30pm; ⓂJordan, exit D) This tiny shop whips up decent meat-filled pastries, hearty dumplings and noodles of the chewy northern variety. Get your carb fix seated in booths or, if the smell of grease gets to you, on the go.

MAMMY PANCAKE
DESSERTS $

Map p314 (媽咪雞蛋仔; 8-12 Carnarvon Rd, Tsim Sha Tsui; egg waffles HK$16-28; ⊙11.30am-9pm Sun-Thu, to 10.30pm Fri & Sat; ⓂTsim Sha Tsui, exit D2) This takeaway counter serves up some of Hong Kong's best eggettes, the egg-shaped waffles beloved by local children and adults alike. Get them in classic plain, or in inventive flavours such as green tea, chestnut, sweet potato or pork floss. Or pig out with a waffle sandwich oozing with peanut butter and condensed milk. Expect a 15-minute wait for your treat.

PIERRE HERMÉ
DESSERTS $

Map p314 (☑852 2155 3866; www.pierreherme.com/hk; Shop 2410, Level 2, Harbour City, 7-27 Canton Rd, Tsim Sha Tsui; macarons HK$30; ⊙10am-10pm; ⓂTsim Sha Tsui, exit C3) Sweet, tender and transient like young love, the legendary macarons of this French confectioner feature dazzling flavour pairings, all beautifully named. Jardin Dans Les Nuages (Garden in the Clouds) is 'chocolate and smoked salt', which translates on the tongue as a hint of smokiness in velvety chocolate.

YUM CHA
DIM SUM $

Map p316 (飲茶; ☑852 2751 1666; http://yumchahk.com; 3/F 20-22 Granville Rd, Tsim Sha Tsui; meals HK$100-250; ⊙11.30am-3pm & 6-11pm; ⓂTsim Sha Tsui, exit B2) Adorable, animal-shaped dumplings and buns are just begging to be Instagrammed at Yum Cha, one of the newer players on Hong Kong's dim-sum scene. Barbecue pork buns are adorned with tiny piggy faces, custard buns are anthropomorphic eggs, and bird-shaped pineapple puffs are served in ornate cages. There's also a full menu of Cantonese fare, rendered with a modern twist.

SWEET DYNASTY CANTONESE, DESSERTS $

Map p314 (糖朝; ☑852 2199 7799; Shop A, Basement, Hong Kong Pacific Centre, 28 Hankow Rd, Tsim Sha Tsui; meals HK$70-300; ⊗8am-midnight Mon-Thu, 8am-1am Fri, 7.30am-1am Sat, 7.30am-midnight Sun; ⓘ; MⓉTsim Sha Tsui, exit A1) Sweet Dynasty's extensive menu encompasses a plethora of casual Cantonese dishes, but the desserts, noodles and congee, for which they became famous years ago, are still the best. The restaurant is clean and modern, but gets crowded when busy.

CHANGWON KOREAN $

Map p316 (莊園韓國料理; ☑852 2368 4606; 1 Kimberly St, Tsim Sha Tsui East; meals HK$100-200; ⊗noon-5am; MⓉTsim Sha Tsui, exit B1) One of the oldest and most authentic Korean restaurants in town, Chang Won makes delectable beef ribs, seafood pancakes and cold noodles, and the staff are generous with side dishes. But the toilet is not for the faint-hearted.

HUNGRY KOREAN KOREAN $

Map p314 (☑852 2730 5577; http://hungry korean.com; 24-38 Ashley Rd, Tsim Sha Tsui; meals HK$30-60; ⊗noon-midnight) The most popular of this Korean fast casual chain's five locations, there's almost always a line here for cheap and tasty *bibimbap, gim bap* (Korean-style sushi), spicy chicken wings and kimchi pancakes. Don't worry, it moves fast.

CITY'SUPER SUPERMARKET, FOOD COURT $

Map p314 (www.citysuper.com.hk; Shop 3001, Gateway Arcade, Harbour City Level 3, 25-27 Canton Rd, Tsim Sha Tsui; ⊗10am-10pm; MⓉTsim Sha Tsui, exit C2) This posh Japanese supermarket chain has international groceries and a food court serving a plethora of Asian cuisines, including udon, Korean stone pot rice and Taiwanese dumplings, as well as some of the best Hokkaido-style soft-serve ice cream in town.

★ YÈ SHANGHAI DIM SUM $$

Map p314 (夜上海; ☑852 2376 3322; www. elite-concepts.com; 6th fl, Marco Polo Hotel, Harbour City, Canton Rd, Tsim Sha Tsui; meals HK$400-800; ⊗11.30am-2.30pm & 6-10.30pm; ⓘ; MⓉTsim Sha Tsui, exit C2) The name means 'Shànghǎi Nights'. Dark woods and subtle lighting inspired by 1920s Shànghǎi fill the air with romance. The modern Shanghainese dishes are also exquisite. The only exception to this Jiāngnán harmony is the Cantonese dim sum being served at lunch, though that too is wonderful. Sophisticated Yè Shanghai has one Michelin star.

★ DIN TAI FUNG TAIWANESE, NOODLES $$

Map p314 (鼎泰豐; ☑852 2730 6928; www.din taifung.com.hk; Shop 130, 3rd fl, Silvercord, 30 Canton Rd, Tsim Sha Tsui; meals HK$120-300; ⊗11.30am-10.30pm; ⓘ; MⓉTsim Sha Tsui, exit C1) Whether it's comfort food or a carb fix you're craving, the juicy Shanghai dumplings and hearty northern-style noodles at this beloved Taiwanese chain will do the trick. Queues are the norm and there are no reservations, but service is excellent. Must-eats include the famous *xiao long bao* (soup dumplings), fluffy steamed pork buns and the greasy-but-oh-so-good fried pork chop.

★ SPRING DEER NORTHERN CHINESE $$

Map p316 (鹿鳴春飯店; ☑852 2366 4012; 1st fl, 42 Mody Rd, Tsim Sha Tsui; meals HK$80-500; ⊗noon-3pm & 6-11pm; MⓉEast Tsim Sha Tsui, exit N2) Hong Kong's most authentic northern-style roasted lamb is served here. Better known is the Peking duck, which is very good. That said, the service can be about as welcoming as a Běijīng winter, c 1967. Booking is essential.

★ WOO COW HOTPOT $$

Map p316 (禾牛薈火焗館; Great Beef Hot Pot; ☑852 3997 3369; 1st & 2nd fl, China Insurance Bldg, 48 Cameron Rd, Tsim Sha Tsui; meals HK$350-600; ⊗5.30pm-2am; MⓉTsim Sha Tsui, exit B3) Indecisive gluttons will scream at the mind-blowing hotpot choices here – 200 ingredients (the majority fresh or homemade), 20 kinds of broth (from clam soup to fancy herbal concoctions) and an embarrassment of condiments (all-you-can-dip)! There's no escaping the menu either – the lights are too bright! Now onto the sashimi options... Booking essential.

SEN HOTPOT RESTAURANT CANTONESE $$

Map p318 (千鍋居; ☑852 2377 2022; 1st fl, Liberty Mansion, 26E Jordan Rd, Tsim Sha Tsui; meals HK$300; ⊗11.30am-3pm & 5.30pm-1am; MⓉJordan, exit A) A wallet-friendly misnomer, Sen specialises in dishes served in pots, rather than 'hotpot' aka steamboat, though that is available too. Rustic cuisine evokes dew-fresh ingredients in heart-warming combos

– and this modern eatery fares well, notably with the braised goose. That said, it's noisy, unlike the portraits of old Hong Kong gracing its walls. Enter from Temple St.

GAYLORD INDIAN $$

Map p314 (爵樂印度餐廳; ☑852 2376 1001; 1st fl Ashley Centre, 23-25 Ashley Rd, Tsim Sha Tsui; meals from HK$250; ⊘noon-3pm & 6-11pm; ☑; Ⓜ Tsim Sha Tsui, exit E) Dim lighting and live sitar music set the scene for enjoying the excellent rogan josh, dhal and other favourite dishes at Hong Kong's oldest – and Kowloon's classiest – Indian restaurant, which has been operating since 1972. There are lots of vegetarian choices as well. Though pricier than other Indian places in town, the cosy alcoves and attentive service more than compensate.

DONG LAI SHUN CHINESE $$

Map p316 (東來順; ☑852 2733 2020; www.rghk.com.hk; B2, The Royal Garden, 69 Mody Rd, Tsim Sha Tsui; meals HK$250-1500; ⊘11.30am-2.30pm & 6-10.30pm; ☎ ⓗ; Ⓜ East Tsim Sha Tsui, exit P2) Besides superbly executed Northern Chinese dishes, the phonebook of a menu here also features Shanghainese, Sichuanese and Cantonese favourites. But Dong Lai Shun is best known for its mutton hotpot, which involves dunking paper-thin slices of mutton into boiling water and eating it with sesame sauce. The atmosphere is a little formal but the service is warm.

HING KEE RESTAURANT CANTONESE $$

Map p314 (避風塘興記; ☑852 2722 0022; 1st fl, Bowa House, 180 Nathan Rd, Tsim Sha Tsui; meals HK$380-1200; ⊘6pm-5am; Ⓜ Jordan, exit D) This celebrity haunt is run by a feisty fisherman's daughter who's known for her brilliant dishes prepared the way they were on sampans. The signature crabs smothered in a mountain of fried garlic are a wonder to taste and behold. The service can be a little edgy. Be sure you know the price of every dish before you order.

AL MOLO ITALIAN $$

Map p314 (☑852 2730 7900; www.diningconcepts.com.hk; Shop G63, Ocean Terminal, 7-23 Canton Rd, Harbour City, Tsim Sha Tsui; meals HK$360-700; ⊘noon-10.30pm; ⓗ; ⛴ Star Ferry, Ⓜ East Tsim Sha Tsui, exit J) The Hong Kong venture of New York–based chef and restaurateur Michael White has brick walls, iron fittings and an alfresco area where you can savour homemade semolina pasta with sea-

food accompanied by the delicious views of the Tsim Sha Tsui harbourfront. Lunch sets start from HK$150.

FOOK LAM MOON CANTONESE, DIM SUM $$$

Map p316 (福臨門; ☑852 2366 0286; www.fooklammoon-grp.com; Shop 8, 1st fl, 53-59 Kimberley Rd, Tsim Sha Tsui; meals HK$400-2000; ⊘11.30am-2.30pm & 6-10.30pm; Ⓜ Tsim Sha Tsui, exit B1) Locals call FLM 'celebrities' canteen'. But even if you're not rich and famous, FLM will treat you as if you were. The huge menu contains costly items such as abalone, which would shoot your bill up to at least HK$1000 per head. But no one will snub you if you stick to the dim sum (from HK$60 a basket), which is divine and available only at lunch.

GADDI'S FRENCH $$$

Map p314 (☑852 2696 6763; www.peninsula.com; 1st fl, The Peninsula, 19-21 Salisbury Rd, Tsim Sha Tsui; set lunch/dinner HK$500/2000; ⊘noon-2.30pm & 7-10.30pm; Ⓜ Tsim Sha Tsui, exit E) Gaddi's, which opened just after WWII, was the kind of place where wealthy families went to celebrate special occasions. Today the classical decor may be a tad stuffy and the live Filipino band gratuitous, but the food – traditional French with contemporary touches – is without a doubt still some of the best in town.

T'ANG COURT CANTONESE, DIM SUM $$$

Map p314 (唐閣; ☑852 2375 1133; www.hongkong.langhamhotels.com; 1st fl, Langham Hotel, 8 Peking Rd, Tsim Sha Tsui; lunch HK$300-2000, dinner HK$500-2000; ⊘noon-2.30pm & 6-10.30pm; ⓗ; Ⓜ Tsim Sha Tsui, exit L4) As befitting its name T'ang Court, with two Michelin stars, has mastered the art of fine Cantonese cooking. Deep-pile carpets, heavy silks and mindful staff contribute to a hushed atmosphere. If that seems too formal, rest assured the polished service will make you feel right at home, like an emperor in his palace. The signature baked oysters with port requires pre-ordering.

SUN TUNG LOK CANTONESE, DIM SUM $$$

Map p314 (新同樂; ☑852 2152 1417; www.suntunglok.com.hk; 4th fl, Miramar Shopping Centre, 132 Nathan Rd, Tsim Sha Tsui; lunch HK$250-3000, dinner HK$500-5000; ⊘11.30am-3pm & 6-10.30pm; Ⓜ Tsim Sha Tsui, exit B2) Crowned with two Michelin stars, elegant Sun Tung Lok (c 1969) proudly upholds the fine traditions of Cantonese cooking. It's evident in the dim sum (available at lunch), which food critics hail as the best in town, and dishes such as braised abalone, which are a litmus test of culinary skill. STL is pricey but sets are available and dim sum come in half-baskets.

STEAK HOUSE
INTERNATIONAL $$$

Map p316 (☑852 2313 2323; https://hongkong-ic.intercontinental.com; InterContinental Hong Kong, 18 Salisbury Rd, Tsim Sha Tsui; meals HK$700; ⊙6-11pm Mon-Fri, noon-2.30pm & 6-11pm Sat & Sun; 🚼; MEast Tsim Sha Tsui, exit J) At this first-rate steakhouse, the imported beef exhilarates, and there are trimmings to enhance your experience such as a flight of eight exotic salts, multiple mustards and fancy steak knives. The extravagant salad bar (HK$398 per person) is a meal in itself; and the desserts are awesome, but beware: they're huge even by American standards!

KIMBERLEY CHINESE RESTAURANT
CHINESE $$$

Map p316 (君怡閣中菜廳; ☑852 2369 8212; M fl, Kimberley Hotel, 28 Kimberley Rd, Tsim Sha Tsui; meals HK$300-600; ⊙11am-3pm & 6-11pm; MTsim Sha Tsui, exit B1) This restaurant is famous for the Kimberley Pig – a 30-day piglet stuffed with sticky rice that's been cooked with shallots and garlic, then roasted whole. Each piglet (HK$900) will feed at least five hungry people. You need to order it two days in advance, and pay a (negotiable) deposit of HK$200 the day before. Still hungry? Try the beef ribs.

🍴 Yau Ma Tei

⭐ SUN SIN
NOODLES $

Map p318 (新仙清湯腩; ☑852 2332 6872; 37 Portland St, Yau Ma Tei; meals HK$40-65; ⊙11am-midnight; MYau Ma Tei, exit B2) A Michelin-praised brisket shop in a 'hood known for brothels, Sun Sin has kept quality up and prices down despite its laurels. The succulent cuts of meat are served in a broth with radish, in a chunky tomato soup, or as a curry. At peak times, makeshift tables are available upstairs for those who prize food over comfort.

NATHAN CONGEE AND NOODLE
NOODLES $

Map p318 (彌敦粥麵家; ☑852 2771 4285; 11 Saigon St, Yau Ma Tei; meals HK$60; ⊙7.30am-11.30pm; MJordan, exit B2) This low-key eatery

has been making great congee and noodles for the last half-century. Order a side of fritters (to be dunked into congee and eaten slightly soggy), tackle a pyramidal rice dumpling, or conquer the blanched fish skin tossed with parsley and peanuts.

HING KEE RESTAURANT
CANTONESE $

Map p318 (興記菜館; ☑852 2384 3647; 19 Temple St, Yau Mei Tei; ⊙6pm-1am; MYau Ma Tei, exit C) Previously a roadside stall that started out by whipping up hearty claypot rice and oyster omelettes (HK$20) for night revellers and triads, Hing Kee now serves the same under a roof but without the atmosphere.

OSAMA TONY
SHANGHAINESE, DUMPLINGS $

&Map p318 (☑852 2755 5090; 122 Woo Sung St, Jordan; meals HK$40-80; ⊙noon-11pm; MJordan, exit A) We're not sure how it chose its strange English name, but this cosy little spot serves some of Kowloon's best and cheapest *xiao long bao* (soup dumplings), as well as to-die-for crispy radish cakes and heaped plates of Shanghai-style noodles and fried rice.

AUSTRALIA DAIRY COMPANY
CAFE $

Map p318 (澳洲牛奶公司; ☑852 2730 1356; 47-49 Parkes St, Jordan; meals HK$30-50; ⊙7.30am-11pm Wed-Mon; MJordan exit C2) Long waits and rude service are the standard at this beloved Hong Kong *cha chaan teng* (tea house), famed for its scrambled egg sandwiches, macaroni and ham soup, and milk pudding. An experience to be had.

MIDO CAFÉ
CAFE $

Map p318 (美都餐室; ☑852 2384 6402; 63 Temple St, Yau Ma Tei; meals HK$40-90; ⊙9am-10pm; MYau Ma Tei, exit B2) This retro *cha chaan tang* (tea house; 1950) with mosaic tiles and metal latticework stands astride a street corner that comes to life at sundown. Ascend to the upper floor and take a seat next to a wall of iron-framed windows overlooking Tin Hau Temple – its atmosphere is what makes it Kowloon's most famous tea cafe, despite passable food and service.

BBQ LOBSTER
BARBECUE $

Map p318 (龍蝦燒; ☑852 2374 9888; 7 Man Ying St, Ferry Point, Yau Ma Tei; skewers HK$12-35; ⊙5pm-3am; 🌱; MJordan, exit A) The most comfortable of three neighbouring branches, this buzzing eatery lures Kowloon gluttons with scrumptious grilled skewers that are 30% to 50% cheaper than the same in

Soho. With fresh seven-inch prawns at only HK$17 each and vegetarian options aplenty, indulgence is the norm. In between sticks, cleanse your palate with a sip of Hoegaarden or a zesty white.

✕ Mong Kok

TIM HO WAN, THE DIM SUM SPECIALISTS
DIM SUM $

(添好運點心專門店; 9-11 Fuk Wing St, Sham Shui Po; meals HK$40-200; ⏰8am-10pm; ⓂSham Shui Po, exit B1) A former Four Seasons dim-sum chef re-creates his magic in the first budget dim-sum eatery to receive a Michelin star. Get a ticket when you arrive and a table should be available in under 30 minutes. The barbecue pork bun is famed across Asia. There's a branch (p72) in Central.

GOOD HOPE NOODLE
NOODLES $

Map p318 (好旺角麵家; ☑852 2384 6898; Shop 5-6, 18 Fa Yuen St, Mong Kok; meals HK$30-90; ⏰11am-12.45am; ⓂMong Kok, exit D3) This 40-year-old shop has retained its Michelin commendation and fan following. Now the al dente egg noodles, bite-sized wontons and silky congee that have won hearts for decades continue to be cooked the old way, but are served in neat, modern surrounds.

ONE DIM SUM
DIM SUM $

Map p319 (一點心; ☑852 2789 2280; Shop 1 & 2, Kenwood Mansion, 15 Playing Field Rd, Mong Kok; meals HK$35-60; ⏰11am-1am; ⓂPrince Edward, exit A) This cheery place is known for all-day, bang-for-the-buck dim sum. Customers place orders by ticking their selections of 45 items. There's always a line, but the wait is usually under 30 minutes. Nonpeak hours are 3pm to 5pm, and 9pm to midnight.

KUNG WO TOFU FACTORY
DESSERT $

(公和荳品廠; ☑852 2386 6871; 118 Pei Ho St, Sham Shui Po; meals HK$8-30; ⏰9am-9pm; ⓂSham Shui Po, exit B2) A charming 50-year-old shop of a brand established in 1893, Kung Wo wears its name proudly in red clerical script. Regulars come for fresh soy milk, pan-fried tofu and sweet tofu pudding, made the traditional way from beans ground using a hand-operated millstone. The silky tofu has nutty notes, and the hue is off-white – reassuringly imperfect, just like the service.

✕ New Kowloon

CHI LIN VEGETARIAN
VEGETARIAN, CHINESE $

(志蓮素齋, 龍門樓; Long Men Lou; ☑852 3658 9388; 60 Fung Tak Rd, Nan Lian Garden; meals from HK$200; ⏰noon-9pm Mon-Fri, 11.30am-9pm Sat & Sun; ✗; ⓂDiamond Hill, exit C2) Tasty vegetarian food and a location behind a waterfall make dining here a superb way to begin or end your visit to Chi Lin Nunnery and Nan Lian Garden. The elegant Song Cha Xie (p148) nearby specialises in the art of Chinese tea drinking. Be sure to reserve ahead, especially on weekends.

CHEONG FAT
THAI, NOODLES $

(昌發泰國粉麵屋; ☑852 2382 5998; 27 South Wall Rd, Kowloon City; noodles from HK$30; ⏰noon-11.30pm) Blasting music videos in this hole-in-the-wall eatery set the rhythm as you slurp up the tasty Chiang Mai noodles. The open kitchen has appetising cooked dishes on display too, such as pork trotters with preserved vegetables. To get to Kowloon City, take minibus 25M from Kowloon Tong station (exit B2).

KOWLOON TANG
CHINESE, DIM SUM $$

(九龍廳; ☑852 2811 9398; www.kowloontang.com; 3rd fl, roof deck, Elements Mall, 1 Austin Rd W, Tsim Sha Tsui; meals HK$300-2000; ⏰noon-10.30pm; ✗; ⓂKowloon, exit U3) Sophisticated Kowloon Tang serves impeccable Cantonese dishes, including a few Dongguan classics, a laudable Peking duck and an impressive selection of Western-style desserts in an art deco-inspired setting.

> **LOCAL KNOWLEDGE**
> ## LEI YUE MUN VILLAGE
> Popular seafood venue Lei Yue Mun has around two dozen restaurants lining a winding road that overlooks a typhoon shelter. Once you've settled down in a restaurant, go outside and pick your dinner from one of the stalls with live seafood tanks, making sure you know how much you're paying and for what, before committing. The restaurant will take care of the rest. Expect to pay upwards of HK$800 per person for a meal.
>
> After leaving Yau Tong MTR station (exit A2), follow Cha Kwo Ling Rd and Shung Shun St south for 15 minutes or catch green minibus 24M from outside the station.

LUNG MUN SEAFOOD
RESTAURANT
SEAFOOD $$$

(龍門海鮮酒家; ☎852 2717 9886; www.lung
mun.com.hk; 20 Hoi Pong Rd W, Lei Yue Mun; meals
HK$800-2000; ⊙noon-10.30pm) Founded in
1967, this is one of the oldest and most ele-
gant restaurants in the seafood restaurant-
filled village of Lei Yue Mun (p145). Lobster
baked with cheese and fried mantis shrimp
with salt and pepper are the specialities.

LUNG YUE RESTAURANT
SEAFOOD $$$

(龍如海鮮酒樓; ☎852 2348 6332; 41 Hoi Pong
Rd Central, Lei Yue Mun; meals HK$800-2000;
⊙11.30am-11pm) A veteran restaurant in the
fishing village of Lei Yue Mun (p145), Lung
Yue is known for its skills in steaming fish
and abalone.

SEA KING GARDEN
RESTAURANT
SEAFOOD $$$

(海皇園林酒家; ☎852 2348 1408, 852 2348
1800; 39 Hoi Pong Rd Central, Lei Yue Mun; meals
HK$800-2000; ⊙noon-10pm; ⊕Lei Yue Mun) In
the fishing village of Lei Yue Mun (p145),
this restaurant has a dated feel with an in-
door garden and pool where turtles are kept.
Expect Cantonese seafood classics such as
grouper with garlic and ginger, and salt and
pepper fried shrimp.

ROBATAYAKI
JAPANESE $$$

(爐端燒日本餐廳; ☎852 2996 8438; http://
kowloon.harbourgrand.com; Ground fl, Harbour
Grand Kowloon Hotel, 2 Harbour Front, 22 Tak Fung
St, Whampoa Gardens, Hung Hom; lunch/dinner
from HK$350/500; ⊙noon-2pm & 6-10.30pm;
⊠minibus 5) At this farmhouse-style restaurant, Japanese skewers are grilled by chefs
seated on a wooden deck surrounded by a
display of fresh ingredients. To order, just
point at what you want; the chef will scoop
it up on a wooden paddle, cook it, and serve
it back to you on the same device. Minibus
5 from Hankow Rd (Tsim Sha Tsui) has a
final stop at Whampoa bus terminus. The
hotel's three-minute walk away.

🍷 DRINKING &
NIGHTLIFE

🍸 Tsim Sha Tsui

★INTERCONTINENTAL
LOBBY LOUNGE
BAR

Map p316 (☎852 2721 1211; www.hongkong-
ic.intercontinental.com; Hotel InterContinental
Hong Kong, 18 Salisbury Rd, Tsim Sha Tsui; ⊙7am-
12.30am; ☎; ⓂEast Tsim Sha Tsui, exit J) Soaring plate glass and an unbeatable waterfront location make this one of the best
spots to soak up the Hong Kong Island skyline and take in the busy harbour, although
you pay for the privilege. It's also an ideal
venue from which to watch the evening
light show at 8pm.

★AQUA
BAR

Map p314 (☎852 3427 2288; www.aqua.com.hk;
29 & 30th fl, 1 Peking Rd, Tsim Sha Tsui; ⊙4pm-
2am, happy hour 4-6pm; ☎; ⓂTsim Sha Tsui,
exit L5) When night falls, you'll know why
this uberfashionable bar has dim illumination and black furniture – the two-storey,
floor-to-ceiling windows command sweeping views of the Hong Kong Island skyline
that come to life after sundown. The tables
by the windows are awesome for bringing a
date. On the weekends, a DJ spins hip hop
and lounge jazz.

TAPAGRIA
BAR

Map p314 (☎852 2147 0111; www.tapagria.hk;
18th fl, The One, 100 Nathan Rd, Tsim Sha Tsui;
⊙noon-midnight Sun-Thu, to 1.30am Fri & Sat;
ⓂTsim Sha Tsui, exit A2) Less crowded than
many of Kowloon's 'million-dollar view'
bars, this slinky Spanish-inflected spot has
some three dozen different sangrias on the
menu, from a lychee and elderflower version made with Cava to one with chocolate
and banana liqueurs combined with straw-
berries. Get a patio table to take in the skyline from the 18th floor.

BUTLER
COCKTAIL BAR

Map p316 (☎852 2724 3828; 5th fl, Mody House,
30 Mody Rd, Tsim Sha Tsui; drinks around
HK$200; ⊙6.30pm-3am Mon-Fri, to 2am Sat &
Sun; ⓂEast Tsim Sha Tsui, exit N2) A cocktail
and whisky heaven hidden in the residential part of Tsim Sha Tsui. You can flip
through its whisky magazines as you watch
the experienced bartenders create magical
concoctions with the flair and precision of
a master mixologist in Ginza. We loved the
cocktails made from fresh citruses. A discreet and welcome addition to the Tsim Sha
Tsui drinking scene.

FELIX BAR
BAR

Map p314 (☎852 2315 3188; 28th fl, Peninsula Hong Kong, Salisbury Rd, Tsim Sha Tsui;
⊙5.30pm-1.30am; ⓂTsim Sha Tsui, exit E) Enjoy
the fabulous view at this Philippe Starck–
designed bar in Hong Kong's poshest hotel.
Even the bathrooms have beautiful views.

AMUSE BAR

Map p316 (☑852 2317 1988; 4 Austin Ave, Tsim Sha Tsui; ☺5pm-4am Mon-Fri, 6pm-4am Sat, 6pm-3am Sun; ☎; Ⓜ Jordan, exit D) An airy bistro-like bar frequented by white-collar locals and university students who come for their draught beers, decent wines and funky cocktails. The best seats are the leather couches next to a row of large windows; the communal table is great if you want to meet people, and the banquettes make for intimate tête-à-têtes.

TAPAS BAR BAR

Map p316 (☑852 2733 8756; www.shangri-la. com; Lobby, Kowloon Shangri-La, 64 Mody Rd, Tsim Sha Tsui; ☺3.30pm-1am Mon-Fri, from noon Sat & Sun; ☎; Ⓜ East Tsim Sha Tsui, exit P1) An intimate vibe and bistro-style decor make this a good place to unwind over champagne, tapas and the sports channel after a day of sightseeing. A table in the alfresco area will let you smoke and take in harbour views, visible beyond a river of cars.

VIBES LOUNGE

Map p314 (☑852 2315 5999; www.themirahotel. com; 5th fl, Mira Hong Kong, 118 Nathan Rd, Tsim Sha Tsui; ☺5pm-midnight Sun-Wed, 5pm-1am Thu-Sat; ☎; Ⓜ Tsim Sha Tsui, exit B1) This open-air lounge bar comes with plush seating, exotic cabanas and random greenery. You can take your pick from their 'molecular' cocktails, which feature liquid nitrogen and foam, or smoke a fruit-flavoured shisha. From 8pm daily (except Sunday), a resident DJ spins groovy tunes from his station.

UTOPIA BAR

Map p314 (☑852 3188 0816; 26th fl, Hon Kwok Jordon Centre, 7 Hillwood Rd, Tsim Sha Tsui; ☺5pm-2am Mon-Thu, to 3am Fri & Sat, to 1am Sun; ☎; Ⓜ Jordan, exit D) A favourite haunt of young local office workers, Utopia has good views but doesn't charge you for them. The drinks list of 50 Old and New World bottles, and draught beer, is also reasonably priced. There's a dart board if you're bored. Happy hour runs from 5pm to 9pm and midnight to late Monday to Thursday, plus all day Sunday.

NED KELLY'S LAST STAND PUB

Map p314 (☑852 2376 0562; 11A Ashley Rd, Tsim Sha Tsui; ☺11.30am-2am, happy hour 11.30am-9pm; Ⓜ Tsim Sha Tsui, exit L5) Named after a gun-toting Australian bushranger, Ned's is one of Hong Kong's oldest pubs. Most of the expat regulars here (and there are many) are drawn to the laid-back atmosphere and the Dixieland jazz band that plays and cracks jokes between songs. The bar is filled with old posters, rugby shirts and Oz-related paraphernalia.

KING LUDWIG BEER HALL BEER HALL

Map p316 (☑852 2369 8328; www.kingparrot. com; 32 Salisbury Rd, Tsim Sha Tsui; ☺noon-1am Sun-Thu, to 2am Fri & Sat; Ⓜ East Tsim Sha Tsui, exit K) This busy place with antler lighting fixtures is popular with visiting Germans and others hankering after fried pork knuckle and German beer on tap, including Maisel's Weiss. It's just under the Middle Road Children's Playground (p138).

🍴 Yau Ma Tei & Mong Kok

★**KUBRICK BOOKSHOP CAFÉ** CAFE

Map p318 (☑852 2384 8929; www.kubrick. hk; Shop H2, Prosperous Garden, 3 Public Square St, Yau Ma Tei; ☺11.30am-9.30pm; Ⓜ Yau Ma Tei, exit C) The airy bookshop-cafe attached to the Broadway Cinematheque (p149) serves decent coffee and simple eats, attracting an eclectic, arty crowd. While waiting for your cuppa, you can browse the shop's strong collection of art, film and cultural studies titles.

BOO BAR

Map p318 (☑852 2736 6168; 5th fl, Pearl Oriental Tower, 225 Nathan Rd, Jordan; ☺7pm-2am Sun-Thu, to 4am Fri, 9pm-4am Sat, happy hour 7-9pm; Ⓜ Jordan, exit C1) This low-key gay bar with a karaoke jukebox seems to attract huggable 'bear' types in the local gay community; there's a DJ every Saturday from 9pm.

KNOCKBOX COFFEE COMPANY COFFEE

Map p319 (☑852 2781 0363; http://knockbox coffee.hk; 21 Hak Po St, Mong Kok; ☺11am-10pm Mon-Thu, to 11pm Fri-Sun, last orders 9pm; ☎; Ⓜ Mong Kok, exit E) This tiny cafe in hectic Mong Kok offers good espresso-based coffees, and the baristas are ready to share their encyclopaedic knowledge of beans. If you're hungry, there's fish and chips, cakes and other cafe food.

🍴 New Kowloon

OZONE BAR

(☑852 2263 2263; www.ritzcarlton.com; 118th fl, ICC, 1 Austin Rd, Tsim Sha Tsui; ☺5pm-1am Mon-Wed, to 2am Thu, to 3am Fri, 3pm-3am Sat, noon-midnight Sun; 🛜; Ⓜ Kowloon, exit U3) Ozone is the highest bar in Asia. Its imaginative interiors, created to evoke a cyberesque Garden of Eden, have pillars resembling chocolate fountains in a hurricane and a myriad of refracted glass and colour-changing illumination. Equally dizzying is the wine list, with the most expensive bottle selling for over HK$150,000. Offers potential for a once-in-a-lifetime experience, in more ways than one.

Oh, that temptingly empty corner table? That's HK$10k just to sit there.

SONG CHA XIE TEA

(松茶榭; Pavilion of Pine & Tea; ☑ 852 3658 9390; 60 Fung Tak Rd, Nan Lian Garden; tea leaves from HK$150; ⊙ noon-6.30pm; Ⓜ Diamond Hill, exit C2) This elegant tea pavilion has long wooden corridors and intimate alcoves, which provide the serenity required for savouring good Chinese tea. Every table comes with a teapot, and the proper drinking utensils. If you're hungry, there are a couple of vegetarian dim sum on offer. The pavilion is inside Nan Lian Garden (p134).

ENTERTAINMENT

★ CANTON SINGING HOUSE LIVE MUSIC

Map p318 (艷陽天; 49-51 Temple St, Yau Ma Tei; HK$20; ⊙ 3-7pm & 8pm-5am; Ⓜ Yau Ma Tei, exit C) The oldest and most atmospheric of the singalong parlours, Canton resembles a film set with its mirror balls and glowing shrines. Each session features 20 singers, all with fan following. Patrons tip a minimum of HK$20 (per patron) if they like a song.

Even if you don't, it's nice to tip every now and then for the experience – just slip your money into a box on stage. For HK$100, you can sing a song.

★ HIDDEN AGENDA LIVE MUSIC

(☑ 852 9170 6073; www.hiddenagenda.hk; 2A, Wing Fu Industrial Bldg, 15-17 Tai Yip St, Kwun Tong; Ⓜ Ngau Tau Kok, exit B6) Hong Kong's best-known music dive has the setting (former warehouse), line-up (solid indie acts) and elusiveness (it's out of the way) all other dives wish they had. Located in the gritty industrial hub of Kwun Tong (about a five-block walk from the MTR), Hidden Agenda is synonymous with underground music. The entrance has a small metal gate that's open after-hours.

XXX LIVE MUSIC

Map p318 (☑ 852 9156 2330; www.xxxgallery.hk; Unit A, Kin Luen Factory Bldg, 89-91 Larch St, Tai Kok Tsui, Kowloon; Ⓜ Sheung Wan, exit A2) This underground arts space features bare concrete and indie music performances, as well as art exhibitions. Opening hours are irregular. Check the website for upcoming events.

DADA LIVE MUSIC

Map p316 (www.dadalounge.com.hk; 2nd fl, Luxe Manor, 39 Kimberley Rd, Tsim Sha Tsui; ⊙ 11am-2am Mon-Sat, to 1am Sun; 🛜; Ⓜ Tsim Sha Tsui, exit B1) Upstairs in a quirky hotel, Dada is an intimate cocktail bar decked out with florid wallpaper, plush velvet seats and a couple of Dalí-esque paintings. Jazz and blues bands play to a professional mid-30s crowd a few times a month.

JYUT WAN GO ZO LIVE MUSIC

Map p318 (粵韻歌座; Yuèyùn Gēzuò; 53-57 Temple St, Yau Ma Tei; HK$20; ⊙ 3.30-7.30pm & 8pm-4am; Ⓜ Yau Ma Tei, exit C) This long-standing singalong place is large and slightly shabby, but the women here are sweet and persuasive. For HK$50, you can make a dedication or sing with them.

TONGTHREE LIVE MUSIC

Map p319 (妖物唐三; https://www.facebook.com/tongthree; 2nd fl, 716 Shanghai St, Mong Kok; Ⓜ Prince Edward, exit C2) This atmospheric studio and artists' hideout on the 3rd floor of a Chinese tenement building, or *tong lau*, stages cultural events several times a month. Its charming turn-of-the-century setting is the backdrop for live gigs, poetry readings, dance performances and movie screenings. See the Facebook page for the latest.

LEE SHAU KEI SCHOOL OF CREATIVITY ARTS CENTRE LIVE PERFORMANCE

(香港兆基創意書院文化藝術中心; www.creativehk.edu.hk/artscentre; 135 Junction Rd, Kowloon City; 🚌 11D, 11K, 75K, 85, 891, Ⓜ Lok Fu, exit B) This out-of-the-way performance-arts academy has a rich cultural program that covers music, film and a book fair. Though some events are meant for students, many are professional and interestingly experimental in nature, such as noise concerts by internationally renowned artists. See the calendar online for what's on.

ON AND ON THEATRE WORKSHOP THEATRE

(前進進戲劇工作坊; ☑ 852 2503 1630; www.onandon.org.hk; Unit 7, Cattle Depot Artist Village,

TEMPLE STREET'S SINGALONG PARLOURS

A highlight of Yau Ma Tei is its old-fashioned singalong parlours (歌廳). These origi-
nated 20 years ago to offer shelter to street singers on rainy days.

Most parlours have basic set-ups – tables, a stage and Christmas lights for an
upbeat atmosphere. All have their own organist and a troupe of freelance singers –
women who'll keep you company and persuade you to make a dedication or sing along
with them for a fee. Their repertoire ranges from Chinese operatic extracts to English
oldies. You'll see many regulars at these places – kooky types from the neighbourhood; old men who drink from whisky flasks and know all the dames...

It's more fun to go after 9pm. As parlours don't provide food, you're welcome to
order delivery. Some sell beer but you can also get your own from convenience stores.

63 Ma Tau Kok Rd, To Kwa Wan; 🚌106, 12A, 5C,
101, 111) This independent theatre group at
the Cattle Depot Artist Village (p140) puts
on thought-provoking works by local and
international playwrights and runs workshops for professional actors. Their website
has more.

HONG KONG CULTURAL
CENTRE   THEATRE, MUSIC
Map p314 (香港文化中心; www.lcsd.gov.hk; 10
Salisbury Rd, Tsim Sha Tsui; ⊙9am-11pm; 🚇; Ⓜ East
Tsim Sha Tsui, exit L6) Hong Kong's premier arts
performance venue, this world-class cultural
centre contains a 2085-seat concert hall with
an impressive Rieger pipe organ, plus two
theatres and rehearsal studios.

BROADWAY CINEMATHEQUE   CINEMA
Map p318 (百老匯電影中心; ☑852 2388 3188;
Ground fl, Prosperous Gardens, 3 Public Square St,
Yau Ma Tei; Ⓜ Yau Ma Tei, exit C) The place for
new art-house releases and rerun screenings. The Kubrick Bookshop Café (p147)
next door serves decent coffee and simple
meals.

🛍 SHOPPING

🛍 Tsim Sha Tsui

⭐ K11 SELECT   ACCESSORIES, CLOTHING
Map p316 (Shop 101, K11 Mall, 18 Hanoi Rd, Tsim
Sha Tsui; ⊙10am-10pm) In the K11 (p149)
mall, this shop gathers the best of Hong
Kong designers in one spot. Look for theatrical clothing from Daydream Nation,
founded by a pair of Hong Kong siblings,
and unisex accessories from Kapok.

⭐ RISE SHOPPING
ARCADE   CLOTHING
Map p316 (利時商場; 5-11 Granville Circuit,
Tsim Sha Tsui; ⊙3-9pm; Ⓜ Tsim Sha Tsui, exit
B2) Bursting the seams of this minimall is
cheap streetwear from Hong Kong, Korea
and Japan, with a few knock-offs chucked
in for good measure. Patience and a good
eye could land you purchases fit for a Vogue
photo shoot. It's best visited between 4pm
and 8.30pm when most of the shops are
open.

K11 ART MALL   MALL
Map p316 (18 Hanoi Rd, Tsim Sha Tsui; Ⓜ East Tsim
Sha Tsui, exit D2) With international clothing
and accessories brands plus some edgier
local offerings, K11 features exhibition
spaces for local artists, hence its 'art mall'
title. The basement is a sweet-lover's paradise, with a global array of chocolate shops.
It's right above the MTR station.

SWINDON BOOKS   BOOKS
Map p314 (☑852 2366 8001; www.swindonbooks.
com/; 13-15 Lock Rd, Tsim Sha Tsui; ⊙9am-6pm
Mon-Fri, to 1pm Sat; Ⓜ Tsim Sha Tsui, exit A1) This
is one of the best locally run bookshops in
the city, with an excellent range and knowledgeable staff. Strong on local books and
history in particular.

HARBOUR CITY   MALL
Map p314 (www.harbourcity.com.hk; 3-9 Canton
Rd, Tsim Sha Tsui; ⊙10am-10pm; Ⓜ Tsim Sha Tsui,
exit C1) This is an enormous place, with 700
shops, 50 food and beverage outlets and
five cinemas. Outlets are arrayed in four
separate zones: for kids, sport, fashion, and
cosmetics and beauty. Almost every major
brand is represented. Massively crowded on
weekends.

CURIO ALLEY
GIFTS & SOUVENIRS

Map p314 (btwn Lock & Hankow Rds,Tsim Sha Tsui; ⏰10am-8pm; Ⓜ Tsim Sha Tsui, exit C1) This is a fun place to rummage for name chops, soapstone carvings, fans and other Chinese bric-a-brac. It's found in an alleyway between Lock and Hankow Rds, just south of Haiphong Rd.

HEAVEN PLEASE
CLOTHING

Map p316 (☎852 2311 9533; www.heavenplease. com; 7th fl, Kolling Centre, 77-79 Granville Rd, Tsim Sha Tsui; ⏰1-9pm Mon-Sat, 2-8pm Sun; Ⓜ Tsim Sha Tsui, exit B2) Lady Gaga meets punk Lolita at this fun place. The designers are liberal with the lace and the '80s glam. Even if you don't want the whole rack on you, the pieces will add whimsical touches to any classic wardrobe. Stiff-collars and strait-jackets won't be caught dead here, but who needs them anyway? Building entrance on Chatham Rd South.

PREMIER JEWELLERY
JEWELLERY

Map p314 (愛寶珠寶有限公司; ☎852 2368 0003; Shop G14-15, ground fl, Holiday Inn Golden Mile Shopping Mall, 50 Nathan Rd, Tsim Sha Tsui; ⏰10am-7.30pm Mon-Sat, to 4pm Sun; Ⓜ Tsim Sha Tsui, exit G) This third-generation family firm is directed by a qualified gemologist and is one of our favourite places to shop. The range isn't huge but if you're looking for something particular, give Premier Jewellery a day's notice and a selection will be ready in time for your arrival. Staff can also help you design your own piece.

BIZET
SHOES

Map p316 (☎852 3621 0878; www.bizetleather. com; Room 1610, 16th fl, Beverley Commercial Centre, 87-105 Chatham Rd S, Tsim Sha Tsui; ⏰11.30am-7.45pm Mon-Fri, 12.30-7pm Sat; Ⓜ Tsim Sha Tsui, exit B2) Everyone has heard of Gucci, but Italy also makes chic, hand-crafted footwear for the mid-market that is little known overseas. Bizet's owner orders quality shoes directly from Italian artisans for her small, but exquisite, women's collection. Everything from ballerina flats and Oxfords to peek-a-boo sandals and combat boots at prices modest for the '100% made in Italy' label.

BROWN'S TAILOR
CLOTHING

Map p314 (☎852 3996 8654; www.brownstailor. com; Unit E, 2nd fl, Comfort Bldg, 88 Nathan Rd, Tsim Sha Tsui; ⏰11am-7pm Mon-Fri, to 6.30pm Sat; Ⓜ Tsim Sha Tsui, exit B1) Chic Brown's

Tailor belongs to a new generation of bespoke tailoring shops for men. They're adept at both making traditional gentlemen's attire and instilling modern elements into a classic look. Depending on the fabric used, a suit can cost you anywhere between HK$4200 and HK$18,000.

🏠 Yau Ma Tei & Mong Kok

⭐ SHANGHAI STREET
MARKET

Map p318 (上海街; Yau Ma Tei; Ⓜ Yau Ma Tei, exit C) Wander Kowloon's kitchen district for food-related souvenirs such as wooden mooncake moulds, chopsticks, woks and ceramic teapots.

⭐ LADIES' MARKET
MARKET

Map p319 (通菜街, 女人街; Tung Choi Street Market; Tung Choi St; ⏰noon-11.30pm; Ⓜ Mong Kok, exit D3) The Tung Choi Street market is a cheek-by-jowl affair offering cheap clothes and trinkets. Vendors start setting up their stalls as early as noon, but it's best to get here between 1pm and 6pm when there's much more on offer. Beware, the sizes stocked here tend to suit the lissom Asian frame. A terrific place to soak up local atmosphere.

⭐ YUE HWA CHINESE PRODUCTS EMPORIUM
DEPARTMENT STORE

Map p318 (裕華國貨; ☎852 3511 2222; www.yue hwa.com; 301-309 Nathan Rd, Jordan; ⏰10am-10pm; Ⓜ Jordan, exit A) This five-storey behemoth is one of the few old-school Chinese department stores left in the city. Gets here include silk scarves, traditional Chinese baby clothes and embroidered slippers, jewellery both cheap and expensive, pretty patterned chopsticks and ceramics, plastic acupuncture models and calligraphy equipment (to name a few). The top floor is all about tea, with various vendors offering free sips. Food is in the basement.

⭐ CHAN WAH KEE CUTLERY STORE
HOMEWARES

Map p318 (陳華記刀莊; ☎852 2730 4091; 278D Temple St, Yau Ma Tei; ⏰11am-6pm Thu-Tue; Ⓜ Jordan, exit C2) At this humble shop, octogenarian Mr Chan, one of Asia's few remaining master knife-sharpeners, uses nine different stones to grind each blade, and alternates between water and oil. If you bring him your blade, he charges between

HK$100 and HK$600 with a three-month wait. But if you buy from him, and he has a great selection, he'll do it there and then.

Prices range from HK$200 for a small paring knife to around HK$2000 for a Shun knife. His customers include chefs, butchers, tailors and homemakers from all over the world. He's had clients send him Japanese willow knives for his magic touch. Choppers, cleavers, slicers, paring knives, even scissors – he's done them all. Find his shop close to Bowring St.

HONG KONG READER
BOOKS

Map p319 (序言書室; ☎852 2395 0031; www. hkreaders.com; 7th fl, 68 Sai Yeung Choi St S, Mong Kok; ⊙2pm-midnight; MMong Kok, exit D3) Run by a handful of young people, this is a bilingual bookstore-cafe with an intellectual bent. If you're looking for the likes of Derrida or Milosz, this is the place to go. Check the website for the latest literary readings, though most are conducted in Cantonese. Hong Kong Reader is above a 1010 telecommunications shop.

APLIU STREET FLEA MARKET
MARKET

(鴨寮街; Apliu St, btwn Nam Cheong & Yen Chow Sts, Sham Shui Po; ⊙noon-midnight; MSham Shui Po, exit A1) A geek's heaven, this flea market specialises in all things digital and electronic. The market spills over into Pei Ho St.

JADE MARKET
MARKET

Map p318 (玉器市場; Battery St & Kansu St, Yau Ma Tei; ⊙10am-6pm; MYau Ma Tei, exit C) The covered Jade Market, split into two parts by Battery St, has hundreds of stalls selling all varieties and grades of jade. But unless you really know your nephrite from your jadeite, it's not wise to buy expensive pieces here. Some of the best gets here are not jade at all, but pretty, vintage-y ceramic bead necklaces and bracelets, or coloured wooden beads with double happiness signs.

TAK HING DRIED SEAFOOD
FOOD

Map p318 (德興海味; ☎852 2780 2129; 1 Woo Sung St, Yau Ma Tei; ⊙9am-7.30pm; MYau Ma Tei, exit C) One of the very few honest dried-seafood stores in the area, this delightful old corner establishment has glass jars stuffed with dried scallops, crocodile meat and bird's nests, though you might prefer the figs, cashews, candied lotus seeds and ginseng.

SINO CENTRE
MALL

Map p318 (信和中心; 582-592 Nathan Rd, Mong Kok; ⊙10am-10pm; MYau Ma Tei, exit A2) This shabby go-to place for all things related to Asian animation and comics gives a taste of local culture. Its tiny shops carry new and back issues of Japanese manga, action figures, retro video games and other kidult bait that attracts a largely male following.

SIN TAT PLAZA
MALL

Map p319 (83 Argyle St, Mong Kok; ⊙11am-10pm; MMong Kok, exit D2) Popular with locals, Sin Tat Plaza on busy Argyle St is dedicated to mobile phones of all persuasions, including a Chinese-made phone that doubles as a lighter! It's also where you go to get your phone fixed and unlocked.

LANGHAM PLACE MALL
MALL

Map p319 (朗豪坊; ☎852 3520 2800; www.lang hamplace.com.hk/en/; 8 Argyle St, Mong Kok; ⊙11am-11pm; MMong Kok, exit C3) This 15-storey supermall has some 300 shops that stay open till as late as 11pm, making it popular with local teens. Smaller, funkier, more local brands occupy the top floors, with bigger names down below. The focal point of the mall is the high-tech Digital Sky, where special events take place.

MONG KOK COMPUTER CENTRE
ELECTRONICS

Map p319 (旺角電腦中心; www.mongkokcc. com/; 8-8A Nelson St, Mong Kok; ⊙1-10pm; MMong Kok, exit D3) Prices at this computer mall are cheap but language can be a barrier, and you'll see more finished products than computer components.

PROTREK
SPORTS & OUTDOORS

Map p318 (保捷行; www.protrek.com.hk; 5 Tung Fong St, Yau Ma Tei; ⊙11.30am-9pm; MYau Ma Tei, exit C) This reliable shop with branches all over town is arguably your best bet for outdoor gear that will see you through from sea to summit. It runs training courses on outdoor activities as well. The English-speaking staff is very helpful.

New Kowloon

★GOLDEN COMPUTER ARCADE & GOLDEN SHOPPING CENTER
ELECTRONICS

(黃金電腦商場, 高登電腦中心; www.golden arcade.org; 146-152 Fuk Wa St, Sham Shui Po; ⊙11am-9pm; MSham Shui Po, exit D2) Occupying different floors of a building opposite Sham Shui Po MTR station, these are *the* places to go for low-cost computers and peripherals. Golden Computer Arcade comprises the basement and ground floor; Golden Shopping Centre, the 1st floor. The 3Cs are generally considered the best shops – Centralfield (Golden Shopping Centre), Capital (Golden Computer Arcade) and Comdex (both places).

CHEUNG SHA WAN ROAD   MARKET
(長沙灣道; Cheung Sha Wan Rd, Sham Shui Po; ⊙10am-6.30pm Mon-Fri, to 4pm Sat; MSham Shui Po, exit C1) This long road is a riot of shops selling fabrics, trimmings, buttons, ribbons and other raw materials, as well as prêt-à-porter clothing. You'll bump into fashion designers here.

VIVIENNE TAM   FASHION & ACCESSORIES
(☑852 2265 8381; www.viviennetam.com; LG1 Shop 05, Festival Walk, Kowloon Tong; ⊙11am-8.30pm Sun-Thu, to 9pm Fri & Sat; MKowloon Tong, exit C2) This enduring brand from New York–based designer Tam, who was trained in Hong Kong, sells eminently wearable, feminine – but also streetwise – women's foundation pieces, light gossamer dresses and slinky tops, plus a range of accessories.

ELEMENTS   MALL
(圓方; www.elementshk.com; 1 Austin Rd W, West Kowloon; ⊙11am-9pm; MKowloon, exit U3) Inside the ICC (p136), Kowloon's most upmarket shopping mall comprises five pleasant sections each decorated according to one of the five natural elements. Other thoughtful touches include good nursing facilities and helpful staff. Austin Rd West is an area built on reclaimed land that's connected to Austin Rd in Tsim Sha Tsui at its eastern end.

SPORTS & ACTIVITIES

COUNTRY & MARINE PARKS
AUTHORITY   PARK
(☑852 2150 6868; www.afcd.gov.hk/english/country/cou_vis/cou_vis.html) Has information about visiting Hong Kong's various country and marine parks.

HONG KONG
DOLPHINWATCH   WILDLIFE WATCHING
Map p314 (香港海豚觀察; ☑852 2984 1414; www.hkdolphinwatch.com; 15th fl, Middle Block,

1528A Star House, 3 Salisbury Rd, Tsim Sha Tsui; adult/child HK$420/210; ⊙cruises Wed, Fri & Sun) Hong Kong Dolphinwatch was founded in 1995 to raise awareness of Hong Kong's wonderful pink dolphins and promote responsible ecotourism. It offers 2½-hour cruises to see them in their natural habitat. About 97% of the cruises result in the sighting of at least one dolphin; if none are spotted, passengers are offered a free trip.

WATER TOURS   BOATING
Map p314 (☑852 2926 3868; www.watertours.com.hk; 6th fl Carnarvon Plaza, 20 Carnarvon Rd, Tsim Sha Tsui) Offers six different tours of the harbour on junk-style boats, as well as dinner and cocktail cruises. Prices range from HK$260 (HK$170 for children aged two to 12 years) for the Morning Harbour Cruise, to HK$350 (HK$260 for children) for the Symphony of Lights Cruise and HK$900 (HK$700 for children) for the Aberdeen Dinner Cruise.

BIG BUS COMPANY   BUS
Map p314 (☑852 3102 9021; www.bigbustours.com; Unit KP-38, 1st fl, Star Ferry Pier, Tsim Sha Tsui; adult/child from HK$450/400; ⊙9am-6pm) A good way to get your bearings in the city is on the hop-on, hop-off, open-topped double-deckers. Three tours are available: the Kowloon Route takes in much of the Tsim Sha Tsui and Hung Hom waterfront; the Hong Kong Island Route explores Central, Admiralty, Wan Chai and Causeway Bay; and the Green Tour goes to Stanley Market and Aberdeen.

PENINSULA ACADEMY   COURSE
Map p314 (☑852 2696 6693; www.peninsula.com; The Peninsula, Salisbury Rd, Tsim Sha Tsui; dim-sum class HK$2000; MTsim Sha Tsui) Offers various luxury classes, from traditional Chinese arts and crafts to understanding fashion. Especially popular is a 1½-hour dim sum–making class, which includes lunch.

WING CHUN YIP MAN MARTIAL ARTS
ATHLETIC ASSOCIATION   MARTIAL ARTS
Map p314 (葉問國術總會; ☑852 2723 2306; www.yipmanwingchunasso.com; 54 3/F Mirador Mansion, 58 Nathan Rd, Tsim Sha Tsui; MTsim Sha Tsui, exit E) The cost for three lessons a week (two or three hours each) for a month is HK$500. A six-month intensive course (six hours a day, six days a week) is around HK$5000, depending on the student.

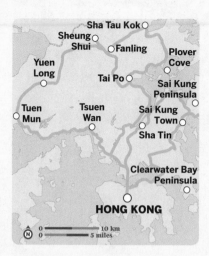

Sha Tau Kok
Sheung Shui
Fanling
Plover Cove
Yuen Long
Tai Po
Sai Kung Peninsula
Tuen Mun
Tsuen Wan
Sai Kung Town
Sha Tin
Clearwater Bay Peninsula
HONG KONG

0   10 km
0   5 miles

New Territories

Tsuen Wan p156
Home to some of Hong Kong's most important monasteries.

Tuen Mun p158
Visit at leisure the temples and monasteries that dot the landscape.

Yuen Long p159
Hong Kong Wetland Park, laid-back Pak Nai and old walled villages.

Fanling & Sheung Shui p161
A heaven for history buffs, with fortified villages and historic ruins.

Tai Po p163
Lively markets and temples, plus an encyclopaedia of flora and fauna.

Plover Cove p165
Plover Cove is where you go to hike, hike, hike or bike, bike, bike!

Sha Tin p166
A New Town with a historical feel, temples and a heritage museum.

Sai Kung Peninsula p169
Beautiful beaches and deserted coves, and half of Hong Kong Global Geopark.

Clearwater Bay Peninsula p172
The name says it all – beaches with crystal-clear water.

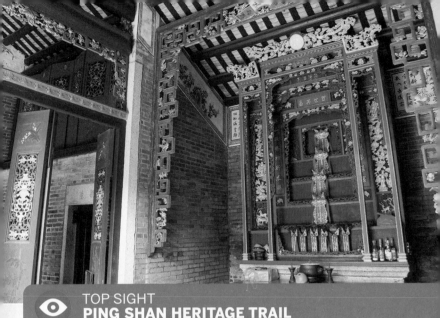

TOP SIGHT
PING SHAN HERITAGE TRAIL

This meandering 1km trail through three old but lively villages in northwestern New Territories features 12 thoughtfully restored historic buildings and a museum at Ping Shan dedicated to the powerful Tang clan, the founders of the spectacular 500-year-old Ping Shan village. The Tangs are believed to be some of the Hong Kong's earliest immigrants.

Start with the **Ping Shan Tang Clan Gallery** (屏山鄧族文物館; ☎852 2617 1959; Hang Tau Tsuen, Ping Shan, Yuen Long; ⏰10am-5pm Tue-Sun; ☒Ping Shan) FREE at the eastern end of the trail. Housed in a former police station, the gallery showcases the history of the Tangs. The colourful collections include a traditional sedan chair, ritual wares and a giant wooden bed. The building itself was constructed in 1899 and was a colonial outpost to monitor 'untoward' villagers.

Leaving the Tang Clan Gallery, retrace your steps to Ping Ha Rd and turn right. The small **Hung Shing Temple** is on your right-hand side, followed by **Ching Shu Hin Chamber** and **Kun Ting Study Hall** when you turn right again.

North of Hung Shing Temple, Shu Hin Chamber and Kun Ting Study Hall are the Tang Clan Ancestral Hall (p160) and **Yu Kiu Ancestral Hall**, two of Hong Kong's largest ancestral halls. The Tangs justifiably brag about them, especially the one that bears their name, as it follows a three-halls-two-courtyards structure indicative of the clan's prestigious status in the imperial court.

There are some more temples and an old well ahead. At the end of the heritage trail is small, three-storey **Tsui Sing Lau Pagoda** (聚星樓; Ping Ha Rd, Ping Shan Heritage Trail; ⏰9am-1pm, 2-5pm Wed-Sun; ☒Tin Shui Wai) FREE, the only surviving ancient pagoda in Hong Kong.

DON'T MISS

➡ Ping Shan Tang Clan Gallery

➡ Tang Clan Ancestral Hall

➡ Yu Kiu Ancestral Hall

PRACTICALITIES

➡ 屏山文物徑

➡ ☎852 2617 1959

➡ Hang Tau Tsuen, Ping Shan, Yuen Long

➡ ⏰ancestral halls & Tsui Sing Lau Pagoda 9am-1pm & 2-5pm Wed-Mon

➡ Ⓜ Tin Shui Wai, exit E

HONG KONG GLOBAL GEOPARK

The breathtaking, Unesco-listed Hong Kong Global Geopark (p155) spans 50 sq km across the eastern and northeastern New Territories and comprises two regions of spectacular rock formations – volcanic (140 million years) and sedimentary (400 million years ago). The best way to experience either region is by joining a guided boat tour. R2G, the Recommended Geopark Guide System (http://hkr2g.net), has more information.

The beautiful Sai Kung Volcanic Rock Region features interlocking hexagonal volcanic rock columns with a honeycomb-shaped cross-section lined up in tilting clusters like fingers pointing at the sky. They may cover an entire rock face like the pipes of a giant organ, or stick out above a secluded bay like a metaphor for the city.

The formations are similar to the grey basaltic lava formations in Giant's Causeway in Northern Ireland, but Hong Kong's acidic, silica-rich rocks are a luminous yellow, which is rare and looks stunning against the blue of the sea and, on a sunny day, the sky.

The columns were made by lava and volcanic ash that cooled and contracted after violent volcanic eruptions in the Cretaceous Period. In some places, including this region's only walkable section at High Island Reservoir East Dam (p172), you can see rocks buckled by gravity before they managed to cool completely.

You'll also get to visit old villages, including 400-year-old Hakka walled village **Lai Chi Wo** (荔枝窩; hakkahomelcw@gmail.com).

DON'T MISS

➡ Sea stacks and sea arches
➡ Red siltstone and secluded islands

PRACTICALITIES

➡ 香港地質公園
➡ www.geopark.gov.hk

Tsuen Wan

Explore

The industrial and residential New Town of Tsuen Wan is nothing special, but its outskirts can be rewarding, especially if you are an early bird.

Eating yum cha in the morning at one of the teahouses in Chuen Lung village is an experience. After breakfast, hikers usually continue up to Tai Mo Shan Country Park. If you want to see vibrant temples, head back to the town centre and take a minibus bound for the serene Western Monastery and colourful Yuen Yuen Institute, the latter stuffed with all manner of deities; or make a pilgrimage to Chuk Lam Sim Monastery.

Do not miss the Hakka-themed Sam Tung Uk Museum before you head back to the MTR station.

The Best...

⇒**Sight** Western Monastery (p156)

⇒**Place to Sleep** Campus Hong Kong (p226)

⇒**Place to Eat** Yue Kee Roasted Goose Restaurant (p158)

Top Tip

Tak Wah Park in the centre of town, with ancient trees and footbridges over ponds, is an ideal spot to take a break from the hustle and bustle of Tsuen Wan.

Getting There & Away

⇒**Bus** Many buses from around the New Territories arrive at **Tsuen Wan Bus Terminus** (under Tsuen Wan West MTR station; MTsuen Wan West, exit A1), including bus 60M from Tuen Mun and 68M from Yuen Long. **Bus 51** (on Tai Ho Rd overpass, Tsuen Wan; MTsuen Wan, exit A1) from Tai Mo Shan and Kam Tin stops along Tai Ho Rd. The main bus station is opposite the MTR on Castle Peak Rd (exit A2), but buses and green minibuses, including **minibus 80** (Chuen Lung St, Tsuen Wan; MTsuen Wan, exit B1) and **minibuses 81 and 85** (Shiu Wo St, Tsuen Wan; MTsuen Wan, exit B1) pick up and disgorge passengers throughout the New Town.

⇒**MTR** Tsuen Wan MTR station is on the Tsuen Wan line; it's on Sai Lau Kok Rd, with the Luk Yeung Galleria shopping centre above it. Tsuen Wan West station is on the West Rail line.

Need to Know

⇒**Area Code** ⏺852

⇒**Location** 11km northwest of Kowloon Peninsula

⇒**Last train to Kowloon** Leaves 2.30am from Tsuen Wan station; 12.24am from Tsuen Wan West station.

⊙ SIGHTS

WESTERN MONASTERY   BUDDHIST MONASTERY
(西方寺; ⏺852 2411 5111; Lo Wai Rd, Sam Dip Tam, Tsuen Wan; ⏱8.30am-5.30pm; ☒green minibus 81) **FREE** This Buddhist monastery built in the '70s is a tranquil spot in which to pass the time. The main building, styled as a Chinese palace, lies behind a statue of the Bodhisattva at the entrance. Further behind is a two-storey building where, depending on the time of day, you may witness scores of monks chanting mantras. It's topped by a nine-storey pagoda, which, like the rest of the complex, calls to mind a set from a period movie.

To reach the monastery, take minibus 81 from Shiu Wo St. A taxi from the MTR station will cost around HK$50.

YUEN YUEN INSTITUTE   RELIGIOUS CENTRE
(圓玄學院; ⏺852 2492 2220; Lo Wai Rd, Sam Dip Tam, Tsuen Wan; ⏱8.30am-5pm; ☒green minibus 81) **FREE** Stuffed with vivid statuary of Taoist and Buddhist deities plus Confucian saints, the Yuen Yuen Institute, in the hills northeast of Tsuen Wan, gives a fascinating look into Hong Kong's tripartite religious system. The main building is a replica of the Temple of Heaven in Běijīng. On the upper ground floor are three Taoist immortals seated in a quiet hall; walk down to the lower level to watch as crowds of faithful pray and burn offerings to the 60 incarnations of Taoist saints lining the walls.

To reach the institute, take minibus 81 from Shiu Wo St, two blocks due south of Tsuen Wan MTR station (exit B1). A taxi from the MTR station will cost around HK$50.

CHUK LAM SIM MONASTERY   BUDDHIST MONASTERY
(竹林禪苑; ⏺852 2416 6557; Fu Yung Shan Rd, Tsuen Wan; ⏱9am-5pm; ☒green minibus 85) In a bucolic setting, the large Chuk Lam Sim (Bamboo Forest) Monastery was completed in 1932 when (legend has it) Tou Tei, the earth god, told an elderly monk to build it,

Tsuen Wan

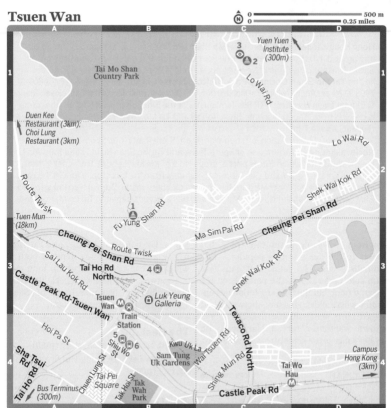

and he carved it out of a hillside with six disciples. The second hall features three of the largest golden Buddhas in the territory. Locals come to worship the four-faced Brahma (Phra Phrom) statue from Thailand, going round in circles in prayer – clockwise or anti-clockwise depending on the request.

The monastery is northeast of Tsuen Wan MTR station. To reach it, take green minibus 85 from Shiu Wo St.

✖ EATING

CHOI LUNG
RESTAURANT CANTONESE, CHA CHAAN TANG $
(彩龍茶樓; ☑852 2415 5041; 2 Chuen Lung village, Route Twisk; dim sum from HK$12; ⏰5.30am-3pm; ☐minibus 80 from Tsuen Wan) This 40-year-old establishment near the village entrance uses spring water to make tofu dessert. It's self-service – pick your dim sum from the kitchen, make your tea, and

Tsuen Wan

plonk yourself down on a plastic stool. The best time to go is between 8am and 10am when the widest choices are available and the bustling atmosphere makes you feel you're starting the day right.

DUEN KEE
RESTAURANT CANTONESE, CHA CHAAN TANG $
(端記茶樓; ☑852 2490 5246; 57-58 Chuen Lung village, Route Twisk; dim sum from HK$12; ⏰6am-2pm; ☐minibus 80 from Tsuen Wan) Not

TAI MO SHAN

Hong Kong's tallest mountain is Tai Mo Shan (957m). Several hiking trails thread up and around it, but you'll need to bring your own food and water. The Countryside Series *North-east & Central New Territories* map is the one you want for this area.

The **Tai Mo Shan Country Park Visitor Centre** (大帽山郊野公園遊客中心; ☎852 2498 9326; cnr Route Twisk & Tai Mo Shan Rd; ⏰9.30am-4.30pm Mon, Wed-Sun, closed Tue; 🚌51 from Tsuen Wan West MTR Bus Terminus) is at the junction of Route Twisk (the name is derived from 'Tsuen Wan into Shek Kong') and Tai Mo Shan Rd, which is crossed by the MacLehose Trail.

The nearest MTR station is Tsuen Wan. From there, catch bus 51 on Tai Ho Rd North, alighting at the junction of Route Twisk and Tai Mo Shan Rd in Tsuen Kam Au. Follow Tai Mo Rd, which forms part of stage No 9 of the MacLehose Trail, east to the summit. On the right-hand side, about 45 minutes from the bus stop, a fork in the road leads south along a concrete path to the Sze Lok Yuen Hostel. Bus 64 also links Tai Mo Shan with Yuen Long and Tai Po Market, and bus 25K runs between Tai Po Market and Tai Mo Shan.

far from Choi Lung Restaurant (p157) but closer to the fields is this popular – and no-frills – yum-cha joint. You can have dim sum under one of the parasols on the ground floor, but the true attraction lies upstairs where older villagers show off their caged birds while sipping tea. The homegrown watercress served blanched with oyster sauce is the signature vegetable here.

⭐**YUE KEE ROASTED GOOSE RESTAURANT**   CANTONESE $$
(裕記大飯店; ☎852 2491 0105; www.yuekee.com.hk/en; 9 Sham Hong Rd, Sham Tseng; meals HK$150-500; ⏰11am-11pm; 🚌minibus 302 from Tai Wo Hau MTR) In an alley lined with roast-goose restaurants, 54-year-old Yue Kee is king. Order gorgeous plates of coppery-skinned charcoal-roasted goose (half is plenty for four people) and sample house specialities including soy-braised goose web (feet), wine-infused goose liver, and stir-fried goose intestines. If that's not your speed, there are plenty of standard Cantonese dishes on offer. Book ahead.

Tuen Mun

Explore

Industrial-residential Tuen Mun is not a particularly attractive part of Hong Kong, but several historic temples make it worth the trek. If you want to stretch your legs, walk uphill to Tsing Shan Monastery and enjoy the sweeping views of Tuen Mun

Valley; lazybones can head to Miu Fat Monastery and Ching Chung Temple, both of which are conveniently served by light rail.

Foodwise, try the local speciality, roast goose, in the neighbourhood of Shem Tseng, or seafood along the coast.

The Best...

➡**Sight** Tsing Shan Monastery (p159)
➡**Place to Eat** Sam Shing Hui Seafood Market (p159)

Top Tip

If you're travelling to Tuen Mun from Tsuen Wan, Kowloon or Hong Kong Island by bus, sit on the upper deck on the left side for spectacular views of the Tsing Ma Bridge.

Getting There & Away

➡**Bus** Bus 60M from Tsuen Wan MTR station (exit A3) travels along the coast to Tuen Mun.

➡**Ferry** Services to Tuen Mun ferry pier arrive from Tung Chung, Sha Lo Wan and Tai O (all on Lantau). Ferries to the airport, Tung Chung and Tai O on Lantau depart from the pier to the southwest of the town centre.

➡**Light Rail** Tuen Mun is towards the southern end of the useful light-rail network. Other major points include Tin Shui Wai, Yuen Long and Siu Hong. The station is linked to the MTR station.

➡**MTR** Tuen Mun is on the West Rail line.

Need to Know
➡ **Area Code** ☑852
➡ **Location** 30km northwest of Kowloon Peninsula
➡ **Last train to Kowloon** Leaves 12.15am from Tuen Mun West Rail station.

SIGHTS

TSING SHAN MONASTERY   BUDDHIST MONASTERY
(青山禪院; ☑852 2441 6666; www.tsingshan monastery.org.hk; Tsing Shan Monastery Path; ⊙24hr; 🚈610, 615, 615P) Also known as Castle Peak Monastery, this temple complex perched on the hill of Castle Peak is the oldest in Hong Kong. Founded by Reverend Pui To (literally, 'travelling in a cup') 1500 years ago, the complex you see today was rebuilt in 1926. Check out shrines and temples for different deities and Bodhisattvas, including one to Pui To in a grotto, as you ascend the hill. Some of these have slid into dilapidation; nonetheless they're imbued with a spooky charm.

The temple was also one of the shooting locations for the Bruce Lee classic *Enter the Dragon*. To reach here, board light-rail line 610, 615 or 615P and alight at Tsing Shan Tsuen. From there, follow the sign to Tsing Shan Monastery Path, which is due west of the station. The steep path to the entrance of the monastery is a 30-minute hike.

MIU FAT MONASTERY   BUDDHIST MONASTERY
(妙法寺; ☑852 2461 8567; 18 Castle Peak Rd, Tuen Mun; ⊙9am-5pm; 🚈line 751) Miu Fat Monastery in Lam Tei, due north of Tuen Mun town centre, is one of Hong Kong's most eccentric Buddhist complexes, second to Sha Tin's 10,000 Buddhas Monastery (p168). The main hall features, with true '70s flamboyance, not only dragons coiled over pillars, but huge stone elephants. Inside there's a golden likeness of Buddha and three larger statues of Lord Gautama. You can't miss the new extension, a 45m tower resembling a huge lotus blossom – it even glows at night.

This is an active monastery; you'll see brown-robed nuns in droves. To get here take light-rail line 751 from the Tuen Mun or Town Centre stops to Lam Tei station. The complex is on the opposite side of Castle Peak Rd; cross over the walkway and

walk north 150m. Bus 63X, from the Mong Kok MTR station, also stops in front of the monastery.

CHING CHUNG TEMPLE   TAOIST TEMPLE
(青松觀, Ching Chung Koon; ☑852 2462 1507; www.daoist.org; Tsing Chung Path, Tsing Chung Koon Rd, Tuen Mun; ⊙7am-6pm; 🚈line 505) Green Pine Temple (c 1950) is a Taoist temple complex northwest of Tuen Mun town centre. With a polychromatic palette, gnarly bonsai trees, florid murals and an ornate rock garden, it's visually quite busy, yet surprisingly peaceful to be in. The main temple is dedicated to Lu Dongbin, a Taoist immortal who likened a righteous man to the hardy and humble pine, and features lanterns given by Běijīng's Imperial Palace. A **Bonsai Festival** is held here in April or May.

Ching Chung Temple is directly opposite Ching Chung light-rail station. To reach it from the Tuen Mun or Town Centre stations, catch line 505.

EATING

SAM SHING HUI SEAFOOD MARKET   SEAFOOD $$
(三聖墟海鮮市場; Sam Shing St, Castle Peak Bay, Tuen Mun; meals HK$250-500; ⊙10am-10pm; 🚌minibus 140M from Tsing Yi) Along Castle Peak Beach, this busy working seafood market sits adjacent to rows of *dai pai dong* (food stalls), as well as fancier enclosed establishments, ready to cook up whatever you've picked. This is like Sai Kung seafood feasting, but without the tourists and with no English spoken (but pointing and smiling should get you going – just be sure to ask for prices first).

Yuen Long

Explore
Yuen Long is an important transport hub and a gateway to the Mai Po Marshes and the nearby walled villages.

Bring your binoculars and set off early for Mai Po. Morning hours are the best time to go birdwatching. If you didn't manage to book a guided tour to Mai Po, Hong Kong Wetland Park is a more than worthy substitute. Then head back to town, enjoy lunch

WORTH A DETOUR

MAI PO NATURE RESERVE

The stunning 270-hectare **Mai Po Nature Reserve** (米埔自然保護區; ☑852 2526 1011; www.wwf.org.hk; Mai Po, Sin Tin, Yuen Long; ⊗9am-5pm; ⊇76K from Sheung Shui East Rail or Yuen Long West Rail stations) consists of floating boardwalks and trails through mangroves and mud flats, and is dotted with a dozen hides (towers or huts from where you can watch migrating birds, both common and rare, up close without being observed). See it by joining one of several guided tours run by the **World Wide Fund for Nature Hong Kong** (WWF; www.wwf.org.hk), which manages the reserve; you can book online. Three-hour tours (HK$120, or HK$100 for those over 65 or students under 18) depart the visitor centre at 9.30am, 10am, 10.30am, 1.30pm, 2pm and 2.30pm on Saturdays, Sundays and public holidays, and are led by bilingual guides when there are English-speakers present.

in Dai Wing Wah, sampling some walled-village dishes, after which you could visit one or two of those fortified hamlets in Kat Hing Wai and Shui Tau Tsuen.

An even better place to spend an hour or two in the afternoon is along the popular Ping Shan Heritage Trail. Watching the sunset in Pak Nai at the westernmost edge of Hong Kong is an unforgettable experience. Afterwards, a seafood dinner in Lau Fau Shan is the best way to end the day.

....

The Best...

➤**Sight** Hong Kong Wetland Park (p160)

➤**Place to Watch Sunset** Pak Nai (p161)

➤**Place for Sweets** Hang Heung (p161)

....

Top Tip

There are several bird hides in Hong Kong Wetland Park. The mudflat hide at the end of the mangrove boardwalk is where you can see the greatest variety of birds.

....

Getting There & Away

➤**Bus** From Yuen Long West Bus Terminal on Kik Yeung Rd, bus 968 leaves for Tin Hau on Hong Kong Island; bus 76K calls at Mai Po, Pak Wo Rd in Fanling and Choi Yun Rd in Sheung Shui.

➤**Green minibus** Buses 35 and 33 from Tai Fung St travel respectively to Lau Fau Shan and Pak Nai via Ping Shan.

➤**MTR** Yuen Long, Long Ping and Tin Shui Wai stations are on the West Rail line; Ping Shan station is on the light-rail line.

....

Need to Know

➤**Area Code** ☑852

➤**Location** 30km northwest of Kowloon Peninsula

➤**Last Train to Kowloon** Leaves 12.26am from Yuen Long West Rail station.

⊙ SIGHTS

PING SHAN HERITAGE TRAIL   VILLAGE

See p154.

★HONG KONG WETLAND PARK   PARK

(香港濕地公園; ☑852 3152 2666; www.wetlandpark.gov.hk; Wetland Park Rd, Tin Shui Wai; adult/concession HK$30/15; ⊗10am-5pm Wed-Mon; ♿; ⊇967, ⊇705, 706) This 60-hectare ecological park is a window on the wetland ecosystems of northwest New Territories. The natural trails, bird hides and viewing platforms make it a handy and excellent spot for birdwatching. The futuristic grass-covered headquarters houses interesting galleries (including one on tropical swamps), a film theatre, a cafe and a viewing gallery. If you have binoculars, bring them; otherwise be prepared to wait to use the fixed points in the viewing galleries and hides.

TANG CLAN ANCESTRAL HALL   NOTABLE BUILDING

(鄧氏宗祠; Hang Tau Tsuen, Ping Shan, Yuen Long; ⊗9am-1pm & 2-5pm Wed-Sun; Ⓜ Tin Shui Wai, exit E) **FREE** The sense of dignified grandiosity is unmistakable at Hong Kong's most magnificent ancestral hall (c 1273). The spaces and ornaments are larger than life, but keep to an understated palette. Basin feasts (consisting of layers of food piled in a basin) thrown in the courtyards here by the Tangs are famous, as are the fashion shows by one of their best-known members – William Tang, a fashion designer who created uniforms for Dragon Air, the MTR and the HK International Airport.

PAK NAI
BEACH

(白泥; ☐ 33 minibus from Tin Shui Wai MTR) Literally 'white mud', Pak Nai is one of the best places to see the sunset in Hong Kong. This 6km stretch of coastline is dotted with mangroves, fish ponds, farms, shacks and muddy beaches sprinkled with oyster shells. Sunset can be watched from most parts of Deep Bay Rd (it continues as Nim Wan Rd after Upper Pak Nai), the only road meandering along the coastline.

Green minibus 33 goes from Yuen Long via Lau Fau Shan. Check Hong Kong Observatory (www.hko.gov.hk) for sunset times.

KAT HING WAI
VILLAGE

(吉慶圍; ☐ 64K) This tiny village is 500 years old and was walled during the early years of the Ming dynasty (1368–1644). It contains just one main street, off which a host of dark and narrow alleyways lead. There are quite a few new buildings and retiled older ones in the village. A small temple stands at the end of the street. Visitors are asked to make a donation when they enter the village; put the money in the coin slot by the entrance.

You can take photographs of the Hakka women in their traditional black trousers, tunics and distinctive bamboo hats with black cloth fringes, but they'll expect you to pay (around HK$10).

To get here from Yuen Long, get off bus 64K at the first bus stop on Kam Tin Rd, cross the road and walk east for 10 minutes. Alternatively, take a taxi from Kam Sheung Rd West Rail station for about HK$28.

✕ EATING

HO TO TAI NOODLE SHOP
NOODLES $

(好到底麵家; ☐ 852 2476 2495; 67 Fau Tsoi St, Yuen Long; wonton noodles HK$30; ⊗ 8am-8pm; ⊠ Tai Tong Rd) This 60-year-old Yuen Long institution is one of the world's cheapest Michelin restaurants. It is best known for the fresh Cantonese egg noodles and shrimp roe noodles that it churns out daily. Foodies from all corners come to slurp the delightful wonton noodles. An English menu is available from the cashier. The haunt is a three-minute walk south of Tai Tong Rd light-rail station.

HANG HEUNG
BAKERY $

(恆香老餅家; ☐ 852 2479 2141; www.hangheung. com.hk; 64 Castle Peak Rd, Yuen Long; ⊗ 10am-10pm; Ⓜ Yuen Long, exit B) Hong Kongers are familiar with the gold lettering on red paper boxes that have been stained by lard from the warm and crumbly Chinese pastries inside. Often they're 'wife cakes' – flaky moons of sweetened wintermelon and white lotus seed paste. But they can also be date paste cakes or egg rolls. Of all of Hang Heung's branches, this old shop in red and gold is the best.

DAI WING WAH
HAKKA $

(大榮華; ☐ 852 2476 9888; 2nd fl, Koon Wong Mansion, 2-6 On Ning Rd; dishes HK$80-400; ⊗ 6am-11.30pm; ⊠ Tai Tong Rd) The brainchild of celebrated chef Leung Man-to, Dai Wing Wah is most famous for its walled-village dishes. Leung sources local ingredients from small farms and producers whenever possible, and complements them with his innovations in cooking. Must-eats include lemon-steamed grey mullet, smoked oysters and steamed sponge cake with demarara sugar.

From Tai Tong Rd light-rail station, walk north along Kuk Ting St then turn left on to Sai Tai St. You'll see the restaurant sitting 30m away.

Fanling & Sheung Shui

••••••••••••••••••••••••••••••••••••

Explore

Begin with a visit to the Fung Ying Sin Temple, which is just a stone's throw from Fanling East Rail station. After a vegetarian lunch in the temple, head to Lung Yeuk Tau Heritage Trail for some village immersion.

For the more adventurous, off-the-beaten-path options include the seldom-visited walled village of Ping Kong, or the village of Sha Tau Kok, where Japanese pillboxes from WWII lie intact in the (still) unspoilt countryside.

••••••••••••••••••••••••••••••••••••

The Best...
➡ **Sight** Fung Ying Sin Temple (p162)
➡ **Place to Eat** Sun Hon Kee (p162)
➡ **Activity** Lung Yeuk Tau Heritage Trail (p162)

••••••••••••••••••••••••••••••••••••

Top Tip

Some walled villages along the Lung Yeuk Tau Heritage Trail are private properties; be discreet and use common sense when visiting.

Getting There & Away

➡ **Bus** Most onward travel connections depart from the East Rail stations. Bus 76K to Yuen Long and Mai Po Marshes departs from Pak Wo Rd in Fanling and Choi Yun Rd in Sheung Shui. Bus 77K to Ping Kong stops at Yuen Long Jockey Club Rd in Fanling and Po Shek Wu Rd in Sheung Shui.

➡ **Green minibus** Bus 58K heads to Ping Kong from San Wan Rd in Sheung Shui.

➡ **MTR** Take the MTR to Fanling and Sheung Shui East Rail stations.

Need to Know

➡ **Area Code** ☑852

➡ **Location** Fanling and Sheung Shui are in north-central New Territories, much closer to the mainland (5km) than to Tsim Sha Tsui (20km).

➡ **Last Train to Kowloon** Leaves 12.26am from Yuen Long West Rail station.

 SIGHTS

TAI FU TAI MANSION   HISTORIC BUILDING

(大夫第; San Tin, Yuen Long; ⊙9am-1pm & 2-5pm Wed-Mon; ☑76K) Located between Yuen Long and Sheung Shui, this splendid Mandarin-style building complex dating from 1865 is eclectically fused with Western design. Members of the Man clan, another powerful family in the New Territories, lived here for well over a century until they moved out in 1980. The courtyard is encircled by stone walls with a guarded checkpoint. Inside, auspicious Chinese symbols are found in the woodcarvings along with art-nouveau glass panels, and there is a European fountain.

Board bus 76K in Sheung Shui and get off at the San Tin stop.

FUNG YING SIN TEMPLE   TAOIST TEMPLE

(蓬瀛仙館; ☑852 2669 9186; www.fysk.org; 66 Pak Wo Rd, Fanling; ⊙8am-6pm Ⓜ Fanling) This brightly coloured Taoist temple perched on a hillside opposite Fanling MTR station is one of Hong Kong's most important Taoist temples. It was founded in 1926 and has been meticulously renovated over the years. There are wonderful exterior murals of Taoist immortals, an orchard terrace, a wall inscribed with Laozi's Dao Dejing (Classic of the Dao and of Virtue), and a **vegetarian restaurant**

(⊙11am-5pm; Ground & 1st fl, Bldg A7). There's a columbarium behind the temple.

 EATING

KWAN KEE BEEF BALLS & PORK KNUCKLES   NOODLES $

(群記牛肉丸豬手; ☑852 2675 6382; 5 Luen Cheong St, Luen Wo Hui, Fanling; meals HK$50; ⊙11am-5.45pm) There's always a wait at this unpretentious shop for the bouncy beef balls and the chewy, collagen-laden pork knuckles served in light-blue plastic bowls and (optional) drizzled with aromatic homemade chilli sauce. They sell out fast and customers may be asked to return an hour later for the next batch.

SUN HON KEE   HAKKA, CANTONESE $$

(新漢記; ☑852 2683 0000; 5 Luen Wo Rd, Fanling; mains HK$88-288; Ⓜ Fanling, exit C) Well-executed Hakka cuisine, known for its use of preserved ingredients as well as stews and braises, is on offer at this busy two-floor restaurant. Dishes tend to be boldly flavoured, as they're meant to go with rice. Try the chicken cooked in yellow wine (黃酒煮雞), braised pork belly (客家炆豬肉), and pan-seared squid with shallots (紅蔥爆吊桶). Best with rice...or beer.

 SPORTS & ACTIVITIES

LUNG YEUK TAU HERITAGE TRAIL   HERITAGE WALK

(龍躍頭文物徑; ☑54K) This 4.5km-long trail northeast of Fanling meanders through five relatively well-preserved walled villages, home to the Tang clan. The oldest (800 years), most attractive and most intact village is **Lo Wai**, identifiable by its 1m-thick fortified wall. Unfortunately, it's not open to the public. Admire the exterior, before continuing to the more welcoming villages of **Tung Kok Wai** to the northeast and **Sun Wai** towards the trail's northern end.

Other attractions here include the **Tang Chung Ling Ancestral Hall** and the adjacent **Tin Hau temple**. The ancestral hall was built during the Ming dynasty, and the dragon motif that you'll see on some of the spirit tablets inside the building was a symbol of the clan's royal status. The temple houses two bronze bells; one is from 1695, the other, 1700. **Shek Lo**, literally 'stone cottage' and built in 1925, is an eclectic mix of colonial and traditional Chinese architectural styles. The cottage appears to be permanently locked, but it can be seen clearly from the east of **Tsung Kyam church**, the start of the trail.

To get there from Fanling station (exit C), take the green minibus 54K and ask to be dropped at Tsung Kyam church (Shun Him Tong in Cantonese).

Tai Po

Explore

Formed from two former market towns on either side of the Lam Tsuen River, Tai Po has a lively waterfront downtown ringed by housing estates and, beyond, rolling rural hills. On offer are quirky temples, a cute railway museum and several nature areas. But the best thing about this ever-changing region is the street life. Barter for lychees in the crowded street markets, queue for tofu or noodles at hole-in-the-wall stalls, or watch proud parents photograph their babies toddling along the pedestrian bridge crossing the river. This is old-school Hong Kong living at its finest.

The Best...
➡ **Sight** Tai Po Market (p163)
➡ **Place to Eat** Yat Lok Barbecue Restaurant (p165)
➡ **Activity** Cycling from Tai Po to Plover Cove Reservoir

Top Tip
Tai Po has a number of markets and nature sanctuaries that are more than worth a visit, so wake up early!

Getting There & Away
➡ **Bus** Bus 71K runs between the Tai Wo and **Tai Po Market Transport Interchange** (Nga Wan Rd, outside Tai Po Market MTR station, exit A3) while **Bus 72** (Po Heung St, Tai Po) makes stops in Tai Wo and Tai Po.

➡ **Green minibus** For onward travel, start at Tai Po Market East Rail station, or from Heung Sze Wui St, take bus 20K for San Mun Tsai; catch bus 25K at Tsing Yuen St to get to Ng Tung Chai for Tai Mo Shan.

➡ **MTR** Take the MTR to Tai Po Market or Tai Wo East Rail stations.

Need to Know
➡ **Area Code** ✆852
➡ **Location** 13km to the Hong Kong–China border at Lo Wu; 18km north of Kowloon Peninsula
➡ **Last Train to Kowloon** Leaves 12.42am from Tai Wo East Rail station; 12.45am from Tai Po Market East Rail station.

⊙ SIGHTS

TAI PO MARKET　　　　　　MARKET
(大埔街市; Fu Shin St, Tai Po; ☺6am-8pm; Ⓜ Tai Wo) Not to be confused with the MTR station of the same name, this street-long outdoor wet market is one of the most winning in the New Territories. Feast your eyes on a rainbow of fruit and vegetables, tables lined with dried seafood, elderly women hawking

WORTH A DETOUR

TAI PO KAU NATURE RESERVE

The thickly forested 460-hectare **Tai Po Kau Nature Reserve** (大埔滘自然護理區; Tai Po Rd; 🚍70, 72) is Hong Kong's most extensive woodlands. It is home to many species of butterflies, amphibians, birds, dragonflies and trees, and is a superb place in which to enjoy a quiet walk. The reserve is crisscrossed with four main tracks ranging in length from 3km to 10km, plus a short nature trail of less than 1km. If possible, avoid the reserve on Sunday and public holidays, when the crowds descend upon the place.

The reserve is well served by buses. Bus 70 passes through Jordan and Mong Kok on its way here. Bus 72 can be used to get here from the nearby Sha Tin and Tai Po Market East Rail stations. A taxi from Tai Po Market East Rail station will cost around HK$30, and from the University East Rail station about HK$45.

Tai Po

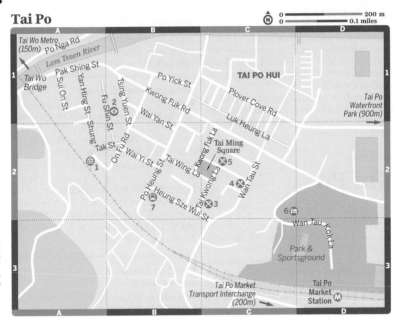

Tai Po

◎ Sights
1 Hong Kong Railway Museum A2
2 Tai Po Market B1

✖ Eating
3 Ah Po Tofu C2
4 Kwan Kee C2
5 Yat Lok Barbecue Restaurant.............C2

▣ Sleeping
6 Green Hub...C2

ℹ Transport
7 Bus 72 Stop..B2

glutinous Hakka rice cakes, and stalls selling fresh aloe and sugar cane juices.

TAI PO WATERFRONT PARK   PARK
(大埔海濱公園; ⊘Insect House 8am-7pm, tower from 7am, park 24hr; 72A, 73, 73X, 75X, 271, 275R, 275S, 275, 74K) Hong Kong's largest and arguably most beautiful public park has tree-fringed lawns for picnics and kite-flying, an amphitheatre with white sail-canopies, a cycling track along Tolo Harbour from where you can watch dragon boat races during the Dragon Boat Festival, and an **Insect House**. The highlight is a

quirky lookout tower resembling a rocket in a hoop skirt. It has telescopes with which to view the harbour and high rises in the distance, and the dystopian '70s industrial landscape of **Tai Po Industrial Estate**.

KADOORIE FARM &
BOTANIC GARDEN   WATERFALL, GARDEN
(梧桐寨瀑布、嘉道理農場暨植物園; ☎852 2483 7200; www.kfbg.org.hk; Lam Kam Rd; aged 12-59/5-11 HK$30/15, below 5 & over 60 free; ⊘9.30am-5pm; 64K) Kadoorie Farm & Botanic Garden, southwest of Ng Tung Chai, is primarily a conservation and teaching centre, but the gardens are especially lovely, with many indigenous birds, animals, insects and plants in residence. You can reach the farm most easily on bus 64K.

HONG KONG RAILWAY MUSEUM   MUSEUM
(香港鐵路博物館; ☎852 2653 3455; www.heritagemuseum.gov.hk/eng/museums/railway.aspx; 13 Shung Tak St; ⊘10am-6pm Wed-Mon; ; ⓜTai Wo) **FREE** Housed in the former Tai Po Market train station (built in 1913 in traditional Chinese style), this small museum is a fun stop for trainspotters and families with train-crazy kids. There are a few exhibits about the history of the Hong Kong railways, but the real draws are the historical train carriages open to visitors.

EATING

★ YAT LOK BARBECUE RESTAURANT
CANTONESE $

(一樂燒臘飯店; ☑852 2656 4732; 5 Tai Ming Lane; meals HK$50-180; ◐11am-11pm; Ⓜ Tai Po Market, exit A2) Glossy roast goose with shatteringly crisp skin and a pillow of succulent fat is the order of the day at this one-Michelin-star, family-run eatery, which counts celebrity chef Anthony Bourdain among its many fans. *Char siu* (roast pork) is a bit dry, so focus on the bird. Chinese menu only, but friendly servers will help you order.

KWAN KEE
NOODLES $

(群記清湯腩; ☑852 2638 3071; 26 Tai Ming Lane,Tai Po Market, Tai Po; meals from HK$45; ◐1-8pm Mon-Sat; Ⓜ Tai Po Market, exit A2) The beef brisket in clear broth at this hole-in-the-wall is not only as good as the ones at celebrity shops, but also can be ordered in cuts you wouldn't get elsewhere, such as tender, collagen-jammed beef cheek and unctuous beef tongue. If sticking to brisket, chewy *song lahm* (爽腩), a cut near the flank, is a perennial favourite. Prepare to queue for a seat.

AH PO TOFU
DESSERTS $

(亞婆豆腐花; Shop 2A, Tai Kwong Lane, Tai Po; tofu pudding HK$8; ◐10am-8pm; Ⓜ Tai Po Market, exit A2) You'll recognise this beloved *dau fu fa* (sweet silky tofu pudding) shop by the line snaking down the busy pedestrian street. Sprinkle on palm sugar to taste, then eat while standing before returning the bowl to the counter.

🏃 SPORTS & ACTIVITIES

NG TUNG CHAI WATERFALL
HIKING

(梧桐寨瀑布; 🚌64 from Tai Po Market MTR) The scenic area around the Ng Tung Chai Waterfall is a retreat from the bustle of downtown Tai Po. Reach the series of streams and waterfalls by bus 64K from Tai Po Market East Rail station, and get off at Ng Tung Chai stop. Enter the eponymous village and hike through the bamboo groves towards the **Man Tak Monastery** (萬德苑), which can be reached in 30 minutes. From the monastery, hike uphill for 20 minutes and you'll see the waterfalls sliding down.

Plover Cove

Explore

Plover Cove has only two themes: hiking and cycling. Large parts of it are designated Geopark areas, so you'll see rugged rocks and mineral marvels, especially around Plover Cove Reservoir. Plan a full day here. For an easy walk, the 4.4km Pat Sin Leng Nature Trail is a good alternative.

The Best...
➡ **Place to Eat** Chung Shing Thai Restaurant (p166)
➡ **Activity** Biking around Plover Cove Reservoir (p166)

Getting There & Away
➡ **Bus** Take bus 75K (and additionally 74K or 275R on Sundays and holidays) from Tai Po Market East Rail station in Tai Po.
➡ **Green minibus** Bus 20C passes Tai Po Market East Rail station and Heung Sze Wui St in Tai Po on its way to Plover Cove.

Need to Know
➡ **Area Code** ☑852
➡ **Location** 12km northeast of Tai Po
➡ **Plover Cove Country Park Management Centre** (船灣郊野公園管理中心; ☑852 2665 3413; Tai Mei Tuk; ◐9.30am-4.30pm)
➡ **Last Train to Kowloon** Leaves at 12.45am from Tai Po Market East Rail station.

👁 SIGHTS

TSZ SHAN MONASTERY
MONASTERY

(慈山寺; ☑852 2123 8666; www.tszshan.org; 88 Universal Gate Rd, Tai Po; ◐9.30am-5pm; Ⓜ Tai Po Market, Tai Wo) Tsz Shan Monastery spans 46,000 sq metres and took 12 years and HK$1.5 billion to complete. It's state-of-the-art but gracefully cloaked in Tang-dynasty antiquity. Inside its shell of *zitan* wood is a steel structure that does away with the need for pillars and interlocking eave brackets often associated with Tang architecture, giving a cleaner look. Tsz Shan does not entertain walk-ins. Book online as close to a month ahead as possible. Slots are quickly snapped up once released for booking.

EATING

CHUNG SHING THAI RESTAURANT   THAI $

(忠誠茶座泰國菜; ☑852 2664 5218; 69 Tai Mei Tuk Village,Ting Kok Rd, Tai Po; meals from HK$150; ⏱noon-3pm & 6-10.30pm) Arguably the best restaurant in Plover Cove and Tai Mei Tuk food-wise, though not the most atmospheric, loud and busy Chung Shing serves up hearty satays, grilled meats, curries and Thai salads. Al fresco here means dining in air-conditioned comfort behind vinyl covers. Book ahead or go early. It gets crazy at meal times.

SPORTS & ACTIVITIES

★PLOVER COVE RESERVOIR   OUTDOORS

(船灣淡水湖; ▣75K) Part of Hong Kong Geopark, this reservoir was completed in 1968, in a very unusual way. Rather than build a dam across a river, of which Hong Kong has very few, a barrier was erected across the mouth of a great bay. The sea water was siphoned out and fresh water was pumped in. The area around the reservoir is glorious hiking and cycling country, and well worth a full day's exploring.

The village of **Tai Mei Tuk**, the springboard for most of the activities in the Plover Cove area, is about 6km northeast of Tai Po Market MTR station. Bicycles can be rented at several locations in Tai Mei Tuk, including Lung Kee Bikes. A bicycle track along the coast runs from Tai Mei Tuk to Chinese University (p168) at Ma Liu Shui. Ting Kok Rd in **Lung Mei Village** is also where you'll find a row of restaurants.

You can also take a stroll along the dam of Plover Cove Reservoir, accessible via a path next to **Bradbury Jockey Club Youth Hostel** (☑852 2662 5123; 66 Tai Mei Tuk Rd; ▣75K), and watch people cycling and flying kites. It's beautiful at sunset. The dam is also a popular venue for watching comet showers. Plover Cove Reservoir was the world's first lake to be built from the sea and the idea is said to have come from the then governor while on a leisurely boat trip in this beautiful area.

The Plover Cove Country Park Management Centre, a short distance further east from the car park on Ting Kok Rd, is where the Pat Sin Leng Nature Trail to Bride's Pool starts.

PAT SIN LENG NATURE TRAIL   HIKING

(八仙嶺自然教育徑; ▣75K) This excellent 4.4km-long trail, which should take from two to 2½ hours, leads from the Plover Cove Country Park Management Centre at Tai Mei Tuk and heads northeast for 4km to **Bride's Pool**; there are signboards numbered 1 to 22, so there is little danger of getting lost. The scenery is excellent and the two waterfalls at Bride's Pool are delightful, but the place gets packed on the weekend.

You can either return to Tai Mei Tuk via Bride's Pool Rd on foot or catch green minibus 20C, which stops at Tai Mei Tuk before carrying on to Tai Po Market MTR station.

Those looking for a more strenuous hike can join stage No 9 of the **Wilson Trail** at Tai Mei Tuk on the Plover Cove Reservoir and head west into the steep Pat Sin Leng range of hills to **Wong Leng Shan** (639m). The trail then carries on westward to **Hok Tau Reservoir** and **Hok Tau Wai** (12km, four hours).

LUNG KEE BIKES   CYCLING

(龍記單車; ☑852 2662 5266; Tai Mei Tuk Village, Ting Kok Rd, Tai Po; bicycle rental per hr HK$10-40, per day HK$40-100; ⏱9.30am-7.30pm; ▣75K) Bicycles can be rented at Tai Mei Tuk at several locations, including Lung Kee Bikes. A track along the coast runs from Tai Mei Tuk to Chinese University at Ma Liu Shui.

Sha Tin

Explore

You're likely to arrive in New Town Plaza, a claustrophobic mall connected to Sha Tin MTR station, if you visit this busy part of the New Territories. There are three noteworthy religious establishments in the area – 10,000 Buddhas Monastery, Po Fook Hill columbarium and Che Kung Temple. The town's other key drawcard is the Heritage Museum, where you can relive Hong Kong's past in a range of thoughtfully constructed exhibitions.

If you'd rather have some raw outdoor action, then time your visit with one of the rip-roaring weekend race days at the beautifully set Sha Tin Racecourse.

Sha Tin

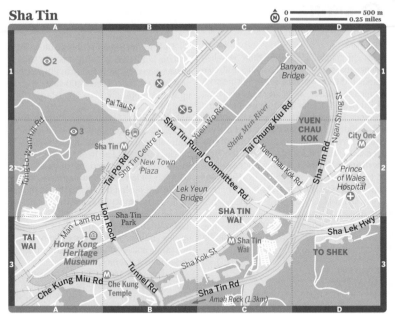

N 0 ─────── 500 m
0 ─────── 0.25 miles

The Best...

➜**Sight** Hong Kong Heritage Museum (p168)

➜**Place to Win Big** Sha Tin Racecourse (p169)

➜**Place to Eat** Sha Tin 18 (p169)

Top Tip

On race days, admission to the Sha Tin Racecourse is free from around 3pm (roughly halfway through the afternoon program).

Getting There & Away

➜**Bus** Buses into and out of Sha Tin leave from/terminate at **New Town Plaza Bus Terminus** (新城市中心巴士總站). Bus 182 links Sha Tin with Wan Chai, Admiralty and Central. Bus 170 connects Sha Tin East Rail bus station with Causeway Bay and Aberdeen. Bus 299 shuttles between Sha Tin and Sai Kung.

➜**MTR** Sha Tin, Tai Wai and Racecourse stations are on the East Rail line; Che Kung Temple station is on Ma On Shan line.

Sha Tin

Need to Know

➜**Area Code** ☎852

➜**Location** 12km north of Kowloon Peninsula

➜**Last Train to Kowloon** Leaves at 12.57am from Sha Tin East Rail station.

◉ SIGHTS

HONG KONG HERITAGE MUSEUM
MUSEUM

(香港文化博物館; ☑852 2180 8188; www.heritagemuseum.gov.hk; 1 Man Lam Rd; adult/concession HK$10/5, Wed free; ⊙10am-6pm Mon & Wed-Sat, to 7pm Sun; ⽥; Ⓜ Che Kung Temple, exit A) Southwest of Sha Tin town centre, this spacious, high-quality museum inside an ugly building gives a peek into local history and culture. Highlights include a **children's area** with interactive play zones, the **New Territories Heritage Hall** with mock-ups of traditional minority villages, the **Cantonese Opera Heritage Hall**, where you can watch old operas with English subtitles, and an elegant **gallery** of Chinese art. There's also a **Bruce Lee exhibit**, with some 600 items of the kung fu star's memorabilia on display until July 2018.

10,000 BUDDHAS MONASTERY
TEMPLE

(萬佛寺; ☑852 2691 1067; ⊙10am-5pm; Ⓜ Sha Tin, exit B) FREE Built in the 1950s, this quirky temple actually contains more than 10,000 Buddhas. Some 12,800 miniature statues line the walls of the main temple and dozens of life-sized golden statues of Buddha's followers flank the steep steps leading to the complex. There are several halls and pavilions, as well as a nine-storey pagoda. It's kitsch but so unlike any other temple in Hong Kong that it's worth the uphill hike to visit.

The temple is about 500m northwest of Sha Tin MTR station. To reach it, take exit B at the MTR station and walk down the ramp, passing a series of traditional houses at Pai Tau village on the left. Take the left onto Pai Tau St, and turn right onto Sheung Wo Che St. At the end of this road, a series of signs in English will direct you to the left along a concrete path and through bamboo groves to the first of some 400 steps leading up to the temple.

AMAH ROCK
LANDMARK

(望夫石; Lion Rock Country Park; Ⓜ Tai Wai) This oddly shaped boulder southwest of Sha Tin carries a legend. For many years a fisherman's wife would stand on this spot in the hills above **Lion Rock Country Park**, watching for her husband to return from the sea while carrying her baby on her back. One day he didn't come back – and she waited and waited. The gods apparently took pity on her and transported her to heaven on a lightning bolt, leaving her form in stone. Today it's a great day hike.

As you take the MTR south from Sha Tin to Kowloon, Amah Rock is visible to the east (on the left-hand side) up on the hillside after Tai Wai East Rail station, but before the train enters the tunnel.

TAO FONG SHAN CHRISTIAN CENTRE
ARCHITECTURE

(道風山基督教叢林; ☑852 2694 4038; 33 Tao Fong Shan Rd, Sha Tin) FREE A representative of the 'Chinese Revival' architectural style like St Mary's Church (p104), Tao Fung Shan is a Protestant retreat centre, seminary and hostel with Chinese architectural features. In 1929, Karl Ludvig Reichelt, a Norwegian Lutheran missionary who was passionate

---

WORTH A DETOUR

UNIVERSITY SIGHTS

Chinese University of Hong Kong (香港中文大學; ☑852 2609 7000; www.cuhk.edu.hk; Ⓜ University, exit A) has its main campus in Sha Tin. If you are in this neck of the woods, it's worth making time to see the university's **art museum** (香港中文大學文物館; ☑852 3943 7416; www.cuhk.edu.hk/ics/amm; Institute of Chinese Studies, Central Campus; ⊙10am-5pm, closed public holidays; Ⓜ University, exit A) FREE. The four-floor **East Wing Galleries** house a permanent collection of Chinese paintings and calligraphy, but it is the ceramics and jade objets d'art that are especially worth inspecting, including 2000-year-old bronze seals and a large collection of jade flower carvings. The **West Wing Galleries** stage five to six special exhibitions each year.

Other than that, the **lotus pond** in Chung Chi Campus (you'll see it when you step out of the train station) is a photogenic spot, especially when the lotuses are blooming in spring; and the **Pavilion of Harmony** (合一亭) in hilly New Asia Campus offers panoramic views of Tolo Harbour.

A shuttle bus from University station travels through the campuses. The bus runs every 20 to 30 minutes daily and is free.

about Buddhism, bought land on a hill in Sha Tin and commissioned Danish architect Johannes Prip-Möller to design the complex.

SHA TIN RACECOURSE

RACECOURSE

(沙田賽馬場; www.hkjc.com; Penfold Park; race-day public stands HK$10; Ⓜ️Racecourse) Northeast of Sha Tin town centre is Hong Kong's second racecourse, which can accommodate up to 80,000 punters. Races are usually held on Sunday afternoon (and sometimes on Saturday and public holidays) from September to early July; a list of race meetings is available on the website.

The Racecourse East Rail station, just west of the track, opens on race days only.

EATING

FOODY

TAIWANESE, INTERNATIONAL $

(伙食工業; ☎️852 3586 0863; Shop 3, ground fl, Leader Industrial Centre, 57-59 Au Pui Wan St, Fo Tan; meals HK$80-180; ◷noon-6pm Mon, to 10.30pm Tue-Sun) Taiwanese-style noodles and fried chicken as well as pastas and burgers served in a spacious, shabby chic cafe decorated with retro furniture and vintage objects. The food is decent though not exceptional, but slouchy chairs and friendly service make it a great place for chilling. Taiwanese R&B is played during the day, with occasional gigs by singer-songwriter types at night. Entrance is on Fo Tan Rd.

SHING KEE

DAI PAI DONG, CANTONESE $

(盛記; ☎️852 2692 6611; Shop 5, Lek Yuen Estate Market; meal from HK$80; ◷6am-4pm & 7-11pm; 🚌83K from Sha Tin New Town Plaza, Ⓜ️Sha Tin) Tucked into the oldest public housing estate in Sha Tin, this 30-year-old establishment is no ordinary *dai pai dong* (food stall). It resembles a gallery, with black-and-white photos on the wall, CDs, toys, and potted plants in other corners. All of which, including the chairs, were picked up from public wheelie bins and recycled by the owner.

Noodles are served in the daytime. In the evening, it turns into a popular hotpot joint, with several dozens of broths on offer. To get there, take bus 83K, or it's a 15-minute walk northeast from Sha Tin station.

LUNG WAH HOTEL RESTAURANT

CANTONESE $

(龍華酒店; ☎️852 2691 1828; www.lungwah hotel.hk; 22 Ha Wo Che; pigeon HK$98; ◷11am-11pm; Ⓜ️Sha Tin, exit B) Shatin's first postwar hotel (c 1951) is where Bruce Lee is said to have stayed during the filming of *The Big Boss*. The hotel closed in 1985 and this dated restaurant frequented by nostalgic Hong Kongers remains. It's still 1971 here – there are peacocks kept in cages and old men come to play mah-jong. The roast pigeon is delicious, but service can be surly.

To reach the hotel, walk north for 10 minutes along the railway line after exiting the Sha Tin MTR station.

★SHA TIN 18

CANTONESE, CHINESE $$

(沙田18; ☎️852 3723 7932; www.hongkong. shatin.hyatt.com; 18 Chak Cheung St, Hyatt Regency Hong Kong; meals HK$300-700; ◷11.30am-3pm & 5.30-10.30pm; Ⓜ️University) The Peking duck (whole HK$785, half HK$500) here has put this hotel restaurant, adjacent to the Chinese University, in the gastronomic spotlight. Book your prized fowl 24 hours in advance, and tantalise your taste buds in three ways – pancakes with the crispy skin, meat and leeks, duck soup and wok-fried minced duck. The Asian fusion desserts here are also famous.

Sai Kung Peninsula

• •

Explore

The rugged and massive Sai Kung Peninsula is an outdoor-pursuits paradise. The hiking is excellent here – the MacLehose Trail runs right across it. Sai Kung town is a good base for exploring the easily accessible countryside. This eclectic waterfront town has a cluster of restaurants and is also a stopping point and transport hub to and from the surrounding countryside. A *kaido* (small, open-sea ferry) trip to one or more of the little offshore islands and their secluded beaches is recommended.

• •

The Best...

➡ **Sight** Hong Kong Global Geopark (p155)

➡ **Place to Eat** Loaf On (p171)

➡ **Place to Drink** Classifieds (p171)

Sai Kung Town

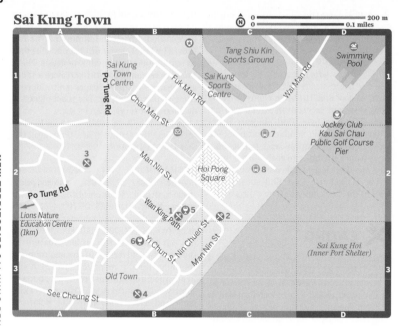

Sai Kung Town

Top Tip

Near the Sai Kung town pier, you'll find one of the liveliest fish markets in Hong Kong, where fishers sell their catch directly from their boats.

Getting There & Away

➡ **Bus** To/from Sai Kung town, bus 299 connects to Sha Tin East Rail station, bus 92 to Diamond Hill and Choi Hung, bus 96R (Sunday and public holidays) connects to Wong Shek, Hebe Haven, and Choi Hung and Diamond Hill MTR stations, while bus 792M calls at Tseung Kwan O and Tiu Keng Leng MTR stations. Bus 94 goes to Wong Shek. Village Bus 29R runs from Chan Man St in Sai Kung town to Sai Wan Pavilion. The **bus terminus** (Sai Kung Waterfront Park) is on the waterfront.

➡ **Green minibus** To/from Sai Kung town, buses 1A, 1M and 1S (12.30am to 6.10am) connect with Hebe Haven and Choi Hung MTR station. The **minibus terminus** (小巴總站; Sai Kung Waterfront Park) is on the waterfront.

Need to Know

➡ **Area Code** ☏852

➡ **Location** 21km northeast of Kowloon

➡ **Sai Kung Country Park Visitor Centre** (西貢郊野公園遊客中心; ☏852 2792 7365; Tai Mong Tsai Rd, Sai Kung Peninsula; ⊗9.30am–4.30pm Wed-Mon; ⊟94) In Pak Tam Chung, by the road from Sai Kung town.

➡ **Last Train to Kowloon** Leaves at 12.20am from Tseung Kwan O station, 12.22am from Tiu Keng Leng MTR station.

SIGHTS

HONG KONG GLOBAL GEOPARK PARK
See p155.

SAI KUNG TOWN AREA
(西貢市中心; 92, M Choi Hung, minibus 1A, 1M, 299, M Sha Tin East Rail) Sai Kung Peninsula is one of the last havens left in Hong Kong for hikers, swimmers and boaters, and most of it is one beautiful 7500-hectare country park. A short journey to any of the beach islands off Sai Kung town is rewarding. Small ferry boats depart from the waterfront. There are also boats moored along the waterfront selling seafood. Though prices may not be cheaper than in the markets, the atmosphere is unbeatable.

The **MacLehose Trail**, a 100km route across the New Territories, begins at Pak Tam Chung on the Sai Kung Peninsula. On top of this, Sai Kung town boasts excellent Chinese seafood restaurants, especially along the attractive waterfront.

LIONS NATURE EDUCATION CENTRE OUTDOORS
(獅子會自然教育中心; 852 2792 2234; www.lnec.gov.hk; Pak Kong; 9am-5pm Wed-Mon; ; 92) FREE One of the best kid-pleasing destinations around, this 34-hectare attraction, 2km northwest of Hebe Haven, is Hong Kong's first nature education centre. It comprises everything from an arboretum, a medicinal plants garden and an insectarium to a mineral and rocks corner and a shell house. The **Dragonfly Pond**, which boasts up to a quarter of the more than 100 dragonfly species found in Hong Kong, is the star of the show.

EATING

HONEYMOON DESSERT DESSERTS $
(滿記甜品; 852 2792 4991; Units B&C, 10A Po Tung Rd, Sai Kung; desserts from HK$20; 1pm-2.45am; 1) This shop specialises in Chinese dessert concoctions made with nuts, pulses and root vegetables, or with fruit, coconut milk and sago. It also – famously – whips up crêpes and puddings with durian. If the pungent fruit does not float your boat, there are versions with mango and banana.

ALI OLI BAKERY CAFE EUROPEAN, BAKERY $
(852 2792 2655; 11 Sha Tsui Path, Sai Kung; pastries from HK$20, all-day breakfast HK$90; 8am-7.30pm; 1) This bakery is a favourite with hikers, with simple sandwiches on European-style homemade bread, and pies and preserves. Breakfast and set lunches are also offered here and are best enjoyed at its outdoor tables. Service can be patchy.

★LOAF ON CANTONESE, SEAFOOD $$
(六福菜館; 852 2792 9966; 49 See Cheung St, Sai Kung; dishes from HK$100; 11am-11pm; 1) The motto here is: eat what they hunt. This three-storey Michelin-star restaurant is where fish freshly caught from Sai Kung waters in the morning lands on customers' plates by midday. The signature fish soup and steamed fish sell out fast. There is no English signage, but it's identifiable by a lone dining table set outside and the shiny brass sign. Reservations recommended.

CHUEN KEE SEAFOOD RESTAURANT SEAFOOD $$$
(全記海鮮館; 852 2792 6938; 87-89 Man Nin St, Sai Kung; seafood meals from HK$350; 7am-11pm; 1) Any Hong Kong seafood place worth its salt serves fresh marine life. The difference between Chuen Kee and low-key shops is the sheer range of fish, crustaceans and molluscs available here – all displayed alive at the entrance of course. The preparation is similar, but you'll get goods unseen elsewhere, such as palm-length mantis shrimp, king crab and foot-long razor clams.

DRINKING & NIGHTLIFE

CLASSIFIED WINE BAR
(852 2529 3454; 5 Sha Tsui Path, Sai Kung; 8am-midnight) Classy Classified is the place to go in Sai Kung for good wine and cheese. Wooden communal tables and open frontage make it ideal for people-watching, too.

STEAMERS BAR
(852 2792 6991; www.steamerssaikung.com; 66 Yi Chun St, Sai Kung; 9am-2am, happy hour 2-8pm Mon-Fri; 1) Steamers is graced with a blissful alfresco bar area where you can chill with some excellently blended cocktails and bar grub.

🏃 SPORTS & ACTIVITIES

★ HIGH ISLAND RESERVOIR EAST DAM
HIKING

(萬宜水庫東壩) A reservoir built in the 1970s, the South China Sea, and 14 million-year-old volcanic rocks make this one of Hong Kong's most breathtaking places. High Island East Dam is in the only part of Hong Kong Global Geopark that's reachable on foot, and the only place where you can touch the hexagonal rock columns. The scenery is surreal and made even more so by the presence of thousands of huge dolosse blocks (huge cement barriers shaped like jacks) placed along the coast to break sea waves.

Hong Kong's second reservoir built by sealing off the coast with dams – Plover Cove was the first – High Island was constructed to provide fresh water to the territory when mainland China shut down supply during the 1967 riots. It was designed by Binnie & Partners of London and constructed by an Italian company, Vianini Lavori. At the southern end of East Dam, you'll see a giant dolos block in sky blue. It's a memorial erected by Vianini Lavori to those who died on the project. Nearby there's a slab of concrete that commemorates, in Chinese and English, the inauguration of the reservoir in 1978. The construction of the reservoir had one unintentional effect – it made a part of what 30 years later became Hong Kong Global Geopark accessible on foot. Off the coast of the southern end of the dam is Po Pin Chau (literally, Broken-Sided Island), a massive sea stack with rock columns all over its face like a giant pipe-organ.

★ TAI LONG WAN HIKING TRAIL
HIKING

(大浪灣遠足郊遊徑; 🚌village bus 29R) The northern end of Sai Kung Peninsula has several wonderful hikes that will take you through some of Hong Kong's most pristine scenery. The breathtaking 12km Tai Long Wan Hiking Trail, which starts from the end of Sai Wan Rd and passes through beautiful coves including Sai Wan, Tai Long Wan and Chek Keng, is a perennially popular option. On weekdays you're likely to have the trail to yourself. The walk takes five to six hours.

Take the village bus 29R at Chan Man Rd (the stop is in front of McDonald's), get off at the last stop – Sai Wan Ting (西灣亭), literally West Bay Pagoda – and start the hike there. Departures are more frequent on Sundays and public holidays. A taxi ride will be less than HK$160. The trail ends at Pak Tam Au, from where you can catch a minibus back to Sai Kung town.

CHONG HING WATER SPORTS CENTRE
WATER SPORTS

(創興水上活動中心; 🚌852 2792 6810; www.lcsd.gov.hk/en/watersport/hiring/hiring_craft/hiri_book1.html; West Sea Cofferdam, High Island Reservoir, Sai Kung; canoe, dinghy & board hire per hr HK$20-30) Government-run watersports centre with a vast artificial lake, a campsite and **Astropark** (天文公園; 🚌852 2792 6810; http://astropark.hk.space.museum; ⏲24hr). You can hire crafts for sailing, canoeing and windsurfing, or book tents for HK$7 to HK$24 a day. It also operates canoe tours to sea caves.

Bring your passport. Take bus route 94, 96R or 698R to Wong Shek Pier, or green minibus 7 from Sai Kung to Hoi Ha or 9 from Sai Kung to Lady MacLehose Holiday Village in Pak Tam Chung. From both, a 15-minute taxi ride should take you to the centre.

HOI HA WAN MARINE PARK
OUTDOORS

(海下灣海岸公園; 🚌1823; Hoi Ha; 🚌green minibus 7) A rewarding 6km walk here starts from the village of Hoi Ha, part of the Hoi Ha Wan Marine Park, a 260-hectare protected area blocked off by concrete booms from the Tolo Channel and closed to fishing vessels. There are mangroves along the coast, coral growing in abundance underwater, starfish and Nemo's friends.

Snorkels, masks and kayaks can be rented from **Wan Hoi Store** (🚌852 2328 2169) on the beach. Green minibus 7 makes the run from Sai Kung town daily, with the first departure at 8.25am and the last at 6.45pm. A taxi from there will cost around HK$130.

Clearwater Bay Peninsula

....

Explore

Tseung Kwan O, accessible via the MTR station of the same name, is the springboard to the Clearwater Bay Peninsula. There are several wonderful beaches for whiling away an afternoon. The most beautiful and popular are Clearwater Bay First Beach and Clearwater Bay Second Beach. They are often packed with local weekenders during the warmer months.

The Clearwater Bay Country Park offers some easy but exceptional walks with sweeping views of the bay. The secluded Tai Miu Temple, dedicated to the goddess of heaven, is best visited during Tin Hau's Birthday Festival in April or May. Seafood lovers will not want to miss Po Toi O village: this is where you can enjoy sumptuous seafood and home-style cooking at its best.

The Best...

→**Sight** Joss House Bay Tin Hau Temple (p173)

→**Beach** Clearwater Bay Second Beach (p173)

→**Place to Eat** Seafood Island (p173)

Top Tip

Early birds shouldn't miss the breathtaking sunrise that can be watched from Clearwater Bay Second Beach. The first minibus leaves at 6am.

Getting There & Away

→**Bus** Bus 91 runs from Diamond Hill and Choi Hung MTR stations to Tai Au Mun.

→**Green minibus** Bus 103M runs between Tseung Kwan O MTR station and Clearwater Bay. Bus 103 runs to Kwun Tong ferry pier, and bus 16 to Po Lam MTR station.

Need to Know

→**Area Code** ☑852

→**Location** 15km east of Tsim Sha Tsui, Kowloon; Junk Bay (Tseung Kwan O) is to the west of the peninsula and Clearwater Bay (Tsing Sui Wan) sits to the east; Joss House Bay (Tai Miu Wan) lies to the south

→**Clearwater Bay Country Park Visitor Centre** (清水灣郊野公園遊客中心; ☑852 2719 0032; ☺9.30am-4.30pm, closed Tue; ☐91 from Choi Hung to Tai Au Mun)

→**Last train to Kowloon** Leaves at 12.16am from Po Lam MTR station.

◉ SIGHTS

JOSS HOUSE BAY TIN HAU TEMPLE TEMPLE
(糧船灣天后古廟; ☑852 2519 9155; ☺8am-5pm; minibus 16) This far-flung temple along Tai Au Mun Rd is the largest, oldest and one of the most important Tin Hau temples in the territory, hence its nickname 'Big Temple' (大廟, 'Tai Miu'). It features protruding eaves,

two miniature boats, and a large courtyard where fishermen often dry silver bait. It was built in 1266 by Fujianese salt traders to thank the deity for saving them during a storm and has been restored four times.

CLEARWATER BAY BEACHES BEACH
(清水灣一灘和二灘; ☐91) **FREE** From Tai Au Mun, Tai Au Mun Rd leads south to two fine, sandy beaches: **Clearwater Bay First Beach** (清水灣一灘) and, a bit further southwest, **Clearwater Bay Second Beach** (清水灣二灘). In summer try to go during the week, as both beaches get very crowded on the weekend.

 ## EATING

SEAFOOD ISLAND CANTONESE, SEAFOOD $$
(海鮮島海鮮酒家; ☑852 2719 5730; Shop B, 7 Po Toi O Chuen Rd; meals from HK$180; ☺11am-11pm) Crustaceans of every kind are on full display at this energetic restaurant hidden in discreet Po Toi O village. A totally non-luxe setting but with no-nonsense fare, Seafood Island is famed for its squid sashimi and razor clams. It's more a group activity to dine here. Grab a couple of friends and enjoy all the treats on offer.

🏃 SPORTS & ACTIVITIES

CLEARWATER BAY COUNTRY PARK OUTDOORS
(清水灣郊野公園; ☐103) The heart of the country park is **Tai Au Mun**, from where trails go in various directions, through the Clearwater Bay Country Park Visitor Centre (p173) to the southeast in Tai Hang Tun. Take Lung Ha Wan Rd north from Tai Au Mun to the beach at **Lung Ha Wan** (Lobster Bay) and return via the 2.3km **Lung Ha Wan Country Trail**.

CLEARWATER BAY GOLF & COUNTRY CLUB GOLF
(清水灣高爾夫球鄉村俱樂部; ☑852 2335 3700; www.cwbgolf.org; 139 Tau Au Mun Rd, Clearwater Bay; greens fees HK$1600-2200; ☐91) A 27-hole course at the tip of Clearwater Bay in the New Territories. Nonmembers can play here on weekday mornings except public holidays and Wednesdays. Tee-off time is from 9.30am to 11.30am.

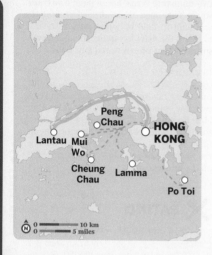

Outlying Islands

Lamma p176

The quickest island escape from downtown Hong Kong, laid-back Lamma exudes a bohemian charm and is home to many a commuter who prefers more space and greenery.

Lantau p180

The largest of the islands boasts bountiful sights and recreational possibilities: country parks, hiking trails, fishing villages, beaches, monasteries and the unmissable Big Buddha.

Cheung Chau p188

Think seafood and seafaring culture on this bustling isle with great windsurfing beaches and temples dedicated to water deities. The annual Bun Festival is a highlight.

TOP SIGHT
PO LIN MONASTERY & BIG BUDDHA

No trip to Hong Kong is complete without visiting Ngong Ping Plateau for the seated Tian Tan Buddha statue, the biggest of its kind in the world. It can be seen aerially as you fly into Hong Kong, or on a clear day from Macau, but nothing beats coming up close and personal with this much-loved spiritual icon over 500m up in the western hills of Lantau.

Commonly known as the 'Big Buddha', the Tian Tan Buddha is a representation of Lord Gautama some 23m high (or 26.4m with the lotus), or just under 34m if you include the podium. It was unveiled in 1993, and still holds the honour as the tallest seated bronze Buddha statue in the world. It's well worth climbing the 268 steps for a closer look at the statue and the surrounding views. The Buddha's birthday, a public holiday in April or May, is a lively time to visit when thousands make the pilgrimage. Visitors are requested to observe some decorum in dress and behaviour. It is forbidden to bring meat or alcohol into the grounds.

On the second level of the podium is a small **museum** containing oil paintings and ceramic plaques of the Buddha's life and teachings.

Po Lin Monastery, a huge Buddhist complex built in 1924, is more of a tourist honeypot than a religious retreat, attracting hundreds of thousands of visitors a year and it's still being expanded. Most of the buildings you'll see on arrival are new, with the older, simpler ones tucked away behind them. Po Lin Vegetarian Restaurant (p186) in the monastery is famed for its inexpensive but filling vegetarian food.

The most spectacular way to get to the plateau is by the 5.7km **Ngong Ping 360** (昂平360 纜車; Map p181; adult/child/concession one way HK$130/65/90, return HK$185/95/130; ⊙10am-6pm Mon-Fri, 9am-6.30pm Sat, Sun & public holidays), a cable car linking Ngong Ping with the centre of Tung Chung (downhill and to the north). The journey over the bay and the mountains takes 25 minutes, with each glassed-in gondola carrying 17 passengers. The upper station is at the skippable theme-park-like Ngong Ping Village just west of the monastery.

DON'T MISS

➡ Tian Tan Buddha
➡ Ngong Ping 360

PRACTICALITIES

➡ 寶蓮禪寺
➡ Map p181. C3
➡ ☑852 2985 5248
➡ Lantau Island
➡ ⊙9am-6pm

Lamma

Explore

Lamma, Hong Kong's laid-back 'hippie island', is easily recognisable at a distance by the three coal chimneys crowning its hilly skyline. The chimneys stand out so much because Lamma, home to 6000 or so, is otherwise devoid of high-rise development. Here it's all about lush forests, hidden beaches and chilled-out villages connected by pedestrian paths. You won't see any cars here, but be prepared for spotting the odd snake.

Most visitors arrive in the main town of Yung Shue Wan, a counterculture haven popular with expats.

The Best...

➧**Sight** Lo So Shing Beach (p178)

➧**Place to Eat** Rainbow Seafood Restaurant (p179)

➧**Place to Drink** Island Bar (p179)

Top Tip

Want huge swaths of the island all to yourself? Visit on a weekday to avoid the weekend crowds.

Getting There & Away

➧**Ferry** Run from **Yung Shue Wan pier** to pier 4 of Central's Outlying Islands ferry terminal, **Pak Kok Tsuen** and Aberdeen; they also go from **Sok Kwu Wan** pier to pier 4 of Central's Outlying Islands ferry terminal, **Mo Tat Wan** and Aberdeen.

Need to Know

➧**Area Code** ☑852
➧**Location** 3km across the East Lamma

Lamma

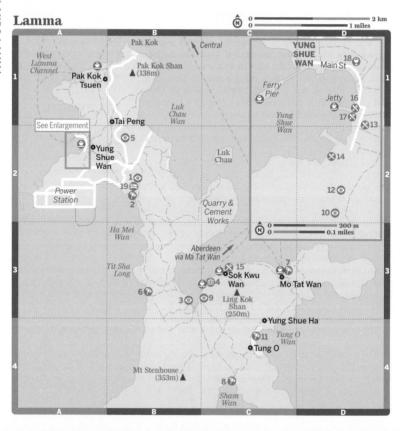

Channel from Aberdeen. There are two main settlements on the island: Yung Shue Wan to the northwest and Sok Kwu Wan on the east coast of the island.

➡ **Last Ferry to Central** 11.30pm from Yung Shue Wan; 10.40pm from Sok Kwu Wan.

◉ SIGHTS

HERBOLAND FARM

(📞852 9094 6206; off Hung Shing Yeh beach; ⊙10am-5pm; 🚢Yung Shue Wan) Nestled in the leafy fringes of Hung Shing Yeh beach is Herboland, the first organic herb farm in the territory. Stroll past fragrant bushes of rosemary and verbena, or choose from more than 40 types of herbal tea in the farm's blissful tea garden.

YUNG SHUE WAN VILLAGE

(榕樹灣; 🚢Yung Shue Wan) Yung Shue Wan (Banyan Tree Bay) may be the largest settlement on the island, but it remains a small village with little more than a car-free main street following the curve of the bay. Despite encroaching development, the village has somehow managed to retain more than a whiff of rustic charm. The main street is lined with cafes, bars, veggie stalls and new-age shops, all popular with locals and tourists alike.

At the southern end of the bay, look for a small Tin Hau Temple (p177) dating from the late 19th century, with a pair of eccentric Western lion statues guarding the entrance.

HUNG SHING YEH BEACH

(🚢Yung Shue Wan) A 25-minute walk southeast from the Yung Shue Wan ferry pier, Hung Shing Yeh beach is the most popular beach on Lamma. Arrive early in the morning or on a weekday and you'll probably find it deserted, though you may find the view of the power station across the bay takes some getting used to. The beach is protected by a shark net and has toilets, showers and changing rooms. There are a few restaurants and drinks stands nearby, open in season.

TIN HAU TEMPLE TEMPLE

(天后廟; Yung Shue Wan) This totally renovated Tin Hau Temple dates back to 1826.

SHAM WAN BEACH

(Deep Bay; ⊙closed Jun-Oct; 🚢Sok Kwu Wan) Sham Wan is a beautiful bay in the south of the island that can be reached from Tung O Wan by clambering over the hills. A trail on the left about 200m up the hill from Tung O Wan leads south to this small and sandy beach. Don't come here from June to October, when Hong Kong's endangered green turtles nest and the beach is closed to the public.

LAMMA FISHERFOLK'S VILLAGE MUSEUM, VILLAGE

(漁民文化村; 📞852 2982 8585; http://lamma fisherfolks.com.hk; 2nd fl, 20 Sok Kwu Wan First St, Sok Kwu Wan; adult/child HK$80/60; ⊙10am-6pm; 🚢) This 2000-sq-metre floating museum and theme park on a raft showcases the fishing culture and history of the traditional fishery industry in Hong Kong. Fishing tools and model vessels are on display, including a real 60-year-old junk. You can also try your hand at angling and rope weaving.

TUNG O WAN BEACH

(🚢Sok Kwu Wan) Long coveted by developers as a prime location for new condos and marina facilities, unspoiled Tung O Wan is still holding out against the might of the property dollar thanks to the combined resistance of local residents and environmentalists from other shores. Ringed by a long sandy beach, this small and secluded bay makes a rewarding detour while walking to Sok Kwu Wan from Yung Shue Wan or from Sok Kwu Wan itself.

Just before the Tin Hau Temple at the entrance to Sok Kwu Wan, follow the signposted path to the right southward, up and over the hill to the tiny village of Tung O. The walk takes about 30 minutes over a rugged landscape, and the first half is a fairly strenuous climb up steps and along a path.

MO TAT WAN   BEACH

(🚢Sok Kwu Wan) The clean and relatively uncrowded beach at Mo Tat Wan is a mere 20-minute coastal path walk east of Sok Kwu Wan village. Mo Tat Wan is OK for swimming, but has no lifeguards. You can also reach it by *kaido* (small open-sea ferry) from Aberdeen, which continues on to Sok Kwu Wan.

LO SO SHING   BEACH

(🚢Yung Shue Wan) Lo So Shing beach is the most beautiful stretch of sand on Lamma, a small gold crescent fringed by thickly forested hills. Since getting here requires some walking, it's often practically deserted, even on weekends.

To get here, head south from Hung Shing Yeh beach. The path climbs steeply until it reaches a Chinese-style pavilion. You'll pass a second pavilion that offers splendid sea views; from here a path leads from the Family Trail down to Lo So Shing.

SOK KWU WAN   VILLAGE

(索罟灣; 🚢Sok Kwu Wan) Though still a small settlement (population 500), Lamma's secondary village of Sok Kwu Wan supports at least a dozen waterfront seafood restaurants popular with boaters. The small harbour is filled with rafts from which cages are suspended and fish are farmed. It's a lovely place to end your Family Trail walk with a seafood feast and a few cold beers.

Sok Kwu Wan's peaceful vibe may not last much longer, as there are plans for a new housing development in the village's abandoned quarry. The high-rise apartments would house some 5000 residents, nearly doubling Lamma's population.

KAMIKAZE CAVES   CAVE

(神風洞; 🚢Sok Kwu Wan) The three so-called Kamikaze Caves, grottoes measuring 10m wide and 30m deep, were built by the occupying Japanese forces to house motorboats wired with explosives to disrupt Allied shipping during WWII. They were never used. You'll pass the caves when entering Sok Kwu Wan from the south (ie from the Family Trail linking this village with Yung Shue Wan).

LAMMA WINDS   LANDMARK

(南丫風采發電站; ⏰7am-6pm; 🚢Yung Shue Wan) Standing in elegant contrast to that carbon dioxide–belching, coal-fired power station, Lamma's giant wind turbine, dramatically positioned atop the ridge just southeast of Tai Peng old village, makes a stirring sight (although in reality it is something of a white elephant generating far less power than was hoped for). There's a small **exhibition centre** on wind power, but there's not much else to do here other than admire its feathered blades scything the breeze.

To reach it, follow the paths from Yung Shue Wan up to Tai Peng old village and turn right once you hit the concrete roadway linking the power station with Pak Kok.

 EATING

BOOKWORM CAFE   CAFE $

(南島書蟲; ☎852 2982 4838; 79 Main St, Yung Shue Wan; meals from HK$80; ⏰9am-9pm Fri-Wed; @🖥; 🚢Yung Shue Wan) 🌱 Vegetarian foodies are in heaven at Bookworm, the granddaddy of Hong Kong's healthy and ecoconscious dining scene. Tasty dishes include the dhal and salad combo, goat's cheese sandwich and shepherdess pie, which all pair well with the carefully selected organic wines. The cafe is also a second-hand bookshop.

BEST KEBAB & PIZZA   TURKISH $

(☎852 2982 0902; 4 Yung Shue Wan Back St, Yung Shue Wan; meals from HK$40; ⏰2-10pm Mon-Fri, noon-10pm Sat; 🚢Yung Shue Wan) This small, unpretentious Turkish-run eatery serves exactly what it says on the tin. The pizza, lamb chops and sizzling shish kebab are what the local residents rave about. Wash them down with freshly brewed Turkish coffee and fruit teas.

WORTH A DETOUR

PENG CHAU

Backwater Peng Chau does not possess much wow factor but it is perhaps the most traditionally Chinese of the Outlying Islands, with narrow alleyways, crowded housing, a covered wet **market** (坪洲街市) near the ferry pier, a couple of small but important temples, and interesting shops selling everything from humble household goods to religious paraphernalia. Come any day and you can count on hearing the clatter of mah-jong tiles and Cantonese opera tunes leaking from old transistors that act as a soundtrack to this sleepy getaway.

Climbing the steps to Finger Hill (95m), the island's highest point, offers some light exercise and excellent views. To get here from the ferry pier, walk up Lo Peng St, turn right at the Tin Hau temple (天后廟), containing a century-old 2.5m-long whale bone blackened by incense smoke, and walk south along Wing On St. This gives way to Shing Ka Rd, and Nam Shan Rd leads from here east up to Finger Hill. It's an easy half-hour walk.

Peng Chau Heritage Trail (www.greenpengchau.org.hk) Follow the signs around Peng Chau to see the ghostly remains of the island's past life as an industrial hub. Though it may seem hard to believe, this was once one of Hong Kong's major industrial centres, with a large match factory and a lime kiln. All that remains today are picturesque ruins. Don't miss the cool octagonal well just off the town square.

Les Copains d'Abord (☏852 9432 5070; Lo Peng St; cheese & meat plates from HK$80; ⊙11am-9pm) Don't leave Peng Chau without sipping a glass of *vin rouge* and nibbling a plate of charcuterie under parasols at Les Copains d'Abord, an incongruously located, French-owned wine bar and cafe. Opening hours can be erratic. Don't be surprised if it's closed for a neighbourhood party; it's that kind of place. You'll find it on the island's main square straight up from the pier.

WATERFRONT INTERNATIONAL $
(☏852 2982 1168; 58 Main St, Yung Shue Wan; meals from HK$90; ⊙9am-2am; ⊛Yung Shue Wan) With great views and lapping waves a few steps from the terrace, this restaurant is both a popular breakfast joint and sundowner spot. Traditional British and Italian fare is served here, as is straightforward Indian grub.

★**RAINBOW SEAFOOD
RESTAURANT** CHINESE, SEAFOOD $$
(天虹海鮮酒家; ☏852 2982 8100; www.rainbowrest.com.hk; Shops 1A-1B, ground fl, 23-25 First St, Sok Kwu Wan; meals from HK$180; ⊙10am-10.30pm; ⊛Sok Kwu Wan) Gigantic Rainbow may boast 800 seats but you still need to book ahead for prime hours. Steamed grouper, lobster and abalone are the specialities at this waterfront restaurant. You have the option of being transported by its own ferries from Central pier 9 or Tsim Sha Tsui Public Pier; call or check its website for sailings.

**TAI HING SEAFOOD
RESTAURANT** CANTONESE, SEAFOOD $$
(大興海鮮酒家; ☏852 2982 0339; 53 Main St, Yung Shue Wan; meals from HK$250; ⊙lunch & dinner) The unassuming Tai Hing enjoys a stream of return customers for its honest home cooking. Lamma native Cheong Gor is the heart and soul of this semiprivate kitchen. Tell him your budget and he will pick the best seasonal seafood for you. Four hundred dollars (per head) will get you a veritable seafood extravaganza. Reservations recommended.

🍷 DRINKING & NIGHTLIFE

ISLAND BAR BAR
(⊙5pm-late Mon-Fri, noon-late Sat & Sun, happy hour 5-8pm; ⊛Yung Shue Wan) The closest bar to Yung Shue Wan's ferry pier, this place is a favourite with older expats and hosts the best jam sessions on the island.

7TH AVENUE BAR
(7 Main St, Yung Shue Wan; ⊙noon-late; ⊛Yung Shue Wan) Though the city-sounding name doesn't match Lamma's rural ambience, this new kid on the block has a welcoming atmosphere with hookahs and outdoor seating, thanks to the young entrepreneur who runs it. All food and booze is reasonably priced.

Lantau

Explore

The sheer size of Lantau, Hong Kong's largest island, makes for days of exploration. The north tip of the island, home to the airport, Disneyland and the high-rise Tung Chung residential and shopping complex, is highly developed. But much of the rest of Lantau is still entirely rural. Here you'll find traditional fishing villages, empty beaches and a mountainous interior crisscrossed with quad-burning hiking trails.

Most visitors come to Lantau to visit Mickey or see the justly famous 'Big Buddha' statue, but be sure you get beyond the north side for a taste of a laid-back island where cows graze in the middle of the road, school kids gather seaweed with their grandparents in the shallow bays, and the odd pangolin is said to still roam the forested hillsides.

The Best...

➡**Sight** Po Lin Monastery & Big Buddha (p175)

➡**Place to Eat** Mavericks (p185)

➡**Place to Sleep** Tai O Heritage Hotel (p227)

Top Tip

There are only 50 taxis serving the whole island. Have the call-service numbers ready, especially after hours.

Getting There & Away

➡**Bus** Bus S1 connects Lantau's Tung Chung and the airport. Bus N11 connects Tung Chung and Central, while bus N21 connects Tung Chung with Kowloon.

➡**Ferry** Major services from Central (www.nwff.com.hk) leave from pier 6 at the Outlying Islands ferry terminal for Mui Wo. Ferries also depart from Chi Ma Wan (also on Lantau), Cheung Chau and Peng Chau for Mui Wo. Chi Ma Wan is served by the inter-island ferry from Mui Wo, Cheung Chau and Peng Chau. There are also ferries between Tung Chung and Tuen Mun in the New Territories and ferries between Discovery Bay and Central.

➡**MTR** The Tung Chung MTR line runs between Central and Lantau, and is the main way (other than the Mui Wo ferry) visitors access Lantau from Hong Kong Island.

Need to Know

➡**Area Code** ☑852

➡**Location** 8km west of Hong Kong Island. The most inhabited town, Tung Chung, is on the northern coast, while Mui Wo, the second-largest settlement, is on the eastern coast. The airport is directly north of Tung Chung.

➡**Last Ferry to Central** 11.30pm from Mui Wo

◉ SIGHTS

◉ North Lantau

PO LIN MONASTERY & BIG BUDDHA BUDDHIST MONASTERY
See p175.

HONG KONG DISNEYLAND AMUSEMENT PARK
Map p181 (香港迪士尼樂園; ☑852 183 0830; http://park.hongkongdisneyland.com; adult/child one-day ticket HK$539/385; ⊙10am-8pm Mon-Fri, to 9pm Sat & Sun; ⊛; Ⓜ Disney Resort Station) Ever since it claimed Hong Kong in 2005, Disneyland has served as a rite of passage for the flocks of Asian tourists who come daily to steal a glimpse of one of America's most famous cultural exports. It's divided into seven areas – Main Street USA, Tomorrowland, Fantasyland, Adventureland, Toy Story Land, Mystic Point, and Grizzly Gulch – but it's still quite tiny compared to the US version, and most of the attractions are geared towards families with small children.

Most of the rides are appropriate for all but the smallest kids. Highlights include the goofy-scary tour through the Mystic Manor, and classics such as 'It's a Small World' and the Mad Hatter teacups. Adrenalin junkies have only a few true thrills – the whipping-through-utter-darkness Space Mountain roller coaster in Tomorrowland, the Big Grizzly Mountain coaster in Grizzly Gulch, and the stomach-dropping RC Racer half-pipe coaster in Toy Story Land. The Iron Man Experience 3D motion simulator opens late 2016.

While most of Hong Kong Disney is essentially a scaled-down version of the American Disneyland, there are a number of nods to Chinese culture. Disney consulted a feng-shui master when building the park, and ended up moving the entrance 12 degrees to

Lantau

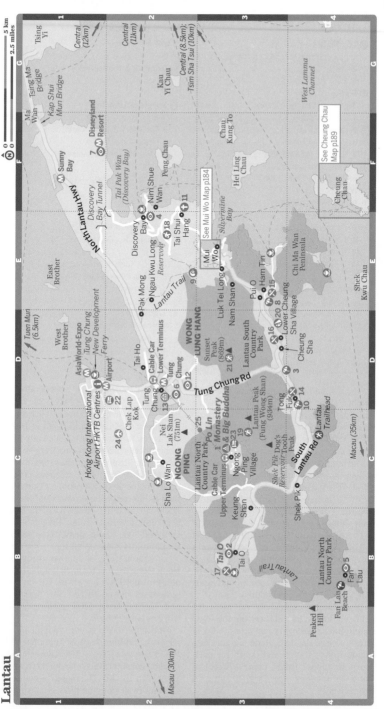

Lantau

avoid *chi* slipping into the ocean. The lucky number eight is repeated throughout the park (the Western mining town of Grizzly Gulch was said to be founded on 8 August 1888), and Canto-pop singer Jacky Cheung is the park's official spokesperson.

The hungry will never be far from a snack or a sit-down meal, whether Eastern (dried squid, fish balls on a stick, dim sum) or Western (burgers, cotton candy, muffins). And you'll certainly never be far from a souvenir shop.

There's a parade daily through Main Street at 3.30pm, and a music, light and fireworks show centred on Sleeping Beauty's Castle nightly at 8pm. As in any Disney theme park, costumed characters wander around ready to be greeted by excited children.

Disneyland is linked by rail with the MTR at Sunny Bay station on the Tung Chung line; passengers just cross the platform to board the dedicated train for Disneyland Resort station and the theme park. Journey times from Central/Kowloon/Tsing Yi stations are 24/21/10 minutes respectively.

TRAPPIST MONASTERY CHRISTIAN MONASTERY
Map p181 (神樂院; ☏852 2987 6292; Tai Shui Hang; ⛴kaido from Peng Chau or Discovery Bay) Northeast of Mui Wo and south of Discovery Bay is the Roman Catholic Lady of Joy Abbey, better known as the Trappist Monastery. The Trappists gained a reputation as one of the most austere religious communities in the Roman Catholic Church and the Lantau congregation was established at Peking in the 19th century. All of the monks here now are local Hong Kongers. Their medieval-style stone chapel is a peaceful spot for quiet contemplation.

The monastery is known throughout Hong Kong for its cream-rich milk, sold in half-pint bottles everywhere, but the cows have been moved to the New Territories and Trappist Dairy Milk is now produced in Yuen Long.

One of the nicest ways to visit the monastery is by hiking the three hours from Mui Wo to Discovery Bay – just follow the well-marked coastal trail at the northern end of Tung Wan Tau Rd. The monastery makes a good halfway stopping place. You can then have dinner at Discovery Bay and catch a ferry back to Central.

DISCOVERY BAY

AREA

Map p181 (⛴ Discovery Bay) With a fine stretch of sandy beach ringed by luxurious condominiums, 'DB' is a dormitory suburb on Lantau's northeastern coast for professionals who commute to Central. There is no pressing need to visit except to ogle at residents in their converted golf carts, which cost HK$200,000 a pop, or perhaps to eat dinner and watch the nightly Disneyland fireworks, visible across the water.

There are a handful of decent restaurants in **Discovery Bay Plaza** (愉景灣廣場), just up from the ferry pier and the central plaza. The 27-hole Discovery Bay Golf Club (p188) is perched in the hills to the southwest.

Buses make the run to and from Tung Chung and the airport at Chek Lap Kok via the Discovery Bay Tunnel and the North Lantau Hwy. A trail leading from the golf course will take you down to Silvermine Bay and the rest of Lantau in a couple of hours.

TUNG CHUNG FORT & BATTERY

HISTORIC BUILDING

Map p181 Annals record a settlement at Tung Chung as early as the Ming dynasty. There are several Buddhist establishments in the upper reaches of the valley, but the main attraction here is Tung Chung Fort, which dates back to 1832, when Chinese troops were garrisoned on Lantau. The Japanese briefly occupied the fort during WWII. Measuring 70m by 80m and enclosed by granite-block walls, it retains six of its muzzle-loading cannons pointing out to sea.

About 1km to the north are the ruins of Tung Chung Battery, which is a much smaller fort built in 1817. All that remains is an L-shaped wall facing the sea, with a gun emplacement in the corner. The ruins were only discovered in 1980, having been hidden for about a century by scrub.

HAU WONG TEMPLE

TEMPLE

Map p181 (侯王廟) Facing Tung Chung Bay is this double-roofed temple, founded at the end of the Song dynasty. It contains a bell dating from 1765 that's inscribed by the Qing dynasty emperor Qian Long.

TUNG CHUNG

AREA

Map p181 (🚌3M from Mui Wo, 11 from Tai O, 23 from Ngong Ping, Ⓜ Tung Chung) Before 1994 Tung Chung, on Lantau's northern coast,

was an inaccessible farming village. Less than four years later, it was transformed into a new town and a new airport was added to nearby Chek Lap Kok. Today Tung Chung has the largest population on the island, with a 760-hectare residential estate served by the MTR. Most people come here to shop at the Citygate Outlets, but there are some interesting historical sights in the vicinity too.

⊙ Mui Wo

MUI WO

VILLAGE

(⛴ Mui Wo) Mui Wo (Plum Nest) was Lantau's largest settlement before Tung Chung was born. Today this sleepy town functions as a shopping, eating and transport hub for the island's south side. The big draw is **Silvermine Bay beach** (銀礦灣), a decent stretch of sand with toilets and changing facilities just east of town. There's also a wet market with several seafood restaurants, as well as a number of local bars and eateries.

There are several decent places to stay and eat in Mui Wo. Friendly Bicycle Shop (p188) near the Park 'n' Shop supermarket rents bikes.

SILVERMINE BAY BEACH

BEACH

Map p184 (銀礦灣; 🚻; ⛴ Mui Wo) Just east of Mui Wo town, Silvermine Bay beach is a popular spot for day trippers. The long, wide beach fringed by houses and a few small hotels is not the most pristine, but it's nice enough for an afternoon of sun and surf. There are changing facilities and lifeguards, but only in season (April to October).

SILVERMINE WATERFALL

WATERFALL

Map p181 (⛴ Mui Wo) If time allows, hike from Mui Wo town to Silvermine Waterfall (銀礦瀑布), near the old Silvermine Cave northwest of town (the cave was mined for silver in the 19th century but has now been sealed off). The waterfall is quite a spectacle when it gushes during the rainy season, usually from May through October. The walk to the waterfall from Mui Wo is about 3km; head westward along Mui Wo Rural Committee Rd and then follow the marked path north.

BUTTERFLY HILL WATCHTOWER

HISTORIC BUILDING

Map p184 (蝴蝶山更樓) This granite watchtower was built in the late 19th century for

Mui Wo

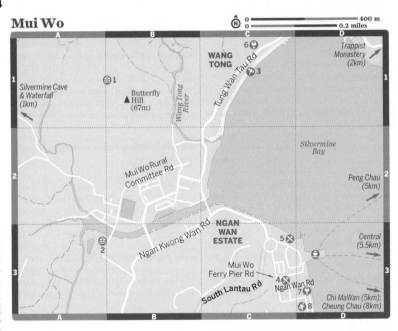

Mui Wo

◎ Sights

1 Butterfly Hill Watchtower B1
2 Luk Tei Tong Watchtower A3
3 Silvermine Bay Beach C1

✖ Eating

4 Bahçe C3
5 Mui Wo Cooked Food
    Centre C3

🍷 Drinking & Nightlife

6 China Beach Club C1
7 China Bear D3

◆ Sports & Activities

8 Friendly Bicycle Shop D3

defence against pirates, and now makes for
a scenic ruin.

LUK TEI TONG
WATCHTOWER   HISTORIC BUILDING

Map p184 (鹿地塘更樓) Once a fortification
against pirates, this 19th-century tower
makes for a photogenic ruin, with vines
bursting forth from its windows.

◉ South Lantau Road

FAN LAU   AREA

Map p181 Only accessible on foot, Fan Lau
(Divided Flow), a small peninsula on the
southwestern tip of Lantau, has a couple of
good beaches and the remains of **Fan Lau
Fort**, built in 1729 to protect the channel
between Lantau and the Pearl River estuary from pirates. It remained in operation
until the end of the 19th century and was
restored in 1985. The sea views from here
are sterling.

To the southeast of the fort is an **ancient
stone circle**. The origins and age of the
circle are uncertain, but it probably dates
from the neolithic or early Bronze Age and
may have been used in rituals.

To get here from Tai O, walk south from
the bus station for 250m and pick up section 7 of the coastal Lantau Trail (p187), a
distance of about 8km. The trail then carries on to the northeast towards Shek Pik
for another 12km, where you can catch bus
1 back to Mui Wo.

CHEUNG SHA   BEACH

Map p181 (🚌3M from Mui Wo) Cheung Sha
(Long Sand) is Hong Kong's longest beach,
stretching more than 3km on the southern

coast of Lantau. It's divided into 'upper' and 'lower' sections; a trail over a hillock links the two. Upper Cheung Sha, with occasional good surf, is the prettier and longer beach, and boasts changing facilities and a snack bar. Lower Cheung Sha has a beachfront restaurant and a water-sports centre. This is said to be the best windsurfing beach in Hong Kong, especially from November to March.

PUI O
BEACH

Map p181 (🚌3M from Mui Wo) Along South Lantau Rd is a succession of beaches that attract surfers, beach-goers and retirees alike. Just 5km southwest of Mui Wo, Pui O has a decent beach, but as it's the closest one to Mui Wo it can get very crowded. The village has several restaurants, holiday flats galore and, in season, stalls renting bicycles.

TONG FUK
BEACH

Map p181 (🚌3M from Mui Wo) The beach at Tong Fuk is not Lantau's nicest, but the village has holiday flats, several shops and restaurants, and its distance from Mui Wo means it's usually quite peaceful. To the northwest is the not-so-scenic sprawl of Ma Po Ping Prison.

⊙ Tai O

★TAI O
VILLAGE

Map p181 (🚌1 from Mui Wo, 11 from Tung Chung, 21 from Ngong Ping) On weekends, droves of visitors trek to the far-flung west coast of Lantau to see a fascinating way of life. Here in Tai O, historical home to the Tanka boat people, life is all about the sea. Houses are built on stilts above the ocean, sampans ply the dark-green waterways, and elderly residents still dry seafood on traditional straw mats and make the village's celebrated shrimp paste.

Tai O is built partly on Lantau and partly on a tiny island about 15m from the shore. Until the mid-1990s the only way to cross was via a rope-tow ferry pulled by elderly Hakka women. That and the large number of sampans in the small harbour earned Tai O the nickname 'the Venice of Hong Kong'. Though the narrow iron Tai Chung footbridge now spans the canal, the rope-tow ferry is resurrected on some weekends and holidays: drop HK$1 in the box as you disembark.

Some of the tiny, traditional-style village houses still stand in the centre, including some of Tai O's famed stilt houses (p185) on the waterfront. There are a few houses that escaped a fire in 2000, plus a number of shanties, their corrugated-iron walls held in place by rope, and houseboats that haven't set sail for years.

The main activity for visitors in Tai O is simply wandering the back alleys, photographing the stilt houses, strolling the long causeway, and buying seafood at the crowded street markets.

Note that taxis out of Tai O are essentially nonexistent, and weekend afternoons mean long queues for buses headed back to Mui Wo and Tung Chung.

STILT HOUSES
HISTORIC BUILDING

Map p181 (🚌1 from Mui Wo, 11 from Tung Chung, 21 from Ngong Ping) Tai O's remaining stilt houses and the local **Kwan Tai Temple** (關帝廟; Map p181; ⊙8am-6pm), dedicated to the god of war, are on Kat Hing St. To reach them, cross the bridge from the mainland to the island, walk up Tai O Market St and go right at the Fook Moon Lam restaurant.

There are a couple of other temples here too, including an 18th-century one erected in honour of Hung Shing, patron of fisherfolk; it's on Shek Tsai Po St, about 600m west of the Fook Moon Lam restaurant.

OLD TAI O POLICE STATION
HISTORIC BUILDING

Map p181 (舊大澳警署; Tai O Heritage Hotel; ☎852 2985 8383; www.taioheritagehotel.com; Shek Tsai Po St; ⊙tours 3pm & 4pm; 🚌1 from Mui Wo, 11 from Tung Chung, 21 from Ngong Ping) **FREE** At the end of Shek Tsai Po St stands the beautifully restored colonial-style Old Tai O Police Station. Built in 1902, the former marine police station was originally set up to protect the surrounding waters from pirate activity. In 2012, the restored building was reopened as the charming Tai O Heritage Hotel. Even if you aren't staying here, it's worth joining the free guided tour; online reservations are a must.

EATING

★MAVERICKS
BURGERS, INTERNATIONAL $

Map p181 (☎852 5402 4154; Pui O beach; meals from HK$100; ⊙5.30-11.30pm Fri, 11.30am-11.30pm Sat & Sun; 🚌1 from Mui Wo) 🍃 Sunburned beach-goers gather for house-made

THE PINK DOLPHINS OF THE PEARL RIVER

Between 100 and 200 misnamed Chinese white dolphins *(Sousa chinensis)* – they are actually bubble-gum pink – inhabit the coastal waters around Hong Kong, finding the brackish waters of the Pearl River estuary to be the perfect habitat. Unfortunately these glorious mammals, which are also called Indo-Pacific humpback dolphins, are being threatened by environmental pollution, and their numbers are dwindling. **Hong Kong Dolphinwatch** (p152) was founded in 1995 to raise awareness of these wonderful creatures and promote responsible ecotourism. It offers 2½-hour cruises to see the pink dolphins in their natural habitat three times a week, year-round. Guides assemble in the lobby of the **Kowloon Hotel Hong Kong** (www.harbour-plaza.com/kowloon) in Tsim Sha Tsui at 9am for the bus to Tung Chung via the Tsing Ma Bridge, from where the boat departs; the tours return at 1pm.

sausages and burgers on artisan buns at this hip surf-themed weekend spot, right on the water in Pui O. Many of the veggies are grown on the restaurant's own farm, the meat and dairy used are hormone-free, and menus are printed on recycled bamboo paper. Wash your meal down with a locally brewed Young Master Ale.

PO LIN VEGETARIAN
RESTAURANT   VEGETARIAN $
Map p181 (寶蓮禪寺齋堂; ☑852 2985 5248; Ngong Ping; set meals regular/deluxe HK$60/100; ☺11.30am-4.30pm; ☑) The famous Po Lin monastery (p175) has a reputation for inexpensive but substantial vegetarian food. The restaurant is located in the covered arcade to the left of the main monastery building. Buy your ticket there or at the ticket office below the Tian Tan Buddha statue. Sittings take place every half-hour.

GALLERY   INTERNATIONAL, PIZZERIA $
Map p181 (☑852 2980 2582; 26 Tong Fuk Village; meals from HK$80; ☺6pm-1am Mon-Sat, noon-1am Sun; ☑3M from Mui Wo) This laid-back alfresco spot in the poky little village of Tong Fuk has some of Hong Kong's better steaks, at way-better-than-Central prices. Ideal for a post-hike feast. Pizzas get high marks as well.

MUI WO COOKED FOOD
CENTRE   CANTONESE, SEAFOOD $
Map p184 (next to ferry pier, Mui Wo; meals from HK$50; ☺6am-2am, hours vary; ☑Mui Wo) Next to the Mui Wo ferry pier, this smallish centre has a handful of seafood restaurants with tables overlooking the water. Wah Kee is the pick for Cantonese-style seafood.

SOLO   CAFE $
Map p181 (☑852 9153 7453; 86 Kat Hing St, Tai O; meals from HK$40; ☺11am-6pm Mon-Sat; ☑1

from Mui Wo) Framed by a backdrop of stilt houses and lush mountains, this sunny terrace right on the water invites lazy afternoons spent enjoying coffee. The tiramisu and the apple crumble with ice cream are as tempting as its fresh roasted coffee.

BAHÇE   TURKISH $
Map p184 (☑852 2984 0222; Shop 19, ground fl, Mui Wo Centre, 3 Ngan Wan Rd, Mui Wo; mains from HK$95; ☺11am-10.30pm Mon-Fri, 9.30am-10.30pm Sat & Sun; ☑Mui Wo) Near the ferry pier is this small, busy place where locals and expats alike opt to eat at its outdoor tables in the warmer months. Chow down on heaping plates of savoury lamb, felafel, hummus, *fattoush* (a pita bread and vegetable salad) and more before hitting the beaches or taking the ferry back to Central.

STOEP RESTAURANT   SOUTH AFRICAN $$
Map p181 (☑852 2980 2699; 50 Lower Cheung Sha Wan Rd; meals from HK$85; ☺11am-10pm Tue-Sun; ☑1 from Mui Wo) This Mediterranean-style restaurant is just set back from Cheung Sha beach, with decent meat and fish dishes and a South African *braai* (barbecue). Be sure to book on the weekend.

TAI O LOOKOUT   FUSION $$
Map p181 (☑852 2985 8383; www.taioheritage-hotel.com; Tai O Heritage Hotel, Shek Tsai Po St, Tai O; dishes from HK$100; ☺7.30am-10pm; ☑1 from Mui Wo, 11 from Tung Chung, 21 from Ngong Ping) The rotating ceiling fans, wooden booths and tiled floor of this rooftop glass-house restaurant ooze old-world charm, and no one would blame you if you came to just sip coffee and chill. But the food – fried rice tossed with Tai O's famous shrimp paste, cheesecake with local mountain begonia – is well rated, too.

🍷 DRINKING & NIGHTLIFE

CHINA BEACH CLUB   BAR

Map p184 (📞852 2983 8931; 18 Tung Wan Tau Rd, Silvermine Bay beach; ◷noon-11pm Fri-Sun; 🚇Mui Wo) This cheerful restaurant has an airy rooftop and balcony overlooking Silvermine Bay beach. Chill over a home-style Greek moussaka or just kick back with a cocktail or beer. The two-for-one cocktail 'hour' can go on well into the night.

HEMINGWAY'S   BAR

Map p181 (📞852 2987 8855; Shop G9, D'Deck, Discovery Bay; ◷noon-1am Mon-Fri, to 2am Sat; 🚢) Sleek and somewhat corporate-feeling, this Caribbean restaurant and bar is always packed with Disco Bay expats sipping rum cocktails and eating plates of jerk chicken. Its umbrella-topped patio tables are a lovely place to watch the water.

CHINA BEAR   PUB

Map p184 (📞852 2984 9720; Ground fl, Mui Wo Centre, Ngan Wan Rd, Mui Wo; ◷10am-2am, happy hour 5-9pm Mon-Fri, 5-8pm Sat & Sun; 🚇Mui Wo) The most popular expat pub-restaurant in Mui Wo, China Bear boasts a wonderful open bar facing the water. It's right by the ferry terminal, making it the perfect spot for your first and last beer in Mui Wo.

🏃 SPORTS & ACTIVITIES

LANTAU PEAK   HIKING

Map p181 (Fung Wong Shan) Known as Fung Wong Shan (Phoenix Mountain) in Cantonese, this 934m-high peak is the second-highest in Hong Kong after Tai Mo Shan (957m) in the New Territories. The view from

the summit is absolutely stunning, and on a clear day it's possible to see Macau 65km to the west. Watching the sun rise from the peak is a popular choice among hardy hikers. Some choose to stay at the Ngong Ping SG Davis Hostel (p227) and leave around 4am for the two-hour summit push.

If you're hiking Lantau Peak as a day trip, take the MTR to Tung Chung, then take bus 3M to Pak Kung Au (tell the driver where you're getting off beforehand). From here, you'll follow the markers for section 3 of the Lantau Trail (p187), ascending the peak then descending the steps into Ngong Ping. This 4.5km route takes about three hours.

SUNSET PEAK   HIKING

Map p181 (Tai Tung Shan) Hong Kong's third-highest peak (869m) is a good sweaty climb with lovely panoramic views of the surrounding mountains. Plan for three hours. The ambitious can combine it with Lantau Peak (this is popularly known as the 'two peak challenge'). Check out the creepy 'ghost houses' near the peak – ruins of British holiday bungalows from colonial days.

To get to the start, take the ferry to Mui Wo and bus 1 towards Pui O. Get off the bus just before the top of the hill where there's a fenced trailhead and noticeboard with the Lantau Trail map. This section ends at Pak Kung Au, where the Lantau Peak section begins. From here catch a bus back to Mui Wo, or on to Tung Chung and the MTR.

LANTAU TRAIL   HIKING

The Lantau Trail is a 70km circular trail beginning and ending in Mui Wo. It's divided into 12 sections ranging from 2.5km to 10.5km, some of which can be done alone, others of which must be hiked together. While a few sections are relatively flat, others are among the hillier (and most spectacular) hikes in Hong Kong.

WORTH A DETOUR

PO TOI

A solid favourite of weekend holidaymakers with their own seagoing transport, Po Toi is the largest of a group of five islands – one is little more than a huge rock. Hong Kong's territorial border lies just 2km to the south.

There's some decent walking on Po Toi, a tiny **Tin Hau temple** across the bay from the pier, and, on the southern coast, rock formations that (supposedly) look like a palm tree, a tortoise and a monk, and some mysterious **rock carvings** resembling stylised animals and fish. You can see everything here in an hour.

Ming Kee Seafood Restaurant (明記海鮮酒家; 📞852 2849 7038, 852 2472 1408; ◷11am-11pm) is one of a handful of restaurants in the main village and is by far the most popular with day trippers. Make sure you book ahead on the weekend.

OUTLYING ISLANDS LANTAU

FRIENDLY BICYCLE SHOP   CYCLING

Map p184 (老友記單車專門店; ☑852 2984 2278; 18A Mui Wo Ferry Pier Rd, Mui Wo; bike rental per hr HK$30; ◷10am-6pm Wed-Mon) Rent bikes at this Mui Wo shop. To get here, turn left out of the ferry pier and follow the sea road.

SHEK PIK RESERVOIR TO TAI O   HIKING

Sections 8 and 7 (in that order) of the Lantau Trail (p187) are a long but relatively flat walk along Lantau's southwestern hillsides and down into Tai O fishing village. You'll pass a postcard-pretty beach and, with a quick 30-minute detour, the ruins of Fan Lau Fort and a Tin Hau temple. If you time it right, you can have a sunset seafood feast in Tai O before catching the bus back to Tung Chung. Plan for five hours.

To get to the trailhead, take the ferry to Mui Wo and catch a Tai O–bound bus. Alight just after Shek Pik Reservoir on your right.

BOAT TOURS   BOATING

Map p181 (Tai O; ☐1 from Mui Wo, 11 from Tung Chung, 21 from Ngong Ping) As soon as you step off the bus in Tai O you'll be greeted by offers of 'dolphin tours'. While you're unlikely to spot one of the increasingly rare pink dolphins (p186), this can be a nice chance to tour the village waterways. Always agree on a price beforehand – expect to pay about HK$20 per person for a 20-minute trip.

HONG KONG SHAOLIN WUSHU
CULTURE CENTRE   MARTIAL ARTS

Map p181 (香港少林武術文化中心; ☑852 2985 8898; http://shaolincc.org.hk; Shek Tsai Po St, Tai O; courses from HK$650) Located outside the centre of Tai O is this low-key martial-arts school, one of the few in Hong Kong that runs intensive short courses for curious first-timers; check the website. On-site accommodation is available. It's next to the Hung Shing Temple.

DISCOVERY BAY GOLF CLUB   GOLF

Map p181 (愉景灣高爾夫球會; ☑852 2987 7273; www.dbgc.hk; Valley Rd, Discovery Bay; nonmember green fees weekday/weekend HK$2300/4500; ◉Discovery Bay) Perched high on a hill, this 27-hole course has impressive views of the Outlying Islands.

LONG COAST
SEASPORTS   WINDSURFING, KAYAKING

Map p181 (☑852 8104 6222; www.longcoast.hk; 29 Lower Cheung Sha Village; ◷10am-sunset Mon-Fri, 9am-sunset Sat & Sun) This water-sports centre has its own lodge and campground and offers windsurfing, sea kayaking and wakeboarding. Day-long windsurfing lessons are HK$1500, while a single kayak rents for HK$70/210 for an hour/half-day.

Cheung Chau

Explore

This small, dumb-bell–shaped island is a popular getaway thanks to its beaches and its cute downtown lined with snack shops and incense-filled temples. Come here for an afternoon of temple touring, noshing on fish balls and exploring the rocky coastline. Or stay for a weekend at one of the many holiday rentals and treat yourself to a day of windsurfing lessons followed by an alfresco seafood dinner at one of several harbourside restaurants.

The Best...

➡ **Place to Eat** Kam Wing Tai Fish Ball Shop (p191)

➡ **Place to Drink** Hing Kee Beach Bar (p191)

➡ **Activity** Cheung Chau Windsurfing Centre (p191)

Top Tip

During the Bun Festival, it's wise to take a ferry to Mui Wo, and then take the inter-island ferry to Cheung Chau to avoid the long wait on Central ferry pier.

Getting There & Away

➡ **Ferry** Services from Central leave from pier 5 of the Outlying Islands **ferry terminal** (regular one hour, fast ferry 45 minutes). Ferries can also be taken from Mui Wo and Chi Ma Wan on Lantau and from Peng Chau. Additionally, regular *kaido* operate between Cheung Chau village (Sampan Pier) and **Sai Wan** (☑852 2560 9929) in the south of the island.

Need to Know

➡ **Area Code** ☑852

➡ **Location** Just off the southeast coast of Lantau Island.

➡ **Last Ferry to Central** 11.45pm Monday to Saturday, 11.30pm Sunday and public holidays

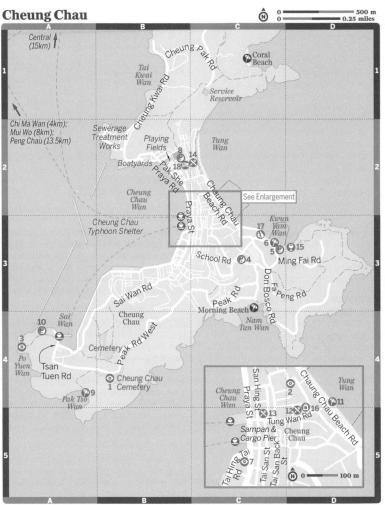

◉ SIGHTS

PAK TAI TEMPLE   TAOIST TEMPLE
(北帝廟; ☎852 2981 0663; ⊙7am-5pm;
🚢Cheung Chau) This colourfully restored
temple from 1783 is the epicentre of the annual Cheung Chau Bun Festival, held in late
April or early May. The most important and
oldest temple on the island, it is dedicated
to the Taoist deity Pak Tai, the 'Supreme
Emperor of the Dark Heaven', military protector of the state, guardian of peace and
order, and protector of fisherfolk.

Legend tells that early settlers from
Canton province brought an image of Pak

Tai with them to Cheung Chau and, when
the statue was carried through the village,
Cheung Chau was spared the plague that
had decimated the populations of nearby
islands. A temple dedicated to the saviour
was built six years later.

CHEUNG CHAU VILLAGE   VILLAGE
(🚢Cheung Chau) The island's main settlement lies along the narrow strip of land
connecting the headlands to the north
and the south. The waterfront is a bustling
place and the maze of streets and alleyways
that make up the village are filled with
old Chinese-style houses and tumbledown

Cheung Chau

shops selling everything from plastic buckets to hell money and other combustible grave offerings. The streets close to the waterfront are pungent with the smell of incense and fish hung out to dry in the sun.

TUNG WAN
BEACH

Tung Wan beach, east of the ferry pier, is not Cheung Chau's prettiest beach but it's the longest and most popular. The far southern end of Tung Wan is a great area for windsurfing. There are plenty of facilities here, as well as lifeguard stations overlooking the roped-off swimming area.

PAK TSO WAN
BEACH

(Italian Beach) If you are visiting the nearby cemetery, it's worth dropping down to Pak Tso Wan (known by local Westerners as 'Italian Beach'), a sandy, isolated spot that is good for swimming.

KWUN YAM WAN
BEACH

East of the ferry pier and just south of Tung Wan beach is Kwun Yam Wan, a quiet spot

LOCAL KNOWLEDGE

SAMPAN RIDES

A great way to see the harbour and soak up the fishing-village atmosphere is to charter a sampan for half an hour (expect to pay HK$70 to HK$120 depending on the day, the season and the demand). Most sampans congregate around the cargo pier in Cheung Chau village, but virtually any small boat you see in the harbour can be hired as a water taxi. Just wave and two or three will come forward. Agree on the fare first.

popular with windsurfers. Go up the footpath and look for the sign to the Fa Peng Knoll. From the knoll you can walk down to signposted Don Bosco Rd; it leads due south to rocky Nam Tam Wan (aka 'Morning Beach'), where swimming is possible.

KWAN KUNG PAVILION
TAOIST TEMPLE

(關公忠義亭前面; Kwun Yan Wan Rd) This small temple houses a 2.5m statue of the god Kwan Kung, a Han dynasty general, made from a whole camphor tree.

SAI WAN TIN HAU TEMPLE
TAOIST TEMPLE

This small 200-year-old temple is dedicated to Tin Hau, goddess of the sea, a most important deity for a sea-centric island like Cheung Chau.

KWUN YAM TEMPLE
TAOIST TEMPLE

This small temple is dedicated to Kwun Yam, the goddess of mercy. A footpath uphill from the southeastern end of Kwun Yam Wan will lead you here.

CHEUNG PO TSAI CAVE
CAVE

(張保仔洞; ⊠Cheung Chau) This 'cave' – in truth not much more than a hole in some rocks – on the southwestern peninsula of the island is said to have been the favourite hideout of the notorious pirate Cheung Po Tsai, who once commanded a flotilla of 600 junks and had a private army of 4000 men. He surrendered to the Qing government in 1810 and became an official himself, but his treasure is said to remain hidden here.

It's a 2km walk from Cheung Chau village along Sai Wan Rd, or take a *kaido* (adult/child from HK$3/2) from the cargo ferry pier to the pier at Sai Wan. From here the walk is less than 200m (uphill).

CHEUNG CHAU BUN FESTIVAL

Taking place over four days in late April or early May, the **Cheung Chau Bun Festival** (www.cheungchau.org) is one of Hong Kong's unique cultural experiences. Honouring the Taoist god Pak Tai, the festival involves days of parades, music and sweet buns galore. The main event is the scramble up the 'bun tower' – whoever grabs the top bun first wins.

Bun towers consist of bamboo scaffolding up to 20m high covered with sacred rolls. If you visit Cheung Chau a week or so before the festival, you'll see the towers being built in front of Pak Tai Temple (p189). At midnight on the designated day, hundreds of people clamber up the towers to snatch buns for good luck. The higher the bun, the greater the luck. In 1978 a tower collapsed under the weight of climbers, injuring two dozen people. The race didn't take place again until it was revived – with strict safety controls – in 2005.

The third day of the festival features a procession of floats, stilt walkers and people dressed as characters from Chinese legends and opera. Most interesting are the colourfully dressed 'floating children' who are carried through the streets on long poles, cleverly wired to metal supports hidden under their clothing. The supports include footrests and a padded seat.

Offerings are made to the spirits of all the fish and livestock killed and consumed over the previous year. During the festival, the whole island goes vegetarian.

CEMETERY   CEMETERY

Peak Rd is the main route to the island's cemetery in the southwest; you'll pass several pavilions along the way built for coffin bearers making the hilly climb.

MARKET   MARKET

(⊙6am-8pm) You'll find plenty of dried seafood, plus staples such as vegetables, rice and meat, at this traditional food market.

EATING & DRINKING

KAM WING TAI FISH BALL SHOP   CHINESE $
(甘永泰魚蛋; ☑852 2981 3050; 106 San Hing St; balls HK$10-15; ⊙10am-8pm; ⛴Chueng Chau) The long line snaking along the alley says something about this celebrated pit stop. Hakka-style snack balls of minced fish and meat are served piping hot. A stick of chewy assorted balls is highly recommended.

KWOK KAM KEE CAKE SHOP   BAKERY $
(郭錦記餅店; ☑852 2986 9717; 46 Pak She St; buns from HK$4; ⊙6am-7pm; ⛴Cheung Chau) This 40-year-old bakery supplies *ping on bao* (peace and prosperity buns), round white buns with a lucky red stamp, for the Bun Festival. Get fresh buns, filled with sesame paste, lotus-seed paste or red-bean paste, at 2pm daily. No English sign – look for the line.

HOMETOWN TEAHOUSE   JAPANESE $
(故鄉茶寮; ☑852 2981 5038; 12 Tung Wan Rd; sushi from HK$16; ⊙11.30am-9pm; ⛴Cheung Chau) Run by an amiable Japanese couple, this tiny backstreet eatery floods with both locals and visitors who come for its sushi and red-bean pastries, served through a walk-up window.

HING KEE BEACH BAR   BAR
(興記士多; ☑852 2981 3478; Kwun Yam Wan beach; ⊙10am-8pm; ⛴Cheung Chau) This hole-in-the-wall drinking spot at quiet Kwun Yam Wan beach is a store-and-bar combo, and a popular hang-out for villagers and those in the know. Auntie Hing (the owner) makes great grub with her home-grown herbs.

SHOPPING

MYARTS   ACCESSORIES, CRAFT
(☑852 2332 9985; 3 Tung Wan Rd; ⊙11am-6pm; ⛴Cheung Chau) This hip little spot stands out for its fun Hong Kong–made jewellery and accessories. Look for earrings shaped like Hong Kong egg tarts, handmade ukuleles painted with dragons and koi by an expat artisan, and arty hand-drawn postcards.

SPORTS & ACTIVITIES

CHEUNG CHAU WINDSURFING CENTRE   WINDSURFING
(☑852 2981 8316; http://ccwindc.com.hk; Kwun Yam Wan beach; ⊙10am-6pm) Day-long beginner classes cost HK$1500; sign up a week ahead). Windsurfers, kayaks and stand-up paddleboards for rent.

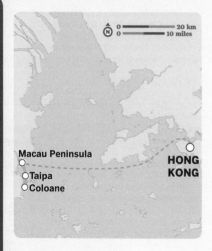

0　20 km
0　10 miles

Macau Peninsula

Taipa
Coloane

HONG
KONG

Macau

Macau Peninsula p194

Lying 65km to the west of Hong Kong, Macau is a city of duality. Its fortresses, churches and the culinary traditions of its former Portuguese colonial masters speak to a uniquely Mediterranean style on the China coast. These are intermixed with the customs, alleys, temples and shrines of its Chinese heritage. On the other hand, the Special Administrative Region (SAR) of Macau is the 'Vegas of the East', the only place in China where gambling is legal.

The Islands: Taipa, Coloane & Cotai p210

Taipa was once two islands that were slowly joined together by silt from the Pearl River. A similar physical joining has happened to Taipa and Coloane because of land reclamation from the sea. The new strip of land joining the two islands is known as Cotai (from Coloane and Taipa). Taipa has rapidly urbanised and it's hard to imagine that just a few decades ago it was an island of duck farms and boat yards. The small island of Coloane was a haven for pirates until 1910. Today it retains Macau's old way of life, though luxurious villas are finding their way onto the island.

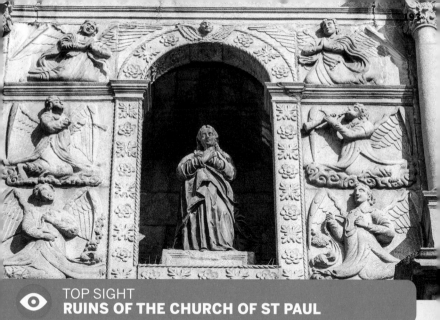

YOKO_KEN_CHAN / SHUTTERSTOCK ©

◉ TOP SIGHT
RUINS OF THE CHURCH OF ST PAUL

Also known as 'the Gate to Nowhere', the ruins of the Church of St Paul are the most treasured icon in Macau. Once a Jesuit church in the early 17th century, all that remains of it now are the facade and the stairway. However, with its statues, portals and engravings that effectively make up a sermon in stone, it's one of the greatest monuments to Christianity in Asia.

The church was designed by an Italian Jesuit and built in 1602 by Japanese Christian exiles and Chinese craftsmen. After the expulsion of the Jesuits, a military battalion was stationed here. In 1835 a fire erupted in the kitchen of the barracks, destroying everything, except what you see today.

The facade has five tiers. At the top is a dove, representing the Holy Spirit, surrounded by stone carvings of the sun, moon and stars. Beneath that is a statue of the infant Jesus accompanied by the implements of the Crucifixion. In the centre of the third tier stands the Virgin Mary being assumed bodily into heaven along with angels and two flowers: the peony, representing China, and the chrysanthemum, representing Japan. Just below the pediment, on the right side of the facade, is a dragon surmounted by the Holy Virgin. To the right of the Virgin is a carving of the tree of life and the apocalyptic woman (Mary) slaying a seven-headed hydra; the Japanese *kanji* next to her reads: 'The holy mother tramples the heads of the dragon'.

The facade is approached by six flights of 11 stairs each, with an attractive balustrade running up each side.

The small Museum of Sacred Art & Crypt (p199) contains carved wooden statues, silver chalices and oil paintings, as well as the remains of Vietnamese and Japanese Christians martyred in the 17th century.

DON'T MISS
➡ Facade details
➡ The stairway
➡ Museum of Sacred Art
➡ Crypt & ossuary

PRACTICALITIES
➡ 大三巴牌坊, Ruinas de Igreja de São Paulo
➡ Map p200, D1
➡ Travessa de São Paulo
➡ admission free
➡ 🚌8A, 17, 26, disembark at Luís de Camões Garden

Macau Peninsula

Explore

While many visitors automatically equate 'Macau' with 'gambling', the historic Macau Peninsula is far more about history than blackjack. The Peninsula is the city's busy core, with dense working neighbourhoods, charming colonial buildings (and, yes, some casinos too – mostly the smaller, older ones). It's here that you'll come to see the city's top historic attractions, vestiges of its past as a Portuguese colony. It's also the heart of Macau's burgeoning arts scene, with a growing number of cool cafes and galleries to peruse.

The Best...

➡ **Sight** Ruins of the Church of St Paul (p193)

➡ **Place to Eat** Clube Militar de Macau (p206)

➡ **Place to Drink** Macau Soul (p207)

Top Tip

All the big-name casinos have free shuttle services to and from the ferry terminals, the border gate and the airport. Anyone can use these buses – no questions asked. You'll see them outside the ferry terminals and the casinos. Ask for a timetable at the casinos.

Need to Know

➡ **Area Code** ✆853

➡ **Location** Sixty kilometres southwest of Hong Kong.

➡ **Tourist Office** (✆853 8397 1120, tourism hotline 853 2833 3000; www.macautourism.gov. mo; Edificio Ritz, Largo de Senado; ⊗9am-1pm & 2.30-5.35pm Mon-Fri)

MACAU PENINSULA & ISLANDS TRANSPORT

For information on getting to, from and around Macau Peninsula, see p264. For getting around the islands, see p210.

SIGHTS

⊙ Central Macau Peninsula

RUINS OF THE CHURCH OF ST PAUL   RUINS
See p193.

ST JOSEPH'S SEMINARY & CHURCH   CHURCH
Map p200 (聖若瑟修院及聖堂, Capela do Seminario Sao Jose; Rua do Seminario; ⊗church 10am-5pm; ☐9, 16, 18, 28B) St Joseph's, which falls outside the tourist circuit, is one of Macau's most beautiful models of tropicalised baroque architecture. Consecrated in 1758 as part of the Jesuit seminary (not open to the public), it features a white-and-yellow facade, a scalloped entrance canopy (European) and the oldest dome, albeit a shallow one, ever built in China. The most interesting feature, however, is the roof, which features Chinese materials and building styles.

ST LAZARUS CHURCH DISTRICT   AREA
Map p200 (瘋堂斜巷, Calcada da Igreja de Sao Lazaro; www.cipa.org.mo; ☐7, 8) A lovely neighbourhood with colonial-style houses and cobbled streets makes for some of Macau's best photo-ops. Designers and other creative types like to gather here, setting up shop and organising artsy events.

MANDARIN'S HOUSE   HISTORIC BUILDING
Map p196 (鄭家大屋, Caso do Mandarim; ✆853 2896 8820; www.wh.mo/mandarinhouse; 10 Travessa de Antonio da Silva; ⊗10am-5.30pm Thu-Tue; ☐28B, 18) **FREE** Built around 1869, the Mandarin's House, with over 60 rooms, was the ancestral home of Zheng Guanying, an influential author-merchant whose readers included emperors, Dr Sun Yatsen and Chairman Mao. The compound features a moon gate, tranquil courtyards, exquisite rooms and a main hall with French windows, all arranged in that labyrinthine style typical of certain Chinese period buildings. There are guided tours in Cantonese on weekend afternoons.

SIR ROBERT HO TUNG LIBRARY   LIBRARY
Map p200 (何東圖書館; 3 Largo de St Agostinho; ⊗10am-7pm Mon-Sat, 11am-7pm Sun; ☐9, 16, 18) This charming building founded in the 19th century was the country retreat of the late

tycoon Robert Ho Tung, who purchased it in 1918. The colonial edifice, featuring a dome, an arcaded facade, Ionic columns and Chinese-style gardens, was given a modern extension by architect Joy Choi Tin Tin not too long ago. The new four-storey structure in glass and steel has Piranesi-inspired bridges connecting to the old house and a glass roof straddling the transitional space.

LEAL SENADO
HISTORIC BUILDING

Map p200 (民政總署大樓; ☑853 2857 2233; 163 Avenida de Almeida Ribeiro; ☺9am-9pm Tue-Sun; ☐3, 6, 26A, 18A, 33, disembark at Almeida Ribeiro) Facing Largo do Senado is Macau's most important historical building, the 18th-century 'Loyal Senate', which houses the Instituto para os Assuntos Cívicos e Municipais (IACM; Civic and Municipal Affairs Bureau). It is so-named because the body sitting here refused to recognise Spain's sovereignty during the 60 years that it occupied Portugal. In 1654, a dozen years after Portuguese sovereignty was re-established, King João IV ordered a heraldic inscription to be placed inside the entrance hall, which can still be seen today.

Inside the entrance hall is the **IACM Temporary Exhibition Gallery** (民政總署臨時展覽廳; Map p200; ☑853 8988 4100) **FREE**. On the 1st floor is the Senate Library.

SENATE LIBRARY
LIBRARY

Map p200 (民政總署圖書館; ☑853 2857 2233; Leal Senado, 163 Avenida de Almeida Ribeiro; ☺1-7pm Tue-Sat; ☐3, 6, 26A, 18A, 33, disembark at Almeida Ribeiro) **FREE** Located in the Leal Senado, Macau's oldest and most lavish library is a beautiful adaptation of the 18th-century library in the Convento de Mafra outside Lisbon, which was built between 1717 and 1730 by German architect Fredrico Ludovice. Though much smaller, with only two rooms, it features a baroque style with scrolling on the ceiling, and dark wood bookcases surmounted by cartouches. The library's 19,000-book collection includes antique publications in Portuguese, French and English.

MONTE FORT
FORT

Map p200 (大炮台, Fortaleza do Monte; ☺7am-7pm; ☐7, 8, disembark at Social Welfare Bureau) Just east of the ruins, Monte Fort was built by the Jesuits between 1617 and 1626 as part of the College of the Mother of God. Barracks and storehouses were designed to allow the fort to survive a two-year siege, but the cannons were fired only once, during

---

① BROWSING IN THE OLD CITY

Browsing through the shops in the old city, specifically on crumbly Rua dos Ervanários and Rua de Nossa Senhora do Amparo near the Ruins of St Paul, can be a great experience. You can also look for antiques or replicas at shops on or near Rua de São Paulo, Rua das Estalagens and Rua de São António. Rua de Madeira and Rua dos Mercadores, which lead up to Rua da Tercena and its flea market, have shops selling mah-jong tiles and bird cages.

---

the aborted attempt by the Dutch to invade Macau in 1622. Now the cannons on the south side are trained at the gaudy Grand Lisboa Casino like an accusing finger.

On the outside of the southeastern wall, about 6m from the ground, under a cannon, is a sealed rectangular opening. This was a door used by soldiers patrolling the old city wall, which was connected to the fort at a right angle.

CHURCH OF ST DOMINIC
CHURCH

Map p200 (玫瑰堂, Igreja de São Domingos; Largo de São Domingos; ☺10am-6pm; ☐3, 6, 26A) Smack in the heart of Macau's historic centre, this sunny yellow baroque church with a beautiful altar and a timber roof was founded by three Spanish Dominican priests from Acapulco, Mexico, in the 16th century, though the current structure dates from the 17th century. It was here, in 1822, that the first Portuguese newspaper was published on Chinese soil. The former bell tower now houses the **Treasury of Sacred Art** (聖物寶庫, Tresouro de Arte Sacra; Map p200; Largo de São Domingos; ☺10am-6pm) **FREE**, an Aladdin's cave of ecclesiastical art and liturgical objects exhibited on three floors.

LOU KAU MANSION
HISTORIC BUILDING

Map p200 (盧家大屋, Casa de Lou Kau; ☑853 8399 6699; 7 Travessa da Sé; ☺9am-7pm Tue-Sun; ☐3, 4, 6A, 8A, 19, 33) **FREE** Built around 1889, this Cantonese-style mansion with southern European elements belonged to merchant Lou Wa Sio (aka Lou Kau), who also commissioned the Lou Lim Ieoc Garden (p203). Behind the grey facade, an intriguing maze of open and semi-enclosed spaces blurs the line between inside and outside. The flower-and-bird motif on the roof can also be found in the Mandarin's House and A-Ma Temple.

Macau Peninsula

N

0   500 m
0   0.25 miles

Av Norte da Amizade

Rotunda da Amizade

Av do Noroeste

Rua de Maio

Rua dos Pescadores

Ruado Canal Novo

Cemetery

Reservoir

Av Norte do Hipódromo

Av Leste do Hipódromo

Montanha Russa Garden

Estrada de Ferreira do Amaral

Guia Hill
12

Guia Hill

Flora Garden
47

Travessa do Túnel

Rua de Sidónio Pais

AFA (Art for All Society)
1

Travessa de Praia

36

44

Rua Um (Bairro Iao Hon)

Rua Dois

14

Av do Conselheiro Ferreira de Almeida

Rua de Silva Mendes

29

16

30

31

45

Tap Seac Square

Kee Kwan Motor Road Co (200m)

Av de Artur Tamagnini Barbosa

E do Arco

15

24

48

40

Av do Coronel Mesquita

35

34

26

28

Rua de Francisco Xavier Pereira

Av do Almirante Lacerda

Av Horta e Costa

Rua de Bras da Rosa

Rua da Entre Campos

Travessa da Corda

Estrada de Coelho do Amaral

Rua de Almirante Costa Cabral

9

Sun Yat Sen Memorial Park

Av do Conselheiro Borja

CHINA

Canal das Patos

Ilha Verde

Rua da Ribeira do Patane

Rua de Santo António

17

8

23

10

Rua de Tomás Vieira

See Central Macau Peninsula Map (p200)

Inner Harbour

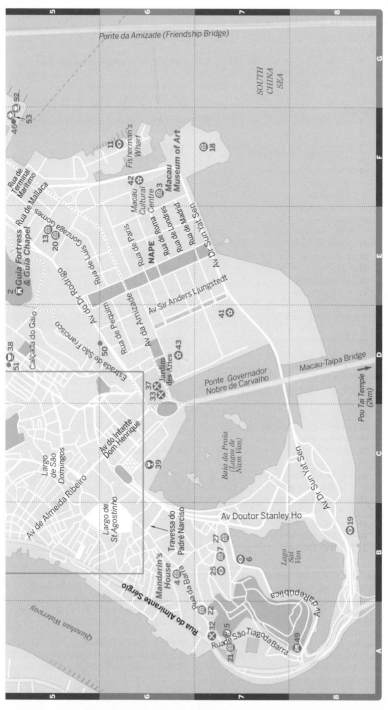

MACAU MACAU PENINSULA

Ponte da Amizade (Friendship Bridge)

SOUTH CHINA SEA

Rua de Terminal Marítimo

Rua de Malaca

Guia Fortress & Guia Chapel

Fisherman's Wharf

Macau Cultural Centre

Macau Museum of Art

NAPE

Rua de Paris
Rua de Roma
Rua de Londres
Rua de Madrid

Rua de Luís Gonzaga Gomes

Av do Dr Rodrigo

Rua de Pequim

Av da Amizade

Av Sir Anders Ljungstedt

Av do Dr Sun Yat Sen

Calçada do Gaio

Estrada de São Francisco

Jardim das Artes

Ponte Governador Nobre de Carvalho

Macau-Taipa Bridge

Pou Tai Temple (2km)

Av do Infante Dom Henrique

Largo de São Domingos

Baía da Praia (Lagos de Nam Van)

Av de Almeida Ribeiro

Largo de St Agostinho

Travessa do Padré Narciso

Av Doutor Stanley Ho

Av do Dr Sun Yat Sen

Mandarin's House

Rua da Barra

Lago Sai Van

Av da República

Rua do Almirante Sérgio

Rua de São Tiago da Barra

Quinshan Waterway

Macau Peninsula

Traditional craft workers often practise their art here during weekdays. Free guided tours in Chinese on weekends.

STREET OF HAPPINESS STREET
Map p200 (福隆新街; Rua da Felicidade; 🚍3, 6, 26A) Not far west of Largo do Senado is Rua da Felicidade (Street of Happiness). Its shuttered terraces were once Macau's main redlight district. Several scenes from *Indiana Jones and the Temple of Doom* were shot here. The government has plans to repaint the famous red shutters in the original colour – green. But whether it's wise to change the distinguishing feature of so iconic a landmark remains to be seen.

MACAU WINE MUSEUM MUSEUM
Map p196 (Museu do Vinho de Macau; ☎853 8798 4188; Basement, CAT, 431 Rua de Luís Gonzaga Gomes; wine tasting MOP$15; ⊙10am-8pm Wed-Mon; 🚍1A, 3, 10, 10B, 10X, 23, 28A) **FREE** Over

1100 types of wine are on display at the only museum in Macau where beverages are allowed. About 90% of these are of Portuguese origin, including the oldest bottle – the Porto 1815. For MOP$15, you can have a tasting of selected bottles. There is also a rundown of Portugal's various wine regions, and a (rather bland) display of wine racks, barrels, presses and tools.

MUSEUM OF THE HOLY HOUSE OF MERCY
MUSEUM

Map p200 (仁慈堂博物館, Núcleo Museológico da Santa Casa da Misericórdia; ☑853 2857 3938; www.scmm.mo; 2 Travessa da Misericórdia; adult/child MOP$5/free; ⊙10am-noon, 2.30-5pm Tue-Sun; ☑3, 6, 26A) In the heart of Largo do Senado is Macau's oldest charitable institution (c 1569). The house once sheltered orphans and prostitutes in the 17th and 18th centuries. Today it's a museum with an eclectic collection that includes religious sculptures, ancient porcelain, and the skull of its founder and Macau's first bishop, Dom Belchior Carneiro.

MACAU MUSEUM
MUSEUM

Map p200 (澳門博物館, Museu de Macau; ☑853 2835 7911; www.macaumuseum.gov.mo; 112 Praceta do Museu de Macau; admission MOP$15, 15th of month free; ⊙10am-5.30pm Tue-Sun; ☑7, 8, disembark at Social Welfare Bureau) This interesting museum inside Monte Fort will give you a taste of Macau's history. The 1st floor introduces the territory's early history and includes an elaborate section on Macau's religions. Highlights of the 2nd floor include a recreated firecracker factory and a recorded reading in the local dialect by Macanese poet José dos Santos Ferreira (1919–93). The top floor focuses on new architecture and urban-development plans.

CHURCH OF ST LAWRENCE
CHURCH

Map p200 (聖老楞佐教堂, Igreja de São Lourenço; Rua de São Lourenço; ⊙10am-5pm Tue-Sun, 1-2pm Mon; ☑9, 16, 18, 28B) One of Macau's three oldest churches, St Lawrence was originally constructed of wood in the 1560s, then rebuilt in stone in the early 19th century. The neoclassical church has a magnificent painted ceiling and one of its towers once served as an ecclesiastical prison. Enter from Rua da Imprensa Nacional.

CHURCH OF ST AUGUSTINE
CHURCH

Map p200 (聖奧斯定教堂, Igreja de Santo Agostinho; 2 Largo de St Agostinho; ⊙10am-6pm; ☑3, 4, 6, 26A) The foundations of this church date from 1586 when it was established by Spanish Augustinians, but the present structure was built in 1814. The high altar has a statue of Christ bearing the cross, which is carried through the streets during the Procession of the Passion of Our Lord on the first Saturday of Lent, followed by thousands of devotees.

HONG KUNG TEMPLE
TEMPLE

Map p200 (康公廟; cnr Rua das Estalagens & Rua de Cinco de Outubro; ⊙8am-6pm; ☑3, 6, 26A) This peaceful, 200-year-old temple is dedicated to Li Lie, a Han-dynasty general. The boat-shaped sculpture in the main hall is used to offer wine to the deities during religious festivities.

ALBERGUE SCM
HISTORIC BUILDING

Map p200 (仁慈堂婆仔屋, Albergue da Santa Casa da Misericórdia or Old Ladies' House; ☑853 2852 2550; 8 Calcada da Igreja de Sao Lazaro; ⊙noon-7pm Wed-Mon; ☑7, 8) Once known as the Old Ladies' House, this was a shelter for Portuguese refugees from Shànghǎi in WWII and later a home for elderly women. It's now run by an art organisation, Albergue SCM, which organises cultural events and art exhibitions here. The two yellow colonial-style buildings sit in a poetic courtyard with magnificent old camphor trees.

MUSEUM OF SACRED ART & CRYPT
MUSEUM

Map p200 (天主教藝術博物館和墓室, Museu de Arte Sacra e Cripta; Travessa de São Paulo; ⊙9am-6pm; ☑8A, 17, 26, disembark at Luís de Camões Garden) FREE This small museum behind the Ruins of the Church of St Paul (p193) contains polychrome carved wooden statues, silver chalices, monstrances and oil paintings, including a copy of a 17th-century painting depicting the martyrdom of 26 Japanese Christians by crucifixion at Nagasaki in 1597.The adjoining crypt contains the remains of Asian Christian martyrs. Also here is the tomb of Alessandro Valignano, the Jesuit who founded the College of the Mother of God and is credited with establishing Christianity in Japan.

PAWNSHOP MUSEUM
HISTORIC BUILDING

Map p200 (典當業展示館, Espaço Patrimonial – Uma Casa de Penhores Tradicional; ☑853 2892 1811; 396 Avenida de Almeida Ribeiro; ⊙10.30am-7pm, closed 1st Mon of month; ☑2, 3, 7, 26A) FREE This museum housed inside the former Tak Seng On (virtue and success) pawnshop offers an atmospheric glimpse into Macau's pawnshop business, which dates back to the Qing dynasty. Built in 1917, it comprises an office, a lobby and an

Central Macau Peninsula

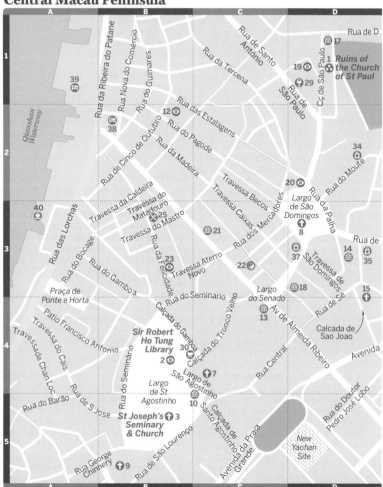

eight-storey, fortress-like tower. On display is equipment from the original establishment, safes where goods were stored and financial records.

TAP SEAC GALLERY
GALLERY

Map p196 (塔石藝文館, Galeria Tap Seac; www.macauart.net/ts; 95 Avenida Conselheiro Ferreira de Almeida; ⏰10am-9pm; 🚌) The gallery building features a European-style facade and Moorish arched doors and hosts excellent contemporary art exhibitions. The original patio in the middle of the house has been kept, which creates a light-filled, relaxing setting.

TAP SEAC SQUARE
SQUARE

Map p196 (塔石廣場, Praca do Tap Seac; 🚌7, 8) This beautiful square surrounded by important historic buildings from the 1920s was designed by Macanese architect Carlos Marreiros. Marreiros also created the Tap Seac Health Centre, a contemporary interpretation of Macau's neoclassical buildings.

MACAU CATHEDRAL
CHURCH

Map p200 (大堂(主教座堂), A Sé Catedral; Largo da Sé; ⏰8am-6pm; 🚌3, 6, 26A, 18A) East of Largo do Senado is this cathedral, consecrated in 1850 and rebuilt in 1937 in concrete. It's not a particularly attractive structure,

Belchior Carneiro

Estrada do Cemitério

Calcada da Igreja de Sao Lazaro

St Lazarus Church District

Rua de Sao Miguel

Rua de Sao Roque

Pedro Nolasco da Silva

Travessa dos Anjos

Rua do Campo

Rua Formosa

da Praia Grande

St Francis Garden

Av de D. João IV

Av da Praia Grande

Rua de Escola Comercial

Av do Infante Dom Henrique

Avenida de Lisboa

NA TCHA TEMPLE   TEMPLE

Map p200 (哪吒廟; 6 Calçada de Sao Paulo; ◷8am-5pm; ☐3, 4, 6A, 8A, 18A, 19) There's no better symbol of Macau's cultural diversity than Na Tcha Temple sitting quietly beside a major Christian monument – the Ruins of the Church of St Paul. Built around 1888, it's dedicated to the child god of war to halt the plague occurring at that time. The wall outside, often said to be a section of Macau's old city walls, in fact belonged to the former St Paul's College located at the ruins.

G32   HISTORIC BUILDING

Map p200 (☎853 2834 6626; 32 Rua de Sao Miguel; ◷free guided tours 2.30-5pm Sat & Sun; ☐7, 8) This three-storey tenement building has been restored as a middle-class Macanese home from the 1960s and '70s, with wooden floorboards, floral wallpaper and retro furniture. A narrow staircase takes you to the roof, where you'll see a unique skyline formed by Chinese buildings, Unesco-protected monuments and casino kitsch.

TAI FUNG TONG ART HOUSE   HISTORIC BUILDING

Map p200 (大瘋堂藝舍; ☎853 2835 3537; 7 Calçada de São Lazaro; ◷2-6pm Tue-Sun; ☐7, 8) **FREE** Featuring a mix of Chinese and European architectural styles, this unusual-looking mansion was built almost a century ago by a philanthropist. It's now occupied by a nonprofit that promotes the area's Chinese heritage. The house has a collection of traditional Chinese artefacts and a calligrapher is sometimes here to demonstrate ink-and-brush calligraphy.

CHINESE READING ROOM   NOTABLE BUILDING

Map p200 (八角亭圖書館; Rua de Santa Clara; ◷9am-noon & 7pm-midnight; ☐2A, 6A, 7A, 8) This former drinks booth (c 1926), known as the 'Octagonal Pavilion' in Chinese, is a library with red windows and a slip of a staircase linking the two floors. It's a serene place people go to read newspapers for free.

NU WA TEMPLE   TEMPLE

Map p200 (女媧廟; cnr Rua das Estalagens & Travessa dos Algibebes; ◷9am-5pm; ☐3, 6, 26A) This tiny temple in a faded yellow building, built in 1888, was consecrated to the serpent-like Nu Wa – the Chinese equivalent of Gaia, the creator goddess. Unlike most other divinities worshipped in Macau, Nu Wa does not offer services associated with the sea. Instead she gives divine assistance to marital and fertility matters. Her likeness

though it has some notable stained-glass windows. It's very active during major Christian festivals and holy days in Macau.

SAM KAI VUI KUN TEMPLE   TAOIST TEMPLE

Map p200 (三街會館; 10 Rua Sui do Mercado de São Domingos; ◷8am-6pm; ☐3, 4, 6A, 26A) Literally 'a community hall for three streets', this temple was a meeting place for merchants and an adjudication court, before the Chinese Chamber of Commerce came into existence in 1912. It's dedicated to Kwan Yu, the god of war and justice. It gets particularly busy in May, June and July when locals celebrate three festivals in the god's honour.

Central Macau Peninsula

sits among those of other deities in the cluttered and smoky temple.

DOM PEDRO V THEATRE   HISTORIC BUILDING
Map p200 (崗頂劇院, Teatro Dom Pedro V; ☑853 2893 9646; Calçada do Teatro, Largo de St Agostinho; ◎10am-6pm Wed-Mon; 🚌3, 4, 6A, 8A, 19) This green-and-white colonnaded, neoclassical theatre is the oldest (1858) Western-style theatre in China, and remains an important cultural venue for the Macanese community.

⦿ Northern Macau Peninsula

GUIA FORTRESS & GUIA CHAPEL   FORT, CHURCH
Map p196 (東望洋炮台及聖母雪地殿聖堂, Fortaleza da Guia e Capela de Guia; ◎fortress 6am-6pm, chapel 10am-5.30pm; 🚌2, 2A, 6A, 12, 17, 18, Flora Garden stop) **FREE** As the highest point on the peninsula, Guia Fort affords panoramic views of the city and, when the air is clear, across to the islands and China. At the top is the stunning Chapel of Our Lady of Guia, built in 1622 and retaining almost 100% of its original features, including some of Asia's most important frescoes. Next to it stands the oldest modern **lighthouse** on the China coast (1865) – an attractive 15m-tall structure that is closed to the public.

You could walk up, but it's easier to take the Guia cable car that runs from the entrance of Flora Gardens (p203), Macau's largest public park.

AFA (ART FOR ALL SOCIETY)   GALLERY
Map p196 (全藝社; ☑853 2836 6064; www.afamacau.com; 3rd fl, Edifício da Fabrica de Baterias N E National, 52 Estrada da Areia Preta; ◎noon-7pm Mon-Sat; 🚌8, 8A, 18A, 7) Macau's best contemporary art can be seen at this nonprofit gallery, which has taken Macau's art world-

wide and holds monthly solo exhibitions by Macau's top artists. AFA is near the Mong Há Multi-Sport Pavilion. Disembark from the bus at Rua da Barca or Rua de Francisco Xavier Pereira. Alternatively, it's a 20-minute walk from Largo do Senado.

CASA GARDEN   HISTORIC BUILDING
Map p196 (東方基金會會址; 13 Praça de Luís de Camões; ⊙garden 9.30am-6pm daily, gallery open only during exhibitions 9.30am-6pm Mon-Fri; ☐8A, 17, 26) One of the oldest buildings in the city, this beautiful colonial villa was built in 1770. It was the headquarters of the British East India Company when it was based in Macau in the early 19th century. Today it's home to a small gallery that mounts interesting art exhibitions. Visitors can wander the slightly forlorn gardens.

FLORA GARDENS   GARDENS
Map p196 (Jardim da Flora; Travessa do Túnel; ⊙8am-6pm, cable car closed Mon) The former grounds of a Portuguese mansion, this European-style garden is known for its cable car, which travels the short distance up Guia Hill, the highest point in the city and home to Guia Fortress & Guia Chapel. The park's tiny zoo is quite sad by global standards.

CEMETERY OF ST MICHAEL THE ARCHANGEL   CEMETERY
Map p196 (西洋墳場, Cemitério de São Miguel Arcanjo; 2a Estrada do Cemitério; ⊙8am-6pm; ☐7, 7A, 8) This cemetery, northeast of Monte Fort, contains tombs and sepulchres that can only be described as baroque ecclesiastical works of art. Near the main entrance is the **Chapel of St Michael** (聖彌額爾小堂, Capela de São Miguel; Map p196; ⊙10am-6pm), a doll-sized, mint-green church with a tiny choir loft and pretty porticoes.

LOU LIM IEOC GARDEN   GARDENS
Map p196 (盧廉若公園, Jardim Lou Lim Ieoc; 10 Estrada de Adolfo de Loureiro; ⊙6am-9pm; ☐2, 2A, 5, 9, 9A, 12, 16) Locals come to this lovely Suzhou-style garden to practise taichi, play Chinese music or simply relax among its lotus ponds and bamboo groves. The Victorian-style **Lou Lim Ieoc Garden Pavilion** (Map p196; 盧廉若公園, Pavilhão do Jardim de Lou Lim Ieoc; ⊙9am-7pm Tue-Sun) was where the Lou family received guests, including Dr Sun Yatsen, and is now used for art exhibitions and recitals during the Macau International Music Festival in late October/November.

MACAO TEA CULTURE HOUSE   MUSEUM
Map p196 (澳門茶文化館, Caultura do Chá em Macau; ☑853 2882 7103; Lou Lim Ieoc Garden, Avenida do Conselheiro Ferreira de Almeida; ⊙9am-7pm Tue-Sun; ☐2, 2A, 5, 9, 9A, 12, 16) FREE Adjacent to the picturesque Lou Lim Ieoc Garden (p203), this museum introduces tea-drinking culture with exhibits of teapots and 'tea paintings'. The latter were produced by foreign and local painters (sometimes in a collaborative relationship) for sale to Westerners in China's trade ports. The museum is housed in a colonial mansion with southern European features and a Chinese tiled roof. There's free tea tasting every Saturday and Sunday from 3pm to 4pm.

LUÍS DE CAMÕES GARDEN & GROTTO   GARDENS
Map p196 (白鴿巢公園, Jardim e Gruta de Luís de Camões; Praça de Luís de Camões; ⊙6am-10pm; ☐8A, 17, 26) This relaxing garden with dappled meandering paths is dedicated to the one-eyed poet Luís de Camões (1524–80), who is said to have written part of his epic *Os Lusíadas* in Macau, though there is little evidence that he ever reached the city. You'll see a bronze bust (c 1886) of the man here. The wooded garden attracts a fair number of chess players, bird owners and Chinese shuttlecock kickers. The **Sr Wong Ieng Kuan Library** (白鴿巢公園黃營均圖書館; Map p196; ☑853 2895 3075; ⊙8am-8pm Tue-Sun) is also here.

SUN YAT SEN MEMORIAL HOUSE   MUSEUM
Map p196 (國父紀念館, Casa Memorativa de Doutor Sun Yat Sen; ☑853 2857 4064; 1 Rua de Silva Mendes; ⊙10am-5pm Wed-Mon; ☐2, 2A, 5, 9, 9A, 12) FREE This mock Moorish house (c 1910) commemorates Dr Sun Yatsen's (1866–1925) brief stay in Macau, where he gathered support to overthrow the Qing dynasty. You'll see documents and personal belongings of the 'Father of the Chinese Republic'. Interestingly Sun himself had never lived in the house, though it was built by his son, and his first wife Lu Muzhen lived here until she died in 1952.

OX WAREHOUSE   ARTS CENTRE
Map p196 (牛房倉庫, Armazem de Boi; ☑853 2853 0026; http://oxwarehouse.blogspot.com; cnr Avenida do Coronel Mesquita & Avenida do Almirante Lacerda; ⊙noon-7pm Wed-Mon; ☐4, 5, 25, 26A, 33) FREE This atmospheric former slaughterhouse is run by a nonprofit that hosts contemporary exhibitions, workshops and performances by local and visiting

MACAU MACAU PENINSULA

artists. Much of the work is engagingly experiential. Even if nothing's on, the architecture of the old buildings here makes it worthwhile to come for a peek.

CHURCH OF ST ANTHONY CHURCH

Map p196 (聖安多尼教堂, Igreja de Santo António; cnr Rua de Santo António & Rua do Tarrafeiro; ⊙7.30am-5.30pm; ⏹8A, 17, 26) This stern-looking grey stone church, built from 1558 to 1608 and renovated in 1930, is one of Macau's oldest, and the Jesuits' earliest headquarters. The local Portuguese used to hold wedding ceremonies here, hence the church's name in Cantonese: Fa Vong Tong (Church of Flowers).

OLD PROTESTANT CEMETERY CEMETERY

Map p196 (基督教墳場, Antigo Cemitério Protestante; 15 Praça de Luís de Camões; ⊙8.30am-5.30pm; ⏹8A, 17, 26) As church law forbade the burial of non-Catholics on hallowed ground, this cemetery was established in 1821 as the last resting place of (mostly Anglophone) Protestants. Among those interred here are Irish-born artist George Chinnery (1774–1852), and Robert Morrison (1782–1834), the first Protestant missionary to China and author of the first Chinese-English dictionary.

LIN FUNG TEMPLE BUDDHIST TEMPLE

Map p196 (蓮峰廟, Lin Fung Miu; Avenida do Almirante Lacerda; ⊙7am-5pm; ⏹1A, 8, 8A, 10, 28B) Dedicated to Kun Iam, the Goddess of Mercy, this Temple of the Lotus was built in 1592, but underwent several reconstructions from the 17th century. It used to host mandarins from Guǎngdōng province when they visited Macau. The most famous of these imperial visitors was Commissioner Lin Zexu, who was charged with stamping out the opium trade.

RED MARKET MARKET

Map p196 (紅街市大樓, Mercado Almirante Lacerda; cnr Avenida do Almirante Lacerda & Avenida Horta e Costa; ⊙7.30am-7.30pm; ⏹23, 32) Designed by Macanese architect Júlio Alberto Basto, this three-storey art-deco building with a clocktower houses a lively wet market. It was so-named because of the red bricks used in its construction.

KUN IAM TEMPLE BUDDHIST TEMPLE

Map p196 (觀音廟, Templo de Kun Iam; 2 Avenida do Coronel Mesquita; ⊙7am-5.30pm; ⏹1A, 10, 18A, stop Travessa de Venceslau de Morais) Macau's oldest temple was founded in the 13th century, but the present structures date back to 1627. Its roofs are embellished with porcelain figurines and its halls are lavishly decorated. Inside the main one stands the likeness of Kun Iam, the Goddess of Mercy; to the left of the altar is a statue of a bearded *arhat* rumoured to represent Marco Polo. The first Sino-American treaty was signed at a round stone table in the temple's terraced gardens in 1844.

ROTUNDA DE CARLOS DA MAIA SQUARE

Map p196 The lively Three Lamps district, known for its Burmese immigrant community, encompasses a series of streets packed with vendors and street food. It centres on the Rotunda de Carlos da Maia square.

◉ Southern Macau Peninsula

MACAU MUSEUM OF ART MUSEUM

Map p196 (澳門藝術博物館, Museu de Arte de Macau; ☑853 8791 9814; www.mam.gov.mo; Macau Cultural Centre, Avenida Xian Xing Hai; adult/child MOP$5/2, Sun free; ⊙10am-6.30pm Tue-Sun; ⏹1A, 8, 12, 23) This excellent five-storey museum has well-curated displays of art created in Macau and China, including paintings by Western artists like George Chinnery, who lived in the enclave. Other highlights are ceramics and stoneware excavated in Macau, Ming- and Qing-dynasty calligraphy from Guǎngdōng, ceramic statues from Shíwān (Guǎngdōng) and seal carvings. The museum also features 19th-century Western historical paintings from all over Asia, and contemporary Macanese art.

PENHA HILL AREA

Map p196 (西望洋山, Colina da Penha; ⏹6, 9, 16) Towering above the colonial villas along Avenida da República is Penha Hill, the most tranquil and least-visited area of the peninsula. From here you'll get excellent views of the central area of Macau. Atop the hill is the **Bishop's Palace** (主教府; Map p196), built in 1837 and a residence for bishops (not open to the public), and the **Chapel of Our Lady of Penha** (主教山小堂, Ermida de Nossa Senhora da Penha; Map p196; ⊙9am-5.30pm; ⏹6B, 9, 16, 28B), once a place of pilgrimage for sailors.

AVENIDA DA REPÚBLICA AREA

Map p196 (⏹6, 9, 16) Avenida da República, along the northwest shore of Sai Van Lake, is Macau's oldest Portuguese quarter. There are several grand colonial villas not open to the public here. The former Bela Vista Hotel, one of the most-storied hotels in Asia, is now the **Residence of the Portuguese Consul-General** (葡國駐澳門領事官邸; Consulado-Geral de Portugal em Macau; Map p196; Rua do Boa Vista). Nearby is the ornate **Santa Sancha Palace**, once the residence of Macau's Portuguese governors, and now used to accommodate state guests. Not too far away are beautiful, abandoned art deco–inspired buildings.

MACAU TOWER   LANDMARK

Map p196 (澳門旅遊塔, Torre de Macau; ☑853 2893 3339; www.macautower.com.mo; Largo da Torre de Macau; observation deck adult/child MOP$135/70; ⊙10am-9pm Mon-Fri, 9am-9pm Sat & Sun; ☑9A, 18, 23, 26, 32) At 338m, Macau Tower looms above the narrow isthmus of land southeast of Avenida da República. You can stay put on the observation decks on the 58th and 61st floors, or challenge yourself to some gravity-defying sport: the tower hosts a climbing wall, a bungee platform (said to be the highest commercial bungee jump in the world), a sky walk around the rim of the tower and more.

MACAO SCIENCE CENTRE   MUSEUM

Map p196 (澳門科學館; www.msc.org.mo; Avenida Dr Sun Yat Sen; adult/child MOP$25/15, planetarium MOP$60; ⊙10am-6pm Fri-Wed; ♿; ☑3A, 8, 10A, 12) In an IM Pei–designed silvery spiral of a building on the waterfront, this modern science museum is one of Macau's best places to take kids. Fourteen exhibition areas have fun, hands-on exhibits on subjects ranging from music to robotics. The 3D planetarium is always a hit.

MARITIME MUSEUM   MUSEUM

Map p196 (海事博物館, Museu Marítimo; ☑853 2859 5481; www.museumaritimo.gov.mo; 1 Largo do Pagode da Barra; adult MOP$3-10, child free; ⊙10am-5.30pm Wed-Mon; ☑1, 2, 5, 6B, 7, 10) The highlights here are the interactive displays detailing the maritime histories of Portugal and China, the artefacts from Macau's seafaring past, and the mock-ups of boats – including the long, narrow dragon boats used during the Dragon Boat Festival – and a Hakka fishing village.

GRAND PRIX MUSEUM   MUSEUM

Map p196 (大賽車博物館, Museu do Grande Prémio; ☑853 8798 4108; Basement, CAT, 431 Rua de Luís Gonzaga Gomes; ⊙10am-8pm Wed-Mon; ☑1A, 3, 10) FREE Cars from the Macau Formula 3 Grand Prix, including the bright-red Triumph TR2 driven by Eduardo de Carvalho that won the first Grand Prix in 1954, are on display here, while simulators let you test your racing skills.

From early 2017, the museum is scheduled to close for two to three years for a complete renovation.

MOORISH BARRACKS   HISTORIC BUILDING

Map p196 (Calcada da Barra, Barra Hill; ☑18, 28) These former barracks (c 1874) were designed by an Italian in a neoclassical style inspired by Moorish architecture to accommodate Muslim Indian policemen from Goa. The confusion of Muslims with Moors was due to the fact that dated Cantonese refers to Indians as 'moh loh cha', and 'moh loh' is a transliteration of 'Moorish'. You can't enter the building, now occupied by the Macau Maritime Administration.

MACAU CULTURAL CENTRE   NOTABLE BUILDING

Map p196 (澳門文化中心, Centro Cultural de Macau; ☑853 2870 0699; www.ccm.gov.mo; Avenida Xian Xing Hai; ⊙9am-7pm Tue-Sun; ☑1A, 8, 12, 23) This US$100-million, 45,000-sq-metre contemporary concrete structure is the territory's prime venue for cultural performances, from dance to theatre to multimedia shows. Creative Macau (p205), an art space that runs exhibitions and poetry readings, is on the ground floor.

CREATIVE MACAU   GALLERY

Map p196 (創意空間; ☑853 2875 3282; www.creativemacau.org.mo; Ground fl, Macau Cultural Centre, Avenida Xian Xing Hai; ⊙2-7pm Mon-Sat; ☑1A, 8, 12, 23) This space managed by a nonprofit organisation aims at promoting and enhancing the potentials of Macau's creative industries. You'll find here exhibitions of works by a spectrum of industries, from advertising and architecture to publishing and fashion design.

A-MA TEMPLE   TAOIST TEMPLE

Map p196 (媽閣廟, Templo de A-Ma; Rua de São Tiago da Barra; ⊙7am-6pm; ☑1, 2, 5, 6B, 7) A-Ma Temple was probably already standing when the Portuguese arrived, although the present structure may date from the 16th century. It was here that fisherfolk once came to replenish supplies and pray for fair weather. A-Ma, aka Tin Hau, is the goddess of the sea, from which the name Macau is derived. It's believed that when the Portuguese asked the name of the place, they were told 'A-Ma Gau' (A-Ma Bay). In modern Cantonese, 'Macau' (Ou Mun) means 'gateway of the bay'.

FISHERMAN'S WHARF AREA

Map p196 **FREE** Is that a volcano you see from the ferry window while arriving at the Macau terminal? Why yes, that's Fisherman's Wharf, the beyond-cheesy theme park/dining/shopping complex along the waterfront. The area features buildings made to resemble various landmarks from history and mythology: a mock Colosseum, a Babylonian-themed casino, a half-timbered shopping strip resembling Ye Olde Bavaria. Perpetually empty, the Wharf is only recommendable for kitsch fans seeking bizarro photo opportunities.

EATING

★ LUNG WAH TEA HOUSE CANTONESE $

Map p196 (龍華茶樓; ☑853 2857 4456; 3 Rua Norte do Mercado Aim-Lacerda; dim sum from MOP$14, tea MOP$10, meals MOP$50-180; ☉7am-2pm; ⊛; ☐23, 32) There's grace in the retro furniture and the casual way it's thrown together in this airy Cantonese teahouse (c 1963). Take a booth by the windows overlooking the Red Market, where the teahouse buys its produce every day. There's no English menu; just point and take. Lung Wah sells a fine array of Chinese teas.

O PORTO MACANESE $

Map p196 (☑853 2859 4643; 17 Travessa da Praia; meals MOP$160; ☉noon-2pm & 6-10pm Thu-Tue; ⊛; ☐2, 10, 12) Not to be confused with O Porto Interior on Rua do Almirante Sérgio, this modest place serves decent and affordable Macanese dishes, with a few luxuries: chequered tablecloths, football paraphernalia and warm service. It's near the steps leading to Mong Há Hill.

CHEONG KEI CANTONESE $

Map p200 (祥記麵家; ☑853 2857 4310; 68 Rua da Felicidade; noodles MOP$20-55; ☉11.30am-11.30pm; ☐3, 6, 26A) Peak-time queues at the door even before the Michelin recommendation are a clue that this long-standing noodle joint has a loyal following. Try the

noodles tossed with shrimp roe. There are just a few communal tables; be prepared to bump elbows with the locals.

NGA HEONG BURMESE $

Map p196 (雅馨緬甸餐廳; ☑853 2855 2711; 27 Rua De Fernao Mendes Pinto; mains MOP$25-45; ☉7.30am-6.30pm; ☐23, 32) In Macau's Three Lamps district, an area known for its Burmese immigrants, this popular two-floor greasy spoon dishes out home-style Burmese classics like coconut chicken noodles, braised pig ear salad and shrimp paste–fragrant greens. There's an English menu with pictures.

★ CLUBE MILITAR DE MACAU PORTUGUESE $$

Map p200 (陸軍俱樂部; ☑853 2871 4000; 975 Avenida da Praia Grande; meals MOP$150-400; ☉1.45-2.30pm & 7-10.30pm Mon-Fri, noon-2.30pm & 7-10pm Sat & Sun; ☐6, 28C) Housed in a distinguished colonial building, with fans spinning lazily above, the Military Club takes you back in time to a slower and quieter Macau. The simple and delicious Portuguese fare is complemented by an excellent selection of wine and cheese from Portugal. The MOP$153 buffet is excellent value. Reservations are required for dinner and weekend lunches.

A LORCHA MACANESE, PORTUGUESE $$

Map p196 (船屋葡國餐廳; ☑853 2831 3193; www.alorcha.com; 289 Rua do Almirante Sérgio; meals MOP$300-500; ☉12.30-2.30pm & 6.30-10.30pm Wed-Mon; ⊛; ☐1, 5, 10) 'The Sailboat' is listed in every guidebook. One reason for its popularity is its walking distance to A-Ma Temple. Don't expect outstanding creativity, but solid Portuguese and Macanese fare. Portions are generous.

★ GUINCHO A GALERA PORTUGUESE $$$

Map p196 (葡國餐廳; ☑853 8803 7676; www.hotelisboa.com; 3rd fl, Hotel Lisboa, 2-4 Avenida de Lisboa; meals MOP$550-1800; ☉noon-2.30pm & 6.30-10.30pm; ☐3, 10) The international branch of Portugal's famous Fortaleza do Guincho, this luxuriously decorated restaurant brings Portuguese haute cuisine to Macau. The menu features well-executed classical dishes, with a couple of Macanese additions. Set meals are available at lunch (from MOP$310) and dinner (from MOP$630).

MACAU MACAU PENINSULA

EATING PRICE RANGES

$	Less than MOP$200
$$	MOP$200 to MOP$400
$$$	More than MOP$400

ROBUCHON AU DÔME
FRENCH $$$

Map p200 (☑853 8803 7878; www.grandlisboa hotel.com; 43rd fl, Grand Lisboa Hotel, Avenida de Lisboa; lunch/dinner set menu from MOP$598/1688; ☺noon-2.30pm & 6.30-10.30pm; ☑3, 10) Encased in a glass dome, this is arguably the most tastefully decorated of the casino restaurants. As one of two Macau restaurants with three Michelin stars, it has everything you associate with the celebrated Robuchon name: fine decor, exquisite Gallic creations and impeccable service. The 8000-bottle wine cellar is one of the best in Asia.

TIM'S KITCHEN
CHINESE $$$

Map p196 (桃花源小廚; ☑853 8803 3682; www.hotelisboa.com; Shop F25, East Wing, Hotel Lisboa, 2-4 Avenida de Lisboa; meals MOP$300-1500; ☺noon-2.30pm & 6.30-10.30pm; ☑3, 6, 26A) At Tim's, with one Michelin star, fresh ingredients are meticulously prepared using methods that preserve or highlight their original flavours, resulting in dishes that look simple but taste divine – a giant 'glass' prawn shares a plate with a sliver of Chinese ham; a crab claw lounges on a cushion of wintermelon surrounded by broth.

EIGHT
CANTONESE $$$

Map p200 (8餐廳; ☑853 8803 7788; www.grand lisboahotel.com; 2nd fl, Grand Lisboa Hotel, Avenida de Lisboa; meals MOP$160-1500; ☺lunch 11.30am-2pm Mon-Sat, brunch 10am-3pm Sun, dinner 6.30-10.30pm; ☑3, 10, 28B) With water (a symbol for money) cascading down the wall, crystal-dripping chandeliers and an auspicious numeral for a name, the Eight can only belong to a casino. Granted, it's a stellar restaurant set apart from similar places by its solid dim sum, the chef's creativity and three Michelin stars. Getting a table is almost impossible without a reservation.

LA PALOMA
SPANISH, MEDITERRANEAN $$$

Map p196 (芭朗瑪餐廳; ☑853 2837 8111; www.saotiago.com.mo; 2nd fl, Pousada de São Tiago, Avenida da República; meals MOP$250-800; ☺7am-11pm; ☑9) 'The Dove' sits on the foundations of a 17th-century fortress – one of Macau's most romantic spots and a welcome change from the casino restaurants. Hence any meal or drink here – be it a protracted Spanish feast under modern chandeliers or a glass of *vinho do porto* (port wine) on the terrace – should be accompanied by a walk around the premises.

MACAU CHOW

A typical Macanese menu features an enticing stew of influences from Chinese and South Asian cuisines, and the cooking of former Portuguese colonies in Africa, India and Latin America. Coconut, tamarind, chilli, jaggery (palm sugar) and shrimp paste can all feature.

A famous Macanese speciality is *galinha africana* (African chicken), made with coconut, garlic and chillies. Other popular dishes include *casquinha* (stuffed crab), *minchi* (minced meat cooked with potatoes and onions) and *serradura* (a milk pudding).

You'll find Portuguese dishes here too, such as *arroz de pato* (rice with duck confit) and *leitão assado no forno* (roasted suckling pig).

🍷 DRINKING & NIGHTLIFE

★ MACAU SOUL
BAR

Map p200 (澳感廊; ☑853 2836 5182; www.macausoul.com; 31a Rua de São Paulo; ☺3-10pm Wed & Thu, to midnight Fri-Sun; ☑8A, 17, 26) An elegant haven in wood and stained glass, where twice a month a jazz band plays to a packed audience. On most nights, though, Thelonious Monk fills the air as customers chat with the owners and dither over their 430 Portuguese wines. Opening hours vary; phone ahead.

★ SINGLE ORIGIN
COFFEE

Map p196 (單品; ☑853 6698 7475; 19 Rua de Abreu Nunes; coffee MOP$35; ☺11.30am-8pm Mon-Sat, 2-7pm Sun; 🛜; ☑2, 4, 7, 7A, 8) This airy corner cafe opened by coffee professional Keith Fong makes a mean shot of espresso. You can choose your poison from a daily selection of 10 beans from various regions. If you can't decide, the well-trained baristas are more than happy to help.

LION'S BAR
CLUB

Map p196 (☑853 8802 2375; www.mgm macau.com/lion-bar; MGM Grand, Avenida Dr Sun Yat Sen; ☺7pm-5am Thu-Tue) Sleekly dressed revellers dance to the house DJ and band at this open-till-5am bar and club in the MGM Grand, your best bet for Vegas-style debauchery in Macau.

TERRA COFFEE HOUSE
CAFE

Map p200 (⌖853 2893 7943; 1 Largo de St Agostinho; ⊙11am-8pm; 🛜; 🚌9, 16) This tiny haven overlooking pretty St Augustine Sq will make you forget you're only a five-minute walk away from heaving Largo do Senado. Stop here for a strong and carefully crafted cuppa after visiting the nearby Sir Robert Ho Tung Library (p194).

SKY 21 LOUNGE
LOUNGE

Map p196 (⌖853 2822 2122; www.sky21macau. com; 21st fl, AIA Tower, 215a-301 Avenida Comercial de Macau; ⊙6.30pm-2am Sun-Thu, to 3am Fri & Sat, happy hour 5-9pm; 🛜; 🚌18, 23, 32) Zen and cyber come together in this sleek lounge-bar with alfresco seating and panoramic views. It has a DJ and live jazz on some days of the week, and special parties on Saturdays.

CINNEBAR
BAR

Map p196 (霞酒廊; ⌖853 8986 3663; Ground fl, Wynn Macau, Rua Cidade de Sintra, Novos Aterros do Porto Exterior; ⊙3pm-1am Sun-Thu, to 2am Fri & Sat; 🛜; 🚌8, 10A, 23) Cinnebar has a fantastic combination of swish and casual: classy surroundings indoors and a relaxed atmosphere in its outdoor seating area around the swimming pool. Some exotically blended cocktails are served in this lobby bar.

☆ ENTERTAINMENT

★ LIVE MUSIC ASSOCIATION
LIVE MUSIC

Map p196 (LMA; 現場音樂協會; www.facebook. com/LMA.Macau; 11b San Mei Industrial Bldg, 50 Avenida do Coronel Mesquita; 🚌3, 9, 32, 12, 25) The go-to place for indie music in Macau, this excellent dive inside an industrial building has hosted local and overseas acts, including Cold Cave, Buddhistson, Mio Myo and Pet Conspiracy. See the website for what's on. Macau indie bands to watch out for include WhyOceans (www.why oceans.com) and Turtle Giant (www.turtle giant.com).

WYNN MACAU CASINO
CASINO

Map p196 (永利娛樂場; ⌖853 2888 9966; www.wynnmacau.com; Wynn Macau, Rua Cidade de Sintra, Novos Aterros do Porto Exterior; 🚌8, 10A) Despite the outdoor 'Performance Lake', which gives a fountain show every 15 minutes to the tune of 'Money Makes the World Go Round' or Chinese tunes, the Wynn is one of Macau's more tranquil casino complexes. The gaming floors are relatively hushed, as is the small posh shopping

area. Less quiet is the *Dragon of Fortune* show in the Rotunda atrium, where every half an hour a golden animatronic dragon emerges from the floor breathing smoke. Other draws for the non-gambler include a 24-carat gold tree that rises from the floor on the half hour, and an aquarium full of moon jellyfish.

MGM GRAND MACAU
CASINO

Map p196 (澳門美高梅; www.mgm.mo; Grande Praça, Avenida Dr Sun Yat Sen; 🚌8, 3A, 12) With softly lit casino floors and a bland up-market shopping mall, you might think the MGM is less flashy than its brethren. But then you walk into the Grande Praça, a vast domed indoor plaza based on the streets of old Lisbon, centred on a ceiling-high tube-shaped aquarium of tropical fish.

SANDS CASINO
CASINO

Map p196 (⌖853 2888 3330; www.sandsmacao. com; Largo de Monte Carlo 203; 🚌8, 3A, 12) One of the peninsula's older international casinos, the Sands' gaming floors have a somewhat dated, midrange-hotel-lobby vibe. Within walking distance of the ferry dock, it has fewer entertainment and dining options than the Cotai casinos.

RUI CUNHA FOUNDATION
CULTURAL CENTRE

Map p200 (官樂怡基金會, Fundacao Rui Cunha; ⌖853 2892 3288; http://ruicunha.org; 749 Avenida da Praia Grande; ⊙gallery 10am-7pm; 🚌2A, 6A, 7A, 8) From its airy venue in the heart of the peninsula, this foundation promotes the Macau identity through a carefully curated series of art exhibitions, literary readings and recitals. These are held alongside thought-provoking seminars on Macau's legal and social systems.

SUN NEVER LEFT – PUBLIC ART PERFORMANCE
LIVE MUSIC

Map p200 (黃昏小叙-街頭藝術表演; www. cipa.org.mo; Rua de Sao Roque; ⊙3-6pm Sat & Sun; ♿; 🚌7, 8) Every weekend, artists at St Lazarus Church District set up shop on the picturesque Rua de Sao Roque, selling art and handicrafts. Buy coffee from a nearby cafe and sip it as you browse and enjoy the live music.

GRAND LISBOA CASINO
CASINO

Map p200 (新葡京; ⌖853 2838 2828; www. grandlisboa.com; Avenida de Lisboa, Macau Peninsula; 🚌3, 10) A golden lotus-shaped tower, the delightfully tacky Grand Lisboa has become the landmark by which people navigate the peninsula's streets. Its four gaming floors are always jam-packed with serious gamblers. Less populated is the free daily 'Crazy Paris' cabaret dance show at the bar.

 SHOPPING

MACAU DESIGN CENTRE GIFTS & SOUVENIRS
Map p196 (✆853 2852 0335; www.dcmacau. com/en; Travessa da Fabrica 5; ⊙11am-7pm; 🚌1A, 2, 6A, 8, 8A, 10, 12, 19, 22, 28B, 28BX, 28C, 34) In a gritty working-class neighbourhood, this shop/gallery/exhibition space showcases Macau designers. Look out for handmade ceramics, high-quality leather bags, trendy clothes, framed graphics and more.

LIVRARIA PORTUGUESA BOOKS, GIFTS
Map p200 (Portuguese Bookstore; ✆853 2851 5915; Rua do São Domingos 18; ⊙11am-7pm; 🚌3, 4, 6A, 8A, 19, 33) Right in the heart of Macau's historic district, this two-storey bookshop carries both English and Portuguese titles, including some hard-to-find Macanese cookbooks. It also stocks gift items, like imported Portuguese soaps and perfumes. Founded more than 30 years ago, it's one of the few places in Macau where you can reliably hear Portuguese spoken.

MERCEARIA PORTUGUESA FOOD
Map p200 (✆853 2856 2708; www.mercearia portuguesa.com; 8 Calçada da Igreja de São Lazaro; ⊙1-9pm Mon-Fri, noon-9pm Sat & Sun; 🚌7, 8) The charming Portuguese corner shop opened by a film director and actress has a small but well-curated selection of provisions, which includes honey, chinaware, wooden toys and jewellery from Portugal – gorgeously packaged and reasonably priced.

PINTO LIVROS BOOKS
Map p200 (邊度有書; http://blog.roodo.com/ pintolivros; 1a Veng Heng Bldg, 31 Largo do Senado; ⊙11.30am-11pm; 🚌3, 6, 26A) This upstairs reading room overlooking Largo do Senado has a decent selection of titles in art and culture, a few esoteric CDs and two resident cats.

FUTURA CLASSICA COSMETICS
Map p200 (✆853 2835 8378; 1A Calçada da Rocha; ⊙noon-8pm; 🚌3, 6, 26 A, 18A, 33) This dizzyingly sweet-smelling shop is the Asian distributor of Claus Porto, a Portuguese brand of luxury soap and beauty products. It's a great place to shop for souvenirs. Prices range from MOP$50 to MOP$1000.

WORKER PLAYGROUND CLOTHING
Map p196 (✆853 2875 7511; Ground fl, Edificio Cheung Seng, 83a Avenida do Conselheiro Ferreira de Almeida; ⊙3-10pm; 🚌) Worker Playground makes solid-quality baseball jackets, biker pants, and fashionably androgynous garments for men and women. The brand pays tribute to the old Workers' Stadium, a nostalgic landmark that was razed to make way for the Grand Lisboa Casino.

MACAO FASHION GALLERY CLOTHING
Map p200 (澳門時尚廊; ✆853 2835 3341; www.macaofashiongallery.com; 47 Rua de São Roque; ⊙10am-8pm Tue-Sun; 🚌7, 8) This place comprises a boutique on the ground floor displaying the creations of Macau designers and a (underwhelming) gallery on the upper floors with exhibitions that change every three months and showcase fashion-related artefacts.

LINES LAB CLOTHING
Map p200 (www.lineslab.com; Shop A3, 8 Calçada da Igreja de São Lazaro; ⊙1-8pm Tue-Sun; 🚌7, 8) Two Lisbon-trained designers opened this boutique in the Old Ladies' House art space and created edgy Macau-inspired clothes and bags for it.

 SPORTS & ACTIVITIES

GUIA HILL HIKING CIRCUIT HIKING
Map p196 There are two trails on Guia Hill in central Macau Peninsula that are good for a stroll or jog. The **Walk of 33 Curves** (1.7km) circles the hill; inside this loop is the shorter **Fitness Circuit Walk**, with 20 exercise stations. You can access these by the Guia cable car.

AJ HACKETT ADVENTURE SPORTS
Map p196 (✆853 988 8656; http://macau. ajhackett.com; Largo da Torre de Macau; ⊙11am-7.30pm, later on Fri & Sat & during summer) New Zealand–based AJ Hackett organises all kinds of adventure climbs, bungee jumps and more on the Macau Tower.

GRAY LINE TOURS
Map p196 (✆853 2833 6611; www.grayline.com. hk; Room 1015, ground fl, Macau Ferry Terminal; 10hr tour adult/child 3-11 MOP$1275/1200 incl ferry to Hong Kong) Quality tours organised by the Macau Government Tourist Office and tendered to agents take around 10 hours.

The Islands: Taipa, Coloane & Cotai

Explore

The islands of Taipa, Cotai and Coloane are more like one big island these days, thanks to land reclamation. Head to Taipa for dining and shopping in the narrow streets of old Taipa Village. Visit the new area of Cotai (created by infilling marsh between Taipa and Coloane, hence the name) to gamble and gawk at the biggest casinos on earth. Go south to Coloane for beachy getaways and long Portuguese lunches.

The Best...

➡**Sight** Taipa Houses-Museum (p210)
➡**Place to Eat** António (p214)
➡**Place to Drink** Macallan Whisky Bar & Lounge (p215)

Top Tip

Cycling is a great way to see Taipa and Coloane. In Taipa, 有記士多 on 11 Rua dos Negociantes, near Pak Tai Temple, has bikes for rent. In Coloane, Dang Rang (東榮單車行) on Rua do Meio, does the same.

Getting There & Away

➡**Shuttle** Free shuttle buses run from the ferry terminals and the border gates to the casinos of Cotai; anyone can ride, not just hotel guests.

➡**Bus** Public bus 25 goes all the way from the Peninsula's northern border gate, through Taipa and Cotai and all the way to Coloane; 26A covers a similar route.

➡**Taxi** There are plenty of taxi queues around the casinos in Cotai, but expect long lines and refusals to take you to far-flung locations (ie Coloane).

Need to Know

➡**Area Code** ☑853
➡**Location** Taipa is 2.5km from Macau Peninsula and 39.3km away from Hong Kong; Cotai is 3km from Macau Peninsula and 39.3km from Hong Kong; Coloane is 5.6km from Macau Peninsula and 39.3km from Hong Kong.

➡**Tourist Office** (澳門旅遊局; Macau Government Tourism Office; ☑853 2886 1418; www.macautourism.gov.mo; Macau International Airport; ◷10am-10pm) There is a MGTO information counter at the Taipa Temporary Ferry Terminal.

◉ SIGHTS

◉ Taipa

TAIPA VILLAGE   VILLAGE

(☐22, 26, 33) The historical part of Taipa is best preserved in this village in the south of the district. An intricate warren of alleys hold traditional Chinese shops and some excellent restaurants, while the broader main roads are punctuated by colonial villas, churches and temples. Rua do Cunha, the main pedestrian drag, is lined with vendors hawking free samples of Macanese almond cookies and beef jerky, and tiny cafes selling egg tarts and serradura pudding. Avenida da Praia, a tree-lined esplanade with wrought-iron benches, is perfect for a leisurely stroll.

TAIPA HOUSES-MUSEUM   MUSEUM

(龍環葡韻住宅式博物館, Casa Museum da Taipa; ☑853 2882 7103; Avenida da Praia, Carmo Zone, Taipa village; adult/student MOP$5/2, child & senior free, Sun free; ◷10am-5.30pm Tue-Sun; ☐11, 15, 22, 28A, 30, 33, 34) The pastel-coloured villas (c 1921) here were the summer residences of wealthy Macanese. House of the Regions of Portugal showcases Portuguese costumes. House of the Islands looks at the history of Taipa and Coloane, with displays on traditional industries, such as fishing and the manufacture of fireworks. Macanese House offers a snapshot of life in the early 20th century.

MUSEUM OF TAIPA & COLOANE HISTORY   MUSEUM

(路氹歷史館, Museu da História da Taipa e Coloane; ☑853 2882 5361; Rua Correia da Silva, Taipa; adult/student MOP$5/2, child & senior free, Tue free; ◷10am-5.30pm Tue-Sun; ☐11, 15, 22, 28A, 30, 33, 34) This museum has a display of excavated relics and other artefacts on the 1st floor, while the 2nd floor contains religious objects, handicrafts and architectural models.

Taipa

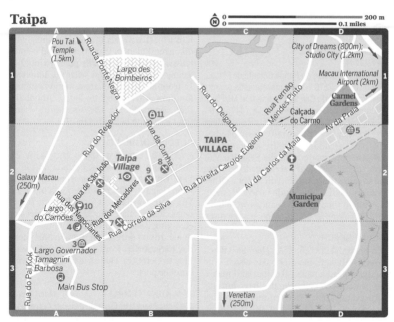

PAK TAI TEMPLE
TAOIST TEMPLE

(Rua do Regedor; 🚌22, 28A, 26) Pak Tai Temple sits quietly in a breezy square framed by old trees. It is dedicated to a martial deity – the Taoist God (Tai) of the North (Pak) – who defeated the Demon King who was terrorising the universe. A pair of Chinese lions guards the entrance to the temple. On the third day of the third lunar month each year, Cantonese opera performances take place here.

CHURCH OF OUR LADY OF CARMEL
CHURCH

(Igreja de Nossa Senhora de Carmo; Rue da Restauração, Taipa village; 🚌22, 28A, 26) Built in 1885, this lovely yellow neoclassical church stands on a hill overlooking the harbour, scenic Taipa village and the pastel-coloured Taipa Houses-Museum. If you visit on a weekend, you can expect to see dozens of couples shotting their wedding photos here.

POU TAI TEMPLE
BUDDHIST TEMPLE

(菩提禪院; Pou Tai Un; 5 Estrada Lou Lim Ieok; ⏱9am-6pm; 🚌21A, 22, 25, 25X, 26A, 28A) A picturesque temple founded in the 19th century by Buddhist monks, Pou Tai has an enormous bronze statue of Lord Gautama

Taipa

◎ Top Sights
1 Taipa Village......................................B2

◎ Sights
2 Church of Our Lady of Carmel...........C2
3 Museum of Taipa & Coloane History...A3
4 Pak Tai Temple.................................A3
5 Taipa Houses-Museum.....................D2

✖ Eating
6 A Petisqueira...................................A2
7 António..B3
8 O Santos...B2
9 Tai Lei Loi...B2

◉ Drinking & Nightlife
10 Old Taipa Tavern.............................A2

◉ Shopping
11 Cunha Bazaar..................................B1

in its main hall, and prayer pavilions and orchid greenhouses scattered around the complex. The monks also operate a vegetarian restaurant (p213).

⊙ Coloane

MACAU GIANT PANDA PAVILION   ZOO

(大熊貓館, Pavihao do Panda Gigante de Macau; ☏853 2833 7676; www.macaupanda.org.mo; Seac Pai Van Park, Coloane; admission MOP$10; ⊘10am-1pm & 2-5pm Tue-Sun; ☒; ☐15, 21A, 25, 26, 26A, 50) Coloane offers a convenient and inexpensive opportunity to see pandas. The pair of cuddly ones are kept inside a purpose-built pavilion inside Seac Pai Van Park (p212). There are six hour-long viewing sessions daily, from 10am to 4pm. Other animals on display include peacocks, monkeys and a toucan. Twin pandas were born here this summer and have been a big draw.

HÁC SÁ BEACH   BEACH

(黑沙海灘; ☐21A, 25, 26A) Hác Sá (Black Sand) is Macau's most popular beach. The sand is indeed a blackish colour and makes the water look somewhat dirty, but it's natural. Lifeguards are on duty from May to October. The stalls just off the beach rent out parasols for MOP$60 a day, with a MOP$100 deposit (but you'll need to bring your parasol back).

CHAPEL OF ST FRANCIS XAVIER   CHURCH

(聖方濟各教堂, Capela de São Francisco Xavier; Rua do Caetano, Largo Eduardo Marques, Coloane;

LOCAL KNOWLEDGE

COLOANE'S STILT HOUSES

Macau was a fishing village before gambling was legalised in the mid-19th century. Now the only vestiges of that idyllic past are found in Coloane.

Along the coastline, on Rua dos Navegantes in Coloane's old fishing village, there are a few stilt houses and shipyards. These huts of colourful corrugated metal, extending like chunky chopsticks out into the harbour, were once landing spots for house boats. A couple have been turned into dried seafood shops, such as Loja de Peixe Tong Kei (棠記魚舖) at Largo do Cais, the square just off the charming old pier of Coloane.

From the square, take the slope to the right of the Servicos de Alfangega building. After two minutes, you'll see the cavernous cadaver of a shipyard, also on stilts.

⊘10am-8pm; ☐15, 21A, 25, 26A) This chapel built in 1928 contains paintings of the infant Christ with a Chinese Madonna, and other reminders of Christianity and colonialism in Asia. It's a quirky place painted in yellow and embellished with red lanterns. In front of the chapel are a monument and fountain surrounded by four cannonballs that commemorate the successful – and final – routing of pirates in 1910.

CHEOC VAN BEACH   BEACH

(竹灣海灘; Estrada de Cheoc Van; ☐21A, 25, 26A) About 1.5km down Estrada de Cheoc Van, which runs east and then southeast from Coloane village, is the beach at Cheoc Van (Bamboo Bay). It's smaller but somewhat cleaner than Hác Sá beach. There are changing rooms and toilets and, in season, lifeguards on duty (from 10am to 6pm Monday to Saturday, from 9am to 6pm Sunday, May to October). There's also a large public outdoor pool.

TAM KUNG TEMPLE   TAOIST TEMPLE

(譚公廟; Avenida de Cinco de Outubro, Coloane village; ⊘8.30am-5.30pm; ☐15, 21A, 25, 26A) This temple is dedicated to Tam Kung, a Taoist god of seafarers. Inside the main altar is a long whale bone carved into a model of a dragon boat. To the left of the main altar is a path leading to the roof, which has views of the village and waterfront.

A-MA STATUE & TEMPLE   MEMORIAL

(媽祖像及媽祖廟, Estátua da Deusa A-Ma; Estrada do Alto de Coloane; ⊘temple 8am-7.30pm) Atop Alto de Coloane (176m), this 20m-high white jade statue of the goddess who gave Macau its name was erected in 1998. It's the best part of a touristy 'cultural village', which also features **Tian Hou Temple**. A free bus runs from the A-Ma ornamental entrance gate (媽祖文化村石牌坊) on Estrada de Seac Pai Van (bus 21A, 25, 50) half-hourly from 8am to 6pm. You can also reach both by following the Coloane Trail (p216; Trilho de Coloane) from Seac Pai Van Park.

COLOANE LIBRARY   LIBRARY

(路環圖書館; Rua de Cinco de Outubro, Coloane; ⊘1-7pm Mon-Sat; ☐21A, 25, 26A) This buttercup-yellow mini Grecian temple, built in 1917, still functions as a public library.

SEAC PAI VAN PARK   PARK

(石排灣郊野公園; Estrada de Seac Pai Van; ⊘8am-6pm Tue-Sun, aviary 9am-5pm Tue-Sun; ☐21A, 26A, 50) **FREE** At the end of Cotai, this

Coloane

⊙ N
0 _____ 400 m
0 _____ 0.2 miles

COLOANE VILLAGE

Estrada do Campo

7 6

Rua Da Tassara

10

Rua da Cordoaria

5
1
3

Av de Cinco de Outubro

Rua do Estaleiro

Av da Republica

Lai Chi Wan

4

Largo Tam Kong Miu

Seac Pai Van Park

Seac Pai Van Park

Alto de Coloane (170m)

Estrada de Cheoc Van

8

2

Cheoc Van Bay (Bamboo Bay)

9

Hác Sá Beach (2km);
Macau Golf & Country Club (2.5km)

SOUTH CHINA SEA

Shuttle to A-Ma Cultural Village (800m);
Macau Giant Panda Pavilion (1.2km);
Seac Pai Van Park (1.2km);
A-Ma Statue & Temple (2.2km)

20-hectare park, built in the wooded hills on the western side of the island, has somewhat unkempt gardens, the Macau Giant Panda Pavilion (p212), a lake with swans and other waterfowl, and a walk-through aviary.

✖ EATING

✖ Taipa

★ **TAI LEI LOI**　　　　　　　　CHINESE $
(大利来; ☑853 2882 7150; www.taileiloi.com.mo; 42 Rua dos Clérigos, Taipa village; buns MOP$40; ☺8am-6pm; ◈; ☒22, 26) South China's most famous pork-chop bun is made here – a shop founded in 1960 as a street stall by the mother of the current owner. Succulent slices of pork (or slivers of fish) are coupled with warm, chewy buns that emerge from the oven daily at 2pm sharp.

POU TAI TEMPLE RESTAURANT　　　　　　CHINESE $
(5 Estrada Lou Lim leok, Taipa; meals MOP$40-120; ☺11am-8pm Mon-Sat, 9am-9pm Sun; ◢◈) The two vegetarian restaurants (one more formal, one more casual), set in Pou Tai Temple (p211) in northern Taipa, are a great find.

Coloane

A PETISQUEIRA　　　　　　　PORTUGUESE $$
(葡國美食天地; ☑853 2882 5354; 15 Rua de São João, Taipa village; meals MOP$150-500; ☺12.30-2.15pm & 6.45-10pm Tue-Sun; ◈; ☒22, 28A) Set in an obscure alley, 'The Snackery' is an amicable place with myriad Portuguese choices. It serves its own *queijo fresca da casa* (homemade cheese). Try the *bacalao* (cod) five ways, and baked seafood with rice.

BANZA
PORTUGUESE $$

(百姓餐廳; ☑853 2882 1519; 154a & b, G & H, Block 5, Edificio Nam San Garden, Avenida de Kwong Tung, Taipa; meals MOP$200-500; ⊘noon-3pm & 6.30-11pm Tue-Sun; ☐11, 16, 28A) Off the beaten track, this welcoming place run by a Portuguese former lawyer is known for its well-executed fish dishes and Portuguese classics. If you'd like, Banza could also recommend a bottle from its interesting selection of Portuguese wines.

O SANTOS
PORTUGUESE $$

(☑853 2882 7508; www.osantoscomidaportuguesa.com; 20 Rua da Cunha, Taipa village; meals MOP$200-350; ⊘noon-3pm & 6-10pm Wed-Mon; 🖋; ☐22, 26) Despite its location on the touristy Rua da Cunha, charming O Santos keeps its standards up. Patrons have been coming back for the chicken and rice in blood and friendly banter with the owner (a former naval chef) for 20 years.

★ANTÓNIO
PORTUGUESE $$$

(安東尼奧; ☑853 2888 8668; www.antoniomacau.com; 7 Rua dos Clérigos, Taipa village; meals MOP$350-1200; ⊘noon-midnight; ☐22, 26) The cosy mahogany-framed dining room, the meticulously thought-out menu and the entertaining chef, António Coelho, all make this the go-to place for traditional Portuguese food. If you can only try one Portuguese restaurant in Macau, make it this one. The octopus salad, homemade sausage (served flaming) and the African chicken are exceptional.

🍴 Coloane

★CAFÉ NGA TIM
MACANESE $

(雅憩花園餐廳; Rua do Caetano, Coloane village; mains MOP$70-200; ⊘noon-1am; 🖋; ☐21A, 25, 26A) We love the Chinese-Portuguese food, the small-town atmosphere, the view of the Chapel of St Francis Xavier, the prices and the owner – a guitar- and *erhu*-strumming ex-policeman named Feeling Wong.

HON KEE COFFEE
CAFE $

(Estrada de Lai Chi Vun; mains MOP$15-30; ⊘7.30am-6pm) Amid the atmospheric abandoned shipyard just north of Coloane village, this idiosyncratic *cha chaan teng* (a Southern Chinese-style greasy spoon specialising in coffee, tea and breakfast) is a cult hit among young Macanese. Crowd into the high-ceilinged shanty to slurp

sweet dense coffee and snack on fluffy white toast drizzled with condensed milk.

LORD STOW'S BAKERY
BAKERY $

(澳門安德魯餅店; 1 Rua da Tassara; egg tarts MOP$9; ⊘7am-10pm Thu-Tue, to 7pm Wed) Though the celebrated English baker Andrew Stow has passed away, his cafe (9 Largo do Matadouro) and Lord Stow's Bakery keep his memory alive by serving his renowned *pastéis de nata* – a warm egg-custard tart (MOP$9) – and cheesecake (MOP$14) in unusual flavours, including black sesame and green tea.

BARBECUE STALLS NEAR HÁC SÁ BEACH
BARBECUE $

(Rua de Hác Sá Long Chao Kok, Coloane; skewers MOP$15-45; ⊘11am-3pm; 🖋; ☐21A, 25, 26A) Just off Hác Sá beach is a row of barbecue stalls – some with tables – emitting the mouthwatering aromas of grilled meat and seafood.

★RESTAURANTE FERNANDO
PORTUGUESE $$

(法蘭度餐廳; ☑853 2888 2264; 9 Hác Sá beach; meals MOP$150-270; ⊘noon-9.30pm; 🖋; ☐21A, 25, 26A) Possibly Coloane's most famous restaurant, sprawling Fernando's contains two separate dining rooms and a large courtyard bar area. Devoted customers and travellers pack the chequered-tablecloth-covered tables to chow on plates of garlicky clams, golden roast suckling pig, and piles of codfish rice. Expect lines during peak lunch and dinner times, especially on weekends. Cash only.

ESPACO LISBOA
PORTUGUESE, MACANESE $$$

(里斯本地帶; ☑853 2888 2226; 8 Rua das Gaivotas, Coloane village; meals MOP$250-800; ⊘noon-10.30pm; 🖋; ☐21A, 25, 26A) The home-style dishes here are solidly good, but what makes this two-storey restaurant in Coloane village unique is the combination of Portugal-inspired decor and a Chinese village house – in other words, the space (*espaco*).

DRINKING & NIGHTLIFE

OLD TAIPA TAVERN
PUB

(好客鄉村餐廳; 21 Rua dos Negociantes, Taipa village; 🖾; ☐22, 28A, 26) A location near the Pak Tai Temple makes laid-back OTT a sublime spot to down and beer and watch the comings and goings in the centre of Taipa village.

★MACALLAN WHISKY BAR & LOUNGE
BAR

(☑853 8883 2221; www.galaxymacau.com; 203, 2nd fl, Galaxy Hotel, Cotai; ⏰5pm-1am Mon-Thu, to 2am Fri & Sat; 🚌25, 25X) Macau's best whisky bar is a traditional affair featuring oak panels, Jacobean rugs and a real fireplace. The 400-plus whisky labels include representatives from Ireland, France, Sweden and India, and a 1963 Glenmorangie. The pre-9pm happy hour means you get your age in years discounted as a percentage from your drink (30 years old = 30 percent off).

CLUB CUBIC
CLUB

(☑853 6638 4999; www.cubic-cod.com; 2105-02, Level 2, City of Dreams, Estrada do Istmo, Cotai; ⏰11.30pm-6am Mon-Sat; 🚌50, 35) The massive and flashy Club Cubic at the Hard Rock Hotel has themed rooms and a large disco ball. There are DJs mixing a variety of tunes, including hip hop, techno and Korean pop, pumped out of the club's top-notch sound system.

☆ ENTERTAINMENT

★VENETIAN
CASINO

(澳門威尼斯人度假村酒店; ☑853 2882 8877; www.venetianmacao.com; 🚌25, 26A) Said to be one of the 10 largest buildings in the world, The Venetian is 980,000 sq metres of what might be described as Casino Gothic architecture, packed to the gills with busloads of goggle-eyed tourists. Features include some 3000 hotel suites, a full-sized arena, an onsite medical and plastic surgery clinic and more than 500,000 sq ft of gaming floor. Its centrepiece is the Grand Canal Shoppes, an indoor mall surrounding three enormous curved canals, where gondoliers push boats of tourists through pool-blue waters while singing opera. The ceiling is painted and lit to resemble the sky at dusk, the shops are housed behind Venetian-style facades, and wandering magicians dressed like carnival revellers entertain the crowds. Surreal.

★HOUSE OF DANCING WATER
THEATRE

(水舞間; ☑853 8868 6688; http://thehouse ofdancingwater.com; City of Dreams, Estrada do Istmo, Cotai; tickets MOP$580-1480; 🚌50, 35) 'The House of Dancing Water', Macau's most expensively made show, is a breathtaking melange of stunts, acrobatics and theatre designed by Franco Dragone, the former director of Cirque du Soleil. The magic revolves around a cobalt pool the size

ℹ EVENTS & TICKETS

The website www.macau.com has events listings and a ticket-booking service. You can also book tickets to most events through **Macau Ticket** (Map p196; ☑853 2855 5555; www. macauticket.com; 71b Avenida Conselheiro Ferreira de Almeida) and Cotai Ticketing (www.cotaiticketing.com).

The monthly events calendar for upmarket entertainment is *Destination Macau*, available at Macau Government Tourist Office outlets and larger hotels.

of several Olympic-sized swimming pools. Over, around, into and under this pool a cast of 80 perform hair-raising stunts dressed in glorious costumes.

GALAXY MACAU
CASINO

(澳門銀河綜合渡假城; ☑853 2888 0888; www.galaxymacau.com; Avenida Marginal Flor de Lotus, Cotai; 🚌25, 26A) Towering over Cotai like an alien palace out of *Star Wars*, the ginormous gold-and-white Galaxy is one of the most extravagant megacasinos in the city (and that's saying something). It contains six hotels, more than 100 restaurants and kilometres of upmarket shopping, as well as a movie theatre, Chinese foot massage spa and a jaw-dropping rooftop wave pool and lazy river (for hotel guests only). The brightly lit game floors tinkle with the sounds of dice and slot machines all night long. Mere gawkers can enjoy lobby violinists, wandering dance troupes and a fountain that lights up and sings once an hour.

STUDIO CITY
CASINO

(☑853 8865 8888; www.studiocity-macau.com; Estrada Flor de Lotus, Cotai; ♿; 🚌25, 26A) You can recognise this new casino from afar by the figure-8-shaped 'Golden Reel' at its centre, a double Ferris wheel with views across the Cotai Strip. This Hollywood-themed casino complex is one of Macau's more family-friendly, with a Warner Brothers–themed indoor kiddie amusement park and a (very entertaining) Batman flight-simulation ride (MOP$150). Beyond the fully loaded casino, you'll find a 1600-room hotel, a mall, a house magic show and a food court designed to look like old Macau.

CITY OF DREAMS
CASINO

(新濠天地; ☑853 8868 6688; www.city ofdreamsmacau.com; Estrada do Istmo, Cotai;

BRIGHT LIGHTS, SIN CITY

A gambling mecca since the 19th century, Macau has lately been sprouting glitzy megacasinos like mushrooms after a rain. The change began when casino mogul Stanley Ho's monopoly ended in 2002 and Las Vegas operators set up shop in competition. There are now more than 30 casinos in Macau, their total gaming revenue surpassing all of the world's major gambling jurisdictions combined. Macau Peninsula has most of the older, smaller casinos, while the newly infilled Cotai area is home to the new breed of casino-hotel-shopping-entertainment behemoths.

Table games are the staple at casinos here – mostly baccarat, then roulette and a dice game called *dai sai* (big small). You'll hardly hear any whooping and clunking – slot machines make up only 5% of total casino winnings (versus Vegas' 60%). Drunks are also hard to come by, as Chinese players believe that booze dulls their skill. Over 80% of gamblers and 95% of high rollers come from mainland China. The latter play inside members-only rooms where the total amount wagered on any given day can exceed a small country's GDP.

For recreational players, the only thing to watch out for is harassment by tip hustlers – scam artists who hang around tables acting like your new best friend. They may steal your chips, nag you for a cut or try to take you to a casino that will tip them for bringing clients.

Casinos are open 24 hours. To enter, you must be 21 years or older and neatly dressed.

25, 26A) Opened in 2009, this megacasino features three hotels, several dozen restaurants, a mall and several theatres, as well as nearly half a million square feet of gaming floor. Check out the 3D projection shows in the Bubble Dome Theatre (MOP$50) or the digital mermaids swimming along the walls of the virtual aquarium.

 SHOPPING

★ **CUNHA BAZAAR** GIFTS & SOUVENIRS

(www.cunhabazaar.com; Rua do Cunha 33-35, Taipa village; ☺9.30am-10pm) This four-storey shop on the corner of Taipa village's Rua do Cunha pedestrian street has the motherlode of made-in-Macau gifts, T-shirts, candies and more. You'll find traditional foods like almond cookies and jerky on the ground floor; the 1st floor is dedicated to goods bearing the image of Macau's own Soda Panda, a perpetually grumpy cartoon panda who likes to do Macanese things like eat egg tarts and play roulette. The remaining two floors are dedicated to leather goods, ceramics, notebooks and sketches by local designers.

🏃 SPORTS & ACTIVITIES

TAIPA TRAIL HIKING HIKING

The **Little Taipa Trail** (Trilho de Taipa Pequena) is a 2km-long circuit around a hill (111m) in northwestern Taipa, reachable via Estrada Lou Lim Ieok. The 2.2km-long **Taipa Trail** (Trilho de Taipa Grande) rings Taipa Grande, a 160m-high hill at the eastern end of the island. You can access the trail via a short paved road off Estrada Colonel Nicolau de Mesquita.

COLOANE TRAIL HIKING

Coloane's (and Macau's) longest trail, the 8100m **Trilho de Coloane**, begins in the mid-section of Estrada do Alto de Coloane and winds around the island. (To get there, take bus 21A and get off at stop Estrada do Campo, then enter Estrata Militar across the road; after 600m, turn right.) You can make a detour to Alto de Coloane (170m) to see the A-Ma Statue (p212).

The shorter **Coloane Northeast Trail** (Trilho Nordeste de Coloane), near Ká Hó, runs for 3km. Other trails that offer good hiking are the 1.5km **Altinho de Ká Hó Trail** and **Circuito da Barragem de Hác Sá**, which both loop around the reservoir to the northwest of Hác Sá beach.

MACAU GOLF & COUNTRY CLUB GOLF

(澳門高爾夫球鄉村俱樂部; ☎853 2887 1188; www.macaugolfandcountryclub.com; 1918 Estrada de Hác Sá, Coloane; ☒15) One of three tournament courses in greater China, the scenic 18-hole, par-71 course connected to the Westin Resort has special weekday tee times for non-members. The driving range allows players to hit balls into the South China Sea.

Sleeping

Hong Kong's accommodation runs the gamut from hostels with tiny rooms to opulent suites. In a city where real estate is the price of gold, money makes all the difference: you'll be spoiled for choice with the range of luxurious places. Midrange options are less mind-blowing but adequate, and in the budget range pickings get thinner.

Facilities

All rooms have air-conditioning, and all but the cheapest rooms have private bathrooms, in-room wi-fi and cable TV in English. Most places have computers for guests' use. All indoor areas of hostels and hotels are supposed to be nonsmoking.

Top-End Hotels

Hong Kong's luxury hotels are locked in an arms race for the dollars of affluent travellers. Their weapons are star restaurants, lavish spa complexes and smooth service. Prices for top-of-the-range hotels start from close to HK$2000 per room. A few of them offer comfort, amenities and service that compete with or surpass that of the world's finest five-star hotels.

Midrange Hotels

New places continue to emerge that are uniquely cool to look at and easy on the pocket, with rates hovering between HK$1000 and HK$2000 and dipping to budget range in the low season. Rooms at these places tend to be smallish and come with wi-fi connection, limited cable TV, and room service.

Guesthouses

Dominating the lower end of the accommodation market are guesthouses, usually a block of tiny rooms squeezed into a converted apartment. Often several guesthouses operate out of the same building. Some offer dormitory accommodation for those on tight budgets.

Though rooms are small, many places are clean and cheerily shabby or neat and austere. All have air-con and most have TVs and phones. Anything under HK$900 should be considered budget.

Depending on the season, try to negotiate a better deal, as a lot of places will be eager to fill empty rooms. Most guesthouses offer free wi-fi.

Hostels & Campsites

The Hong Kong Youth Hostels Association (p267) maintains seven hostels affiliated with Hostelling International (HI). It also sells HKYHA and HI cards. If you haven't applied for membership in your own country, visit the HKYHA office or the hostels to do so. Be sure to take along a visa-sized photo and ID.

All HKYHA hostels have separate toilets and showers for men and women, and cooking facilities. They provide blankets, pillows and sheet bags. Most have lockers available.

Prices for a bed in a dormitory range from HK$75 to HK$250 a night, depending on the hostel.

The Country & Marine Parks Authority (p152) maintains 41 basic campsites in the New Territories and Outlying Islands.

SLEEPING

NEED TO KNOW

Price Ranges: Hong Kong
Nightly rates for a double room:

$ Less than HK$900

$$ HK$900–1900

$$$ More than HK$1900

Monthly rates for a one-bedroom apartment:

$ Less than HK$15,000

$$ HK$15,000–25,000

$$$ More than HK$25,000

Price Ranges: Macau
Breakfast is usually included in the rates for hotels marked $$ and $$$.

$ Less than MOP$700

$$ MOP$700-2000

$$$ More than MOP$2000

Taxes
Most midrange and top-end hotels and a small number of budget places add 10% service and 3% government tax to your bill.

Useful Websites
Lonely Planet (lonelyplanet.com/china/hong-kong/hotels) Hostels, B&B and hotel listings, and an online booking service.

Hong Kong Hotels Association (www.hkha.org)

Discover Hong Kong (www.discoverhongkong.com)

Asia Travel (www.hongkonghotels.com)

Traveller Services (香港旅遊; www.traveller.com.hk)

Hong Kong Tourism Board (www.discoverhongkong.com)

Lonely Planet's Top Choices

Peninsula Hong Kong (p225) World-class luxury and colonial elegance at the harbour end of Tsim Sha Tsui.

TUVE (p221) A tiny paradise for design fans in a pleasant neighbourhood full of restaurants.

Hotel Indigo (p222) Large, colourful rooms, attentive staff and a fabulous bar in a lively part of Wan Chai.

Campus Hong Kong (p226) Brand new student hostel with premium views and the luxuries of a top-notch hotel.

Upper House (p223) A Zen-like atmosphere, yoga on the lawn and warm service overlooking the hills in Admiralty.

Hyatt Regency Tsim Sha Tsui (p225) A self-assured veteran offering comfort and understated luxury from a prime location.

Best by Budget

$
Campus Hong Kong (p226) Live like royalty in a student hostel (if you manage to book a room, that is) in Tsuen Wan.

YesInn (p221) A quirky, super-friendly international hostel.

$$
TUVE (p221) Sleek, industrial-chic rooms, an artsy reception area and helpful staff in Tin Hau.

Twenty One Whitfield (p222) Clean, bright rooms available for daily and monthly stays in Tin Hau.

$$$
Peninsula Hong Kong (p225) One of the most elegant and richly storied hotels in Asia.

Hotel Indigo (p222) Chinese-inspired design, state-of-the-art facilities and exceptional service make this a winner.

Best for Design

TUVE (p221) It's all about design here, from the beds to the soft drink bottles in the mini-fridge.

Madera Hong Kong (p226) Boldly coloured, whimsical decor reminiscent of the movie sets of Pedro Almodóvar.

Mira Moon (p222) Taking a famous Chinese legend to new and creative heights.

Landmark Mandarin Oriental (p220) The subtle elegance associated with the Mandarin Oriental name infuses every nook and corner.

Where to Stay

NEIGHBOURHOOD	FOR	AGAINST
HONG KONG ISLAND: CENTRAL	close to the Star Ferry pier, famous skyscrapers and luxury malls; within walking distance of bars and eats; good transport links	the narest eats, sleeps, bars and shops are pricey; gets quiet after office hours.
HONG KONG ISLAND: THE PEAK & THE NORTHWEST	in the thick of the nightlife and dining action; close to the Peak and the historic sites in Sheung Wan	sloping topography, hence more trips uphill and down; districts further west are quiet and away from the action
HONG KONG ISLAND: WAN CHAI & THE NORTHEAST	good for Hong Kong Park, Happy Valley Racecourse and shopping; abundant eating and drinking options; great transport links	Wan Chai and Causeway Bay are traffic-choked and crowded; districts further east are a little worn and far away
HONG KONG ISLAND: ABERDEEN & THE SOUTH	great for Aberdeen Typhoon Shelter, Stanley Market, Horizon Plaza, swimming and hiking around Repulse Bay and Shek O	not central, frequent traffic jams near Aberdeen Tunnel, limited sleeps, eats, bars and shops
KOWLOON	convenient for Museum of Art and of History, best views of the harbour; great for shopping, eating, even 'slumming'; cool mix of old and new, highbrow and lowheel; great transport links	crowded and traffic-choked around Nathan Rd; some areas can be touristy and/or a little seedy
NEW TERRITORIES	fewer crowds, fresher air; handy for outdoor sports, nature tours, walled villages; prices generally lower	far from the action; fewer eats, sleeps, bars and shops; little to do at night
OUTLYING ISLANDS: LAMMA, LANTAU & CHEUNG CHAU	laid-back vibe, nice setting, good for seafood on Lamma, windsurfing on Cheung Chau, hiking the Lantau Trail and loads of beaches	longer time spent commuting; fewer eats, sleeps, bars and shops; activities dependent on weather
MACAU	close to the historic center and the casino action; luxury hotels often far cheaper than Hong Kong	few decent ultra-budget options beyond two government-run hostels far from the city centre

🛏 Hong Kong Island: Central

⭐ HELENA MAY
HOTEL $

Map p298 (梅夫人婦女會主樓; ☐852 2522 6766; www.helenamay.com; 35 Garden Rd, Central; s/d HK$580/760, studio per month HK$16,300-21,240; ☐23) If you like the peninsula's colonial setting but not its price tag, this grand dame could be your cup of tea. Founded in 1916 as a social club for single European women, it is now a private club for women of all nationalities and a hotel with 43 creaky but charming rooms. Rooms are women-only; studios are open to men.

Rooms are in the main building and have shared bathrooms, while the rent-by-the-month studios are in an adjacent building. You must be 18 or above to stay at the Helena May. The building is a stone's throw from the Peak Tram Terminus and the Zoological & Botanical Gardens.

All guests pay a HK$180 membership fee, plus a HK$120 monthly subscription.

⭐ MANDARIN ORIENTAL
LUXURY HOTEL $$$

Map p298 (文華東方酒店; ☐852 2522 0111; www.mandarinoriental.com/hongkong; 5 Connaught Rd, Central; r HK$3655-7400, ste HK$6120-65,000; @☎≋; MCentral, exit J3) The venerable Mandarin has historically set the standard in Asia and continues to be a contender for the top spot, despite competition from the likes of the Four Seasons. The styling, service, food and atmosphere are stellar throughout and there's a sense of gracious, old-world charm. The sleek **Landmark Oriental** (Map p298; ☐852 2132 0088; www.mandarinoriental.com/landmark; 15 Queen's Rd, Central; r HK$5470-9000, ste HK$9300-45,000; @☎≋; MCentral, exit D1), just across the way, offers modern luxury, but with a business vibe.

FOUR SEASONS
LUXURY HOTEL $$$

Map p298 (四季酒店; ☐852 3196 8888; www.fourseasons.com/hongkong; 8 Finance St, Central; r HK$4800-8100, ste HK$9800-65,000; @☎≋; MHong Kong, exit F) The Four Seasons arguably edges into top place on the island for its amazing views, pristine service, and its location close to the Star Ferry Pier, Hong Kong station, and Sheung Wan. Also on offer are palatial rooms, a glorious pool and spa complex, and award-winning restaurants Caprice (p74) and Lung King Heen (p74).

🛏 Hong Kong Island: The Peak & the Northwest

⭐ BISHOP LEI INTERNATIONAL HOUSE
HOTEL $

Map p304 (宏基國際賓館; ☐852 2868 0828; www.bishopleihtl.com.hk; 4 Robinson Rd, Mid-Levels; s/d/ste from $550/700/1250; @≋; ☐23 or 40) This hotel in residential Mid-Levels, though out of the way, provides a lot of bang for your buck. It boasts good service, a swimming pool, a gym and proximity to the Zoological & Botanical Gardens. The standard single and double rooms are small. It's worth paying a little more for the larger, harbour-facing rooms, which offer good views of the skyline and the cathedral from high up. Buses to Central and Wan Chai stop in front of the hotel.

⭐ 99 BONHAM
BOUTIQUE HOTEL $$

Map p304 (☐852 3940 1111; www.99bonham.com; 99 Bonham Strand, Sheung Wan; r from HK$1300; @☎; MSheung Wan, exit A2) This hotel has 84 unusually large rooms (for Hong Kong). They are stylishly minimalist, featuring a palette of white, black and grey. The hotel also has a small gym, a business centre, and a rooftop terrace where you can take in the resplendent views. There's no hotel restaurant, but an abundance of eateries await just out the door.

OVOLO NOHO
HOTEL $$

Map p302 (香港奧華·時尚精品酒店–蘇豪; ☐852 3423 3286; www.ovolohotels.com/en/; 286 Queen's Rd Central, Sheung Wan; r from HK$1300; @☎; MSheung Wan, exit D1) In the hip 'NoHo' (North of Hollywood Rd) neighbourhood, this friendly little hotel showers guests with freebies, including breakfast, minibar, use of a small gym, self-service laundry, and booze every evening in the 24-hour lounge. All 60 smoke-free rooms, some with connecting doors, are clean and compact (14 to 18 sq metre), with low beds and a minimalist Japanese-influenced design.

LAN KWAI FONG HOTEL
BOUTIQUE HOTEL $$

Map p302 (蘭桂坊酒店@九如坊; ☐852 3650 0000; www.lankwaifonghotel.com.hk; 3 Kau U Fong, Central; r/ste from HK$1500/5000; @☎; MSheung Wan, exit E2) This well-located hotel (not to be confused with Hotel LKF) is closer to Soho than Lan Kwai Fong. The Chinese decor with a contemporary twist adds an interesting touch to the reasonably spacious digs. The service is top-notch.

★POTTINGER
BOUTIQUE HOTEL $$$

Map p302 (☑852 2308 3188; www.thepottinger. com; 74 Queen's Rd Central, enter from Stanley St, Central; r from HK$2700, ste from HK$4200; Ⓜ Central D2) Smack in the heart of Central, this unobtrusive new boutique hotel has 86 airy, white-and-cream rooms with subtle Asian touches – carved wooden screens, calligraphy work, black-and-white photos of old Hong Kong. The Envoy, the Pottinger's excellent hotel bar, has a colonial theme, with dark panelling and afternoon high tea, a tribute to Sir Henry Pottinger, Hong Kong's first governor and the hotel's namesake.

PUTMAN
APARTMENT $$$

Map p302 (☑852 2233 2233; www.theputman. com; 202-206 Queen's Rd, Central; ste from HK$3000; @🛜📶; Ⓜ Sheung Wan, exit A or E) Behind the art deco–inspired glass facade, this designer outfit has three cool-toned studios for shorter stays and 25 one-bedroom flats for long-term rental. Each flat occupies an entire storey and the floor-to-ceiling windows allow a lot of natural light. You also get space (the flats are 120 sq metre and the studios are 30 to 40 sq metre) and impeccable taste here. The kitchens come with designer cooking utensils, crockery, stemware and laundry facilities. Prices include membership to a gym nearby.

MERCER
BOUTIQUE HOTEL $$$

Map p302 (尚圜; ☑582 2922 9988; 29 Jervois St, Sheung Wan; r/ste from HK$2000/2800; @🛜✉; Ⓜ Sheung Wan, exit A2) There are 55 rooms at this modern, conveniently located hotel. Decked out in beige with lots of mirrored surfaces, they offer a host of freebies – wi-fi, minibar, local calls and breakfast, and – for the suites – coffee machines. There's a small gym and lap pool for the sporty, and dozens of restaurants on the surrounding blocks.

HOTEL LKF
HOTEL $$$

Map p302 (隆堡蘭桂坊酒店; ☑852 3518 9688; www.hotel-lkf.com.hk; 33 Wyndham St, Central; r HK$2100-3200, ste from HK$3500; @🛜; Ⓜ Central, exit D2) Located on the upper, flatter section of Wyndham St, Hotel LKF is arguably the best gateway to the Lan Kwai Fong action, but is far enough above it not to be disturbed by it. It has high-tech rooms in muted tones and they brim with all the trimmings you'll need: fluffy bathrobes,

espresso machines and free bedtime milk and cookies. The hotel has a small gym, and there are several high-end restaurants in the building.

🛏 Hong Kong Island: Wan Chai & the Northeast

★YESINN
HOSTEL $

Map p310 (☑852 2213 4567; www.yesinn.com; 2nd fl, Nan Yip Bldg, 472 Hennessy Rd, Causeway Bay; dm HK$159-469, r HK$199-459; Ⓜ Causeway Bay, exit F2) This funky, vibrant hostel attracts backpackers from all over the world, as evidenced by their signatures on the building's chalkboard paint ceiling. There are both female and mixed dorms, and private rooms, all brightly painted. The small reception area is made up for by the excellent roof deck, sometimes the site of hostel-sponsored barbecues.

The hostel entrance is at the side of the building on the corner. Private rooms are in a building across the street. The neon, shopping and late-night sushi of Causeway Bay are a two-minute walk away. YesInn has sister hostels in Fortress Hill and Kowloon.

CHECK INN
HOSTEL $

Map p308 (卓軒旅舍; ☑852 2955 0175; www. checkinnhk.com; Room A, 3rd fl, Kwong Wah Mansion, 269-273 Hennessy Rd, Wan Chai; dm HK$160-200, r HK$450-600; 🛜; Ⓜ Wan Chai, exit A2) Twelve basic dorms (female and mixed) and four simple en suite rooms in an old, centrally located building. The reception and hang-out area (2nd floor) is cosy and spacious, featuring books and coffee next to a wall of windows. The knowledgeable staff hosts two or three free tours a week for guests, who just need to pay for food and transport.

The top bunk in some dorms may be a little too close to the ceiling for comfort. Try to book a middle bunk if possible.

★TUVE
BOUTIQUE HOTEL $$

Map p310 (☑852 3995 8800; www.tuve.hk; 16 Tsing Fung St, Tin Hau; from HK$980; @🛜; Ⓜ Tin Hau, exit A1) From the dungeon-like entrance to the noir-ish reception area with black iron grille and the brass-and-concrete slab that is the front desk, everything here spells design. Industrial glam continues in the rooms where concrete walls are discreetly highlighted with gold foil, and grey-and-white marble plays off against oak and wired glass, and all are grounded by immaculate white linen and excellent service.

Tuve's design was inspired by a series of hauntingly beautiful photos of Lake Tuve in Sweden. Even the drinks in the minibar were handpicked by its owner, a product designer, for their compliance with overall aesthetics. Design fanatics will have a field day here, but if your idea of holiday lodging involves lots of colours, curves and fluff, it may not be for you.

TWENTY ONE
WHITFIELD   HOTEL, SERVICED APARTMENT $$

Map p310 (第二十一威菲路酒店; ☑852 3994 8585; 21 Whitfield Rd, Causeway Bay; r daily HK$800-3000, monthly HK$27,000-31,000; @🛜; MTin Hau, exit A2) The 54 welcoming and compact rooms are available for daily and monthly stays. Besides daily cleaning service, long-stayers also get an electric stove, simple crockery, twice-a-week linen service, and free use of the laundry room. There are two rooms to each floor – similar, but apartment B has more closet space. Views from the 29th floor up are stunning.

The hotel is slightly closer to Fortress Hill MTR station than to Tin Hau, but is easier to find from the latter. When you get out of the Tin Hau MTR exit, look for an HSBC sign down the road. The street next to HSBC is Whitfield Rd.

MIRA MOON   BOUTIQUE HOTEL $$

Map p308 (問月酒店; ☑852 2643 8888; www.miramoonhotel.com; 388 Jaffe Rd, Wan Chai; r HK$1500-3000; 🛜; MWan Chai, exit A1) 🏝 Decor at this 91-room boutique hotel riffs on the Chinese fairy-tale of the Moon Goddess and the Jade Rabbit – stylised rabbit wall art, oversized Chinese lanterns, graphic peony floor mosaics. For all the hotel's hipness, its staff is warm and helpful, and the architecture is ecofriendly to boot. Special offers are available, including a package for (well, of course) honeymooners.

It's all about the details here. Freestanding bath-tubs in the 'Half Moon' and 'Full Moon' rooms are to die for, while the more budget-friendly 'New Moon' rooms offer walk-in showers. All rooms come with a phone, which guests can take with them for free 3G and local and international calls. Free soy milk and soda are in the minifridge, and the room's iPad connects to the TV. Amenities include a 24-hour gym, a Spanish-Chinese fusion tapas restaurant and a house DJ.

DORSETT WANCHAI   HOTEL $$

Map p308 (灣仔帝盛酒店; ☑852 3552 1111; www.dorsett.com; 387-397 Queen's Rd E, Wan Chai; r/ste from HK$1000/3200; @🛜🛗; MCauseway Bay, exit A) Cosmopolitan Hotel has undergone a complete renovation and changed its name to Dorsett Wanchai. All 54 bright and modernised rooms come with warm service and thoughtful amenities, which include smartphones for guests. Kids will enjoy the themed family rooms. The views here are unusual: a cemetery to the south and a racecourse to the east.

Dorsett Wanchai is actually closer to Queen's Rd East in Wan Chai than to Causeway Bay, but there's a shuttle service to the latter as well as 15 other places. Look for online deals for as much as 35% off. Sister hotel **Cosmo** (Map p308; ☑852 3552 8388; www.cosmohotel.com.hk; 375-377 Queen's Rd E, Wan Chai; r/ste from HK$900/3400; 🛗🛜; MCauseway Bay, exit A) is down the block.

CITY GARDEN HOTEL
HONG KONG   HOTEL $$

(城市花園酒店; ☑852 2887 2888; www.citygarden.com.hk; 9 City Garden Rd, North Point; r HK$800-2800; @🛜; MFortress Hill, exit A) Only five minutes' walk from Fortress Hill MTR station, this exceptionally well-turned-out business hotel also boasts large rooms (by local standards), good service, free and fast wi-fi and a generous discounting policy. Enter from the corner of Electric Rd and Power St.

★HOTEL INDIGO   BUSINESS HOTEL $$$

Map p308 (☑852 3926 3888; www.ihg.com; 246 Queen's Rd E, Wan Chai; dm HK$2000-3800, ste HK$4500-6000; @🛜🏊; MWan Chai, exit A3) Excitingly located near markets and hipster hang-outs, Indigo has slightly over-the-top modern Chinese decor and 138 large-ish, tech-forward, and very comfortable rooms. A dragon-shaped heat-absorbing grid covers its exterior, giving texture to sceneries framed by the rooms' floor-to-ceiling windows. The rooftop pool has views of the hills and, dizzyingly – the courteous staff will remind you – the street below.

Choose an upper-floor 'deluxe' room for the best views and more natural light. Indigo also has a small 24-hour gym, a meeting room seating eight, a quaint cafe that makes attractive use of the eponymous colour, and Skybar (p113), which has killer views.

★**UPPER HOUSE** BOUTIQUE HOTEL **$$$**

Map p306 (☑852 2918 1838; www.upperhouse.com; 88 Queensway, Pacific Pl, Admiralty; r/ste from HK$5000/17,000; @ 🛜; MAdmiralty, exit F) Every corner here spells zen-like serenity: the understated lobby, the sleek ecominded rooms, the elegant sculptures, the warm and discreet service, and the manicured lawn where guests can join free yoga classes. Other pluses include a free and 'bottomless' minibar, a 24-hour gym, and easy access to Admiralty MTR station. The cafe is famous for its afternoon tea.

Guests of the Upper House can pay to use the pool facilities of nearby hotels. This is a superb alternative to luxury options in Central and Admiralty, if you don't mind fewer luxuries.

ISLAND SHANGRI-LA HONG KONG LUXURY HOTEL **$$$**

Map p306 (港島香格里拉大酒店; ☑852 2877 3838; www.shangri-la.com; Supreme Court Rd, Pacific Pl, Admiralty; r/ste from HK$3200/7200; @ 🛜 ⛱; MAdmiralty, exit F, via Pacific) This monolithic hotel offers plush digs with an early-'90s vibe. Comfortable (though not particularly chic) rooms are matched by a good gym, a swimming pool and excellent service. Take a quick ride up the bubble lift that links the 39th and 56th floors; you'll catch a glimpse of the hotel's signature 60m-high painting: a mountainous Chinese landscape that's quite impressive.

EAST HONG KONG BUSINESS HOTEL **$$$**

(香港東隅; ☑852 3968 3808; www.east-hong kong.com; 29 Taikoo Shing Rd, Taikoo Shing, Quarry Bay; r/ste from HK$1750/5100; @ 🛜 ⛱; MTai Koo, exit D1) This sleekly cool business hotel, a favourite of media and publishing professionals, has 345 clean, bright rooms decorated with contemporary art and minimalist furniture. Corner harbour-view rooms, commanding good views, cost more than rooms on the lower floors which look on to buildings nearby. The 32nd-floor bar, Sugar (p115), is spectacular for sunset cocktails.

J PLUS BY YOO BOUTIQUE HOTEL **$$$**

Map p310 (香港J Plus精品酒店; ☑852 3196 9000; www.jplushongkong.com/en; 1-5 Irving St, Causeway Bay; r HK$1300-2500; @ 🛜; MCauseway Bay, exit F) This stylish boutique hotel occupies a prime location in Causeway Bay within walking distance of bus, tram and MTR stations. Littered with designer furniture (or their lookalikes), the rooms are small, but clean and modern. Some taxi drivers may not know it, so tell them you're going to the Regal hotel, which is right across the street.

🛏 Hong Kong Island: Aberdeen & the South

★**T HOTEL** HOTEL **$$**

(T酒店; ☑852 3717 7388; www.vtc.edu.hk/thotel; VTC Pokfulam Complex, 145 Pok Fu Lam Rd, Pok Fu Lam; r/ste from HK$1040/2760; @ 🛜; 🚌7, 91 from Central, 973 from Tsim Sha Tsui) Ah, we almost don't want to tell you about this gem! The 30-room T in the serene neighbourhood of Po Fu Lam is entirely run by students of the hospitality training institute. The young trainees are attentive, cheerful and eager to hone their skills. Rooms, all on the 6th floor, are sparkling and spacious, and offer ocean or mountain views.

The suites, larger than many serviced apartments, come with guest toilets and a kitchenette. The food and beverage outlets, run by the famous culinary school in the complex, provide excellent Chinese and international meals.

OVOLO SOUTHSIDE BOUTIQUE HOTEL **$$**

Map p312 (Ovolo 南區; ☑85221651000; www.ovolo hotels.com; 64 Wong Chuk Hang Rd, Wong Chuk Hang; r HK$800-$1400; 🚌73, 973, 42, 171, 99) Converted from a warehouse, Ovolo Southside complements its industrial setting with sleek decor. Views of the hills from the upper floors, mostly attentive service, happy-hour perks, and a free mini-bar more than make up for small rooms and bathrooms.

L'HOTEL ISLAND SOUTH HOTEL **$$**

Map p312 (如心南灣海景酒店; ☑852 3968 8888; www.lhotelislandsouth.com; 55 Wong Chuk Hang Rd, Aberdeen; r/ste from HK$1900/3500; @ 🛜; 🚌73, 973, 42, 171, 99) L'Hotel Island South, 2km from Ocean Park (p122), echoes its views of Aberdeen Harbour and the hills with a rippling facade and ocean- and nature-themed decor. The comfortable rooms come with a selection of pillows; the more affordable ones have wooden flooring. Staff are very accommodating. Prices for a standard room can drop to well under HK$1000.

There are also long-stay packages, starting from HK$10,000 for 14 consecutive nights and from HK$18,000 for 30 consecutive nights.

🛏 Kowloon

⭐ SALISBURY
HOTEL $

Map p314 (香港基督教青年會; ☎852 2268 7888; www.ymcahk.org.hk; 41 Salisbury Rd, Tsim Sha Tsui; dm HK$360, s/d/ste from HK$1200/1360/2200; ⊛@🎇⊠; ⓂTsim Sha Tsui, exit E) If you can manage to book a room at this fabulously located YMCA hotel, you'll be rewarded with professional service and excellent exercise facilities. Newly renovated rooms and suites are comfortable but simple, so keep your eyes on the harbour: that view would cost you five times as much at the Peninsula next door. The dormitory rooms are a bonus, but restrictions apply.

The four-bed dorm rooms are meant for short-stay travellers, hence no one can stay there more than 10 nights in a 30-day period, and walk-in guests aren't accepted if they've been in Hong Kong for more than seven days; check-in is at 2pm. The same restrictions do not apply to the other rooms at the Salisbury. Sports enthusiasts will love it here – the hotel has a 25m swimming pool, a fitness centre, and a climbing wall.

⭐ URBAN PACK
HOSTEL $

Map p314 (休閒小窩; ☎852 2732 2271; www. urban-pack.com; Unit 1410, 14th fl, Haiphong Mansion, 99-101 Nathan Rd, Tsim Sha Tsui; dm HK$200-500, r from HK$500, apt from HK$700; 🎇; ⓂTsim Sha Tsui, exit A1) If your idea of a great hostel involves a chilled vibe, lots of interaction with fellow travellers, and bar-hopping with the owners, Urban Pack is *the* place for you. Run by two friendly Canadian-Chinese, Albert and Jensen, Urban Pack also offers solid dorms (mixed and women's), as well as new private rooms and suites.

Sophisticated showering facilities (rain showers anyone?), free coffee, and even a massage chair are an extra bonus.

⭐ MARINER'S CLUB
HOTEL $

Map p316 (海員之家; ☎852 2368 8261; www.the marinersclubhk.org; 11 Middle Rd, Tsim Sha Tsui; s/d without bathroom from HK$370/520, with bathroom from HK$550/750, ste from HK$1140; @🎇⊠; ⓂEast Tsim Sha Tsui, exit K) The Mariner's Club, overlooking the Middle Road Children's Playground, offers a lazy, old-world charm, as well as a first-rate swimming pool. The hotel has 100 rooms – 30 new (with wi-fi, on the 4th and 5th floors), and 70 old (austere-looking with retro furniture). Anyone can book this great budget option, but you'll be asked for mariner's ID or proof of shipping-company employment at check-in.

We've had reports that they're not very strict about this. Prices for shipping companies are about HK$80 more for each category.

INNSIGHT
GUESTHOUSE $

Map p314 (悠悠客舍; ☎852 2369 1151; www. innsight.hk; 3rd fl, 9 Lock Rd, Tsim Sha Tsui; s HK$380-570, d HK$490-780; @🎇; ⓂTsim Sha Tsui, exit H) A fabulous location, warmly decorated (though tiny) rooms and a cosy kitchenette are the strengths here. Owner Carmen makes an effort to please, even providing free shampoo and bath gel, which makes it easy to overlook the fact that the showers are not encased in stalls. If you want a wider bed, ask for a Comfort Double.

CARITAS BIANCHI LODGE
GUESTHOUSE $$

Map p318 (明愛白英奇賓館; ☎852 2388 1111; www.caritas-chs.org.hk/eng/bianchi_lodge. asp; 4 Cliff Rd, Yau Ma Tei; s HK$750-1350, d & tw HK$960-1600, f HK$1600-2100; 🎇; ⓂYau Ma Tei, exit D) This 90-room guesthouse run by a Catholic NGO is just off Nathan Rd (and a stone's throw from Yau Ma Tei MTR station), but the rear rooms are quiet and some have views of King's Park. All rooms are clean with private bathrooms. The wait for lifts can be long, especially at night. Breakfast is included in the rates.

KNUTSFORD HOTEL
HOTEL $$

Map p316 (樂仕酒店; ☎852 2377 1180; www.ace sitehotel.com; 8 Observatory Ct, Tsim Sha Tsui; s HK$1000, d HK$1200-1800; 🎇; ⓂTsim Sha Tsui, exit B1) The 28 coffin-sized rooms here feel quite airy, thanks to a savvy use of glass and whites. The service, by contrast, can be nonchalant. The hotel is in a quiet corner of Tsim Sha Tsui's old residential quarter, yet close to the watering holes of Knutsford Tce. Tall people will find the beds cramped.

CITYVIEW
HOTEL $$

Map p318 (城景國際; ☎852 2771 9111; www. thecityview.com.hk; 23 Waterloo Rd, Yau Ma Tei; r/ tr/ste from HK$880/1560/1400; @🎇⊠; ⓂYau Ma Tei, exit A2) All 422 rooms at this YMCA-affiliated hotel are clean and smart, featuring mellow colour tones and stylish fabrics. The service is also impeccable. The hotel occupies a quiet corner between Yau Ma Tei and Mong Kok. It's a short stroll from Yau Ma Tei Theatre (p50) and the Yau Ma Tei Wholesale Fruit Market (p138).

★PENINSULA HONG KONG

HOTEL $$$

Map p314 (香港半島酒店; ☎852 2920 2888; www.peninsula.com; Salisbury Rd, Tsim Sha Tsui; r/ste from HK$4000/6000; @🛜🗶; MTsim Sha Tsui, exit E) Lording it over the southern tip of Kowloon, Hong Kong's finest hotel exudes colonial elegance. Your dilemma will be how to get here: landing on the rooftop helipad or arriving in one of the hotel's 14-strong fleet of Rolls Royce Phantoms. Some 300 classic European-style rooms sport wi-fi, CD and DVD players, as well as marble bathrooms.

Many rooms in the 20-storey annexe also offer spectacular harbour views; in the original building you'll have to make do with the glorious interiors. There's a top-notch spa and swimming pool, and Gaddi's (p143) is one of the best French restaurants in town.

★HYATT REGENCY TSIM SHA TSUI

HOTEL $$$

Map p316 (尖沙咀凱悅酒店; ☎852 2311 1234; http://hongkong.tsimshatsui.hyatt.com; 18 Hanoi Rd, Tsim Sha Tsui; r/ste from HK$2150/3600; @🛜🗶; MTsim Sha Tsui, exit D2) Top marks to this classic that exudes understated elegance and composure. Rooms are plush and relatively spacious, with those on the upper floors commanding views over the city. Black-and-white photos of Tsim Sha Tsui add a thoughtful touch to the decor. The lobby gets crowded at times, but the helpful and resourceful staff will put you at ease.

INTERCONTINENTAL HONG KONG

HOTEL $$$

Map p316 (香港洲際酒店; ☎852 2721 1211; www.intercontinental.com; 18 Salisbury Rd, Tsim Sha Tsui; r from HK$6000-9000, ste from HK$11,000; @🛜🗶; MTsim Sha Tsui, exit F) Occupying arguably the finest waterfront spot in the territory, the InterContinental tilts at modernity while bowing to colonial

SLEEPING KOWLOON

CHUNGKING MANSIONS

Say 'budget accommodation' and 'Hong Kong' in one breath and everyone thinks of Chungking Mansions. Built in 1961, CKM is a labyrinth of homes, guesthouses, Indian restaurants, souvenir stalls and foreign-exchange shops spread over five 17-storey blocks in the heart of Tsim Sha Tsui. According to anthropologist Gordon Mathews, it has a resident population of about 4000 and an estimated 10,000 daily visitors. More than 120 different nationalities – predominantly South Asian and African – pass through its doors in a single year.

Though standards vary significantly, most of the guesthouses at CKM are clean and quite comfortable. It's worth bearing in mind, however, that rooms are usually the size of cupboards and you have to shower right next to the toilet. The rooms typically come with air-con and TV and, sometimes, a phone. Many guesthouses can get you a Chinese visa quickly, most have internet access and some have wi-fi and laundry service.

Bargaining for a bed or room is always possible, though you won't get very far in the high season. You can often negotiate a cheaper price if you stay more than, say, a week, but never try that on the first night – stay one night and find out how you like it before handing over more rent. Once you pay, there are usually no refunds.

Though there are dozens of ever-changing hostels in Chungking Mansions, some reliable ones include **New China Guesthouse** (新欣欣賓館; Map p314; ☎852 9489 3891; http://newchinaguesthouse.com; Flat D7, 9th fl, D Block; r from HK$230; 🛜; MTsim Sha Tsui, exit D1), **Park Guesthouse** (百樂賓館; Map p314; ☎852 2368 1689; fax 2367 7889; Flat A1, 15th fl, A Block; s from HK$250, d from HK$450, without bathroom HK$200; 🛜; MTsim Sha Tsui, exit D1), **Holiday Guesthouse** (Map p314; ☎852 2316 7152, 852 9121 8072; fax 2316 7181; Flat E1, 6th fl, E Block; s HK$250-600, d HK$350-700; @🛜; MTsim Sha Tsui, exit D1) and **Dragon Inn** (龍滙賓館; Map p314; ☎852 2368 2007; www.dragoninn.info; Flat B5, 3rd fl, B Block; s HK$180-400, d HK$360-680, honeymoon rooms HK$660, tr HK$480, q HK$520; 🛜; MTsim Sha Tsui, exit D1).

Movie buffs note: it was at nearby Mirador Mansion – and not Chungking Mansions – where Wong Kar-wai filmed most of *Chungking Express* (1994).

traditions, such as a fleet of navy-blue Rolls Royces, doormen liveried in white and incessant brass polishing. The emphasis on service ensures a lot of return customers, from rock stars to business VIPs. The lobby lounge bar (p146) has the best views in Hong Kong.

RITZ-CARLTON HONG KONG — HOTEL $$$

(麗思卡爾頓酒店; ☎852 2263 2263; www.ritzcarlton.com; 1 Austin Rd W, Tsim Sha Tsui; r HK$5000-9900, ste from HK$9000; 🛜🛆; Ⓜ Kowloon, exit C1 or D1) Sitting on Kowloon Station, this out-of-the-way luxury hotel is the tallest hotel on earth (lobby's on the 103rd floor). To echo the theme of excess, the decor is over the top with imposing furniture and a superfluity of shiny surfaces, the service is stellar, **Tin Lung Heen** (天龍軒; ☎852 2263 2270; meals HK$400-1700; 🕘noon-2.30pm & 6-10.30pm; Ⓜ Kowloon, exit U3) serves top-notch Chinese food, and the views on a clear day are mind-blowing.

MADERA HONG KONG — BOUTIQUE HOTEL $$$

Map p318 (木的地酒店; ☎852 2121 9888; www.hotelmadera.com.hk; 1-9 Cheong Lok St, Yau Ma Tei; r HK$1700-4000, ste HK$4200-$9000; Ⓜ Jordan, exit B1) A spirited addition to Kowloon's accommodation options, Madera is close to the Temple Street Night Market and the Jordan MTR station. The decent-sized rooms are decorated in neutral tones accented with the bold, vibrant colours of Spanish aesthetics. Madera (meaning 'wood') also has a mini art gallery exhibiting retro Hong Kong artefacts, a hypoallergenic floor, and a tiny, but adequate, gym room.

🛏 New Territories

★CAMPUS HONG KONG — HOSTEL $

(☎852 2945 1111; www.campushk.com; 123 Castle Peak Rd, Yau Kom Tau, Tsuen Wan; dm HK$190-260, r HK$700-1000; 🛆; Ⓜ Tsuen Wan) Fabulous hostel for university students that also entertains backpackers whenever rooms are available, but especially during the summer months. The 48 rooms with four beds each feature nifty communal and study spaces, kitchenette and shower. It's part of a serviced apartment complex (Bay Bridge Hong Kong) and hostels guests also get to enjoy the sea views, the fitness room and the swimming pool.

Weekly rates are HK$1200 to HK$1500 per room, and monthly HK$5000 (over six months) or HK$5500 (under six months). There's free shuttle bus service to Tsuen Wan MTR station. At exit B of Tsuen Wan MTR station, turn right and ascend some stairs to Tai Ho Road North and you'll see the shuttle bus station for Bay Bridge Hong Kong.

★GREEN HUB — HOSTEL $

Map p164 (綠匯學苑; ☎852 2996 2800; www.greenhub.hk; 11 Wan Tau Kok Lane, Tai Po; s/tw/tr from HK$400/650/900; 🛜; Ⓜ Tai Po Market, exit A2) 🌿 This fabulous hostel is part of the re-purposed Old Tai Po Police Station complex now run by Kadoorie Farm. Guest rooms have high ceilings and double-tiled roofs. Only four come with air-conditioners; the rest rely on fans and natural ventilation. The canteen, open from 10am to 3.30pm, prepares vegetarian meals with local, Fair Trade ingredients. There are monthly barter parties. Booking essential.

The hostel is a 10-minute walk from the metro exit.

TAO FONG SHAN PILGRIM'S HALL — HOSTEL $

Map p167 (道風山雲水堂; ☎852 2691 2739; www.tfssu.org/pilgrim.html; 33 Tao Fong Shan Rd; r with shared bathroom HK$300-460; 🚆Sha Tin, exit B) This Lutheran Church–affiliated hostel, part of the Tao Fong Shan (p168) complex, is set on a peaceful hillside above Sha Tin. The rooms are clean and quiet. The canteen serves simple and healthy meals, but you need to reserve in advance.

At exit B of Sha Tin MTR station, walk down the ramp, passing a series of old village houses on the left. To the left of these houses is a set of steps signposted 'To Fung Shan'. Follow the path all the way to the top. The walk should take around 20 minutes. A taxi from the nearest MTR station in Sha Tin will cost about HK$38, from Tai Wai MTR station less than HK$30.

BRADBURY HALL YOUTH HOSTEL — HOSTEL $

(☎852 2328 2458; www.yha.org.hk; Chek Keng, Sai Kung; dm HK$85-115, campsite HK$20-30; 🚌94, 96R, 698R) This hostel is in the beautiful cove of Chek Keng, where some unspoilt beaches are just a flip-flop's throw away. The dorms are slightly dated but clean, and there's also a campsite. Bring your own tent or rent one for HK$55 (HK$40 for members). To get there, take bus 94 from Sai Kung bus terminal to Pak Tam Au. Walk along stage 2 of the MacLehose Trail towards Chek Keng Village. The walk takes about 40 minutes. A faster way to the hostel is to take bus 96R or 698R to Wong Shek Pier, and then take a scheduled ferry to Chek Keng Pier. The boat journey is about 10 minutes.

GOLD COAST HOTEL
RESORT $$

(黃金海岸酒店; ☑852 2452 8888; www.gold coast.com.hk; 1 Castle Peak Rd, Castle Peak Bay, Gold Coast, Tuen Mun; r HK$700-1700; ✱♠) A large, family-friendly hotel that's part of the Gold Coast complex featuring residences, a mall, an artificial beach and a promenade lined with coconut trees. It has a '90s vibe, but service is warm and the hotel has been updating its facilities. Refurbished rooms and the ones with balconies overlooking the marina are nicer. Don't eat in the hotel.

Gold Coast Hotel offers special packages. Bus K51 departing from Siu Hong MTR station and bus K53 from Tuen Mun MTR station come here.

HYATT REGENCY SHA TIN
HOTEL $$$

(沙田凱悅酒店; ☑852 3723 1234; www.hong kong.shatin.hyatt.com; 18 Chak Cheung St, Sha Tin; r HK$2500-3000, ste HK$3500-12,500; 🚇University) An excellent option if you don't mind being a few MTR stations removed from the action. To make up for that, you get views of Tolo Harbour or the rolling hills of Sha Tin and an exceptional Chinese restaurant. Prices for a standard room could go down to the hundreds during low season, and there are long-stay packages.

🛏 Outlying Islands

CHEUNG CHAU B&B
B&B $

Map p189 (☑852 2986 9990; www.bb cheungchau.com.hk; 12-14 Tung Wan Rd; r Sun-Thu from HK$650, Fri & Sat from HK$780; 🛜; 🚢Cheung Chau) An alternative to the island's only hotel and the rooms offered by kiosks, this B&B (more like a small hotel) has two locations in the village. Some of the brightly painted rooms are quite compact, so look before you commit to make sure you don't get a tiny one. Larger deluxe and family suites are available as well.

CONCERTO INN
HOTEL $$

Map p176 (☑852 2982 1668; www.concertoinn. com.hk; 28 Hung Shing Yeh beach, Hung Shing Yeh; r Sun-Fri from HK$920, Sat from $1068; 🛜; 🚢Yung Shue Wan) This cheerful beachfront

hotel, southeast of Yung Shue Wan, is quite some distance from the action, so you should stay here only if you really want to get away from it all. Rooms for three or four people are actually doubles with a sofa bed or pull-out bed.

NGONG PING SG DAVIS HOSTEL
HOSTEL $

Map p181 (☑852 2985 5610; www.yha.org.hk; Ngong Ping; dm from HK$110, r from HK$400; 🚌2 from Mui Wo, or 21, 23 from Tung Chung) This hostel is near the Tian Tan Buddha statue and is an ideal place to stay if you want to watch the sunrise at Lantau Peak. The hostel is only open to HKYHA/HI cardholders or the guests of a cardholder.

From the Ngong Ping bus terminus, take the paved path to your left as you face the Tian Tan Buddha, pass the public toilets on your right and follow the signs.

ESPACE ELASTIQUE
B&B $$

Map p181 (歸田園居; ☑852 2985 7002; www. espaceelastique.com.hk; 57 Kat Hing St, Tai O; r Sun-Thu HK$680-1450, Fri & Sat HK$880-1750; @🛜✉; 🚌1 from Mui Wo, 11 from Tung Chung, 21 from Ngong Ping) This cosy four-room B&B is one of the best-kept gems on Lantau. All rooms are tastefully decorated; the 2nd-floor double room with a balcony overlooking the main Tai O waterway gets booked up quickly. The friendly owner Veronica provides multilingual travel advice, plus a hearty breakfast in the cafe. The Jacuzzi on the rooftop is a delight.

HONG KONG DISNEYLAND HOTEL
RESORT $$

Map p181 (☑852 3510 6000; www.hongkong disneyland.com; Hong Kong Disneyland, Lantau; r from HK$2500; ♠) Kids will be delighted with this palatial Disney resort, complete with a Mickey-shaped hedge maze, an enormous pool with a twisty water slide, and various kid-centric amenities: a reading hour headlined by Disney characters, a princess boutique and an indoor playroom. Adults should be happy as well with the relatively spacious, Victorian-themed rooms.

★TAI O HERITAGE HOTEL
BOUTIQUE HOTEL $$$

Map p181 (大澳文物酒店; www.taioheritage hotel.com; Shek Tsai Po St, Tai O; r HK$2000-2500; @🛜✉; 🚌1 from Mui Wo, 11 from Tung Chung, 21 from Ngong Ping) Housed in a century-old former police station, this is Lantau's coolest hotel. All nine rooms are handsomely furnished in a contemporary style, offering top-of-the-line comfort. Our favourite is the inspector-office-turned–Sea Tiger Room, the smallest digs (24 sq metre) but with picture windows ushering in the sea breeze.

🛏 Macau

POUSADA DE JUVENTUDE DE CHEOC VAN
HOSTEL $

Map p213 (☑853 2888 2024; Rua de António Francisco, Coloane; dm/tw from MOP$100/160; ❀❄; ☐21A, 25, 26A) This government-run, beachside hostel is excellent value, but conditions apply. You'll need to book at least a week in advance and own an International Youth Card, International Youth Hostel Card or similar. It's closed to tourists in July and August. Don't expect much of a social vibe – most of the guests here are local or Chinese school groups.

★POUSADA DE MONG HÁ
INN $$

Map p196 (澳門望廈迎賓館; ☑853 2851 5222; www.ift.edu.mo; Colina de Mong Há; r MOP$700-1300, ste MOP$1300-1800; ❀❀@❄❅; ☐5, 22, 25) Sitting atop Mong Há Hill near the ruins of a fort built in 1849 is this Portuguese-style inn run by students at the Institute for Tourism Studies. Rooms are well appointed, with some having computers, and the service is attentive. Rates include breakfast. Discounts of 25% to 40% midweek and in low season.

★5FOOTWAY INN
INN $$

Map p200 (五步廊旅舍; ☑853 2892 3118; www.5footwayinn.com; 8 Rua de Constantino Brito; d/tr from MOP$1400/2200; ❀❀❄; ☐1, 2, 10, 5, 7) This Singapore-owned accommodation converted from a love motel has 23 small clean rooms, vibrant paintings in communal areas and excellent English-speaking staff. Rates include a self-service breakfast. It's opposite the Sofitel Macau at Ponte 16, which means you can take the latter's free shuttle buses to and from the ferry terminal.

OKURA
HOTEL $$

(☑853 8883 8883; www.hotelokuramacau.com; Avenida Marginal Flor de Lotus, Cotai; r MOP$1000-5600, ste MOP$3000-20,000; ☐25, 26A) In the Galaxy Macau, this Japanese hotel offers attentive service and subdued

luxury for a price that tends to be among the area's most reasonable. Rooms are large and bathrooms are even larger, complete with heated Japanese toilet seats and free-standing tubs with televisions.

POUSADA DE COLOANE
HOTEL $$

Map p213 (☑853 2882 2143; www.hotelpcoloane.com.mo; Estrada de Cheoc Van, Coloane; r from MOP$750; @❄; ☐21A, 25) This 30-room hotel with its Portuguese-style rooms (all with balconies and sea views) is great value, though some rooms are better maintained than others. And the location above Cheoc Van beach is about as chilled as you'll find. Rates drop considerably midweek. Discounts of 20% to 40% in low season.

SOFITEL MACAU AT PONTE 16
CASINO HOTEL $$

Map p200 (澳門十六浦索菲特大酒店; ☑853 8861 0016; www.sofitelmacau.com; Rua do Visconde Paço de Arcos; r MOP$980-2220, ste from MOP$4500; ❀❀@❄❅; ☐1, 2, 10, 5, 7) This reasonably priced luxury hotel offers some atmospheric views of the sleepy Inner Harbour and the Ruins of the Church of St Paul on the other side. The rooms are large, with contemporary decor and plush, inviting beds.

POUSADA DE SÃO TIAGO
HISTORIC HOTEL $$$

Map p196 (聖地牙哥古堡; ☑853 2837 8111; www.saotiago.com.mo; Fortaleza de São Tiago da Barra, Avenida da República; ste MOP$2800-5400; ❀❀@❄❅❅; ☐6, 9, 28B) Built into the ruins of the 17th-century Barra Fort, the landmark São Tiago is the most romantic place to stay in Macau. No other hotel has such a rich history. All 12 rooms are elegantly furnished suites. Discounts of up to 35% in low season. The restaurant, La Paloma, serves elegant modern Spanish food.

BANYAN TREE
LUXURY HOTEL $$$

(☑853 8883 8833; www.banyantree.com/en/macau; Galaxy, Avenida Marginal Flor de Lotus, Cotai; ste MOP$2880-63,800, villas MOP$23,600-35,100; ☐25, 25X) One of three hotels at the Galaxy Macau, this extravagant resort recreates tropical-style luxury in Macau. All 10 villas come with private gardens and swimming pools, while the suites have huge baths set by the window. If you need more pampering, there's a spa with state-of-the-art facilities.

Understand Hong Kong

Hong Kong Today

Just a decade ago, most Hong Kong residents would say return to Chinese rule in 1997 did not bring many changes, but since then, for many, things have gone downhill. Rising tensions with Běijīng dominate Hong Kong politics and public sentiment, putting the 'One Country, Two Systems' experiment in peril. Běijīng has politicised a city that was known for its political antipathy during 150 years of British rule.

Best on Film

Infernal Affairs (2002) The crime-thriller that inspired Scorsese's *The Departed*.
Election I and II (2005 and 2006) A complex two-part film noir about elections inside a Triad society.
Night and Fog (2010) Auteur Ann Hui's darkly realistic drama on domestic violence and the lives of migrant women.
The Grandmaster (2013) Wong Kar-wai's stylish martial-arts drama about the life of Wing Chun grandmaster Ip Man.
Comrades: Almost a Love Story (1996) Two mainland migrants take a reality check in the maddening city.
Trivisia (2016) Engaging and reflective action crime thriller produced by Johnnie To and Yau Nai-hoi, featuring three new directors.

Best in Print

City at the End of Time: Poems by Leung Ping-kwan (Ed Esther Cheung; 2012) Leung Ping-kwan aka Yesi was Hong Kong's unofficial poet laureate.
The Hungry Ghosts (Anne Berry; 2009) Restless spirits haunt this excellent tale.
Hong Kong: A Cultural History (Michael Ingham; 2007) The definitive title in this category.

The State of Play

Hong Kong has witnessed much political strife since the turn of the decade. Critics of the government have focused on a long list of increasingly intractable issues, from slow democratic reform and the perceived collusion between the government and big businesses, to stifling property prices and the perceived drain on public resources by mainland migrants. The involvement of Běijīng's Hong Kong–based proxies around Leung Chun-ying's ascent to the top post in town marks a definitive dynamics shift in the local political landscape, and serves as an ominous forewarning of worsening political turbulence.

The combination of divisive party politics and the lack of a democratic mandate has caused many to condemn the government as weak, and hopelessly so when faced with vested interests as strong as the largest developers.

Basic Economics

Inflation hit a 16-year high in 2011 and, while it has slowed down since, the truth is that for many, Hong Kong has become a depressingly expensive place to live. The city has more billionaires than most countries, but many more struggle to meet basic levels of subsistence. Despite reasonable economic growth in the past few years, Hong Kong's economy has become increasingly reliant on the financial sector and the spending power of mainland tourists.

A New Era

Once savvy and confident, many Hong Kongers are worried about what they see as Běijīng's attempt at homogenisation. The arrival of mainland visitors has bred discontent among critics as these tourists dominate shopping areas and the resulting rent hikes force traditional shops out of business. Cultural differences between Hong Kongers and mainlanders, and the influx of tariff-dodging parallel traders to border towns are other sources of conflict. But despite the general mood of anxiety, all is not doom and gloom. If anything, these challenges are stirring a strong spirit among many people to defend their core values (namely, the rule of law and civil liberties).

New Waves

Hong Kong's youth are increasingly becoming involved in politics as many believe that the baby-boomers in power cannot represent their interests. They're also coming to the forefront of resistance. In September 2014, protesters – many of them students – took to the streets to speak out against planned reforms to the local electoral system which they claimed would limit the potential for universal suffrage. The protests grew into a thousands-strong pro-democracy campaign known variously as Occupy Central and the Umbrella Movement. The protests lasted for three months and saw semi-permanent tent villages overtake several main arteries in Hong Kong, and sometimes-violent clashes with police. Since then, several student leaders have launched a new political party.

At Lunar New Year 2016, a government crackdown on unlicensed hawkers turned violent as riot police clashed with protesters in an incident that came to be known as the Fishball Riot. Traditionally authorities have turned a blind eye to street-food vendors during the territory's most important festival.

Hong Kong continues to be the only place in China where the crackdown on the Tiān'ānmén pro-democracy uprising of 4 June 1989 can be openly commemorated. As Běijīng desperately searches for a formula of soft power to project on the international stage, the answers it needs may well lie in the rebellious tendencies of its semi-autonomous territory in the south.

Part of the city's growing assertion of its identity is an increasing drive to preserve its heritage. Many Hong Kongers bristle at any perceived threat to the use of Cantonese or traditional Chinese characters, or to the well-being of country parks and old neighbourhoods. Collectives have flowered to document the social history of storied neighbourhoods caught in the tide of urban redevelopment. The perennial tussle for space has also seen the growth of alternative cultural venues and farms. As always, there's more than meets the eye in this pulsating metropolis, which has time and again shown an extraordinary ability to rebound, adapt and excel.

population per sq km

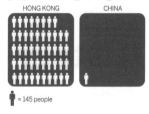

HONG KONG   CHINA

👤 ≈ 145 people

first language
(% of population)

88
Cantonese

5
Putonghua

4
non-Chinese languages

3
other Chinese dialects

if Hong Kong were 100 people

50 would be a form of Chinese folk religion
20 would be Buddhist
14 would be Taoist
7 would be Protestant
5 would be Catholic
3 would be Muslim
1 would be Hindu or Sikh

History

The name Hong Kong came from the Cantonese *heung gawng* ('fragrant harbour'), which was inspired by the sandalwood piled at what is now Aberdeen. In the long scale of history, Hong Kong as we know it today has existed for a mere blink of an eye. But there was a lot going on in the region before that morning in 1841 when British marines clambered ashore and planted the Union flag on the western part of Hong Kong Island.

Early Inhabitants

Archaeologists say Hong Kong's Stone Age inhabitants enjoyed a relatively nutritious diet of iron-rich vegetables, small mammals, shellfish and fish harvested far offshore. Early Chinese historical records call the diverse maritime peoples along China's southeastern coasts the 'Hundred Yue' tribes, which potentially included some of Hong Kong's prehistoric inhabitants.

Hong Kong has supported human life since at least the Middle Neolithic Period (c 4000–2500 BC). Artefacts uncovered at almost 100 archaeological sites in the territory suggest that the inhabitants of these settlements shared similar cultural characteristics to the people who lived in the Pearl River delta. The remnants of Bronze Age habitations (c 1500–220 BC) unearthed on Lamma and Lantau Islands, among other places – as well as the eight extant geometric rock carvings along Hong Kong's coastline – also indicate that these early peoples practised some form of folk religion involving animal worship.

The Five Great Clans

The first of Hong Kong's mighty 'Five Clans' – Han Chinese, whose descendants hold political and economic clout to this day – began settling the area around the 11th century. The first and most powerful of the arrivals was the Tang, who initially settled around Yuen Long (the walled village of Kat Hing Wai is part of this cluster).

The Tang clan was followed by the Hau and the Pang, who spread around present-day Sheung Shui and Fanling. These three clans were followed by the Liu in the 14th century and the Man a century later.

The Cantonese-speaking newcomers called themselves *bun day* (Punti), meaning 'indigenous' or 'local' – something they clearly were not. They looked down on the original inhabitants, the Tanka, many of whom had been shunted off the land and had moved onto the sea to live on boats.

TIMELINE	4000–1500 BC	214 BC	AD 1000–1400
	Small groups of Neolithic hunter-gatherers and fisherfolk settle in coastal areas; a handful of tools, pottery and other artefacts are the only remnants left by these nomads.	Chinese emperor Qin Shi Huang conquers present-day Guǎngxī, Guǎngdōng and Fújiàn after a long period of war. Hong Kong comes under greater cultural influence from the north.	Hong Kong's Five Clans – Tang, Hau, Pang, Liu and Man – settle in what is now the New Territories and build walled villages in the fertile plains and valleys.

An Imperial Outpost

Clinging to the southern edge of the Chinese province of Canton (now Guǎngdōng), the peninsula and islands that became the territory of Hong Kong counted only as a remote pocket in a neglected corner of the Chinese empire.

The Punti flourished until the struggle that saw the moribund Ming dynasty (1368–1644) overthrown. The victorious Qing (1644–1911), angered by the resistance put up by southerners loyal to the old order, enforced evacuation inland of all the inhabitants of China's southeastern coastal area, including Hong Kong, in the 1660s.

More than four generations passed before the population was able to recover to its mid-17th-century level, boosted in part by the influx of the Hakka (Cantonese for 'guest people'), who moved here in the 18th century and up to the mid-19th century. A few vestiges of their language, songs, folklore and cooking survive, most visibly in the wide-brimmed, black-fringed bamboo hats sported by Hakka women in the New Territories.

The discovery of coins and pottery from the Eastern Han dynasty (AD 25–220) on Lantau and at several important digs, including a tomb at Lei Cheng Uk in central Kowloon, attests to the growing Han influence in Hong Kong at the start of the first millennium.

Arrival of the Outer Barbarians

For centuries the Pearl River estuary had been an important trading artery centred on the port of Canton (now Guǎngzhōu). Some of the first foreign traders (or 'outer barbarians') were Arab traders who entered – and sacked – the settlement as early as the 8th century AD. Similarly, the Ming emperors regarded their subjects to the south as an utterly uncivilised bunch. It was therefore fitting that the Cantonese should trade with the 'outer barbarians'.

Regular trade between China and Europe began in 1557 when Portuguese navigators set up a base in Macau, 65km west of Hong Kong. Dutch traders came in the wake of the Portuguese, followed by the French. British ships appeared as early as 1683 from the East India Company concessions along the coast of India, and by 1711 the company had established offices and warehouses in Guǎngzhōu to trade for tea, silk and porcelain.

In 1276 the boy emperor Duan Zong and his younger brother, Bing, were forced to flee to Hong Kong as the Mongols swept aside the remaining army of the Song dynasty. After Mongol ships defeated the tattered remnants of the imperial fleet on Pearl River, the dynasty was definitively ended.

The First Opium War & British Hong Kong

China did not reciprocate Europe's voracious demand for its products, for the most part shunning foreign-manufactured goods. The foreigners' ensuing trade deficit was soon reversed, however, after the British discovered a commodity that the Chinese did want: opium.

The British, with a virtually inexhaustible supply of the drug from the poppy fields of India, developed the trade aggressively. Consequently,

1557	1644	1683	1757
Portuguese navigators set up a base in Macau, and are followed by Dutch and then French traders. Regular trade begins between China and Europe.	The Ming dynasty (1368–1644) is overthrown by the Qing dynasty, which reigns until 1911.	British East India Company ships begin to arrive, and by 1711 the company has established offices and warehouses in Guǎngzhōu, to trade for tea, silk and porcelain.	An imperial edict restricts European trade to the cohong (local merchants guild) in Guǎngzhōu; growing discontent with the trading system sets the stage for the First Opium War.

opium addiction spread out of control in China, and the country's silver reserves became perilously drained.

In late 1838 Emperor Dao Guang (r 1820–50) appointed Lin Zexu, governor of Húnán and Húběi and a Mandarin of great integrity, to stamp out the opium trade. His rather successful campaign would ultimately lead to the First Opium War (or First Anglo-Chinese War) of 1839–42.

In January 1841 a naval landing party hoisted the British flag at Possession Point (now Possession St) on Hong Kong Island. Subsequently, the Treaty of Nanking abolished the monopoly system of trade, opened five 'treaty ports' to British residents and foreign trade, exempted British nationals from all Chinese laws and ceded the strategically useful island of Hong Kong to the British 'in perpetuity'.

Hong Kong, with its deep, well-sheltered harbour, formally became a British possession on 26 June 1843, and its first governor, Sir Henry Pottinger, took charge. A primitive, chaotic and lawless settlement soon sprang up.

> Today's Triads still recite an oath of allegiance to the Ming, but their loyalty these days is to the dollar rather than the vanquished Son of Heaven.

> Alarmed by the spread of addiction and the silver draining from the country to pay for opium, the Qing emperor issued an edict in 1799 banning the trade of opium in China. The ban had little effect and the lucrative trade continued.

Growing Pains

What would later be called the Second Opium War (or Second Anglo-Chinese War) broke out in October 1856. The victorious British forced the Chinese to sign the Convention of Peking in 1860, which ceded Kowloon Peninsula and Stonecutters Island to Britain. Britain was now in complete control of Victoria Harbour and its approaches.

As the Qing dynasty slid into major chaos towards the end of the 19th century, the British government petitioned China to extend the colony into the New Territories. The June 1898 Convention of Peking handed Britain a larger-than-expected slice of territory that included 235 islands and ran north to the Shumchun (Shēnzhèn) River, increasing the colony's size by 90%.

A Sleepy Backwater

While Hong Kong's major trading houses, including Jardine Matheson and Swire, prospered from their trade with China, the colony hardly thrived in its first few decades. Fever, bubonic plague and typhoons threatened life and property, and at first the colony attracted a fair number of criminals and vice merchants.

Gradually Hong Kong began to shape itself into a more substantial community. Nonetheless, from the late 19th century right up to WWII, Hong Kong lived in the shadow of the treaty port of Shànghǎi, which had become Asia's premier trade and financial centre – not to mention its style capital.

1773	1799	1841	1842
Opium smuggling to China skyrockets after the British East India Company monopolises production and export of Indian opium.	China's silver reserves drain rapidly as opium addiction sweeps through China. The Qing emperor issues an edict banning opium trade in the country.	British marines plant the Union flag on the western part of Hong Kong Island, claiming the land for the British Crown.	China cedes Hong Kong Island to Britain.

The colony's population continued to grow thanks to the waves of immigrants fleeing the Chinese Revolution of 1911, which ousted the decaying Qing dynasty and ushered in several decades of strife, rampaging warlords and famine. The Japanese invasion of China in 1937 sparked another major exodus to Hong Kong's shores.

Hong Kong's status as a British colony would offer the refugees only a temporary haven. The day after Japan attacked the US naval base at Pearl Harbor on 7 December 1941, its military machine swept down from Guăngzhōu and into Hong Kong.

Conditions under Japanese rule were harsh, with indiscriminate killings of mostly Chinese civilians; Western civilians were incarcerated at Stanley Prison on Hong Kong Island. Many Hong Kong Chinese fled to Macau, administered by neutral Portugal.

'Albert is so amused at my having got the island of Hong Kong', wrote Queen Victoria to King Leopold of Belgium in 1841. At the time, Hong Kong was little more than a backwater of about 20 villages and hamlets.

The Road to Boomtown

After Japan's withdrawal from Hong Kong, and subsequent surrender in August 1945, the colony looked set to resume its hibernation. But events both at home and on the mainland forced the colony in a new direction.

The Chinese Civil War (1945–49) and the subsequent communist takeover of China caused a huge number of refugees – both rich and poor – to flee to Hong Kong. The refugees brought along capital and cheap labour, which would prove vital to Hong Kong's economic take-off. On a paltry, war-torn foundation, local and foreign businesses built a huge manufacturing (notably textiles and garments) and financial services centre that transformed Hong Kong into one of the world's great economic miracles.

Hong Kong's stability received a hard battering at the height of the Cultural Revolution in 1967, as local pro-communist groups instigated a series of anti-colonial demonstrations, strikes and riots. The violence soon mushroomed into bombings and arson attacks, and the colony's economy was paralysed for months. The riot came to an end in December 1967, when Chinese Premier Zhou Enlai ordered the pro-communist groups to stop.

In the early years of British Hong Kong, opium dens, gambling clubs and brothels proliferated; just a year after Britain took possession, an estimated 450 prostitutes worked out of two-dozen brothels, including a fair number of foreign prostitutes clustered in Lyndhurst Tce, which today is home to a hip bar scene.

A Society in Transition

After the 1967 crisis the colonial government initiated a series of reforms to alleviate social discontent and to foster a sense of belonging to Hong Kong. In the next decade the government introduced more labour laws, and invested heavily in public housing, medical services, education and recreational activities for youth.

1860	1894	1895	1898
Under the Convention of Peking, China cedes Kowloon Peninsula and Stonecutters Island to Britain, giving Britain complete control of Victoria Harbour and its approaches.	Bubonic plague breaks out in Hong Kong, killing 2500 of mainly local Chinese; trade suffers badly.	Future Chinese national hero Sun Yatsen plots an insurrection in southern China from his base in Hong Kong; it fails and the British ban Sun from the territory.	China hands the New Territories to Britain on a 99-year lease, which begins on 1 July 1898 and ends at midnight on 30 June 1997.

Although Hong Kong's stock market collapsed in 1973, its economy resumed its upward trend later in the decade. The 'Open Door' policy of Deng Xiaoping, who took control of China in the confusion after Mao Zedong's death in 1976, revived Hong Kong's role as the gateway to the mainland and it boomed. By the end of the 1980s, Hong Kong was one of the richest places in Asia, second only to Japan in terms of GDP per capita.

The 1997 Question

Few people gave much thought to Hong Kong's future until 1979, when the governor of Hong Kong, Murray MacLehose, raised the issue with Deng Xiaoping on his first official visit to Běijīng. Britain was legally bound to hand back only the New Territories – not Hong Kong Island and Kowloon, which had been ceded to it forever. However, the fact that nearly half of Hong Kong's population lived in the New Territories by that time made it an untenable division.

It was Deng Xiaoping who decided that the time was ripe to recover Hong Kong, forcing the British to the negotiating table. The views of Hong Kong people were not sought. The inevitable conclusion laid to rest the political jitters and commercial concerns that in 1983 had seen the Hong Kong dollar collapse and subsequently be pegged to the US dollar.

Despite soothing words from the Chinese, British and Hong Kong governments, over the next 13 years the population of Hong Kong was to suffer considerable anxiety over the possible political and economic consequences of the handover due in 1997.

In the early 1970s, the construction of the first three 'New Towns' (Sha Tin, Tsuen Wan and Tuen Mun) commenced, marking the start of a massive and unprecedented public-housing program that would, and still does, house millions of Hong Kong people.

One Country, Two Systems

Under the Sino-British Joint Declaration on the Question of Hong Kong of December 1984, Hong Kong would be reborn as a Special Administrative Region (SAR) of China. This meant its capitalist system would be permitted to continue, while across the border China's version of socialism would continue. The Chinese catchphrase for this was 'One Country, Two Systems'.

The Basic Law for Hong Kong, the future SAR's constitution, preserved Hong Kong's English common-law judicial system and guaranteed the right of property and ownership, as well as other key civil liberties. The SAR would enjoy a high degree of autonomy with the exception of foreign affairs and matters of defence.

Despite these assurances, many families and individuals had little faith in a future Hong Kong under Chinese rule, and a so-called brain drain ensued when tens of thousands left the colony for the US, Canada, Australia and NZ towards the end of the 1980s.

1911	1937	1941	1962
The colony's population expands as large groups of immigrants flee the Chinese Revolution on the mainland.	Pouncing on a country weakened by a bloody civil war, Japan invades China; as many as 750,000 mainlanders seek shelter in Hong Kong over the next three years.	British forces surrender to Japanese forces on Christmas Day; the population in Hong Kong is more than halved during almost four years of Japanese occupation.	The great famine caused by the Great Leap Forward in China drives 70,000 people to flee into Hong Kong in less than three months.

Tiān'ānmén & Its Aftermath

The concern of many Hong Kong people over their future turned to out-and-out fear on 4 June 1989, when the Chinese army killed pro-democracy demonstrators in Běijīng's Tiān'ānmén Square.

Tiān'ānmén was a watershed for Hong Kong. Sino-British relations deteriorated, the stock market fell 22% in one day and a great deal of capital left the territory for destinations overseas.

The Hong Kong government sought to rebuild confidence by announcing plans for a new airport and shipping port in what was the world's most expensive (HK$160 billion or US$20.6 billion) infrastructure project of the day.

The Tiān'ānmén protests had strengthened the resolve of those people who either could not or would not leave, giving rise to the territory's first official political parties. In a bid to restore credibility, the government introduced a Bill of Rights in 1990 and the following year gave Hong Kong citizens the right to choose 18 of the 60 members of the Legislative Council (LegCo), which until then had essentially been a rubber-stamp body chosen by the government and special-interest groups.

Hong Kong is the only place under Chinese rule that still mourns those killed in 1989. Every year on 4 June, tens of thousands of people gather at Victoria Park to attend a candlelight vigil held in commemoration of those who lost their lives.

Democracy & the Last Governor

One of the first parties to emerge was the United Democrats of Hong Kong, led by outspoken democrats Martin Lee and Szeto Wah. The pair, initially courted by China for their anti-colonial positions and appointed to the committee that drafted the Basic Law, subsequently infuriated Běijīng by publicly burning copies of the proto-constitution in protest over Tiān'ānmén. China denounced them as subversives.

Chris Patten, Hong Kong's 28th – and last – British governor, arrived in 1992, pledging that democracy reforms would be sped up. China reacted by levelling verbal attacks at Patten and threatening the post-1997 careers of any pro-democracy politicians or officials. When these tactics failed, China targeted Hong Kong's economy. Talks on certain business contracts and infrastructure projects straddling 1997 suddenly came to a halt, including the new airport program.

Sensing that it had alienated even its supporters in Hong Kong, China backed down and in 1994 gave its blessing to the new airport at Chek Lap Kok. It remained hostile to direct elections, however, and vowed to disband the democratically elected legislature after 1997. It eventually did what it said by installing an interim rubber-stamp body which would serve until June 1998.

As for the executive branch of power, China organised an 'election' in December 1996 to select Hong Kong's first post-colonial leader. But

Following the Tiān'ānmén Square protests of 1989, an underground smuggling operation, code-named Yellow Bird, was set up in Hong Kong to spirit many activists to safety overseas. Meanwhile Hong Kong–based Chinese officials who had criticised the killings were either removed from their posts or sought asylum in the West.

1967	1971	1976	1982
Riots and bombings by pro-communist groups rock Hong Kong; armed Chinese militia cross the border, killing five policemen and penetrating 3km into the New Territories before pulling back.	A former child actor called Bruce Lee lands his first adult leading role in the kung fu film *The Big Boss*; it becomes a smash around the world.	Deng Xiaoping takes control of China after Mao Zedong's death, and revives Hong Kong's role as the gateway to the mainland.	British PM Margaret Thatcher visits Běijīng to begin talks on Hong Kong's future. Two years of closed-door wrangling between the Chinese and British ensues.

Tung Chee Hwa (1937–), the Shànghǎi-born shipping magnate hand-picked to be the SAR's first chief executive, won approval by retaining Patten's right-hand woman, Anson Chan, as his chief secretary and Donald Tsang as financial secretary.

On the night of 30 June 1997, the handover celebrations held in the purpose-built extension of the Hong Kong Convention & Exhibition Centre in Wan Chai were watched by millions of people around the world. Chris Patten shed a tear while Chinese President Jiang Zemin beamed and Prince Charles was outwardly stoic (but privately scathing, describing the Chinese leaders in a diary leaked years later to the British tabloids as 'appalling old waxworks').

So the curtain fell on a century and a half of British rule, and the new Chief Executive Tung summed up Chinese feelings about the handover with the words: 'Now we are masters of our own house'.

Hong Kong Post-1997

Almost as soon as the euphoria of the 1997 handover faded, things started going badly in Hong Kong. The financial crisis that had rocked other parts of Asia began to be felt in Hong Kong at the end of 1997. A strain of deadly avian flu saw the city slaughter more than one million chickens.

CHINA'S HONG KONG INVASION PLAN

The peaceful agreement that eventually settled the status of Hong Kong was by no means a foregone conclusion in the decades leading up to it. The key negotiators have since revealed just how touchy China felt about Hong Kong and how close it came to retaking the territory by force.

Margaret Thatcher, the British prime minister who negotiated the deal, said later that Deng Xiaoping, then China's leader, told her he 'could walk in and take the whole lot this afternoon'.

She replied that China would lose everything if it did. 'There is nothing I could do to stop you,' she said, 'but the eyes of the world would now know what China is like.'

Lu Ping, the top Chinese negotiator, recently confirmed that this was no bluff on Deng's part. Deng feared that announcing the date for the 1997 handover would provoke serious unrest in Hong Kong, and China would be compelled to invade as a result.

According to Lu, China had also been hours away from invading during 1967, at the height of the chaotic Cultural Revolution, when a radical faction of the People's Liberation Army (PLA) was poised to invade the British colony during pro-communist riots. The invasion was called off only by a late-night order from Premier Zhou Enlai to the local army commander, Huang Yongsheng, a radical Maoist who had been itching to invade.

1984	1989	1990	1997
Hong Kong's future is sealed in the Sino-British Joint Declaration on the Question of Hong Kong; the city's capitalist system will continue after 1997.	More than a million Hong Kong people march in support of the pro-democracy movement in Běijīng; the Chinese army kills protesting students in and around Tiān'ānmén Square.	The government introduces a Bill of Rights and in 1991 gives Hong Kong citizens the right to choose 18 of the 60 members of the Legislative Council (LegCo).	The rain falls, Chris Patten cries and Hong Kong returns to Chinese sovereignty; avian flu breaks out, leaving six dead. Tung Chee Hwa is sworn in as Hong Kong's first chief executive.

The credibility of the SAR administration was severely damaged in 1999 when the government challenged a High Court ruling that upheld residency rights for China-born offspring of Hong Kong citizens, regardless of the parents' residency status at the time of the child's birth. The ruling was based on certain clauses of the Basic Law, and the government calculated that it would potentially make 1.67 million people from the mainland eligible for right of abode in the territory. The SAR administration appealed to the standing committee of the National People's Congress (NPC), China's rubber-stamp parliament, to reinterpret these clauses. The NPC complied, and ruled that at least one parent must already have acquired permanent residency status at the time of the birth.

As a result, the mainland stands accused of interfering in Hong Kong's judicial independence via intrusion into the city's legal system, and the apparent withholding of universal suffrage from Hong Kong citizens. Clearly the mainland government wields huge influence, but in the first few years after the handover (at least up until the historic 500,000-strong anti-government protests of 1 July 2003, which changed Běijīng's stance on Hong Kong), it largely chose to tread lightly, honouring the spirit of the handover agreement to a great extent.

The Clamour for Democracy

Tung Chee Hwa's first term is remembered as much for his confusing housing policy, which many blamed for a sustained fall in property prices, as for such vacuous infrastructure proposals as a Chinese medicine port. Despite his poor standing in the polls, Tung was returned for a second five-year term in March 2002.

Controversy continued to dog his time in office, however, most notably in March 2003, with the government's failure to contain the Severe Acute Respiratory Syndrome (SARS) epidemic at an early stage, provoking a torrent of blame. The outbreak killed 299 people, infected 1755 and all but closed Hong Kong down for weeks.

In July 2003 the government caused further controversy when it tried to turn Article 23 of the Basic Law into legislation; the National Security Bill raised fears that Hong Kong's press freedom and civil liberties would be undermined. In the face of massive public protests – of 500,000 people or more – the government shelved the bill indefinitely.

In March 2005 Tung announced his resignation as chief executive. His replacement was the bow-tie-wearing chief secretary Sir Donald Tsang, who had continuously served as Hong Kong's financial secretary from before the handover up to 2001, when he became the city's number-two public official.

In the wake of the Tiān'ānmén Square protests, local Hong Kong people with money and skills made a mad dash to emigrate to any country that would take them. During the worst period more than 1000 people were leaving each week, especially for Canada and Australia.

HISTORY THE CLAMOUR FOR DEMOCRACY

2003	**2009**	**2010**	**2011**
SARS all but shuts down Hong Kong for weeks. The Closer Economic Partnership Agreement with the mainland government provides favourable business opportunities.	Hong Kong's population exceeds seven million and the unemployment rate grows to almost 5% in the face of the world's worst economic crisis since the Great Depression.	LegCo approves HK$66.9 billion for the Hong Kong portion of the Guǎngzhōu–Hong Kong high-speed rail link, following 25 hours of heated debate.	A minimum wage of HK$28 per hour takes effect, and inflation hits a 16-year high.

Compared to Tung, Tsang was a welcome replacement for both the Běijīng powerbrokers and the Hong Kong public. In 2007 Tsang was easily re-elected with Běijīng's blessing. However, he soon suffered an erosion of public confidence when he was seen to renege on a series of promises, including delaying a highly anticipated consultation on reforming the electoral process for the chief executive and legislature to make the 2012 polls more democratic.

The clamour for democracy reached a crescendo in 2010 as two landmark political events took place in successive months. In May five pro-democracy lawmakers were re-elected to LegCo after they collectively resigned four months earlier in the hope that the resulting by-elections would serve as a de-facto referendum on universal suffrage. The pro-Běijīng parties boycotted the contests, however, and the quintet's campaign came unstuck, even though they could claim to have been returned to the chamber by a respectable vote.

The pro-democracy parties had in fact been divided over the political strategy behind the forced by-elections, and the long-running differences among the key players imploded the following month when the biggest of them all, the Democratic Party, sided with the government in a new political reform package that would see LegCo earn a slightly increased percentage of popularly elected seats at the expense of delayed universal suffrage for the entire legislature and for the election of Hong Kong's chief executive.

The calls for democracy have continued since, most notably around the election – by a 1200-member body of predominantly pro-Běijīng notables – of the SAR's fourth chief executive in March 2012. Leung Chun-ying, a stalwart in Hong Kong politics with impeccably close links to Běijīng, defeated the long-time hopeful and former civil-service chief Henry Tang.

In June 2014 an unofficial referendum on making the election of the city's CE more democratic garnered votes from more than 787,000 Hong Kong residents – the equivalent of more than 22% of the city's 3.5 million registered voters. Following this, on 1 July 2014, an estimated 510,000 people turned out for a pro-democracy protest march on the anniversary of the handover, though the police put the figure at 98,600.

A measure of just how successful the handover had generally been came in a 2007 BBC interview with Margaret Thatcher. Marking the 10th anniversary of the handover of Hong Kong from Britain to China, Thatcher, to her own surprise, deemed China's overall performance a success.

A Changed City?

Visitors returning to Hong Kong since July 1997 would see and feel little material difference walking around the city today. Perhaps the most striking thing for returning visitors from the West is the influx of a new breed of visitor: mainland Chinese, who now make up nearly 70% of the territory's visitor numbers.

2011	2012	2014	2014
Public hospitals stop accepting reservations from pregnant mainland women through year's end; immigration officials block 1930 heavily pregnant women from crossing the border.	Property surveyor Leung Chun-ying begins a five-year term as the fourth Hong Kong SAR chief executive after beating former civil-service head Henry Tang in a scandal-plagued election.	Archaeological finds at an MTR site in East Kowloon show that Hong Kong's history in the Sung dynasty may have been far richer than had been popularly believed.	Tens of thousands of pro-democracy protesters take to the streets in what becomes known as the Umbrella Movement, a civil disobedience campaign against reforms limiting universal suffrage.

In many ways Hong Kong has benefited from closer ties with the mainland. The growth in Hong Kong's tourism would have been impossible without the influx of mainland tourists, and the Closer Economic Partnership Agreement signed with the mainland government in 2003 provided favourable business opportunities to Hong Kong's investors and industries.

However, the seemingly headlong rush for the Chinese tourist dollar, with the attendant proliferation of luxury stores in areas such as Causeway Bay and Canton Rd in Tsim Sha Tsui, has pushed up shop rentals across the board, fuelling inflation and taking many small traders off Hong Kong's once accommodating streetscape. Similarly, the property market, flush with cash from mainland speculators, has become prohibitively expensive for ordinary folk. Of most concern to many Hong Kong people are the tens of thousands of mainland Chinese migrants who have poured into the city in the past decade or so. Worries abound that the influx is putting a strain on Hong Kong's public services and there are fears that the cultural – and material-wealth – differences between locals and 'mainlanders' could provide more fodder for both sensationalist and sobering news headlines in the years to come.

While closer ties with the mainland have often been met with uneasy feelings, might history one day identify an equal and opposite reaction going on? Hong Kong's dazzling success and core values arguably exert 'soft' power that influences thinking on the mainland. It might be hard to measure, but in the enclave that sheltered and inspired the fathers of powerful mainland movements (Sun Yatsen and Zhou Enlai), it should not be dismissed.

What is certain is that, two decades on from the handover, Hong Kong people are asking questions about their identity more intensely than ever as Hong Kong and mainland China, for better or worse, increasingly intertwine.

Hong Kong's latest political star is 17-year-old Joshua Wong, convenor of Scholarism, a pressure group that famously organised the anti-national education protests in 2012. Wong is now fighting for civil nomination in the 2017 CE election.

HISTORY A CHANGED CITY?

2014	2015	2016
A massive crowd (180,000 according to organisers; 99,500 to police) turns out for the 25th anniversary of the 4 June candlelight vigil marking the Tiān'ānmén demonstration in 1989.	Five booksellers connected with a publisher of books banned on the mainland go missing; one resurfaces in Hong Kong and asks the police to end their investigation into his missing-person case.	At Lunar New Year, a government crackdown on unlicensed hawkers turns violent as riot police clash with protesters in Mong Kok.

Arts

Hong Kong's arts scene is more vibrant than its reputation suggests. There are musical ensembles of all persuasions, an assortment of theatre groups, Chinese and modern dance troupes, and numerous art organisations. The West Kowloon Cultural District is one of Asia's most ambitious cultural projects. Government funds allow organisers to bring in top international performers, and the number of international arts festivals hosted here seems to grow each year.

Art

Hong Kong is one of the three most important art auction centres in the world, along with New York and London. Theoretically, it can only get stronger, given that China has already surpassed the US as the world's largest market for art and antiques. Despite some industry concern about the ability of the Chinese market to promote stable, long-term growth, Hong Kong will continue to ride the bull wave nimbly – and with gusto – for as long as the overheated market keeps its lid on. Art Basel (p30), the world's premier art fair, launched a Hong Kong edition in 2013; **Hong Kong Art Walk** (www.hongkongartwalk.com; ☉Mar) is an annual event that runs alongside it, involving dozens of galleries in town.

Contemporary Hong Kong art tends not to bother too much with grandiose narratives about nationhood and religion, preferring to take an introverted view of the world and expressing visions of Chinese-ness and increasingly Hong Kong–ness outside of the national frame.

The opening of the M+, tentatively slated for 2019, will definitely be a highlight of Hong Kong's cultural arena in the not too distant future. The M+ is a museum for 20th- and 21st-century visual culture, and is part of the West Kowloon Cultural District (WKCD), the city's most ambitious arts development project to date. However, both the museum and the WKCD have been plagued by a series of leadership losses, the latest involving M+'s executive director, Lars Nittve, who chose not to renew his contract when it expired in January 2016.

The best sources for information on Hong Kong and Asian art are *Asian Art News* (www.asianartnews.com), the free monthly *Art Map* (www.artmap.com.hk), the **Asia Art Archive** (Map p304; ☑852 2815 1112; www.aaa.org.hk; 11th fl, Hollywood Centre, 233 Hollywood Rd, Sheung Wan; ☉10am-6pm Mon-Sat) and the Hong Kong International Association of Art Critics (www.aicahk.org).

Top Museums for Hong Kong Art

Hong Kong Museum of Art (Tsim Sha Tsui)

Hong Kong Arts Centre (Wan Chai)

Asia Society Hong Kong (Admiralty)

Roots

In general, Chinese painters of the past were interested in traditional forms and painting processes – not necessarily composition and colour. Brush strokes and the utensils used to produce them are of vital importance and interest. In traditional Chinese art, change for the sake of change was never the philosophy or the trend; Chinese artists would compare their work with that of the master and judge it accordingly.

The influential Lingnan School of Painting, founded by the water-colourist Chao Shao-an (1905–98) in the 1930s and relocated to Hong Kong in 1948, attempted to move away from this tradition. It combined traditional Chinese, Japanese and Western artistic methods to produce a rather decorative style, and dominated the small art market in Hong Kong for the next two decades.

The most distinct group of painters and sculptors to appear in Hong Kong were the proponents of the New Ink Painting movement who came to prominence in the late 1960s. Most had strong links to China or its cultural heritage. The movement aimed at reconciling Chinese and Western ideas by steering traditional Chinese ink painting towards abstract expressionism. Lui Shou-kwan (1919–75), who arrived in Hong Kong in 1948, was the earliest and the best known of the New Ink Painting artists. Lui worked for the Yau Ma Tei ferry as a pier inspector and taught in his spare time. Speaking no English, his only experience of the West was through pictures and books borrowed from the British Council library. Many of the artists who became associated with the movement were his students.

The only major artist to break free of the dominant style of the era was Luis Chan (1905–95). Born in Panama, Chan came to Hong Kong at the age of five, where he learnt to paint from art magazines and a correspondence course. Stylistically, Chan was a loner with no apparent allegiance to any painting tradition. He was also a genius who, particularly in his post-1960s works, transformed Hong Kong into a fantastical realm of dreams and hallucinations. His 1976 painting *Ping Chau* is a bizarre interpretation of the somnolent outlying island that is at once puzzling and endearing.

Antonio Mak's work employs much visual 'punning'. In his *Bible from Happy Valley* (1992), a racehorse is portrayed with a wing-like book made of lead across its back. The word 'book' in Cantonese has the same sound as 'to lose (at gambling)'.

Avant-Garde

The 1980s and '90s saw the coming of age of artists born after WWII, many of whom had received their training abroad. Less burdened by the need to reconcile East and West, they devoted their efforts to defining avant-garde art, often through Western mediums. They were also politically engaged. Wong Yan-kwai, a painter educated in France, was arguably the most influential artist of that period and is still one of the most accomplished today. His powerful paintings in vibrant colours are free of any social or historical context. Wong's mural graces Club 71 in Central.

London-trained Antonio Mak (1951–94) is Hong Kong's most famous contemporary sculptor and is known for his figurative pieces in cast bronze. He focused on the human figure as well as on animals important in Chinese legend and mythology (eg horses and tigers), and was greatly influenced by Rodin.

Salisbury Gardens, leading to the entrance of the Hong Kong Museum of Art in Tsim Sha Tsui, is lined with modern sculptures by contemporary Hong Kong sculptors. Dotted among the greenery of Kowloon Park is Sculpture Walk, with 30 marble, bronze and other weather-resistant works by both local and overseas artists, including a bronze by Mak called *Torso* and one by Britain's late Sir Eduardo Paolozzi (1924–2005) called *Concept of Newton*.

Contemporary

Compared to their predecessors, Hong Kong's young artists – those born in the '70s and '80s – take a more internalised view of the world. They are overwhelmingly unfussed with orthodox Chinese culture and older generations' attempts to amalgamate East and West. Instead, they're often looking for – or perhaps, trying to retrieve – something that is uniquely Hong Kong. Nonetheless, their works show eloquence in a host of mediums, from Wilson Shieh's cheeky urban paintings using Chinese gōngbǐ (fine-brush) techniques to Jaffa Lam's sculpture installations.

Chow Chun-fai's background across a wide spectrum of media has seen him work between different art forms, such as photographs from classical paintings, or paintings from films. Adrian Wong's playful works involve his family connections to prominent names in the local entertainment industry, and indigenous superstitions. Kacey Wong's exciting installations can usually move about and invariably involve some kind of Hong Kong theme or common household treasure recast in a jovial light. His *Sleepwalker* (2011) contraption imbues the bunk bed – an indispensable fixture in Hong Kong's tight living spaces – with life and speaks to a mass aspiration, or doomed desperation, for a more humane habitat.

Photography

Hong Kong is endowed with internationally competitive photographers, and some of their works can be seen in the Hong Kong Heritage Museum (p168), Blindspot Gallery (p38), AO Vertical Art Space (p107) and during the excellent biennial **Hong Kong Photo Festival** (香港國際攝影節; www.hkphotofest.org).

Working in black and white, documentary photographer Yau Leung (1941–97) captured some of the most stunning and iconic images of 1960s Hong Kong, while art photographer So Hing-keung focuses on the shadows, figurative and literal, of the city in creations known for their psychological depth. Hong Kong–born, London-based visual artist Kurt Tong explores his multi-layered identity, family heritage and memories through thoughtful documentary photography. *In Case it Rains in Heaven* (2010), his best-known project, is presented like a high-end shopping catalogue of stylised portraits of paper-made objects burnt as offerings for the deceased. The combustible items honoured by Tong run the gamut of modern human desires in Chinese societies.

There are only about four Tsang Tsou-choi works left on Hong Kong's streets today (with three subject to the mercy of the elements), but you won't miss the concrete pillar that bears his imperial treatise at the Star Ferry pier in Tsim Sha Tsui.

Street Art & Other Arts

Street graffiti was almost non-existent or largely unrecognised in Hong Kong until the passing in 2007 of the self-proclaimed 'King of Kowloon' (aka Tsang Tsou-choi), who for decades had smothered the city with his trademark rambling, childlike calligraphy that cursed the Queen of England for 'usurping' his rightful land. His irrepressible daily reveries and inimitable visual style eventually inspired many artists and designers, and won him exhibitions both at home and abroad.

Street art has noticeably grown in Hong Kong since, perhaps with the King's benediction. This trend in part stems from a new-found confidence among a younger generation of artists to express their dissatisfaction with the social problems of the day using means that are more open and combative. The website Hong Kong Street Art (http://hkstreetart.com) shows where you can see samples of the genre.

HKWalls (http://hkwalls.org) is an annual street-art festival held around March that showcases the works of local and international artists on the streets of Hong Kong. Unlike much of the graffiti you see in town, the organisers of HKWalls actually seek approval from businesses to use their walls before covering them with art. Events have been held in Sheung Wan and Sham Shui Po in 2015 and 2016.

After the April 2011 arrest in mainland China of the prominent artist and activist Ai Weiwei, a number of artists in Hong Kong came forth with a dose of creative surprise to raise public awareness of his case and to rally for his release. Most memorably, Ai-inspired graffiti stencils appeared on pavements, overpasses and walls for five nights straight around the city, thanks to a lone operator known only as 'Tangerine'.

Street Art Movement is a group that stages seemingly impromptu gallery shows in the most ordinary of common spaces. In 2012 the group organised an art ride along the Tsuen Wan line on the MTR, sketching and clipping their finished drawings onto laundry lines that they strung up inside the train carriages as fresh interest poured in at every station.

Contemporary ceramics is another field in which Hong Kong artists enjoy an edge beyond the city's borders. Fiona Wong, one of the city's best-known ceramic artists, makes life-sized sculptural works of clothing, shoes and other familiar items.

The Leisure and Cultural Services Department (www.lcsd.gov.hk) regularly stages free arts and entertainment shows at its venues throughout the territory.

ARTS MUSIC

Music

Hong Kongers may not be quick to get up and jive when music is played, but they certainly enjoy music – in their homes, the air-conditioned comfort of a concert hall or a casual bar or karaoke lounge. Thanks to the city's mixed heritage, you'll find a decent range of music, from Eastern to Western, and classical to contemporary.

Western Classical

Western classical music is very popular in Hong Kong. The territory boasts the Hong Kong Philharmonic Orchestra, the Hong Kong Sinfonietta and the City Chamber Orchestra of Hong Kong. Opportunities to see big-name soloists and major orchestras abound throughout the year, especially during the Hong Kong Arts Festival (p50). The **Hong Kong International Piano Competition** (http://chshk.brinkster.net), with its star-studded jury, is held every three years in October/November. The Hong Kong Academy for Performing Arts (www.hkapa.edu) has free concerts almost daily.

Jazz

The best times to experience world-class jazz in the city are during the Hong Kong International Jazz Festival (p51) and the Hong Kong Arts Festival (p50). Hong Kong also has a small but zealous circle of local musicians, including the 17-piece Saturday Night Jazz Orchestra (www.saturdaynight-jazz.com), which plays big-band sounds every month. Other names to watch out for include guitarist Eugene Pao, the first local jazz artist to sign with an international label, and pianist Ted Lo, who has played with Astrud Gilberto and Herbie Hancock.

Traditional Chinese

You won't hear much traditional Chinese music on the streets of Hong Kong, except perhaps the sound of the doleful *dī-daa*, a clarinet-like instrument played in funeral processions; the hollow-sounding *gú* (drums) and crashing *luó* (gongs) and *bat* (cymbals) at lion dances; the *èrhú*, a two-stringed fiddle favoured by beggars for its plaintive sound; or strains of Cantonese opera wafting from the radio of a minibus driver. You can sample this kind of music, albeit in a form adapted to a symphony-orchestra model, at concerts given by the Hong Kong Chinese Orchestra (www.hkco.org). For more authentic fare, catch a Chinese opera or check out the Temple Street Night Market, where street performers deliver operatic excerpts.

The website www.renditions.org has excellent info on Chinese literature published in English. Hong Kong University Press (www.hkupress.org) also publishes works by local Chinese writers.

Canto-Pop

Hong Kong's home-grown popular-music scene is dominated by 'Canto-pop' – compositions that often blend Western rock, pop and R&B with Chinese melodies and lyrics. Rarely radical, the songs invariably deal with such teenage concerns as unrequited love and loneliness; to many they sound like the American pop songs of the 1950s. The music is slick and eminently singable – thus the explosion of karaoke bars throughout the territory. Attending a Canto-pop concert is to see the city at its sweetest and most over the top, with screaming, silly dancing, day-glo wigs and enough floral tributes to set up a flower market.

Canto-pop scaled new heights from the mid-1980s to mid-1990s and turned singers such as Anita Mui, Leslie Cheung, Alan Tam, Priscilla Chan and Danny Chan into household names in Hong Kong and among Chinese communities around the world. The peak of this Canto-pop golden age came with the advent of the so-called Four Kings: thespian/singer Andy Lau, Mr Nice Guy Jacky Cheung, dancer-turned-crooner Aaron Kwok and teen heart-throb Leon Lai.

It never quite reached that altitude again. Subsequent arrivals such as Beijing waif Faye Wong, Sammi Cheung, Kelly Chen and proto-hunk Nicholas Tse took their turns on the throne for a time. But today most stars are a packaged phenomenon. Singers from the mainland and Taiwan – singer/songwriter Jay Chou is one example – are competing with local stars and gaining new fans here, and the strongest influences on local music are now coming from Japan and Korea. There are also acts making their marks from the edge of the mainstream, such as Ellen Lo and Eman Lam, two 'urban folk' singer-songwriters, and My Little Airport, a dapper act whose irreverent multilingual lyrics are often speckled with cute Chinglish.

Theatre

The Cantonese opera Sunbeam Theatre seems to face a closure crisis every few years when its lease expires. The most recent crisis, in February 2012, was averted only when a group of private benefactors intervened at the last minute.

Much, though not all, theatre in Hong Kong is Western in form, if not content. Traditional Chinese theatre can still be experienced, but Western theatre has been very influential. Most productions are staged in Cantonese, and a large number are new plays by Hong Kong writers. The fully professional Hong Kong Repertory Theatre (www.hkrep. com) and Chung Ying Theatre Company (www.chungying.com) put on Cantonese productions, very often with English titles. Theatre du Pif (www.thtdupif.com), formed by a professional Scottish-Chinese couple, puts on innovative works incorporating text, movement and visuals, in English and/or Cantonese. Hong Kong Players (www.hongkongplayers. com), consisting of expatriate amateurs, mounts classical and modern productions in English, while Zuni Icosahedron (www.zuni.org.hk) creates conceptual multimedia works known for their experimental format.

Among the more popular venues are the Fringe Club theatres in Central. The Hong Kong Cultural Centre, Hong Kong Academy for the Performing Arts, Hong Kong City Hall and the Hong Kong Arts Centre all host foreign productions, ranging from large-scale Western musicals to minimalist Japanese theatre.

Chinese Opera

Chinese opera *(hei kuk)*, one of the three oldest dramatic art forms in the world, is a colourful, cacophonous spectacle featuring music, singing, martial arts, acrobatics and acting. Admittedly, it can take some getting used to. Female characters, whether played by men or women, sing in falsetto. The instrumental accompaniment often takes the form of drumming, gonging and other unmelodious punctuation. And the whole affair can last four to six hours. But the costumes are splendid and the plots are adapted from legends and historical tales with universal themes. If you happen to attend a performance by a leading Cantonese opera troupe such as Chor Fung Ming, you'll experience some of the best moments of Chinese opera.

Cantonese opera *(yuet-kek)* is a regional variety of Chinese opera that flourished in Hong Kong, particularly in the 1950s when opera virtuosi fleeing China composed and performed a spate of original works in the territory. But eventually the limelight shifted to the sleek, leather-clad kid on the block – cinema – and things have been going downhill for Cantonese opera ever since. A shortage of performance venues is a problem. At present there are only two venues, Sunbeam Theatre in North Point and the recently restored Yau Ma Tei Theatre, dedicated to the promotion and development of Chinese opera.

The best way to experience Cantonese opera is by attending a 'performance for the gods' *(sun kung hei)* in a temporary theatre. During major Chinese festivals, such as the Lunar New Year, Mid-Autumn Festival and Tin Hau Festival, rural communities invite troupes to perform. The performances usually take place on a makeshift stage set up in a temple or a bamboo shed, and it is a jovial, laid-back event for the whole family that lasts several days.

For a more formal experience, try the Hong Kong Arts Festival (p50). Ko Shan Theatre (www.lcsd.gov.hk/CE/CulturalService/KST) also has Cantonese opera offerings. But the most reliable venue for opera performances year-round is Sunbeam Theatre, while Yau Ma Tei Theatre is expected to also develop an active show calendar on the other side of the harbour. At other times, you might stumble upon a performance at the Temple Street Night Market nearby.

You can also check out the enlightening Cantonese-opera display at the Hong Kong Heritage Museum (p168), where the Hong Kong Tourist Board (HKTB) offers a Chinese-opera appreciation course every Saturday from 2.30pm to 3.45pm.

Other varieties of Chinese opera being performed in Hong Kong by local and/or visiting troupes include Peking opera, a highly refined form that uses almost no scenery but different kinds of traditional props; and Kun opera, the oldest form and one designated a Masterpiece of the Oral and Intangible Heritage of Humanity by Unesco.

A Xiqu Centre, a top-notch venue for the performance, production, education and research of Chinese opera will open in 2018 in the West Kowloon Cultural District.

Literature

Liu Yichang (b 1918), Hong Kong's most respected senior writer, is the author of the stream-of-consciousness novella *Tête-bêche* which inspired Wong Kar-wai's *In the Mood for Love.*

Hong Kong has long suffered from the misconception that it does not have a literature of its own, but, in fact, the city has seen a thriving microclimate in the vast landscape of Chinese literature, where the same sun shining on other parts of China has spawned distinct smells, textures and voices.

From the 1920s to the 1940s, Hong Kong was a haven for Chinese writers on the run. These émigrés continued their writing here, their influence lasting until the 1970s when the first generation of writers born and/or raised locally came into their own. The relative creative freedom offered by the city has spawned works in a variety of genres and subjects, from prose poems to experimental novels, from swordplay romance to life as a make-up artist for the dead.

Hong Kong Collage: Contemporary Stories and Writing (ed Martha PY Cheung; 1998) is an important collection of fiction and essays by 15 contemporary local writers. *To Pierce the Material Screen: an*

TRANSLATED HONG KONG FICTION

The Cockroach and Other Stories (1995) by Liu Yichang Liu Yichang (b 1918), Hong Kong's most respected senior writer, is believed to have written the first stream-of-consciousness novel in Chinese literature. 'The Cockroach' is a Kafkaesque exploration of psychology and philosophy. In 'Indecision', a woman is torn between staying in Hong Kong and returning to her mad husband in Shànghǎi.

Islands and Continents: Short Stories (2007) by Leung Ping-kwan Anti-heroes enter the limelight against the background of Hong Kong history. In 'Postcolonial Affairs of Food and the Heart', a man devours the culinary and erotic delights of other cultures in a bid to find his identity. Leung has also published the bilingual *Travelling with a Bitter Melon: Selected Poems (1973–98)*.

Love in a Fallen City: And Other Stories by Eileen Chang Chang (1920–95) is considered by some to be the best modern Chinese writer. In the title story set during WWII, a divorcée pursues a liaison with a playboy from Shànghǎi to Hong Kong. Director Ann Hui made it into a film starring Chow Yun-fat. Chang also wrote *Lust, Caution*, a tale of love and espionage, which was adapted for film by Ang Lee.

My City: A Hong Kong Story (1993) by Xi Xi This novel offers a personal vision of Hong Kong in the '60s and '70s through the lives of a telephone repairman, his family, friends and, come to think of it, pineapples and stationery. *Asia Weekly* ranked it one of the top 100 works of 20th-century Chinese fiction.

Renditions Nos 47 & 48: Hong Kong Nineties (1997) Two writers to watch in this collection of 1990s Hong Kong fiction are Wong Bik-wan (b 1961) and Dung Kai-cheung (b 1969). Wong, a flamenco dancer, writes with a violent passion. 'Plenty and Sorrow' is a tale about Shànghǎi, with a chunk of cannibalism thrown in. Dung re-creates the legend of the Father of Chinese Agriculture in 'The Young Shen Nong'.

Anthology of Twentieth Century Hong Kong Literature (ed Eva Hung; 2008) is a two-volume anthology featuring established figures, younger names and emerging voices, and spans 75 years. In *From the Bluest Part of the Harbour: Poems from Hong Kong* (ed Andrew Parkin; 1996), 12 modern poets reveal the emotions of Hong Kong people in the run-up to 1997. For critical articles on Hong Kong literature, check out the special Hong Kong issue (winter 2008) of the *Journal of Modern Literature in Chinese* (Lingnan University of Hong Kong).

The major literary festival in the city is the Hong Kong Literary Festival (p30), which is usually, but not always, held in November. **Cha** (http://www.asiancha.com), Hong Kong's home-grown literary journal, features poetry, prose and photography about Asia.

Cinema

Once known as the 'Hollywood of the Far East', Hong Kong was for decades the third-largest motion-picture industry in the world (after Mumbai and Hollywood) and the second-largest exporter. Now it produces a few dozen films each year, down from well over 200 in the early 1990s. Yet Hong Kong film continues to play an important role on the world cinema stage as it searches for a new identity in the Greater China market.

Martial Arts

Hong Kong cinema became known to the West when a former child actor appeared as a sinewy hero in a kung fu film. But before Bruce Lee unleashed his high-pitched war cry in *The Big Boss* (1971), the kung fu genre was alive and kicking. The *Wong Fei-hung* series, featuring the adventures of a folk hero, has been named by the *Guinness Book of Records* as the longest-running cinema serial dedicated to one man, with roughly a hundred episodes made from 1949 to 1970 alone. The works of the signature directors of the period – Chang Cheh, whose macho aesthetics seduced Quentin Tarantino, and King Hu, who favoured a more refined style of combat – continue to influence films today.

The One-Armed Swordsman (1967), directed by Chang Cheh, was one of the first of a new style of martial-arts films featuring male heroes and serious bloodletting.

Jackie Chan & Jet Li

The decade after Lee's death saw the leap to stardom of two martial artists: Jackie Chan and Jet Li. Chan's blend of slapstick and action, as seen in *Snake in the Eagle's Shadow* (1978), a collaboration with action choreographer Yuen Wo-ping (who choreographed the action on *Crouching Tiger, Hidden Dragon* and *The Matrix*), became an instant hit. He later added stunts to the formula, resulting in the hits *Police Story* and the *Rush Hour* series. Li garnered international acclaim when he teamed up with director Tsui Hark in *Once Upon a Time in China* (1991). Despite his reputation for tampering with a print just hours before its premiere, Tsui introduced sophisticated visuals and rhythmic editing into the martial-arts genre, most notably in Hong Kong's first special-effects extravaganza, *Zu: Warriors from the Magic Mountain* (1983). As a producer, he helped to create John Woo's gangster classic *A Better Tomorrow* (1986).

Contemporary Martial Arts Films

Fast forward to the 21st century, when a Bruce Lee craze briefly returned on the 35th anniversary of his death with the release of *Ip Man* (2008), a fawning semi-speculative biopic of Lee's mentor. A sequel, *Ip Man 2* (2011), was more chop socky and less solemn, though the nationalist-hero treatment still applied, with a Sinophobic British pugilist in post-war Hong Kong replacing Japanese soldiers as the enemy. Also cashing in on Lee's revived legend is *Bruce Lee, My Brother* (2010), a coming-of-age comedy based on a published recollection of childhood memories that the master's siblings shared of their famous brother. Similarly nostalgic is *Gallants* (2010), a retro comedy in which various kung fu stars of yesteryear pay a feisty homage to an old genre. The low-budget film won

APHOTOSTORY / SHUTTERSTOCK ©

Avenue of Stars (p136)

Best Picture at the 2011 Hong Kong Film Awards. *Ashes of Time Redux* (2008) is a shorter cut of Wong Kar-wai's haunting 'non-action action movie' of the same name from 1994.

New Wave

Tsui Hark belonged to the New Wave, a group of filmmakers of the late 1970s and '80s who grew up in Hong Kong, and were trained at film schools overseas as well as in local TV. Their works had a more contemporary sensibility, unlike those of their émigré predecessors, and were more artistically adventurous.

Ann Hui, Asia's top female director, is a New Waver who has won awards both locally and overseas. *Song of the Exile* (1990), a tale about the marriage between a Japanese woman and a Chinese man just after the Sino-Japanese War, won Best Film at both the Asian Pacific Film Festival and the Rimini Film Festival in Italy.

International Acclaim

The 1990s saw Hong Kong gaining unprecedented respect on the global film-festival circuit. Besides Ann Hui, Wong Kar-wai received Best Director at the Cannes Film Festival for *Happy Together* in 1997. Auteur of the cult favourite *Chungking Express* (1994), Wong is famous almost as much for his elliptical mood pieces as for his disregard of shooting deadlines. In the same year, Fruit Chan bagged the Special Jury Prize at the Locarno International Film Festival with *Made in Hong Kong*, an edgy number shot on film stock Chan had scraped together while working on other projects.

Tough Times & New Directions

Due to changes in the market, in the 1990s the Hong Kong film industry sank into a gloom from which it has not recovered. The return to China also presented problems related to censorship and self-censorship. But

The 1970s saw the start of another trend spearheaded by actor-director-screenwriter Michael Hui, who produced comedies satirising the realities and dreams of Hong Kong people. *Games Gamblers Play* (1974) was the highest grossing film of its time, even surpassing the movies of Bruce Lee.

there have been sunny patches, too. *Infernal Affairs* (2002), directed by Andrew Lau and Alan Mak, made such an impact on its release that it was heralded as a box-office miracle, though it suffered some loss in translation in Martin Scorsese's remake, *The Departed*. *Election* (2005) and *Election 2* (2006), by master of Hong Kong noir Johnnie To, also enjoyed immense critical and box-office success.

Echoes of the Rainbow (2010), a rather maudlin tale about the battling spirit of Hong Kong people in the turbulent 1960s, won a Crystal Bear at the Berlin Film Festival. Meanwhile, veteran thespian Deanie Ip won the Best Actress award at the Venice Film Festival for her role as a traditional housemaid in Ann Hui's *A Simple Life* (2011), an elegant drama about ageing and loneliness.

The past few years have also seen a string of big-budget Hong Kong–China collaborations, most notably the *Ip Man* series and *Bodyguards and Assassins* (2009), a story of anti-Qing intrigue set in 1905 Hong Kong. The trend of growing cooperation with the wealthy – and lucrative – Chinese market looks set to take hold as local filmmakers seek new ways to finance their celluloid (or digital) fantasies.

That said, despite budgetary constraints, local films by new directors, like *Wong Ka-yan* (2015) and *Weeds on Fire* (2016), and *Trivisa* (2016) managed to garner critical acclaim, signalling a brighter future for Hong Kong cinema. Adding to this is Financial Secretary John Tsang's announcement that an extra HK$20 million will be injected into the Film Development Fund to subsidise distribution and promotion of locally made Cantonese films.

Ten Years, a dystopian indie film offering a vision of Hong Kong in 10 years' time with with freedoms diminishing as the mainland authorities exert increasing influence, was voted Best Film at the Hong Kong Film Awards. As the film is banned on the mainland, it is believed that the triumph was due less to the film's artistic merit than to it being a statement that Hong Kong cinema will not bow to fear.

Film Festivals & Awards

The Hong Kong International Film Festival (p51), now in its third decade, is the best in Asia and boasts a laudable if precarious balance of art-house choices and titles offering red-carpet opportunities. The Hong Kong Film Awards is also among the most respected in this part of the world. The Hong Kong Film Archive is a treasure trove of Hong Kong films and resources on them.

Hong Kong in Film

Hong Kong has been the setting of many Western-made films, including: *Love is a Many-Splendored Thing* (1955), starring William Holden, and Jennifer Jones as his Eurasian doctor paramour, with great shots on and from Victoria Peak; *The World of Suzie Wong* (1960), with Holden again, and Nancy Kwan as the pouting bar girl from Wan Chai; and *The Man with the Golden Gun* (1974), with Roger Moore as James Bond and filmed partly in a Tsim Sha Tsui topless bar. More recently, in *The Dark Knight* (2008), Christian Bale's Batman performed one of his trademark escapes from Two International Finance Centre (although a planned scene in which the superhero would drop from a plane into the harbour was axed after the film's producers found the water quality could pose a potential health danger). An excellent source for spotting familiar locations is the two-part freebie *Hong Kong Movie Odyssey Guide* from the Hong Kong Tourist Board (HKTB).

Once Upon a Time in China (1991) is the first of Tsui Hark's five-part epic that follows folk hero Wong Fei-hung (Jet Li) as he battles government officials, gangsters and foreign entrepreneurs to protect his martial-arts school in 19th-century China.

The Warlords (2007), directed by Peter Chan, is a period war film about sworn brothers forced to betray one another by the realities of war – showing it's possible to please both Hong Kong and mainland audiences.

Days of Being Wild (1990), set in the 1960s, is a star-studded piece directed by Wong Kar-wai and steered along by the characters' accounts of seemingly mundane events. It won Best Picture at the 1991 Hong Kong Film Awards.

Architecture

Welcome to the most dazzling skyline in the world. We defy you not to be awed as you stand for the first time at the harbour's edge in Tsim Sha Tsui and see Hong Kong Island's majestic panorama of skyscrapers march up those steep, jungle-clad hills. This spectacle arises from the rapidity of construction in Hong Kong, where buildings are knocked down and replaced with taller, shinier versions almost while your back is turned. The scarcity of land, the strains of a growing population and the rapacity of developers – as well as the opportunism of the common speculator – drive this relentless cycle of destruction and construction.

Heritage Preservation

Neo-Classical Buildings

....

Former Legislative Council Building (Central)

....

Hung Hing Ying Building, University of Hong Kong (The Mid-Levels)

Modernism

....

Bank of China Buildings (Central)

....

Lippo Centre (Admiralty)

....

International Finance Centre (Central)

....

Hong Kong & Shanghai Banking Corporation Building (Central)

....

Hong Kong International Airport (Lantau)

The government's lack of interest in preserving architecturally important buildings went almost entirely unregretted by most until very recently. The destruction of the iconic Star Ferry Terminal in Central marked a surprising reversal in public apathy. Heartfelt protests greeted the wrecking balls in late 2006, but to no avail.

However, in the wake of the protests, the government announced that the Streamline Moderne–style Wan Chai Market would be partially preserved (though a luxury apartment tower has risen over it).

Meanwhile the nearby Pawn, a flashy drinking hole converted from four old tenements and a century-old pawn shop, is a running sore with heritage activists who argue that the Urban Renewal Authority has short-changed the public by refusing to list the building's rooftop terrace as an unrestricted public space. Similarly, the former Marine Police Headquarters in Tsim Sha Tsui, now yet another hotel-cum-shopping centre, has disappointed many after the original landscape was razed.

There have been some bright spots, however, most notably when the government stopped the demolition of the magnificent King Yin Lei (1937), a private, Chinese Renaissance–style mansion on Stubbs Rd over Happy Valley. Even more significantly, the government launched in 2008 a scheme for the 'revitalisation' of historic monuments, which allows NGOs to pitch for the use of these buildings. The nascent program has already seen the restoration of the Old Tai O Police Station and the distinctive pre-WWII shophouse Lui Seng Chun.

Despite these positive examples of heritage preservation, the reality remains that the imperatives of the property market, in the name of urban redevelopment, continue to dictate the city's future and its connection with the past. The deep, protracted uncertainty over the fate of the West Wing of the former Government Secretariat in Central – a fine model of understated elegance and a vital place of contact between the former colonial administration and the people – shows that no building in Hong Kong, no matter how valued its architectural and historical heritage, is truly safe from the bulldozers.

Traditional Chinese Architecture

About the only examples of 19th-century Chinese architecture left in urban Hong Kong are the popular Tin Hau temples, including those at Tin Hau near Causeway Bay, Aberdeen, Stanley and Yau Ma Tei. Museums in Chai Wan and Tsuen Wan have preserved a few 18th-century Hakka village structures. More substantial physical reminders of the past lie in the New Territories and the Outlying Islands, where walled villages, fortresses and even a 15th-century pagoda can still be seen.

East-Meets-West Architecture

Largely the preserve of the wealthy and the religious, fusion architecture has appeared in Hong Kong since the 1920s.

The abandoned Shek Lo Mansion in Fanling (1925) resembles a Kaiping *diāolóu* (a fortified tower that blends Chinese and Western architectural elements) across the border in Guǎngdōng. The Anglican St Mary's Church is a somewhat comical Orientalist exercise from 1937 while a Tao Fung Shan Christian centre features Buddhist-inspired buildings designed by a Dane.

Tai Hang's Lin Fa Kung is a small Kwun Yum temple with a unique octagonal design and side entrances reminiscent of a medieval Catholic chapel.

Colonial Architecture

Most of the colonial architecture left in the city is on Hong Kong Island, especially in Central, such as the former Legislative Council building (1912) and Government House, residence of all British governors from 1855 to 1997. In Sheung Wan there is Western Market (1906), and in the Mid-Levels the Edwardian-style Old Pathological Institute, now the Hong Kong Museum of Medical Sciences (1905). The Old Stanley Police

Pre-Colonial Buildings

Tsui Sing Lau Pagoda (Yuen Long)

Tang Ancestral Hall (Yuen Long)

Yu Kiu Ancestral Hall (Yuen Long)

Sam Tung Uk Museum (Tsuen Wan)

ARCHITECTURE TRADITIONAL CHINESE ARCHITECTURE

DORASON / SHUTTERSTOCK ©

Tin Hau Temple, Sai Kung, New Territories

Station (1859) and nearby Murray House (1848) are important colonial structures on the southern part of Hong Kong Island.

The interesting **Hong Kong Antiquities & Monuments Office** (Map p314; ☑852 2721 2326; www.amo.gov.hk; 136 Nathan Rd, Tsim Sha Tsui; ⊙9am-5pm Mon-Sat; ⓂTsim Sha Tsui, exit A2), located in a British schoolhouse that dates from 1902, has information and exhibits on current preservation efforts.

Victorian & Edwardian Buildings

Central Police Station (Soho)

Nam Koo Terrace (Wan Chai)

Kam Tong Hall (The Mid-Levels)

Western Market (Sheung Wan)

Contemporary Architecture

Hong Kong's verticality was born out of necessity – the scarcity of land and the sloping terrain have always put property at a premium in this densely populated place. Some buildings, such as Central Plaza and International Commercial Centre, have seized height at all costs; a privileged few, such as the Hong Kong Convention & Exhibition Centre and the windowless Hong Kong Cultural Centre, have pulled off audacious moves to go horizontal.

Internationally celebrated modern architecture in the city includes the Hong Kong & Shanghai Banking Corporation building in Central and the Hong Kong International Airport in Chep Lap Kok (opened in 1998) – both by English architect Norman Foster, in Late-Modern high-tech style – as well as IM Pei's soaring symphony of triangular geometry that is the Bank of China Tower.

For more on Hong Kong's contemporary architecture, pick up a copy of the illustrated pocket guide *Skylines Hong Kong*, by Peter Moss (2006), or the more specialist *Hong Kong: A Guide to Recent Architecture* (1998), by Andrew Yeoh and Juanita Cheung.

Distinctively Urban Vistas

For thrill-seekers, a seemingly ordinary tram ride across the northern shore of Hong Kong Island often feels more like an impossible hurtle through an endless canyon of high-rises. Indeed, similar psychogeography can be experienced in much of urban Hong Kong. While the bulk of the buildings here may be uninspired office and apartment blocks sprouting cheek by jowl throughout the territory, there are perverse spectacles to be found as various forms of the built environment routinely challenge conventional notions of scale and proportion to achieve their purpose.

Revitalised Heritage

Lui Seng Chun (Sham Shui Po)

Béthanie (Pok Fu Lam)

Explosives Magazine (Admiralty)

Mei Ho House Youth Hostel (Sham Shui Po)

A classic example is the tumbledown Oceanic Mansion (1010–30 King's Rd), a forbidding cliff of pulverised dwellings that soars above a tight, sloping bend in the shadows of a country park in Quarry Bay. Near the western end of the tramline in Kennedy Town, Hill Rd Flyover is a towering urban racetrack that lures traffic from the rarefied heights of Pok Fu Lam to the siren call of Central, *Blade Runner*–like.

The same sense of space or freedom can rarely be manufactured by the many luxury real-estate projects you will see in Hong Kong, however, even if they've been romantically given names such as Sorrento, Leguna Verde or Cullinan. Tiny living spaces remain the norm in this city.

Those interested in the future of the city's urban landscape can visit the **City Gallery** (展城館; Map p298; ☑852 3102 1242; www.infrastructuregallery.gov.hk; 3 Edinburgh Pl, Central; ⊙10am-6pm Wed-Mon; ⓂCentral, exit K).

Religion & Belief

Hong Kong is arguably the only city in China where religious freedom is both provided for by the law and respected in practise. Almost everyone here is brought up on certain spiritual beliefs, even though these may not always add up to the profession of a religion. And most of the time, they don't – Hong Kongers are not a particularly religious bunch.

Early Influences

The city's early inhabitants were fishers and farmers who worshipped a mixed bag of deities – some folk, some Taoist, notably the Kitchen God, the Earth God, and the Goddess of the Sea (Tin Hau). Many sought divine protection by symbolically offering their children to deities for adoption. All villages have ancestral shrines. Traditional practices are alive in Hong Kong today, often colourfully intertwined with those of imported religions including Buddhism and Christianity.

Confucianism

For 2000 years the teachings of Confucius (551–479 BC) and the subsequent school of thought called Confucianism informed the familial system and all human relationships in imperial China. Yet in the revolutionary fervour of the 20th century, the philosophy that was the bedrock of Chinese civilisation was blamed for a host of evils from feudal oppression and misogyny to all-round backwardness.

> Some 80% of funeral rites in Hong Kong are presided over by Taoist priests. These are noisy affairs with cymbals and *suona* (a Chinese reed instrument). Some have elaborate rituals featuring props from coins to flaming swords that are meant to ensure the soul lets go of its worldly relationships.

Family Ethos

Traditionally, Confucian doctrines helped Chinese rulers to maintain domestic order. Emperors led by 'mandate of heaven'; government positions were filled by top-scoring candidates on exams in the Confucian classics. For historical reasons, Confucianism in this institutionalised form never existed in Hong Kong. Yet Confucian values are at the core of familial and social relationships in the former British colony. Two pillars of Confucian thought are respect for knowledge and filial piety. Hong Kong parents attach huge importance to academic performance; youngsters are trained to work hard as well as to treat parents and teachers with courtesy. Many adults live with their folks (though this is related to the city's exorbitant rent); almost everyone is expected to provide for their parents, though whether they do is another matter.

Buddhism

Buddhism is Hong Kong's dominant religion. It was first introduced here in about the 5th century, when the monk Pui To set up a hermitage in the western New Territories. The area, a stop on the ancient route linking Persia, Arabia and India to Guǎngzhōu, is regarded as the birthplace of Buddhism in the territory.

Although a tiny fraction of the population is purely and devoutly Buddhist, about a million practise some form of the religion, and use its funeral and exorcism rites. Generally speaking, the ritual of taking refuge in the Three Jewels (Buddha, Darma, Sangha) is regarded as the Buddhist initiation rite. Some followers abstain from meat on certain days of the month, others for longer periods. Very few are strict vegetarians.

A small Parsee community migrated to Hong Kong from Mumbai in the early colonial period. Despite their small number, the Parsees' influence has been great. At one time, three of the 13 board members of HSBC were Parsee. It was also a Parsee who founded the Star Ferry.

Life, Afterlife

Buddhist organisations here do not play an active political role, unlike some of their counterparts in Southeast Asia. They focus instead on providing palliative care and spiritual services. Every year on Remembrance Day (11 November), they hold a ceremony for the souls of the victims of the two World Wars and the Japanese invasion. Buddhist funerals are dignified affairs that can be quite elaborate, with some ceremonies lasting 49 days – the time it purportedly takes an average soul to find the conditions for its rebirth. Prayers are chanted every seven days to help the soul find rebirth in a higher realm ('happy human' versus 'cockroach', for instance). On the seventh day, souls are believed to revisit their homes. Everyone in the family stays in their room to avoid crossing paths with the loved one.

Taoism

Taoism is an indigenous Chinese religion more than 2000 years old. Though never declared a national faith, its presence is ubiquitous in most aspects of Chinese life. Unlike evangelical religions stressing crusading and personal conversion, Taoism simply offers its services, whether it's treatment for illness or protection from evil spirits, to everyone within its locale.

There are about 30,000 Muslims of various nationalities in Hong Kong. The city's earliest Muslims were seamen who settled in the area around Lower Lascar Row in Central. Subsequent Muslim migrants from South Asia were known to take up posts in the British colony's disciplinary forces.

Liturgical Function

The Hong Kong horseracing season, and all construction and filming projects, are preceded by Taoist rituals to appease the nature deities and ensure good feng shui. Necromancy, which strives for harmony between humanity and nature, is a practise influenced by Taoism. During the first two weeks of the Lunar New Year, millions of all creeds and faiths pay their respects at Taoist temples. Taoist priests preside over the majority of funeral rites in Hong Kong.

Christianity

Hong Kong's Christian community has more than 800,000 followers, with Protestants outnumbering Roman Catholics and having more young believers. About a third of the Catholics are Filipina domestic helpers. Most churches offer services in Cantonese and English, and some also in Tagalog.

Christianity has been in Hong Kong since the mid-19th century. In the early days, the Hong Kong Catholic Church provided support to the missionaries travelling to and from China, and served the Catholics in the British Army as well as Portuguese merchants and their families from Macau. In the ensuing decades, both Catholics and Protestants began working for the local community, founding schools, hospitals and welfare organsations. These services were, as they are now, open to followers and non-followers alike.

Survival Guide

Transport

ARRIVING IN HONG KONG

Most international travellers arrive and depart via Hong Kong International Airport. Travellers to and from mainland China can use ferry, road or rail links to Guǎngdōng and points beyond. Hong Kong is also accessible from Macau via ferry or helicopter.

More than 100 airlines operate between Hong Kong International Airport and some 190 destinations around the world. Flights include from New York (16 hours), Los Angeles (14 hours), Sydney (9½ hours), London (13 hours) and Běijīng (3½ hours). There are regular buses connecting Hong Kong with major destinations in neighbouring Guǎngdōng province. Twelve trains run daily from Hong Kong to Guǎngzhōu (two hours), and trains to Běijīng (24 hours) and Shànghǎi (19 hours) run on alternate days. Visas are required to cross the border to the mainland.

Regularly scheduled ferries link the China Ferry Terminal in Kowloon and/or the Hong Kong-Macau Ferry Terminal on Hong Kong Island with a string of towns and cities on the Pearl River Delta, including Macau. Trips take two to three hours.

Flights, cars and tours can be booked online at lonely planet.com.

Air

There are flights between Hong Kong and around 50 cities in mainland China, including Běijīng, Chéngdū, Kūnmíng and Shànghǎi. One-way fares are a bit more than half the return price. The national carrier is **Air China** (☑852 3970 9000; www. airchina.hk).

Other carriers include:

Cathay Pacific (Map p314; www.cathaypacific.com; 7th fl The Cameron, 33 Cameron Rd, Tsim Sha Tsui; Ⓜ Tsim Sha Tsui, exit A2) From Hong Kong, with connections to Cape Town, Port Elizabeth and Durban.

Dragonair (www.dragonair. com) Owned by Cathay Pacific, Dragonair specialises in regional flights and flies to 20 cities in mainland China.

Hong Kong Airlines (☑852 3151 1888; www.hongkong airlines.com) Budget airline specialis in regional routes, including 22 cities in mainland China.

Hong Kong International Airport

Designed by British architect Sir Norman Foster, the **Hong Kong International Airport** (HKG; Map p181; ☑852 2181 8888; www.hkairport.com) is on Chek Lap Kok, a largely reclaimed area off Lantau's northern coast. Highways, bridges (including the 2.2km-long Tsing Ma Bridge, one of the world's longest suspension bridges) and a fast train link the airport with Kowloon and Hong Kong Island.

The two terminals have a wide range of shops, restaurants, cafes, ATMs and moneychangers, incuding:

Hong Kong Hotels Association (香港酒店業協會; HKHA; Map p181; ☑852 2769 8822, 852 2383 8380; www.hkha. org; Hong Kong International Airport; ⊘7am-midnight) Counters are located inside the Buffer Halls. HKHA deals with midrange and top-end hotels only and does not handle hostels, guesthouses or other budget accommodation.

China Travel Service (中國旅行社, CTS; ☑customer service 852 2998 7333, tour hotline 852 2998 7888; www.ctshk.com; ⊘7am-10pm) Has four counters in the terminals, including one in Arrivals Hall A that issues **China** (Map p314; ☑852 2315 7171; www.ctshk.com; 1/F Alpha House, 27-33 Nathan Rd, Tsim Sha Tsui; ⊘9am-7pm Mon-Fri, 9am-5pm Sat & Sun; Ⓜ Tsim Sha Tsui, exit D1) visas (normally takes one working day).

Transport from the Airport

AIRPORT EXPRESS

Airport Express line (☑852 881 8888; www.mtr. com.hk; one way Central/Kowloon/Tsing Yi HK$100/90/60;

TRANSPORT ARRIVING IN HONG KONG

CLIMATE CHANGE & TRAVEL

Every form of transport that relies on carbon-based fuel generates CO_2, the main cause of human-induced climate change. Modern travel is dependent on aeroplanes, which might use less fuel per kilometre per person than most cars but travel much greater distances. The altitude at which aircraft emit gases (including CO_2) and particles also contributes to their climate change impact. Many websites offer 'carbon calculators' that allow people to estimate the carbon emissions generated by their journey and, for those who wish to do so, to offset the impact of the greenhouse gases emitted with contributions to portfolios of climate-friendly initiatives throughout the world. Lonely Planet offsets the carbon footprint of all staff and author travel.

⊙every 10min) is the fastest (and most expensive, other than a taxi) way to get to and from the airport.

Departures

From 5.54am to 12.48am for Central, calling at Kowloon station in Jordan, Tsing Yi island en route; the full trip takes 24 minutes. Tickets are available from vending machines at the airport and train stations.

Fares

Return fares for Central/Kowloon/Tsing Yi, valid for a month, cost HK$180/160/110. Children three to 11 years pay half-price. An Airport Express Travel Pass allows three days of unlimited travel on the MTR and Light Rail and one-way/return trips on the Airport Express (HK$250/350).

Shuttle buses

Airport Express also has two shuttle buses on Hong Kong Island (H1 and H2) and five in Kowloon (K1 to K5), with free transfers for passengers between Central and Kowloon stations and major hotels. The buses run every 12 to 20 minutes between 6.12am and 11.12pm. Schedules and routes are available at Airport Express and MTR stations and on the Airport Express website.

BUS

There are good bus links to/from the airport. These buses have plenty of room for luggage, and announcements are usually made in English, Cantonese and Mandarin notifying passengers of hotels at each stop. For more details on the routes, check the Transport section at www.hkairport.com.

Departures

Buses run every 10 to 30 minutes from about 6am to between midnight and 1am. There are also quite a few night buses (designated 'N').

Fares

Major hotel and guesthouse areas on Hong Kong Island are served by the A11 (HK$40) and A12 (HK$45) buses; the A21 (HK$33) covers similar areas in Kowloon. Bus drivers in Hong Kong do not give change, but it is available at the ground transport centre at the airport, as are Octopus cards. Normal returns are double the one-way fare. Unless otherwise stated, children aged between three and 11 years and seniors over 65 pay half-fare.

Tickets

Buy your ticket at the booth near the airport bus stand.

LIMOUSINE

There are limousine service counters in the arrivals hall and at the ground transportation centre, including **Parklane Limousine Service** (☑852 2730 0662; www.hongkonglimo.com) and **Intercontinental Hire Cars** (☑852 3193 9332; www.trans-island.com.hk). In a car seating up to four people, expect to pay HK$650 to HK$850 to destinations in Hong Kong Island and urban Kowloon and

from HK$600 to HK$1500 to the New Territories.

Car & Motorcycle

Hong Kong's transport system is so far-reaching and efficient that you will not need your own vehicle unless getting stuck in traffic is your idea of fun.

Coaches to Mainland China

CTS Express Coach (Map p298;☑852 2764 9803; http://ctsbus.hkcts.com)
Eternal East Cross-Border Coach (Map p314;☑852 3760 0888, 852 3412 6677; www.eebus.com; 13th fl, Kai Seng Commercial Centre, 4-6 Hankow Rd, Tsim Sha Tsui; ⊙7am-8pm) Mainland destinations from Hong Kong include Dōngguǎn, Fóshān, Guǎngzhōu, Huìzhōu, Kāipíng, Shēnzhèn's Bǎoān airport and Zhōngshān.

Ferry

Chu Kong Passenger Transport Company (☑852 2858 3876; www.cksp.com.hk) provides regularly scheduled ferries that link the **China Ferry Terminal** (中港碼頭; Map p314; China Hong Kong City, 33 Canton Rd, Tsim Sha Tsui) in Kowloon and/or the **Hong Kong–Macau Ferry Terminal** (Shun Tak Centre; Map p304; Shun Tak Centre,

200 Connaught Rd, Sheung Wan) on Hong Kong Island with a string of towns and cities on the Pearl River Delta.

Mainland destinations from Hong Kong include:

Shékǒu One hour

Shùndé Two hours

Zhàoqìng Four hours

Zhōngshān 1½ hours

Zhūhǎi 70 minutes

A fast ferry service called the **SkyPier** (☑852 2215 3232) links Hong Kong airport with nine Pearl River Delta destinations: Shēnzhèn Shékǒu, Shēnzhèn Fúyǒng, Dōngguǎn, Zhōngshān, Zhūhǎi, Guǎngzhōu Nánshā, Guǎngzhōu Lianhuashan, Macau (Maritime Ferry Terminal) and Macau (Taipa). The service enables travellers to board ferries directly without clearing Hong Kong customs and immigration. Book a ticket prior to boarding from the ticketing counter located at Transfer Area E2 at least 60 minutes before ferry departure time. Take the Automated People Move to the ferry terminal.

Train

One-way and return tickets for Běijīng and Shànghǎi can be booked 30 to 60 days in advance at MTR stations in Hung Hom, Mong Kok East, Kowloon Tong and Sha Tin, and at Tourist Services at Admiralty station.

There are direct rail links between Hung Hom and both Shànghǎi and Běijīng. Trains to Běijīng West train station (hard/soft/deluxe sleeper from HK$601/934/1191) depart on alternate days at 3.15pm, arriving at 3.13pm the following day. Trains to Shànghǎi (hard/soft/deluxe sleeper from HK$530/825/1039) also depart on alternate days at 3.15pm, arriving at 10.22am the following day.

GETTING AROUND HONG KONG

Hong Kong is small and crowded, and public transport is the only practical way to move people. The ultramodern Mass Transit Railway (MTR) is the quickest way to get to most urban destinations. The bus system is extensive and as efficient as the traffic allows, but it can be bewildering for short-term travellers. Ferries are fast and economical and throw in spectacular harbour views at no extra cost. Trams serve the purpose if you're not in a hurry.

For information on Octopus travel cards, see p263.

Bicycle

Cycling in urbanised Kowloon or Hong Kong Island would be suicide, but in the quiet areas of the islands (including southern Hong Kong Island) and the New Territories, a bike can be a lovely way to get around. It's more recreational than a form of transport, though – the hilly terrain will slow you down (unless you're mountain biking). Be advised that shops and kiosks renting out bicyles tend to run out early on weekends if the weather is good.

Wong Kei (旺記單車; ☑852 2662 5200; Ting Kok Rd, Tai Mei Tuk) offers bicycle hire.

Boat

Despite Hong Kong's comprehensive road and rail public-transport system, the territory still relies very much on ferries to get across the harbour and to reach the Outlying Islands. The cross-harbour Star Ferry services are faster and cheaper than buses and the MTR. They're also great fun and afford stunning views. While Lantau can be reached by MTR and bus, for the other Outlying

Islands ferries remain the only game in town.

Star Ferry

You can't say you've 'done' Hong Kong until you've taken a ride on a **Star Ferry** (天星小輪; Map p298; ☑852 2367 7065; www.starferry.com.hk; adult HK$2.50-3.40, child HK$1.50-2.10; ⊙every 6-12min, 6.30am-11.30pm; Ⓜ Hong Kong, exit A2), that wonderful fleet of electric-diesel vessels with names like *Morning Star, Celestial Star* and *Twinkling Star*.

There are two Star Ferry routes, but by far the most popular is the one running between Central (Pier 7) and Tsim Sha Tsui. Quite frankly, there's no other trip like it in the world. Star Ferry also links Wan Chai with Tsim Sha Tsui.

The coin-operated turnstiles do not give change, but you can get change from the ticket window or use an Octopus card.

Outlying Island Ferries

Regular ferry services link the main Outlying Islands to Hong Kong. Fares are reasonable and the ferries are comfortable and usually air-conditioned. They have toilets, and some have a basic bar that serves snacks and cold drinks. The ferries can get very crowded on Saturday afternoon and all day Sunday, especially in the warmer months.

Ferry Services

Three separate ferry companies operate services to the Outlying Islands from the ferry terminal in Central. Another, Tsui Wah Ferry Service, offers services to less-visited but scenic spots.

Discovery Bay Transportation Services (www.dbcommunity. hk) Fast-speed regular ferries between Central (Pier 3) and Discovery Bay on Lantau Island.

Hong Kong & Kowloon Ferry (HKKF; ☑852 2815 6063; www. hkkf.com.hk) Serves destinations on Lamma Island and Peng Chau only.

New World First Ferry
(NWFF; Map p298;☑852 2131 8181; www.nwff.com.hk; Ⓜ Hong Kong, exit A1 or A2) Boats sail to/from Cheung Chau, Peng Chau and Lantau Island, and connect all three via an interisland service (regular/deluxe class/fast ferry HK$13.20/20.70/25.80), every 1¾ hours from 6am to 10.50pm.

Tsui Wah Ferry Service (翠華旅遊有限公司;☑852 2527 2513, 852 2272 2022; www.traway.com.hk) Slower ferries from Ma Liu Shui (15 minutes' walk from the University MTR station) to Tap Mun and Sai Kung Peninsula (twice daily); Ma Liu Shui to Tung Ping Chau (only on weekend and public holidays); and Aberdeen to Po Toi Island (on Tuesday, Thursday, Saturday and Sunday).

Bus

Hong Kong's extensive bus system will take you just about anywhere in the territory. Since Kowloon and the northern side of Hong Kong Island are so well served by the MTR, most visitors use the buses primarily to explore the southern side of Hong Kong Island, the New Territories and Lantau Island.

Departures

Most buses run from 5.30am or 6am until midnight or 12.30am, though there are smaller numbers of night buses that run from 12.45am to 5am or later.

Fares

Bus fares cost HK$4 to HK$46, depending on the destination. Fares for night buses cost from HK$7 to HK$32. You will need exact change or an Octopus card.

Bus Stations

On Hong Kong Island the most important bus stations are **Central** (Map p298; Exchange Sq; Ⓜ Hong Kong, exit A1 or A2) and **Admiralty** (Map p306; ground fl, United Centre, 95 Queensway, Admiralty; Ⓜ Admiralty, exit D). From these stations you can catch buses to Aberdeen, Repulse Bay, Stanley and other destinations on the southern side of Hong Kong Island.

In Kowloon the **Star Ferry bus terminal** (Map p314) has buses heading up Nathan Rd and to the Hung Hom train station.

Most parts of Lantau Island are served by the **New Lantau Bus** (☑852 2984 9848; www.newlantaobus.com). Major bus stations are located in Mui Wo ferry terminal and Tung Chung MTR station.

Route Information

Figuring out which bus you want can be difficult, but **City Bus** (☑852 2873 0818; www.nwstbus.com.hk) and **New World First Bus** (☑852 2136 8888; www.nwstbus.com.hk), owned by the same company, plus **Kowloon Motor Bus** (KMB; ☑852 2745 4466; www.kmb.hk) provide user-friendly route search on their websites. KMB also has a route app for smartphones.

Car & Motorcycle

Hong Kong's maze of one-way streets and dizzying expressways isn't for the fainthearted. Traffic is heavy and finding a parking space is difficult and very expensive. If you are determined to see Hong Kong under your own steam, do yourself a favour and rent a car with a driver.

Road Rules

Vehicles drive on the left-hand side of the road in Hong Kong, as in the UK, Australia and Macau, but *not* in mainland China. Seat belts must be worn by the driver and all passengers, in both the front and back seats. Police are strict and give out traffic tickets at the drop of a hat.

Driving licences

Hong Kong allows most foreigners over the age of 18 to drive for up to 12 months with a valid licence from home. It's still a good idea to carry an International Driving Permit (IDP) as well. Car-rental firms accept IDPs or driving licences from your home country. Drivers must usually be at least 25 years of age.

Car Hire

Ace Hire Car (☑852 2572 7663, 24hr 852 6108 7399; www.acehirecar.com.hk; Flat F, 1st fl, Nam Wing Bldg, 49-51A Sing Woo Rd, Happy Valley; 🚌1 from Des Voeux Rd Central) Hires out chauffeur-driven Mercedes Benz for HK$250 per hour (minimum two to five hours, depending on location).

Avis (Map p308;☑852 2511 9338; www.avis.com.hk; Shop 2 & 3, ground fl, Centre Point, 181-185 Gloucester Rd, Wan Chai; ⊙10am-7pm; Ⓜ Causeway Bay, exit C) Hires out cars for a day/weekend/week starting from HK$930/1200/1500, nearly double on weekends. A chauffeur-driven Toyota is HK$600 per hour.

Minibus

Minibuses are vans with no more than 16 seats. They come in two varieties: red and green:

Red minibuses (HK$7 to HK$40) Cream-coloured with a red roof or stripe; pick up and discharge passengers wherever hailed or asked to stop along fixed routes. Destination and price displayed on a card propped up on windscreen, but often only written in Chinese.

You usually hand the driver the fare when you get off, and change is given. You can use your Octopus card on certain routes.

Green minibuses (HK$3 to HK$24) Cream-coloured with a green roof or stripe; these make designated stops. You must put the exact fare in the cash box when you get in or you can use your Octopus card. Two popular routes are the 6 (HK$6.40) from Hankow Rd in Tsim Sha Tsui to Tsim Sha Tsui East and Hung Hom station in Kowloon, and the 1 (HK$10) to Victoria Peak from next to Hong Kong station.

MTR

The **Mass Transit Railway** (MTR; ☑852 2881 8888; www. mtr.com.hk) is the name for Hong Kong's rail system comprising underground, overland and Light Rail (slower tram-style) services. Universally known as the 'MTR', it is clean, fast and safe, and transports around four million people daily.

Though it costs slightly more than bus travel, the MTR is the quickest way to get to most destinations in Hong Kong.

Train

There are around 90 stations on nine underground and overland lines, and a Light Rail network that covers the northwest New Territories. Smoking, eating and drinking are not permitted in MTR stations or on the trains, and violators are subject to a fine of HK$5000.

DEPARTURES
Trains run every two to 14 minutes from around 6am to sometime between midnight and 1am.

EXITS
MTR exit signs use an alpha-numerical system and there can be as many as a dozen to choose from. You may find yourself studying the exit table from time to time and scratching your head. There are maps of the local area at each exit.

FARES
Tickets cost HK$8 to HK$35, but trips to stations bordering mainland China (Lo Wu and Lok Ma Chau) can cost up to HK$60. Children aged between three and 11 years and seniors over 65 pay half-fare. Ticket machines accept notes and coins and dispense change.

TICKETS
Once you've passed through the turnstile to begin a journey you have 90 minutes to complete it before the ticket becomes invalid. If you have underpaid (by mistake or otherwise), you can make up the difference at an MTR service counter next to the turnstile.

PEAK HOURS
If possible, it's best to avoid the rush hours: 7.30am to 9.30am and 5pm to 7pm weekdays.

Light Rail Lines

The MTR's Light Rail system is rather like a modern, air-conditioned version of the trams in Hong Kong, but it's much faster. It runs in the northwest New Territories.

DEPARTURES
Operates from about 5.30am to between 12.15am and 1am. Trams run every four to 12 minutes, depending on the line and time of day.

FARES
HK$5.50 to HK$8, depending on the number of zones (from one to five) travelled; children and seniors over 65 pay from HK$3 to HK$4.

TICKETS
Buy single-journey tickets from vending machines on the platforms. There are no gates or turnstiles and customers are trusted to validate tickets or Octopus cards when boarding and exiting.

Taxi

Hong Kong taxis are a bargain compared with those in other world-class cities. With more than 18,000 cruising the streets of the territory, they're easy to flag down, except during rush hour, when it rains or during the driver shift-change period (around 4pm daily).

Taxis are colour-coded:

Red with silver roofs Urban taxis – those in Kowloon and on Hong Kong Island. Can go anywhere except Lantau.

Green with white tops New Territories taxis.

Blue Lantau taxis.

Red In New Territories take these if your destination is in Hong Kong, Kowloon or the city centres of the new towns in New Territories.

Availability

When a taxi is available, there should be a red 'For Hire' sign illuminated on the

TAXI FARES

TYPE OF TAXI	FIRST 2KM (HK$)	EVERY ADDITIONAL 200M & MINUTE OF WAITING
Urban taxi (red)	22	HK$1.60 (HK$1 if fare exceeds HK$78)
New Territories taxi (green)	18.50	HK$1.40 (HK$1 if fare exceeds HK$60.50)
Lantau taxi (blue)	17	HK$1.40 (HK$1.20 if fare exceeds HK$143)

meter that's visible through the windscreen. At night the 'Taxi' sign on the roof will be lit up as well. Taxis will not stop at bus stops or in restricted zones where a yellow line is painted next to the kerb.

Complaints

Though most drivers are scrupulously honest, if you feel you've been ripped off, take down the taxi or driver's licence number (usually displayed on the sun visor in front) and contact the Transport Complaints Unit hotline (www.info.gov. hk/tcu/complaint) or the **Transport Department hotline** (☑852 2804 2600; www.td.gov.hk/en/contact_us/ index.html) to lodge a complaint. Be sure to have all the relevant details: when, where and how much.

Fees

There is a luggage fee of HK$5 per bag, but (depending on the size) not all drivers insist on this payment. It costs an extra HK$5 to book a taxi by telephone. There are no extra late-night charges and no extra passenger charges. Passengers must pay the toll if a taxi goes through the many Hong Kong harbour or mountain tunnels or uses the Lantau Link to Tung Chung or the airport. Though the Cross-Harbour Tunnel costs only HK$10, you'll have to pay HK$20 if, say, you take a Hong Kong taxi from Hong Kong Island to Kowloon. If you manage to find a Kowloon taxi returning 'home', you'll pay only HK$10. (It works the other way round as well, of course.)

Lost property

If you leave something behind in a taxi, call the **Road Co-op Lost & Found hotline** (☑852 187 2920; www. yp.com.hk/taxi/); most drivers turn in lost property.

HAILING A CROSS-HARBOUR TAXI

Hailing a cross-harbour taxi can be a frustrating task. There are three main ways to snag one:

➡ Look for a taxi with its lights on, but its 'Out of Service' sign up. This generally means the taxi is looking for a cross-harbour fare.

➡ Find a (rare) cross-harbour taxi stand.

➡ Hail a cab with a sort of 'walk like an Egyptian' gesture, snaking your arm as if in imitation of a wave. Taxis potentially interested in cross-harbour fares will stop to negotiate.

Language

Some taxi drivers speak English well; others don't know a word of English. It's never a bad idea to have your destination written down in Chinese.

Paying

Try to carry smaller bills and coins; most drivers are hesitant to make change for HK$500.

Seat belts

The law requires that everyone in a vehicle wears a seat belt. Both driver and passenger(s) will be fined if stopped by the police and not wearing a seat belt, and most drivers will gently remind you to buckle up before proceeding.

Tipping

You can tip up to 10%, but most Hong Kong people just leave the little brown coins and a dollar or two.

Tickets & Passes

Octopus Card (www.octopus cards.com) A rechargeable smartcard valid on the MTR and most forms of public transport. It also allows you to make purchases at retail outlets across the territory (such as convenience stores and supermarkets). The card costs HK$150 (HK$70 for children and seniors), which includes a HK$50 refundable deposit and HK$100 worth of travel. Octopus fares are about 5% cheaper than ordinary fares on the MTR. You can buy one and recharge at any MTR station.

Airport Express Travel Pass (one way/return HK$250/350) As well as travel to/from the airport, it allows three consecutive days of unlimited travel on the MTR.

MTR Tourist Day Pass (adult/ child 3-11yr HK$65/35) Valid on the MTR for 24 hours after the first use.

Tourist Cross-Boundary Travel Pass (1/2 consecutive days HK$85/120) Allows unlimited travel on the MTR and two single journeys to/from Lo Wu or Lok Ma Chau stations.

Tram

Hong Kong's venerable old trams, operated by **Hong Kong Tramways** (☑852 2548 7102; www.hktramways. com; fares HK$2.30; ◷6am-midnight), are tall, narrow double-deckers. They are slow, but they're cheap and a great way to explore the city. Try to get a seat at the front window on the upper deck for a first-class view while rattling through the crowded streets.

For a flat fare (dropped in a box beside the driver as you disembark, or use an Octopus card) you can rattle along as far as you like over 16km

MACAU PENINSULA TRANSPORT

Most travellers arrive in Macau by ferry from Hong Kong. If you are coming from mainland China, you can take the ferry or a bus from Guǎngdōng, or fly from select cities in mainland China.

Macau International Airport is connected to a limited number of destinations in Asia. If you are coming from outside Asia and destined for Macau, your best option is to fly to Hong Kong International Airport and take a ferry to Macau without going through Hong Kong customs.

Nationals of Australia, Canada, the EU, New Zealand and most other countries (but not US citizens) can purchase their China visas at Zhūhǎi on the border, but it will ultimately save you time if you get one in advance. These are available in Hong Kong or in Macau from **China Travel Service** (中國旅行社; Zhōngguó Lǚxíngshè; CTS; Map p196; ☑853 2870 0888; www.cts.com.mo; Nam Kwong Bldg, 207 Avenida do Dr Rodrigo Rodrigues; ⏲9am-6pm), usually in one day.

Bus

Public buses and minibuses run by TCM (www.tcm.com.mo) and **Transmac** (☑853 2827 1122; www.transmac.com.mo) operate from 6am until shortly after midnight. Fares – MOP$3.20 on the peninsula, MOP$4.20 to Taipa Village, MOP$5 to Coloane Village and MOP$6.40 to Hác Sá beach – are dropped into a box upon entry (exact change needed), or you can pay with a Macau Pass, which can be purchased from various supermarkets and convenience stores. The card costs MOP$130 at first purchase, which includes a refundable deposit of MOP$30. A minimum of MOP$50 is required to add money to the card each time. Expect buses to be very crowded.

The *Macau Tourist Map* has a full list of bus company routes and it's worth picking one up from one of the Macau Government Tourist Office (MGTO) outlets. You can also check the routes online. The two most useful buses on the peninsula are buses 3 and 3A, which run between the ferry terminal and the city centre, near the post office. Both continue up to the border crossing with the mainland, as does bus 5, which can be boarded along Avenida Almeida Ribeiro. Bus 12 runs from the ferry terminal, past the Lisboa Hotel and then up to Lou Lim Ioc Garden and Kun Iam Temple. The best services to Taipa and Coloane are buses 21A, 25 and 26A. Buses to the airport are AP1, 26, MT1 and MT2.

Ferry

Macau's main ferry terminal, **Macau Maritime Ferry Terminal** (外港客運碼頭; Terminal Marítimo de Passageiros do Porto Exterior; Map p196; Outer Harbour, Macau), is in the outer harbour.

TurboJet (Map p196; ☑bookings 852 2921 6688, in Hong Kong 852 790 7039, information 852 2859 3333; www.turbojet.com.hk; economy/superclass Mon-Fri HK$153/315, Sat & Sun HK$166/337, night crossing HK$189/358) has the most sailings to Hong K. The one-hour trip departs from the Hong Kong–Macau Ferry Terminal and Macau Maritime Ferry Terminal; see TurboJet's website for services to Hong Kong International Airport.

CotaiJet (☑853 2885 0595; www.cotaijet.com.mo; weekday fare to Hong Kong regular/1st class MOP$154/267) departs every half-hour from 7.30am to midnight, and runs between the Taipa Temporary Ferry Terminal and Hong Kong–Macau Ferry Terminal; a feeder shuttle-bus service drops off at destinations along the Cotai Strip. Check CotaiJet's website for services to Hong Kong International Airport.

Sampans & ferries Boats (MOP$12.50, hourly 8am to 4pm) run to Wānzái from a small pier near where Rua das Lorchas meets Rua do Dr Lourenço Pereira Marques. MOP$20 departure tax.

Yuet Tung Shipping Co (粵通船務有限公司; Map p200; ☑853 2893 9944, 853 2877 4478; www.ytmacau.com; Point 11A Inner Harbour, Inner Harbour Ferry Terminal) has ferries connecting Macau's Taipa temporary ferry terminal (MOP$238, 1½ hours, seven times daily) with Shékǒu in Shēnzhèn on mainland China and Shēnzhèn airport. Ferries also leave from Macau maritime ferry terminal (MOP$30, every half-hour, 8am to 4.15pm) for Wānzái in Zhūhǎi.

of track, 3km of which wends its way into Happy Valley. There are six routes but they all move on the same tracks along the northern coast of Hong Kong Island. The longest run (Kennedy Town–Shau Kei Wan, with a change at Western Market) takes about 1½ hours.

Hong Kong Tramways also offers an hour-long TramOramic tour, which lets you experience the city on an open-top, faux-vintage tram. An audio guide is available, souvenirs are for sale on board, and there are displays of vintage tickets and tram models. Three departures daily; check the website for details.

Peak Tram

The **Peak Tram** (Map p298; ☑852 2522 0922; www.thepeak.com.hk; Lower Terminus, 33 Garden Rd, Central; one-way/return adult HK$28/40, child 3-11yr & seniors over 65yr HK$11/18; ⊙7am-midnight; Ⓜ Central, exit J2) is not really a tram but a cable-hauled funicular railway that has been scaling the 396m ascent to the highest point on Hong Kong Island since 1888. It is thus the oldest form of public transport in the territory. It's such a steep ride that the floor is angled to help standing passengers stay upright.

The Peak Tram runs every 10 to 15 minutes from 7am to midnight. The lower terminus is behind the St John's Building. The upper tram terminus is in the **Peak Tower** (128 Peak Rd, Victoria Peak). Avoid going on Sunday and public holidays when there are usually long queues. Octopus cards (p263) can be used.

Between 10am and 11.40pm, open-deck (or air-conditioned) bus 15C (HK$4.20, every 15 to 20 minutes) takes passengers between the bus terminus near Central Ferry Pier 7 and the lower tram terminus.

TOURS

Hong Kong has a profusion of organised tours. There are tours available to just about anywhere in the territory and they can make good a option if you have limited time, want more in-depth knowledge in a short time, or don't want to deal with public transport. Some are standard excursions covering major sights, while others may give you a deeper experience of a neighbourhood. There are also speciality tours such as food tours, WWII tours and architecture tours.

Hong Kong Tourism Board (香港旅遊發展局; Map p314; Star Ferry Concourse, Tsim Sha Tsui; ⊙8am-8pm; 🚢Star Ferry) has recommendations, and tours run by individual companies can usually be booked at any HKTB branch.

Harbour Tours

The easiest way to see the full extent of Victoria Harbour from sea level is to join a circular **Star Ferry Harbour Tour** (天星小輪; Map p298; ☑852 2367 7065; www.starferry.com.hk; ⊙every 6-12min, 6.30am-11.30pm; Ⓜ Hong Kong, exit A2), of which there are a number of different options. Most of the tours depart from the Star Ferry Pier in Tsim Sha Tsui, but there are also departures from the piers at Central and Wan Chai; see the website for details.

Single daytime round trip Departs hourly between 11.55pm and 5.55pm daily; costs HK$95 for adults and HK$86 for concessions (children aged three to 12 years, seniors over 65).

Night round trip departs at 5.55pm and 8.55pm and is HK$175 for adults and HK$158 concessions.

Symphony of Lights Harbour Cruise Departs at 7.15pm or 7.55pm depending on

the season and takes in the nightly sound-and-light show over Victoria Harbour; it costs HK$200 for adults, HK$180 concessions.

Some operators offer tours with drinks, food and even buffet.

Hong Kong Ferry Group (☑852 2802 2886; www.cruise.com.hk; adult/child from HK$350/250) Offers two harbour cruises in a large boat with buffet dinner and live band performance; it costs HK$350 for adults and HK$250 for children.

Jaspa's Party Junk (☑852 2869 0733; http://www.casteloconcepts.com; adult HK$700, child HK$150-500) Boat for up to 40 people with a minimum booking of 14. Prices are per person and include all drinks and food.

Water Tours (Map p314; ☑852 2926 3868; www.watertours.com.hk; 6th fl Carnarvon Plaza, 20 Carnarvon Rd, Tsim Sha Tsui) Six different tours of the harbour, as well as dinner and cocktail cruises, are available. Prices range from HK$260 (HK$170 for children aged two to 12 years) for the Morning Harbour & Noon Day Gun Firing Cruise, to HK$350 (HK$260 for children) for the Harbour Lights and HK$900 (HK$700 for children) for the Aberdeen Dinner Cruise.

Nature Tours

Eco Travel (綠恆生態旅遊;☑852 3105 0767; www.ecotravel.hk) This eco-travel company offers tours exploring Hong Kong's fishing and ocean culture, wetlands tours, a nature bike tour, and a trip to the Geopark of the northern New Territories. Some are only in Cantonese – check ahead regarding English availability.
Hong Kong Dolphinwatch

(香港海豚觀察; Map p314; ☑852 2984 1414; www.hkdol phinwatch.com; 15th fl, Middle Block, 1528A Star House, 3 Salisbury Rd, Tsim Sha Tsui; adult/child HK$420/210; ☺cruises Wed, Fri & Sun) ✍ Offers 2½-hour cruises to see dolphins in their natural habitat every Wednesday, Friday and Sunday year-round. About 97% of the cruises result in the sighting of at least one dolphin; if none are spotted, passengers are offered a free trip. Guides assemble in the lobby of the Kowloon Hotel in Tsim Sha Tsui at 9am for the bus to Tung Chung via the Tsing Ma Bridge, from where the boat departs; the tours return at 1pm.

Kayak & Hike (☑852 9300 5197; www.kayak-and-hike. com) The seven-hour Sai Kung Geopark kayak tour provides an exciting option for exploring the beauty of Sai Kung. It takes you to a kayak base at nearby Bluff Island in a speedboat, from where you paddle to a beach to enjoy swimming and snorkelling. Departs 8.45am at Sai Kung old pier (HK$800 per person). You need to pack your lunch.

Recommended Geopark Guide System (http://www. hkr2g.net/en_index.htm) The government's R2G website has trained guides and agency recommendations for tours of Hong Kong Global Geopark.

Walk Hong Kong (☑852 9187 8641; www.walkhongkong. com) Offers a range of hiking tours to some of most beautiful places in Hong Kong, includ-ing deserted beaches in Sai Kung (HK$800 per person, 8½ hours), Dragon's Back in Shek O (HK$500, four hours) and WWII battlefields (HK$500, half-day), as well as half-day local market tours (HK$450).

City & Culture Tours

Big Bus Company (Map p314; ☑852 3102 9021; www.bigbus tours.com; Unit KP-38, 1st fl, Star Ferry Pier, Tsim Sha Tsui; adult/child from HK$450/400; ☺9am-6pm) A good way to get your bearings in the city is on the hop-on, hop-off, open-topped double-deckers. Three tours are available: the Kowloon Route takes in much of the Tsim Sha Tsui and Hung Hom waterfront; the Hong Kong Island Route explores Central, Admiralty, Wan Chai and Causeway Bay; and the Green Tour goes to Stanley Market and Aberdeen.

Big Foot Tours (☑852 6075 2727; www.bigfoottour.com) Small group tours tailored to your interests get behind the scenes of daily Hong Kong life. Itineraries can focus on food, architecture, nature or

whatever strikes your fancy. Four-hour tours are about HK$700 per person, depending on group size.

Gray Line (☑852 2368 7111; www.grayline.com.hk; adult/ child 3-11yr from HK$530/430) Has a one-day tour taking in Man Mo Temple, Victoria Peak, Aberdeen and Stanley Market.

Heliservices (☑852 2802 0200; www.heliservices.com. hk; ☺9am-before sunset) If you hanker to see Hong Kong from on high (and hang the expense), Heliservices has chartered Aero-spatiale Squirrels for up to five passengers. A 15-minute tour that takes in the Hong Kong skyline is HK$1999 per seat.

Splendid Tours & Travel (☑852 2316 2151; www. splendid.hk; adult/child from HK$490/390) Runs several half-day tours and one full-day tour to Lantau Island, Sai Kung, and various bays on Hong Kong Island. Tours start from HK$490 per person.

Sky Bird Tours (☑852 2736 2282; www.skybird.com.hk) A traditional lifestyle tour. Learn all about taichi, feng shui and Chinese tea with a four-hour tour (HK$460 per person). Tours depart 7.30am from the Excelsior Hotel in Causeway Bay and 7.45am from the Salisbury YMCA in Tsim Sha Tsui on Mon-day, Wednesday and Friday.

Directory A–Z

Discount Cards
Hostel Card

If you arrive without a Hostelling International (HI) card, you can apply for one at the **Hong Kong Youth Hostels Association** (香港青年旅舍協會; HKYHA; ☑852 2788 1638; www.yha.org.hk; Shop 118, 1st fl, Fu Cheong Shopping Centre,Shum Mong Rd, Sham Shui Po; HI card under/over 18yr $70/150; ⊗9am-7pm Mon-Fri, 10am-5pm Sat; Ⓜ Nam Cheong, exit A) or at any affiliated hostel. There are seven HI-affiliated hostels in Hong Kong, mostly in remote locations in the New Territories.

Seniors Card

Most museums are either free or half-price for those over 60. Most forms of public transport offer a 50% discount to anyone over 65. A passport or ID with a photo should be sufficient proof of age.

Student, Youth & Teacher Cards

Hong Kong Student Travel, based at **Sincerity Travel** (永安旅遊; Map p314; ☑852 2730 2800; www.hkst.com.hk/; Room 833-8343, Star House, Salisbury Rd, Tsim Sha Tsui; ⊗9.30am-8pm Mon-Sat, noon-6pm Sun; ⛴Star Ferry), can instantly issue you any of the following cards for HK$100. Make sure you bring your student ID or other credentials along with you.

International Student Identity Card (ISIC, www.wysetc.org) Provides discounts on some transport and admission to museums and other sights.

International Youth Travel Card (IYTC) Gives similar discounts to the ISIC card for anyone aged under 26 but not a student.

International Teacher Identity Card (ITIC) Holders may enjoy discounts at certain bookshops.

Hong Kong Museums Pass

This pass allows multiple entries to seven of Hong Kong's museums. Passes are valid for seven consecutive days, cost HK$30 and are available from **Hong Kong Tourism Board** (香港旅遊發展局; Map p314; Star Ferry Concourse, Tsim Sha Tsui; ⊗8am-8pm; ⛴Star Ferry) outlets and participating museums.

Embassies & Consulates

About 120 countries have representative offices in Hong Kong, including over 60 consulates-general, 60 consulates and six 'officially recognised bodies'. These include:

Australian Consulate (Map p308;☑852 2827 8881; http://hongkong.china.embassy.gov.au; 23rd fl, Harbour Centre, 25 Harbour Rd, Wan Chai; ⊗9am-5pm Mon-Fri; Ⓜ Wan Chai, exit C)

British Consulate (Map p306; ☑852 2901 3000; www.gov.uk/government/world/hong-kong; 1 Supreme Court Rd, Admiralty; ⊗8.30am-5.15pm Mon-Fri; Ⓜ Admiralty, exit F)

Canadian Consulate (Map p298;☑852 3719 4700; 5th fl, Tower 3, Exchange Square, 8 Connaught Place, Central; Ⓜ Central, exit A)

French Consulate (Map p306;☑852 3196 6100; www.consulfrance-hongkong.org; 26th fl, Tower II, Admiralty Centre, 18 Harcourt Rd, Admiralty; Ⓜ Admiralty, exit C2)

German Consulate (Map p306; ☑852 2105 8788; www.hong kong.diplo.de; 21st fl, United Centre, 95 Queensway, Admiralty; Ⓜ Admiralty, exit C2)

Indian Consulate (Map p306; ☑852 3970 9900; www.cgihk. gov.in; Unit A, 16th fl, United Centre, 95 Queensway, Admiralty; ⊗9am-5.30pm Mon-Fri)

Irish Consulate (Map p298; ☑852 2527 4897; www.dfa.ie/irish-consulate/hong-kong; 33 Des Voeux Rd Central, Sheung Wan; ⊗10am-noon & 2.30-4.30pm Mon-Fri; Ⓜ Central)

Japanese Consulate (Map p298;☑852 2522 1184; www.hk.emb-japan.go.jp; 46-47th fl, 1 Exchange Sq, 8 Connaught Pl, Central; Ⓜ Central, exit D1)

Kazakhstani Consulate (Map p304;☑general enquiries 852 2548 3841, visa application 852 2548 3773; www.consul-kazakh

stan.org.hk; Unit 3106, 31 fl, West Tower, Shun Tak Centre, 200 Connaught Rd Central, Sheung Wan; ⊗visa applications 10am-1pm (drop-off), 3-5pm (pick-up) Mon, Wed, Fri)

Laotian Consulate (Map p304; ☑852 2544 1186; 14th fl, Arion Commercial Centre, 2-12 Queen's Rd West, Sheung Wan)

Nepalese Consulate (Map p316; ☑852 2369 7813; 715 China Aerospace Tower, Concordia Plaza, 1 Science Museum Rd, Tsim Sha Tsui; ⓂHung Hom, exit D1)

Netherlands Consulate (Map p298; ☑852 2599 9200; http://hongkong.nlconsulate.org; Room 2402B, 24th fl, 23 Harbour Rd, Great Eagle Centre)

New Zealand Consulate (Map p308; ☑852 2525 5044; www.eit.ac.nz; Room 6501, 65th fl, Central Plaza, 18 Harbour Rd, Wan Chai; ⊗8.30am-1pm, 2-5pm Mon-Fri; ⓂWan Chai, exit C)

US Consulate (Map p298; ☑852 2523 9011; 26 Garden Rd, Central; ⓂCentral, exit J2)

Electricity

220V/50Hz

Emergency

| Police emergency | ☑999 |
| Police | ☑852 2527 7177 |

Health

The occasional avian- or swine-flu outbreak notwithstanding, health conditions in the region are good. Travellers have a low risk of contracting infectious diseases compared to much of Asia. The health system is generally excellent. However, observe good personal and food hygiene and take antimosquito measures to prevent infectious diseases such as dengue fever. If your health insurance doesn't cover you for medical expenses abroad, consider supplemental insurance.

Environmental Hazards

MOSQUITOES
These are prevalent in Hong Kong. You should always use insect repellent during warm and hot weather, and if you're bitten use hydrocortisone cream to reduce swelling.

CENTIPEDES
Lamma Island is home to large red centipedes, which have a poisonous bite that causes swelling and discomfort in most cases, but can be more dangerous (and supposedly in very rare cases deadly) for young children.

WILD BOARS & DOGS
Wild boars and aggressive dogs are a minor hazard in some of the more remote parts of the New Territories. Wild boars are shy and retiring most of the time, but are dangerous when they feel threatened, so give them a wide berth and avoid disturbing thick areas of undergrowth.

SNAKES
There are many snakes in Hong Kong, and some are deadly, but you are unlikely to encounter any. Still, always take care when bushwalking, particularly on Lamma and Lantau Islands. Go straight to a public hospital if bitten; private doctors do not stock antivenene.

Required Vaccinations
There are no required vaccinations for entry into Hong Kong, unless you will be travelling to the mainland or elsewhere in the region.

Health Insurance
Visitors without a Hong Kong Identity card can use public hospitals by paying private market rates, which are multiple times the normal rate. However, if you have the appropriate supporting documents, many private health insurances reimburse these fees.

A health insurance plan with international coverage may allow you to receive inpatient medical and certain surgical treatments in Hong Kong, but do check with your insurer about coverage of outpatient services, ie services that do not require overnight stay in hospital.

Tap Water
Hong Kong tap water conforms to World Health Organization standards and is considered safe to drink, though many locals prefer bottled for reasons of flavour and prestige.

Medical Services
The standard of medical care in Hong Kong is generally excellent but expensive. Always take out travel insurance before you travel. Healthcare is divided into public and private, and there is no interaction between the two.

PRACTICALITIES

Media

➡ The main English-language newspaper in the city is the *South China Morning Post* (www.scmp.com). A daily broadsheet that has always toed the government line, both before and after the handover, it has the largest circulation and is read by more Hong Kong Chinese than expatriates.

➡ Other options include *Hong Kong Standard* (www.thestandard.com.hk) and *Hong Kong Economic Journal* (www.ejinsight.com).

➡ The Běijīng mouthpiece *China Daily* (www.chinadaily.com.cn) also prints an English-language edition.

➡ Hong Kong has its share of English-language periodicals, including a slew of homegrown (and Asian-focused) business-related magazines. *Time*, *Newsweek* and the *Economist* are all available in their current editions.

Smoking

All indoor areas of eateries are now smoke-free. The ban does not apply to unsheltered outdoor spaces.

Weights & Measures

Although the international metric system is in official use in Hong Kong, traditional Chinese weights and measures are still common. At local markets, meat, fish and produce are sold by the *léung*, equivalent to 37.8g, and the *gàn* (catty), which is equivalent to about 600g. There are 16 *léung* to the *gàn*. Gold and silver are sold by the *tael*, which is exactly the same as a *léung*.

CLINICS

There are many English-speaking general practitioners, specialists and dentists in Hong Kong, who can be found through your consulate, a private hospital or the *Yellow Pages*. If money is tight, take yourself to the nearest public-hospital emergency room and be prepared to wait.

The general enquiry number for hospitals is ☑2300 6555.

HOSPITALS & EMERGENCY ROOMS

In the case of an emergency, all ambulances (☑999) will take you to a government-run public hospital where, as a visitor, you will be required to pay a hefty fee for using emergency services. Treatment is guaranteed in any case; people who cannot pay immediately will be billed later. While the emergency care is excellent, you may wish to transfer to a private hospital once you are stable.

HONG KONG ISLAND

Queen Mary Hospital (瑪麗醫院;☑852 2255 3838; www3.ha.org.hk/qmh; 102 Pok Fu Lam Rd, Pok Fu Lam; ☐30x, 55, 90B, 91) Public.

Ruttonjee Hospital (律敦治醫院; Map p308;☑852 2291 2000; www.ha.org.hk; 266 Queen's Rd E, Wan Chai; Ⓜ Wan Chai, exit A3) Public.

KOWLOON

Hong Kong Baptist Hospital (瑪嘉烈醫院;☑852 2339 8888; 222 Waterloo Rd, Kowloon Tong) Private.

Princess Margaret Hospital (瑪嘉烈醫院;☑852 2990 1111; www.ha.org.hk; 2-10 Princess Margaret Hospital Rd, Lai Chi Kok) Public.

Queen Elizabeth Hospital (伊利沙伯醫院; Map p318; ☑852 2958 8888; 30 Gascoigne Rd, Yau Ma Tei; ☐112, Ⓜ Jordan, exit C1) Public.

NEW TERRITORIES

Prince of Wales Hospital (威爾斯親王醫院; Map p167; ☑852 2632 2211; 30-32 Ngan Shing St, Sha Tin). Public.

PHARMACIES

➡ Pharmacies are abundant; they bear a red-and-white cross outside and there should be a registered pharmacist available inside.

➡ Many medications can be bought over the counter without a prescription, but always check it is a known brand and that the expiry date is valid.

➡ Birth-control pills, pads, tampons and condoms are available over the counter in pharmacies, as well as in stores such as Watson's and Mannings.

Internet Access

Getting online in Hong Kong is a breeze.

Increasingly available in hotels and public areas, including the airport, public libraries, key cultural and recreational centres, large parks, major MTR stations, shopping malls and almost all urban cafes and bars. You can also get a free 60-minute PCCW Wi-Fi pass, available at HKTB visitor centres.

You can also purchase a PCCW account online or at convenience stores and PCCW stores, and access the internet via any of PCCW's 7000-plus wi-fi hot spots in Hong Kong.

If you don't have a computer there are a few options where you can log on.

Central Library (香港中央圖書館; Map p310; ☑852 3150 1234; www.hkpl.gov.hk; 66 Causeway Rd, Causeway Bay; ⊘10am-9pm Thu-Tue, 1-9pm Wed; Ⓜ Tin Hau, exit A1) Free access.

Pacific Coffee Company (Map p314; ☑852 2735 0112; www. pacificcoffee.com; Shop L121, The One, 100 Nathan Rd, Tsim Sha Tsui; ⊘7am-midnight Mon-Thu, 7am-1am Fri & Sat, 8am-midnight Sun) Internet is free for customers. There are dozens of other branches throughout Hong Kong.

Left Luggage
MTR TRAIN & FERRY
Left-luggage lockers/ services are in major stations, including Hung Hom station, Kowloon station and Hong Kong station; the West Tower of Shun Tak Centre in Sheung Wan, from where the Macau ferry departs; and the China ferry terminal in Tsim Sha Tsui. Lockers cost between HK$20 and HK$30 per hour (depending on size).

AIRPORT
The Hong Kong International Airport provides a **left-luggage service** (☑852 2261 0110; www.hongkongairport. com/eng/passenger/arrival/ t1/baggage/left-baggage.html; Level 3, Terminal 2, Hong Kong International Airport; per hr/day HK$12/140; ⊘5.30am-1.30am).

ACCOMMODATION
Most hotels and even some guesthouses and hostels

have left-luggage rooms and will let you leave your gear behind, even if you've already checked out and won't be staying on your return. There is usually a charge for this service, so be sure to inquire first.

Legal Matters
➜ Carry your passport all the time. As a visitor, you are required to show your identification if the police request it.

➜ *All* forms of narcotics are illegal in Hong Kong. Whether it's heroin, opium, 'ice', ecstasy or marijuana, the law makes no distinction. If police or customs officials find dope or even smoking equipment in your possession, you can expect to be arrested immediately.

➜ If you run into legal trouble, contact the **Legal Aid Department** (☑24hr hotline 852 2537 7677; www.lad.gov.hk), which provides residents and visitors with representation, subject to a means and merits test.

Maps
Most popular trails have maps at the starting point and bilingual signs along the trails. If you're heading for any of Hong Kong's four major trails, you can get a copy of the trail map produced by the Country & Marine Parks Authority, which is available at the Map Publication Centres.

Money
ATMs are widely available. Credit cards are accepted in most hotels and restaurants; some budget places only take cash.

ATMs
➜ Most ATMs are linked up to international money systems such as Cirrus, Maestro, Plus and Visa Electron.

➜ Some of HSBC's so-called Electronic Money machines offer cash withdrawal facilities for Visa and MasterCard holders.

➜ American Express (Amex) cardholders have access to Jetco ATMs and can withdraw local currency and travellers cheques at Express Cash ATMs in town.

Changing Money
Hong Kong has no currency controls; locals and foreigners can bring, send in or take out as much money as they like. No foreign-currency black market exists in Hong Kong; if anyone on the street does approach you to change money, assume it's a scam.

BANKS
Hong Kong banks generally offer the best rates, though two of the biggest ones (Standard Chartered Bank and Hang Seng Bank) levy a HK$50 commission for each transaction for those who don't hold accounts. Avoid HSBC, which levies HK$100. If you're changing the equivalent of several hundred US dollars or more, the exchange rate improves, which usually makes up for the fee.

MONEYCHANGERS
Licensed moneychangers, such as Chequepoint, abound in touristed areas, including Tsim Sha Tsui. While they are convenient (usually open on Sundays, holidays and late into the evenings) and take no commission per se, the less-than-attractive exchange rates offered are equivalent to a 5% commission. These rates are clearly posted, though if you're changing several hundred US dollars or more you might be able to bargain for a better rate. Before the actual exchange is made, the moneychanger is required by law to give you a form to sign that clearly shows the amount due to you, the exchange rate and any service charges.

Try to avoid the exchange counters at the airport or in hotels, which offer some of the worst rates in Hong Kong.

Credit Cards

The most widely accepted cards are Visa, MasterCard, Amex, Diners Club and JCB – pretty much in that order. It may be an idea to carry two, just in case.

Some shops add a surcharge to offset the commission charged by credit companies, which can range from 2.5% to 7%. In theory, this is prohibited by the credit companies, but to get around this many shops will offer a 5% discount if you pay with cash.

If a card is lost or stolen, you must inform both the **police** (☎852 2527 7177; www.police.gov.hk) and the issuing company as soon as possible; otherwise you may have to pay for the purchases that have been racked up on your card.

American Express (☎emergency 852 2811 6122, general card info 852 2277 1010; www. americanexpress.com/hk/)

Diners Club (☎852 2860 1888; www.dinersclub.com)

MasterCard (☎800 966 677; www.mastercard.com)

Visa (☎800 900 782; www. visa.com.hk) Might be able to help you should you lose your Visa card, but in general you must deal with the issuing bank in the case of an emergency.

Denominations

The local currency is the Hong Kong dollar (HK$), which is divided into 100 cents. Bills are issued in denominations of HK$10, HK$20, HK$50, HK$100, HK$500 and HK$1000. There are little copper coins worth 10¢, 20¢ and 50¢, silver-coloured HK$1, HK$2 and HK$5 coins, and a nickel and bronze HK$10 coin.

Three local banks issue notes: HSBC (formerly the Hong Kong & Shanghai Bank), the Standard Chartered Bank and the Bank of China (all but the HK$10 bill).

Opening Hours

The following list summarises standard opening hours.

Banks 9am to 4.30pm or 5.30pm Monday to Friday, 9am to 12.30pm Saturday.

Museums 10am to between 5pm and 9pm; closed Monday, Tuesday or Thursday.

Offices 9am to 5.30pm or 6pm Monday to Friday (lunch hour 1pm to 2pm).

Restaurants 11am to 3pm and 6pm to 11pm.

Shops Usually 10am to 8pm.

Post

Hong Kong Post (www.hong kongpost.com) is generally excellent; local letters are often delivered the same day they are sent and there is Saturday delivery. The staff at most post offices speak English, and the green mail boxes are clearly marked in English.

Receiving Mail

If a letter is addressed c/o Poste Restante, GPO Hong Kong, it will go to the GPO on Hong Kong Island. Pick it up at counter No 29 from 8am to 6pm Monday to Saturday only. If you want your letters to go to Kowloon, have them addressed as follows: c/o Poste Restante, Tsim Sha Tsui Post Office, 10 Middle Rd, Tsim Sha Tsui, Kowloon. Overseas mail is normally held for two months and local mail for two weeks.

Sending Mail

On Hong Kong Island, the **General Post Office** (中央郵政局; Map p298; 2 Connaught Pl, Central; ⊗8am-6pm Mon-Sat, 9am-5pm Sun; MHong Kong Station, exit A1 or A2) is just east of the Hong Kong station. In Kowloon, the **Tsim Sha Tsui Post Office** (尖沙咀郵政局; Map p314; Ground & 1st fl, Hermes House, 10 Middle Rd, Tsim Sha Tsui; ⊗9am-6pm Mon-Sat, to 2pm Sun; MEast Tsim Sha Tsui, exit L1) is just east of the southern end of Nathan Rd. Post office branches elsewhere keep shorter hours and usually don't open on Sunday.

You should allow five to six days for delivery of letters, postcards and aerogrammes to Europe, Australia and the US.

Courier Services

Many MTR stations have DHL outlets, including the **MTR Central branch** (Map p298; ☎852 2877 2848; www. dhl.com.hk/en.html; MTR Central) next to exit H, and the **MTR Admiralty branch** (Map p308; ☎852 2400 3388; www.dhl.com.hk; Shop G2, Great Eagle Centre, 23 Harbour Rd, Wan Chai; ⊗24hr, closed Sat; MWan Chai, exit C) next to exit E.

Postal Rates

Local mail is HK$1.70 for up to 30g.

Airmail letters and postcards for the first 20/30g are HK$2.90/5.50 to most of Asia and HK$3.70/6.50 to the rest of the world – and HK$150 and HK$160 respectively per kilogram thereafter. Aerogrammes are HK$2.50 to Asia and HK$3.70 to the rest of the world.

Speedpost

Letters and small parcels sent via Hong Kong Post's Speedpost (www.hongkong post.com/speedpost) should reach any of 210 destinations worldwide within two days and are automatically registered. Speedpost rates vary enormously according to destination; every post office has a schedule of fees and a timetable.

Public Holidays

Western and Chinese culture combine to create an interesting mix – and number – of public holidays in Hong Kong. Determining the exact date of some of them is tricky, as there are traditionally two calendars in use: the Gregorian solar (or Western) calendar and the Chinese lunar calendar.

New Year's Day 1 January

Chinese New Year 28–31 January 2017, 16–19 February 2018

Easter 14–17 April 2017, 30 March–2 April 2018

Ching Ming 5 April 2017, 5 April 2018

Labour Day 1 May

Buddha's Birthday 3 May 2017, 22 May 2018

Dragon Boat (Tuen Ng) Festival 30 May 2017, 18 June 2018

Hong Kong SAR Establishment Day 1 July

Mid-Autumn Festival 4 October 2017, 24 September 2018

China National Day 1 October

Chung Yeung 28 October 2015, 17 October 2018

Christmas Day 25 December

Boxing Day 26 December

Telephone

As in the rest of the world, public telephones are increasingly rare.

International Calls & Rates

To make a phone call to Hong Kong, dial your international access code, Hong Kong's country code, then the eight-digit number.

The 'country' code for Hong Kong is ☑852. To call someone outside Hong Kong, dial ☑001, then the country code, the local area code (you usually drop the initial zero if there is one) and the number.

Phone rates are cheaper from 9pm to 8am on weekdays and throughout the weekend. If the phone you're using has registered for the IDD 0060 service, dial ☑0060 first and then the number; rates will be cheaper at any time.

Local Calls & rates

All local calls in Hong Kong are free. However, hotels charge from HK$3 to HK$5 for local calls.

Mobile Phones

Any GSM-compatible mobile (cell) phone can be used in Hong Kong.

Mobile phones have coverage everywhere, including in the harbour tunnels and on the MTR.

Service providers, including **PCCW** (Map p298; Ground fl, 113 Des Voeux Rd, Central; ☺10am-8.30pm Mon-Sat, 11am-8pm Sun; Ⓜ Hong Kong Station, exit A1 or A2), have mobile phones and accessories along with rechargeable SIM cards for sale from HK$98. Local calls cost between 6¢ and 12¢ a minute (calls to the mainland are about HK$1.80/minute).

Phonecards

You can make an International Direct Dial (IDD) call to almost anywhere in the world, but you'll need a phonecard to do so. They are available at PCCW stores, 7-Eleven and Circle K convenience stores, Mannings pharmacies or Vango supermarkets.

Time

➡ Hong Kong Time is eight hours ahead of London (GMT); 13 hours ahead of New York (EST); the same time as Singapore, Manila and Perth; and two hours behind Sydney (AEST).

➡ Hong Kong does not have daylight-saving time.

Toilets

Hong Kong has a vast number of public toilets. All MTR stations have toilets, but finding them sometimes requires asking. Markets, villages and parks also have facilities. Equip yourself with tissues, though, as they are often out of toilet paper.

Almost all public toilets have access for people with disabilities, and baby-changing shelves in both men's and women's rooms.

Tourist Information

Hong Kong Tourism Board (香港旅遊發展局; Map p314; www.discoverhongkong. com; Star Ferry Concourse, Tsim Sha Tsui; ☺8am-8pm; ⛴ Star Ferry) has helpful and welcoming staff, and reams of information – most of it free. Also sells a few useful publications.

In addition to the office at the Star Ferry Visitor Concourse, HKTB has visitor centres at the **airport** (Map p181; Chek Lap Kok; ☺7am-11pm), in Halls A and B on the arrivals level in Terminal 1 and the E2 transfer area); at **The Peak** (港島旅客諮詢 及服務中心; Map p310; www. discoverhongkong.com; Peak Piazza, The Peak; ☺11am-8pm; Peak Tram), between the Peak Tower and the Peak Galleria; and at the border to **mainland China** (羅湖旅客 諮詢及服務中心; 2nd fl, Arrival Hall, Lo Wu Terminal Bldg; ☺8am-6pm).

China Travel Service has four counters at the **airport** (中國旅行社, CTS; ☑customer service 852 2998 7333, tour hotline 852 2998 7888; www. ctshk.com; ☺7am-10pm).

Outside these centres, and at several other places in the territory, you'll be able to find iCyberlink screens, from which you can conveniently access the HKTB website and database 24 hours a day.

VISAS FOR CHINA

Everyone except Hong Kong Chinese residents must have a visa to enter mainland China. Visas can be arranged by **China Travel Service** (中國旅行社, CTS; ☑customer service 852 2998 7333, tour hotline 852 2998 7888; www.ctshk.com; ☺7am-10pm), the mainland-affiliated agency; a good many hostels and guesthouses; and most Hong Kong travel agents.

At the time of writing, holders of Canadian, Australian, New Zealand and most EU passports – but not USA ones – can get a single visa on the spot for around HK$150 at the Lo Wu border crossing, the last stop on the MTR's East Rail. This visa is for a maximum stay of five days within the confines of the Shēnzhèn Special Economic Zone (SEZ). The queues for these visas can be interminable, so it is highly recommended that you shell out the extra money and get a proper China visa before setting off, even if you're headed just for Shēnzhèn. If you have at least a week to arrange your visa yourself, you can go to the **Visa Office of the People's Republic of China** (Map p308; ☑call 10-11am & 3-4pm Mon-Fri 852 3413 2424, recorded info 852 3413 2300; www.fmcoprc.gov.hk; 7th fl, Lower Block, China Resources Centre, 26 Harbour Rd, Wan Chai; ☺9am-noon & 2-5pm Mon-Fri; ⓂWan Chai, exit A3). For further details see www.fmprc.gov.cn.

Travel Agencies

The following are among the most reliable agencies and offer the best deals on air tickets:

Concorde Travel (Map p302; ☑852 2526 3391; www.concorde-travel.com; 7th fl, Galuxe Bldg, 8-10 On Lan St, Central; ☺9am-5.30pm Mon-Fri, to 1pm Sat)

Forever Bright Trading Limited (Map p316; ☑852-2369 3188; www.fbt-chinavisa.com.hk; Rm 916-917, Tower B, New Mandarin Plaza, 14 Science Museum Rd, Tsim Sha Tsui East, Kowloon; ☺8.30am-6.30pm Mon-Fri, to 1.30pm Sat; ⓂEast Tsim Sha Tsui, exit P2)

Traveller Services (☑852 2375 2222; www.traveller.com.hk; 18E, Tower B, Billion Centre, 1 Wang Kwong Rd, Kowloon Bay; ☺9am-6pm Mon-Fri, to 1pm Sat)

Travellers with Disabilities

People with mobility issues have to cope with substantial obstacles in Hong Kong, including the stairs at many MTR stations, as well as pedestrian overpasses, narrow and crowded footpaths, and steep hills. On the other hand, some buses are accessible by wheelchair, taxis are never hard to find, most buildings have lifts (many with Braille panels) and MTR stations have Braille maps with recorded information. Wheelchairs can negotiate the lower decks of most ferries.

Easy Access Travel (香港社會服務聯會; ☑852 2855 9360; www.rehabsociety.org.hk; Ground fl, HKSR Lam Tin Complex, 7 Rehab Path, Lam Tin; ⓂLam Tin, exit D1) Offers tours and accessible transport services.

Transport Department (www.td.gov.hk) Provides guides to public transportation, parking and pedestrian crossing for people with disabilities.

Visas

Visas are not required for the following:

➜ British passport holders for stays up to 180 days – or 90 days for citizens of British Dependent Territories and British Overseas citizens

➜ citizens of Australia, Canada, the EU, Israel, Japan, New Zealand and the USA for stays up to 90 days

➜ holders of many African (including South African), South American and Middle Eastern passports for visits of 30 days or less.

Anyone wishing to stay longer than the visa-free period must apply for a visa before travelling to Hong Kong.

If you require a visa, you must apply beforehand at the nearest Chinese consulate or embassy; see www.fmprc.gov.cn/eng/wjb/zwjg.

Visa extensions must be applied for in person at the **Hong Kong Immigration Department** (Map p308; ☑852 2824 6111; www.immd.gov.hk; 2nd fl, Immigration Tower, 7 Gloucester Rd, Wan Chai; ☺8.45am-4.30pm Mon-Fri, 9-11.30am Sat; ⓂWan Chai, exit C) seven days from visa expiry.

If you plan to visit mainland China, you must have a visa.

You can check all visa requirements at www.immd.gov.hk/en/services/hk-visas/visit-transit/visit-visa-entry-permit.html.

Language

Cantonese is the most popular Chinese dialect in Hong Kong and the surrounding area. Cantonese speakers can read Chinese characters, but will pronounce many characters differently from a Mandarin speaker.

Several systems of Romanisation for Cantonese script exist, and no single one has emerged as an official standard. In this chapter we use Lonely Planet's pronunciation guide designed for maximum accuracy with minimum complexity.

Pronunciation
Vowels

a	as the 'u' in 'but'
ai	as in 'aisle' (short sound)
au	as the 'ou' in 'out'
ay	as in 'pay'
eu	as the 'er' in 'fern'
eui	as in French *feuille* (eu with i)
ew	as in 'blew' (short and pronounced with tightened lips)
i	as the 'ee' in 'deep'
iu	as the 'yu' in 'yuletide'
o	as in 'go'
oy	as in 'boy'
u	as in 'put'
ui	as in French *oui*

Consonants

In Cantonese, the ng sound can appear at the start of a word. Practise by saying 'sing along' slowly and then do away with the 'si'.

WANT MORE?

For in-depth language information and handy phrases, check out Lonely Planet's *China phrasebook*. You'll find it at **shop. lonelyplanet.com**, or you can buy Lonely Planet's iPhone phrasebooks at the Apple App Store.

Note that words ending with the consonant sounds p, t, and k must be clipped in Cantonese. You can hear this in English as well – say 'pit' and 'tip' and listen to how much shorter the 'p' sound is in 'tip'.

Many Cantonese speakers, particularly young people, replace an 'n' sound with an 'l' if a word begins with it – náy (you), is often heard as láy. Where relevant, this change is reflected in our pronunciation guides.

Tones

Cantonese is a language with a large number of words with the same pronunciation but a different meaning, eg gwàt (dig up) and gwàt (bones). What distinguishes these homophones is their 'tonal' quality – the raising and the lowering of pitch on certain syllables. Tones in Cantonese fall on vowels (a, e, i, o, u) and on the consonant n.

To give you a taste of how these tones work, we've included them in our red pronunciation guides in this chapter – they show six tones, divided into high and low pitch groups. High-pitch tones involve tightening the vocal muscles to get a higher note, whereas low-pitch tones are made by relaxing the vocal chords to get a lower note. The tones are indicated with the following accent marks:

à	high
á	high rising
a	level
à	low falling
á	low rising
a	low

Basics

Hello.	哈佬。	hàa·ló
Goodbye.	再見。	joy·gin
How are you?	你幾好啊嗎？	láy gáy hó à maa
Fine.	幾好。	gáy hó

Excuse me. (to get attention)	對唔住 。	deui·ng·jew
Excuse me. (to get past)	唔該借借 。	ng·gòy je·je
Sorry.	對唔住 。	deui·ng·jew
Yes.	係 。	hai
No.	不係 。	ng·hai
Please ...	唔該……	ng·gòy ...
Thank you.	多謝 。	dàw·je
You're welcome.	唔駛客氣 。	ng·sái haak·hay

What's your name?
你叫乜嘢名？　láy giu màt·yé méng aa

My name is ...
我叫……　ngáw giu ...

Do you speak English?
你識唔識講
英文啊？　láy sik·ng·sik gáwng
yìng·mán aa

I don't understand.
我唔明 。　ngáw ng mìng

Accommodation

campsite	營地	yìng·day
guesthouse	賓館	bàn·gún
hostel	招待所	jiù·doy·sáw
hotel	酒店	jáu·dim

Do you have a ... room?	有冇…… 房？	yáu·mó ... fáwng
single	單人	dàan·yàn
double	雙人	sèung·yàn

How much is it per ...?	一……幾多 錢？	yàt ... gáy·dàw chín
night	晚	máan
person	個人	gaw yàn

air-con	空調	hùng·tiù
bathroom	沖涼房	chùng·lèung·fáwng
bed	床	chàwng
cot	BB床	bi·bì chàwng
window	窗	chèung

Directions

Where's ...?
……喺邊度？　... hái bìn·do

What's the address?
地址係？　day·jí hai

KEY PATTERNS

To get by in Cantonese, mix and match these simple patterns with words of your choice:

When's (the next tour)?
(下個旅遊團)
係幾時？　(haa·gaw léui·yàu·tèwn hai) gáy·sì

Where's (the station)?
(車站)喺邊度？　(chè·jaam) hái·bìn·do

Where can I (buy a padlock)?
邊度可以
(買倒鎖)？　bin·do háw·yí (máai dó sáw)

Do you have (a map)?
有冇(地圖)？　yáu·mó (day·tò)

I need (a mechanic).
我要(個整車
師傅) 。　ngáw yiu (gaw jíng·chè sì·fú)

I'd like (a taxi).
我想(坐的士) 。　ngáw séung (cháw dik·sí)

Can I (get a stand-by ticket)?
可唔可以(買
張(後補飛)呀？　háw·ng·háw·yí (máai jèung hau·bó fày) aa

Could you please (write it down)?
唔該你(寫落嚟)？ng·gòy láy (sé lawk lài)

Do I need (to book)?
駛唔駛(定飛
先呀？　sái·ng·sái (deng·fày sìn) aa

I have (a reservation).
我(預定)咗 。　ngáw (yew·deng) jáw

behind	後面	hau·min
left	左邊	jáw·bìn
near ...	……附近	... fu·gan
next to ...	……旁邊	... pàwng·bìn
on the corner	十字路口	sap·ji·lo·háu
opposite	對面	deui·min
right	右邊	yau·bìn
straight ahead	前面	chìn·min
traffic lights	紅綠燈	hùng·luk·dàng

Eating & Drinking

What would you recommend?
有乜嘢好介紹？　yáu màt·yé hó gaai·siu

What's in that dish?
呢道菜有啲乜嘢？　lày do choy yáu dì màt·yé

That was delicious.
真好味 。　jàn hó·may

Cheers!
乾杯！　gàwn·bui

I'd like the bill, please.
唔該我要埋單 。　ng·gòy ngáw yiu màai·dàan

I'd like to book a table for ...	我想 訂張檯 ……嘅。	ngáw séung deng jèung tóy ... ge
(eight) o'clock	(八) 點鐘	(bàat) dím·jùng
(two) people	(兩)位	(léung) wái

I don't eat ...	我唔吃……	ngáw ǹg sik ...
fish	魚	yéw
nuts	果仁	gwáw·yàn
poultry	雞鴨鵝	gài ngaap ngàw
red meat	牛羊肉	ngàu yèung yuk

Key Words

appetisers	涼盤	lèung·pún
baby food	嬰兒食品	yìng·yi sik·bán
bar	酒吧	jáu·bàa
bottle	樽	jèun
bowl	碗	wún
breakfast	早餐	jó·chàan
cafe	咖啡屋	gaa·fè·ngùk
children's menu	個小童 菜單	gaw siú·tung choy·dàan
(too) cold	(太)凍	(taai) dung
dinner	晚飯	máan·fáan
food	食物	sik·mat
fork	叉	chàa
glass	杯	buì
halal	清真	chìng·jàn
high chair	高凳	gò·dang
hot (warm)	熱	yit
knife	刀	dò
kosher	猶太	yàu·tàai
local specialities	地方 小食	day·fàwng siú·sik
lunch	午餐	ńg·chàan
market	街市	gàai·sí
main courses	主菜	jéw·choy
menu (in English)	(英文) 菜單	(yìng·màn) choy·dàan
plate	碟	díp
restaurant	酒樓	jáu·làu
(too) spicy	(太)辣	(taai) laat
spoon	羹	gàng
supermarket	超市	chiù·sí
vegetarian food	齋食品	jàai sik·bán

Meat & Fish

beef	牛肉	ngàu·yuk
chicken	雞肉	gài·yuk
duck	鴨	ngaap
fish	魚	yéw
lamb	羊肉	yèung·yuk
pork	豬肉	jèw·yuk
seafood	海鮮	hóy·sìn

Fruit & Vegetables

apple	蘋果	pìng·gwáw
banana	香蕉	hèung·jiù
cabbage	白菜	baak·choy
carrot	紅蘿蔔	hùng·làw·baak
celery	芹菜	kàn·choy
cucumber	青瓜	chèng·gwàa
fruit	水果	séui·gwáw
grapes	葡提子	pò·tài·jí
green beans	扁荳	bín·dau
lemon	檸檬	ling·mùng
lettuce	生菜	sàang·choy
mushroom	蘑菇	màw·gù
onion(s)	洋蔥	yèung·chùng
orange	橙	cháang
peach	桃	tó
pear	梨	láy
pineapple	菠蘿	bàw·làw
plum	梅	muì
potato	薯仔	sèw·jái
spinach	菠菜	bàw·choy
tomato	番茄	fàan·ké
vegetable	蔬菜	sàw·choy

Other

bread	麵包	min·bàau
egg	蛋	dáan
herbs/spices	香料	hèung·liú
pepper	胡椒粉	wù·jiù·fán
rice	白飯	baak·faan
salt	鹽	yìm
soy sauce	豉油	si·yàu
sugar	砂糖	sàa·tàwng
vegetable oil	菜油	choy·yàu
vinegar	醋	cho

SIGNS

入口	Entrance
出口	Exit
廁所	Toilets
男	Men
女	Women

Drinks

beer	啤酒	bè·jáu
coffee	咖啡	gaa·fè
juice	果汁	gwáw·jàp
milk	牛奶	ngàu·láai
mineral water	礦泉水	kawng·chèwn·séui
red wine	紅葡萄酒	hùng·pò·tò·jáu
tea	茶	chàa
white wine	白葡萄酒	baak·pò·tò·jáu

Emergencies

Help!	救命!	gau·meng
Go away!	走開!	jáu·hòy
I'm lost.	我蕩失路。	ngáw dawng·sàk·lo
I'm sick.	我病咗。	ngáw beng·jáw

Call a doctor!
快啲叫醫生! — faai·dì giu yì·sàng

Call the police!
快啲叫警察! — faai·dì giu gíng·chaat

Where are the toilets?
廁所喺邊度? — chi·sáw hái bìn·do

I'm allergic to ...
我對⋯⋯過敏。 — ngáw deui ... gaw·mán

Shopping & Services

I'd like to buy ...
我想買⋯⋯ — ngáw séung máai ...

I'm just looking.
睇下。 — tái haa

Can I look at it?
我可唔可以睇下? — ngáw háw·ng·háw·yí tái haa

How much is it?
幾多錢? — gáy·dàw chín

That's too expensive.
太貴啦。 — taai gwai laa

Can you lower the price?
可唔可以平啲呀? — háw·ng·háw·yí pèng dì aa

There's a mistake in the bill.
帳單錯咗。 — jeung·dàan chaw jáw

QUESTION WORDS

How?	點樣?	dím·yéung
What?	乜嘢?	màt·yé
When?	幾時?	gáy·sì
Where?	邊度?	bìn·do
Who?	邊個?	bìnz·gaw
Why?	點解?	dím·gáai

ATM	自動提款機	ji·dung tài·fún·gày
credit card	信用卡	seun·yung·kàat
internet cafe	網吧	máwng·bàa
post office	郵局	yàu·gúk
tourist office	旅行社	léui·hàng·sé

Time & Dates

What time is it?	而家幾點鐘?	yi·gàa gáy·dím·jùng
It's (10) o'clock.	(十)點鐘。	(sap)·dím·jùng
Half past (10).	(十)點半。	(sap)·dím bun

morning	朝早	jiù·jó
afternoon	下晝	haa·jau
evening	夜晚	ye·máan
yesterday	寢日	kàm·yat
today	今日	gàm·yat
tomorrow	听日	tìng·yat

Monday	星期一	sìng·kày·yàt
Tuesday	星期二	sìng·kày·yi
Wednesday	星期三	sìng·kày·sàam
Thursday	星期四	sìng·kày·say
Friday	星期五	sìng·kày·ńg
Saturday	星期六	sìng·kày·luk
Sunday	星期日	sìng·kày·yat

January	一月	yàt·yewt
February	二月	yi·yewt
March	三月	sàam·yewt
April	四月	say·yewt
May	五月	ńg·yewt
June	六月	luk·yewt
July	七月	chàt·yewt
August	八月	baat·yewt
September	九月	gáu·yewt
October	十月	sap·yewt
November	十一月	sap·yàt·yewt
December	十二月	sap·yi·yewt

Transport

Public Transport

boat	船	sèwn
bus	巴士	bàa·sí
plane	飛機	fày·gày

NUMBERS

1	一	yàt
2	二	yi
3	三	sàam
4	四	say
5	五	ńg
6	六	luk
7	七	chàt
8	八	baat
9	九	gáu
10	十	sap
20	二十	yi·sap
30	三十	sàam·sap
40	四十	say·sap
50	五十	ńg·sap
60	六十	luk·sap
70	七十	chàt·sap
80	八十	baat·sap
90	九十	gáu·sap
100	一百	yàt·baak
1000	一千	yàt·chìn

taxi	的士	dìk·sí
train	火車	fáw·chè
tram	電車	dịn·chè

When's the ... (bus)?
……（巴士） ... (bàa·sí)
幾點開？ gáy dím hòy
first 頭班 tàu·bàan
last 尾班 máy·bàan
next 下一班 haa·yàt·bàan

A ... ticket to (Panyu).
一張去 yàt jèung heui
（番禺）嘅 (pùn·yèw) ge
……飛。 ... fày
1st-class 頭等 tàu·dáng
2nd-class 二等 yi·dáng
one-way 單程 dàan·chìng
return 雙程 sèung·chìng

What time does it leave?
幾點鐘出發？ gáy·dím jùng chèut·faa

Does it stop at ...?
會唔會喺 wuí·ńg·wuí hái
……停呀？ ... tìng aa

What time does it get to ...?
幾點鐘到……？ gáy·dím jùng do ...

What's the next stop?
下個站 haa·gaw jaam
叫乜名？ giu màt méng

I'd like to get off at ...
我要喺…… ngáw yiu hái ...
落車 。 lawk·chè

Please tell me when we get to ...
到……嘅時候， do ... ge sị·hau
唔該叫聲我 。 ǹg·gòy giu sèng ngáw

Please stop here.
唔該落車 。 ǹg·gòy lawk·chè

aisle	路邊	lo·bìn
cancelled	取消	chéui·siù
delayed	押後	ngaat·hau
platform	月台	yéwt·tòy
ticket window	售票處	sau·piu·chew
timetable	時間表	sị·gaan·biú
train station	火車站	fó·chè·jaam
window	窗口	chèung·háu

Driving & Cycling

I'd like to hire a ... 我想租 ngáw séung jò
架…… gaa ...
4WD 4WD fàw·wiù·jàai·fù
bicycle 單車 dàan·chè
car 車 chè
motorcycle 電單車 dịn·dàan·chè

baby seat	BB座	bi·bì jaw
diesel	柴油	chàai·yàu
helmet	頭盔	táu·kwài
mechanic	修車師傅	sàu·chè sì·fú
petrol	汽油	hay·yàu
service station	加油站	gàa·yàu·jaam

Is this the road to ...?
呢條路係唔係去 làu tịu lo hai·ǹg·hai heui
……㗎？ ... gaa

Can I park here?
呢度泊唔泊得 làu·do paak·ǹg·paak·dàk
車㗎？ chè gaa

How long can I park here?
我喺呢度可以 ngáw hái làu·do háw·yí
停幾耐？ tìng gáy·loy

Where's the bicycle parking lot?
喺邊度停單車？ háy·bin·do tìng dàan·chè

The car/motorbike has broken down at ...
架車/電單車 gaa chè/dịn·dàan·chè
係……壞咗 。 hái ... waai jáw

I have a flat tyre.
我爆咗肽 。 ngáw baau·jáw tàai

I've run out of petrol.
我冇晒油 。 ngáw mó saai yáu

I'd like my bicycle repaired.
我想修呢架車 。 ngáw séung sàu làu gaa chè

GLOSSARY

arhat – Buddhist disciple freed from the cycle of birth and death

bodhisattva – Buddhist striving towards enlightenment

cha chaan tang – local tea cafe serving Western-style beverages and snacks and/or Chinese dishes

cheongsam – a fashionable, tight-fitting Chinese dress with a slit up the side (*qípáo* in Mandarin)

dai pai dong – open-air eating stall, especially popular at night, but fast disappearing in Hong Kong

dim sum – literally 'touch the heart'; a Cantonese meal of various tidbits eaten as breakfast, brunch or lunch and offered from wheeled steam carts in restaurants; see also yum cha

dragon boat – long, narrow skiff in the shape of a dragon, used in races during the Dragon Boat Festival

feng shui – Mandarin spelling for the Cantonese *fung sui* meaning 'wind water'; the Chinese art of geomancy that manipulates or judges the environment to produce good fortune

Hakka – a Chinese ethnic group who speak a different Chinese language than the Cantonese; some Hakka people still lead traditional lives as farmers in the New Territories

hell money – fake-currency money burned as an offering to the spirits of the departed

HKTB – Hong Kong Tourism Board

junk – originally Chinese fishing boats or war vessels with square sails; die-sel-powered, wooden pleasure yachts, which can be seen on Victoria Harbour

kaido – small- to medium-sized ferry that makes short runs on the open sea, usually used for nonscheduled services between small islands and fishing villages; sometimes spelled kaido

kung fu – the basis of many Asian martial arts

mah-jong – popular Chinese game played among four persons using tiles engraved with Chinese characters

MTR – Mass Transit Railway

nullah – uniquely Hong Kong word referring to a gutter or drain and occasionally used in place names

Punti – the first Canton-ese-speaking settlers in Hong Kong

sampan – motorised launch

that can only accommodate a few people and is too small to go on the open sea; mainly used for interharbour transport

SAR – Special Administrative Region of China; both Hong Kong and Macau are now SARs

SARS – Severe Acute Respiratory Syndrome

si yau sai chaan – 'soy sauce Western'; a cuisine that emerged in the 1950s featuring Western dishes of various origins prepared in a Chinese style

taichi – slow-motion shad-ow-boxing and form of exer-cise; also spelt tai chi or t'ai chi

tai tai – any married woman but especially the leisured wife of a businessman

Tanka – Chinese ethnic group that traditionally lives on boats

Triad – Chinese secret society originally founded as patriotic associations to protect Chinese culture from the influence of usurping Manchus, but today Hong Kong's equivalent of the Mafia

wan – bay

wet market – an outdoor market selling fruit, vegetables, fish and meat

yum cha – literally 'drink tea'; common Cantonese term for dim sum

MENU DECODER

Fish & Shellfish

baau·yew	鮑魚	abalone
daai·haa	大蝦	prawn
haa	蝦	shrimp
ho	蠔	oyster
lung haa	龍蝦	rock lobster
yau·yew	魷魚	squid
yew	魚	fish
yew chi	魚翅	shark's fin
yew daan	魚蛋	fish balls, usually made from pike

Meat & Poultry

gai	雞	chicken
jew sau	豬手	pork knuckle
jew·yuk	豬肉	pork
ngaap	鴨	duck
ngau yuk	牛肉	beef
ngaw	鵝	goose
paai guat	排骨	pork spareribs
yew jew	乳豬	suckling pig

Pastries

bo lo baau	菠蘿包	pineapple bun
gai mei baau	雞尾包	cocktail bun

Rice & Noodle Dishes

baak·faan	白飯	steamed white rice
chaau·faan	炒飯	fried rice
chaau·min	炒麵	fried noodles
faan	飯	rice
fan·si	粉絲	cellophane noodles or bean threads
haw·fan	河粉	wide, white, flat rice noodles that are usually pan-fried
juk	粥	congee
min	麵	noodles
sin·haa haa wan·tan	鮮蝦餛飩	wontons made with prawns
wan·tan min	餛飩麵	wonton noodle soup

Sauces

gaai laat	芥辣	hot mustard
ho yau	蠔油	oyster sauce
laat jiu jeung	辣椒醬	chilli sauce
si yau	豉油	soy sauce

yau·jaa·gwai 油炸鬼 'devils' tails'; dough rolled and fried in hot oil

Soups

aai yuk suk mai gang	蟹肉粟米羹	crab and sweet corn soup
baak·choy tawng	白菜湯	Chinese cabbage soup
daan faa·tawng	蛋花湯	'egg flower' (or drop) soup; light stock into which a raw egg is dropped
dung·gwaa tawng	冬瓜湯	winter-melon soup
wan·tan tawng	餛飩湯	wonton soup
yew·chi tawng	魚翅湯	shark's-fin soup
yin waw gang	燕窩羹	bird's-nest soup

Vegetarian Dishes

chun gewn	春卷	vegetarian spring rolls
gai lo may	雞滷味	mock chicken, barbecued pork or roast duck
gam gu sun jim	金菇筍尖	braised bamboo shoots and black mushrooms
law hon jaai	羅漢齋	braised mixed vegetables
law hon jaai yi min	羅漢齋伊麵	fried noodles with braised vegetables

Cantonese Dishes

baak cheuk haa	白灼蝦	poached prawns served with dipping sauces
chaa siu	叉燒	roast pork
ching chaau gaai laan	清炒芥蘭	stir-fried Chinese broccoli
ching jing yew	清蒸魚	whole steamed fish served with spring onions, ginger and soy sauce
geung chung chaau haai	薑蔥炒蟹	sautéed crab with ginger and spring onions
haai yuk paa dau miu	蟹肉扒豆苗	sautéed pea shoots with crab meat
ho yau choi sam	蠔油菜心	*choisum* with oyster sauce
ho yau ngau yuk	蠔油牛肉	deep-fried spare ribs served with coarse salt and pepper
jaa ji gai	炸子雞	crispy-skin chicken
jiu yim yau·yew	椒鹽魷魚	squid, dry-fried with salt and pepper
mui choi kau yuk	霉菜扣肉	twice-cooked pork with pickled cabbage
sai laan faa daai ji	西蘭花帶子	stir-fried broccoli with scallops
siu ngaap	燒鴨	roast duck
siu yew gaap	燒乳鴿	roast pigeon
siu yew jew	燒乳豬	roast suckling pig
yìm guk gai	鹽焗雞	salt-baked chicken, Hakka-style

Dim Sum

chaa siu baau	叉燒包	steamed barbecued-pork buns
cheung fan	腸粉	steamed rice-flour rolls with shrimp, beef or pork

ching chaau si choi	清炒時菜	fried green vegetable of the day
chiu·jau fan gwaw	潮州粉果	steamed dumpling with pork, peanuts and coriander
chun gewn	春卷	fried spring rolls
fan gwaw	粉果	steamed dumplings with shrimp and bamboo shoots
fu pay gewn	腐皮卷	crispy tofu rolls
fung jaau	鳳爪	fried chicken feet
haa gaau	蝦餃	steamed shrimp dumplings
law mai gai	糯米雞	sticky rice wrapped in a lotus leaf
paai gwat	排骨	small braised spare ribs with black beans
saan juk ngau yuk	山竹牛肉	steamed minced-beef balls
siu maai	燒賣	steamed pork and shrimp dumplings

Chiu Chow Dishes

bing faa gwun yin	冰花官燕	cold, sweet bird's-nest soup served as a dessert
chiu·jau lo Oseui ngaw	潮州滷水鵝	Chiu Chow braised goose
chiu·jau yew tong	潮州魚湯	aromatic fish soup
chiu·jau yi min	潮州伊麵	pan-fried egg noodles served with chives
dung jing haai	凍蒸蟹	cold steamed crab
jin ho beng	煎蠔餅	oyster omelette
sek lau gai	石榴雞	steamed egg-white pouches filled with minced chicken
tim·sewn Ohung·siu haa/ haai kau	甜酸紅燒蝦 蟹球	prawn or crab balls with sweet, sticky dipping sauce

Northern Dishes

bak·ging tin ngaap	北京填鴨	Peking duck
chong baau yeung yuk	蔥爆羊肉	sliced lamb with onions served on sizzling platter
gaau·ji	餃子	dumplings
gon chaau ngau yuk si	乾炒牛肉絲	dried shredded beef with chilli sauce
haau yeung·yuk	烤羊肉	roast lamb
sewn laat tong	酸辣湯	hot-and-sour soup with shredded pork (and sometimes congealed pig's blood)

Shanghainese Dishes

baat bo faan	八寶飯	steamed or pan-fried glutinous rice with 'eight treasures', eaten as a dessert
chong yau beng	蔥油餅	pan-fried spring onion cakes
chung·ji wong yew	松子黃魚	sweet-and-sour yellow croaker with pine nuts
daai jaap haai	大閘蟹	hairy crab (an autumn and winter dish)
fu gwai gai/ hat yi gai	富貴雞/ 乞丐雞	'beggar's chicken'; partially deboned chicken stuffed with pork, Chinese pickled cabbage, onions, mushrooms,ginger and other seasonings, wrapped in lotus leaves, sealed in wet clay or pastry and baked for several hours in hot ash

gon jin say gwai dau	乾煎四季豆	pan-fried spicy string beans
hung·siu si·ji·tau	紅燒獅子頭	Braised 'lion's head meatballs' – over-sized pork meatballs
jeui gai	醉雞	drunken chicken
lung jeng haa jan	龍井蝦仁	shrimps with 'dragon-well' tea leaves
seung·hoi cho chaau	上海粗炒	fried Shànghǎi-style (thick) noodles with pork and cabbage
siu lung baau	小籠包	steamed minced-pork dumplings

Sichuan Dishes

ching jiu ngau yok si	青椒牛肉絲	sautéed shredded beef and green pepper
daam daam min	擔擔麵	noodles in savoury sauce
gong baau gai ding	宮爆雞丁	sautéed diced chicken and peanuts in sweet chilli sauce
jeung chaa haau ngaap	樟茶烤鴨	duck smoked in camphor wood
maa ngai seung sew	螞蟻上樹	'ants climbing trees'; cellophane noodles braised with seasoned minced pork
maa paw dau fu	麻婆豆腐	stewed tofu with minced pork and chilli
say·chewn ming haa	四川明蝦	Sichuan chilli prawns
wui gwaw yuk	回鍋肉	slices of braised pork with chillies
yew heung ke ji	魚香茄子	sautéed eggplant in a savoury, spicy sauce

Behind the Scenes

SEND US YOUR FEEDBACK

We love to hear from travellers – your comments keep us on our toes and help make our books better. Our well-travelled team reads every word on what you loved or loathed about this book. Although we cannot reply individually to your submissions, we always guarantee that your feedback goes straight to the appropriate authors, in time for the next edition. Each person who sends us information is thanked in the next edition – the most useful submissions are rewarded with a selection of digital PDF chapters.

Visit **lonelyplanet.com/contact** to submit your updates and suggestions or to ask for help. Our award-winning website also features inspirational travel stories, news and discussions.

Note: We may edit, reproduce and incorporate your comments in Lonely Planet products such as guidebooks, websites and digital products, so let us know if you don't want your comments reproduced or your name acknowledged. For a copy of our privacy policy visit lonelyplanet.com/privacy.

OUR READERS

Many thanks to the travellers who used the last edition and wrote to us with helpful hints, useful advice and interesting anecdotes: Carl Möller, Dan Nelson, Dan Stevens, Daniëlle Wolbers, David Moffett, Graeme Swaddle, James Cowcher, Kathryn Rosie, Kirsten Hansen, Kiwi Wong, Peter Allen.

WRITER THANKS

Emily Matchar

Thanks to Megan Eaves and the rest of the LP team for their terrific work. Thanks to the Hong Kong Tourism Board and the Macau Government Tourism Office for their assistance. Thanks to Marie Kobler for all her extremely helpful Lamma Island suggestions and to Michael Johnson for his expert food advice. Thanks also, of course, to my husband, Jamin Asay, for accompanying me on so many restaurant, bar and hotel explorations.

Piera Chen

Thanks to the Lonely Planet team, and to my friends Janine Cheung and Yuen Ching-sum for their generous assistance. Thanks also to my husband Sze Pang-cheung and daughter Clio for their patience and wonderful support.

ACKNOWLEDGEMENTS

Cover photograph: Traditional Chinese junk boat in Victoria Harbour, Hong Kong, Comezora/Getty ©

THIS BOOK

This 17th edition of Lonely Planet's *Hong Kong* guidebook was researched and written by Emily Matchar and Piera Chen, who also wrote the previous edition. The 15th edition was written by Piera Chen and Chung Wah Chow. This guidebook was produced by the following:

Destination Editor Megan Eaves
Product Editors Kate Mathews, Susan Paterson
Senior Cartographer Julie Sheridan
Book Designers Virginia Moreno, Wendy Wright
Assisting Editors Judith Bamber, Kate Chapman, Pete Cruttenden, Grace Dobell, Samantha Forge,

Helen Koehne, Lauren O'Connell, Simon Williamson
Cover Researcher Naomi Parker
Thanks to Cheree Broughton, Jennifer Carey, Neill Coen, Daniel Corbett, Jane Grisman, Liz Heynes, Andi Jones, Lauren Keith, Claire Naylor, Karyn Noble, Ellie Simpson, Tony Wheeler

Index

✕ EATING

INDEX EATING

Hong Kong Maps

Sights

- Beach
- Bird Sanctuary
- Buddhist
- Castle/Palace
- Christian
- Confucian
- Hindu
- Islamic
- Jain
- Jewish
- Monument
- Museum/Gallery/Historic Building
- Ruin
- Shinto
- Sikh
- Taoist
- Winery/Vineyard
- Zoo/Wildlife Sanctuary
- Other Sight

Activities, Courses & Tours

- Bodysurfing
- Diving
- Canoeing/Kayaking
- Course/Tour
- Sento Hot Baths/Onsen
- Skiing
- Snorkelling
- Surfing
- Swimming/Pool
- Walking
- Windsurfing
- Other Activity

Sleeping

- Sleeping
- Camping

Eating

- Eating

Drinking & Nightlife

- Drinking & Nightlife
- Cafe

Entertainment

- Entertainment

Shopping

- Shopping

Information

- Bank
- Embassy/Consulate
- Hospital/Medical
- Internet
- Police
- Post Office
- Telephone
- Toilet
- Tourist Information
- Other Information

Geographic

- Beach
- Gate
- Hut/Shelter
- Lighthouse
- Lookout
- Mountain/Volcano
- Oasis
- Park
- Pass
- Picnic Area
- Waterfall

Population

- Capital (National)
- Capital (State/Province)
- City/Large Town
- Town/Village

Transport

- Airport
- Border crossing
- Bus
- Cable car/Funicular
- Cycling
- Ferry
- Metro/MTR/MRT station
- Monorail
- Parking
- Petrol station
- Skytrain/Subway station
- Taxi
- Train station/Railway
- Tram
- Underground station
- Other Transport

Note: Not all symbols displayed above appear on the maps in this book

Routes

- Tollway
- Freeway
- Primary
- Secondary
- Tertiary
- Lane
- Unsealed road
- Road under construction
- Plaza/Mall
- Steps
- Tunnel
- Pedestrian overpass
- Walking Tour
- Walking Tour detour
- Path/Walking Trail

Boundaries

- International
- State/Province
- Disputed
- Regional/Suburb
- Marine Park
- Cliff
- Wall

Hydrography

- River, Creek
- Intermittent River
- Canal
- Water
- Dry/Salt/Intermittent Lake
- Reef

Areas

- Airport/Runway
- Beach/Desert
- Cemetery (Christian)
- Cemetery (Other)
- Glacier
- Mudflat
- Park/Forest
- Sight (Building)
- Sportsground
- Swamp/Mangrove

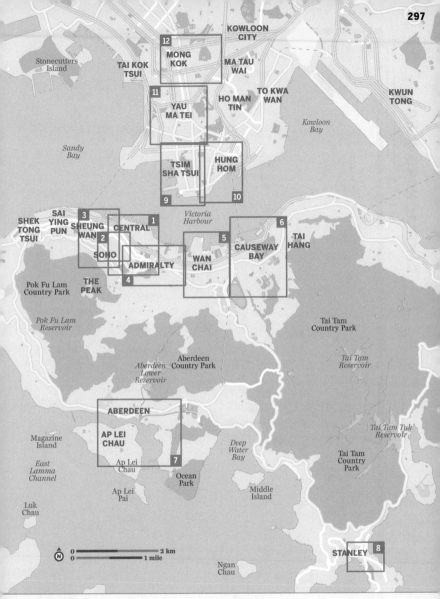

CENTRAL HONG KONG

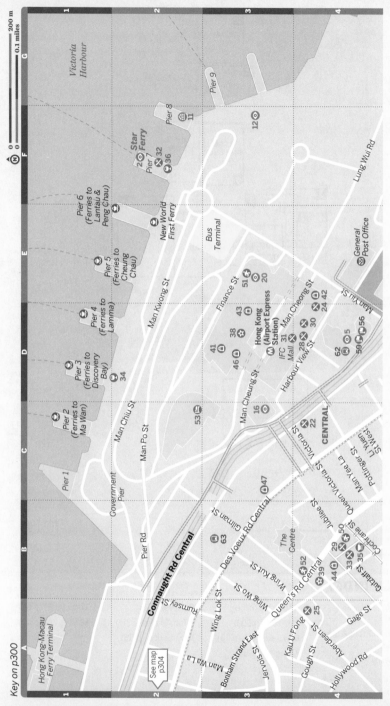

Key on p300

200 m
0.1 miles

Hong Kong–Macau
Ferry Terminal

Victoria
Harbour

Pier 1

Pier 2
(Ferries to
Ma Wan)

Pier 3
(Ferries to
Discovery
Bay)

Pier 4
(Ferries to
Lamma)

Pier 5
(Ferries to
Cheung
Chau)

Pier 6
(Ferries to
Lantau &
Peng Chau)

Star
Ferry
Pier 7

Pier 8

Pier 9

Government
Pier

New World
First Ferry

Bus
Terminal

Finance St

Hong Kong
(Airport Express
Station)

IFC
Mall

Man Cheong St

Harbour View St

Man Kwong St

Man Chiu St

Man Po St

Man Cheung St

Victoria St

Li Yuen St West

Li Yuen St East

Man Yee La

Pottinger St

CENTRAL

Lung Wui Rd

Man Yui St

General
Post Office

Connaught Rd Central

Pier Rd

Rumsey St

Des Voeux Rd Central

Gilman St

Wing Kut St

Wing Lok St

Wing Wo St

Jervois St

Bonham Strand East

Queen's Rd Central

Jubilee St

Cochrane St

Gutzlaff St

Cochrane St

The
Centre

Kau U Fong

Aberdeen St

Gough St

Gage St

Hollywood Rd

See map
p304

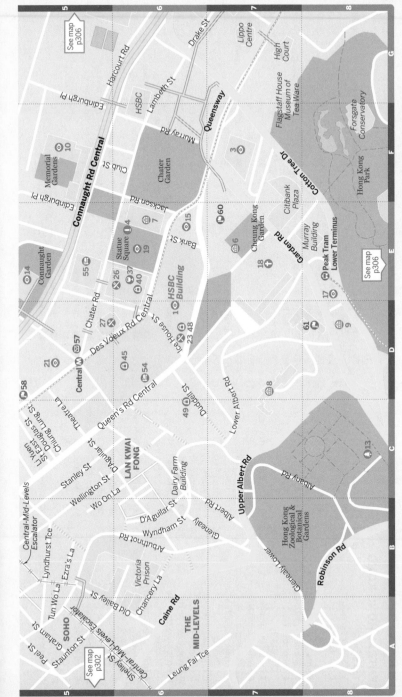

See map p306

See map p306

See map p302

LAN KWAI FONG & SOHO *Map on p302*

LAN KWAI FONG & SOHO

Key on p301

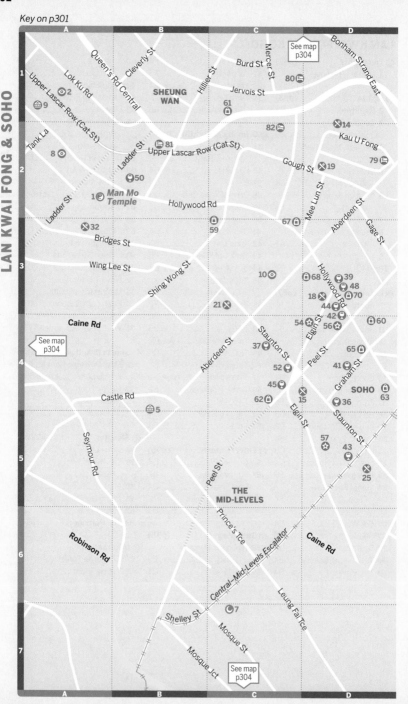

LAN KWAI FONG & SOHO

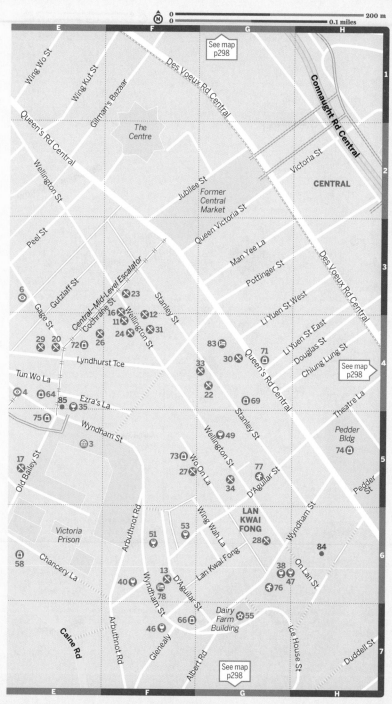

SHEUNG WAN

N
0 ——————— 200 m
0 ——————— 0.1 miles

Victoria Harbour

1

Kennedy Town
(2km)

West Fire Service St

Chung Kong Rd

Connaught Rd West

Des Voeux Rd West

Connaught Rd Central

2

Western Districts

Ko Shing St

Queen St

10 ✕

Bonham Strand West

New Market St

Wing Lok St

Connaught Rd Central

29

9

26 ✛

Sheung Wan Ⓜ

Cleverly St

Hillier St

Man Wa La

12

30 ✕

SHEUNG WAN

19 ✕

Morrison St

21

27

Bonham Strand East

4

3

8 ◉

Queen's Rd West

Hollywood Rd

New St

Hollywood Road Park

Possession St

Queen's Rd Central

16

14

Burd St

Jervois St

Western District Community Centre
(500m)

Hospital Rd

Po Yan St

6 ◉

11 ✕

22

13 ✕

15

7

20

Sai St

Tung St

23

Lok Ku Rd

Hollywood Rd

Sai Ying Pun Community Complex (100m);
University of Hong Kong (1.5km);
Queen Mary Hospital (3km)

Pound La

3

Tai Ping Shan St

24

18

Po Hing Fong

Blake Garden

4

Breezy Path

Caine Rd

Bonham Rd

17

Caine La

2

Tank La

Bridges St

Shing Wong St

Staunton St

Aberdeen St

Caine Rd

5

Conduit Rd

Park Rd

Castle Rd

5 ✕

Seymour Rd

Peel St

Elgin St

THE MID-LEVELS

6

Robinson Rd

Shelley St

Leung Fai Tce

Central–Mid-Levels Escalator

See Lan Kwai Fong & Soho Map p302

7

Lugard Rd

Pok Fu Lam Country Park

Victoria Peak

Robinson Rd

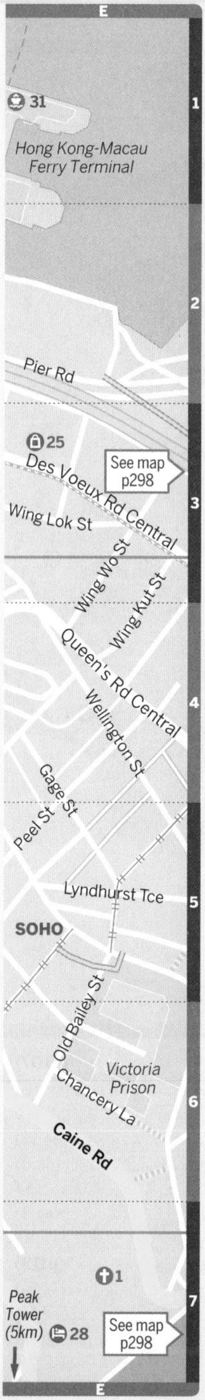

SHEUNG WAN

31

Hong Kong-Macau Ferry Terminal

Pier Rd

25

Des Voeux Rd Central

Wing Lok St

Wing Wo St

Wing Kut St

Queen's Rd Central

Wellington St

Gage St

Peel St

Lyndhurst Tce

SOHO

Old Bailey St

Victoria Prison

Chancery La

Caine Rd

1

Peak Tower (5km) 28

See map p298

See map p298

E

ADMIRALTY

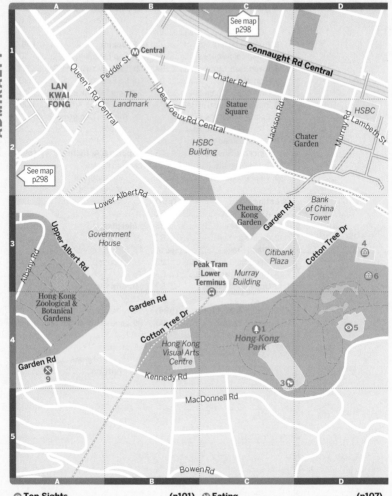

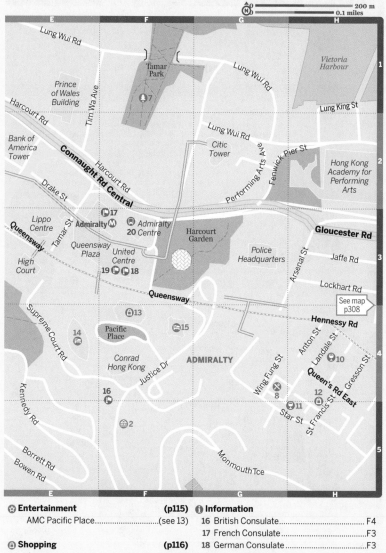

WAN CHAI

Victoria
Harbour

Tsim Sha Tsui
(1km)

3 ⓘ

Expo Dr

Hong Kong Convention
& Exhibition Centre
(New Wing)

Expo Dr

Expo Dr Central

Expo Dr East

54 ⓗ

Convention Ave

Hung Hing Rd

Bus Station

Hong Kong
Convention &
Exhibition Centre

Great Eagle
Centre
48 ✉

Harbour
Centre
47 ⓗ

Wan Chai
Sports
Ground

15 ⓗ 27 ✕ⓗ

Harbour Rd

Harbour Rd

Sun
Hung Kai
Centre
35 ⓗ

33 ☆

Convention Ave

Wan Chai
Tower

Central
Plaza

Fleming Rd

37 🔒

Causeway
Centre

Tonnochy Rd

34 ⓗ

Revenue
Tower

49 ●

50 🏛

52 ●

Harbour Dr

24 ✕

Gloucester Rd

See map
p306

WAN
CHAI

Jaffe Rd

Fleming Rd

36 ✪

Fenwick St

Jaffe Rd
28 ✪ 26

O'Brien Rd

Lockhart Rd

Stewart Rd

42 🏛

Lockhart Rd

Lockhart Rd
Market

18 ✕

Heard St

20 ✕

25 ✕

Wan Chai Ⓜ

Hennessy Rd

19 ✕

Johnston Rd

2 🔒

13 ✕

40 ⓗ

O'Brien Rd

Thomson Rd

Fleming Rd

14 ✕
17 🔒 38

Wan Chai Rd

21 ✕

Tai Wong St
East

Johnston Rd

Cross La

Wood Rd

22 ✕

Ship St

11 ✕

Lun Fat St

29 ✕

Swatow St

Stone Nullah La

Tai Wo Rd

51 ✚

Burrows St

10 ✕

Amoy St

Lee Tung St

39 ✕

Cross St

23 🏛

MORRISON
HILL

Wan Chai
Park

Queen's Rd

43 🏛

Ship St

5 ⛵

Tai Wong St
West

30 ✕

Spring Garden La

45 🏛

41 🔒

Stubbs Rd

6 🅿

Hopewell
Centre

Fung Wong Terr

Queen's Rd East

7 ◉

Kennedy Rd

31 ⓗ

1 ◉
9 ◉

32 ◉

Lung On St

Wan Chai Gap Rd

Kennedy St

8 ◉

St Margaret's
College

HAPPY
VALLEY

Lovers' Rock (700m);
King Yin Lei (1.5km)

Hung Hing Rd

Marsh Rd

Gloucester Rd

●53

Jaffe Rd

⊜46

Marsh Rd

Lockhart Rd

Hennessy Rd   16 ⊗

12 ⊗

Wan Chai Rd

See map
p310

Sung Tak St

Wong Nai Chung Rd

East
⊜44

Happy
Valley
Racecourse

CAUSEWAY BAY

N

0   500 m
0   0.25 miles

A | **B** | **C** | **D**

Hong Kong
Film Archive
(3.5km)

Victoria
Harbour

Eastern Corridor Island Rd

Watson Rd

King Ming Rd

Whitfield Rd

Causeway Bay
Typhoon Shelter

1

44

8

Gordon Rd

Kellett
Island

Causeway
Bay

Victoria Park Rd

Tsing Fung St

Victoria
Park

Hing Fat St

Cargo
Handling
Basin

Cross-Harbour Tunnel

4

6

Gloucester Rd

29

Causeway Rd

18

9

Houston
St

World
Trade
Centre

Paterson St

21

Causeway Bay
Sports
Ground

11

Jaffe Rd

Cannon St

Paterson St

CAUSEWAY
BAY

Lockhart Rd

32

37

16

47

39

Sugar St

46

7

26

Hennessy Rd

Causeway
Bay

31

Percival St

Kai Chiu Rd

Yee Wo St

Shelter St

24

45

27

Garden Rd

40

Yun Ping Rd

Irving St

Leighton Rd

St Mary's
Church

36

15

20

Russell St

10

42

19

School
St

38

34

17

Hysan Ave

35

23

30

22

28

Lee
Theatre
Plaza

Leighton Rd

Haven St

Caroline Hill Rd

Cotton Path

Ka Ning Path

SO KON PO

Sun Wui
Rd

Leighton Rd

CAROLINE HILL

Broadwood Link Rd

Eastern Hospital Rd

Sports Rd

LEIGHTON
HILL

41

South China
Association
Stadium

Hong Kong
Football Club

Wong Nai Chung Rd

25

Ventris Rd

Stadium Path

Hong
Kong
Stadium

2

F11 Photographic
Museum (400m)

See map
p308

A | **B** | **C** | **D**

CAUSEWAY BAY

North Point (600m);
Island East (2km)

Fortress
Hill Ⓜ

Shell St

Mercury St
13 ⊗

Electric Rd

King's Rd

Wing Hing St

Lau Li St

Tin Hau Temple Rd

Yacht St

43 🚌

Tin
Hau Ⓜ

⊙ 5

Tung Lo Wan Rd

School St

King St

14 ⊗ 12

Wun Sha St

Brown St

Tai Hang Rd

Tai Hang Rd

TAI
HANG

ABERDEEN

N 0 0.25 miles / 0 500 m

Pok Fu Lam Village (2.3km); Kennedy Town (5.5km)

Hong Kong Trail (1km)

Wong Chuk Hang Rd

Heung Yip Rd

Welfare Rd

Shum Wan Rd

Ocean Park (750m); Cable Car (750m)

Sham Wan

Aberdeen Harbour

Aberdeen Main Rd

Yue Kwong Rd

Aberdeen Main Rd

Aberdeen Praya Rd

Tung Sing Rd

Chengtu St

ABERDEEN

AP LEI CHAU

Hung Shing St

Main St

Ap Lei Chau

Ap Lei Chau Praya Rd

Ap Lei Chau Bridge Rd

Lei Tung Estate Rd

Lee Wing St

Lee Nam Rd

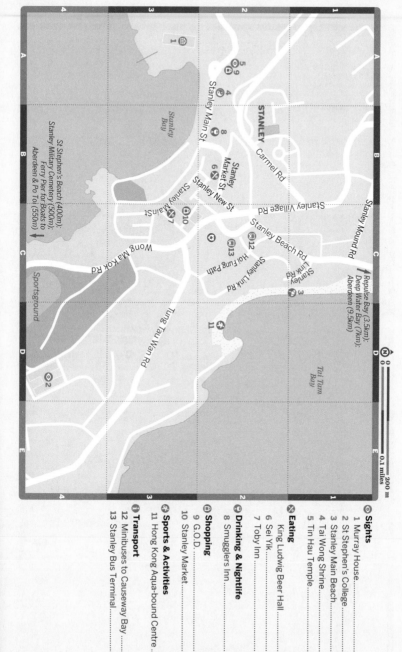

STANLEY

TSIM SHA TSUI

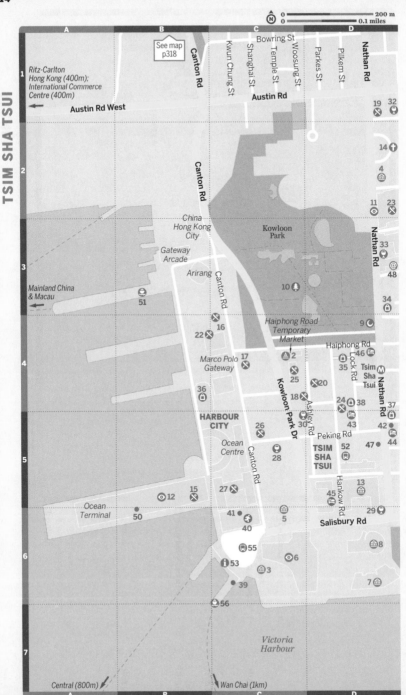

0   200 m
0   0.1 miles

A   **B**   **C**   **D**

Ritz-Carlton
Hong Kong (400m);
International Commerce
Centre (400m)

Bowring St

Canton Rd

Kwun Chung St

Shanghai St

Temple St

Woosung St

Parkes St

Pilkem St

Nathan Rd

Austin Rd

← Austin Rd West

1

19 ⊗   32 ⊟

14 ⊕

4 ⊞

Canton Rd

11 ◎   23 ⊗

Nathan Rd

2

China
Hong Kong
City

Kowloon
Park

Gateway
Arcade

Arirang

Canton Rd

33 ⊟

@
48

← Mainland China
& Macau

51 ⊟

10 ⊕

34 ⊟

3

9 ⊕

Haiphong Road
Temporary
Market

Haiphong Rd

46 ⊟

22 ⊗   16 ⊗

⊕ 2

35 ⊟

Lock Rd

Tsim
Sha Ⓜ
Tsui

Marco Polo
Gateway

17 ⊗

25 ⊗

Kowloon Park Dr

20 ⊗

24 ⊟   38 ⊟

Nathan Rd

37 ⊟

36 ⊟

18 ⊗

Ashley Rd

30 ⊟   43 ⊟

42 ●
44 ⊟

4

HARBOUR
CITY

26 ⊗

Peking Rd

TSIM
SHA
TSUI

52 ⊟

47 ●

Ocean
Centre

28 ⊟

Canton Rd

13 ⊟

45 ⊟

Hankow Rd

5

◎ 12   15 ⊟

27 ⊗

29 ⊟

Ocean
Terminal

50 ●

41 ●
40 ⊕

5 ⊞

Salisbury Rd

55 ⊟

8 ⊞

ⓘ 53

◎ 6

3 ⊞

7 ⊞

39 ●

6

56 ⊟

Victoria
Harbour

7

Central (800m) ↙   ↓ Wan Chai (1km)

A   **B**   **C**   **D**

See map
p318

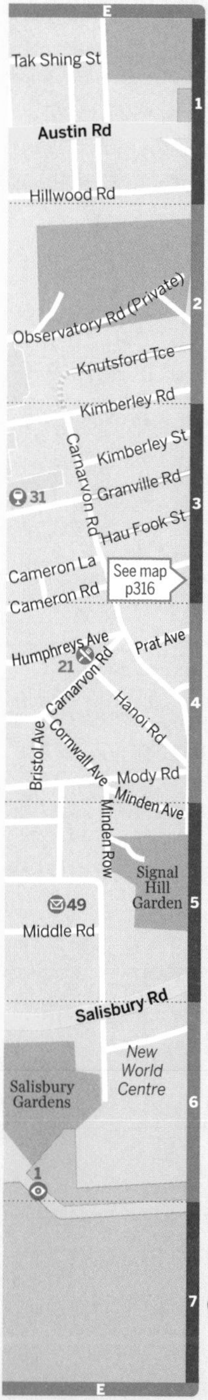

TSIM SHA TSUI

Tak Shing St

Austin Rd

Hillwood Rd

Observatory Rd (Private)

Knutsford Tce

Kimberley Rd

Kimberley St

Granville Rd

Carnarvon Rd

Hau Fook St

Cameron La

Cameron Rd

See map p316

Humphreys Ave

Carnarvon Rd

Prat Ave

Hanoi Rd

Bristol Ave

Cornwall Ave

Mody Rd

Minden Ave

Minden Row

Signal Hill Garden

Middle Rd

Salisbury Rd

New World Centre

Salisbury Gardens

31

21

49

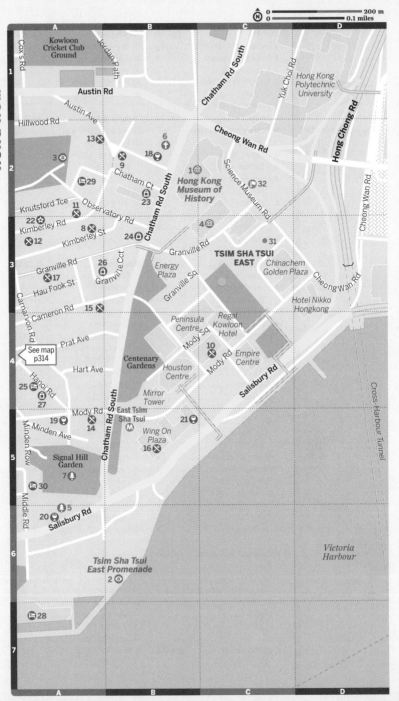

0 — 200 m
0 — 0.1 miles

A

Cox's Rd

Kowloon
Cricket Club
Ground

Jordan Path

Austin Rd

Austin Ave

Hillwood Rd

13 ✕

3 ◉

9 ✕

29 🍴

Knutsford Tce

11 ✕

22 ✿

Kimberley Rd

8 ✕

12 ✕

Kimberley St

Granville Rd

17 ✕

Hau Fook St

Cameron Rd

15 ✕

Carnarvon Rd

Prat Ave

Hart Ave

25 🍴

27

Hanoi Rd

19 🍴

14 ✕

Minden Ave

Minden Row

Signal Hill
Garden

7 ♨

30 🛏

20 🍴

5 ♨

Salisbury Rd

Middle Rd

Tsim Sha Tsui
East Promenade

2 ◉

28 🛏

B

Chatham Rd South

6 ✝

18 ✕

Chatham Ct

23 🔒

Observatory Rd

26 🔒

Granville Cct

Peninsula
Centre

Centenary
Gardens

Houston
Centre

Mirror
Tower

Mody Rd

East Tsim
Sha Tsui Ⓜ

Wing On
Plaza

16 ✕

C

Chatham Rd South

Cheong Wan Rd

1 🏛
**Hong Kong
Museum
of History**

Science Museum Rd

4 🏛

Granville Rd

**TSIM SHA TSUI
EAST**

Energy
Plaza

Granville Sq.

Granville St

Regal
Kowloon
Hotel

10 ✕

Mody Rd

Empire
Centre

21 🍴

Salisbury Rd

D

Chatham Rd South

Yuk Choi Rd

Hong Kong
Polytechnic
University

Hong Chong Rd

Cheong Wan Rd

32 🍴

31 ●

Chinachem
Golden Plaza

Cheong Wan Rd

Hotel Nikko
Hongkong

Cross-Harbour Tunnel

Victoria
Harbour

See map
p314

1

2

3

4

5

6

7

YAU MA TEI

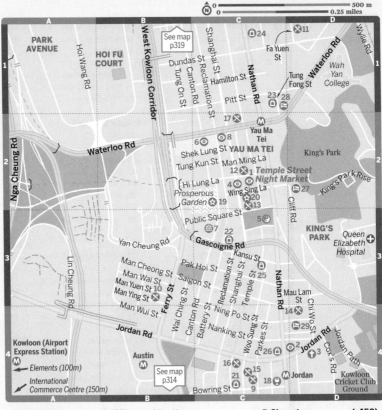

MONG KOK

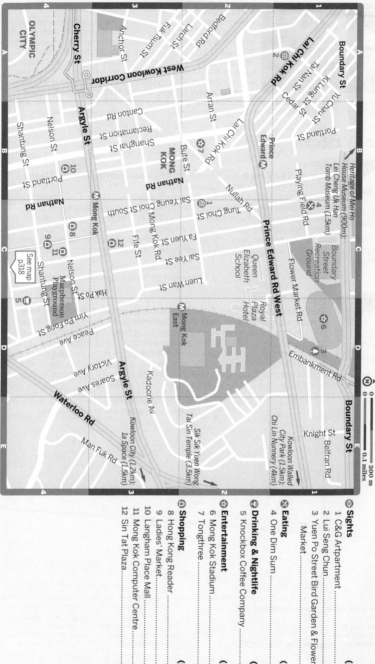

Our Story

A beat-up old car, a few dollars in the pocket and a sense of adventure. In 1972 that's all Tony and Maureen Wheeler needed for the trip of a lifetime – across Europe and Asia overland to Australia. It took several months, and at the end – broke but inspired – they sat at their kitchen table writing and stapling together their first travel guide, *Across Asia on the Cheap*. Within a week they'd sold 1500 copies. Lonely Planet was born.

Today, Lonely Planet has offices in Franklin, London, Melbourne, Oakland, Dublin, Beijing and Delhi, with more than 600 staff and writers. We share Tony's belief that 'a great guidebook should do three things: inform, educate and amuse'.

Our Writers

Emily Matchar

Central, The Peak & the Northwest, Kowloon, Outlying Islands, Macau A native of Chapel Hill, North Carolina, Emily first caught Relapsing Travel Fever during a high-school semester abroad in Argentina. To date, Emily has contributed to some two dozen Lonely Planet guides. She also writes about culture, travel, politics and food for the *New York Times*, *The Washington Post*, *The New Republic*, *The Atlantic*, *Men's Journal*, *Outside*, *Gourmet* and many more. When she's not busy rating Memphis barbecue joints, wandering around night markets in Laos, or tramping in New Zealand, she can be found chowing down on dumplings in her adopted city of Hong Kong.

Read more about Emily at:
http://auth.lonelyplanet.com/profiles/ematchar

Piera Chen

Plan Your Trip, Wan Chai & the Northeast, Aberdeen & the South, New Territories, Understand Hong Kong, Survival Guide When not on the road, Piera divides her time between hometown Hong Kong, Taiwan and Vancouver. She has authored more than a dozen travel guides and contributed to as many travel-related titles. Piera has a BA in Literature from Pomona College. Her early life was peppered with trips to Taiwan, China and Southeast Asia , but it was during her first trip to Europe that dawn broke. She remembers being fresh off a flight, looking around her in Rome, thinking, 'I want to be doing this everyday.' And she has.

Read more about Piera at:
http://auth.lonelyplanet.com/profiles/pierachen

Published by Lonely Planet Global Limited
CRN 554153
17th edition – May 2017
ISBN 978 1 78657 442 8
© Lonely Planet 2017   Photographs © as indicated 2017
10 9 8 7 6 5 4 3 2 1
Printed in Singapore